The Jewish Political Tradition

EDITORS Michael Walzer

Menachem Lorberbaum

Noam J. Zohar

The Jewish Political Tradition

VOLUME I *Authority*

EDITORS

Michael Walzer

Menachem Lorberbaum

Noam J. Zohar

COEDITOR

Yair Lorberbaum

Yale University Press

New Haven and London

Published with assistance from the Castle Fund, endowed by John K. Castle to honor his ancestor the Reverend James Pierpont, one of Yale's original founders, and administered by the Program in Ethics, Politics, and Economics at Yale University.

Designed by Sonia L. Shannon. Set in Bembo type by Tseng Information Systems, Inc., Durham, North Carolina. Printed in the United States of America by Edwards Brothers, Ann Arbor, Michigan.

The Library of Congress has cataloged the hardcover edition as follows:
The Jewish political tradition / editors, Michael Walzer, Menachem Lorberbaum, Noam J. Zohar.
p.   cm.
Includes bibliographical references and indexes.
Contents: v. 1. Authority.
ISBN 0-300-07822-6 (alk. paper)
1. Jews—Politics and government.   2. Judaism and politics.   3. Judaism and state.   4. Leadership—Religious aspects—Judaism.   I. Walzer, Michael.
II. Lorberbaum, Menachem, 1958– .   III. Zohar, No'am.
DS140 .J475   2000
320'.088'296—dc21   99-059743

A catalogue record for this book is available from the British Library.
The paper in this book meets the guidelines for permanence and durability of the Committee on Production Guidelines for Book Longevity of the Council on Library Resources.

ISBN 0-300-10201-1 (pbk. : alk. paper)
10   9   8   7   6   5   4   3   2

". . . we see it as in a dream."—Psalm 126:1

To the *halutzim*—the pioneers—who paved the roads connecting dream and reality

Contents

Contents for Volumes I–IV

Volume IV. Politics in History

Foreword

The quest for spiritual meaning is often identified with a "leap of the alone to the Alone," with the religious experience of lonely men and women of faith. The biblical roots of the Jewish tradition, however, point toward a different conception, in which the central focus of spiritual life is on community. The covenant with God is mediated through a collective drama, the story of a nation deprived of freedom and dignity for generations, delivered from its bondage, and brought into a covenant with God. Only by participating in the collective liberation from Egypt can the individual grasp the meaning of a life rooted in the revelation at Sinai.

History and collective memory are definitive categories in the biblical tradition. The covenant is enacted day after day through the ethical, ritual, and political forms of community.

Israel's loss of sovereignty and its exile from the land did not mean the end of this community. Rabbinic Judaism developed a comprehensive way of life mediated by explicit and precise legal norms that sustained the collective thrust of Judaic spirituality. Prayers were formulated in the plural; important segments of religious worship were conditioned upon a quorum of ten; the celebration of the Shabbat and the festivals was simultaneously familial and communal. The *kahal* provided both a site and a structure for the common life.

In response to this strong collective orientation, many modern Jewish religious thinkers sought to rescue and reinstate the individual by infusing Judaic spirituality with an existentialist passion. Their aim was to shift the focus of the Jew's religious imagination from Moses—the prophet as political and legislative leader—to Abraham and the patriarchs, that is, to religious figures who could mediate the intensity of the individual's experience before God.

But with the establishment of the state of Israel—the third Jewish commonwealth—Jewish thinkers have to address again the central issues of collective existence. Their challenge is to formulate a spiritual vision suited

xiii

to the new social realities of sovereignty in the world. The complexity of the ethical and political issues that surface within the emerging Israeli democracy require a language rooted in the historical experience of the Jewish people but capable also of shaping the common life of a modern state.

Because of national renewal and empowerment, Jews are no longer living metaphors for the "other," the "stranger," the eternal victim. They now wield power in a sovereign state, and so they cannot conceal their moral failures by blaming others. The rebirth of Israel provides the Jewish people with a public arena where they themselves must take charge, drawing on the strength of their tradition to give a direction to political life and a content to popular aspiration. Now Jewish values must come to grips with Jewish power.

Judaism isn't confined to the privacy of the synagogue, the family, or the academy of learning. It is now being tested in the public square and the political assembly, where the hard questions that face self-governing nations cannot be ignored. There is no escaping to the privacy of the inner soul or to some spiritual sanctuary separated from the mundane issues of everyday life: poverty, social welfare, unemployment, relations with strangers, tolerance, pluralism, security, and justice. Given the compromises that a full political life requires, how can Jews retain a compelling moral vision?

If public life in Israel cannot derive moral strength and critical insight from the tradition; if the private and public domains, the worlds of the individual and the citizen, are totally isolated from one another, then the Jewish people will lose their sense of history and identity. If the language of politics is void of personal meaning, and the language of private life void of political idealism, we will forfeit a historic opportunity to build a society that overcomes the modern tendency to separate self-realization and communal commitment.

These volumes on the Jewish political tradition fill a pressing need: they aim to retrieve a Jewish political discourse concerned with issues like authority, distributive justice, membership, and welfare. They help correct the mistaken notion that the Jewish tradition was concerned only with ritual celebration, laws of purity, daily worship, the study of Torah. They make the political arguments that have gone on for more than three millennia accessible, so that readers can gain a new appreciation of the traditional meaning of covenantal engagement—which encompassed not only the life of worship but also the building of a just and compassionate community.

David Hartman

Preface and Acknowledgments

The Jewish Political Tradition has its origin in a conference on Jewish philosophy, religion, and politics, sponsored by the Shalom Hartman Institute in Jerusalem, that has been convened every year since 1983. Its participants are political theorists, philosophers, law professors, and historians brought together with scholars of the Talmud and of Jewish literature generally. The discussions have ranged widely, but have come back again and again to political questions of the sort that we have tried to engage in these volumes. The idea of a "reader with commentaries" arose out of the conference discussions, where we read texts together and argue about what the texts mean and what value their arguments have. From the beginning, the project has had strong support—intellectual, financial, and logistical—from the faculty and staff of the Hartman Institute. We are especially grateful for David Hartman's guidance and encouragement.

The first, rough proposal for a book on Jewish political thought was circulated by Michael Walzer in 1987. Menachem Lorberbaum joined in launching the project in 1989 and played the major role in fleshing out the proposal and producing the first long list of readings; he is responsible for the translations of our medieval and modern texts. Noam Zohar has worked on the project since 1991, helping to revise, supplement, and reorganize the list and undertaking the translation of all our talmudic and midrashic texts. Yair Lorberbaum has been involved since 1993 in further revisions and reorganizations. The introductory essays for all the chapters were drafted by Michael Walzer and then rewritten with the benefit of comments and criticisms from the other coeditors. Headnotes and footnotes were the primary responsibility of Menachem Lorberbaum and Noam Zohar; the glossaries were the primary responsibility of Yair Lorberbaum—in all cases, with the advice and criticism of the others. The choice of commentators was a joint responsibility. We are grateful to Michael Fishbane for writing one of the introductory essays to the work as a whole.

Originally recruited as a translator of medieval texts, Ari Ackerman has also functioned as a key adviser on many other textual matters and has taken responsibility for the consistency of all our translations. A host of other friends and colleagues have helped with advice and criticism, telling us about their favorite texts, advising us on editorial matters of all sorts. We mention here only a few whose support was critically important to us: Menachem Brinker, Moshe Halbertal, and Sidney Morgenbesser.

The project has required and received a great deal of financial support. The Institute for Advanced Study in Princeton, where Michael Walzer is a professor, provided funds to bring each of the coeditors to Princeton for two or three years of residence and research. A grant from the Gladys Delmas Foundation sustained our work for a critical year. The National Endowment for the Humanities paid for most of the translations and a good deal of the final editing of the texts. The Castle Fund at Yale University provided a subsidy for the publication of all four volumes of *The Jewish Political Tradition.* We are deeply indebted to the men and women who manage these institutions and funds, a number of whom have taken a sympathetic interest in our work; without them we could not have seen it through to completion. We can single out only two of them here: Patricia Labalme of the Delmas Foundation and Ian Shapiro of the Castle Fund committee at Yale.

We are honored by the participation of the commentators whose critical essays appear in these volumes. Their contributions express a strong commitment to our larger enterprise—to make this tradition of political thought vivid and accessible, a subject for engagement as well as study.

We are also the appreciative beneficiaries of the Yale Judaica Series, whose fine translations we have used whenever they were available. Ivan Marcus, general editor of the series, has even permitted us to publish translations in progress, with the agreement of the translators.

Grateful acknowledgment is made for permission to reprint selections from the following books and journals:

Albo, Joseph. *Book of Principles,* trans. Isaac Husik (Philadelphia, 1929); reprinted with the permission of the Jewish Publication Society.
Barak, Aharon. "The Legal Revolution: Protected Fundamental Rights" (Hebrew), *Mishpat u-Mimshal* (Haifa University Law and Government Review), 1992.
Bergman, Samuel Hugo. "The Absolute Duty to God." In *Dialogical Philosophy*

from Kierkegaard to Buber (Albany: State University of New York Press, 1991); first published in Hebrew by the Bialik Institute, Jerusalem, in 1974, under the title *Ha-Philosophyah Ha-Dialogit me-Kierkegaard ad Buber,* and printed here with permission of the Hebrew publisher.

Buber, Martin. *Israel and the World* (New York: Schocken, 1948); reprinted by permission of the Balkin Agency, copyright 1948, 1963.

Cohen, Hayyim. "Issues Relating to the Fundamental Law of Human Dignity" (Hebrew), *Ha-Praklit: Sefer Yovel* (The Lawyer: Jubilee Volume), 1993.

Cohen, Herman. *Reason and Hope: Selections from the Jewish Writings of Herman Cohen,* trans. Eva Jospe (New York: W. W. Norton, 1971); copyright 1971 by the B'nai B'rith Commission on Adult Education.

Dessler, Eliyahu. *Mikhtav me-Eliyahu* (Tel Aviv: Committee for the Publication of the Writings of Rabbi E. E. Dessler, 1955), vol. 1; reprinted with the permission of the Committee for the Publication of the Writings of Rabbi E. Dessler.

Einhorn, David. "Responsum on Free Inquiry and Rabbinic Office." In W. Gunther Plaut, *The Rise of Reform Judaism: A Sourcebook of Its European Origins* (New York: World Union for Progressive Judaism, 1963); reprinted with the permission of the publisher.

Elon, Menachem. "The Legal Method in Legislation" (Hebrew), *Iyunei Mishpat* (Tel Aviv University Law Review), 1993; reprinted with the permission of Menachem Elon.

Hirsch, Samson Raphael. *Collected Writings* (Jerusalem and New York: Feldheim Publishers, 1993).

Josephus. *Against Apion.* In *Josephus,* vol. I, trans. H. St. J. Thackeray (Cambridge: Harvard University Press, 1926); reprinted by permission of the publishers and the Loeb Classical Library.

Kook, Abraham Isaac. *Orot* (1961), *Mishpat Cohen* (1966), and *Orot ha-Kodesh* (1964) (Jerusalem: Mossad Harav Kook).

Leibowitz, Yeshayahu. *Judaism, Human Values, and the Jewish State,* trans. Eliezer Goldman et al. (Cambridge: Harvard University Press, 1992); world copyright by Schocken Publishing House, Ltd., Tel Aviv, Israel.

Maccabees, trans. Jonathan A. Goldstein (Garden City, N.Y.: Doubleday, 1976);

copyright 1976 by Doubleday; used by permission of Doubleday, a division of Bantam Doubleday Dell Publishing Group, Inc.

Maimonides. *The Guide of the Perplexed,* trans. Shlomo Pines (Chicago: University of Chicago Press, 1963); copyright 1963 by the University of Chicago.

Mendelssohn, Moses. *Jerusalem,* trans. Alan Arkush (Hanover and London: University Press of New England, 1983); copyright 1983 by Trustees of Brandeis University, Brandeis University Press, by permission of the University Press of New England.

Modena, Leon (attrib.). *Kol Sakhal.* In Talya Fishman, *Shaking the Pillars of Exile* (Stanford: Stanford University Press, 1997); reprinted with the permission of the publishers; copyright 1997 by the Board of Trustees of the Leland Stanford Junior University.

Rabbi Meir of Rothenberg, ed. and trans. I. Agus (Hoboken, N.J.: Ktav Publishing House, 1970).

Spinoza, Baruch. *Theological-Political Treatise,* trans. Samuel Shirley (Leiden: E. J. Brill, 1991).

The Wisdom of Ben Sira, trans. Alexander DiLella and Margaret Skeham (Garden City, N.Y.: Doubleday, 1987); copyright 1987 by Doubleday; used by permission of Doubleday, a division of Bantam Doubleday Dell Publishing Group, Inc.

Selections from the following texts are reprinted with the permission of the Yale Judaica Series and Yale University Press:

Elijah ben Moses Basyatchi. *Adderet Eliyahu.* From *Karaite Anthology,* ed. and trans. Leon Nemoy, 1952.

Halevi, Judah. *The Kuzari,* trans. Lawrence Berman and Barry S. Kogan, forthcoming; used with the permission of Barry S. Kogan.

Maimonides. *The Code of Maimonides, Book Eleven: The Book of Torts,* trans. H. Klein, 1954.

Maimonides. *The Code of Maimonides, Book Fourteen: The Book of Judges,* trans. Abraham M. Hershman, 1949.

Maimonides. *Sefer ha-Madda* (The Book of Knowledge), trans. Bernard Septimus, forthcoming; used with the permission of the translator.

Saadia Gaon. *The Book of Beliefs and Opinions,* trans. Samuel Rosenblatt, 1948.

Salmon ben Jeroham. *Book of the Wars of the Lord.* From *Karaite Anthology,* ed. and trans. Leon Nemoy, 1952.

Sifre on Deuteronomy, trans. Reuven Hammer, 1986.

The staff of Yale University Press have been helpful and supportive ever since we first approached them. The Press's readers provided detailed suggestions, many of which we have adopted. John Covell has been an astute and kindly shepherd at the Press, and Mary Pasti a wonderfully effective manuscript editor.

The editors take this joyful occasion to record their debt to the members of their four families, who have provided abiding love and steadfast support for the past many years. Taken together, we have one living grandparent, seven living parents, nine brothers and sisters, four spouses, thirteen children, and two grandchildren. So we have a strong sense of the familial character that Jewish politics sometimes takes and an even stronger sense that there is a world beyond politics, a world of infinite human value, which good political arrangements ought to protect. We intend this book to serve all our generations.

Introduction: The Jewish Political Tradition

The association of politics with the state is pervasive in Western thought. Without statehood, sovereignty, and coercive power, there doesn't appear to be anything like political agency, nor, therefore, any point to the standard political questions: Who are the legitimate and authoritative agents? Where does their authority come from? Over what group of people does this authority extend? For what purpose, subject to what limits, is it exercised? One can answer these questions with regard to many different agents and groups, from ancient Assyrians to modern Americans. One can answer them with regard to the Israelites of the biblical age and again with regard to the citizens of the reestablished Israeli state. But with regard to the Jews, so it is commonly believed, no answers are possible; the questions don't arise. After the great revolt against Rome was suppressed and the Temple destroyed in 70 C.E., there was no Jewish state for almost two thousand years; there were no sovereign agents, no coercive powers, no politics to think about — hence, no political thought. For many writers, Jews and non-Jews alike, the apolitical condition of the Jews is, or was, the most interesting thing about them.

But politics is pervasive, with or without state sovereignty. The Jewish communities of the diaspora managed to organize a common life — first in Babylonia, then in Egypt, Syria, and Rome, then across all of Europe and North Africa. They made political choices about the distribution of power and influence; they developed and even enforced a set of laws, taxed their members for the sake of security, welfare, religion, and education, and maintained relations of one sort or another with the non-Jewish authorities. They sought to limit the uses of power by both Jews and non-Jews and to guard against its corrupting effects. All this required ideas as well as actions, arguments as well as decisions. Nor were the ideas and arguments limited to the immediate and highly constrained life of the scattered exilic communities. Jews also remembered their earlier political history — David's kingdom and its successors and the priestly regime of the Second Commonwealth — and they dreamed of a messianic renewal.

So there arose a tradition of thought, theological and legal rather than autonomously political in form, but political in substance nonetheless. Its point of departure is always the Hebrew Bible, understood as the revealed word of God. But since writers in the diaspora could not recapitulate the experience represented in that text, they were forced into a radical reinterpretation or, better, a series of reinterpretations, of its meaning. Embodied in the Talmud, in midrashic collections of legends and parables, retellings and expansions of the biblical narrative, in commentaries on the Bible and the Talmud, in legal responsa, and only occasionally and incompletely in philosophical treatises, this interpretive tradition never took on the firm shape of a doctrine or theory. Nonetheless, it does display certain characteristic modes of thought—themes, concerns, tendencies, and internal tensions—and it is these that we propose as objects of study and sources of enlightenment.

One of the internal tensions is an ambivalence about politics itself. Understood as a form of human coping with physical need, social conflict, and natural disaster, the political enterprise was already disparaged by the biblical prophets, who seem to enjoin radical trust in God as an alternative to "wisdom" or policy. In exile, this disparagement took a different, though related, form: the conviction that politics was mostly a matter of war and conquest, killing and being killed, and that God had set Israel apart from all those hostile and fatal engagements, destined it for a different existence. Politics was for the gentiles. This argument represented a kind of accommodation to, even a justification for, the exile. But it was never the only or the dominant view among Jewish writers, and it was belied by the everyday practice of law and politics—and by the reflections on this practice that make up a significant part of Jewish literature.

What makes this body of work a distinct and more or less unified tradition, and what marks its limits, is its intertextuality. A long series of writers have addressed political questions by referring themselves to the same authoritative texts and to the critical events on which these texts are focused: the exodus from Egypt, the Sinai revelation and covenant, the winning of the land, the establishment of the monarchy in the time of Saul and David, and then the conquests and revolts, the wars and civil wars, that brought destruction, loss, and exile. And the same writers, despite their radical dispersion and the absence of all modern means of communication, refer endlessly to one another, agree and disagree with each other's interpretations of both texts and events. Reference and cross-reference constitute the tradition, although it is crucial to its unity that these Jewish writers also have a roughly similar experience of politics: until the nineteenth-century emancipation admitted many of them to citizenship in the lands where they lived, they were everywhere noncitizens, subject to gentile rule, locked into communities that were subordinate, precarious, and vulnerable.

Writers who opted out of the referential system and who avoided or escaped the common experience are not part of the Jewish political tradition, even if they are still Jews writing about politics. Karl Marx on the class struggle, Sigmund Freud on transference and political leadership, Emile Durkheim on socialism and "moral education," Georg Simmel on the philosophy of money—these texts do not fall within the tradition. Baruch Spinoza's political theology does, despite his excommunication, for Spinoza writes always with the tradition in mind: the Hebrew Bible is his first text; the greatest of medieval Jewish philosophers, Moses Maimonides, is his crucial reference. Modern secular writers like Ahad Ha'am (Asher Ginsberg) and Micha Josef Berdichevsky, schooled in the communities of eastern Europe, still know the tradition and work within it, or at least start from it—even if one of their purposes is an antitraditionalist critique: criticism is a form of engagement. Many of their successors, by contrast, are largely ignorant and entirely disengaged.

The tradition as a whole is our subject in these volumes, and our purpose with regard to it is threefold.

First, *retrieval:* we want to make its central texts and arguments available to new generations of students and potential participants. Years of reading and consultation have gone into this effort: we have sought advice, studied texts, circulated lists, studied more texts. Never before has the tradition been looked at systematically from this perspective, with our specific set of questions about political agency and authority in mind. The resulting selection is the product, necessarily partial and incomplete, of a process of discovery, bringing familiar texts into new contexts, bringing obscure and neglected texts into the political light.

Second, *integration:* we want to take this body of Jewish thought out of its intellectual ghetto and to begin an examination of the ways in which it follows, parallels, and strains against Greek, Arabic, Christian, and secularist modes of thought. "Begin" is the relevant word here, for it is our intention that the interpretations and comparisons presented in these volumes be read as a challenge to further work.

Third, *criticism:* we want to join the arguments that have characterized the tradition and to carry them forward—or, better, to argue among ourselves and to encourage others to argue about which of them can usefully be carried forward under the modern conditions of emancipation and sovereignty.

Jewish writing about politics commonly takes a legal form. Political issues take shape as legal cases and are addressed in the idiom of the law, even when what is at stake is conduct outside the legal frame: the necessary prudence of political leaders, judicial discretion, or action in emergencies. Theology and, for some writers, philosophy provide a critical background for the legal arguments, without which many of the most interesting cannot be understood. But the tradition includes very few treatises explicitly devoted to political philosophy or political theology. Its most characteristic genre is the commentary.

The biblical texts already feature a kind of internal interpretive process through which revealed law is applied, elaborated, and revised. Because the law is divinely revealed, it can never be repudiated or abandoned. But the radical text-centeredness of the tradition derives only in part from the centrality of revelation; it has a second source in the loss of every other center, the absence for so much of Jewish history of a land, a shrine, and a state. The key texts, Bible and Talmud, function as a surrogate home; they are read as all-embracing collections of laws and stories—in constant need, however, of exegesis and refinement, as a home might be of refurnishing and repair. These they receive in reiterated fashion, in successive generations. Certain commentaries achieve classical status and are commented on in turn; the continuity of the tradition is manifest in commentary on commentary.

But two other genres also figure significantly in this as in all legal literatures: first, the *code,* which is mostly an effort to summarize the legal consequences of the commentaries so far (though Maimonides in the fourteen books of his *Mishneh Torah* aims to stop the interpretive flow and to present a definitive account of the law-as-it-always-will-be); and second, the *responsa,* the answers of authoritative rabbis—their authority most often derives from learning and piety, not from any official position—to legal questions. Responsa are applications of the law and often revisions or modifications of it, and so are likely to figure in the arguments of future commentators and codifiers. The thousands of medieval and early modern "questions and answers" are a major source for the history of exilic political and social life. Historians will no doubt find the questions more interesting than the answers, for they are full of the detail of everyday experience: familial disputes; arguments over inheritance; economic conflicts having to do with loans, partnerships, and taxes; communal regulations; dealings with non-Jews, and so on. In these volumes we are inevitably focused on the answers, which often contain general statements about how families are organized, how far the authority of the community reaches, and what membership means.

Commentaries, codes, and responsa still play a major part in the modern period, but they are supplemented now by new genres—essays, articles, pamphlets, books in the contemporary style. Party publicists, journalists, lay intellectuals, and professors join the ranks of the rabbis and sages. We include all of them here, always subject to the criterion of intertextuality. Still, editorial choices among twentieth-century authors and texts are very difficult. For earlier periods, we are simply recognizing the important writers; for our own time, we are participating in the process of deciding which writers are important. Sometimes we have looked only for representative figures without primary regard for their reputations or intellectual strength. But mostly we have tried to include those figures whose work, we believe, will continue to be read (and commented on).

Very few of the texts reprinted here come from the vast body of Jewish mystical writings. But this relative absence does not have the usual reasons. It does not reflect a rationalist effort to suppress this part of the tradition, in the style of the nineteenth-century German *Wissenschaft des Judentums.* It does not derive from a commitment to Judaism as a "religion of reason." We do not mean to deny the central role of mysticism in Jewish history; nor do we mean to conceal the extent to which it is intertwined with halakhic (legal) discourse. Many of the writers presented here as legal scholars addressing political questions were also deeply engaged with the literature of mysticism (Kabbalah). Many kabbalists were, and are, politically engaged.

Yet it is hard to specify the political meaning of these engagements. On questions having to do with the community and its everyday problems, legal writers friendly to mysticism do not argue differently from legal writers hostile to mysticism. There is as great a range of difference within each group as between them—and it is the same range. Nor is it at all common that anything we can recognize as a political issue is explicitly addressed in a mystical text. (One important exception to this rule is the argument of nineteenth-century hasidic writers about the authority of their charismatic leaders, the *tzaddikim.*) It isn't the case that mystical interests or commitments systematically pushed people toward an antipolitical position, or toward political quietism, or toward political radicalism, though each of these possibilities is realized among some writers.

With regard to the big issues of Jewish political thought—election or "chosenness," the holiness of the Land of Israel, the experience of exile, and the hope for redemption—mysticism may have inclined people in certain directions, toward particular doctrines. Curiously, it may have led some writers toward a biological view of divine election (as if Jews were a species apart) and a material view of the holiness of the Land of Israel (as if the soil itself were hospitable to prophecy). Views of this sort are fully represented in these volumes. But they are not entailed by mysticism, and their centrality to the mystical tradition will surely be disputed, especially by scholars friendly to the tradition. In any case, insofar as questions about election, say, are *argued,* the arguments are most likely to take legal or philosophical forms. So they commonly do in our texts—and, as readers will quickly see, our own commentaries take these forms exclusively. In a sense, then, these volumes represent only one part of the tradition. But so far as politics is concerned, this is surely the dominant part.

Our own account of the tradition is organized as an anthology of texts with commentaries. The texts are gathered under thirty headings (chapter titles) that represent a compromise between the categories and divisions most appropriate to the tradition and those most familiar to students of modern political theory—with the balance tilted toward the tradition. Hence, headings like "political obligation" or "individual rights" do not appear in these volumes, for they would require an artificial and inevitably suspect extraction of texts from their legal and doctrinal (as well as their historical) contexts. Writers in the tradition do not address subjects like these in any direct way, although questions about obligations and rights figure obliquely in many of their arguments (the general index can be used to locate these oblique engagements).

Although a scheme of this kind can be, and should be, historically sensitive, its primary aim is not historical verisimilitude. The texts are arranged (roughly) chronologically in each chapter to suggest an ongoing discussion of the issues at hand. That there actually is a discussion of this kind is evidenced by the way the writers stand self-consciously within the tradition and continually refer to its classical writings. But they also live in a particular time and place; they are faithful to local customs and practices; and they are often deeply involved in local political struggles and intellectual debates. We can only rarely capture these local engagements in a work of this sort. They are the province of the historian, and readers interested in them should consult one of the standard histories. We highlight only the larger, recurrent issues, the long-term responses (or the ongoing arguments about how to respond) to reiterated political and intellectual challenges. This is the province of the political theorist, who can also ask what characteristic form these issues and responses take and what we have to learn from them. How should we engage with and carry on this tradition of thought? What in it needs to be criticized, or revised, or abandoned?

There is another verisimilitude that we cannot achieve: an anthology is a collection of excerpts, and there are many writers—perhaps especially philosophers like Maimonides, Spinoza, Moses Mendelssohn, and Franz Rosenzweig—whose range and complexity cannot be represented by passages extracted from the body of their work. We get their perspective or opinion on a particular issue; we miss the intricate connectedness of their opinions on many different issues. In representing the tradition as a whole, however, excerpts, even very short excerpts, are often entirely appropriate. Isolated biblical verses and rabbinic aphorisms, stories, legal maxims, conversational exchanges, and questions are the building blocks of traditional dis-

course, quoted again and again, sometimes to begin an argument, sometimes
to move it along, sometimes as a clinching conclusion. We reprint many of
these: texts that have become prooftexts or standard references. They are like
William Blake's grain of sand, in which it is possible to find the whole world.

    The number and precision of our headings is obviously artificial;
the subjects we mean to mark off in fact overlap; the best location of a particular text is sometimes indeterminate. Our frequent cross-references suggest the seamlessness of arguments that we have been forced to divide. Nonetheless, the thirty headings should make sense to students of the tradition,
and the four main groupings (volumes) have strong and sufficient reasons.
    We begin with *Authority* because the tradition itself begins with
God's authority, with divine rule and divine revelation. Exactly how much
room there is for human authority and decision making is always a question.
Rule by one, or some, or many human beings over all the others is always
under a cloud—though there are repeated efforts to bring it into the sun. For
Jews the clouds were especially dark after the exile and the long experience
of foreign domination. The typical Jewish attitude toward political authority
is suspicion. But this doesn't lead, as in modern liberal theory, to a defense of
constitutionalism. Liberal governments are not only limited but also legitimate, and most Jewish writers in exile find it very difficult to acknowledge
a full-scale political legitimacy—for this can come, and will come, they believe, only with the messianic kingdom. Here and now, only the authority
of the rabbis escapes suspicion, but that is probably because theirs was an
authority without political power—and it was the rabbis, and until modern times hardly anyone else, who wrote about these questions. In any case,
politics was never their chief interest. Although Maimonides quotes Aristotle's "Man is a political animal," there isn't much evidence that many Jews
thought of themselves in that way.
    How to explain the importance of politics, how to justify the exer-
cise of power—these are hard questions for Jewish writers. But even if an-
swering such questions was not for them an urgent task, the answers they
provide are often penetrating and valuable. We have highlighted especially
the emphasis on consent, not only because of its contemporary interest but
also because of its early appearance and frequent reiteration in Jewish

thought. Even the authority of God's law is often said to rest on a certain kind of consent. Once again, it is necessary to stress that this claim doesn't press Jewish writers toward some version of liberal democracy, but (along with monotheism itself and the hatred of idolatry) it does make all the varieties of political authoritarianism difficult to defend.

Membership is our second major theme. Who is a Jew? isn't only a contemporary question; it has been a central issue in Jewish life since the Babylonian exile of the sixth century B.C.E., when the Jews—the name dates from that time—were first forced to constitute themselves as a community of faith, which is to say, a community without territorial boundaries. From then on, the standard political questions of citizenship and naturalization, loyalty and treason, take forms appropriate to a religion. It is necessary to talk of conversion and apostasy, orthodoxy and heresy. But it is a peculiarity of Jewish history that these new terms still have national and political implications. Indeed, there is a sense in which the loss of state power gave national identity an enhanced value. The enhancement is already visible in biblical texts—dating (probably) from the years in Babylonia or the period immediately after—about the election and mission of Israel. Both of these required perseverance in the law, and the law required in turn a pattern of communal organization and a structure of authority that was as much political as religious.

The discussion of *Community* follows naturally, to explain what members have in common and how they organize their common life. After the fall of the Second Commonwealth, Jews lived under the authority of semi-monarchic patriarchs (in Roman Palestine) and exilarchs (in Sasanian and Muslim Babylonia), but we know almost nothing about how—or whether—this authority was exercised in everyday life. The most important political structure of the exile emerged only gradually, in western Europe and North Africa: this was the *kahal,* a small autonomous or semiautonomous community (ordinary *kehillot* ranged from ten families to a few hundred in size, although by the early modern period there were much larger urban centers). The miracle of Jewish politics is the persistence of this formation over many centuries—a common regime with a common legal system, reiterated across a wide range of countries, in very different circumstances, without the benefit of (and sometimes in opposition to) state power.

Jewish discussions of welfare, taxation, communal government, and the judicial process invariably begin from the Bible, and the crucial talmudic rules and regulations reflect the political experience of Palestine in the first centuries of the Common Era and of Babylonia during the next four centuries. But many of the most important arguments on all these issues relate specifically to the *kahal,* and we have focused a great deal of attention on that political community. The *kahal* is both historically and symbolically important; it is the polis of exilic Jewry—the actual site of an untheorized and undervalued politics that is nonetheless vigorously enacted and endlessly debated. The Jews did not choose, and never celebrated, the decentered politics of the exile, but, within the limits set by their relative powerlessness, they made it work. And that achievement is, in our view, one of the most compelling features of their political tradition.

Our last theme is the idea of *Politics in History* that gives to all the debates about authority, membership, and communal life their larger significance, situating them within a world-historical perspective. Here the focus of our study shifts to a political/theological understanding of secular time and eternity, mundane geography and the space of holiness—an understanding whose sources lie in the biblical texts and which has been profoundly influential for Christianity and Islam as well as for Judaism. Its crucial terms (for the Jews) are "exile" and "redemption," and the critical political questions that it poses are, first, how the Jews, collectively and individually, ought to accommodate themselves to exilic life and, second, whether there is any practical work incumbent upon them, things that ought to be done, for the sake of redemption: Is there, can there be, a redemptive politics? But there is another question, which is not posed within the literature of the tradition but rather by it, and then, more concretely, by recent Jewish history: Is there a middle term between exile and redemption, a political condition that avoids both messianic pretension and the undervalued politics of the exile? We ask this last question only at the end of these volumes.

The texts we have selected and arranged are accompanied, in a style that fits the tradition we mean to represent, by commentaries. These were written by contemporary political and social theorists and moral philosophers and by scholars in Jewish studies with related interests who were asked to join the arguments of the texts—not simply to describe or contextualize them. They do this in their own historical or analytical fashion; the point of the commentaries, however, is not history or analysis but rather engagement with a set of issues. We want to display the tradition as a *continuing* argument. That doesn't mean that every traditional argument warrants continuation. Traditions survive through a series of partial abandonments and partial innovations—rejections, revisions, and renewals—as well as through faithful perseverance. Our commentaries represent all these possibilities.

Two forms of commentary, however, are not represented here: the pious/apologetic and the scholarly/detached. The reasons for avoiding these two should be obvious from the texts themselves. Although both these forms no doubt make their appearance in traditional literature, they are not dominant there. Writing a commentary is an act of engagement, and this commonly is, and always should be, a critical engagement, an effort to get or set things right. For commentators who regard the founding texts as religiously authoritative, this critical effort is often indirect. But it is entirely possible, and often very effective, to address by indirection the questions that we have posed to all our commentators: Is this a good argument? Should it be continued, elaborated, improved, amended, or discarded? Responding to these questions, they bring all their resources to bear: their (very different) knowledge of Jewish texts and of modern philosophy, their (very different) political commitments and experiences. So they serve the second and third purposes of this work, integration and criticism; they expose the tradition (as it was regularly exposed in the past) to the challenge of contemporary understandings and convictions.

Michael Walzer

The Selection, Translation, and Presentation of the Texts

To portray the Jewish political tradition, we have gleaned arguments, stories, interpretations, and commentaries from many different works of different genres, few of which are dedicated solely to political issues. The very nature of the Jewish tradition—and of Rabbinic Judaism in particular—demands close attention to its manifold forms and contexts. The interplay over many centuries of biblical law, monarchic epics, and prophetic critiques; Rabbinic fables, disputes, and legal reinterpretations; medieval communal ordinances, codes, and philosophical writings; and the rediscoveries and re-readings of all these in the course of the modern upheavals of emancipation and Zionism—this is our subject.

Many of the selections are "classics": doctrinal statements or arguments that became centerpieces of subsequent discourse and yet are unavailable to this day except in the original Hebrew (or a rabbinic admixture of Hebrew and Aramaic). Others were chosen because they reflect important themes or institutions; most commonly, they represent (what came to be regarded as) mainstream positions, but frequently they represent salient minority opinions as well. In preserving both the winning and the losing sides of many arguments, we follow the editorial tradition of what might be called a Jewish "politics of knowledge," as attested in the Mishnah (Eduyot 1:5 [€7, §2]). Where a similar point is expressed in several texts, we preferred as a rule adding another example of the work of a figure who has appeared before in our pages rather than introducing a single text from yet another author—so that readers will gain some real familiarity with at least a few major authors.

Besides these substantive criteria, there were considerations pertaining to the form of the texts. Wherever possible, we sought to avoid selections of either extreme brevity or great length. In addition, we excluded some important texts that we judged to be too intricate or cumbersome to be made accessible in a book of this kind.

Rabbinic Texts

The textual world of the Jewish tradition is complex and, for the unaccustomed reader, often more than a little bewildering. A comprehensive orientation is provided below in Michael Fishbane's introductory essay. At this point, we offer only a brief overview of the main texts and their interrelations.

All Jewish traditional discourse relates to the Hebrew Bible as its canon. Initially, Rabbinic teachings were expounded and transmitted in connection with the biblical books. Thus the *Mekhilta* follows many parts of Exodus line by line, just as the *Sifre* follows Numbers and Deuteronomy. Since the same legal topic is often addressed in more than one biblical location, there was a need to organize the material according to subject, independently of Scripture. The Mishnah—a concise collection of Rabbinic legal teachings (and arguments)—was redacted by Rabbi Judah "the Prince" early in the third century C.E., organized in six "orders," which are further divided into tractates, chapters, and individual clauses (each of which is also called a mishnah—not capitalized).

The Mishnah became the core document of Rabbinic Judaism, and its redaction marks the end of the era of the *tannaim*. A supplementary collection of the teachings of the *tannaim*, the Tosefta, as well as both the Jerusalem and the Babylonian Talmuds, follows the order of the Mishnah. The talmudic discussions (*sugyot,* sing. *sugya*) take the mishnaic clauses as their point of departure but often also revolve around independent statements and traditions of the *amora'im.* Unlike the Mishnah, which focuses almost exclusively on *halakhah,* the Talmud also incorporates much aggadic material. In talmudic times aggadic collections were also compiled for many books of the Bible—primarily the *Midrash Rabbah* series for the Pentateuch.

Subsequent generations continued to study the Bible directly and to produce commentaries thereon, although they often consulted and quoted talmudic interpretations. The halakhic tradition focused, however, on the Babylonian Talmud (BT), which was considered authoritative—yet whose *sugyot* rarely conclude with decisions in the myriad controversies that they record and elaborate. Initially the intricate Hebrew-Aramaic talmudic discussions were barely decipherable even by the learned, and rulings based on the Talmud were rendered centrally by the Babylonian Geonim, the heads of academies. By the eleventh century, however, the Jewish world had become strongly decentralized. Rashi's classic line-by-line commentary finally made the talmudic text widely accessible. Much of medieval talmudic scholarship was written in the form of commentaries or "novellae"—that is, new interpretive insights and discussions—relating to the talmudic text. Rashi's contemporary Yitzhak Alfasi produced the first major code of talmudic law. Alfasi's abridgement of the Talmud still closely followed the talmudic tractates. It was Maimonides' *Mishneh Torah* (MT) that first provided an independent reordering of Rabbinic *halakhah,* restated with all arguments resolved, in fourteen "books." Another such scheme, including only the sections of *halakhah* that apply "in these times" (i.e., in exile), was designed by Jacob b. Asher in his "Four Columns" (*Tur,* pl. *turim*); this scheme was also adopted by Joseph Karo in his influential *Shulhan Arukh.*

These various codes themselves became focuses of study and comment. Karo's code, for example, is based on his own extensive commentaries on both Maimonides' *Mishneh Torah* (*Kesef Mishneh*) and the *Tur* (*Bet Yosef*). Even halakhic works not directly addressing the clauses of the codes, such as the numerous collections of responsa, are normally loosely organized according to the four "columns" of the *Tur.*

The works mentioned in this overview, as well as many others, constitute the rabbinic (with a small *r*) tradition. We have reserved the capitalized adjective "Rabbinic" for the classical period of the *tannaim* and *amora'im,* collectively "the Rabbis." The generic (lowercase) "rabbis" refers, accordingly, to the agents of the tradition over the generations.

The Translations

Many of the selections are from works not yet translated into English (nor, as a rule, into any other language). This is true especially of the responsa literature, which is the main repository for legal and "constitutional" Jewish writing, both medieval and modern, and for the bulk of the medieval codes. Of the five classical codes (Alfasi, Maimonides, Rosh, *Tur,* and *Shulhan Arukh*), only Maimonides' *Mishneh Torah* and the *Shulhan Arukh* have been partially rendered into English, and this without their accompanying commentaries. The same holds true for all medieval commentaries and novellae on the Talmud.

With regard to medieval philosophical tracts, the situation is generally better: many of the basic texts have already appeared in English. We have used reliable English versions whenever they are available. Indeed, we are fortunate to have been able to choose passages from the excellent translations of the Yale Judaica Series, including (with the agreement of the translators and the assistance of the editor of the series, Ivan Marcus) some translations not yet published. In all these cases, we have omitted the translators' footnotes and added our own so that the annotation of texts is consistent throughout the book.

Although many translations exist of Rabbinic works, they are often not readily usable for our work—for two main reasons.

1. The quality of the published translations is not always acceptable. The pioneering Soncino translation of the Talmud (the first volumes appeared in 1935) provides an English text that sounds ponderous and awkward to the contemporary ear and, more problematically, contains numerous inexactitudes or outright mistakes. Newer translations, all of them incomplete at this time, offer a more contemporary and readable English, but their loyalty to the exact wording or sense of the original is uneven. For a work like this one, which concentrates on a relatively few selected texts, loose or free translations are not helpful; we need something closer to a strict accounting of the original.

2. Because the picture we draw in each chapter depends on the interconnections among component selections, there is a crucial issue of terminological consistency. The texts constitute a tradition (so we argue) in the sense that their authors constantly refer to earlier texts and to their own contemporaries, and they do so both by explicit citation and by implicit allusions in their choice of words. Much, perhaps most, of this interplay would be hopelessly obscured by mixing passages from different translations of the works on which we draw. With respect to the Soncino Talmud, again, there are innumerable inconsistencies in translating the same term as it appears in different places—due mostly to the independent work of the scholars entrusted with the various tractates.

Apart from the importance of cross-referencing for appreciating both the details and the larger picture, inconsistent translations often render an argument totally incomprehensible. Where a commentator's interpretation or the legal point of a responsum depends on a specific connotation or turn of phrase, a compatible translation of the primary text is indispensable.

But new translations of rabbinic material come at a price: they differ from the complete editions readily available to the larger public. We have therefore made use of existing translations and standard editions whenever possible: most importantly, the Yale Judaica Series editions of the *Sifre* and the *Mishneh Torah* and the new Jewish Publication Society translation of the Hebrew Bible (1985), but also many other texts, medieval and modern. The cost is an occasional sacrifice of consistency. A partial remedy is provided by the glossary of terms, which offers the range of meanings carried by some protean Hebrew words. A complementary tool is the general index, through which the reader will be able to trace significant appearances of some important Hebrew concepts (e.g., *tikkun olam*).

In rare cases, we have altered the translation of a particular word; in such instances, our departure from the published translation is explicitly noted.

Presentation of the Texts

Rabbinic texts are both condensed in substance and elliptical in style. In our translations we have striven to reflect this character of the originals. At the same time, we have provided some minimal expansion, always in brackets within the translated text. In doing so we follow the traditional mode of studying the Talmud: one finger on the talmudic text and one finger on Rashi's commentary, which since the first printing of the Talmud (Venice, 1520–23) has appeared alongside the text and which has guided our own expansions and annotations. Occasionally we have inserted a line or two from Rashi directly into the text, in brackets, as follows: [*Rashi*: . . .]. Where we have used existing translations, brackets indicate additions by the translators; any additions we have made are marked as editors' notes (—Eds.).

Individual selections are preceded by headnotes. These serve to provide background information (historical, legal, and conceptual) and to suggest connections among the texts. Biographical information on particular authors and on the more important persons or groups mentioned in the selections may be found in the glossary of names. Where particular points in the text or the translation require elaboration, this is offered in accompanying footnotes. As a rule, the notes serve simply to clarify the texts. Citations in the introductions and commentaries are given in parentheses.

In some cases, we preserve the original Hebrew term (sometimes the Aramaic term) in transliteration, either beside or instead of an English equivalent. Non-English words are italicized (in lowercase), and recurring terms are explained in the glossary of terms. We have resorted to transliteration in cases where the Hebrew term is in common use and where it carries multiple meanings. In these latter cases an English translation would necessarily involve distinct terms, and the thread of the tradition would be lost. In addition, transliteration of the Hebrew sometimes draws the reader's attention to significant semantic links between key terms; these are elaborated in the glossary. In transliteration we generally follow the ("nonscientific") form adopted in the *Encyclopedia Judaica*. Hebrew names are reproduced as precisely as possible. For both terms and the names of some individuals, however, we depart from this practice if another form is in common English usage. Reference to certain figures is often by acronym. We transliterate the Hebrew acronym and regard it as a proper name, capitalizing only the first letter.

All omissions are indicated by three ellipsis points. Brackets indicate all manner of additions to the original. Parentheses are used to indicate references (for example, to biblical texts) and sometimes to mark off a phrase in the original language, when this is the best way to convey the author's meaning. This practice is in line with our more general practice of adding punctuation, mostly absent in ancient and medieval texts.

Citations are given to specific editions when appropriate. We consulted standard critical editions where available, as listed:

Mechilta D'Rabbi Ismael, ed. H. S. Horovitz and I. A. Rabin (Jerusalem: Wahrmann, 1970, 2d edition).

Mekilta De-Rabbi Ishmael, ed. and trans. J. Z. Lauterbach (Philadelphia: Jewish Publication Society, 1933–35).

Midrash Debarim Rabbah, ed. S. Liebermann (Jerusalem: Wahrmann, 1974, 3d edition).

Siphre D'be Rab [Numbers], 2d edition, ed. H. S. Horovitz (Jerusalem: Wahrmann, 1966).

The Tosefta, ed. S. Liebermann (New York: Jewish Theological Seminary of
America, 1955–88).

Tosephta, ed. M. S. Zuckermandel (Trier, 1881).

Many traditional works, from the Mishnah to rabbinic responsa and
novellae, are available in numerous editions (including electronic versions),
and we saw no reason to refer the reader to one edition and its pagination
rather than to another. Instead, we follow the practice that is common for
biblical citations, providing references by section (and subsection, when appropriate) in accordance with the original or traditional division of a work.
As a rule, the original subdivisions of a text are reproduced in the body of
the readings. We depart from this rule only for the biblical readings, for including the verse numbers would detract too much from the natural flow of
the texts. But here, too, we remain true to the Hebrew, for in the traditional
scrolls there is no division into chapters or verses.

The Translators

The work of translation in this volume—as for the project as a
whole—has been a collective effort. The contributions of those who translated texts from various languages and of experts who helped verify specific
translations are acknowledged in notes to the relevant texts. Final editing
of all translations was done jointly by Menachem Lorberbaum and Noam
Zohar.

Ancient Rabbinic texts were translated mostly by Noam Zohar. On
many matters of Rabbinic usage, we had the privilege of consulting with
Shlomo Naeh. Modern texts and medieval responsa were translated mostly
by Menachem Lorberbaum. Rabbinic commentaries were translated mostly
by Ari Ackerman, who also translated some of the responsa. In addition,
Ari Ackerman helped in verifying the consistency of language and form
throughout.

Menachem Lorberbaum and Noam J. Zohar

Law, Story, and Interpretation:
Reading Rabbinic Texts

The guiding framework of rabbinic practice is a political order founded upon a divine covenant and its obligations. This covenant, of biblical origin, establishes the community as a sacral fellowship under God. All legitimate actions have coherence and integrity within this order, whereas illegitimate actions disrupt and desacralize the polity. According to Scripture, the prophet Moses first mediated between the divine and human realms as a founding legislator; in due course rabbinic tradition proclaimed itself the heir of this legislation, and has deliberated its contents for more than two millennia. Tradition is therefore the cumulative construction of belief and practice that actualizes the founding revelation for the ongoing community. Indeed, tradition is the evolving shape (or shapes) of the ancient covenant, embracing every sphere of life and placing it under divine dominion.

With the historical unfolding of Jewish life from biblical times to the present, the ancient covenant has been challenged by changing values and circumstances. New actions and rulings were developed—naturally, as life was lived in fluid faithfulness to covenantal regulations, and deliberately, as the biblical text was explicated in light of living circumstances and legal gaps. The result of the natural development was customary practice, all or part of which could be legitimated by Scripture. The result of the deliberate development was an accretion of commentaries and regulations that could serve as expressions of tradition in different circles and times. Each type produced distinct genres of rules and practices. The tradition is the accumulation of these genres, and often their agglutination and harmonization. In addition to the Hebrew Bible, the foundation document of the covenant, there are the scriptural expositions of legal and homiletical Midrash, the abstract rulings collected in the canonical Mishnah or in extra-canonical collections like the Tosefta, as well as the collation of all such materials in the two Talmuds (Jerusalem and Babylonian). The analytical syntheses of talmudic rules by the tosafists, the abstract or annotated codes of Sephardic and Ashkenazic legists, the novellae of jurists and theorists, and the ongoing answers (responsa) to halakhic queries are typical of activities continuing through the Middle Ages to the present time.

The details of this literary corpus are voluminous, vibrant testimony to the enduring self-consciousness of Jews as a covenantal community. With practical wisdom, if no little irony, the principle that "the *halakhah* (or legal norm) follows the latest authorities" kept the scales of jurisprudence tipped toward the present. But this was hardly an evasion of tradition, for "the latest authorities" were always the heirs of an earlier wisdom. The products of rabbinic education and values, these sages tried to regenerate tradition from within, being always attentive to its spirit and letter in new times. A classical homily by Rabbi Eleazar ben Azaria (who flourished toward the end of the first century C.E.) attests to the antiquity and probity of the process. He expounded as follows on Ecclesiastes 12:11, which reads: "The words of the wise are like goads, and like nails well planted are the [words of] masters of assemblies, which are given by one Shepherd."

> Why are the words of the Torah likened to a "goad"? To teach you that just as this goad directs the heifer along its furrow in order to bring life to the world, so the words of the Torah direct those who study them from the paths of death to the paths of life. But [lest you think] that just as the goad is movable so the words of the Torah are movable [and hence impermanent], therefore the text says "nails." And [should you also think] that just as the nail [does not] diminish and does not increase, so too the words of the Torah [do not] diminish and do not increase; therefore the text says "well planted": just as a plant is fruitful and increases, so the words of the Torah are fruitful and increase. "The masters of assemblies": these are the disciples of the wise who sit in manifold assemblies and occupy themselves with the Torah, some declaring [a matter] unclean and others declaring [it] clean, some prohibiting [a matter] and others permitting [it], some disqualifying [a person from giving testimony or acting as a priest] and others declaring [that same one] fit [to serve].

> Now should one say: Given all this, how shall I learn Torah? Therefore the text says: "All of them are given from one Shepherd." One God gave them; one leader uttered them from the mouth of

the Lord of all creation, blessed be He, for it is written: "And God spoke all these words" (Exod. 20:1). In like manner should you make your ear like a hopper and get a perceptive heart to understand the words of those who declare unclean and the words of those who declare clean, the words of those who prohibit and the words of those who permit, [and] the words of those who disqualify and the words of those who declare fit. (BT Hagigah 3b)

This exegetical passage articulates the very basis of covenantal theology: the nature and authority of Torah and the nature and authority of its exposition. It does so through a reinterpretation of Ecclesiastes 12:11 and Exodus 20:1. Indeed, this conjunction of different verses is the essence of classical midrashic homilies, which regularly open with a verse from the Writings (often the Psalms or the wisdom texts) and use it to give new meaning to a passage from the Torah portion prescribed for a given Shabbat. In the present instance, verse 11 from Ecclesiastes 12 is explicated to unfold the ideology that Torah is one, despite its great diversity of content and commentary. And just this truth is presumed to inhere in the pentateuchal proclamation that God spoke "all" these words at Sinai—both the words of Scripture and all their subsequent meanings.

One may sense that Rabbi Eleazar had more than theory in mind. The parsimony and ambiguity of Torah readily lent itself to diverse exegetical possibilities—without which the text could become a dead letter but with which the student was set loose from authoritative restraint. In this homily the danger of exegetical chaos is doubly circumscribed, first by a theology that held the words of Scripture to have multiple meanings and then by a daring anthropology of probity and goodwill. Only thus could the unalterable words of Torah nurture new fruit, and only thus could the work of culture be transformed into covenantal labor. The result was a notion of revelation as fixed and unchanging, yet full and total, and of tradition as fluid and open, yet always partial and contradictory. In the dynamic between revelation and tradition, difference is an inherent feature of human meaning-making. In Rabbi Eleazar's view, such diversity need not destroy Torah or its study; it may, in fact, even be vaunted as necessary for understanding "all" God's words. In this sense, debate is "for the sake of heaven."

Rabbinic literature is grounded in the Hebrew Bible in theory and in fact. Indeed, Scripture provides the foundational framework for the Rabbis' teachings of law and theology. It is the canonical text of instruction, at whose core is the written Torah (called *oraita*)—believed to be divine revelation in every respect. Everything else is oral tradition, however ancient and however related to the written revelation at Sinai. The chain of tradition therefore begins with Moses and his first disciple, Joshua, continues through the elders and prophets to Ezra and the Men of the Great Assembly (after the Babylonian exile), and goes on from them to the sages and their disciples, and the disciples of their disciples, to the present day. In this ideal formulation there are no gaps, only stages in the realization of the tradition of the Rabbis (called *rabbanan*).

Law and narrative are the two main genres of the biblical foundation. Both are traditional, edited genres and part and parcel of the ancient Near Eastern world. This is particularly so for the legal texts found in the Torah, collected over centuries and with different emphases and formulations. They are rooted in Mesopotamian legal traditions with respect to literary forms and many of the specified cases; yet they are also the fruit of an internal Israelite tradition of topics and concerns, one that was successively revised and supplemented in different circles during a half-millennium and more. This diversity of collections and content attests to the vitality of the biblical tradition, yet it also left legal gaps, ambiguities, and duplication of content. Just how was one to "observe" the Sabbath day, and what was "no manner of work"? Was the purchase and sale of a slave (whether native or foreign) administered by the courts or privately? And what about conflicting rules of the Passover sacrifice, or the apparent brutality and injustice of the ancient law of *talion* (retribution, "an eye for an eye")? Clearly, much was left to (oral) judicial discretion and (unwritten) popular custom.

As the traditions of ancient Israel were collected into canonical units, and the units into an authoritative anthology, these sorts of issues demanded theoretical and practical resolution—through the direct explication of Scripture (Midrash), through more abstract formulations of rules (with and without scriptural support), and through customary action. The concurrence of these processes was the natural outgrowth of a living legal culture, giving rise to the wealth of traditions and practices that we largely know about from later sources. The schools of sages entrusted with the more formal work of interpretation and adjudication gradually produced a series of exegetical rules, as well as exemplary collections of discussions and regulations. The norms were named and nuanced, and the evolving result constituted Judaism for those who followed this school or that, one group or another.

Alongside the law and often encasing it are literary units that give expression to the theological and ideological values of the covenant. This pertains particularly to such matters as divine authority and communal obligation, but also to legislative intent (as in making the polity "holy") and contractual consent (enunciated as "we shall do and obey") (Exod. 24:7). It should be added that these vital considerations are not expressed abstractly but in the course of the historical narration; even matters concerning, for example, the nature of the person, the dangers of sedition, or the motivations for compassion or largesse are formulated in and around specific laws, rarely as formal principles for general application. For the late, post-exilic strata of biblical literature (after 538 B.C.E.), this ideological content even included observations on the spiritual or transformative character of the law. The result was the reinforcement of the legal norms by covenantal values, and the generation of cultural ideology by living law. In this way, the Torah provided a vast store of pedagogy for the faithful.

The ancient rabbis deal with legal and theological issues in accordance with oral tradition, stylistic convention, and diversity of opinion; the biblical sources are not always given, depending on genre, and even when they are, they do not always represent the chief features of the formulation. Primary among the classical genres are the Mishnah, Midrash, and Gemara.

The Mishnah is the quintessential collection of tannaitic case law, reflecting legal traditions of the first two centuries of the Common Era; it was edited by Rabbi Judah "the Prince" in the early third century C.E. Its lapidary formulations, attributed to named or unspecified sages, are expressed in abstract terms, with reference to typical situations, and through a hierarchy of topics. Some of the issues and their sequence clearly derive from the biblical legal sources, while others may only be inferred from them but may have arisen independently. Characteristically, these formulations are not linked to Scripture as either derived or justified law; in addition, differences of opinion are simply listed, not compared or justified (although the sequence of presentation often points to the preferred opinions). In the process of collation and publication, a great mass of contemporary material was excluded from the Mishnah. Some of the extraneous teachings (called *baraitot,* sing. *baraita*) are collected in a corpus called the Tosefta, which also includes expansions or clarifications of mishnaic rules.

The Midrash includes legal and homiletical genres (*midrash halakhah* and *midrash aggadah,* respectively). In the legal Midrash of the tannaitic and amoraic periods (first to second and third to fourth centuries C.E., respectively), the topics are linked to passages in the Torah—first, because these texts collect traditions around the sequence of biblical verses; and second, because different opinions and proofs are adduced in the course of the reported discussions. The discussions sometimes start from a fixed point of tradition (itself not clearly related to Scripture) and proceed to debate alternatives with scriptural arguments. In other cases the scriptural formulation is justified by other scriptural rules or potential inferences. The reasoning on which the discussions rest is variously formulated in terms of hermeneutical rules. These include procedures for reasoning a fortiori, from the simple to the complex or the specific to the general (and vice versa), and by analogy (thematic or verbal). The materials are transmitted either in the name of specific sages or anonymously by the editor. Disagreements are not necessarily resolved.

The Gemara is the third major genre of classical Jewish literature. This is the term for the collection of learning found in the Babylonian Talmud, on the topics of the Mishnah, the Midrash, and the extraneous or non-canonical traditions. Built formally around the tannaitic Mishnah, and including a wealth of tannaitic and amoraic citations and discussions, this material extends in named traditions to the late fifth century C.E. and, in subsequent redactional layers known as stammaitic and saboraic, for about two centuries more. The stammaitic contribution is particularly important, because the so-called anonymous (teacher), or *stam,* is the editorial voice of the received collection. Indeed, given the importance of the Babylonian Talmud in the curriculum of the rabbinical academies for fifteen hundred years and its impact on subsequent codes and precedents, it is no exaggeration to say that this anonymous person (or people—for smaller pericopes, called *sugyot,* were edited in different schools) is the formative teacher of Jewish tradition *tout court.* The voluminous corpus far exceeds in cultural impact the shorter and more imperfectly transmitted Jerusalem Talmud (the Talmud of the Land of Israel).

A preliminary characterization of the Gemara must take note of its more formal features. These include, first and foremost, the citation of the Mishnah as the source for discussion, together with a patient and often pains-taking inquiry into its implied biblical sources (to construct the scriptural authority of the ruling) and the legal ramifications to be deduced therefrom. As the mishnaic phrase is analyzed, hypothetical possibilities are broached and their implications weighed, and all this is regularly synthesized (through dialectical reasoning) with diverse traditions bearing on the clarification or harmonization of the subject. Hypothetical cases test the solidity of a pro-posed legal construction and often work to expand or contract the scope of the law, justify a given ruling, or establish new concepts for gray areas of concern.

The *stam* editorially coordinates this discourse and brings the opin-ions of sages and traditions far removed in time and place into one interactive study session. By adroitly adducing opinions and contradictions or assess-ing the strength of a rebuttal, he constructs (even reconstructs) models of textual reasoning of theoretical and practical use to legal students or future theorists. The rhetorical tone moves swiftly and often obscurely between the named traditions and the interlocuting *stam,* creating a rich intergen-erational discourse. Accordingly, if there is a "mind" in the Talmud, it is the mind of the *stam,* who thinks through the traditions, citing and criticizing them through other voices and deliberating their implications with respect to religious action—for all behavior has a legal dimension in the covenantal polity of Judaism. In this respect, the *stam* is the ideal student: capacious in knowledge, probing in analysis, and careful to protect the law or to synthe-size it where necessary. The *stam* thinks with the tradition and its tradents and thereby offers a cognitive model of covenantal hermeneutics. The medieval tosafists build on this method in their conceptual and comparative analyses of the talmudic traditions as a whole.

To gain a concrete sense of Rabbinic hermeneutics in its diverse forms of expression and to appreciate the exegetical patterns of thought in their thick textuality, the following examples are instructive. They have the particular value of displaying the complex interactions between law and ideology in the Rabbinic sources. Given that Rabbinic culture is constructed and justified through its cases, the examples provide a window into its world of meaning-making. Here is the first.

By all standards, the biblical assertion that "God made man in His own image" (Gen.1:27) has been of fundamental importance for Jewish conceptions of the nature of the person and for issues bearing on agency and the value of life. In itself, the meaning of the word "image" is obscure and has led to any number of interpretations in ethical, philosophical, and mystical thought. Ideas range from an insistence on the unique creaturely status of the human person to an emphasis on human rationality or on the mythic character of the human form. This aside, the notion of the divine image is employed as a *Grundnorm* (not itself requiring justification) that establishes a hierarchy in which human life is the supreme value—the pivot of the whole legal system of civil and capital cases.

The first reuse of the principle is an instance of inner-biblical exegesis. It occurs at the end of the flood narrative, in which restored humanity is blessed and promised fertility and worldly power in terms directly borrowed from the creation account chapters earlier; the major revision to be noted is the extension to humans of the right to eat animal flesh in addition to the original diet of grains and greens (see Gen. 9:1–3; compare 1:28–30). This permission to eat "every creature that lives" is itself qualified only by a categorical prohibition "not to eat flesh with its life blood in it"—a further taxonomy of edible creatures is not yet provided. The topic of "life blood" evokes an additional regulation: "But for your own life blood I [God] will require a reckoning: I will require it of every beast; of man, too, I will require a reckoning for human life, of every man for that of his fellow man! Whoever sheds the blood of man, by man shall his blood be shed; for in His image did God make man" (Gen. 9:5–6).

As is evident, this final formulation shifts the focus from food rules (and permissible killing) to capital offenses (and their categorical prohibition by animal or human agency). A clear hierarchy is established, with animal life below all forms of human life and available for consumption without penalty. Moreover, like humans, animals are culpable for killing humans—

and this is because of the principle that human beings are created in the divine image. Because the passage opens with the divine legislator speaking in the first person ("I will require") but shifts in its justification clause to the third person ("for in His image did God make man"), it is clear that the author has cited the theological assertion of Genesis 1:27 and applied it as a principle to legal cases. The older narrative is now reembedded in a later one, whose concerns reflect a complex social order.

Biblical and Rabbinic law go on to qualify the degrees of culpable agency (for animals and persons) and to explicate the penalties (and permissible substitutions) that may be assessed after judgment. Rabbinic law also takes this *Grundnorm* and applies it (with new scriptural sources) in warnings to witnesses about to testify in capital cases. The exegetical justifications for these warnings are striking, and show how a legal narrative may incorporate values fundamental to the polity. The text is found in Mishnah Sanhedrin (4:5), dealing with courts and procedures.

> How do [the judges] admonish the witnesses in capital cases? They would bring them in and admonish them [thus]: "Perhaps you are about to offer [testimony] based on supposition, hearsay, or what one witness told another; or [you would say,] 'We have heard it from a reliable person'; or perhaps you do not know that we shall eventually subject you to a thorough interrogation and investigation. You should [therefore] know that the laws governing property cases [*mamonot*] do not [extend] equally to capital ones. In property cases a person makes payment and [thereby] achieves atonement, [whereas] in capital cases [guilt for] the blood [*dam,* of the falsely convicted person] and his [unborn] offspring is held against [the witness] for all time. For so we find in the case of Cain, who killed his brother, as it is said: 'The bloods of your brother cry' (Gen. 4:10). It does not say 'The *blood* [*dam*] of your brother' but 'The *bloods* [*demey*] of your brother'—[that is,] his blood and the blood of his offspring for all time. . . . Therefore Adam was created alone, to teach you that whoever destroys a single life is deemed by Scripture as if he had destroyed a whole world; and whoever saves a single life is deemed by Scripture as if he had saved a whole world."

Three components of this legal extract are immediately obvious: the concise, lapidary form of mishnaic expression; the rhetorical, homiletical form of midrashic argumentation; and the multivoiced, embedded quality of the tradition. To begin with the last, one must note the levels of direct and indirect speech. The mishnah is in the voice of the scholastic redactor addressing himself to judges who will appraise the witnesses of their task and its implications. The redactor gives words to the judges and imagines (through indirect speech) the thinking of a witness, and then cites Scripture, whose authoritative voice is made applicable through midrashic exegesis. The instructive tenor of the primary voice is then gradually and fundamentally subsumed by the didactic voice of the judges, who draw their conclusions with a direct voice ("Therefore Adam was created alone, *to teach you*").

The mishnaic account is characteristically formulaic and precise. The terminology is completely Rabbinic, even when drawn from biblical prototypes. The reference to "interrogation and examination" (*derishah ve-hakirah*) is a case in point. These nouns reflect the development of abstract legal concepts in rabbinic jurisprudence—even though they ultimately derive from verbal usage in Scripture. Both terms occur in Deuteronomy 13:15, in connection with the investigation of reported apostasy; only the first is found in Deuteronomy 19:15–19, though significantly in the context of a regulation requiring the investigation of witnesses. Clearly the mishnaic procedure has a biblical past, even though the precise biblical procedures are unknown.

One may further observe that this warning to witnesses before their examination establishes testimony as a legal act with consequences. By informing them of the factors bearing on unacceptable evidence, the judges make the witnesses responsible for their statements. Such fundamental categories as agency and foreknowledge are often embedded in the judicial procedures themselves, and their scope and meaning must be explicated from these sources. The deduction and testing of such abstractions is the work of talmudic reasoning.

The midrashic component of the judges' warning demonstrates other features of interest. Primary among them is the invocation of a scriptural source to support the theological assertion about the long-term effects of a death caused by false testimony. In making the point, the judge functions as a homilist—first asserting his theological claim and then justifying it through exegesis. The hermeneutical procedure used here is straightforward. It first observes a lexical or stylistic anomaly in Scripture, then, instead of explaining it away as mere metaphor or rhetorical excess, treats it literally and, by this unexpected move, affirms the theological point. In this case the initiating oddity is the use of the plural noun "bloods" in the case of Cain's murder. Since it is unlikely that the idea of transgenerational guilt is sponsored by this tenuous exegesis, one may assume that the idea came first and its justification second. In the conclusion to the admonition, a related theological claim is made that each person is created alone in order to show that whoever saves or destroys an individual saves or destroys a "whole world." This assertion is apparently linked to the same piece of scriptural exegesis. The main difference between the two teachings is that now the positive aspects of true testimony are stressed: it may in fact save a life, even a world. Remarkably, this broad admonition was subsequently parochialized. In some sources, the formulation "a single *Israelite* life" replaced "a single life," and this version is now found in printed editions of the Mishnah.

The concern for moral probity emphasized by the judicial instruction puts the potential witness in mind of the moral implications of his actions. The point is pivotal. After a series of supplementary explanations as to why a person is created singly, the judges' admonition continues with the theme of civic responsibility.

> And perhaps you [witnesses] would [further] say: "Why should we [get involved in] this trouble?" Has it not already been written, "He being a witness, who has either seen or known of the matter, if he does not give report, then he shall bear his iniquity" (Lev. 5:1)? And if perhaps you would [also] say, "Why should we become accountable for this [convicted] person's blood [*dam*]?" has it not already been written, "When the wicked perish there is rejoicing" (Prov. 11:10)?

As earlier, when the judge stressed the need for probity in dealing with capital cases, so now the conscience of the witness is appealed to. A member of the community cannot evade involvement in difficult cases—either because of a desire to avoid sticky issues or because of the moral weight that such duties impose. Indeed, covenantal politics requires the individual to transcend self-interest and serve the system of justice—if not initially on the basis of eager compliance, then at least because of the authority and assurances of Scripture. In these cases the sources are simply cited. No further explanation is necessary.

As a living guide to judges, this mishnah simultaneously conveys deep cultural values. What is particularly striking is the explicit evocation of fundamental norms of the law: the unique value of each human life, and the responsibility of each person to bear true and active witness to this ideal within the community. The judges uphold these norms, but the sources of the norms lie deeper, in the words of Scripture as cited and interpreted by the sages. This is the ultimate basis of the political theology of Judaism.

A second example takes us in a different hermeneutical direction. As the guardians and teachers of Scripture, the Rabbis were often faced with authoritative but noxious or outmoded rules—and this required bold reinterpretation. Indeed, in many respects, classical Rabbinic law emerges as a massive reinscription of Scripture. The law of *talion* is a case in point. It has long been a crucial but difficult topic, bearing as it does on the rationale for retributive justice. At issue is the principle and practice of compensation for bodily injury, the measure of just exchange for death and damages. Biblical law provides a drastic formulation. Surely the language of "life for life, eye for eye, tooth for tooth, hand for hand, foot for foot, burn for burn, wound for wound, bruise for bruise" (Exod. 21:23–25) seems to leave little room for reinterpretation—particularly if one regards this list as literal and comprehensive or as literal and paradigmatic. So construed, it articulates a series of vicious penalties that would sorely test the limits of social restraint (where administered through self-help) or judicial power (where administered through the courts); and it seemingly offers no mitigating mechanisms for accident, third-party involvement, double jeopardy, and the like.

Perhaps in part for these reasons, and also because of the highly rhetorical style of the list, one might suppose that the biblical rule was never intended to be taken literally, but rather enumerates a rhetorical list of bodily injuries (*x* for *x*; *y* for *y*) to suggest that all torts must be suitably compensated for, and in a way corresponding to the degree or effect of the specific wound involved—for example, the loss of a foot would require compensation for immediate and long-range economic loss due to the permanent disability and for such other medical or social matters (like stigmatization) as may be pertinent. Now there is no way to determine how the rule was read and applied in ancient Israel, but it is fair to say that some such construction of its meaning would seem to underlie the following mishnah, in which injuries are clearly and without qualification rectified by the assessment of financial penalties.

> One who injures his fellow is liable on five counts: Damage, Pain, Cure, Idleness, and Shame.
>
> What is the [liability for] Damage? If he blinded his eye, or cut off his hand, or broke his leg—he is considered as though he were a slave on sale in the market, and is assessed: how much was he worth, and how much is he worth [now]?
>
> Pain: If he burned him with a skewer or [stabbed him] with a nail, even upon his fingernail, where no bruise is produced, they estimate how much a person such as this would want to receive in order to endure such pain.
>
> Cure: In the wake of the injury, he must cure him. . . .
> (Mishnah Bava Kama 8:1)

This excerpt is sufficient to show the shift in style and substance between the biblical rules and the Rabbinic regulations. In particular, the mishnah is formulated as a list that gives advice to judges; therefore, typical issues are mentioned in the different cases, and there is no attempt at a comprehensive formulation. Nor is everything in the fivefold list of possible indemnifications mentioned in Scripture. Whereas damage to limbs or other bodily parts is covered by the biblical rule of *talion,* and the categories of medical costs and loss of income (cure and idleness) are biblical as well (Exod. 21:19), the issues of pain and shame (or indignity) are Rabbinic innovations. In any event, Scripture is not quoted in this excerpt in support of the rules (although it is adduced later in connection with indirect injuries), and there is no justification whatever for the use of monetary compensation in all cases of injury. The fact that just assessments have their own difficulties—particularly in the slippery cases of indignity, where the compensation varies "according to both the person causing shame and the person shamed"—is another matter. Clearly, regulating the conditions of bias or fairness was deemed of lesser difficulty than regulating *talion* itself.

The almost complete absence of explicit scriptural justifications of mishnaic rules might lead one to suppose that the written law (Torah) and the Oral Law (tradition) were separate, and that the authority of Rabbinic law lay solely with the jurists. The fact that most of the topics of the Mishnah are indebted to Scripture does not change this point in principle. What is striking in this regard is that when the sages (in legal Midrash and in the Gemara) justify a mishnaic regulation on the basis of Scripture, their procedure is often speculative and its results diverse. Fixed and acknowledged links are not the rule. This is also and notably the case in connection with the arguments adduced from Scripture to justify compensation for injuries. All the pyrotechnics of Rabbinic hermeneutics are necessary to turn the trick. One may also observe a concern to establish regulatory principles. Portions of the opening discussion may suffice to give a sense of the rhetoric involved and of the struggle to justify the received mishnah through scriptural proof. Being aware of this concern also helps explain the often arbitrary choice of one argument over another in a given *sugya* (pericope).

Let us first review the following discussion, which opens the Gemara and comes right after citation of the foregoing mishnah on injuries.

Why so [pay compensation]? "Eye for eye" is what Scripture says; perhaps it is really an eye! No, that is untenable. As has been taught: "Can it be that if he blinded his eye, he blinds his eye; if he cut off his hand, he cuts off his hand; if he broke his leg, he breaks his leg? We learn from what is written, 'one who strikes a person' and 'one who strikes a beast' (Lev. 24:17–21). Just as he who strikes a beast makes payment, so he who strikes a person makes payment.

"If you prefer, it can be argued [thus]: Scripture reads, 'You may not accept a ransom for the life of a murderer who is guilty of a capital crime' (Num. 35:31). For the life of a murderer you may not accept a ransom—but you may accept a ransom for [even] important limbs that will not recover." . . .

What [creates the need for] "If you prefer . . ."? The *tanna* [teacher] was yet concerned over the retort, "What grounds have you for learning from one who strikes a beast? Why not learn from one who strikes a person [i.e., a murderer]?" Well, [against that] one may argue that the inference should be from damages to damages, not from death to damages. Conversely [one may argue that] the inference should be from human to human [victim], not from beast to human. That is why he teaches [further], "If you prefer, it can be argued [thus]: Scripture reads, 'You may not accept a ransom for the life of a murderer.' . . ."

But is that [verse] not required to pronounce that we may not take money from him and let him off?—For that it would be sufficient to write "You may not accept a ransom for [one] who is guilty of a capital crime"; why [add] "the life of a murderer"? This implies, "For the life of a murderer you may not accept a ransom— but you may accept a ransom for [even] important limbs that will not recover." (BT Bava Kama 83b)

This initial portion of an extensive *sugya* deals with the central question raised by the mishnah: How could rabbinic tradition formulate rules about financial compensation when divine writ seems to require physical retaliation? The *stam* steps in and immediately offers a counterargument from the tradition itself ("as has been taught"), in which a verbal analogy in Scripture ("strikes—strikes") is invoked to draw conclusions from the case of striking animals (where compensation is the rule) to that of smiting persons. This argument seems reasonable enough, and the "just . . . so" formulation brings the point to rhetorical closure. Nevertheless, the discussion turns to another proposal ("if you prefer"), drawing large implications regarding injuries from a rule prohibiting ransom for a murderer. The rhetorical logic is even more tenuous in this second case (putting special emphasis on what *is* stated—no ransom for one guilty of murder—in order to draw the inference that payment is permitted for bodily injury); and this time only one biblical text is adduced. The double proof underscores the concern of Rabbinic tradition to prove from Scripture that the literal meaning of *talion* is untenable.

In a characteristic way the *sugya* proceeds to examine the demonstrations, testing the reasonableness and implications of the arguments as well as the force of the scriptural formulations. As can be observed from the foregoing citation, one line of speculation was to query why a second proof was necessary at all and why a biblical verse was chosen that emphasizes only human beings (Num. 35:31). The proposition is put forth that the supplementary proof was invoked to counter a potential weak spot in the first proof, which is grounded in an analogy comparing animals and humans. To that retort we hear a voice claiming that the passage from Numbers really seems to have a different legal bite, and that is to prevent the manslayer from giving a payment of money to the victim's kin and going scot-free. This reading of the verse makes inherent good (and literal) sense, but it is rejected in a way that reinforces the earlier proof. The interlocutor says that if Scripture (i.e., the divine legislator) wished simply to prohibit a murderer from paying his way out of capital punishment, the language of the rule would have been formulated with that point in mind. As it is, the wording seems redundant—"why [does Scripture add] 'the life of a murderer'?" The answer given is that the law wished us to draw an inference about compensation, namely, that a ransom is prohibited in cases of murder but is permissible in cases of damage to limbs. The assumption of this resolution is that the law is formulated in a precise and careful way and that it is the task of tradition to penetrate the intention of the Legislator and draw the proper generalizations and principles for noxious or impenetrable cases.

The tenuous nature of these arguments and assertions is obvious, for every solution is subject to further analysis. In addition, numerous other proposals are considered. They too are sensible and ingenious by turns— invoking in some instances the need for a unified principle of compensation against the potential injustice of physical retribution. Indeed, says Rabbi Dostai, to argue for literal and equal retribution can lead to absurdities or make the law wholly unworkable. Where would justice lie in a case where the eye of one person was big and that of another small—how could one apply the principle of "eye for eye"? Rabbi Shimon bar Yohai even presents the problem of a blind tortfeasor who puts out the eye of his neighbor, and of an armless person who cuts off the arm of another person. If the rule of *talion* be taken literally, how should one act in such case? And on and on— but without either certain resolution or conclusive scriptural warrant.

One may conclude that the entire *sugya* functions at best as a compendium of scholastic solutions in which a defense of tradition is the goal. In fact, the display of tradition at work to justify itself may be its real pedagogical purpose. The culture thus bears witness to its own passion for justice by its repeated attempt to establish fair procedures and rules and to its legal mind by the rigorous scrutiny of its own arguments and assumptions. The *stam* serves here as the mind and voice of past generations and as the hermeneutical model for future students who would learn how to think traditionally. This is arguably the greatest gift of Gemara to the culture.

This hermeneutical diversity brings us back to the pointed query of Rabbi Eleazar ben Azaria, How can one learn Torah if there are many solutions and no final judge? The answers of the rabbinic legal tradition may vary, but they all depend on the virtues of probity and patience and the will to know. These virtues produce a culture of exegetical intensity and debate, of conflicts and contradictions. By producing texts that display its paideia in full view (the interpretations, the debates, and the conflicts), the literary tradition demonstrates publicly the nature and limitations of its exegetical solutions and the way different exegetical procedures justify diverse models of the person and society. The covenantal polity of Judaism is thus shaped by the expansion and contraction of the Torah—through the expansion and contraction of ongoing tradition.

Michael Fishbane

Abbreviations

ℭ	chapter; used to refer to chapters in *The Jewish Political Tradition*
§	selection; used to refer to selections in *The Jewish Political Tradition*
b.	ben/bar (= son of)
BT	Babylonian Talmud
1 Chron.	1 Chronicles
2 Chron.	2 Chronicles
Dan.	Daniel
Deut.	Deuteronomy
Eccles.	Ecclesiastes
Exod.	Exodus
Ezek.	Ezekiel
Gen.	Genesis
Hab.	Habakkuk
Hag.	Haggai
Hos.	Hosea
Isa.	Isaiah
Jer.	Jeremiah
Jon.	Jonah
Josh.	Joshua
JPS	Jewish Publication Society
JT	Jerusalem Talmud
Judg.	Judges
Lam.	Lamentations
Lev.	Leviticus
1 Macc.	1 Maccabees
Mal.	Malachi
Mic.	Micah
MT	*Mishneh Torah* (The Code of Maimonides)
Nah.	Nahum

Neh.	Nehemiah
Num.	Numbers
Obad.	Obadiah
Prov.	Proverbs
Ps.	Psalms
R.	Rabbi/Rav
1 Sam.	1 Samuel
2 Sam.	2 Samuel
Song of Sol.	Song of Solomon
YJS	Yale Judaica Series
Zech.	Zechariah
Zeph.	Zephaniah

The Jewish Political Tradition
VOLUME I Authority

Introduction

Judaism is a God-centered and then a text-centered religion, which is to say that it starts with the boldest and most far-reaching of all authority claims. An omnipotent God has delivered a sacred text. God speaks or at least has spoken; the text can be read. What more is necessary in the way of authority? In fact, God and text are only the beginning, for God requires — this is the Jewish understanding — a people prepared to listen to and obey his words; and the text in which those words are preserved must be interpreted, elaborated, and applied: mere reading is not enough. How is this people to be organized and led? Who will speak for God in its courts, assemblies, and schools? What structure of human authority is required by divine and textual authority? These are the questions that we will address in this first volume of *The Jewish Political Tradition:* they are quintessentially political questions.

We begin with the acceptance of the text by the people, without which — so it appears — God would have gone unheard in the world. Given God's omnipotence, there are many difficulties about this acceptance, amply revealed in the stories and arguments reprinted here. Nonetheless, much hangs on the dramatic moment at Sinai when the people said, "We will do and we will obey." Here the idea of consent enters Jewish thought, where it plays a large and ongoing part — but not the only part. The moral laws of the Torah are not only *revealed* (and freely accepted); they are also, for many Jewish writers, *rational* (hence, necessarily accepted). The precise character of this rationality and whether or how it characterizes the ritual laws — these are questions much debated. But law has in any case a double authority, which is explored in our first two chapters.

After that, we consider the various human agents who have claimed at different points in Jewish history to exercise political or legal authority. Our interest is in the claims; although the chapters follow a rough chronological order, we do not offer a history of authority relations. The agents themselves are best grouped for our purposes into two categories, those who claim to represent, as it were, God and the law, and those who claim to represent the people or the community. Priests, prophets, and sages fall into the first category; ancient kings (some of the time), "the good men of the town," and the democratically elected rulers of contemporary Israel fall into the second. The first set of agents speak for a religious interest, the second, at least potentially, for a secular interest. One critical question, reiterated in different versions in ancient, medieval, and modern texts is whether or, more realistically, how and how far a religious tradition can accommodate secular authority.

Two chapters are anomalous. In our discussion of gentile rulers (C9), we do not present or examine their own claims to rule over their exiled and dispersed Jewish subjects but rather the account of their authority and of the limits of that authority given by Jewish writers. (The chapter on the gentile state is closely connected to Chapter 27, in Volume IV, on the idea of exile.) And we have doubled our discussion of the sages. Because they ruled by arguing among themselves about the meaning and application of the law (as priests and prophets rarely did, at least in public), we have added a chapter (7) on the extent of permissible argument. Readers can get some sense from the texts reprinted there of the critical connection between textual authority and interpretive pluralism.

It is important to stress in advance that there is no single maxim governing authority relations in the Jewish world. There is no single court of appeal when authority is disputed. Popular agreement is always important, though it is as often a limit as it is a foundation. But biblical kingship and priesthood were hereditary; the prophets were divinely called; the sages were, in modern jargon, meritocrats; the "good men" were most often oligarchs. The question of how writers who took the Sinai covenant as their starting point made sense of all this requires a complex and nuanced answer.

Introduction

Many of the central issues of modern consent theory are already posed in biblical and Rabbinic literature. Reading these texts, one has to keep reminding oneself that their authors were not consent theorists and that a covenant with God is not the same thing as a social contract. Contract and convenant indeed have similar effects—creating political unity and moral obligation—and at least some of the writers represented in this chapter seem to believe that the obligation to obey God's law derives, and can only derive, from the people's consent. But God is no equal or near equal, like all the other parties to the social contract; nor do the people, when they consent, "give the law to themselves" (as in Rousseau's version of contract theory)—they accept the law as God gives it. And how free can their acceptance be, when the divine lawgiver is absolute and omnipotent?

In the different midrashic elaborations of the Sinai story, only sampled here, God is sometimes seen persuading the people to accept his law (the prophet Hosea describes him wooing Israel like a lover) and sometimes threatening and coercing them. The first is the more attractive account; the second is theoretically more interesting, for the Rabbis, or some of them, recognize that coerced consent is not morally or legally binding. So they are driven to look for some later occasion when consent is given voluntarily—and they find this only in the next to last chapter of the book of Esther, where the acceptance of the laws of Purim by the exilic community of Persian Jews is taken as a general acceptance of the law itself—for all future time (see Esther 9:27). But they surely don't imagine that Israel was uncommitted and without obligation from the days of Moses to those of Ahasuerus. If that were the case, the prophetic condemnations of Israel for failing to live up to the Sinai covenant would make no sense.

In any case, whether or not God waits upon Israel's consent at Sinai or at any other time, it is clear that he need not wait at all if he does not choose to do so: he can guarantee consent by inscribing his law not on stone tablets but directly on the human heart, as Jeremiah says he will do in the days to come (31:33). Similarly, although this is not taken up in our texts, he can guarantee rejection, as he apparently has in the past, "hardening the heart," for example, of Egypt's pharaoh. And He can compel obedience whether his commandments have been accepted or rejected, as Ezekiel makes clear in the text reprinted below. In a world of absolute power, consent is always problematic.

Nonetheless, it is a matter of considerable importance that God's revelation, according to many writers, must be received and accepted before it is morally binding. In the biblical account, this view is fairly clear, but at Sinai there is also an epiphany—a sudden, overwhelming, and irresistible manifestation of divine power. In the midrashic parables, the Sinai events take on a rather different character. In one midrash, for example, we have God bringing the Israelites out of Egypt and providing water in the desert to win their gratitude: they agree to obey his law because he has proven himself a good king. In another, by contrast, we have God carrying his law from one nation to another; he is a lawgiver who finds no takers until he comes to Israel (but why is Israel so far down his list?). And yet another midrash describes the people assembled at the foot of the mountain to listen to a reading of the law—not just the Ten Commandments but the whole of the Torah—before they accept it. The moment is certainly solemn, but now the epiphany is omitted entirely; God's frightening power is hidden, as if the people can deliberate only in its absence, which is exactly what consent theory would require.

The most striking feature of this Jewish understanding of consent is its historical specificity. Israel does not accept God's law in some imaginary state of nature but at a precise moment in its history and in a real place. To be sure, this moment (after the deliverance from Egyptian bondage) and this place (an uninhabited wilderness) anticipate many of the features of the state of nature—as Spinoza points out. Israel has neither a regime nor a territory, so it is uniquely situated for a freely enacted construction of the political world. But the point of the biblical narrative is that the people are really there; the construction is something that really happened. The people's consent is in no sense hypothetical; it is not the sort of consent that any rational person would give in idealized circumstances; it is the consent that a particular group of men and women actually did give.

They are bound only because they gave it. But they then face the precise difficulty that hypothetical consent is designed to avoid: How can they be sure that subsequent generations will find their consent comprehensible and justified and so reiterate it? The Deuteronomic account of the covenant renewal in Moab just before the crossing of the Jordan into Canaan specifies that the participants include "those who are standing here with us this day . . . and [also] those who are not with us here this day" (29:14). The latter group presumably includes the unborn, all the future children of Israel. But how can they be bound by their parents' consent (or their great-great-grandparents')? Aware, perhaps, of this difficulty, the biblical writers describe periodic renewals of the covenant, not only in Moses' time but also in Joshua's and Josiah's and, at Ezra's instigation, after the return from Babylonia. The importance given to these events testifies to the centrality of consent in the biblical and then also in the Rabbinic imagination.

But how is this consent to be renewed and the obligation sustained after Israel's exile, when no such collective covenanting is possible? This is the question posed by Isaac Abravanel in a time of persecution and mass conversion, when Spanish Jewry endured a "second exile," and then by Maharal of Prague (Judah Loew) in the late sixteenth century, when the memory of the Spanish disaster was still fresh. The answers they gave—legalistic in the first case, metaphysical in the second—reveal the long-term effects of statelessness on Jewish political thought. Although consent may still play a part in the life of the scattered communities of the diaspora, large-scale deliberation and action in common are no longer possible for Israel as a whole. (It is worth noting that consent theory emerged in the West only with the appearance of the modern state.) Perhaps Jewish writers could have worked out an individualist account of consent, focusing on the ritual celebration of holidays like Passover and Simhat Torah or on the acceptance of benefits like the law itself and the satisfaction its observance brings in daily life. But Israel's covenant is collective from the beginning, generating obligations not only between God and humankind but between every Israelite and every other, and an individualist account of this mutuality does not seem possible.

Abravanel is aware of all these difficulties, and his statement of the problem (though not his proposed solution) is a wonderfully explicit and sophisticated expression of consent theory. He isn't very convincing, however, when he goes on to argue that consent doesn't matter very much after all, since Israel is the slave of God, liberated from the pharaoh only for the sake of divine service. If that is so, why did Moses himself, and Joshua, and Josiah, and Ezra, again and again assemble the people and seek their agreement?

Maharal's argument from the "necessity" of the Torah for cosmic order looks back to the more problematic features of medieval philosophy— only a few decades before Hobbes and Spinoza set out on a new path. Arguments of this sort are very hard to understand today (we are too far along that new path). Does Maharal mean that the cosmos is somehow constituted by Israel's acceptance of the law—which cannot therefore be contingent? But he recognizes at the same time that the acceptance must appear contingent, and therefore voluntary, to the people themselves if they are to be bound by it. Mysteriously, it is both necessary and contingent. How, then, are we to account for the frequent disobedience of the biblical Israelites or for the fact of apostasy—among Spanish Jews, for example—where cosmic necessity seems to fall away entirely?

This chapter closes with Spinoza's modernist reinterpretation of the Sinai covenant. For Spinoza, the covenant with God is purely "theoretical," for each Israelite retains an equal right to "consult" God and interpret his commands. The kingdom of God is something very close to anarchy (see Judg. 21:25, discussed in C3: "Everyone did as he pleased"). God can't have subjects of his own, for they would never know for certain, or at least they would never agree on, what he had commanded them to do—unless his words were delivered by some authoritative human being, who would then be their actual sovereign. Israel's polity, therefore, is effectively founded only when the liberated people "transfer" their rights to Moses as the recognized bearer of God's word. After that, individual Israelites are bound to obey Moses—and his successors. Spinoza carefully traces the succession, which lapses when political independence is lost. It would seem to follow from this analysis that there is no obligation at all in the conditions of the exile. Spinoza's argument accounts, obviously, for his own behavior, but it leaves the conviction of his Jewish contemporaries that they still bear the burden of the law spectacularly unaccounted for. Are they bound because they believe themselves bound? That would indeed be a kind of consent, though not quite the kind suggested by that extraordinary moment at Sinai when the people, standing together, committed themselves to God and to one another.

Biblical Covenants

The founding covenant at Sinai is constituted by revelation and consent, the giving of the Torah by God and its acceptance by the people. In the first of our selections, God pronounces the Ten Commandments; in the second, Moses conveys to the people "all the commands of the Lord and all the rules." In both, lawgiving is preceded by mutual avowals of covenantal commitment, with Moses acting throughout as mediator.

Acceptance of the Torah
1. Exodus 19:7–20:18

Moses came and summoned the elders of the people and put before them all that the Lord had commanded him. All the people answered as one, saying, "All that the Lord has spoken we will do!" And Moses brought back the people's words to the Lord. And the Lord said to Moses, "I will come to you in a thick cloud, in order that the people may hear when I speak with you and so trust you ever after." Then Moses reported the people's words to the Lord, and the Lord said to Moses, "Go to the people and warn them to stay pure today and tomorrow. Let them wash their clothes. Let them be ready for the third day; for on the third day the Lord will come down, in the sight of all the people, on Mount Sinai. You shall set bounds for the people round about, saying, 'Beware of going up the mountain or touching the border of it. Whoever touches the mountain shall be put to death: no hand shall touch him, but he shall be either stoned or shot; beast or man, he shall not live.' When the ram's horn sounds a long blast, they may go up on the mountain."

Moses came down from the mountain to the people and warned the people to stay pure, and they washed their clothes. And he said to the people, "Be ready for the third day: do not go near a woman."

On the third day, as morning dawned, there was thunder, and lightning, and a dense cloud upon the mountain, and a very loud blast of the horn; and all the people who were in the camp trembled. Moses led the people out of the camp toward God, and they took their places at the foot of the mountain.

Now Mount Sinai was all in smoke, for the Lord had come down upon it in fire; the smoke rose like the smoke of a kiln, and the whole mountain trembled violently. The blare of the horn grew louder and louder. As Moses spoke, God answered him in thunder. The Lord came down upon Mount Sinai, on the top of the mountain, and the Lord called Moses to the top of the mountain and Moses went up. The Lord said to Moses, "Go down, warn the people not to break through to the Lord to gaze, lest many of them perish. The priests also, who come near the Lord, must stay pure, lest the Lord break out against them." But Moses said to the Lord, "The people cannot come up to Mount Sinai, for You warned us saying, 'Set bounds about the mountain and sanctify it.' " So the Lord said to him, "Go down, and come back together with Aaron; but let not the priests or the people break through to come up to the Lord, lest He break out against them." And Moses went down to the people and spoke to them.

God spoke all these words, saying:

I the Lord am your God who brought you out of the land of Egypt, the house of bondage. You shall have no other gods besides Me.

You shall not make for yourself a sculptured image, or any likeness of what is in the heavens above, or on the earth below, or in the waters under the earth. You shall not bow down to them or serve them. For I the Lord your God am a jealous[1] God, visiting the guilt of the parents upon the children, upon the third and upon the fourth generations of those who reject Me, but showing kindness to the thousandth generation of those who love Me and keep My commandments.

You shall not swear falsely by the name of the Lord your God; for the Lord will not clear one who swears falsely by His name.

Remember the sabbath day and keep it holy. Six days you shall labor and do all your work, but the seventh day is a sabbath of the Lord your God: you shall not do any work—you, your son or daughter, your male or female slave, or your cattle, or the stranger who is within your settlements. For in six days the Lord made heaven and earth and sea, and all that is in them, and He rested on the seventh day; therefore the Lord blessed the sabbath day and hallowed it.

Honor your father and your mother, that you may long endure on the land that the Lord your God is assigning to you.

You shall not murder.

You shall not commit adultery.

You shall not steal.

You shall not bear false witness against your neighbor.

You shall not covet your neighbor's house: you shall not covet your neighbor's wife, or his male or female slave, or his ox or his ass, or anything that is your neighbor's.

---

1. New JPS: "impassioned."

All the people witnessed the thunder and lightning, the blare of the horn and the mountain smoking; and when the people saw it, they fell back and stood at a distance. "You speak to us," they said to Moses, "and we will obey; but let not God speak to us, lest we die." Moses answered the people, "Be not afraid; for God has come only in order to test you, and in order that the fear of Him may be ever with you, so that you do not go astray." So the people remained at a distance, while Moses approached the thick cloud where God was.

The Covenant at Sinai
2. Exodus 24:1–8, 12–18

Then He said to Moses, "Come up to the Lord, with Aaron, Nadab and Abihu, and seventy elders of Israel, and bow low from afar. Moses alone shall come near the Lord; but the others shall not come near, nor shall the people come up with him."

Moses went and repeated to the people all the commands of the Lord and all the rules; and all the people answered with one voice, saying, "All the things that the Lord has commanded we will do!" Moses then wrote down all the commands of the Lord.

Early in the morning, he set up an altar at the foot of the mountain, with twelve pillars for the twelve tribes of Israel. He designated some young men among the Israelites, and they offered burnt offerings and sacrificed bulls as offerings of well-being to the Lord. Moses took one part of the blood and put it in the basins, and the other part of the blood he dashed against the altar. Then he took the record of the covenant and read it aloud to the people. And they said, "All that the Lord has spoken we will faithfully do!" Moses took the blood and dashed it on the people and said, "This is the blood of the covenant that the Lord now makes with you concerning all these commands." . . .

The Lord said to Moses, "Come up to Me on the mountain and wait there, and I will give you the stone tablets with the teachings and commandments which I have inscribed to instruct them."[2] So Moses and his attendant Joshua arose, and Moses ascended the mountain of God. To the elders he had said, "Wait here for us until we return to you. You have Aaron and Hur with you; let anyone who has a legal matter approach them."

When Moses had ascended the mountain, the cloud covered the mountain. The Presence of the Lord abode on Mount Sinai, and the cloud hid it for six days. On the seventh day He called to Moses from the midst of the cloud. Now the Presence of the Lord appeared in the sight of the Israelites as a consuming fire on the top of the mountain. Moses went inside the cloud and ascended the mountain; and Moses remained on the mountain forty days and forty nights.

The biblical narrator clearly viewed the covenant originally made at Sinai as requiring periodic reiterations and renewals. The first two of these take place a generation after Sinai, at two of the nation's formative moments: just before entering into the land (§3) and upon apportioning the land at the conclusion of the conquest (§4). After the destruction of the First Commonwealth early in the sixth century B.C.E., some of the Judean exiles in Babylonia apparently doubted the continued validity of the covenant and sought assimilation. In response, the prophet Ezekiel (§5) proclaimed God's uncompromising commitment to uphold his covenant whether the people agreed or not.

The Covenant at Moab

3. Deuteronomy 29:1, 9–28; 30:11–20

Moses summoned all Israel and said to them: . . .

You stand this day, all of you, before the Lord your God—your tribal heads, your elders and your officials, all the men of Israel, your children, your wives, even the stranger within your camp, from woodchopper to waterdrawer—to enter into the covenant of the Lord your God, which the Lord your God is concluding with you this day, with its sanctions; to the

---

2. Deut. 10:1–4 makes explicit reference to "Ten Commandments."

end that He may establish you this day as His people and be your God, as He promised you and as He swore to your fathers, Abraham, Isaac, and Jacob. I make this covenant, with its sanctions, not with you alone, but both with those who are standing here with us this day before the Lord our God and with those who are not with us here this day.

Well you know that we dwelt in the land of Egypt and that we passed through the midst of various other nations; and you have seen the detestable things and the fetishes of wood and stone, silver and gold, that they keep. Perchance there is among you some man or woman, or some clan or tribe, whose heart is even now turning away from the Lord our God to go and worship the gods of those nations—perhaps there is among you a stock sprouting poison weed and wormwood. When such a one hears the words of these sanctions, he may fancy himself immune, thinking, "I shall be safe, though I follow my own willful heart"—to the utter ruin of moist and dry alike. The Lord will never forgive him; rather will the Lord's anger and jealousy[3] rage against that man, till every sanction recorded in this book comes down upon him, and the Lord blots out his name from under heaven.

The Lord will single them out from all the tribes of Israel for misfortune, in accordance with all the sanctions of the covenant recorded in this book of Teaching [torah]. And later generations will ask—the children who succeed you, and foreigners who come from distant lands and see the plagues and diseases that the Lord has inflicted upon that land, all its soil devastated . . . just like the upheaval of Sodom and Gomorrah, Admah and Zeboiim, which the Lord overthrew in His fierce anger—all nations will ask, "Why did the Lord do thus to this land? Wherefore that awful wrath?" They will be told, "Because they forsook the covenant that the Lord, God of their fathers, made with them when He freed them from the land of Egypt; they turned to the service of other gods and worshiped them, gods whom they had not experienced and whom He had not allotted to them. So the Lord was incensed at that land and brought upon it all the curses recorded in this book. The Lord uprooted them from their soil in anger, fury, and great wrath, and cast them into another land, as it is this day."[4]

3. New JPS: "passion."
4. New JPS: "is still the case."

Concealed acts concern the Lord our God; but with overt acts, it is for us and our children ever to apply all the provisions of this Teaching [*torah*]. . . .

Surely, this Instruction [*mitzvah*] which I enjoin upon you this day is not too baffling for you, nor is it beyond reach. It is not in heaven,[5] that you should say, "Who among us can go up to heaven and get it for us and impart it to us, that we may observe it?" Neither is it beyond the sea, that you should say, "Who among us can cross to the other side of the sea and get it for us and impart it to us, that we may observe it?" No, the thing is very close to you, in your mouth and in your heart, to observe it.

See, I set before you this day life and prosperity, death and adversity. For I command you this day, to love the Lord your God, to walk in His ways, and to keep His commandments, His laws, and His rules, that you may thrive and increase, and that the Lord your God may bless you in the land that you are about to enter and possess. But if your heart turns away and you give no heed, and are lured into the worship and service of other gods, I declare to you this day that you shall certainly perish; you shall not long endure on the soil that you are crossing the Jordan to enter and possess. I call heaven and earth to witness against you this day: I have put before you life and death, blessing and curse. Choose life—if you and your offspring would live—by loving the Lord your God, heeding His commands, and holding fast to Him. For thereby you shall have life and shall long endure upon the soil that the Lord your God swore to your ancestors, Abraham, Isaac, and Jacob, to give to them.

The Covenant at Shechem

4. Joshua 24:1–28

Joshua assembled all the tribes of Israel at Schechem. He summoned Israel's elders and commanders, magistrates and officers; and they presented themselves before God. Then Joshua said to all the people, "Thus said the

5. New JPS: "the heavens."

Lord, the God of Israel: In olden times, your forefather—Terah, father of Abraham and father of Nahor—lived beyond the Euphrates and worshiped other gods. But I took your father Abraham from beyond the Euphrates and led him through the whole land of Canaan and multiplied his offspring. I gave him Isaac, and to Isaac I gave Jacob and Esau. I gave Esau the hill country of Seir as his possession, while Jacob and his children went down to Egypt.

"Then I sent Moses and Aaron, and I plagued Egypt with the wonders that I wrought in their midst, after which I freed you—I freed your fathers—from Egypt, and you came to the Sea. But the Egyptians pursued your fathers to the Sea of Reeds with chariots and horsemen. They cried out to the Lord, and He put darkness between you and the Egyptians; then He brought the Sea upon them, and it covered them. Your own eyes saw what I did to the Egyptians.

"After you had lived a long time in the wilderness, I brought you to the land of the Amorites who lived beyond the Jordan. They gave battle to you, but I delivered them into your hands; I annihilated them for you, and you took possession of their land. Thereupon Balak son of Zippor, the king of Moab, made ready to attack Israel. He sent for Balaam son of Beor to curse you, but I refused to listen to Balaam; he had to bless you, and thus I saved you from him.

"Then you crossed the Jordan and you came to Jericho. The citizens of Jericho and the Amorites, Perizzites, Canaanites, Hittites, Girgashites, Hivites, and Jebusites fought you, but I delivered them into your hands. I sent a plague ahead of you, and it drove them out before you—[just like] the two Amorite kings—not by your sword or by your bow. I have given you a land for which you did not labor and towns which you did not build, and you have settled in them; you are enjoying vineyards and olive groves which you did not plant.

"Now, therefore, revere the Lord and serve Him with undivided loyalty; put away the gods that your forefathers served beyond the Euphrates and in Egypt, and serve the Lord. Or, if you are loath to serve the Lord, choose this day which ones you are going to serve—the gods that your forefathers served beyond the Euphrates, or those of the Amorites in whose land you are settled; but I and my household will serve the Lord."

In reply, the people declared, "Far be it from us to forsake the Lord and serve other gods! For it was the Lord our God who brought us and our fathers up from the land of Egypt, the house of bondage, and who wrought those wondrous signs before our very eyes, and guarded us all along the way that we traveled and among all the peoples through whose midst we passed. And then the Lord drove out before us all the peoples—the Amorites—that inhabited the country. We too will serve the Lord, for He is our God."

Joshua, however, said to the people, "You will not be able to serve the Lord, for He is a holy God. He is a jealous God; He will not forgive your transgressions and your sins. If you forsake the Lord and serve alien gods, He will turn and deal harshly with you and make an end of you, after having been gracious to you." But the people replied to Joshua, "No, we will serve the Lord!" Thereupon Joshua said to the people, "You are witnesses against yourselves that you have by your own act chosen to serve the Lord." "Yes, we are!" they responded. "Then put away the alien gods that you have among you and direct your hearts to the Lord, the God of Israel." And the people declared to Joshua, "We will serve none but the Lord our God, and we will obey none but Him."

On that day at Shechem, Joshua made a covenant for the people and he made a fixed rule for them. Joshua recorded all this in a book of divine instruction. He took a great stone and set it up at the foot of the oak in the sacred precinct of the Lord; and Joshua said to all the people, "See, this very stone shall be a witness against us, for it heard all the words that the Lord spoke to us; it shall be a witness against you, lest you break faith with your God." Joshua then dismissed the people to their allotted portions.

The Forced Covenant
5. Ezekiel 20:1–6, 10–22, 30–38

In the seventh year, on the tenth day of the fifth month, certain elders of Israel came to inquire of the Lord, and sat down before me. And the word of the Lord came to me:

O mortal, speak to the elders of Israel and say to them: Thus said the Lord God: Have you come to inquire of Me? As I live, I will not respond to your inquiry—declares the Lord God.

Arraign, arraign them, O mortal! Declare to them the abhorrent deeds of their fathers. Say to them: Thus said the Lord God:

On the day that I chose Israel, I gave My oath to the stock of the House of Jacob; when I made Myself known to them in the land of Egypt, I gave my oath to them. When I said, "I the Lord am your God," that same day I swore to them to take them out of the land of Egypt into a land flowing with milk and honey, a land which I had sought out for them, the fairest of all lands. . . .

I brought them out of the land of Egypt and I led them into the wilderness. I gave them My laws and taught them My rules, by the pursuit of which a man shall live. Moreover, I gave them My sabbaths to serve as a sign between Me and them, that they might know that it is I the Lord who sanctify them. But the House of Israel rebelled against Me in the wilderness; they did not follow My laws and they rejected My rules—by the pursuit of which a man shall live—and they grossly desecrated My sabbaths. Then I thought to pour out My fury upon them in the wilderness and to make an end of them; but I acted for the sake of My name, that it might not be profaned in the sight of the nations before whose eyes I had led them out. However, I swore to them in the wilderness that I would not bring them into the land flowing with milk and honey, the fairest of all lands, which I had assigned [to them], for they had rejected My rules, disobeyed My laws, and desecrated My sabbaths; their hearts followed after their fetishes. But I had pity on them and did not destroy them; I did not make an end of them in the wilderness.

I warned their children in the wilderness: Do not follow the practices of your fathers, do not keep their ways, and do not defile yourselves with their fetishes. I the Lord am your God: Follow My laws and be careful to observe My rules. And hallow My sabbaths, that they may be a sign between Me and you, that you may know that I the Lord am your God.

But the children rebelled against Me: they did not follow My laws and did not faithfully observe My rules, by the pursuit of which man shall live; they profaned My sabbaths. Then I resolved to pour out My fury upon them, to vent all My anger upon them, in the wilderness. But I held back My hand and acted for the sake of My name, that it might not be profaned in the sight of the nations before whose eyes I had led them out. . . .

Now say to the House of Israel: Thus said the Lord God: If you defile yourselves as your fathers did and go astray after their detestable things, and if to this very day you defile yourselves in the presentation of your gifts by making your children pass through the fire to all your fetishes, shall I respond to your inquiry, O House of Israel? As I live—declares the Lord God—I will not respond to you. And what you have in mind shall never come to pass—when you say, "We will be like the nations, like the families of the lands, worshiping wood and stone." As I live—declares the Lord God—I will reign over you with a strong hand, and with an outstretched arm, and with overflowing fury. With a strong hand and an outstretched arm and overflowing fury I will bring you out from the peoples and gather you from the lands where you are scattered, and I will bring you into the wilderness of the peoples; and there I will enter into judgment with you face to face. As I entered into judgment with your fathers in the wilderness of the land of Egypt, so will I enter into judgment with you—declares the Lord God. I will make you pass under the shepherd's staff, and I will bring you into the bond of the covenant. I will remove from you those who rebel and transgress against Me; I will take them out of the countries where they sojourn, but they shall not enter the Land of Israel. Then you shall know that I am the Lord.

Pledging a Renewed Covenant
6. Nehemiah 9:1–8, 24–26, 30–37; 10:1–40

The final covenant recorded in the Bible is that of the exiles who returned from Babylon and now assembled in Jerusalem (scholarly guesses about the date of the assembly mostly focus on the middle years of the fifth century B.C.E., when Judah was under Persian rule). Although its normative content is based upon earlier covenants, this covenant is unique in that it is initiated by humans. It takes the form of a mutual "pledge" (ama-

nah) of the community of Israelites toward God rather than the form of a covenant (berit) presented by God to humans.

On the twenty-fourth day of this month, the Israelites assembled, fasting, in sackcloth, and with earth upon them. Those of the stock of Israel separated themselves from all foreigners, and stood and confessed their sins and the iniquities of their fathers. Standing in their places, they read from the scroll of the Teaching of the Lord their God for one-fourth of the day, and for another fourth they confessed and prostrated themselves before the Lord their God. On the raised platform of the Levites stood Jeshua and Bani, Kadmiel, Shebaniah, Bunni, Sherebiah, Bani, and Chenani, and cried in a loud voice to the Lord their God. The Levites Jeshua, Kadmiel, Bani, Hashabniah, Sherebiah, Hodiah, and Pethahiah said, "Rise, bless the Lord your God who is from eternity to eternity: 'May Your glorious name be blessed, exalted though it is above every blessing and praise!'

"You alone are the Lord. You made the heavens, the highest heavens, and all their host, the earth and everything upon it, the seas and everything in them. You keep them all alive, and the host of heaven prostrate themselves before You. You are the Lord God, who chose Abram, who brought him out of Ur of the Chaldeans and changed his name to Abraham. Finding his heart true to You, You made a covenant with him to give the land of the Canaanite, the Hittite, the Amorite, the Perizzite, the Jebusite, and the Girgashite—to give it to his descendants. And You kept Your word, for You are righteous. . . . The sons came and took possession of the land: You subdued the Canaanite inhabitants of the land before them; You delivered them into their power, both their kings and the peoples of the land, to do with them as they pleased. They captured fortified cities and rich lands; they took possession of houses filled with every good thing, of hewn cisterns, vineyards, olive trees, and fruit trees in abundance. They ate, they were filled, they grew fat; they luxuriated in Your great bounty. Then, defying You, they rebelled; they cast Your Teaching behind their back. They killed Your prophets who admonished them to turn them back to You; they committed great impieties. . . . You bore with them for many years, admonished them by Your spirit through Your prophets, but they would not give ear, so You delivered them into the power of the peoples of the lands. Still, in Your great compassion You did not make an end of them or abandon them, for You are a gracious and compassionate God.

"And now, our God, great, mighty, and awesome God, who stays faithful to His covenant, do not treat lightly all the suffering that has overtaken us—our kings, our officers, our priests, our prophets, our fathers, and all Your people—from the time of the Assyrian kings to this day. Surely You are in the right with respect to all that has come upon us, for You have acted faithfully, and we have been wicked. Our kings, officers, priests, and fathers did not follow Your Teaching, and did not listen to Your commandments or to the warnings that You gave them. When they had their own kings and enjoyed the good that You lavished upon them, and the broad and rich land that You put at their disposal, they would not serve You, and did not turn from their wicked deeds. Today we are slaves, and the land that You gave our fathers to enjoy its fruit and bounty—here we are slaves on it! On account of our sins it yields its abundant crops to kings whom You have set over us. They rule over our bodies and our beasts as they please, and we are in great distress.

"In view of all this, we make this pledge and put it in writing; and on the sealed copy [are subscribed] our officials, our Levites, and our priests.

"On the sealed copy [are subscribed]: Nehemiah the Tirshatha son of Hacaliah and Zedekiah, Seraiah, Azariah, Jeremiah, Pashhur, Amariah, Malchijah, Hattush, Shebaniah, Malluch, Harim, Meremoth, Obadiah, Daniel, Ginnethon, Baruch, Meshullam, Abijah, Mijamin, Maaziah, Bilgai, Shemaiah; these are the priests.

"And the Levites: Jeshua son of Azaniah, Binnui of the sons of Henadad, and Kadmiel. And their brothers: Shebaniah, Hodiah, Kelita, Pelaiah, Hanan, Mica, Rehob, Hashabiah, Zaccur, Sherebiah, Shebaniah, Hodiah, Bani, and Beninu.

"The heads of the people: Parosh, Pahath-moab, Elam, Zattu, Bani, Bunni, Azgad, Bebai, Adonijah, Bigvai, Adin, Ater, Hezekiah, Azzur, Hodiah, Hashum, Bezai, Hariph, Anathoth, Nebai, Magpiash, Meshullam, Hezir, Meshezabel, Zadok, Jaddua, Pelatiah, Hanan, Anaiah, Hoshea, Hananiah, Hasshub, Hallohesh, Pilha, Shobek, Rehum, Hashabnah, Maaseiah, and Ahiah, Hanan, Anan, Malluch, Harim, Baanah.

"And the rest of the people, the priests, the Levites, the gatekeepers, the singers, the temple servants, and all who separated themselves from the peoples of the lands to [follow] the Teaching of God, their wives, sons and daughters, all who know enough to understand, join with their noble brothers, and take an oath with sanctions to follow the Teaching of God, given through Moses the servant of God, and to observe carefully all the commandments of the Lord our Lord, His rules and laws.

"Namely: We will not give our daughters in marriage to the peoples of the land, or take their daughters for our sons.

"The peoples of the land who bring their wares and all sorts of food-stuff for sale on the sabbath day — we will not buy from them on the sabbath or a holy day.

"We will forgo [the produce of] the seventh year, and every out-standing debt.

"We have laid upon ourselves obligations: To charge ourselves one-third of a shekel yearly for the service of the House of our God. . . .

"We have cast lots [among] the priests, the Levites, and the people, to bring the wood offering to the House of our God by clans annually at set times in order to provide fuel for the altar of the Lord our God, as is written in the Teaching [torah].

"And [we undertake] to bring to the House of the Lord annually the first fruits. . . .

"We will bring to the storerooms of the House of our God the first part of our dough, and our gifts [of grain], and of the fruit of every tree, wine and oil for the priests, and the tithes of our land for the Levites. . . .

"We will not neglect the House of our God."

Commentary. The Sinai Covenant: The Argument of Revelation

Ancient Israelite authors almost never wrote propositionally; in-stead, they employed narrative, law, and other conventional literary genres to express their ideas. Even when biblical writers sought to express new con-ceptions of religion, social structure, or human values, their ideas assumed the forms of historical narrative and legal stipulation rather than appearing as the propositional formulations familiar to modern readers. Commentary on the Bible thus becomes an exercise in the recovery of meaning: not only the scholarly task of explaining older language and custom through history, linguistics, and archaeology but also the effort to give the ancient writers their intellectual due by showing how any given text represents an intellectual position. This means reconstructing the argument of the text in its own terms and then engaging it not merely as an ancient but also as a contemporary affirmation. With the narrative of Yahweh's revelation at Mount Sinai, where an argument for a new conception of authority and community is shrouded in the metaphor of a mountain as the site of divine revelation—a mountain itself shrouded in smoke, fire, and cloud—these issues are most acute.

To begin with, what is striking in the biblical account of the Sinai covenant is that the promulgation of law is embedded in a larger narrative, without which it is incomplete: the covenant exists in history. Although the revelation is situated in literary terms as a foundational moment in the history of the nation, from the vantage point of most scholarship, the terminology and concept of "covenant" (*berit*) more likely represent the perspective of later writers associated with the Deuteronomic movement of the seventh century B.C.E. For these writers, the narrative of the Sinai covenant represents an ex post facto statement of first principles. The claim is that Israel was constituted as a people at Sinai when Yahweh revealed himself as the God who enters into a covenantal relationship with his people. The divine proclamation of covenantal law is as much a moment of creation as when God spoke to bring the world into being in Genesis 1. It is through the Sinai covenant that the nation gains its identity and history, both its past as a people redeemed from slavery and its future, which is given in the mandate to minister to the world: "You shall become for me a kingdom of priests and a holy nation" (Exod. 19:6; my translation).

This originary moment—the moral and legal constitution of Israel—is completely separated from the beginning of the narrative within which it is contained: the account of creation in Genesis 1. Neither the nation nor its laws existed from the beginning of time. The election of the nation, whereby it was brought into a special relationship to God, derives from history, not from cosmological destiny. With these premises the ancient Israelite author proposes a very different model of law and national existence than is evident in the older literature of ancient Babylon, for example, which provides probably the closest parallel to the biblical material and which Israelite scribes almost certainly knew, directly or indirectly. Like the account of Sinai, the Laws of Hammurabi (c. 1755 B.C.E.) were embedded in a literary frame that explains their origin and authority: but there, the election of Babylon, with its temple, and the appointment of Hammurabi, its king, represent divine destiny decreed from the beginning of time, independent of human history or agency. All that is assumed as absolute in this ancient Near Eastern literary text is implicitly called into question by the biblical author, who begins with universal history rather than national ideology, who removes destiny from history, who writes Israel out of creation. This writer's account of Sinai entails the radical and utopian argument that the existence of the nation is conditional upon the people's assent and ongoing commitment to the covenant:

> Thus shall you say to the House of Jacob and tell the House of Israel: "You have seen what I have done to Egypt, how I have borne you upon the wings of eagles and brought you to me. Now, if you truly obey me and observe my covenant, then you shall become to me more treasured than all the other peoples, for the entire earth is mine. Indeed, you shall become to me a kingdom of priests and a holy nation!" These are the words that you shall speak to the Israelites. (Exod. 19:3–6; my translation)

Everything hangs upon that introductory "if" (*im*). What is left unsaid is telling: the consequences of disobedience. Perhaps the metaphor of Israel as a vulnerable fledgling carried upon Yahweh's back accounts for the disinclination, in this moment of intimacy, to spell out the "if not." But that alternative is no less present for being unspoken. It is remarkable that the very text that sets forth the idealized beginnings of the nation in divine election simultaneously places that concept under critical scrutiny. The nation's existence is not an absolute end in itself but is contingent upon obedience to moral law. The founding moment is a fragile moment that already contains an implicit challenge and warning. The text's authors, even in their myth of origins, incorporate a notion of critique that seeks to avert chauvinism. Almost certainly, later editors have cast the promise of election in light of the vicissitudes of history. But there is a larger point to be made. The assent necessary for participation in the covenant cannot simply be that onetime original agreement emphasized by the narrator: "The *entire* people answered *simultaneously,* saying: 'All that Yahweh has spoken, we shall do' " (Exod. 19:8; my translation). Assent must continue for each generation within ancient Israel and must finally include the assent of the reader, who is invited to enter the narrative of election and who, in the direct address of the Decalogue, is summoned to participate in the covenant.

History is revealed as covenantal and existence becomes a moral postulate. There is no precedent in the literature of the ancient Near East for an entire nation to be directly addressed by a deity. Although the literary representation of a theophany accompanied by natural phenomena like the trembling of the earth and the quaking of mountains was not original to ancient Israel, any more than the literary genre of law was, an entire cluster of features distinguish Exodus 19–20 from Ugaritic or Babylonian exemplars. Unique in the Sinai narrative is the conception of a god who reveals himself publicly to an entire nation, cutting across boundaries of class, gender, and ethnicity. The divine revelation takes the form of a direct address to the people in which God proclaims his will as the law that constitutes the terms of the covenantal relationship between nation and deity. The form is the content: the direct address to the people requires a human response to the divine initiative. The content is the form: Yahweh reveals the covenant as the structure of human community.

The literary structure of the Decalogue (Exod. 20:2–17) is remarkable. In the divine proclamation of the covenant, God, speaking as "I," directly addresses each Israelite as "Thou," ungrammatically using the intimate singular form rather than the expected plural. Each addressee thereby knows himself or herself to be directly addressed by God. Within the narrative structure, each former slave, who previously lacked all sense of history and community, acquires an "I" at Sinai. The transformation of the slave into a person in narrative terms points to the direct address as requiring a personal response—the creation of a moral self—on the part of the reader or hearer. But that self is not conceptualized as existing only in a relation of service to the deity. Indeed, there is no mention of the deity in the second half of the Decalogue, which stipulates rather the addressee's duties to other members of the community. The covenant creates the neighbor just as it creates the self. Adherence to the covenant brings into being a community of moral agents. The moral agent is also a historical agent: the future of the nation hangs upon how I treat my neighbor.

The radical argument of this text is that there exists neither fate nor chance: history is contingent upon moral action; there is no theology without history, no duties to God without duties to the neighbor, no self except one that is construed in and through relationships to God and neighbor, no community or polity without covenant and revelation. The dialectical relationship between deity and people fundamental to the notion of covenant carries with it a clear risk of becoming broken, absolutized either into unconditional heteronomy (passive dependence upon the will of God, understood as entirely other, whereby agency and history are lost) or into unconditional agency, which is to say, tyranny (the absolute self independent of all commitment to the other). The repeated reformulations and renewals of the covenant throughout the Bible emphasize how central it was to ancient Israel's political and religious discourse. That it provides the structure of mutuality—for placing self and other in a relationship and for conceiving the polity as a community—warrants the attention of modern readers.

Bernard M. Levinson

Covenant and Consent

Grounds of Obligation
7. *Mekhilta Derabbi Yishmael,* Bahodesh 5, 6

This midrash describes the negotiations between God and Israel leading up to the Sinai covenant. It employs the parable—common in Rabbinic literature—of God as a king and provides typical grounds for establishing obligation to a sovereign.

(5) "I the Lord am your God" (Exod. 20:2). Why were the Ten Commandments not proclaimed at the beginning of the Torah? A parable: what is this

like? Like a human king who entered a province [*medinah*] and said to the people: Shall I reign over you? They replied: Have You conferred upon us any benefit that you should reign over us? What did he do [then]? He built the city wall for them, he brought in the water supply for them, and he fought their battles. [Then] he said to them: Shall I reign over you? They replied: Yes, yes. Similarly, God brought the Israelites out of Egypt, parted the sea for them, sent down the manna for them, brought up the well for them, brought the quails for them [and] fought for them the battle with Amalek. [Then] He said to them: Shall I reign over you? They replied: Yes, yes. . . .

(6) "You shall have no other Gods besides Me" (Exod. 20:3). . . . A parable: A human king entered a province [*medinah*]. His servants said to him: Issue decrees upon the people. He answered: No! Once they have accepted my reign I shall issue decrees upon them. If they do not accept my reign, why should they accept my decrees?

Similarly, God said to Israel: "I the Lord am your God who brought you out of the land of Egypt. You shall have no other gods." He [thus] said to them: "Am I He whose reign you have accepted in Egypt?" They replied: "Yes"; [so He went on]—"Now, just as you have accepted My reign, accept My decrees."

"A Forceful Disclaimer Regarding the Torah"
8. BT Shabbat 88a

The discussion here introduces the bold proposition that Israel's initial acceptance of the Torah was coerced—and therefore not binding. This latter implication is expressed by the term moda'a *(disclaimer), drawing an analogy to a document asserting that coercive pressure has been applied, which serves to annul a deed of sale signed under duress (cf. BT Bava Batra 48b).*

". . . And they took their places at the foot of the mountain"[6] (Exod. 19:17): Rabbi Avdimi b. Hama b. Hasa said, this teaches that the Holy One held the

6. Literally, "under the mountain."

mountain over them like an [overturned] tub and told them: "If you accept the Torah—well and fine; otherwise, you will be buried right there."

Rav Aha b. Jacob said: This furnishes a powerful disclaimer [*moda'a*] regarding the [acceptance of the] Torah. [*Rashi:* So if He arraigns them, demanding "Why have you failed to observe that which you accepted?" they can respond that the acceptance was coerced.]

Rava said: Nevertheless, they reaffirmed its acceptance in the days of Ahasuerus, as written, "The Jews confirmed and accepted" (Esther 9:27)—they confirmed that which they had already accepted.

God's Bound Subjects
9. *Sifre Numbers* 115

This midrash again takes the form of a royal parable and, drawing upon Ezekiel (§5), characterizes the covenant as a relationship of subjection. Its point of departure is the last verse of the biblical text commanding the wearing of ritual fringes, which—like many other commandments—ends by referring to the Exodus.

"Thus you shall be reminded to observe all My commandments and to be holy to your God. I am the Lord your God, who brought you out of the land of Egypt to be your God: I, the Lord your God" (Num. 15:40–41).

Why is the Exodus mentioned in connection with each and every *mitzvah* [commandment]?

A parable: what is this like? Like a king whose friend's son was taken captive. When he redeemed him, he did not redeem him as a freeman but as a slave, so that if the king issues [decrees] and the son resists, he can say to him: "You are my slave!" When they came into the city, [the king] instructed him: "Put my sandals on my feet; carry my garments before me to the bathhouse!" The [friend's] son started pulling away; he then produced the deed and said to him: "You are my slave!"

Similarly, when the Holy One redeemed the seed of Abraham, his friend, He did not redeem them as freemen but as slaves, so that if He issues [decrees] and they resist, He can say to them: "You are My slaves!" When they emerged into the desert, he issued to them some minor *mitzvot* and some major *mitzvot,* such as the Sabbath, incest, fringed garments, and phylacteries. Israel started pulling away; He then said to them: "You are My slaves! It is on this condition that I redeemed you—that I shall issue [decrees] and you obey."

"I, the Lord your God"—Why is this repeated? Is it not written already, "I am the Lord your God, who brought you out of the land of Egypt"? Why write again, "I, the Lord your God"? So that Israel should not say, "What was the point of God commanding us—wasn't it so that we observe [His commandments] and receive a reward? Let us neither observe [His commandments] nor receive a reward!" Just as Israel asked Ezekiel ["Certain elders of Israel came to inquire of the Lord" (Ezek. 20:1)]: "If a slave is sold by his master, is he not then outside his power?" He answered: "Yes." They said to him: "Since God has sold us over to the nations of the world, we are outside His power." He answered them: "If a slave is sold by his master on condition that he be returned [after a time], is he outside his power?"

"And what you have in mind shall never come to pass—when you say, 'We will be like the nations, like the families of the lands, worshiping wood and stone.' As I live—declares the Lord God—I will reign over you with a strong hand, and with an outstretched arm, and with overflowing fury" (Ezek. 20:32–33). "With a strong hand"—that is the plague, as written, "The hand of the Lord will strike" (Exod. 9:3). "And with an outstretched arm"—that is the sword, as written, "A drawn sword in his hand outstretched against Jerusalem" (1 Chron. 21:16). "And with overflowing fury"—that is starvation. Once I have brought upon you these three calamities one after another, I will reign over you against your will—that is why it is repeated, "I, the Lord your God."

Commentary. Covenant and Consent

At Sinai the people of Israel made a covenant with God to obey his law. But why was their consent necessary? Why didn't God simply hand down the law? Social contract theory suggests a possible answer. Obligation arises from consent; people are bound to obey only those authorities and laws they choose for themselves. Since every man is "master of himself," Rousseau argues, "no one can, under any pretext whatever, place another under subjection without his consent" (*Social Contract* IV:ii). As Hobbes writes, there is "no obligation on any man, which ariseth not from some act of his own" (*Leviathan,* chap. 21).

It might be objected that the covenant was no ordinary social contract. Were the people of Israel really free to accept or reject God's law? And even if their consent was freely given, did the act of consent *create* the obligation to obey, or did it recognize and affirm a preexisting obligation? The Rabbis struggle with these questions, but not in a way that reveals a fundamental difference between God's covenant with Israel and other social contracts. To the contrary, their commentaries highlight a tension endemic to consent theory—between consent as a source of obligation and consent as a way of acknowledging an obligation that exists independently of the contract. Their attempts to account for the moral force of the covenant illustrate a paradox that besets all contract arguments: The more compelling the grounds for consenting to a law or political arrangement, the less true it is that the act of consent creates the obligation to obey.

The notion that obligation depends on consent underlies the dispute, in BT Shabbat 88a, about whether Israel's acceptance of the Torah was invalid due to coercion. The Talmud tells us that God secured the agreement of the people by holding the mountain over their heads and threatening to destroy them. Rav Aha b. Jacob argues that this act of coercion undermines the obligation to keep the commandments. Just as a commercial contract signed under duress does not bind, neither does a coerced covenant with God. Rava accepts the premise but finds a way out. The Jews reaffirmed their acceptance in the days of Ahasuerus, he suggests, when they were not in the shadow of the mountain. In voluntarily adopting the *mitzvah* of reading the *megillah* (a *mitzvah* God did not command), they implicitly accepted the entire Torah. Whether or not Rava's solution is convincing, both Rabbis seem to assume that, absent an act of genuine consent, God's law does not bind.

Other commentators reject the consent-based theory of obligation. In *Sifre Numbers* 115, the obligation to keep the *mitzvot* has nothing to do with the covenant, but arises instead from the conditions under which God redeemed the Jews from slavery in Egypt. On this account, the Exodus is not a journey from slavery to freedom but a journey from one master (pharaoh) to another (God). Since God redeemed the Jews as slaves, not as freemen, the issue of consent never arises. He retains the right to issue decrees and they have the obligation to obey.

In *Mekhilta,* Bahodesh 5, 6, the covenant plays a role but not as the source of obligation. Rather than creating the obligation, it expresses or recognizes an obligation to God that preexists (and motivates) the act of consent. The obedience that Israelites owe God arises from all that he has done for them—delivered them from Egypt, divided the sea, sent manna and quails, fought the battle with Amalek, and so on. When he asks to be their king, the people reply, "Yes, yes." But their obligation to him derives less from the fact of their consent than from the considerations that inform their consent. God is not a worthy sovereign because the people consent to his rule; rather, the people consent to his rule because he is a worthy sovereign.

Gratitude for great deeds is not the only reason for accepting God's law. Another is the intrinsic justice or importance of the law itself. Maharal, a sixteenth-century scholar from Prague, invokes the ultimate version of this argument (§14). More than a just scheme of law, the Torah is necessary to the perfection of the universe; in its absence, he maintains, the universe would revert to chaos. However implausible this metaphysical claim may be, it nicely illustrates the paradox of consent theory by offering a limiting case. If no less than the survival of the cosmos is at stake in Israel's acceptance of the Torah, then two consequences follow for the covenant. One is that the people have the most weighty reason imaginable to give their consent. The other is that, given the stakes, their consent is more or less beside the point. The moral importance of free choice pales in the face of the considerations that point to a particular choice. Unlike Rav Aha, Maharal is not troubled in the least by the coercion that God employed when he held the mountain over the people. Far from undermining the moral force of the Torah, this act of coercion expressed God's view that the acceptance of the Torah was necessary, not contingent on a voluntary act.

Maharal's insight into the limits of consent theory can be detached from his metaphysical assumptions. Consider a law of undisputed moral importance, such as a prohibition against a grave violation of human rights. The moral importance of such a law gives people a strong reason to consent to it (as part of their constitution, say, or bill of rights). But it also gives grounds to obey such a law (and perhaps also to force others to obey it) independent of any act of consent. The weightier the reasons for consenting to a law, the less the obligation to uphold it derives from consent. Nations that fail to accept human rights conventions can nevertheless be held responsible for violating them. And if they protest that they have not given their consent, there may be a case for holding a mountain over their heads until they do.

Michael J. Sandel

Offering the Torah to the Nations

10. *Sifre Deuteronomy* 343

Sifre: A Tannaitic Commentary on the Book of Deuteronomy, translated by Reuven Hammer, Yale Judaica Series (New Haven: Yale University Press, 1986), pp. 352–53.

If the main point of Selection 7 is that God's covenant cannot be refused, the argument here suggests that it can be—and actually was.

"And he said: The Lord came from Sinai [and rose from Seir unto them]" (Deut. 33:2). When God revealed Himself to give the Torah to Israel, He revealed Himself not only to Israel but to all the nations. He went first to the children of Esau[7] and asked them, "Will you accept the Torah?" They replied, "What is written in it?" He said to them, "Thou shalt not murder" (Exod. 20:13). They replied that this is the very essence of these people and that their forefather was a murderer, as it is said, "But the hands are the hands of Esau" (Gen. 27:22), and, "By thy sword shalt thou live" (Gen. 27:40). He then went to the Ammonites and the Moabites and asked them, "Will you accept the Torah?" They replied, "What is written in it?" He said, "Thou shalt not commit adultery" (Exod. 20:13). They replied that adultery is their very essence, as it is said, "Thus were both the daughters of Lot with child by their father. [And the first-born bore a son, and called his name Moab . . . and the

---

7. Otherwise named Seir, hence the midrashic rendering of the opening verse.

younger, she also bore a son . . . the father of the children of Ammon]" (Gen. 19:36–38). He went next to the Ishmaelites and asked them, "Will you accept the Torah?" They replied, "What is written in it?" He said, "Thou shalt not steal" (Exod. 20:13). They replied that theft is their very essence and that their forefather was a thief, as it is said, "And he shall be a wild ass of a man" (Gen. 16:12). And thus it was with every other nation—He asked them all, "Will you accept the Torah?" as it is said, "All the kings of the earth shall give Thee thanks, O Lord, for they have heard the words of Thy mouth" (Ps. 138:4). One might think [from this verse] that they heard and accepted [his offer]; therefore Scripture states elsewhere, "And I will execute vengeance in anger and fury upon the nations, because they hearkened not" (Mic. 5:14). It was not enough for them that they did not hearken—they were not even able to observe the seven commandments that the children of Noah had accepted upon themselves,[8] and they cast them off. When the Holy One, blessed be He, saw that, He surrendered them to Israel.[9] A parable: A man took his ass and his dog to the threshing floor and loaded the ass with a *letek* [of grain] and the dog with three *se'ah*. The ass went along [easily], but the dog began to pant, so the man took off a *se'ah* and put it on the ass, and so too with the second and third *se'ah*. So also Israel accepted the Torah, with all of its explanations and details, as well as the seven commandments which the children of Noah had not been able to observe and had cast off. Therefore it is said, ". . . the Lord came from Sinai, and rose from Seir unto them."

The Scope of Covenantal Commitment

Individual Responsibility
11. BT Sotah 37a–b

The Bible describes a ceremony of reaffirming the covenant that includes a public pronouncement of "blessings" and "curses" with respect to the observance of detailed mitz-

---

8. See the discussion of the Noahide laws in ℂ16.
9. This is an attempt to justify the legal privileges granted to Jews over idolaters; see ℂ16.

vot and the Torah generally (see Deut. 27). The Talmud assumes that this took place repeatedly and adds together the various covenants and the different commitments entailed, starting from the original enactment at Sinai and ending with the ceremony following the entry into the Land of Israel. To this number some rabbis add the covenantal undertakings of each Israelite regarding his own obedience and also as a guarantor for his fellows. There are now an astonishing number of covenants.

Our rabbis taught: "Blessed" in general, "blessed" in particular; "cursed" in general, "cursed" in particular; "to study and to teach, to keep and to do"— these are four by four . . . which makes for sixteen. The same [took place also] at Sinai, and at the plains of Moab. . . . Thus there were forty-eight covenants for each *mitzvah* of the Torah. . . .

Rabbi Shimon b. Yehudah of Akko Village said in the name of Rabbi Shimon: With regard to each and every *mitzvah* of the Torah, there were enacted forty-eight covenants by 603,550 [people].[10] [*Rashi:* For each one, as each became a guarantor on behalf of all his brothers.]

Rabbi [Judah the Prince] said: [This implies further that] for each and every Israelite, there were 603,550 [covenants].

What is the issue? Rav Mesharshia said, They disagree with respect to a guarantor for a guarantor. [*Rashi:* Rabbi is arguing that, according to Rabbi Shimon, who seeks to enumerate the covenants of guarantee . . . each of the 600,000 accepted [also] 600,000 covenants on account of the guarantees that his brothers had offered for their fellows.]

The Covenant: Meaning and Intention
12. BT Shevu'ot 29a–b

Tractate Shevu'ot *is devoted to oaths of various kinds. In the discussion below, the question is raised whether an oath binds by the objective meaning of its words or by the*

10. This is the number reported in the census in Num. 1:46. Below in the passage Rashi employs the more conventional number of 600,000 as reported in Exod. 12:37.

speaker's subjective intention. The Talmud cites a midrashic description of the care that Moses took when administering the oath of the covenant to Israel; this seems to show that oaths normally bind according to subjective intentions.

Come and hear: When Moses administered the oath to Israel, he told them, "Note that I am administering this oath to you not in accordance with your determination, but in accordance with God's determination and mine."

Why so? Let him say to them, "Accept that which God commands!" —Is it not because they might intend that as referring to an idol?

—No, it is because idols too are called "gods," as written, "gods of silver . . . gods of gold" (Exod. 20:20).

Then let him say to them, "Accept the Torah!" [But this might be construed as] "[only] one Torah" [excluding the oral Torah].

Then let him say, "Accept the two Torahs!" [But this might be construed as, e.g.,] the Torah [instruction] concerning the *hattat* and the Torah concerning the *asham.*[11]

Then let him say, "Accept the entire Torah!" [But this might be construed as a commitment to refrain only from] idolatry, of which it has been said: "Idolatry is most grievous, for one who denies it affirms the entire Torah" (BT Nedarim 25a). . . .

Then let him say, "Accept all of the *mitzvot!*" [But this might be construed as a commitment to observe the commandment to wear] fringes [upon one's garment], of which it has been said: "The fringes are equivalent to all of the *mitzvot*" (cf. BT Menahot 43b).

Then let him say to them, "Accept the six hundred and thirteen *mitzvot!*"

—Well, and on your view [i.e., even if it is subjective intention that counts], let him say, [only] "in accordance with my determination"; why [add], "in accordance with God's determination"? Rather, [his aim was] that they should have no possibility of annulment.

---

11. The sections concerning these various sacrificial rites are introduced by the term *torah,* "teaching," in Lev. 6–7—e.g., "this is the *torah* of the *hattat*" (6:18).

Future Generations

13. Isaac Abravanel, *Commentary on the Pentateuch,* Deuteronomy 29

Toward the end of the fifteenth century, the Jews in Spain were forced to choose be-
tween converting to Christianity and being expelled from the country. This agonizing
choice and the arguments it occasioned brought a renewed examination of the ongoing
validity of the covenant. Abravanel, one of the many who chose Judaism and expulsion,
here provides (in the course of his biblical commentaries, written in Italian exile) an ex-
ample of the debates that went on in those last years of Jewish communal life in Spain.
Abravanel's commentary is written in a scholastic style of questions and answers.

Eighteen problems arise upon a reasoned examination of this portion. The
first and greatest of them all, which has occasioned an intense struggle among
contemporary scholars in the Kingdom of Aragon, concerns the issue of the
covenant and the words of Scripture "I make this covenant, with its sanctions, not with you alone, but both with those who are standing here with
us this day before the Lord our God and with those who are not with us here
this day."

    Who gave authority to the desert generation whose feet stood at
Sinai to obligate those succeeding them by proclaiming "We will faithfully
do," and to bring them [the following generations] into the covenant of the
Lord, may He be blessed, their God, or to impose upon them an oath which
will never be annulled? [How could they] obligate the following generations
to comply with the entire Torah and the covenant they established, causing
them to be liable for punishment? For this seems to be the import of these
verses, and of all those instances where the sages employ the argument "He
is already under oath from Mount Sinai" (BT Shevu'ot 23b).[12]

    This is, however, completely unreasonable. For the argument from
the nature of fathers and sons [i.e., that they are one and that the undertakings of the fathers obligate the sons] does not hold. For the body [of the
son], in whose being the father has a part, was not present there [at Sinai] ex-

---

12. Concerning, e.g., an individual who takes an oath to act against the Torah. Such an oath is
    void, because the person is already bound by his or her prior oath at Sinai (see C6, §7).

cept in a potential form exceedingly remote from actual existence. And it is
clear that it is not through potential that a man will prevail[13] in binding his
children by oath for all generations. This is certainly true so far as the rational
soul is concerned, in which the father has neither part nor connection.

Thus we find the words of the prophet Ezekiel:

> What do you mean by quoting this proverb upon the soil of Israel,
> "Fathers eat sour grapes and their sons' teeth are blunted"? As I
> live—declares the Lord God—this proverb shall no longer be cur-
> rent among you in Israel. Consider, all souls are Mine; the soul of
> the father and the soul of the son are both Mine. The soul that sins,
> only it shall die. (Ezek. 18:2–4)

This shows that they stand equally before Him, may He be blessed,
without any partnership. Therefore, "the soul that sins, it only shall die"—by
its own iniquity and not by the iniquity of its fathers. And the whole chapter
in Ezekiel shows this. The prophet Jeremiah too has said so. It therefore follows that no punishment should be visited upon the soul of the son because
of the actions of his father—not to speak of his words! And need it be said
for all subsequent generations?

The Rabbis have already said, "A minor convert undergoes immer-
sion under the auspices of the court . . . [but] when they come of age, they
can protest [and annul the conversion]" (BT Ketubot 11a: see C14). Let us reason a fortiori: If in a case where the body was present he may [nevertheless]
protest because he was a minor—how much more so if he was not present
at all! Clearly he should not be obligated by that which the forefathers determined for themselves.

We should not be appeased by what our ancients have said (e.g., in
the Midrash Tanhuma):[14] that all the souls which would ever exist to the end
of all generations were present at that convention, and that they all established this covenant and accepted it upon themselves by a curse and an oath.
This is difficult for the mind to believe. How were those disembodied souls

13. Abravanel is making a pun on the verse "For not by strength shall man prevail" (1 Sam. 2:9):
the biblical word for "strength" (*koah*) took on, in medieval usage, the additional meaning
of "potential."

14. See *Midrash Tanhuma*, edited by Solomon Buber (Vilna, 1883), Nitzavim 8, p. 50.

[bound] to the *mitzvot* which are obligatory only for that combination of soul and body called Man? It is written: "You shall keep My laws and My rules, by the pursuit of which man shall live" (Lev. 18:5)—the dead, however, are free (BT Shabbat 30a), for when body and soul are separated they are no longer Man. Furthermore, the *mitzvot* are bodily obligations, and a person cannot become obligated [to obey them] without being present. . . .

I will now interpret the verses in a manner that will resolve these problems. It is true that according to the law, "A person can be benefited without being present, but cannot be obligated without being present" (BT Ketubot 11a). . . . Surely, however, if a man receives a loan, the obligation to repay it falls upon him and his sons forever. Just as the sons benefit by inheriting their father's property, so too are they obligated to repay both their own and their father's debts, even those incurred before their birth. On similar grounds, the subjugation of a Canaanite slave transfers to his sons . . . for the slave, like other possessions, is purchased with money.

Now it is well known that God, may He be blessed, acquired a right in Israel, inter alia because He released them from "the iron furnace" of Egypt, from the abode of slaves; their persons, their cattle and possessions, were granted by Him and were within His domain, as written, "For it is to Me that the Israelites are slaves; they are my slaves, whom I freed from the land of Egypt" (Lev. 25:55). He [thus] acquired their bodies, as if they were Canaanite slaves, and He also acquired their souls, since he granted them spiritual perfection through giving them His Torah. . . .

That is why, in establishing the [Sinai] covenant, they declared, "All that the Lord has spoken we will faithfully do!" (Exod. 24:7), meaning, With our bodies we shall do and serve as slaves unto their master; and with our souls we shall faithfully believe, like students unto their teacher.

And because God, may He be blessed, wished now to grant them a further benefit, namely, possession of the holy land, it was necessary that they enter a new covenant. For the first [covenant] relates to the subjection of their bodies and the binding of their beliefs, while the second concerns possession of the land. The latter signifies that they did not conquer land by their sword nor inherit it from their fathers. Rather, God gave it to them, not as a gift but as a loan, as written: "The land shall not be sold without reclaim, for the land is Mine" (Lev. 25:23). They [thus] became obligated to serve the master of the land, and not to serve a God beside Him, for this would constitute high treason against Him. . . .

The sons' obligation and inclusion in the parents' covenant is based on the body, on the soul, and on the land in which they dwell. It is not a function of the oath they [the parents] took but of the bondage they accepted when He released them from Egypt, the Torah they accepted, and the chosen land they received as a loan. . . . No doubt at all can arise regarding the obligation of the covenant. Were this covenant like one made between two friends, a covenant of love and loyalty, this great insoluble problem would obtain — namely, how can sons not yet existing be obligated by it? This covenant and oath is, however, an absolute obligation subjugating their bodies and their land, too. How then is it conceivable that their offspring should repudiate it? Can the sons of Canaanite slaves release themselves from the slavery which they were born into and inherited from their fathers? This is the foundation of the covenant and oath which can never be nullified.[15] . . . Now, since the entire foundation of the covenant and of the eternal servitude is the Exodus, it is always mentioned by God and His prophets. And all the holidays of God are in memory of the Exodus, which signifies eternal servitude.

Freedom and Necessity
14. Judah Loew (Maharal of Prague), *Tiferet Yisrael,* Chapter 32

The themes of natural order, the election of Israel, and the nature of exile and redemption pervade Maharal's works. Here, in a selection from Tiferet Yisrael, *written in the early 1580s, he criticizes the consent model of the covenant and offers instead a metaphysical argument for a nonvolitional understanding: it was "necessary" that Israel accept the Torah. Maharal evokes the religious conviction, deeply rooted in the tradition, that the Torah is not merely a body of law but also the very foundation of the cosmos.*

15. Abravanel goes on to quote Ezek. 20:32–38, cited in §5.

He interprets the talmudic passage about God holding the mountain over the people's heads (§8) as a metaphorical expression of this profound religious truth. Maharal cites the passage and continues as follows.

The tosafists have asked: "Had [Israel] not already said, '[All that the Lord has spoken] we will faithfully do'?" (Exod. 24:7). And they answered: "[God was concerned that] when they beheld the great fire [of the theophany] they might recant."

These statements seem baffling. Would Israel recant their acceptance of the Torah, which is an everlasting distinction and credit? What distinction do they merit if you say that perhaps they would recant? Furthermore, should not God have placed the mountain over them if and when they recanted rather than [when they had already accepted]? . . .

However, God held the mountain over them so that Israel would not say: "We accepted the Torah on our own, and had we not willed it we would not have received the Torah." This would not have suited the elevated status of the Torah. For the entire universe is dependent upon the Torah, and if the Torah did not exist, the universe would revert to chaos.[16] It is therefore unfitting that the acceptance of the Torah should be Israel's choice. Rather, the Holy One, Blessed be He, obligated and coerced them to accept the Torah. It could not be otherwise, lest the universe revert to chaos.

And do not reply that ultimately the lifting up of the mountain was redundant, for they had already said, "We will faithfully do." This poses no difficulty, for the principle of the matter was not to ensure that they would not recant. Indeed, why should they recant when they had already said they would faithfully do? The lifting up was necessary in and of itself, for how can the Torah, which is the [completion and] perfection of the entire universe, depend on the fact that Israel chose to accept it? Could the perfection of the universe depend on the contingency that they may or may not accept? He therefore held the mountain over them like an overturned tub so that if they did not accept, there would be their burial.

16. Maharal uses the Hebrew idiom *tohu vavohu,* "unformed and void," from the story of creation in Gen. 1:2. His interpretation follows the continuation of the talmudic discussion in BT Shabbat 88a (§8).

It may also be said that God held the mountain over them . . . so that Israel would not say that there might be—Heaven forbid—an annulment of the acceptance of the Torah. [For one might argue that] since Israel voluntarily accepted the Torah, they can be released from it, for it was not done of necessity but was contingent: they may or may not have accepted. He therefore held the mountain over them . . . as if to say that they must necessarily accept the Torah, and whatever is necessarily so, has no release or annulment, because it is necessary.[17]

. . . [Now,] Rav Aha said that "this furnishes a powerful disclaimer regarding the [acceptance of the] Torah," for, after all, the acceptance . . . was forced. It was therefore not a complete acceptance, for the acceptance of the Torah ought to be voluntary. . . . Regarding this [concern, the Talmud continues]: "Nevertheless, they reaffirmed its acceptance in the days of Ahasuerus, etc." The explanation of this matter is that in the days of Ahasuerus they voluntarily accepted one *mitzvah*. God, may He be Blessed, did not decree this for them; rather, they accepted it of their own accord [by enacting it], and the Holy One, Blessed be He, concurred. . . . Accepting the reading of the *megillah* is a voluntary acceptance of one of the *mitzvot* of the Torah . . . and thus constitutes the voluntary acceptance of the entire Torah. For if they accepted this latest *mitzvah* of reading the *megillah* of their own accord—for who forced them to accept this?—then how much more so the earlier [body] of *mitzvot!* It too was voluntarily accepted. Hence, it is as though the original acceptance of the Torah was voluntary too, for the [ultimate] conclusion proves the original [intention].

This will suffice to explain that the Torah was voluntary on the part of Israel but necessary on God's part, may He be Blessed. It is fitting that all things which complete and perfect the universe be necessary and not contingent, as was explained.

---

17. The Hebrew word *hekhrah* can mean both "necessity" and "compulsion." Maharal plays on these dual meanings.

Covenant as Social Contract

15. Baruch Spinoza, *Theological-Political Treatise,* Chapters 5 and 17

Tractatus Theologico-Politicus, translated by Samuel Shirley (Leiden: E. J. Brill, 1991), pp. 115, 254–56.

Spinoza offers here an analysis of the covenant as a political act, the founding moment of the Israelite state. It follows, then, that in the apolitical conditions of exile and statelessness, this political covenant is no longer binding. Like Abravanel and Maharal, Spinoza writes in the aftermath of the Spanish expulsion. Yet he not only dissents from their views but presents his own in a new critical and philosophical style. Spinoza begins his reconstruction of the ancient Israelite theocracy by referring to an argument he makes earlier in the book, in chapter 5, excerpted below, that the ritual laws were binding and "of practical value only while their state existed" (see ℭ2, §6). We begin by citing this argument.

Chapter 5

That the Hebrews are not bound to practise their ceremonial rites since the destruction of their state is clear from Jeremiah, who, when he saw and proclaimed the imminent ruin of the city, said that God delights only in those who know and understand that he exercises lovingkindness, judgment and righteousness in the earth, and so thereafter only those who know these things are to be deemed worthy of praise (see [Jeremiah] 9:23). This is as much to say that after the destruction of the city God demanded no special service of the Jews and sought nothing of them thereafter except the natural law by which all men are bound. . . . For when they were led away in captivity to Babylon after the first destruction of the city, they straightaway abandoned their observance of ceremonies. Indeed they turned their backs on the entire Mosaic Law, consigned to oblivion the laws of their native land as being obviously pointless, and began to be assimilated to other nations, as Ezra and Nehemiah make abundantly clear. Therefore there is no doubt that, since the fall of their independent state, Jews are no more bound by the Mosaic Law than they were before their state came into being. For while they were living among other nations before the exodus from Egypt, they had no special laws to themselves; they were bound by no law other than the natural law, and doubtless the law of the state in which they dwelt, in so far as that was not opposed to the natural Divine Law.

Chapter 17

We have already said in chapter 5 that, after their departure from Egypt, the Hebrews were no longer bound by the laws of any other nation, but were free to establish new laws as they pleased, and to occupy whatever lands they wished. For after their liberation from the intolerable oppression of the Egyptians, being bound by no covenant to any mortal man, they regained their natural right over everything that lay within their power, and every man could decide afresh whether to retain it or to surrender it and transfer it to another. Finding themselves thus placed in this state of nature, they hearkened to Moses, in whom they placed the greatest confidence, and resolved to transfer their right not to any mortal man, but to God alone. Without much hesitation they all promised, equally and with one voice, to obey God absolutely in all his commands and to acknowledge no other law but that which he should proclaim as such by prophetic revelation. Now this promise, or transference of right to God, was made in the same way as we have previously conceived it to be made in the case of an ordinary community when men decide to surrender their natural right. For it was by express covenant and oath (Exod. 24:7) that they surrendered their natural right and transferred it to God, which they did freely, not by forcible coercion or fear of threats. Furthermore, to ensure that the covenant should be fixed and binding with no suspicion of deceit, God made no covenant with them until they had experienced his wonderful power which alone had saved them, and which alone might save them in time to come (Exod. 19:4–5). For it was through this very belief, that God's power alone could save them, that they transferred to God all their natural power of self-preservation — which they probably thought they themselves had hitherto possessed — and consequently all their right.

It was God alone, then, who held sovereignty over the Hebrews, and so this state alone, by virtue of the covenant, was rightly called the kingdom of God, and God was also called the king of the Hebrews. Consequently, the enemies of this state were the enemies of God; citizens who aimed to seize the sovereignty were guilty of treason against God, and the laws of the state were the laws and commands of God. So in this state civil law and religion — which we have shown to consist only in obedience to God — were one and the same thing; the tenets of religion were not just teachings but laws and commands; piety was looked upon as justice, impiety as crime and injustice. He who forsook his religion ceased to be a citizen and by that alone became an enemy, and he who died for his religion was regarded as having died for his country. In short, there was considered to be no difference whatsoever between civil law and religion. Hence this form of government could be called a theocracy, its citizens being bound only by such law as was revealed by God. However, all this was a matter of theory rather than fact, for in reality the Hebrews retained their sovereign right completely, as will become clear when I describe the manner and method of the government of this state, which I now intend to set forth.

Since the Hebrews did not transfer their right to any other man, but, as in a democracy, they all surrendered their right on equal terms, crying with one voice, "Whatever God shall speak, we shall do" (no one being named as mediator), it follows that this covenant left them all completely equal, and they all had an equal right to consult God, to receive and interpret his laws; in short, they all shared equally in the government of the state. It was for this reason, then, that on the first occasion they all approached God on equal terms to hear what he wished to command. But on this first appearance before God they were so terrified and so thunderstruck at hearing God speak that they thought their last hour had come. So, overwhelmed with fear, they went to Moses again, saying, "Behold, we have heard God speaking in the midst of the fire; now therefore why should we die? For this great fire will surely consume us; if again we are to hear the voice of God, we shall surely die. Go thou near therefore, and hear all that our God shall say. And speak thou (not God) to us. All that God shall speak unto thee, we shall hear and do" (Deut. 5:21–24).

By this they clearly abrogated the first covenant, making an absolute transfer to Moses of their right to consult God and to interpret his decrees. For at this point what they promised was not, as before, to obey all that God should speak to them, but what God should speak to Moses. (See Deut. 5 after the Decalogue, and 18:15–16.) Therefore Moses was left as the sole lawgiver and interpreter of God's laws, and thus also the supreme judge, whom no one could judge, and who alone acted on God's behalf among the Hebrews, that is, held the supreme kingship, since he alone had the right to consult God, to give God's answers to the people, and to compel them to obey. He alone, I say, for if anyone during Moses' lifetime sought to make any proclamation in God's name, even if he were a true prophet he was nevertheless guilty of claiming the supreme sovereignty (Num. 11:28).

Law and Ethics
8. Hermann Cohen, "Affinities Between the Philosophy of Kant and Judaism"
Commentary. Susan Neiman, "Cohen and Kant"

The Binding of Isaac: Mitzvah Supersedes Morality
9. Yeshayahu Leibowitz, "Religious Praxis: The Meaning of Halakhah"

Rejecting the "Suspension of the Ethical"
10. Samuel Hugo Bergman, Two Texts on the Binding of Isaac
Commentary. Avi Sagi, "Between Obedience and Autonomy"

Introduction

At a certain point in the history of most revealed religions, theological understandings of revelation and history come under philosophical scrutiny. Sometimes the scrutiny is internally produced, as appears to be the case in BT Yoma 67b, where the normal conversation of the sages leads them to the question of revelation's content and meaning (although even here, among themselves, they imagine skeptical non-Jewish interlocuters: "Satan and the nations"). Sometimes the scrutiny is externally driven, as in the case of Saadiah Gaon, who wrote under the influence of Arabic and Greek philosophy. But the problems posed are always the same: How much of what God reveals, how much of what his prophets and priests teach, could human beings learn on their own, autonomously, through rational inquiry? If much of revelation's content turns out to be rationally accessible and verifiable, how does one explain or justify what seems wholly irrational? And if one feels the need to provide such explanations, isn't reason, and not revelation, the ultimate authority? These questions open the way for a deeply subversive interrogation of revealed religion. If revelation is (mostly) rational, why is it necessary? What is the advantage of having stood at Sinai and received the Torah from God directly if other men and women, anywhere, at any time, can discover the same laws by themselves? Why bother with a historical narrative if all one needs is a philosophical argument?

Despite this potential subversiveness, it is not an easy matter to deny the rationality of God's law. Indeed, the Bible itself, in the Deuteronomic account of revelation, takes pride in the Torah's rationality, describing it in terms of a cosmopolitan "wisdom": "for that will be proof of your wisdom and discernment to other peoples, who on hearing of all these laws will say, 'Surely, that is a great nation of wise and discerning people'" (4:6). If the wisdom of the Torah is thus universally recognizable, is it also universally accessible? The Deuteronomist draws no such conclusion, but it is surely a possible meaning of this passage that ordinary human reason is sufficient for a righteous life. Why, then, are the Israelites singled out in the biblical narrative? In what sense is the Torah "theirs"?

The texts presented in this chapter offer a variety of answers to these questions. For analytical purposes, we shall divide these answers into two sets, two ideal-typical accounts of revelation and reason. Obviously, no particular text fits either account exactly, but the division will be apparent in the selections that follow. On the one hand, Jewish writers fix limits on reason's reach for the sake of Israel's singularity; on the other hand, they make Israel's Torah into reason's singular fulfillment.

The first account follows the intimation of Yoma, drawing a line between rational social and moral laws and nonrational or mysterious ritual laws—for example, circumcision, sacrifices, *kashrut,* the prohibition of certain mixtures, holidays, and *halitzah* (the lists vary; some of them are highly restricted). The social and moral laws are indeed universally accessible and universally binding; they are included in the more extended versions of the Noahide Code (see the discussion in ℂ16). Israel is not singled out when it is given these laws, for no human society can exist without them. Plato's well-known argument for their necessity, repeated by Augustine, is repeated again by Judah Halevi: "Even a band of robbers cannot avoid adhering to justice in what is [simply] between them. Otherwise, their association would not last" (*Kuzari* 2:48). But this sort of reason and this sort of justice do not make for a "holy nation." Israel's specific connection to God is established by the ritual laws "by means of which the bounty of the divine order reached them." These are not universally accessible or binding; they can't be discovered by thinking about law or divinity or even holiness; circumcision, as Halevi wryly says, has little to do with philosophy.

The covenantal doctrine described in our first chapter may well be assumed in the texts presented here, but it isn't emphasized. Writers like Halevi seem to imagine something closer to a divine capture or conscription of Israel, a miraculous, mysterious bonding. Obeying the ritual laws is a way (*the* way) of enacting this bond and expressing a sense of connectedness to God. Reason has no place here; its place is logically and chronologically prior—preceding the ritual law "[both] in nature and in time," as Halevi says. Before there can be a holy nation, there must be a nation whose members observe the social and moral laws. But here, too, consent is no longer in the foreground, for social and moral laws require only our understanding, not our agreement.

But if this understanding is natural and universal, the question arises again, Why were the social and moral laws included in the Sinai revelation? Why not just the ritual laws, intended for Israel alone? Saadiah, who accepts something like the division of morality and ritual, argues that the social and moral laws were a divine gift—gratuitous, because obedience would be due in any case, and redundant, because human reason could have discovered these laws without divine assistance. But, Saadiah says, the discovery would have taken a long time (and we would probably not have gotten things exactly right); revelation is a shortcut and in that sense the gift of a gracious God. Israel is saved the pain of self-education and is brought, at one stroke, to the full perfection of moral understanding—though not of moral performance: that is left in the uncertain hands of the people.

The second account of revelation's meaning can be read as an expanded and inclusive version of this argument of Saadiah's. Now the division of the law into two wholly separate parts is rejected. All the laws have their reasons, though we see some of these more clearly than others, and we see them only *after* the laws have been revealed. The Torah is an integrated whole, a complex and complete legal system, superior throughout to what other nations provide for themselves. Early on, in Hellenistic Alexandria, Philo interpreted the ritual laws in symbolic and allegorizing terms and so turned them into practical, everyday means of teaching morality and reinforcing moral habits. Maimonides probably had a similar view, treating even the sacrifices as educational performances. His is the supremely rational account of the Torah: 613 commandments (the standard number), each one useful to the

men and women who obey it. God can hardly be imagined to impose useless laws on his chosen people. What appear mysterious or nonrational in the
Torah are only the specific distinctions and designations that are necessary
in any legal system, and arbitrary in all of them. But some commentators
would deny arbitrariness even here: the detailed distinctions and designations are exactly right, they claim, although human reason would have been
incapable of getting them right on its own. This is the view of Albo, who argues that "divine law" is superior to the precepts of the greatest philosophers
(Plato and Aristotle).

We can recognize in this second set of arguments the source or,
more accurately, the earliest manifestation of the modern apologetic descriptions of the ritual commandments. Mostly, these aim at the radical subordination of ritual to moral law, as in Mendelssohn and Hermann Cohen,
turning the concrete practice of religion into a mnemonic device for universal morality or an everyday expression of monotheistic faith (and making
monotheism itself into morality's ultimate guarantee). It is worth noting—
although we won't represent them here—more direct claims for the rationality of ritual, as in twentieth-century descriptions of *kashrut* as a primitive
public health code. Obviously, the rationalism of Maimonides and his followers, and of Mendelssohn and Cohen, is more serious than this, for they
still mean to insist on and inspire strict obedience to the law, whereas many
contemporary apologists mean to make the law look reasonable while at
the same time making obedience unnecessary (we now have better public
health codes). The latter aim is almost certainly better achieved by the more
forthright Spinozan argument that the ritual laws are relevant to and only
obligatory in the polity founded by Moses. Mendelssohn and Cohen write
in opposition to this view, Spinoza's heresy, which must have seemed even
more plausible after the collapse of Jewish communal autonomy.

It is probably in reaction to the modern rationalizations of religious
practice that some Jewish writers, following Kierkegaard (who responded to
Christian apologetics of a similar sort), insist that the Torah is often irrational
and is most authentically divine when it has no social or moral reason at all.
What serves as a focus of this modernist argument, however, is not the ritual
law but the *akedah* (the near sacrifice of Isaac). Here God's incomprehensible
and even, from a human perspective, immoral willfulness is most dramati-

cally revealed. The commandments to avoid certain foods or certain mixtures are, by contrast, morally neutral. Not so the commandment to kill a child. It may be that in both cases the faithful obey, if they obey, for no other reason than that God commands them. But obedience is infinitely harder in the second case, which therefore tests, as Leibowitz argues, their absolute subordination to God's authority. If they protest, even by invoking other divine commands, they claim a right to choose the occasions of their obedience, even an obligation to choose according to reason. Samuel Hugo Bergman argues in the last of our selections that this claim implies the existence of a rational moral standard external to the law—by reference to which we judge the law itself as well as all additional revelations of God's will.

Bergman points to the political meaning of legal rationalism. However hard individual writers work to construct favorable judgments of divine revelation, they appeal nonetheless to an external standard—a Jewish version, perhaps, of natural law. And this law cannot be Israel's alone; it is universally knowable. The claim that the Torah meets this external standard uniquely well, earlier and better than any other legal system, is the claim to be "a light unto the nations" (Isa. 42:6—we have retained the traditional translation). The counterclaim that some part of the law is mysterious, given only to Israel, is a claim to singularity and specialness, made on behalf of "a people that dwells apart" (Num. 23:9)

Natural Law, Reason, and Revelation: Classical Discussions

Comprehensible and Mysterious Laws
1. BT Yoma 67b

The context of this reading is the talmudic discussion of a central element of the temple ritual on the Day of Atonement: sending the he-goat into the wilderness carrying "all the iniquities and transgressions of the Israelites" (Lev. 16:21 [C4, §3]). The Rabbis find this rite greatly puzzling and list it—along with several other laws—among God's "mysterious hukkim [edicts]," contrasted with the more reasonable mishpatim [ordi-

nances]. This twofold classification of God's commandments became central in medieval discussions about Torah and reason.

Our Rabbis taught: "You shall follow my ordinances" (Lev. 18:4) — [this refers to] things which, had they not been laid down, ought to have been laid down, such as: idolatry, incest, bloodshed, robbery, and blasphemy.[1]

". . . And keep my edicts" — [this refers to] things which Satan[2] and the nations disparage, such as: [not] eating pork, [not] wearing *sha'atnez* [a "mixed" garment of wool and linen], releasing the levirate by *halitzah* [a ceremony enabling a widow to marry someone other than her husband's brother], the purification rites of the leper, and the he-goat sent into the wilderness.

You might think these are senseless deeds; therefore it is written, "I am the Lord" — I, the Lord, have issued these edicts; you have no permission to doubt them.

Commentary. God's Reason — What Should Not Be Doubted?

The *hukkim* have no apparent reason. They are characterized as edicts, to be observed simply on God's authority. Yet the final paragraph leaves us wondering: "You might think these are senseless deeds" — but are they, in fact, senseless?

Perhaps, indeed, Satan's ridicule (and that of "the nations") is directed not merely toward the strange laws but toward their author. The giver of Torah is depicted as an arbitrary force; and the Hebrew *tohu* — translated here as "senseless" — may be an allusion to the dark, primordial chaos of Genesis 1.

Our text's retort to this accusation can be read in two very differ-

1. This list corresponds to the bulk of the Noahide laws, which the Rabbis defined as binding all humanity; see C16.
2. Some texts read instead "the evil inclination" — a substitution not uncommon in Rabbinic literature.

ent ways, depending on the nature of the forbidden doubt—or, conversely, the nature of the requisite faith. On one reading, it is precisely the sense of these edicts that we must not doubt; rather, we should trust in the perfect sense of God, who enacted them. Another reading, however, taking the emphasis on authority much farther, would see the very quest for sense as constituting illicit doubt and disloyalty. On this reading, we differ with Satan not in assessing the (ir)rationality of the *hukkim* but in our attitude to their divine author, whom we faithfully love and obey. The *hukkim* may be the most sublime part of Torah, where faith transcends understanding.

On the first view, by contrast, the *hukkim* are no more than a residual category, those commandments whose sense we have (as yet?) failed to appreciate. It is this reading that seems more consonant with the bulk of the talmudic tradition, where determining the sense of God's commandments and the reasoned working out of their details are the main order of the day. Talk of Satanic disparagement, rather than pointing (paradoxically) toward sublime transcendence of reason, would seem to express Rabbinic frustration with the rare instances of commandments whose sense is elusive.

The main body of the Torah may, then, be characterized as *mishpatim:* "things which, had they not been laid down, ought to have been laid down." The Hebrew phrase for this "ought" is *din,* which here means "reason"; the notion that independent reasoning (*din*) can and does produce norms beyond those revealed in Scripture is commonplace in most midrashic discourse. So if God had not legislated these norms, they still would have been called for by reason. Would reason tell us that this is God's will or perhaps simply that this is how we, as humans, must live? The Rabbis do not seem to address this question; indeed, their theistic worldview may have denied the contrast between the two possibilities. If reason informs us that idolatry and robbery are evil, then clearly God forbids them!

Noam J. Zohar

Revelation and Reason

2. Saadiah Gaon, *The Book of Beliefs and Opinions,* Introduction:6; 3:2

The Book of Beliefs and Opinions, translated from the Arabic and the Hebrew by Samuel Rosenblatt, Yale Judaica Series (New Haven: Yale University Press, 1948), pp. 31–33, 141–45.

In the introduction to The Book of Beliefs and Opinions, *Saadiah first raised the central question of the relation between reason and revelation for medieval Jewish philosophy. His belief in the basic compatibility between the two is expressed in his theory of mitzvot. Saadiah divides the commandments into those dictated by reason and those toward which reason is indifferent.*

Introduction:6

Inasmuch as all matters of religious belief, as imparted to us by our Master, can be attained by means of research and correct speculation, what was the reason that prompted [divine] wisdom to transmit them to us by way of prophecy and support them by means of visible proofs and miracles rather than intellectual demonstrations?

To this question we should like to give, with the help of God, exalted be He, an adequate answer. We say, then, [that] the All-Wise knew that the conclusions reached by means of the art of speculation could be attained only in the course of a certain measure of time. If, therefore, He had referred us for our acquaintance with His religion to that art alone, we would have remained without religious guidance whatever for a while, until the process of reasoning was completed by us so that we could make use of its conclusions. But many a one of us might never complete the process because of some flaw in his reasoning. Again, he might not succeed in making use of its conclusions because he is overcome by worry or overwhelmed by uncertainties that confuse and befuddle him. That is why God, exalted and magnified be He, afforded us a quick relief from all these burdens by sending us His messengers through whom He transmitted messages to us, and by letting us see with our own eyes the signs and the proofs supporting them about which no doubt could prevail and which we could not possibly reject. Thus He said: "Ye yourselves have seen that I have talked with you from heaven"

(Exod. 20:19). Furthermore He addressed His messenger in our presence, and made it an obligation to believe him forever, as He said: "That the people may hear when I speak with thee, and may also believe thee forever" (Exod. 19:9).

Thus it became incumbent upon us immediately to accept the religion, together with all that was embraced in it, because its authenticity had been proven by the testimony of the senses. Its acceptance is also incumbent upon anybody to whom it has been transmitted because of the attestation of authentic tradition, as we shall explain. Now God commanded us to take our time with our speculation until we would arrive thereby at these self-same conclusions. We must, therefore, persevere in this standpoint until the arguments in favor of it have become convincing for us, and we feel compelled to acknowledge God's Torah [that has already been authenticated] by what our eyes have seen and our ears have heard.

So, then, even if it should take a long time for one of us who indulges in speculation to complete his speculation, he is without worry. He who is held back from engaging in such an activity by some impediment will, then, not remain without religious guidance. Furthermore women and young people and those who have no aptitude for speculation can thus also have a perfect and accessible faith, for the knowledge of the senses is common to all men. Praised, then, be the All-Wise, who ordered things thus. Therefore, too, dost thou often see Him include in the Torah the children and the women together with the fathers whenever miracles and marvels are mentioned. . . .

It behooves us also to believe that even before the era of the children of Israel, God never left His creatures without a religion fortified by prophecy and miraculous signs and manifest proofs. Whoever witnessed the latter in person was convinced of their authenticity by what he had perceived with his sense of vision. He, again, to whom it was transmitted, was convinced by what he had grasped by means of his sense of hearing. Thus the Torah says about one of these [who lived before the rise of a Jewish nation]: "For I have known him, to the end that he may command his children" (Gen. 18:19).

Chapter 3:2

Now it is fitting that I proceed first to the discussion of the rational precepts of the Torah. I say, then, that divine Wisdom imposed a restraint upon bloodshed among men, because if license were to prevail in this matter, they would cause each other to disappear. The consequence would be, in addition to the pain experienced by the victims, a frustration of the purpose that the All-Wise had in mind with regard to them. For their murder would cut them off from the fulfillment of the function for which He had created them and in the execution of which He had employed them.

Furthermore [divine] Wisdom forbade fornication in order that men might not become like the beasts with the result that no one would know his father so as to show him reverence in return for having raised him. [Another reason for this prohibition was] that the father might bequeath unto his son his possessions just as the son had received from his father the gift of existence. [A further reason was] that a human being might know the rest of his relatives, such as his paternal and maternal uncles, and show them whatever tenderness he was capable of.

Theft was forbidden by [divine] Wisdom because, if it were permitted, some men would rely on stealing the others' wealth, and they would neither till the soil nor engage in any other lucrative occupation. And if all were to rely on this source of livelihood, even stealing would become impossible, because, with the disappearance of all property, there would be absolutely nothing in existence that might be stolen.

Finally, [divine] Wisdom has made it one of its first injunctions that we speak the truth and desist from lying. For the truth is an assertion about a thing as it really is and in accordance with its actual character, whereas telling a lie is making an assertion about a thing that does not correspond to what it really is or to its actual character. Then when the senses, perceiving it, find it to be constituted in one form whilst the soul, reasoning about it, asserts that it is constituted otherwise, these two contrary views set up in the soul will oppose each other, and, on account of their mutual exclusion, the thing will be regarded by the soul as something grotesque.

Let me say next that I have seen some people who are of the opinion that these four principal vices that have been listed above are not at all objectionable. Only that is objectionable in their view which causes them pain and worry and grief, whilst the good is what affords them pleasure and rest. This thesis will be refuted by me at considerable length in the fourth treatise of this book, in the chapter on "justice." I shall, however, cite a portion of that refutation here. . . .

I say, then, that the slaying of an enemy is an act that gives pleasure to the slayer but pain to the slain. Likewise, the taking of another man's possessions or his wife gives pleasure to the robber but pain to the robbed. In the opinion of those who hold this view, however, each of these two acts would have to be regarded as wisdom and folly at one and the same time — as wisdom because it affords pleasure to the murderer or the thief or the adulterer, and as folly because it inflicts pain on his opponent. Now, any theory that leads to such internal contradiction and mutual exclusion must be false. In fact, there are instances in which two such contrary things can both befall one and the same person, as when he eats honey into which some poison has fallen. This is something that gives pleasure and also causes death, and would consequently, according to their theory, have to be considered as wisdom and folly at one and the same time.

Let me proceed further now and discourse about the second general division of the laws of the Torah. This division consists of acts which from the standpoint of reason are optional. Yet the Law has made some of them obligatory and others forbidden, and left the rest optional as they had been. They include such matters as the consecration of certain days from among others, like the Sabbath and the festivals, and the consecration of certain human beings from among others, such as the prophet and the priest, and refraining from eating certain foods, and the avoidance of cohabitation with certain persons, and going into isolation immediately upon the occurrence of certain accidents because of defilement.

But even though the chief reason for the fulfillment of these principal precepts and their derivatives and whatever is connected with them is the fact that they represent the command of our Lord and enable us to reap a special advantage [i.e., future life — Eds.], yet I find that most of them have as their basis partially useful purposes. I see fit, therefore, to note some of these motivations and discuss them, although the wisdom of God, blessed and exalted be He, is above all that.

Now among the benefits accruing from the consecration of certain seasons, by desisting from work on them, there is first of all that of obtaining relaxation from much exertion. Furthermore, it presents the opportunity for the attainment of a little bit of knowledge and a little additional praying. It also affords men leisure to meet each other at gatherings where they can confer about matters of their religion and make public announcements about them, and perform other functions of the same order.

Some of the benefits accruing from consecrating a particular person from among others are that it makes it possible to obtain more knowledge from him and to secure his services as an intercessor. [It] also [enables him] to imbue his fellow-men with the desire for righteousness so that they might thereby attain something like his own eminence. Finally [it permits him] to concern himself with the moral improvement of humanity, since he is qualified for such a task, and other things of this nature.

Among the advantages, again, that result from the prohibition against the eating of [only] certain animals is the prevention of any comparison between them and the Creator. For it is inconceivable that God would permit anything resembling Him to be eaten or, on the other hand, that [the eating of such a being] could cause defilement to man. This precept also serves to keep man from worshiping any of these animals, since it is not seemly for him to worship what has been given to him for food, nor what has been declared unclean for him.

As for the advantages accruing from the avoidance of cohabitation with certain women, those derived from observing this ruling in regard to a married woman are such as we have stated previously. As far as the mother, sister, and daughter are concerned, since the relationship with them is necessarily intimate, the license to marry them would encourage dissoluteness on their part. There exists also the danger, if this were permitted, that men would be fascinated by those of their female relatives who have a beautiful figure, while those possessing homely features would be spurned even by strangers, since the latter would see that the male relatives [of these women] do not desire them.

Some of the benefits accruing from the observance of the laws of uncleanliness and cleanliness are that man is thereby led to think humbly of his flesh, that it enhances for him the value of prayer by virtue of his being cut off therefrom for a while during the period of defilement, that it endears to him the Temple which he was prevented from entering in the state of impurity, and finally that it causes him to dedicate his heart to the fear of God.

Similarly, if one were to follow up most of these revealed precepts, one would discover that they are, to a large extent at least, partially justified and possess much utilitarian value, although the wisdom and the view that the Creator had in mind in decreeing them is far above anything that men can grasp, as Scripture says: "For as the heavens are higher than the earth, so are My ways higher than your ways" (Isa. 55:9).

Social Nomoi and Divine Laws

3. Judah Halevi, *The Kuzari* 1:79; 2:46–49; 3:7, 11

The Kuzari: The Book of Refutation and Proof on Behalf of the Despised Religion, translated by Lawrence Berman and Barry S. Kogan; forthcoming in the Yale Judaica Series (Yale University Press).

In The Kuzari, *Judah Halevi, formulates an anti-rationalist critique of philosophical religion. It takes the form of a dialogue between the pagan king of the Khazars seeking the true religion and representatives of Christianity, Islam, Philosophy, and Judaism, in which the Jewish sage quickly becomes the king's sole interlocutor. The* Kuzari's *critique of philosophy finds expression in its conception of prophecy as central to Jewish identity (cf. C11), and in its theory of the commandments. For Halevi, what distinguishes religion is the quest for the "divine order" (literally, "divine thing,"* inyan ha-elohi *in the Hebrew translation of Halevi's Arabic).*

(1:79) The sage said: Certainly the things that are fit to receive the divine influence are not within the capacity of human beings [to grasp], nor is it possible for them to determine their [specific] quantities and qualities. Moreover, even if people were to know their essential natures, they would not know their [proper] times, places, circumstances, and the means of preparing for them. For that, one would need consummate divine knowledge, explained thoroughly by God. Someone to whom this instruction has come and who conforms to it in accordance with its [specified] limits and conditions, with pure intent, is the faithful person. But someone who has tried to modify things in order to receive that [influence] by means of [his own] ingenuity, reasoning, and opinions [drawn] from what is found in the books of the astrologers [with respect to] summoning the influence of spiritual beings and making talismans is the rebel, because he offers sacrifices and burns incense on the basis of reasoning and conjecture. Thus, he does not know the true character of what is necessary, [nor] how much, in what way, in which place, at what time, through which person, how it should be handled, and many [other] circumstances, which it would take far too long to describe.

He is like the fool who entered the pharmacy of a physician [who was] well-known for his effective medicines. The physician wasn't there, but people would come to that pharmacy seeking help [anyway]. The fool [in turn] would dispense [the contents] of the vials to them without knowing the medicines [they contained] nor even how much [of each] medicine should be dispensed to each individual. Therefore, he killed people by means of the very medicines that might have helped them. Now, if it happened by coincidence that one of them derived some benefit from [the contents of] one of those vials, the people took a liking to it and said that that [one] was the most beneficial [medicine] until it failed them or [until] they accidentally came to regard something else as beneficial, [so that] they also took a liking to it. They didn't know that what is beneficial in itself is only the advice of that learned physician who had prepared those medicines [in the first place], had dispensed them properly, and would instruct the patient to prepare himself with the most appropriate regimen for [taking] each medicine, such as [the right] food, drink, exercise, rest, sleep, [time] awake, air, sedation, and other such things. So, too, people before Moses, except for a few, used to be deceived into [following] astrological and natural nomoi, going from nomos to nomos and from deity to deity. Sometimes they would cling to several of them [at once] and forget the One who prepares them and dispenses them. They used to believe [those nomoi and deities] to be the cause of [all kinds of] benefits, when in themselves they are the cause of [all kinds of] harm, depending on their disposition and preparation. However, what is [truly] beneficial in itself is the divine order, and what is harmful in itself is its absence.

(2:46) The sage said: . . . Do you think that coming close [to God] is simply a matter of being submissive and abasing oneself and [doing] whatever else follows along the same line?

(2:47) The Khazar said: Yes, with justice, that is exactly what I think. I have read it in your books, just as it was taught [in Scripture]: "What does YHWH, your God, demand of you? Only this: To revere YHWH, your God, etc." (Deut. 10:12), and "What YHWH requires of you [only doing justice and loving mercy, and to walk modestly with your God]" (Mic. 6:8), and there are many other [passages] besides those.

(2:48) The sage said: These and similar such things are the intellectual nomoi [laws]. They are the preparation and preamble to the divine religious Law and precede it [both] in nature and in time. They are indispensable for governing any group of human beings, no matter what [it may be], so that even a band of robbers cannot avoid adhering to justice in what is [simply] between them. Otherwise, their association would not last. Now, when Israel's rebelliousness got to the point that they disregarded [even] the intellectual [and] governmental laws—which are [as] indispensable for [the existence of] every group as certain natural things are indispensable for every individual, like eating and drinking, moving and resting, and sleeping and being awake—but nevertheless held fast to the [various] acts of worship pertaining to the sacrifices and other divine commandments, which are based on hearing [i.e., revelation alone], He became satisfied with less from them. Hence, they were told: "If only you kept the laws that [even] the least and lowest groups accept as obligatory, such as adhering to justice and what is good and also acknowledging God's bounty!" For the divine religious Law can only be fulfilled completely after perfect [adherence to] the governmental and intellectual law [has been achieved], and included within the intellectual law is [both] adhering to justice and acknowledging God's bounty.

Accordingly, how is it [acceptable] for someone who neglects this [to offer] sacrifices, and to observe the Sabbath, and circumcision, and other things of that sort that the intellect neither requires nor rejects? They are the [divine] laws by means of which Israel was singled out, [constituting] an addition to the intellectual ones, and by means of which the bounty of the divine order reached them. But then, they did not know how these laws were obligatory, just as they did not know how it happened that the glory of YHWH descended among them, [how] the fire of YHWH consumes their sacrifices, how they heard the Lord's address to them, and how everything that happened to them took place with respect to the [various] things that [people's] intellects cannot bear to think possible—were it not for direct experience and the personally attested spectacle [they saw], which cannot be rejected. Thus, it was because of [a situation] like this that they were addressed [with the words] "What does YHWH require of you" (Mic. 6:8) and "Add your burnt offerings to your other sacrifices" (Jer. 7:21) and other [passages] resembling these. Is it possible for the [true] Israelite to confine himself to "doing justice and loving mercy" (Mic. 6:8), while treating circumcision, the Sabbath, and the rest of the [divine] laws as superfluous, but [still] prosper?

(2:49) The Khazar said: Not according to what you set forth earlier. [For] according to the philosophers' opinion, he only becomes a virtuous man and does not care about which way he [takes to] come close [to God], whether by becoming a Jew, or a Christian, or something else, or by [following] what he [merely] invents for himself. But now we have really gone back to engaging in intellectual speculation, syllogistic reasoning, and arbitrary judgment, whereby all people begin striving to be in accord with religious laws of their own making, insofar as their reasoning has led them to it. But this is absurd.

(3:7) The sage said: The governmental actions and the intellectual nomoi are the things that are known. But the divine [ones], which are added to these in order to be realized within [the] religious community of [the] living God who governs it, are not known until they come from Him in an explicated [and] detailed manner. Indeed, even if the essential characteristics of those governmental and intellectual ones were known, their precise determination is not known; for we know that giving charity and sharing [what we have] are obligatory, and that training the soul by means of fasting and obedience is obligatory. [We also know that] deceit is disgraceful, and promiscuous behavior with women is disgraceful too; as is having intercourse with some [of one's] relatives, whereas honoring [one's] parents is obligatory and whatever [else] resembles that. However, defining [all] that and determining it [in detail] so that it is appropriate for everyone belongs only to

God, exalted be He. As for the divine actions, they are outside the scope of our intellects; but they are also not rejected by the intellect. Rather, the intellect will follow them unquestioningly, just as a person who is sick will follow the physician unquestioningly with regard to his medicines and prescriptions. Don't you see how far circumcision is from syllogistic reasoning and [how] it has no connection with governance? Still, Abraham submitted himself to it, despite the difficulty of the command from the standpoint of nature, when he was one hundred years old, [both] for his own sake and for the sake of his child. It became a sign of the covenant so that the divine order might attach itself to him and to his progeny, as [Scripture] says: "I will establish My covenant between Me and you, and your offspring to come, as an everlasting covenant through the ages to be God to you, etc." (Gen. 17:7).

(3:11) The sage said: The superior man among us observes these [specific] divine laws, I mean, circumcision, the Sabbaths and festivals and their [various] concomitants, which are legislated by God, the observance of [the commandments dealing with] illicit sexual relations, mixed kinds in relation to plants, clothes, and animals, the seventh year and the jubilee year, avoidance of idolatry and all that pertains to it. . . . He complies with whatever is incumbent upon him for every transgression [he commits, whether] unintentional and intentional, by [offering] a sacrifice. . . . In general, he will observe whatever he possibly can of the divine orders [given him] so as to be truthful when he says, "I have neither transgressed nor neglected any of Your commandments" (Deut. 26:13), quite apart from the vows, free-will offerings, and sacred gifts of greeting. . . . These things and others like them are the divine laws, and complete observance of most of them is possible only through the service of the priests [in the Temple].

Now, the governmental laws, for example, consist [in the following]: "You shall not murder; You shall not commit adultery; You shall not steal; You shall not bear [false witness] against your neighbor; honor [your] father and mother" (Exod. 20:12–13); "Love your neighbor [as yourself]" (Lev. 19:18); You too "must befriend the stranger" (Deut. 10:19); "You shall not deal deceitfully or falsely [with one another]" (Lev. 19:11); having nothing to do with usury and [charging] interest (Lev. 25:36), striving to have honest scales, honest weights . . . as well as leaving behind the gleanings, the fallen fruit, and the corners [of one's fields] (Deut. 24:19–21), and whatever [else] resembles this.

The Ends of Divine Law
4. Maimonides, *The Guide of the Perplexed* 3:31, 26–27

The Guide of the Perplexed, translated with an introduction and notes by Shlomo Pines (Chicago: University of Chicago Press, 1963), pp. 523–24, 506–12.

In the chapters below, Maimonides presents the principles of his teleological theory of the rationality of the commandments. Maimonides views religion as a political endeavor, and divine law as the law for the most perfect polity. Central to this theory is a distinction (developed in Guide *2:40; cf. C30) between two types of law: nomos and divine law. The former aims solely at the ordering of society, whereas the latter seeks also to cultivate rational perfection culminating in the knowledge of God. Maimonides goes on to provide a detailed exposition of the commandments in light of these principles (*Guide *3:35–49).*

(3:31) There is a group of human beings who consider it a grievous thing that causes should be given for any law; what would please them most is that the intellect would not find a meaning for the commandments and prohibitions. What compels them to feel thus is a sickness that they find in their souls, a sickness to which they are unable to give utterance and of which they cannot furnish a satisfactory account. For they think that if those laws were useful in this existence and had been given to us for this or that reason, it would be as if they derived from the reflection and the understanding of some intelligent being. If, however, there is a thing for which the intellect could not find any meaning at all and that does not lead to something useful, it indubitably derives from God; for the reflection of man would not lead to such a thing. It is as if, according to these people of weak intellects, man were more perfect than his Maker; for man speaks and acts in a manner that leads to some intended end, whereas the deity does not act thus, but commands us to do things that are not useful to us and forbids us to do things that are not harmful to us. But He is far exalted above this; the contrary is the case—the whole purpose consisting in what is useful for us, as we have explained on the basis of this dictum: "For our good always, that He might preserve us alive, as it is at this day" (Deut. 6:24). And it says: "Which shall hear all these statutes [*hukkim*] and say: Surely this great community is a wise and understanding people" (Deut. 4:6). Thus it states explicitly that even all the statutes [*hukkim*] will show to all the nations that they have been given with wisdom and understanding. Now if there is a thing for which no reason is known and that does not either procure something useful or ward off something harmful, why should one say of one who believes in it or practices it that he is wise and understanding and of great worth? And why should the religious communities think it a wonder? Rather things are indubitably as we have mentioned: every commandment from among these six hundred and thirteen commandments exists either with a view to communicating a correct opinion, or to putting an end to an unhealthy opinion, or to communicating a rule of justice, or to warding off an injustice, or to endowing men with a noble moral quality, or to warning them against an evil moral quality. Thus all [the commandments] are bound up with three things: opinions, moral qualities, and political civic actions.

(3:26) Just as there is disagreement among the men of speculation among the adherents of Law whether His works, may He be exalted, are consequent upon wisdom or upon the will alone without being intended toward any end at all, there is also the same disagreement among them regarding our Laws, which He has given us. Thus there are people who do not seek for them any cause at all, saying that all Laws are consequent upon the will alone. There are also people who say that every commandment and prohibition in these Laws is consequent upon wisdom and aims at some end, and that all Laws have causes and were given in view of some utility. It is, however, the doctrine of all of us—both of the multitude and of the elite—that all the Laws have a cause, though we ignore [i.e., are ignorant of—Eds.] the causes for some of them and we do not know the manner in which they conform to wisdom. With regard to this the texts of the Book are clear: "righteous statutes [*hukkim*] and judgments" (Deut. 4:8); "The judgments of the Lord are true, they are righteous altogether" (Ps. 19:10).

About the statutes designated as *hukkim*—for instance those concerning the mingled stuff, meat in milk, and the sending of the goat—[the Sages], may their memory be blessed, make literally the following statement: "Things which I have prescribed for you, about which you have not the permission to think, which are criticized by Satan and refuted by the Gentiles" (BT Yoma 67b [§1]). They are not believed by the multitude of the Sages to be things for which there is no cause at all and for which one must not seek an end. For this would lead, according to what we have explained, to their being considered as frivolous actions. On the contrary, the multitude of the Sages believe that there indubitably is a cause for them—I mean to say a useful end—but that it is hidden from us either because of the incapacity of our intellects or the deficiency of our knowledge. Consequently there is, in their opinion, a cause for all the commandments; I mean to say that any particular commandment or prohibition has a useful end. In the case of some of them, it is clear to us in what way they are useful—as in the case of the prohibition of killing and stealing. In the case of others, their utility is not clear—as in the case of interdiction of the first products [of trees] and of [sowing] the vineyard with diverse seeds. Those commandments whose utility is clear to the multitude are called *mishpatim* [judgments], and those whose utility is not clear to the multitude are called *hukkim* [statutes]. They always say with regard to the verse: "For it is no vain thing" (Deut. 32:47)— "And if it is vain, it is because of you" (JT Peah 15b); meaning that this legislation is not a vain matter without useful end and that if it seems to you that this is the case with regard to some of the commandments, the deficiency resides in your apprehension. You already know the tradition that is widespread among us according to which the causes for all the commandments, with the exception of that concerning the red heifer,[3] were known to Solomon, and also their [the Rabbis'—Eds.] dictum that God hid the causes for the commandments in order that they should not be held in little esteem, as happened to Solomon with regard to the three commandments whose causes are made clear.[4] . . . What everyone endowed with a sound intellect ought to believe on this subject is what I shall set forth to you: The gener-

3. See Num. 19. In some Rabbinic sources this commandment is listed among the mysterious *hukkim* (cf. §1).
4. Cf. BT Sanhedrin 21b, which refers to the three commandments in the law of kings (Deut. 17:16–17 [C3, §5]).

alities of the commandments necessarily have a cause and have been given because of a certain utility; their details are that in regard to which it was said of the commandments that they were given merely for the sake of commanding something. . . . The true reality of particulars of commandments is illustrated by the sacrifices. The offering of sacrifices has in itself a great and manifest utility, as I shall make clear. But no cause will ever be found for the fact that one particular sacrifice consists in a lamb and another in a ram and that the number of the victims should be one particular number. Accordingly, in my opinion, all those who occupy themselves with finding causes for something of these particulars are stricken with a prolonged madness in the course of which they do not put an end to an incongruity, but rather increase the number of incongruities. Those who imagine that a cause may be found for such like things are as far from truth as those who imagine that the generalities of a commandment are not designed with a view to some real utility. . . .

(3:27) The Law as a whole aims at two things: the welfare of the soul and the welfare of the body. As for the welfare of the soul, it consists in the multitude's acquiring correct opinions corresponding to their respective capacity. Therefore some of them [namely, the opinions] are set forth explicitly and some of them are set forth in parables. For it is not within the nature of the common multitude that its capacity should suffice for apprehending that subject matter as it is. As for the welfare of the body, it comes about by the improvement of their ways of living one with another. This is achieved through two things. One of them is the abolition of their wronging each other. This is tantamount to every individual among the people not being permitted to act according to his will and up to the limits of his power, but being forced to do that which is useful to the whole. The second thing consists in the acquisition by every human individual of moral qualities that are useful for life in society so that the affairs of the city may be ordered. Know that as between these two aims, one is indubitably greater in nobility, namely, the welfare of the soul—I mean the procuring of correct opinions—while the second aim—I mean the welfare of the body—is prior in nature and time. The latter aim consists in the governance of the city and the wellbeing of the states of all its people according to their capacity. This second aim is the more certain one, and it is the one regarding which every effort has been made precisely to expound it and all its particulars. For the first aim can only be achieved after achieving this second one. For it has already been demonstrated that man has two perfections: a first perfection, which is the perfection of the body, and an ultimate perfection, which is the perfection of the soul. The first perfection consists in being healthy and in the very best bodily state, and this is only possible through his finding the things necessary for him whenever he seeks them. These are his food and all the other things needed for the governance of his body, such as a shelter, bathing, and so forth. This cannot be achieved in any way by one isolated individual. For an individual can only attain all this through a political association, it being already known that man is political by nature. His ultimate perfection is to become rational *in actu,* I mean to have an intellect *in actu;* this would consist in his knowing everything concerning all the beings that it is within the capacity of man to know in accordance with his ultimate perfection. It is clear that to this ultimate perfection there do not belong either actions or moral qualities and that it consists only of opinions toward which speculation has led and that investigation has rendered compulsory. It is also clear that this noble and ultimate perfection can only be achieved after the first perfection has been achieved. For a man cannot represent to himself an intelligible [i.e., an object perceived by the intellect—Eds.] even when taught to understand it and all the more cannot become aware of it of his own accord if he is in pain or is very hungry or is thirsty or is hot or is very cold. But once the first perfection has been achieved it is possible to achieve the ultimate, which is indubitably more noble and is the only cause of permanent preservation.

The true Law then, which as we have already made clear is unique— namely, the Law of Moses our Master—has come to bring us both perfections, I mean the welfare of the states of people in their relations with one another through the abolition of reciprocal wrongdoing and through the acquisition of a noble and excellent character. In this way the preservation of the population of the country and their permanent existence in the same order become possible, so that every one of them achieves his first perfection; I mean also the soundness of the beliefs and the giving of correct opinions through which ultimate perfection is achieved.

Three Kinds of Law

5. Joseph Albo, *Book of Principles* 1:7–8

Sefer Ha-Ikarim, translated and edited by Isaac Husik (Philadelphia: Jewish Publication Society, 1946), pp. 78–88.

Following Maimonides' account of the human condition, which necessitates the political organization of society, Albo, influenced by Thomas Aquinas, presents a threefold legal philosophy, distinguishing natural, positive, and divine law. His argument includes a series of homiletic expositions of Psalm 19 in which the praise of the Torah follows a celebration of God's work in nature.

(7) . . . There are three kinds of law, natural, positive or conventional, and divine. Natural law is the same among all peoples, at all times, and in all places. Positive or conventional is a law ordered by a wise man or men to suit the place and the time and the nature of the persons who are to be controlled by it, like the laws and statutes enacted in certain countries among the ancient idolaters, or those who worship God as human reason dictates without any divine revelation. Divine law is one that is ordered by God through a prophet, like Adam or Noah, or like the custom or law which Abraham taught men, instructing them to worship God and circumcising them by the command of God, or one that is ordered by God through a messenger whom He sends and through whom He gives a law, like the Law of Moses.

The purpose of natural law is to repress wrong, to promote right, in order that men may keep away from theft, robbery, and murder, that society may be able to exist among men and every one be safe from the wrongdoer and oppressor. The purpose of conventional or positive law is to suppress what is unbecoming and to promote what is becoming, that men may keep away from the indecent according to human opinion. Herein lies its advantage over natural law, for conventional law also controls human conduct and arranges their affairs with a view to the improvement of human society, even as natural law. The purpose of divine law is to guide men to obtain true happiness, which is spiritual happiness and immortality. It shows them the way they must follow to obtain it, teaches them the true good that they may take pains to secure it, shows them also real evil that they may guard against it, and trains them to abandon imaginary happiness so that they may not desire it and not feel its loss. And in addition it also lays down the rules of right that the political community may be ordered in a proper manner, so that the bad order of their social life may not prevent them from attaining true happiness, which is the ultimate end of the human race to which they are destined by God. Divine law is therefore superior to conventional or positive.

(8) Positive or conventional law is inferior to divine law in many ways. The first is the one we mentioned, namely that positive law controls human conduct in order to maintain a good political society, but it cannot impart true theoretical knowledge, as we shall show in the sequel, so as to give immortality to the soul and enable it to return to the land of life from which it was taken, because positive law deals only with the becoming and unbecoming. Divine law is adequate for this purpose, because it includes both parts upon which human perfection is based, viz., conduct and theory. Divine law embraces the becoming and unbecoming, and it distinguishes between the true and the false, which constitutes the theoretical part. That is why David describes it as perfect, when he says, "The law of the Lord is perfect, restoring the soul" (Ps. 19:8). The meaning is that the positive law is not perfect because it does not deal with true opinions, but divine law is perfect because it embraces perfection in morals and perfection in theory, which are the two parts upon which the perfection of the soul is dependent. Therefore it "restores" the soul to God who gave it, and to the place which was its original home.

Another point of inferiority of the conventional law to divine law is that the former cannot distinguish between the becoming and the unbecoming in all cases. For a thing may seem becoming or unbecoming to us without being so in reality. For just as it is impossible that a man should be born perfect in all the practical arts, though he may have a natural aptitude for some, so it is impossible that one should be born perfect in all good qualities and free from all defect, though he may have a greater tendency to certain qualities than to others. But that he should have all good qualities is impossible.

It becomes clear now that it is impossible for any author of a human code not to show a natural deficiency in some direction, and regard the becoming as unbecoming and the unbecoming as becoming. His testimony concerning the becoming and the unbecoming will therefore not be true. Thus Plato made a grievous mistake, advocating the unbecoming as though it were becoming. For his idea is that all the women of a given class should be held in common by the men of that class. Thus, the wives of the rulers should be common to all the rulers, the wives of the merchants common to all the merchants, and similarly the wives of the men of a given trade or occupation should be common to the men of that trade or occupation. This is a matter which the Torah forbids; even the Noahide law prohibits it, for Abimelech was told, "Behold, thou shalt die, because of the woman whom thou hast taken; for she is a man's wife" (Gen. 20:3), and his excuse was that he did not know she had a husband. Aristotle, as is known, criticized Plato's idea in this matter.

This shows that no human being is able to differentiate correctly between the becoming and the unbecoming, and his opinion on this matter cannot therefore be relied upon. Not to speak of theoretical knowledge, where it is clear that we cannot rely on a human opinion concerning profound problems, such as the creation or eternity of the world, for the human mind is not adequate to know this with certainty. But "The testimony of the Lord is sure, making wise the simple" (Ps. 19:8), for it gives a reliable statement on the problem of the world's origin, and on other important problems, including morals.

Another point of inferiority in conventional law as compared with divine is that it cannot give full satisfaction to those who follow its requirements. The reason is that when a person is in doubt whether the thing he does is sufficient to lead him to the end intended, he cannot feel satisfaction in what he does. But a person who follows the conventional law is precisely in this position. He does not know whether that which the law defines as just is really just or only apparently so. Hence he cannot find satisfaction. He, however, who lives by the divine law knows that what is defined therein as just is really just. Hence he finds satisfaction in his conduct. This is why "The precepts of the Lord are right, rejoicing the heart" (Ps. 19:9).

Another point of inferiority in the conventional law as compared with the divine is this. Conventional law cannot define the specific acts which are proper in the several virtues. It can only make general statements in the same way as a definition can be given of the general only, while the particular can not be defined. Similarly, conventional law can not define particular acts. Thus Aristotle in his *Ethics* says repeatedly in connection with the different virtues that a virtuous act consists in doing the proper thing at the proper time and in the proper place, but he does not explain what is the proper time and the proper place. It is clearly a matter which not everyone is capable of determining. Aristotle also says in various places in the *Ethics* that the proper measure must be maintained in every act, but does not tell us what the proper measure is. It would seem therefore that his opinion was that the determination of this matter must be sought elsewhere.

. . . Again, the author of conventional law is a human being, and therefore cannot determine the becoming and the unbecoming at all times. For those things which pertain to general opinion may change, and that which is now regarded as becoming may be regarded later as unbecoming and vice versa. Thus we find that in the days of Cain and Abel and the ancient times generally, the marriage of a sister was not thought indecent. The same thing was true in the time of Abraham. For Abraham in excusing himself to Abimelech said, "And moreover she is indeed my sister, the daughter of my father, but not the daughter of my mother" (Gen. 20:12). Later the marriage of sisters came to be regarded as indecent. For this reason, the aversion from the unbecoming which is acquired through the conventional law cannot last forever, because it changes with the times. But the divine law, by reason of the fact that it is determined by divine wisdom, declares the becoming and the unbecoming for all time. And therefore the aversion from the unbecoming that is acquired through the divine law is not liable to change or destruction, for it is free from all error and impurity, and can therefore exist forever like silver which is free from all dross, as the Psalmist says: "The words of the Lord are pure words, as silver tried in a crucible on the earth, refined seven times" (Ps. 12:7).

Commentary. Law and Reason

Since the seventeenth century, the central question about reason and revelation has usually been, Is it possible rationally to prove the existence of God? But that isn't the question that these selections address. All these thinkers—even Halevi and Albo, who express some skepticism about the reach of philosophy—philosophized within a classical tradition in which the possibility of establishing the existence of God, at least the God of the philosophers, was assumed. The question they deal with here is what we are to do *after* we have accepted the existence of a supreme being.

Selection 1, from BT Yoma, introduces a distinction that figures in all our selections, between God's *mishpatim* (ordinances), especially those that belong to a rationally defensible (or at least arguable) morality, and God's mysterious *hukkim* (edicts), that is, such specifically religious or ritual commandments as the laws of *kashrut*, the prohibition on wearing *sha'atnez* (mixtures of wool and linen), and circumcision. One of the positions represented here (notably by Judah Halevi) is that with respect to the latter we have to rely entirely on revelation (a rational defense of the *hukkim* is beyond our powers), while our natural intellectual powers do suffice to justify the former. This position is also contested here, notably by Saadiah and Maimonides, who argue that even the ritual edicts have a largely rational justification. However, the debates going on within these selections and between them concern the power (or the impotence) of reason in the area of rationally arguable morality as much as they do the rationality of the ritual commandments. Because the possibility or impossibility of rationally defending our moral commitments is such a live topic today, I shall begin by discussing the positions of these thinkers with respect to that issue.

First, let me say a word about the conception of morality that is at stake here—what BT Yoma calls "things which, had they not been laid down, ought to have been laid down." In certain ways, that conception is a fairly modest one. If these selections are not concerned with the question Can reason prove the existence of God? neither are they concerned with the question Why should I be moral? (which Plato discussed at such length). When Saadiah argues (in §2) against the view that "the good is what affords . . . pleasure and rest," he takes it for granted that the advocates of this hedonistic position are willing to make the maxim "Treat anything that gives pleasure and relief as good and anything that gives pain or worry or grief as evil" a *universal* maxim of conduct (in what we would call a Kantian sense). In effect, Saadiah's argument appeals to the "categorical imperative." Saadiah is saying that the hedonist maxim cannot be universalized without contradiction. A thinker like Plato's Thrasymachus (in book I of *The Republic*), who doesn't set out to defend a universalizable morality is not addressed at all.

The morality that these thinkers describe as accessible to reason (although they differ on the seriousness of our propensity to make mistakes about it) is a morality justified, in the first instance, by its necessity as a means to a certain end—and that end is the maintenance of human society or, more precisely, the maintenance of a minimal set of social goods. These minimal goods are the protection of members from the continual disruption of their lives by violence, theft, fraud, and anarchy, as well as the securing of certain positive goods, in particular the maintenance and support of family life. (Considerations of what is necessary for the support of family life are appealed to, for instance, in the justification or attempted justification of traditional sexual morality by Saadiah.) A stable society that affords its members protection (or at least legal redress) against murder, theft, fraud, and the sorts of sexual improprieties that are supposed to be destructive of family life is not, however, an end in itself for any of these thinkers (this is especially true of Maimonides, whose understanding of the role of morality in religious life is far too complex to be represented in this or any single selection).

Briefly, the reason that we want a society whose members do not have to worry about being enslaved or swindled or robbed or murdered or having their families disrupted is that these goods—freedom from fear of these things happening and the existence of a supportive and cooperative family and community—have to be in place if we are to aspire to being anything *higher* than merely successful social animals. These thinkers quite reasonably take it for granted that we *are* social animals and that one can say something about what the welfare of human beings qua social animals requires; but they do not think that the vocation of human beings is simply to be successful social animals. As religious thinkers, they think our vocation is incomparably higher than that. This thought continues to have considerable validity today: in contemporary language, the preconditions for what John Rawls (in *A Theory of Justice,* 1971) calls a "well-ordered society" are goods that have to be in place if people are to have "life projects" that give meaning and dignity to their lives.

Albo (in §5) interestingly, however, divides what I have called rationally arguable morality into two parts: a part he calls "natural law," which seems to consist of simple universal principles (like the seven Noahide commandments)—for example, "Do not murder," "Do not steal"—which are valid for all societies at all times, and what is here translated as "conventional law" or "positive law," principles that, while having the same rationale as natural law, are adapted to circumstances that may vary from society to society, as well as principles that concern not only what is minimally necessary for social life but also what is necessary for its improvement. Both Albo and Saadiah hold the view, however, that even in the area of rationally arguable morality, revelation is decidedly superior to unaided reason. The arguments they give, though not acceptable to a person who, like myself, rejects the idea of revelation as an inerrant source of knowledge of God's will, are not without interest. Albo cites disagreements between highly intelligent thinkers concerning the best sexual arrangements. Plato, he reminds us, held that the people of each of the major social classes (in the ideal society) ought to have wives in common, which Albo thinks was clearly a mistake. The fact that the wise disagree over what is a good positive law shows, he thinks, that positive or conventional law arrived at by human reason without the aid of revelation will always be marred by serious errors. Of course, an alternative conclusion, one vigorously defended by John Dewey, would be that no moral or political code that human beings are able to make up, *with* or *without* the aid of what they take to be revelation, can be free of error, any more than any scientific theory that human beings make up can be entirely free of error (complete freedom from error is an unreasonable goal). But this was not a possible position for our authors.

In Saadiah, what one finds is perhaps not as extreme a pessimism concerning the powers of reason as Albo's, but rather an epistemic argument for the superiority of revelation over reason. Reason may be able to arrive at rational moral law by "speculation" (i.e., metaphysical inquiry), according to Saadiah, but this is very slow, and even the best philosopher is apt to make mistakes. Revelation gives us a quicker path and an error-free path to what speculation could eventually arrive at. The views of Albo and of Saadiah both presuppose, however, that we possess a revelation with respect to morality that is error-free. Those of us who believe that the human authors of the Bible (however inspired they were) made mistakes with respect to morality—for example, in their attitudes and legislation concerning women, their attitudes and legislation concerning gays, and so on—have to reject this presupposition. But the question they raise—What should we do about the obvious fallibility of our moral opinions?—is still very much with us.

Leaving the area of *mishpatim* or general morality and coming now to the *hukkim,* and particularly the ritual *hukkim,* such as *kashrut, sha'atnez,* and circumcision, here, too, we find a range of opinions. It is obvious that some of the authors, notably Saadiah and Maimonides, wish to give justifications for most, if not all, of the *hukkim* in terms of utility; but the notion of utility that they employ must not be misunderstood. It is not a question of, say, justifying the prohibition on eating pork by arguing that it is a way of avoiding trichinosis. Sometimes, to be sure, practical utility *is* what is at stake, as when Saadiah tells us that "among the benefits accruing from the consecration of certain seasons, by desisting from work on them, there is first of all that of obtaining relaxation from much exertion." But generally the utility cited in connection with obeying a ritual commandment is of a moral or religious nature. For example, Saadiah goes on to say that when we desist from work on the Sabbath or a holiday, this gives us the opportunity to obtain knowledge and to do additional praying. Similarly, we are told that among the benefits accruing from consecrating a particular person from among others is that it enables that person to imbue his fellows with the desire for righteousness. Maimonides' justifications for particular *mitzvot* are regularly of this kind. Ehud Benor, in a fine study of Maimonides' philosophy of religion (*The Worship of the Heart,* 1995), has shown that the Maimonidean rationale for the structure of the *amidah,* the primary daily prayer, has to do with the role of prayer in moral and spiritual education.

For Judah Halevi all such justifications fall short. Only God knows the true reasons for the ritual commandments, and we obey them because Jews are required to do what God has commanded and because it is glorious to obey God. This justification, that they are directly commanded by God, is one that many modern Jews, even religious Jews (e.g., members of the Conservative, Reform, and Reconstructionist movements), cannot accept. Even within Orthodoxy, the Halevi position is an extreme one. David Weiss Halivni, in his book *Peshat and Derash* (1991), has discerned within the tradition a "nonmaximalist view of revelation," according to which what was revealed to Moses on Sinai was not the details of the *hukkim* but only "general principles"—and then the detailed laws and explanations were worked out by human beings on the basis of the principles. And with respect to those ordinances that are "from the rabbis" (*derabbanan*) rather than directly from the Bible, there is a well-known position according to which what God commanded was that the rabbis work out the details by majority vote. The authority of the rabbis to do this is, however, still held to be directly bestowed by God. But Jews who belong to the non-Orthodox movements find it hard to see even the authority of the rabbinate as literally commanded by God.

For such Jews today, even if they cannot accept the details of Maimonides' justification for this or that *mitzvah,* the idea of seeing the rituals that have so long been a part of the Jewish religious tradition and of Jewish life in general as also being (like the rituals of every great religious tradition) a way of *shaping a particular religious sensibility* is one that we can resonate to. So I can resonate to Franz Rosenzweig's idea in "The Builders" that just as many of us can hold on to a (perhaps mystical) sense that there is something to the idea of revelation without associating that something with infallibility or the dictation model, perhaps we can also accept that there is something to the idea of ritual observance as "obeying a command" (or a Command), while recognizing that for different Jews different *mitzvot* will have meaning in this way.

Hilary Putnam

Revelation, Morality, and Ritual: Modern Struggles

Divine Law Is Morality

6. Baruch Spinoza, *Theological-Political Treatise,* Chapters 4–5

Tractatus Theologico-Politicus, translated by Samuel Shirley (Leiden: E. J. Brill, 1991), pp. 104–5, 112–15.

Contrary to Maimonides' and Albo's claim that the purpose of Torah law is human perfection, Spinoza confines its function to political success. For him divine law is entirely

different. It is universally apprehended by human reason, and obedience to it follows
"naturally" from our knowledge of God. Hence the ritual commandments delivered
at Sinai are no part of it; they belong to a kind of divine positive law intended for
Israel alone—and only for Israel conceived as a polity. In making this argument, para-
doxically, Spinoza draws upon Maimonides' claim that worshiping God out of love is
the "practice of truth because it is the truth" (MT Repentance 10:2); so it requires no
worldly motivation.

Chapter 4

. . . Since the love of God is man's highest happiness and blessedness,
and the final end and aim of all human action, it follows that only he observes the Divine Law who makes it his object to love God not through fear
of punishment nor through love of some other thing such as sensual pleasure,
fame, and so forth, but from the mere fact that he knows God, or knows
that the knowledge and love of God is the supreme good. So the sum of the
Divine Law and its chief command is to love God as the supreme good. . . .

The natural Divine Law does not enjoin ceremonial rites, that is, actions which in themselves are of no significance and are termed good merely
by tradition, or which symbolize some good necessary for salvation, or, if
you prefer, actions whose explanation surpasses human understanding. For
the natural light of reason enjoins nothing that is not within the compass of
reason, but only what it can show us quite clearly to be a good, or a means
to our blessedness. The things whose goodness derives only from authority
and tradition, or from their symbolic representation of some good, cannot
perfect our intellect; they are mere shadows, and cannot be counted as actions that are, as it were, the offspring and fruit of intellect and sound mind.
There is no need for me to go further into this matter.

. . . Finally, we see that the supreme reward of the Divine Law is
the law itself, namely, to know God and to love him in true freedom with
all our heart and mind. The penalty it imposes is the deprivation of these
things and bondage to the flesh, that is, an inconstant and irresolute spirit.

Chapter 5

In the previous chapter we showed that the Divine Law, which makes men truly blessed and teaches the true life, is of universal application to all men. Indeed, our method of deducing it from human nature shows that it must be considered as innate in the human mind and inscribed therein, as it were. Now ceremonial observances—those, at least, that are laid down in the Old Testament—were instituted for the Hebrews alone, and were so adapted to the nature of their government that they could not be practiced by the individual but involved the community as a whole. So it is evident that they do not pertain to the Divine Law, and therefore do not contribute to blessedness and virtue. They have regard only to the election of the Hebrews, that is, (as we demonstrated in chapter 3) to their temporal and material prosperity and peaceful government, and therefore could have been of practical value only while their state existed. If in the Old Testament we find them included in God's law, this can only be because they owed their institution to revelation, or to principles revealed therein. However, since reason, be it of the soundest, carries little weight with the common run of theologians, I now intend to confirm by Scriptural authority what we have just demonstrated; and then, for greater clarity, I shall go on to show how and why ceremonial observances served to strengthen and preserve the Jewish state. . . .

The fact that the observance of ceremonies has regard only to the temporal prosperity of the state and in no way contributes to blessedness is . . . evident from Scripture, which for ceremonial observance promises nothing but material advantages and pleasures, while blessedness is promised only for observance of the universal Divine Law. In the five books commonly attributed to Moses the only promise made, as I have already said, is worldly success—honors or fame, victory, riches, life's pleasures, and health. And although these five books contain much about moral teaching as well as ceremonial observance, these passages are not set forth as moral teachings of universal application to all men, but as commands particularly adapted to the understanding and character of only the Hebrew nation, and therefore relating only to the welfare of their state. For example, it is not as a teacher or prophet that Moses forbids the Jews to kill or to steal; it is as a lawgiver or ruler that he issues these commands. He does not justify his precepts by reasoning, but attaches to his commands a penalty, a penalty which can vary, and must vary, to suit the character of each single nation, as we well know from experience. So, too, his command not to commit adultery has regard only to the good of the commonwealth and state. If he had intended this to be a moral precept that had regard not merely to the good of the common-wealth but to the peace of mind and the true blessedness of the individual, he would have condemned not merely the external act but the very wish, as did Christ, who taught only universal moral precepts (see Matt. 5:28). It is for this reason that Christ promises a spiritual reward, not, like Moses, a material reward. For Christ, as I have said, was sent not to preserve the state and to institute laws, but only to teach the universal law. Hence we can readily understand that Christ by no means abrogated the law of Moses, for it was not Christ's purpose to introduce new laws into the commonwealth. His chief concern was to teach moral doctrines, keeping them distinct from the laws of the commonwealth. . . .

But let us return to our theme, and cite other passages of Scrip-ture which promise for ceremonial observance nothing but material bene-fits, reserving blessedness solely for the universal Divine Law. None of the prophets spoke more clearly on this subject than Isaiah. In chapter 58, after his condemnation of hypocrisy he commends the freeing of the oppressed and charity towards oneself and one's neighbor, promising in return, "Then shall thy light break forth as the morning, and thine health shall spring forth speedily, and thy righteousness shall go before thee; the glory of the Lord shall gather thee in" (Isa. 58:8). Then he goes on to commend the Sabbath, too, and for its diligent observance he promises, "Then shalt thou delight thyself in the Lord, and I shall cause thee to ride upon the high places of the earth, and feed thee with the heritage of Jacob, thy father; for the mouth of the Lord hath spoken it" (Isa. 58:14). So we see that, in return for the free-ing of the oppressed and for charity, the prophet promises a healthy mind in a healthy body, and the glory of the Lord even after death;[5] but in return for the observance of ceremonies he promises only the security of the state, prosperity, and material success. . . .

5. Spinoza follows the traditional midrashic rendering of Isa. 58:8; see *Sifre Numbers* 106.

That the Hebrews are not bound to practice their ceremonial rites since the destruction of their state is clear from Jeremiah, who, when he saw and proclaimed the imminent ruin of the city, said that God delights only in those who know and understand that he exercises lovingkindness, judgment, and righteousness in the earth, and so thereafter only those who know these things are to be deemed worthy of praise (see Jer. 9:23).[6] This is as much as to say that after the destruction of the city God demanded no special service of the Jews and sought nothing of them thereafter except the natural law by which all men are bound.

Revelation and Ritual: Beyond Universal Morality

7. Moses Mendelssohn, *Jerusalem,* Section II

Jerusalem, translated by Allan Arkush (Hanover and London: University Press of New England/Brandeis University Press, 1983), pp. 89–134.

Mendelssohn's political purpose in Jerusalem *was to advocate equal rights for Jewish citizens based on an argument for the separation of church and state. But the call for separation invites a challenge regarding the political character of the Mosaic law: "What are the laws of Moses, they ask, if not a system of religious government, of religious power and rights?" (*Jerusalem, p. 56). *Mendelssohn responded to this challenge with an argument that rejects Maimonides' version of divine law without espousing Spinoza's critique of divine positive law. Mendelssohn's position became one of the basic formulations of Judaism in modernity. His attempt to face the challenge of the loss of Jewish communal autonomy, on the one hand, and the new conditions of emancipation, on the other, echo through the subsequent readings in this chapter. Because of this text's pivotal role and the resemblance of its genre to an essay rather than a traditional text, we present it at length. We have included here Mendelssohn's discussions of the character of the Jewish state and the rights of the community in exile rather than cut his argument and move these sections to the relevant chapters (especially ₵9) below.*

6. A clear contrast to *The Guide of the Perplexed* 3:54 (₵30).

I believe that Judaism knows of no revealed religion in the sense in which Christians understand this term. The Israelites possess a divine *legislation*—laws, commandments, ordinances, rules of life, instruction in the will of God as to how they should conduct themselves in order to attain temporal and eternal felicity. Propositions and prescriptions of this kind were revealed to them by Moses in a miraculous and supernatural manner, but no doctrinal opinions, no saving truths, no universal propositions of reason. These the eternal reveals to us and to all other men, at all times, through *nature* and *thing,* but never through *word* and *script.*

    I fear that this may be astonishing, and again seem new and harsh to some readers. Invariably, little attention has been paid to this difference; one has taken *supernatural legislation* for a *supernatural revelation of religion,* and spoken of Judaism as if it were simply an earlier revelation of religious propositions and doctrines necessary for man's salvation. . . .

    I . . . do not believe that the powers of human reason are insufficient to persuade men of the eternal truths which are indispensable to human felicity, and that God had to reveal them in a supernatural manner. Those who hold this view detract from the omnipotence or the goodness of God, on the one hand, what they believe they are adding to his goodness, on the other. He was, in their opinion, good enough to reveal to men those truths on which their felicity depends, but not omnipotent, or not good enough, to grant them the powers to discover these truths themselves. Moreover, by this assertion one makes the necessity of a supernatural revelation more universal than revelation itself. If, therefore, mankind must be corrupt and miserable without revelation, why has the far greater part of mankind lived without *true revelation* from time immemorial? Why must the two Indies wait until it pleases the Europeans to send them a few comforters to bring them a message without which they can, according to this opinion, live neither virtuously nor happily? To bring them a message which, in their circumstances and state of knowledge, they can neither rightly comprehend nor properly utilize? . . .

    Judaism boasts of no *exclusive* revelation of eternal truths that are indispensable to salvation, of no revealed religion in the sense in which that term is usually understood. Revealed *religion* is one thing, revealed *legislation,* another. The voice which let itself be heard on Sinai on that great day did not proclaim, "I am the eternal, your God, the necessary, independent being, omnipotent and omniscient, that recompenses men in a future life according to their deeds." This is the universal *religion of mankind,* not Judaism; and the universal *religion of mankind,* without which men are neither virtuous nor capable of felicity, was not to be revealed there. In reality, it could not have been revealed there, for who was to be convinced of these eternal doctrines of salvation by the voice of thunder and the sound of trumpets? Surely not the unthinking, brutelike man, whose own reflections had not yet led him to the existence of an invisible being that governs the visible. The miraculous voice would not have instilled any concepts in him and, therefore, would not have convinced him. Still less [would it have convinced] the sophist, whose ears are buzzing with so many doubts and ruminations that he can no longer hear the voice of common sense. He demands *rational proofs,* not miracles. . . .

Anyone who did not know this, who was not imbued with these truths indispensable to human felicity, and was not prepared to approach the holy mountain, could have been stunned and overwhelmed by the great and wonderful manifestations, but he could not have been made aware of what he had not known before. No! All this was presupposed; it was, perhaps, taught, explained, and placed beyond all doubt by human reasoning during the days of preparation. And now the divine voice proclaimed: "I am the eternal, your God, who brought you out of Egypt, who delivered you from bondage, etc." (Exod. 20:2). A historical truth, on which this people's legislation was to be founded, as well as laws, was to be revealed here — commandments and ordinances, not eternal religious truths. . . .

Although the divine book that we received through Moses is, strictly speaking, meant to be a book of laws containing ordinances, rules of life, and prescriptions, it also includes, as is well known, an inexhaustible treasure of rational truths and religious doctrines which are so intimately connected with the laws that they form but one entity. All laws refer to, or are based upon, eternal truths of reason, or remind us of them, and rouse us to ponder them. Hence, our rabbis rightly say: the laws and doctrines are related to each other, like body and soul. I shall have occasion to say more about this below, and shall content myself here with presupposing it as a fact, of the truth of which anyone can convince himself if he peruses the laws of Moses for that purpose, even if only in translation. The experience of many centuries also teaches that this divine law book has become, for a large part of the human race, a source of insight from which it draws new ideas, or according to which it corrects old ones. . . . But all these excellent propositions are presented to the understanding, submitted to us for consideration, without being forced upon our belief. Among all the prescriptions and ordinances of the Mosaic law, there is not a single one which says: *you shall believe or not believe.* They all say: *you shall do or not do.* Faith is not commanded, for it accepts no other commands than those that come to it by way of conviction. All the commandments of the divine law are addressed to man's will, to his power to act. . . .

And now I am able to explain more clearly my surmise about the purpose of the ceremonial law in Judaism. . . . Religious and moral teachings were to be connected with men's everyday activities. The law, to be sure, did not impel them to engage in reflection; it prescribed only actions, only doing and not doing. The great maxim of this constitution seems to have been: *Men must be impelled to perform actions and only induced to engage in reflection.* Therefore, each of these prescribed actions, each practice, each ceremony had its meaning, its valid significance; each was closely related to the speculative knowledge of religion and the teachings of morality, and was an occasion for a man in search of truth to reflect on these sacred matters or to seek instruction from wise men. The truths useful for the felicity of the nation as well as of each of its individual members were to be utterly removed from all imagery; for this was the main purpose and the fundamental law of the constitution. . . .

In this original constitution, state and religion were not conjoined, but *one;* not connected, but identical. Man's relation to society and his relation to God coincided and could never come into conflict. God, the Creator and Preserver of the world, was at the same time the King and Regent of this nation; and his oneness is such as not to admit the least division or plurality in either the political or the metaphysical sense. Nor does this monarch have any needs. He demands nothing from the nation but what serves its own welfare and advances the felicity of the state; just as the state, for its part, could not demand anything that was opposed to the duties toward God, that was not rather commanded by God, the Lawgiver and Regent of the nation. Hence, in this nation, civil matters acquired a sacred and religious aspect, and every civil service was at the same time a true service of God. The community was a community of God, its affairs were God's; the public taxes were an offering to God; and everything down to the least police measure was part of the *divine service*. The Levites, who lived off the public revenue, received their livelihood from God. They were to have no property in the land, "for God is their property" (Deut. 18:2). He who must sojourn outside the land serves *foreign gods*. This [statement which occurs] in several places in Scripture[7] cannot be taken in a literal sense. It actually means no more than that *he is subject to alien political laws, which, unlike those of his own country, are not at the same time a part of the divine service.*

The same can be said of the crimes. Every sacrilege against the authority of God, as the lawgiver of the nation, was a crime against the Majesty, and therefore a crime of state. Whoever blasphemed God committed lese majesty; whoever sacrilegiously desecrated the Sabbath implicitly abrogated a fundamental law of civil society, for an essential part of the constitution was based on the establishment of this day. "Let the Sabbath be an eternal covenant between Me and the children of Israel," said the Lord, "a perpetual sign that in six days the Eternal, etc. . . ." (Exod. 31:16–17). Under this constitution these crimes could and, indeed, had to be punished civilly, not as erroneous opinion, not as *unbelief,* but as *misdeeds,* as sacrilegious crimes aimed at abolishing or weakening the authority of the lawgiver and thereby undermining the state itself. Yet, nevertheless, with what leniency were even these capital crimes punished! With what superabundant indulgence for human weakness!

[Here Mendelssohn cites the extensive constraints placed in Rabbinic law upon capital and corporeal punishment; see ℂ23. — Eds.]

Moreover, as the Rabbis expressly state, *with the destruction of the Temple, all corporal and capital punishments and, indeed, even monetary fines, insofar as they are only national, have ceased to be legal.*[8] Perfectly in accordance with my principles, and inexplicable without them! The civil bonds of the nation were dissolved; religious offenses were no longer crimes against the state; and the religion, as religion, knows of no punishment, no other penalty than the one the remorseful sinner *voluntarily* imposes on himself. It knows of no co-

7. E.g., 1 Sam. 26:19.
8. Cf. BT Bava Kama 84a–b; for a fuller discussion see ℂ24.

ercion, uses only the staff [called] *gentleness,* and affects only mind and heart. Let one try to explain rationally, without my principles, this assertion of the rabbis!

But why, I hear many a reader ask, why this prolixity to tell us something that is very well known? Judaism was a hierocracy, an ecclesiastical government, a priestly state, a theocracy, if you will. We already know the presumptions which such an institution permits itself.

By no means! All these technical terms cast the matter in a false light, which I must avoid. Invariably, all we want to do is to classify, to fit things into pigeonholes. Once we know in which pigeonhole a thing is to be placed, we are content, however incomplete the concept we have of it may otherwise be. But why do you seek a generic term for an individual thing, which has no genus, which refuses to be stacked with anything, which cannot be put under the same rubric with anything else? This constitution existed only once; call it the "Mosaic constitution," by its proper name. It has disappeared, and only the Omniscient knows among what people and in what century something similar will again be seen. . . .

I have said that the Mosaic constitution did not persist long in its erstwhile purity. Already in the days of the prophet Samuel, the edifice developed a fissure which widened more and more until the parts broke asunder completely. The nation asked for a visible king as its ruler, a king of flesh and blood, perhaps because the priesthood had already begun to abuse the authority which it had among the people, as Scripture reports about the sons of the High Priest, or perhaps because the splendor of a neighboring royal household dazzled the eyes. In any event, they demanded a "king such as all other peoples have" (1 Sam. 8:6). The prophet, aggrieved by this, pointed out to them the nature of a human king, who had his own requirements and could enlarge them at will, and how difficult it was to satisfy an infirm mortal to whom one has transferred the rights of the Deity. In vain; the people persisted in their resolution, obtained their wish, and experienced what the prophet had threatened them with. Now the constitution was undermined, the unity of interests abolished. State and religion were no longer the same, and a collision of duties was no longer impossible. Still, such a collision must have been a rare occurrence, as long as the king himself not only was of the nation, but also obeyed the laws of the land. But let one follow history through all sorts of vicissitudes and changes, through many good and bad, God-fearing and godless regimes, down to that sad period in which the founder of the Christian religion gave this cautious advice: "Render unto Caesar that which is Caesar's and unto God what is God's" (Matt. 22:21). Manifest opposition, a collision of duties! The state was under foreign dominion, and received its orders from foreign gods, as it were, while the native religion still survived, retaining a part of its influence on civil life. Here is demand against demand, claim against claim. "To whom shall we give? Whom shall we obey?" Bear both burdens—went the advice—as well as you can; serve two masters with patience and devotion. Give to Caesar, and give to God too! To each his own, since the unity of interests is now destroyed.

And even today, no wiser advice than this can be given to the House of Jacob. Adapt yourselves to the morals and the constitution of the land to which you have been removed; but hold fast to the religion of your fathers too. Bear both burdens as well as you can! It is true that, on the one hand, the burden of civil life is made heavier for you on account of the religion to which you remain faithful, and, on the other hand, the climate and the times make the observance of your religious laws in some respects more irksome than they are. Nevertheless, persevere; remain unflinchingly at the post which Providence has assigned to you, and endure everything that happens to you as your lawgiver foretold long ago.

In fact, I cannot see how those born into the House of Jacob can in any conscientious manner disencumber themselves of the law. We are permitted to reflect on the law, to inquire into its spirit, and, here and there, where the lawgiver gave no reason, to surmise a reason which, *perhaps,* depended upon time, place, and circumstances, and which *perhaps,* may be liable to change in accordance with time, place, and circumstances—if it pleases the Supreme Lawgiver to make known to us His will on this matter, to make it known in as clear a voice, in as public a manner, and as far beyond all doubt and ambiguity as He did when He gave the law itself. As long as this has not happened, as long as we can point to no such authentic exemption from the law, no sophistry of ours can free us from the strict obedience we owe to the law; and reverence for God draws a line between speculation and practice which no conscientious man may cross. I therefore repeat my earlier protestation: Weak and shortsighted is the eye of man! Who can say: I have entered into God's sanctuary, gauged the whole system of his designs, and am able to determine its measure, goal, and boundaries? I may surmise, but not pass judgment nor act according to my surmise. If in things human I may not dare to act contrary to the law on the mere strength of my own surmise and legal sophistry, without the authority of the lawgiver or custodian of the law, how much less may I do so in matters divine? Laws that depend on the possession of the Land [of Israel] and institutions governing it carry their exemption with them. Without Temple and priesthood, and outside Judea, there is no scope for either sacrifices or laws of purification or contributions to the priests, insofar as these depend on the possession of the Land. But, personal commandments, duties imposed upon a son of Israel, without regard to the Temple service and landed property in Palestine, must, as far as we can see, be observed strictly according to the words of the law, until it shall please the Most High to set our conscience at rest and to make their abrogation known in a clear voice and in a public manner.

Law and Ethics

8. Hermann Cohen, "Affinities Between the Philosophy of Kant and Judaism"

Reason and Hope, Selections from the Writings of Hermann Cohen, translated by Eva Jospe (New York: W. W. Norton, 1971), pp. 78–83.

Cohen, an important spokesman for both neo-Kantian philosophy and liberal Judaism in late nineteenth- and early twentieth-century Germany, brings the two together here, arguing for the centrality of law and duty in the Jewish religion. Cohen's position should be read in part as an argument against the rejection of the role of law in Judaism by leading Reform rabbis (see C9).

Maimonides was by no means the first . . . to use the Aristotelian rational principle as a guideline for his religious writings. Saadiah, too, had already formulated this rule clearly and distinctly in his *Emunot ve-Deot* [*Beliefs and Opinions*]. For Aristotle, all knowledge is based on the most abstract principle as well as on sense perception. (Despite, if not actually because of, this dualism, he was more comprehensible to the Middle Ages than Kant proved to be to the period immediately following his own. The great minds of his own time, in whatever fields of endeavor, had clearly understood him. But he remained unintelligible to the romanticism that spread soon thereafter because its obscurantism prevented any real confrontation with his thought.) To our ancient thinkers, Aristotle's dualism was rather welcome, though not because of its theoretical ambiguity. But they themselves always emphasize reason and are not in the least concerned with the conflict between reason and sense experience. What matters to them is the distinction between reason and revelation.

This distinction, however, by no means implies a conflict between those two sources of religion. Nor should it lead to the conclusion that revelation has nothing to do with ethics, or that it concerns merely ritual legislation (with the possible inclusion of state legislation). Such a conclusion would not do justice to the high regard in which religious consciousness holds revelation. And ritual legislation, far from conflicting with ethics, is understood to serve as its vehicle. (This is where Paulinism, today as always, becomes subjective and therefore unjust, no matter how correct its judgment about the value of all particularistic religious practices might be in principle.)

Ancient Judaism regards the difference between moral and ritual legislation somewhat like that between pure and practical ethics. Subsequently, both are seen as legitimate subjects of revelation, as is moral reason—though the latter is also considered autonomous. And Saadiah significantly states that no real discussion is possible with anyone who asserts that only the Torah, and not also reason, is a source of ethics. This shows how unreservedly reason is upheld as a controlling principle of the Torah.

Similarly, there is a statement in Bahya ibn Pakuda's *Duties of the Heart* to the effect that man's blind acceptance of revelation as the sole source of knowledge, to the exclusion of his own reasoning power, might well be the work of his evil inclination. Thus, reason, that inexhaustible and indispensable source of all morality, is acknowledged as the inviolable basis of religion. And it would not take too much to go on from here to an acknowledgement of the sovereignty of reason, as long as revelation is not assigned a secondary position and its sovereignty also remains inviolate.

The decisive factor, though, in determining the sovereignty of reason is one's concept of reason's relation to the world of the senses. And here we encounter another affinity between the philosophy of Judaism and that of Kant.

Kant's ethics is characterized, above all, by its rejection of eudae-monism and all its variations. He contends that all eudaemonic moral systems contradict the concept of ethics and that the pure will must never aspire to any kind of happiness. And since Jewish philosophy also unequivocally re-jects the principle of happiness—from Saadiah to Maimonides and beyond— we are surely justified to note, at this point, yet another agreement between the Jewish and the Kantian view.

This opposition to any eudaemonic principle is at once a sign of the Jewish mind's autonomy and ability to systematize, and a most interest-ing symptom of biblical thinking. For it is always the Bible that serves these thinkers as the last criterion by which to judge their own views. Even con-cerning the role of reason they invoke the Torah, which repeatedly speaks of knowledge as fundamental to all matters of the human heart, mind, and volition. "Know this day, and lay it to thy heart . . ." (Deut. 4:39). And in keeping with the spirit of the Torah, they consider even scientific knowledge as a basic requirement for human understanding. For mathematics, astron-omy, and ethics all have a common foundation in reason. And as for the question of eudaemonism, there is an abundance of biblical sources. More telling than any quotes, though, is that basic tenet of faith, the unity of God, whose corollaries are "unity of the heart" and "unity of action."

It would seem that no language has a more meaningful expression to convey the concept of man's integrity than this "unity of the heart." This profound and crystal-clear leitmotif taken from the Psalms—"Make one my heart to fear thy name" (86:11)—also informs our prayers with its harmo-niousness and enhances our Days of Repentance. Unity of the heart is the prerequisite for love and veneration of God. "Unify our hearts so that we may love and venerate Your name" [9]—had Bahya's *Duties of the Heart* disclosed to us no other concept than that of a unity of heart, action, and veneration of God, this alone would suffice to make it a work of considerable value.

Set against the principles of pleasure and happiness is the principle of reason, that reason of volition which overcomes any schism and establishes

9. Taken from the blessings before the reciting of the *shema* in the morning prayer.

the unity of the will. To Kant, however, this kind of unity (namely, unity of heart and mind) would still be suspect as a merely psychological definition. For he seeks to define the moral will by objective, conceptual principles. Refusing to accept the pleasure principle as the causative factor of volition, he posits a logically derived concept as the determining principle of the will: universal law. Morality must be regarded as a law valid for any individual, without exception. True, this law is seen as derived from the autonomy of reason; but reason's only relation to the will is to impose upon it a universal law. We must not be "volunteers of morality." Kant might have learned this expression from a Jewish philosopher or from the Talmud itself: "Greater is the man who acts in obedience to the commandment than without commandment" (BT Kiddushin 31a).

Here, however, we must not overlook an essential difference between the Kantian and Jewish positions. In the final analysis, in Kant, it is reason itself which must create the universal law anew. But in Judaism, the One God would become a useless machine were He not the eternal source of moral law. Judaism simply denies any possible conflict between the concepts of God and of moral reason. Moral law must and can be both: the law of God and the law of reason.

God and His law signify as well as establish a contrast with the individual's egotism and self-centeredness, or simply with his limited horizon. And this interpretation of law constitutes still another affinity between Judaism and Kant. In the final analysis, we have here the ancient idea of men's equality before God, which finds its methodological expression in the concept of a universal law. This same basic concept underlies the original commandment to love one's fellow man. Maybe its correct translation should read: "Love him; he is like you" (Lev. 19:18).

Commentary. Cohen and Kant

Cohen rightly sees the conception of reason's relation to the world of the senses as the decisive factor in determining the sovereignty of reason. Yet for all his enormous insight into Kant, Jewish philosophy, and the fundamental affinities between them, I believe that Cohen misunderstood both philosophies on some aspects of this question. Let us see how the confusion arises.

Cohen views the idea of the nonmaterial nature of God as the fundamental moment in Jewish thought. He often quotes God's answer to Moses—"Tell them: 'I am, that I am' sent you" (Exod. 3:14)—as the basic statement of Judaism's abstract conception of God's nature. Kant, too, saw the prohibition on idolatry as the "most sublime moment in the law of the Jews" (*Critique of Judgment* AK 274). It was clear to Cohen and Kant that the transcendent character of the divine has far-reaching ethical consequences: it points to the absolute duality of the ideal and the material, the "ought" and the "is." True ethics demands that these be kept strictly separate. To attempt to derive what ought to be from what is, is to abdicate reason's responsibility to legislate for experience. For both Kant and Judaism (on Cohen's view), such abdication contains an element not simply of moral weakness but of sacrilege.

Any attempt to treat the given world as a source, or even a full realization, of value, entails a moment of idolatry, forgetting or denying the ideal nature of the law. Pure value cannot be given, it can only be sought. The human task is an unending attempt to make the real approach the rational. Fail to maintain the distinction between the two, and the messianic impulse so crucial for both prophetic Judaism and Kant is lost. Cohen rightly saw that the metaphysical equation of real and rational had straightforward political consequences; his lifelong commitment to socialism, which he viewed as the only legitimate conclusion of both Kant's work and prophetic Judaism, was also a rejection of the Hegelianism that treats the rational as already realized and ends by quietly justifying the Prussian state. For Cohen, this is a denial of what he regards as the genuine religious impulse, the recognition of the transcendent element in value.

Cohen's position on the relation of moral and divine law is deep and brilliant. The identity between the law of reason and the law of God is not just a matter of happy accident (or insistent apologetics). Nor could Cohen, as a rationalist, hold the position that ethics gains any justification or legitimacy through being derived from God's will. The demand that the moral law must be the law of God has rather, I believe, a logical dimension. A genuinely ethical law must be transcendent, deriving from, and embodying, the absolute distinction between ought and is. The Kantian demand that the ethical imperative be essentially different from all others is, for Cohen, fundamentally related to the notion that God's being must be essentially different from all others. Cohen's criticism of pantheism and Christianity is based on their different denials of the idea that God's essence is the very opposite of nature; this thought is, for Cohen, the basis of both religion and morality. Because the moral law must embody the ideal—the opposition to what is— it can have its source only in pure monotheism.

Cohen was surely right to see this, perhaps the deepest feature of reason's relation to the senses, as fundamental to both Kant and many Jewish thinkers. But, poignantly, he develops this feature to a point that, I think, makes his idealism unnecessarily drastic. For Cohen, the nature of the split between ought and is entails that the human condition is one of permanent exile.

This is clearly a strand in the work of Kant, for whom the only truly human fate is perpetually to seek an unconditioned or absolute reality, which it can never attain; and it is equally present in messianic Judaism. But in neither of these is the metaphysical glorification of exile so unequivocal as it is in Cohen.

We see this in his statement that both Kant and Jewish philosophy completely reject eudaemonism, the principle that happiness is the goal of morality. If this rejection means simply that right conduct is independent of, and prior to, any human idea of the good, Cohen's characterization would be unobjectionable. But Cohen goes much further than this and fails to recognize the role played by the idea of the good both in Kant and in Jewish thought. This is evident when he uncharacteristically accepts the common view that Kant's theory of rational faith is the weakest part of his philosophical system. For Kant, of course, the right and the good, justice and human satisfaction, are completely independent of one another; but their very independence demands that they stand in some relation. Kant marvelously attacks those Stoics who, like Cohen, seek to collapse the good into the right by arguing that the only genuine happiness is the consciousness of one's own virtue. Because the right is within our power while the good very often is not, only God can complete the world so that virtue and happiness exist in appropriate relation. (It is this argument that appears in Kant's mature writings, not the common interpretation—rightly rejected by Cohen—that God will correct earthly imbalances in a world beyond our own.) But the demand that the right be completed by the good follows from reason's search for justice—not, as Cohen suggests, from the senses' search for pleasure. If it is reason's right to legislate for experience, independently of what is, it is equally reason's right to hope that experience will come to meet its demands.

Without more concrete hope of fulfillment than that provided by Cohen, it is hard to imagine how we could achieve the integrity he signifies by the expression "unity of the heart." For the point is not simply that we as creatures possessing both reason and sense are subject to the claims of each; rather, given that we are such creatures, it is a demand of reason itself that the right and the good, justice and satisfaction, be balanced. (Indeed, the greatest threat to reason may be posed by violations of justice, which have a great deal to do with the good but very little to do with the senses, as the example of Job suggests. The bitter injustice of which Job speaks—whether his own misfortunes or those of others—is informed by physical pain but hardly reducible to it. The outrage experienced at the death of one's children or the realization of vast inequalities in the lives of rich and poor cannot be seen as a complaint about a lack of sensual pleasure.) As long as the gap between right and good remains as complete as Cohen here suggests, the unity of which he writes seems unattainable.

The extremity of Cohen's idealism leaves us subject to a split within human nature more radical than that foreseen by either of his sources—thus the emphasis in traditional Judaism on both physical needs and community goods: blood and semen, wine and wheat, as well as courts, Torah scrolls, and political restoration. Kant, too, if sometimes less clearly, views the demand for happiness not simply as a concession to weaker elements of human nature, nor even as a qualified good among others, but as a right of reason, provided that reason has fulfilled its own laws.

Kant's solution, which involves giving God final responsibility for the realization of the good, while the responsibility for the right remains with us, is surely not without problems. Yet it is not, pace Cohen, an outdated accident of Kant's thought, but a recognition that the proper connection between the right and the good is a need of reason itself. No such argument is found in the stark formulation of the second portion of the *shema* (Deut.

11:13–21): acknowledge the truth of pure monotheism and the laws that follow from it, and the rains will come in their seasons, bringing corn, wine, and oil. But the echo between Kant and Judaism on just this question is not one that Cohen heard.

Writing on the book of Job, Cohen praises its attack on the assumption that sin and suffering are connected. In this, Kant would have been in full agreement. Yet Cohen goes on to conclude that the consequence of biblical monotheism is that suffering belongs to the essence of humanity, for "the suffering hero Job represents the ideal of the human" (*Der Begriff der Religion im System der Philosophie,* 1915). For Kant, by contrast, the book of Job represents the demand that God, in acknowledging the rightness of Job's claims, correct the imbalance between right and good—and the faith of the righteous man that he will indeed do so. In both his religious and political writings, Cohen appealed to the historical optimism that he saw as the core of Jewish messianism. And it should be emphasized that, unlike most people who spend their lives as university professors, Cohen deserves to be called a tragic hero. Despite his precarious position as the first Jew to be appointed Professor Ordinarius in Germany, Cohen championed both socialism and the rights of east European Jewry—causes hardly calculated to endear him to the reigning powers who had tentatively accepted him. At the same time he argued poignantly for the recognition of deep and essential similarities between the German and Jewish peoples. His death in 1919 spared him the worst of German responses to his argument; his widow, who lived long enough to be deported to Auschwitz, was less fortunate. Yet Cohen's hope was not merely historically misplaced; it was also exclusively ethical: we are to maintain faith in the progressive moral improvement of humankind that is the goal of world history. That Cohen's failure to emphasize other kinds of improvement wasn't merely oversight is underlined by what he took to be the fundamental flaw of the Zionists: "Those guys want to be happy." Reporting the conversation in which this remark was made, Gershom Scholem called it the deepest thing ever said against Zionism. Whether or not one agrees with Scholem, it may well be the deepest thing ever said against Hermann Cohen.

Susan Neiman

The Binding of Isaac: Mitzvah Supersedes Morality

9. Yeshayahu Leibowitz, "Religious Praxis: The Meaning of Halakhah"

Judaism, Human Values, and the Jewish State, edited by Eliezer Goldman, translated by Eliezer Goldman et al. (Cambridge: Harvard University Press, 1992), pp. 12–16.

Leibowitz repeats the line from BT Kiddushin 31a quoted above by Cohen, but gives it a radically different meaning and so sets himself against the whole rationalist tradition in Jewish philosophy. Religious authenticity, he argues, is achieved by the decision to accept the yoke of divine command and not through independent investigations of God's law or the acceptance of certain truth claims.

What is the religious import of Judaism's embodiment in Halakhah? How to understand the peculiar nature of the religious faith for which Halakhah is the only adequate expression?

The first mark of the religion of Halakhah is its realism. It perceives man as he is in reality and confronts him with this reality—with the actual conditions of his existence rather than the "vision" of another existence. Religion is concerned with the status, the function, and the duties of man as constrained by these circumstances. It precludes the possibility of man's shirking his duties by entertaining illusions of attaining a higher level of being. The religion of Halakhah is concerned with man and addresses him in his drab day-by-day existence. The Mitzvoth are a norm for the prosaic life that constitutes the true and enduring condition of man. Halakhic praxis is oriented to the usual and persisting, not to the exceptional, momentary, and fortuitous. The Mitzvoth require observance out of a sense of duty and discipline, not ecstatic enthusiasm or fervor, which may embellish one's life but do not tell how to conduct it. Resting religion on Halakhah assigns it to the prosaic aspects of life, and therein lies its great strength. Only a religion addressed to life's prose, a religion of the dull routine of daily activity, is worthy of the name. This is not to demean the poetic moments, the rare occasions when a man breaks away from the routine, the experience of rising above the self spiritually and emotionally, the deeds performed fervently. It is quite possible that such moments mark the zenith of a human life. Nonetheless, the fundamental and enduring elements of human existence are in life's prose, not in its poetry. Molière's M. Jourdain discovered at the age of forty that he had unwittingly been speaking prose all his life. No one ever claimed to have been talking unwittingly in poetry. Only in full awareness and intention does one compose poetry, and such awareness and intention occur only at rare moments. A religion of values and concentrated intention is the religion of life's poetry, which can only adorn it. The religion of halakhic practice is the religion of life itself.

The Judaism of the Halakhah despises rhetoric, avoids pathos, abjures the visionary. Above all, it rejects the illusory. It does not permit a man to believe that the conditions of his existence are other than they really are. It prevents flight from one's functions and tasks in this inferior world to an imaginary world which is all good, beautiful, and sublime. Not by chance are so many of the Mitzvoth concerned with the body, procreation and birth, food and drink, sexual life, diseases, and the corpse. The largest section of the Mishnah, the first crystallized formulation of the Halakhah, is *Seder Taharoth,* which places man within the squalor of biological existence from which he can never extricate himself.

Most characteristic of the Halakhah is its lack of pathos. The Halakhah does not depend upon the incidence of religious experience and attaches little importance to the psychic urges to perform extraordinary deeds. It strives to base the religious act, even in its highest manifestations, on the permanent habit of performing one's duty. "Greater is he who performs because he has been commanded than one who performs without having been commanded" (BT Kiddushin 31a). Precisely this nonpathetic attitude hides a depth of intense pathos. How unfounded is the imaginary antithesis of the inner religious experience and the formalism of the halakhic praxis, an antithesis so popular amongst the opponents of the religion of Halakhah!

Two types of religiosity may be discerned: one founded in values and beliefs from which follow requirements of action, the other posited on imperatives of action, the observance of which entails values and intention. The religion of values and beliefs is an endowing religion—a means of satisfying man's spiritual needs and of assuaging his mental conflicts. Its end is man, and God offers his services to man. A person committed to such a religion is a redeemed man. A religion of Mitzvoth is a demanding religion. It imposes obligations and tasks and makes of man an instrument for the realization of an end which transcends man. The satisfactions it offers are those deriving from the performance of one's duty. The religious practitioner serves his God *lishmah* [for His own sake—Eds.]—because He is worthy of worship. The two types of religiosity may be found within all religions, but religions differ from one another in the extent to which one type predominates. A religiosity of the first type is characteristic of Christianity. Its symbol, the cross, represents the sacrifice God brought about for the benefit of mankind. In contrast, the highest symbol of the Jewish faith is the stance of Abraham on Mount Moriah, where all human values were annulled and overridden by fear and love of God. The cross represents submission to human nature. The *akedah* (the near-sacrifice of Isaac) is man's absolute mastery over his own nature. "Abraham rose early in the morning and saddled his ass . . . and set out" for the *akedah*. Don Isaac Abravanel, commenting upon Genesis 22:3, explains: "saddled his ass" means that he overcame his materiality, that is, his physical nature—a pun on the phonetically similar "hamor" (ass) and "homer" (matter). This "matter" or nature includes all the benevolent sentiments as well as man's conscience; all the factors in man's makeup which an atheistic humanism regards as "good." In the morning benedictions, recited prior to reading the narrative of the *akedah,* we find the request: "Compel our *Yetzer* [inclination] to subject itself to you"—a request meant to apply to our benevolent as well as to our evil inclinations. This would be a banal supplication were it concerned only with the evil inclinations. It was Abraham who first burst the bounds of the universal human bondage—the bondage of man to the forces of his own nature. Not everyone is Abraham, and not everyone is put to so terrible a test as that of the *akedah*. Nonetheless, the daily performance of the Mitzvoth, which is not directed by man's natural inclinations or drives but by his intention of serving God, represents the motivation animating the *akedah*. From such a standpoint, the question "what does religion offer to me?" must be completely dismissed. The only proper question is: "What am I obligated to offer for the sake of religion?"

In stark contrast to the Jewish religion, oriented as it is to the realities of human existence, stand religions which claim to offer the means of extricating man from the human condition and transporting him spiritually to a state governed by other categories of merit and obligation, of tasks and attainments. The Christian who believes in the event of the year 33 and has faith in it is redeemed; the very elements of his nature are altered. Among other things, he is liberated from the bondage of "the Law." Halakhic Judaism does not recognize such a redemption. The project it sets for man is permanent and endless. No religious attainment may be considered final; the project is never completed. Observance of the Torah in its entirety is merely the training of man for continuation of its observance. No religious achievement can change the human condition or the task.

A tremendous symbolic exemplification of this attitude appears at the close of Yom Kippur. At the end of the Day of Atonement, the culmination of a period of repentance when the people of Israel purify themselves before their father in heaven and are purified by him—at the close of the Ne'ilah service with the public utterance of the verse of Shema and the blowing of the Shofar—the first words of the weekday evening prayer are uttered: "And He is merciful and forgiving of sin." Thus the basic situation of repentant man at the close of the Day of Atonement is exactly what it was the evening before. His sole achievement consists of the great religious effort invested in this day. Immediately after he must begin his preparations toward the next Yom Kippur. The cycle continues until the end of one's life. In like manner one's labor in study of the Torah is not a means for the attainment of any other goal. This very labor is itself the goal. "Until what period of life ought he to study Torah? Until the day of his death."

Halakhah, as an expression of a religiosity which rejects all illusion, does not entertain man with the vision of some target at which he may aim and which, once attained, constitutes the fulfillment of his tasks. No human achievement affects the regime of religious praxis under which one lives from coming of age until death. Performance of the Mitzvoth is man's path to God, an infinite path, the end of which is never attained and is, in effect, unattainable. A man is bound to know that this path never terminates. One follows it without advancing beyond the point of departure. Recognition that the religious function imposed upon man is infinite and never ending is the faith which finds expression in the regularity, constancy, and perseverance in the performance of the Mitzvoth. The circle of religious praxis rotates constantly about its center. "Every day they will appear to you as new,"[10] for after each act the position of man remains as it was before. The

10. Cf. Rashi on Deut. 11:13.

aim of proximity to God is unattainable. It is infinitely distant, "for God is in heaven and you on the earth" (Eccles. 5:1). What then is the substance and import of the performance of the Mitzvoth? It is man's striving to attain the religious goal.

Halakhic observance as a way of life, a fixed and permanent form of human existence, precludes conversion of religion into a means to some ulterior end. Most of the Mitzvoth are meaningless except as expressions of worship. They have no utility in terms of satisfaction of human needs. No man would commit himself to such a way of life if he did not regard the service of God as an end in itself serving no extrinsic purpose. The Halakhah thus addresses a man's sense of duty rather than his emotions and inclinations.

Rejecting the "Suspension of the Ethical"

10. Samuel Hugo Bergman, Two Texts on the Binding of Isaac

Dialogical Philosophy from Kierkegaard to Buber, translated by Arnold A. Gerstein (Albany: State University of New York Press, 1991), pp. 88–90; *Hashamayim ve-Ha'aretz* (Tel Aviv: Shdemot, 1968), pp. 21–28.

Bergman's philosophy stresses direct religious experience, the individual's "meeting" with God, but here he argues for a critical moral examination of all such experiences, including, decisively, Abraham's sense that God called him to sacrifice Isaac. These texts respond specifically to the "suspension of the ethical"—Kierkegaard's notion—but their critique extends also to the religious argument of Leibowitz, above (§9).

The Absolute Duty to God

The question arises whether religion can suspend morality, even temporarily. If this is possible, the religious paradox limits and reduces the legitimizing force of ethics. Moreover, if we wish to be ruled by the divine power, we are forced by religion into solitude, cutting ourselves off from common understanding and from the mundane world. Then, once we have succeeded in liberating ourselves by infinite resignation from attachment to the finite and temporal, it is possible that whatever was sacrificed will be returned to us, miraculously. Kierkegaard discusses the problem of return in his book *Repetition*. Before we discuss the book . . . we must express our criticism of the conclusions Kierkegaard draws from the story of Isaac. There are great dangers in the concept of a suspension of ethics by religion. In our discussion of Kierkegaard's idea of subjective truth, we mentioned the danger of basing truth on man's enthusiasm and feeling, making feeling the criterion of truth. Feeling, he said, isolates man and prevents communication and the creation of community. We must now return once more to this argument. Kierkegaard stresses repeatedly that a person who receives an order from God is isolated and bound to silence because he has heard what others do not. Walter Kaufmann sharply criticizes Kierkegaard in his book *From Shakespeare to Existentialism* by pointing to the way the Talmud discusses the question of the voice of God. In the Talmud a controversy is related between Rabbi Eliezer and other rabbis, in which Rabbi Eliezer relied on the voice of God he heard from heaven:

[Bergman here quotes the story of Rabbi Eli'ezer from BT Bava Metzia 59b, which appears in full, with commentary, in C6, §10. The story culminates in the citation of Deuteronomy 30:12: "It is not in heaven." "What does this mean?" asks the Talmud. "As the Torah has been given from Mount Sinai, we take no heed of a *bat kol* (heavenly voice)—for at Mount Sinai You have already written in the Torah [that we should] decide according to the majority."—Eds.]

In this wonderful story, Rabbi Eliezer relies upon subjective truth given from on high, as did Abraham in Kierkegaard's presentation of him. In contrast, the other rabbis place their trust in objective truth, recorded and shared by all. They rely upon what Kierkegaard called the "universal," or "moral." The rabbis do not agree with Rabbi Eliezer's reliance upon the heavenly voice. They are like the humanists, who defend a common ethic, in contrast to Rabbi Eliezer, who puts his trust in individual religious inspiration. For the rabbis there is no place for a suspension of the universal through religious inspiration, and subsequently they ostracize Rabbi Eliezer for his reliance upon the divine voice against the voice of the majority. Relating this to Kierkegaard's dilemma, we can again formulate the question thus: Was Rabbi Eliezer, as an individual opposing the majority, justified in relying on the personal inspiration he received?

The Binding of Isaac and the Contemporary Person

In the midrashic account,[11] Abraham on his way to Mount Moriah encounters Satan, who appears in this instance as the protector of ethics: as with Kierkegaard, the ethical imperative is here a seductive temptation. Satan seeks to seduce Abraham [into agreeing] that the voice he had heard was not God's but his own. He asks: How can you take this darling youngster, whom you begot at the age of one hundred, and . . . offer him as a burnt-offering? "Tomorrow [God] will say to you: 'You are a murderer, for you have shed his blood.'"

. . . In the midrash, Abraham answers Satan simply "Even so!"—temptation comes up against the iron wall of unphilosophizing faith. In Kierkegaard, he who philosophizes about faith becomes entangled in insoluble problems and willy-nilly arrives at nihilistic conclusions. For it transpires that the ethical imperative (and the same applies to logical truth as well) is valid only so long as God does not abrogate it. "$2 + 2 = 4$" is true only so long as God so wishes; and the Ten Commandments have no higher value than that of the red heifer commandment. The only virtue of the man of faith is passive obedience and observing the commandments—even when he does not understand them. . . .

But . . . this conception of faith reduces to zero the value of man's independent illumination and of his responsible decision, leaving him only the single virtue—great though it is—of obedience. On such a view, humans will never be able to stand on their own.

If we do not wish to follow this path, then we have only the alternative, human path: we trust in the light of reason. . . . Our reason becomes our supreme authority. . . . This trust in man and in the natural light of his reason gives rise to the duty of criticism. Man may and must impose his criticism even upon sacred texts when they conflict with his logical—and, especially, with his moral—reason. . . .

More than once, our moral sense recoils from the biblical story. Thus, for instance, regarding the command to kill all the male children of Moab and all the women who had lain with men (Num. 31:17). Today, after

11. Cf., e.g., *Midrash Rabbah: Genesis* 56:4.

the Holocaust, we have become more sensitive to these verses. The principle must be: whenever the sacred text collides with our moral sense, I must sacrifice the text and not the rational or the emotional [understanding]. When we are told that God has commanded an act that counters our moral feeling we are commanded to reply: God could not have commanded such a thing. On the specific solution in each case—whether we claim that the person delivering the message misunderstood, or whether we correct the wording or adduce special historical circumstances—we will decide ad hoc. The main issue is the freedom of the individual, the responsibility of the individual as the bearer of . . . reason, [which must be] used to examine supreme values.

Commentary. Between Obedience and Autonomy

Leibowitz's position represents a profound revolution in Jewish thought. The prevalent view is that Jewish religion draws together theoretical beliefs about the world, God, and the individual and the practical obligations that make these beliefs concrete. In contrast, Leibowitz begins with a conception of Judaism as a practical regimen. Rather than being the product of a set of beliefs, Judaism shapes reality through a system of religious obligations. He thus moves away from the realm of theory to the realm of halakhic praxis. Leibowitz does not reject the possibility that the religious person may have unique religious experiences. He insists, however, that the cornerstone of religiosity is not experience; it is commandment.

This conception of Judaism as a set of obligations enables Leibowitz to advance several additional claims. First, he views all religious obligations as revolving around a single axis—the worship of God. Hence, the traditional preoccupation with the reasons for the commandments involves a categorical error: assuming that the commandments are merely means for the attainment of certain ends. Unlike the various theories that analyze these ends and the ways the commandments promote them, Leibowitz argues that the halakhic obligation is itself the first datum of Jewish religion and cannot be explained in terms of any further ends.

In Leibowitz's view, Judaism is an "institutionalized religion," exclusively constituted by the obligations themselves. *Halakhah* is a constitutive rather than a regulative law, instituting an independent normative realm of activity rather than controlling an existing sphere of action. This approach implies that the meaning of the Jewish religion is "internal" in the sense that it cannot be derived from theoretical positions but only from an analysis of Judaism as an independently coherent system of obligations.

Second, if religious individuals do indeed organize their lives around religious obligation, then, in Leibowitz's terms, Jewish religion is "theocentric." Note, however, his special use of this term. God is not central as an object of cognition nor as a subject demanding obedience: all this is precluded by the notion of God's transcendence and absolute otherness— a crucial tenet of Leibowitz's thought. His notion of "theocentrism" holds that the Jewish religion is based on obligation toward God—and on nothing, or almost nothing, else. Leibowitz is clear on this issue: "In reflecting and speaking about man's standing before God . . . the believer tries to refer minimally to God, who has no image at all, and makes an effort to direct his religious consciousness to himself as recognizing his duty to his God. That is the practice of the men of *halakhah*" (*Judaism, Human Values and the Jewish State,* 1992). Theocentrism here means that the core of Jewish religion is not human redemption or the good life. The believer is destined to submission and absolute obedience; faith is the acceptance of the yoke of the kingdom of heaven.

Third, from these statements about obligation, God, and the individual's standing, a clear picture emerges regarding the relation between God's command and rational or moral knowledge. Leibowitz endorses a theory of normative conflict between religion and morality. Not only is there sometimes a conflict of obligations between religious and moral commands, but even when the actual obligation is the same, the religious agent performs the act because it has been divinely commanded whereas the moral agent does so because it is a moral duty.

The *akedah* is, for Leibowitz, the quintessential expression of the antithesis between Jewish religion and moral value. He views this act as the supreme religious symbol: renouncing individual values, desires, and natural inclinations in the face of God's command. The effect of this renunciation is to release the believer from the domination of "nature"; *halakhah* is a "revolt against the domination of the blind natural elements over his body and soul. . . . [The Jewish religion is] a rebellion against natural reality. Nature and *halakhah*—these are opposites" (*Judaism, Jewish People, and the State of Israel* [Hebrew], 1975).

Leibowitz thus presumes an absolute contrast between religious obligations and human values, acknowledging at the same time that shaping life in the light of this principle is a process rather than a onetime decision. In terms resembling those of Camus in *The Myth of Sisyphus,* he describes the believer's life as an endless struggle to impose religious obligations upon himself and to abrogate human values.

Although he claims to speak in the name of the empirical Jewish tradition, Leibowitz is actually in confrontation with it. It is a strange contention that the only purpose of *halakhah* is to reduce life to the task of worship. Many halakhic norms are, in fact, concerned with the betterment of human life, both individual and social. More severely, the halakhic tradition does not, and indeed cannot, aim to rescind human knowledge and human values, because these are central to the halakhic process. A common talmudic adage exclaims, "What need have we for scriptural proof? It is *s'vara* [reason or common sense]!" (BT Bava Kama 46b), reflecting the basic assumption that reason is superior to revelation as a way to determine God's will. Any such ranking rules out Leibowitz's interpretation of Judaism.

This last point is addressed in Samuel Hugo Bergman's critique of Kierkegaard. Bergman, a profoundly devout man, upholds a courageous religious claim—in the spirit of the rabbinic commitment to human reason—and gives primacy to moral sense over Scripture. In cases of outright conflict, he insists, the plain meaning of the text must be rejected, whether through reinterpretation or otherwise, for it is impossible that God would command immorality. But to ensure that human beings will not reduce religion to their own values Bergman elsewhere in his essay tempers this religious daring by demanding that believers adopt a posture of "humility and meekness." They thereby convey their awareness "that there are superior forces and revelations that direct [man's] way even when he does not—as yet—understand them."

Bergman and Leibowitz thus present two contradictory models of religious life: submissiveness and total obedience as opposed to autonomy and reliance on human values and human knowledge. These two religious worldviews reflect two basic intuitions of Jewish religion; like many religions, Judaism demands that human beings obey God's command, but it also fosters and promotes an ethos of responsibility and autonomy. Leibowitz takes the religious ideal of obedience to an unacceptable extreme when he claims that Judaism rejects human values and knowledge. In my view, this approach is both alien to the Jewish tradition and incompatible with a fundamental commitment to human autonomy. A world of worship that excludes human reason and moral sense is doubly diminished. Theologically, it becomes unclear why God should have created human beings in his image—with rational and moral capacities—yet then demand that these be excluded from religious life. And existentially, there seems to be little value in a life of worship where one's true self is left behind.

Traditional Judaism indeed requires submission; but this is expressed in the very commitment to the canon of sacred texts—a commitment that finds expression in the process of interpretation. Bergman shows a fundamental awareness of these complexities of traditional commitment. However, in one important sense he exceeds the bounds of traditional Judaism —when he suggests that a text whose plain meaning is immoral can be rejected in some other way than through reinterpretation. In the interpretive process, the believer accepts his submission to God: the sacred text cannot simply be passed over. At the same time, this process embodies the value of reason and of autonomous moral judgment, for interpretation is the activity of discovering in the text meanings that are in line with one's innermost beliefs.

Avi Sagi

Translated from the Hebrew by Batya Stein

Introduction

Biblical Views of Monarchy

The Constitution of Monarchy

Introduction

Throughout history, the rule of one has been the most common form of government—also the most stable, at least in the sense that the "one," however his or her rule ended, was usually succeeded by another "one." In the earliest Israelite political texts, however, God is the one who rules, and he neither requires nor permits any succession. God is Israel's first king. What kind of regime is his kingdom? According to the biblical book of Judges, it has no established institutions or routinized practices. God rules either directly (as at Sinai) or through intermediaries, the *shoftim,* men and women raised up at critical moments to fight Israel's battles and judge the people. The crises are moral or religious in character; the people sin and God sends oppressors to punish them—and then a savior to rescue them. When there is no crisis, no one is raised up; the people apparently rule themselves by themselves; there is no authority structure at all. Theocracy looks very much like anarchy.

Gideon is the prototypical *shofet,* who most clearly expresses the doctrine of God's kingdom, contrasting it with human monarchy: "I will not rule over you myself, nor shall my son rule over you; the Lord alone shall rule over you" (Judg. 8:23). But there is an opposing voice in the book of Judges, expressing a more secular view and looking toward a human king. On this view, anarchy is just anarchy; the repeated crises have a political rather than a moral or religious explanation: "In those days there was no king in Israel; everyone did as he pleased" (Judg. 17:6, 21:25).

When the elders (on behalf of the people) come to Samuel and ask for a king, they are rejecting this anarchic individualism and also the intermittent rule of the judges—and therefore the rule of God, who seems to favor both anarchy and intermittency, as if established hereditary rule would detract from his saving power. God rules only when there are no political institutions. The institution the elders ask for is still, of course, the rule of one, but they are imitating the countries around them when they make their request, not God's singular dominion.

The rule of the "few" (aristocrats or oligarchs) and the "many" (democrats) were hardly considered in Jewish political writings until postbiblical times. Even then—and indeed until the modern age—kingship was the conventionally accepted regime, although the human king always stood in God's shadow. It was always possible to oppose the king's rule by recalling the biblical judges and the words of Gideon and by insisting that God is Israel's only king. This is still the strategy of Martin Buber in the twentieth century, who writes out of a strong sympathy with the anarchists of his own time. (It is useful to compare Buber's rehabilitation of theocracy to Spinoza's reductionist account of it, in ℭ1, §15, according to which there is always a human ruler.)

What marks off monarchy from the rule of God and his judges is the prospect, even if it's not always realized, of institutionalized stability: a central regime with a standing army and hereditary succession. Kings and queens expect to be followed in office by their own children—which is exactly what Gideon insists will not happen in his case. Prophets like Moses and military chiefs like Joshua resemble the judges more than the kings. They claim a more immediate and temporary authority, which they make no effort to pass on, and presumably are not able to pass on, to their bodily heirs; nor do they levy taxes to sustain an administration and army. But the appeal of monarchy lies precisely in its replacement of individuals like these with a *dynasty,* extended across generations, promising strong government, legitimacy, and continuity over time.

The pro-monarchic voice in Judges and the elders in Samuel offer a secular defense of human kingship. Historically, however, the most common justification of monarchic rule is religious in character. The king claims, or royalist writers claim on his behalf, that he is divinely connected. Himself a god or a godlike figure or the elect of the gods, possessed of a "divine right" to rule over his fellows, he does not need to offer any merely prudential defense of his authority. It is this religious background, common to both Egypt and Mesopotamia (and probably, in some more attenuated sense, to Canaan also), that makes the elders' request for an Israelite king in 1 Samuel 8 so striking: although the elders ask to be ruled "like all the nations," they make an essentially secular argument. As God himself tells Samuel, the request is a repudiation of divine rule and divine right. Instead of these two, the elders call into existence, briefly, an autonomous political realm where utilitarian and prudential considerations prevail.

But note that the elders request a monarchy, not a particular monarch. God chooses the first king and thus the dynasty. What the elders want is simply a steady hand for war and justice. They want to be led into battle and judged in peacetime by rulers who are not raised up to deal with some terrible danger but born to and trained for their tasks, who provide continuous rather than intermittent leadership, maintain a standing army, and so on. Kings rule on a time scale cut to the measure of human need; the perspective of divinity, by contrast, does not make for politically reliable government.

This functionalist understanding of monarchy is not elaborated in the biblical texts. Nor are its democratic possibilities followed up. Conceivably, if the elders and people establish a functional monarchy, they could also make sure that kings fulfill their functions. The revolt of the northern tribes against Solomon's son Rehoboam almost fits this model, but the biblical historian makes sure to tell us that God, through his prophet Ahijah, has chosen the new king long before the people do (see §6, from 1 Kings 11–12). The real opposition in the Bible is not democratic versus monarchic but secular versus religious: we see this most clearly in the historical accounts of both the Northern and Southern Kingdoms, whenever kings act for prudential reasons and suffer the rebuke of God's prophets. It is not suggested that the people would do better, but that no human agents can be depended on. Political self-reliance is contrasted by both Hosea in the North and Isaiah in the South with faith in divine help (reiterating the central theme of the Gideon story). Self-reliance is the biblical version of secularism, but some of the prophetic texts suggest that it is also idolatrous: relying on human-made politics (strategies, weapons, diplomacy) is implicitly compared to relying on human-made idols. Here the king becomes an idol worshiper. But monarchy always carries with it another danger—that the king himself becomes the idol.

In the Northern Kingdom, kings without religious legitimacy ("They have set up kings but not by me," says Hosea's God: Hos. 8:4) turned out to be incapable of either steadiness or continuity. Kingship was far more successful in the South, precisely because it was bolstered there by a royalist-religious ideology, a claim of divine connections at both ends, as it were, of the Davidic line: God's choice at the beginning, messianic fulfillment in the last days (it is not clear how much of this ideology predates the Babylonian exile, but it is at least intimated in texts that are probably pre-exilic). Royalist ideology is sufficiently inclusive to take over the covenantal idea, which figures, for example, in Psalm 89. But it can also include descriptions of the king as God's son or at least as God's adopted son (see Psalm 2), which brings kingship dangerously close to Egyptian and Mesopotamian conceptions. This is "like all the nations" with a vengeance! Nonetheless, over the years the high royalism of the house of David was so popular, so powerfully imagined, so much the focus of both memory and hope, as to make divine-right monarchy, always conceived as Davidic rule, the preferred Jewish regime—

even though the Davidites have had no strong presence in Jewish life since the disappearance of Zerubabel in the aftermath of the Babylonian exile and not even any pretended presence since the end of the exilarchy in the early Middle Ages.

Among the intellectual elite, there was always some opposition to monarchic rule, differently expressed in different periods (see, for example, the midrashic discussion of Deuteronomy 17) but focused on some version of Gideon's claim that God was Israel's only king. Isaac Abravanel, perhaps the leading anti-monarchist among Jewish writers, also makes a plausible secular argument against kingly rule, as if replying to the biblical elders. But his most direct reply is religious: the assurance that God will fight Israel's battles, making the king unnecessary. Although he sometimes sounds like a Renaissance republican, Abravanel's hopes are focused on the regime the elders are said to have rejected: the kingship of God. He writes in the immediate aftermath of the expulsion from Spain and looks, like many of his contemporaries, toward an imminent divine intervention in the political world.

There was no popular opposition to kingship after the exile, presumably because there was no actual experience of kingly government; Jewish kings were figments of the Jewish imagination, and they were consistently imagined, across the diaspora, as messianic figures leading Israel back to its own land. Whatever the views of writers like Abravanel, among the people kingship was the decisive and necessary agency of redemptive politics.

But the monarchy of the elders, deriving its authority from its effectiveness, and the monarchy of royalist ideology and messianic hope, deriving its authority from God, are not the only possibilities explored by Jewish writers. Two modifications of these understandings of kingship need to be considered here, the first a "constitutional" version of royalism, the second a radical extension of the elders' program.

Deuteronomy and the talmudic tractate Sanhedrin are the classic texts of Jewish constitutionalism, the only attempts, except for Maimonides' codification of their doctrine in his *Mishneh Torah,* to make of kingship a government under law. (Prophetic rebuke obviously implies a similar subordination, if only in moral terms.) Deuteronomy doesn't yet suggest the institutions necessary to such a project. It simply calls on pious kings to subject themselves to the Torah and to the instruction of its priestly teachers.

Tractate Sanhedrin describes the court of seventy-one, capable in principle of judging kings, but imagines it as an effective restraint only on Davidites, who presumably rule in accordance with the Deuteronomic injunctions—although these injunctions are probably a historical response to Solomon's *mis*rule. When the sages call to mind rulers like those of the Northern Kingdom (or, more vividly, like the Hasmoneans), they do not seem at all confident of the authority of the court. It is not that the court is overruled by divine right; rather, it is overcome by royal power, which is, so the sages, or some of them, suggest, a law unto itself. These kings act, and apparently must be allowed to act, in accordance with Samuel's description of "the way of the king." The court simply steps aside: it doesn't admit the (non-Davidic) king to its deliberations; it doesn't deliberate on the lawfulness of his actions. But the ideal is different. Ideally, Israel should be ruled by a pious king, who accepts limits on his power (although these certainly seem minimal in the later accounts of Meiri and Maimonides), and by a learned court, the two cooperating with one another, their respective jurisdictions not sharply marked out.

By the time of tractate Sanhedrin, this ideal is entirely speculative. And speculation about kings under the law invites speculation about kings outside the law. Curiously, there is no full-scale account of tyranny in post-biblical Jewish literature: because there were no Jewish kings, there were no Jewish tyrants. Discussions of unjust rule focus on gentile rulers and the obedience that Jews owe, or do not owe, in the conditions of the exile. When the rabbis imagine Jewish kings acting outside the law, they are drawn to a different question—not about the injustices that kings commit but about the necessities that they confront.

The voice of the Israelite elders can still be heard in rabbinic texts calling for a government that is, before anything else, effective. It is most clearly heard in the eleventh *derashah* (sermon or essay) of Nissim Gerondi (Ran). We translate about half of the *derashah* here, excerpting at length because it is one of the most explicitly political texts produced by a medieval Jewish writer, and it is frequently quoted. Here the biblical establishment of kingship becomes the entry point for a full discussion of the realities of political life and then for a defense of prudential government. Royal power is the appointed instrument for dealing with "the needs of the hour"—a phrase we shall see again, for it is also used to justify the extraordinary powers of the rabbinic courts. But the courts have prior functions, whereas Gerondi almost seems to regard necessity as the king's *raison d'être*.

If the Torah were practical rather than ideal law, more adapted to the world-as-it-really-is, Israel would presumably have been ruled from the beginning by sages interpreting its provisions. God gave kings to Israel, Gerondi argues, because worldly necessity requires action outside the law. "Needs of the hour" is the rabbinic term for crises or emergencies. But the royal power that these needs legitimate is permanent; Gerondi does not suggest that pious Jews should wait for leaders more specifically raised up by God. Hence politics is set loose from divine providence and law, provided with a (theoretical) autonomy. Gerondi authorizes the king to act even against the Torah whenever he thinks such action necessary to the maintenance of law and order (*tikkun olam*) — although he is still supposed to carry his own copy of the Torah with him and to study it, as Deuteronomy requires, so as to know the laws he turns away from. Gerondi's king seems almost like Machiavelli's prince, who violates the standards of ordinary morality for the common good. There is nothing in Gerondi, however, that resembles Machiavelli's modernist provocation: it is impossible to imagine him telling his Jewish king that he must "learn how not to be good."

Because the king can be conceived in these essentially secularist terms, this doctrine of kingship suggests a traditional rationale for the medieval *kahal* (which is the immediate political context of Gerondi's writing) and perhaps even for the modern Jewish state. We can see this most clearly in the selections from Naftali Berlin (Netziv) in this chapter and from Abraham Isaac Kook in Chapter 10, although these writers carve out the political realm rather differently from Gerondi, avoiding the radicalism of his position. For them it is the needs of every hour that justify first kingly rule and then *any* secular government — because if kings are mere expedients, they can be replaced whenever it is more expedient by presidents or prime ministers or even popular assemblies. The Torah doesn't reach to questions of everyday politics or administration, so it allows room for alternative constitutional arrangements and prudential decision making.

The problem here, whether or not secular rulers are authorized to break the laws of the Torah, is that politics is understood as a realm of discretion without a law of its own. What is it that guides political choice? How do we recognize bad decisions? As we shall see, secular limits are specified most explicitly in the case of gentile kings, though the limits are admittedly not very restrictive. So we might say of the modern state of Israel that it is the joint heir of Jewish and non-Jewish kings—of kings authorized to act outside (or against) the Torah and of kings who naturally do that but who act rightly only insofar as they recognize other constraints on their power. We consider these secular constraints in Chapter 9.

Biblical Views of Monarchy

Gideon's Refusal of Kingship
1. Judges 6:1–6, 11–16, 33–35; 7:1–8, 15–22; 8:22–23

The book of Judges relates the political history of Israel between the conquest of the land and the establishment of the monarchy. It describes a recurring pattern of divine rule: the people sin, God delivers them into the hands of oppressors, they repent and are rescued by a leader ("judge") inspired by God. These chapters on the Gideon episode illustrate the pattern and present the book's ideal of charismatic and temporary leadership.

(6) Then the Israelites did what was offensive to the Lord, and the Lord delivered them into the hands of the Midianites for seven years. The hand of the Midianites prevailed over Israel; and because of Midian, the Israelites provided themselves with refuges in the caves and strongholds of the mountains. After the Israelites had done their sowing, Midian, Amalek, and the Kedemites would come up and raid them; they would attack them, destroy the produce of the land all the way to Gaza, and leave no means of sustenance in Israel, not a sheep or an ox or an ass. For they would come up with their livestock and their tents, swarming as thick as locusts; they and their camels were innumerable. Thus they would invade the land and ravage it. Israel was reduced to utter misery by the Midianites, and the Israelites cried out to the Lord. . . . An angel of the Lord came and sat under the tere-

binth at Ophrah, which belonged to Joash the Abiezrite. His son Gideon was then beating out wheat inside a winepress in order to keep it safe from the Midianites. The angel of the Lord appeared to him and said to him, "The Lord is with you, valiant warrior!" Gideon said to him, "Please, my lord, if the Lord is with us, why has all this befallen us? Where are all His wondrous deeds about which our fathers told us, saying, 'Truly the Lord brought us up from Egypt?' Now the Lord has abandoned us and delivers us into the hands of Midian!" The Lord turned to him and said, "Go in this strength of yours and deliver Israel from the Midianites. I hereby make you My messenger." He said to him, "Please, my lord, how can I deliver Israel? Why, my clan is the humblest in Manasseh, and I am the youngest in my father's household." The Lord replied, "I will be with you, and you shall defeat Midian to a man." . . .

All Midian, Amalek, and the Kedemites joined forces; they crossed over and encamped in the Valley of Jezreel. The spirit of the Lord enveloped Gideon; he sounded the horn, and the Abiezrites rallied behind him. And he sent messengers throughout Manasseh, and they too rallied behind him. He then sent messengers through Asher, Zebulun, and Naphtali, and they came up to meet the Manassites. . . .

(7) Early next day, Jerubbaal—that is, Gideon—and all the troops with him encamped above En-harod, while the camp of Midian was in the plain to the north of him, at Gibeath-moreh. The Lord said to Gideon, "You have too many troops with you for Me to deliver Midian into their hands; Israel might claim for themselves the glory due to Me, thinking, 'Our own hand has brought us victory.' Therefore, announce to the men, 'Let anybody who is timid and fearful turn back, as a bird flies from Mount Gilead.'" Thereupon, 22,000 of the troops turned back and 10,000 remained. "There are still too many troops," the Lord said to Gideon. "Take them down to the water and I will sift them for you there. Anyone of whom I tell you, 'This one is to go with you,' that one shall go with you; and anyone of whom I tell you, 'This one is not to go with you,' that one shall not go." So he took the troops down to the water. Then the Lord said to Gideon, "Set apart all those who lap up the water with their tongues like dogs from all those who get down on their knees to drink." Now those who "lapped" the water into their mouths by hand numbered three hundred; all the rest of the troops got down on their knees to drink. Then the Lord said to Gideon, "I will de-

liver you and I will put Midian into your hands through the three hundred 'lappers'; let the rest of the troops go home." So [the lappers] took the provisions and horns that the other men had with them, and he sent the rest of the men of Israel back to their homes, retaining only the three hundred men. . . . He shouted, "Come on! The Lord has delivered the Midianite camp into your hands!" He divided the three hundred men into three columns and equipped every man with a ram's horn and an empty jar, with a torch in each jar. "Watch me," he said, "and do the same. When I get to the outposts of the camp, do exactly as I do. When I and all those with me blow our horns, you too, all around the camp, will blow your horns and shout, 'For the Lord and for Gideon!'"

Gideon and the hundred men with him arrived at the outposts of the camp, at the beginning of the middle watch, just after the sentries were posted. They sounded the horns and smashed the jars that they had with them, and the three columns blew their horns and broke their jars. Holding the torches in their left hands and the horns for blowing in their right hands, they shouted, "A sword for the Lord and for Gideon!" They remained standing where they were, surrounding the camp; but the entire camp ran about yelling, and took to flight. For when the three hundred horns were sounded, the Lord turned every man's sword against his fellow, throughout the camp, and the entire host fled. . . .

(8) . . . Then the men of Israel said to Gideon, "Rule over us—you, your son, and your grandson as well; for you have saved us from the Midianites." But Gideon replied, "I will not rule over you myself, nor shall my son rule over you; the Lord alone shall rule over you."

Primitive Theocracy

2. Martin Buber, "Biblical Leadership"

Israel and the World: Essays in a Time of Crisis (New York: Schocken, 1948), pp. 128–29. This essay was translated by G. Hort.

The term "theocracy" is postbiblical (see C4). It does, however, facilitate an understanding of biblical conceptions of political rule. This text from Buber, written at about the same time as he was working on his book Kingship of God *(the late 1920s), aims at rehabilitating theocracy as a political idea—even while recognizing its ultimate failure. Following Spinoza, Buber acknowledges that the "kingship of God" requires human agents, but he views those agents positively: the people rule themselves but submit freely to the temporary leadership of a charismatic figure in times of crisis. And for this regime, Buber had a deep sympathy.*

We have a people, and the people is in bondage. A man [Moses] receives the charge to lead it out. That is he whom I have described as the Leader in the original meaning of the word. It is he who serves in a human way as a tool for the act which God pronounces, "I bore you on eagles' wings, and brought you unto myself" (Exod. 19:4). I have already spoken of his life. But in the middle of his life the event takes place in which Moses, after the passage through the Red Sea, intones the song in which the people joins, and which is the proclamation of a King. The words with which the song ends proclaim it: "King shall the Lord be for ever and ever" (Exod. 15:18). The people has here chosen God himself for its King, and that means that it has made a vital and experienced truth out of the tradition of a divine kingdom which was common to all Semitic peoples but which never had been taken quite seriously. The Hebrew leaders are so much in earnest about it, that after the land has been conquered they undertake to do what is "contrary to history": they try to build up a society without a ruling power save only that of God. It is that experiment in primitive theocracy of which the Book of Judges tells, and which degenerates into anarchy, as it is shown by the examples given in its last part.

. . . This type [of leadership] is to be understood as the attempt made by a leading group among the people [who] are dominated by the desire to make actual the proclamation of God as king, and try to induce the people to follow them. This attempt miscarries time and again. Time and again the people, to use the biblical phrase, falls away from God. But we can also express this in the language of history: time and again the people fall apart; it is one and the same thing whichever language we use. The attempt to establish a society under no other dominion than God's—this too can be expressed in the language of history or . . . of sociology: the attempt to establish society on pure voluntarism fails over and over again. The people falls away. This is always succeeded by an invasion by one of the neighboring peoples, and Israel, from a historical point of view fallen apart and disunited, does not stand firm. But in its conquered state it again makes itself subject to the will of God, resolves anew to accept God's dominion, and again a divine mission occurs; there is always a leader whom the spirit lays hold of as it laid hold of Moses. This leader, whose mission is to free the people, is "the Judge," or more correctly, "he who makes it right"; he makes this right exist in the actual world for the people, which after its return to God now again has right on its side, by defeating the enemy. This is the rhythm of the Book of Judges; it might almost be called a tragic rhythm, were it not that the word tragic is so foreign to the spirit of the biblical language.

But in this Book of Judges there is also something being prepared. [As] the experience of failure, of the inability to bring about this intended, naive, primitive theocracy becomes ever deeper, ever stronger grows the demand for a human kingdom.

Requesting a King
3. I Samuel 8

This is the classic account of the establishment of monarchy in Israel. Samuel is the last of the "judges," and the first chapters of the book bearing his name form a bridge between the period of God's rule and the monarchic era. Chapter 8, printed here in its entirety, ends abruptly when Samuel, commanded by God to heed the people's request for a king, sends them home to await their new ruler—but not before he has provided them, also at God's command, with an account of the practice of kings that became a basic text for both defenders and critics of monarchy. Subsequent chapters describe the continuing role of Samuel in the ascension and death of Saul, Israel's first king.

When Samuel grew old, he appointed his sons judges over Israel. The name of his first-born was Joel, and his second son's name was Abijah; they sat as judges in Beer-sheba. But his sons did not follow in his ways; they were bent on gain, they accepted bribes, and they subverted justice.

All the elders of Israel assembled and came to Samuel at Ramah, and they said to him, "You have grown old, and your sons have not followed your ways. Therefore appoint a king for us, to govern us like all other nations." Samuel was displeased that they said "Give us a king to govern us." Samuel prayed to the Lord, and the Lord replied to Samuel, "Heed the demand of the people in everything they say to you. For it is not you that they have rejected; it is Me they have rejected as their king. Like everything else they have done ever since I brought them out of Egypt to this day—forsaking Me and worshiping other gods—so they are doing to you. Heed their demand; but warn them solemnly, and tell them about the practices of any king who will rule over them."

Samuel reported all the words of the Lord to the people, who were asking him for a king. He said, "This will be the practice [*mishpat*] of the king who will rule over you: He will take your sons and appoint them as his charioteers and horsemen, and they will serve as outrunners for his chariots. He will appoint them as his chiefs of thousands and of fifties; or they will have to plow his fields, reap his harvest, and make his weapons and the equipment for his chariots. He will take your daughters as perfumers, cooks, and bakers. He will seize your choice fields, vineyards, and olive groves, and give them to his courtiers. He will take a tenth part of your grain and vintage and give it to his eunuchs and courtiers. He will take your male and female slaves, your choice young men, and your asses, and put them to work for him. He will take a tenth part of your flocks, and you shall become his slaves. The day will come when you cry out because of the king whom you yourselves have chosen; and the Lord will not answer you on that day."

But the people would not listen to Samuel's warning. "No," they said. "We must have a king over us, that we may be like all the other nations: Let our king rule over us and go out at our head and fight our battles." When Samuel heard all that the people said, he reported it to the Lord. And the Lord said to Samuel, "Heed their demands and appoint a king for them." Samuel then said to the men of Israel, "All of you go home."

Commentary. Kingship and Political Agency

The story of 1 Samuel tells how political rule in the form of kingship comes to Israel. Until this dramatic moment, Israel was ruled by prophets and other leaders, raised up by God and marked by sacred and charismatic authority. Now the people of Israel seem to defy God by insisting on a new kind of authority, resembling that of "other nations." The Bible offers other accounts of the origin of kingship, portraying the roles of God and the people rather differently and endowing kingship with sacral authority. Here, the people's demand, encountering God's sovereignty and the prophet's authority, brings into existence a specifically political regime. This tense story, with its definite beginning and end, is foundational in character. Evoking material from other texts but not seeking to compare or reconcile the texts or to take into account scholarship addressing their varying sources, I focus on this politically seminal moment.

The corruption of Samuel's two sons is part of a deeper crisis. That they remain in Beer-sheba, rather than travel the judicial circuit for which Samuel has grown too old, suggests that justice no longer has a pervasive presence in Israel. Moreover, Samuel's conferring of judicial authority on them, a dynastic gesture, evokes an unfavorable contrast with Moses. Acting on the advice of his father-in-law — who might have been thought to favor the claims of kinship — Moses chose as judges "capable men out of all Israel, and appointed them heads over the people" (Exod. 18:25), a rank indifferent to lineage. The crisis is deepened because God seems not to address the problem of succession. In a brief narrative moment, God provided Joshua as Moses' successor (Num. 27:15). And God called Samuel to replace Eli's feeble priesthood when Eli's rebuke of his own corrupt sons was ineffectual (1 Sam. 2:12–36). We do not know how long Samuel's sons have proved unworthy, but the elders seem not to expect God to provide new leadership. They neither ask that Samuel replace his sons with appointments like those made by Moses nor turn to God for new leadership but, in great surprise, demand "a king for us, to govern us like all other nations."

In demanding a king, the elders cede authority they have as patriarchs and rulers of towns, households, and families. It is *their* dependents and possessions that kings may appropriate; *their* sons, subordinate to fathers and elders, who may become the king's officials as "chiefs of thousands and of fifties"—ranks that ignore the ties of lineage, kinship, and household in which the authority of elders is bound. Sons, daughters, fields, vineyards, harvest, servants, cattle—each noun indistinguishably emphasizes the possessive form: what is *yours* as patriarchs and owners will be *his,* the king's, to take for his purposes. Authority is not only redistributed but assumes a new form: kingship.

The elders do not want a particular king but the institution of kingship. Earlier, "the men of Israel," reacting to Gideon's success in war, acclaim him as dynastic ruler: "Rule over us—you, your son and your grandson as well." But their direct attempt to constitute political rule defies God's authority, as Gideon's refusal explains: "I will not rule over you myself, nor shall my son rule over you, the Lord alone shall rule over you" (Judg. 8:22–23). Later, the ruthless and sinful attempt by Gideon's son Abimelech to make himself king—first of Shechem, then of Israel—ends in failure and a humiliating death; the episode reflects the wrongness, in both divine and human terms, of instituting kingship by personal will and conquest (Judg. 9). The elders' demand for a king differs from these flawed precedents; they neither acclaim nor recognize a ruler, but urgently insist that Samuel provide one.

The response that God tells the prophet to make—"listen to the people in everything they say to you" (my translation)—is amazing in substance and form. It inverts the biblical formula, in which the speech of prophets implies imperative command and the people's listening implies obligated obedience. Yet, God says, "it is Me they have rejected as their king." What is the meaning of this rejection, in which God seems to acquiesce?

"It is not you that they have rejected," God tells Samuel. Indeed, Samuel led "Israel as long as he lived" (1 Sam. 7:15), and later "all Israel" emphatically affirms his righteousness (1 Sam. 12:3–5). The elders demand a king in anticipation of the approaching end of Samuel's career. Concerned that the angered prophet not reject Israel, God offers him an analogy: although they demand a king rather than "capable men who fear God" appointed by prophets, Samuel must not reject them—as God has remained with them, though they worshiped false gods, so must Samuel. However, analogy is not equivalence. The sinful worship of false gods is distinct from the elders' demand for a king in response to Samuel's advanced age, his sons' abuses and, implicitly, the tension between prophecy and dynastic succession. Israel has often fallen into the sin of idolatry, for which it has suffered punishment. But kingship is new both to the people and to Samuel. It is the nature of kingship about which God instructs Samuel in commanding him to "warn" and "tell" the elders.

Samuel's vivid description is an account of political rule, not by corrupt or tyrannical kings, but of the "practice" (*mishpat*)—the custom, manner, rights—inherent in kingship. The king has the right and power to draw extensively on the kingdom's resources. He will take a tenth to sustain his court and retinue—unlike the tenth taken by the priests, which sustains the temple service. The elders will become servants or slaves—both are possible understandings of *la'avadim*—but the word stretches toward a new idea, that of the king's subjects. Though he will take a tenth of grain, vintage, and flocks, there are no specified limits to the fields, vineyards, and olive groves the king may seize or to the number of sons, daughters, and slaves he may impress. Yet when Israel "cries out" from exactions by the kings whom they have willed upon themselves, God "will not answer." Why not? Their demand for a king is daring—it pushes past Samuel's shock in asserting a new political agency, expressed in God's telling Samuel to "listen to the people in everything they say." God instructs Israel, through the distressed Samuel, about the rulership of a king as distinct from the governance they have known, by stipulating that He will not answer when the people "cry out." The customary authority of kings, however harsh, is legitimate; having called a king into existence, the people have no right of appeal against his just exactions.

Before this moment, kingship is anticipated four times in the same formula—"in those days there was no king in Israel"—which is always linked with stories of strife and disorder (Judg. 17:6; 18:1; 19:1; 21:25). The last describes the advent of chaos: without a king, "everyone did as he pleased." At the foundational moment, however, no examples of disorder arise; rather, a new political agency responds to a historical juncture. Now the people, no longer the elders alone, repeat and intensify the demand: "No, but there *will* be a king over us" (my translation)—it is emphatic that they are the active agents bringing kingship into existence. At the beginning of human history, God assigned to Adam the power to name all animal life (Gen. 2:19–20), affirming humanity's dominion over living nature. Demanding a king, Israel asserts a political capacity that God has not assigned. Once asserted, it grows: they want a king not only to replace Samuel's sons and, prospectively, Samuel himself but to lead in war: the king is also to "go out at our head and fight our battles."

Rule in justice and in war are equally central to political authority. But in the story, the crises of judicial and military authority are not quite equivalent or symmetrical. At the battle with the Philistines at Mizpah, Samuel's prophecy, sacrifice, and cries to God result in victory, after which "the hand of the Lord was set against the Philistines as long as Samuel lived" (1 Sam. 7:3–15). Samuel has grown old, but the people do not mention the lack of a successor as war leader, matching the elders' concern that Samuel has no successor as judge. Anticipating the problem and concerned over an Ammonite invasion (1 Sam. 12:12), they expand their demand for a king to fill the space of political rule. The foundational drama ends in Samuel's re-counting of this great transition, in which he emphasizes the reversal of the formulaic relationship of prophet and people—"Behold, I listened to your voice in all that you said to me and I set a king over you. Henceforth, the king will go before you" (1 Sam. 12:1–2). Samuel obeys God in both yielding to the people and remaining with them as prophet, becoming the first to rebuke and chastise a king (1 Sam. 13:13–14, 15:24–31). It is a carefully delineated *political* kingship that comes into existence.

What is the story's attitude toward this radical development? The demand for "a king . . . to govern us like all other nations" does not mean that, like idolatry, kingship is intrinsically alien and abhorrent. The rejection of Egypt is so formative for Israel that the category "all the nations" (*kol ha-goyyim*) excludes the exceptional case of Egypt and its divine pharaohs. Nor does the phrase refer to the kings of Mesopotamia, who, though not divine, mediate between their subjects and the gods. Rather, "all the nations" refers to the peoples with which Israel has been in contact since the going out from Egypt—the Canaanite city kings (whom Abimelech imitated in Shechem) and the territorial kings of Moab and Ammon. Before the demand for a king, Samuel cleansed Israel of Canaanite fertility deities, the *be'alim* and *ashtarot,* the most recent examples of Israel's recurrent lapses into paganism (1 Sam. 7:3–4). The foreign model they wish to adopt is political, not religious.

In the very moment at which a distinction between religious and political domains arises in Israel, Samuel abruptly dismisses and disperses the people—"all of you go home." Although kingship enters Israel at the people's insistence, not they but God, acting through the prophet, chooses the king. The people's demand—"give us a king"—is exactly fulfilled. Their unprecedented political agency creates political rule in Israel. Arising in tension with prophetic authority, it is nonetheless justified, for God, while not approving, complies in its creation.

The story differs from foundational accounts of sacral, medieval, or absolutist monarchy, of feudal lordship, and of democratic, nationalist, and communist regimes. Sacred authority, nature, popular sovereignty, ideology—none of these animate the origin of kingship in Israel. Rather, it comes into existence when a people, facing problems of succession and military threat, suddenly demand a form of political rule consistent with God's sovereignty but not originally part of God's design. Acquiescing, God places kingship within the terms of the Sinaitic covenant. Insisting on a new domain of politics, a new political space, the story does not open the way for kingly despotism, because the powers it ascribes to the king, though new in Israel, are not unbounded or arbitrary; nor for democracy, because the people do not rule; nor for popular consent, because the people's creative role, though seminal, is momentary. It does, however, open the way for secular political rule. The struggles that follow between Samuel and Israel's first king, Saul, set the tone for subsequent conflicts of prophets and kings. The story accounts for the coming into being, within the history of a holy people ruled by God, of legitimate and specifically political authority.

Allan Silver

Royalist Theology
4. Psalms 89:21–38

A large part of Psalm 89 is devoted to a "vision": God's proclamation of a special covenant with the house of David. In the Bible this is followed by a plaintive appeal to God that he be true to his promises. The vision itself (reproduced here) is of a piece with several other "royal psalms," which reflect the theological revolution brought about by the establishment of the monarchy. This psalm stresses the intimate relationship between God and the king and the unconditional covenant between them.

I have found David, My servant;
   anointed him with My sacred oil.
My hand shall be constantly with him,
   and My arm shall strengthen him.
No enemy shall oppress him,
   no vile man afflict him.
I will crush his adversaries before him;
   I will strike down those who hate him.
My faithfulness and steadfast love shall be with him;
   his horn shall be exalted through My name.
I will set his hand upon the sea,
   his right hand upon the rivers.
He shall say to Me,
   "You are my father, my God, the rock of my deliverance."
I will appoint him first-born,
   highest of the kings of the earth.
I will maintain My steadfast love for him always;
   My covenant with him shall endure.
I will establish his line forever,
   his throne, as long as the heavens last.
If his sons forsake My Teaching
   and do not observe My commands,
I will punish their transgression with the rod,
   their iniquity with plagues.
But I will not take away My steadfast love from him;
   I will not betray My faithfulness.
I will not violate My covenant,
   or change what I have uttered.
I have sworn by My holiness, once and for all;

> I will not be false to David.
> His line shall continue forever,
> > his throne, as the sun before Me.
> > as the moon, established forever,
> > an enduring witness in the sky.

Commentary. God's Kingship

      Unlike the pagan gods, the God of Israel is a jealous God. While paganism allows the worship of many gods, the God of Israel demands exclusivity, an idea powerfully captured in the biblical metaphor of monogamous marriage between God the husband and Israel the wife. Worshiping other gods is analogous to betrayal, provoking God's deepest jealousy and anger. But what is the extent and meaning of the metaphor when translated from the human to the theological? What is it that has to be preserved as exclusive on the religious side of the metaphor? The clearest candidate is worship: no one is allowed to sacrifice, pray, burn incense, or pour libation except to God; any such act directed to a person, an institution, or another god constitutes idolatry. Ritual is therefore the direct counterpart of the exclusive sexual relationship in monogamous marriage. Yet, as in marriage, the realm of exclusivity is not so easy to carve out. The ambiguities involved in fixing its borders have enormous implications for understanding God's kingship and its relation to politics.

      The problem can be formulated in the following manner: At what point does the ceremonial acceptance of authority in politics become actual worship? For enlightened pagans in Rome, the worship of the emperor—even sacrificial offerings—was a matter of mere civil religion, an expression of loyalty to the state and nothing more. At the other extreme, for the Jewish zealots who led the rebellion against Rome, a routine civic obligation such as paying taxes to the emperor constituted worship of a false god. Where should the line be drawn between authority and deification? Which attributes are exclusive to God such that ascribing them to a political figure or institution establishes a false god? The broader the realm of political gestures, roles, and attributes ascribed exclusively to God, the narrower the possibility that political authority will not be considered idolatrous. What constitutes worship and what counts as deification is therefore at the heart of the problem of God's kingship.

Within the Bible there is a struggle between two understandings of the idea of God's kingship. The one claims that *God is the king;* the other claims that *the king is not a god.* According to the first argument, kingship is an exclusive attribute of God. The transference of the role to a human is tantamount to deification. This is what Gideon told the people when he was asked to establish a royal dynasty: "I will not rule over you myself, nor shall my son rule over you; the Lord alone shall rule over you" (Judg. 8:23). In the same vein, the desire of the elders to establish a monarch at the end of Samuel's life is experienced by God as a betrayal analogous to the worship of other gods: "For it is not you that they have rejected; it is Me they have rejected as their king. Like everything else they have done ever since I brought them out of Egypt to this day—forsaking Me and worshipping other gods—so they are doing to you" (1 Sam. 8:7–8). The only human leadership that is acceptable on such an understanding of God's kingship is the ad hoc noninstitutional leadership of the judges. As charismatic leaders—ancient versions of crisis managers—the judges never established a standing army supported by taxation. Even given their limited role, however, God insisted on making his direct leadership visible. He ordered Gideon to decrease the number of troops amassed for the war against the Midianites: "You have too many troops with you for me to deliver Midian into their hands; Israel might claim for themselves the glory due to Me, thinking, 'Our own hand has brought us victory'" (Judg. 7:2). A further constraint on realpolitik stemming from God's political monopoly can be seen in the prophetic polemic against protective treaties with superpowers like Egypt or Assyria. God is after all the protector and lord, and Israel is his vassal, not Egypt's or Assyria's: "Ha! Those who go down to Egypt for help and rely upon horses! They have put their trust in abundance of chariots, in vast numbers of riders and they have not turned to the Holy One of Israel, they have not sought the Lord" (Isa. 31:1).

At the heart of the God-is-the-king argument lies the idea that political subjection is worship and that investing individuals with royal authority is tantamount to deification. But what kind of political program does such an idea suppose? Anarchism seems to be the modern analogue, and in-

deed in *Kingship of God,* Martin Buber sought to revive the political ideology of God's kingship as sacred anarchy. Buber envisioned Zionism as a
dynamic, noninstitutionalized community of I-thou rather then I-it relationships. The modern criticism of this idea was already suggested in the
Bible itself. Without a state monopoly on the use of force, the weak will be
completely vulnerable. The anarchic "state of nature" will not evolve into a
community of free individuals respecting each other's dignity. Rather, it will
produce complete chaos or the arbitrary rule of the powerful. The last verse
of the book of Judges is the opposition's summary of what can be learned
from the social experiment in anarchism: "In those days there was no king
in Israel; everyone did as he pleased" (Judg. 21:25). When such a community
of sacred anarchy faces threats from organized states with powerful standing armies, as it inevitably must, it quickly collapses. This is why the elders
of Israel make their request: "We must have a king over us, that we may be
like all other nations: Let our king rule over us and go out . . . and fight our
battles" (1 Sam. 8:19–20). Anarchist theorists respond to these challenges by
arguing that the evils produced by organized states pose a far greater danger than the harm done by individuals to each other. Outside threats to the
anarchist community should not be answered by forced conscription and
taxation but by volunteerism, whose spirit will be unmatched by that of any
organized force.

Anarchism needs further discussion; but in any case, the analogy
between its modern version and the biblical kingship of God, though tempting, is misleading. From the perspective of the book of Judges, the void left
by nonhierarchical, noninstitutional leadership is filled by God's ongoing
presence in history. It is not the army of volunteers or the tribunal of the
people that functions instead of established law and order but God himself
who acts as judge, warrior, and redeemer. Volunteerism and civic participation are not the alternatives to hierarchical structure; the people—according to God-is-the-king ideology—assume political responsibility only when
God hides his face because of their sins. In principle they have only to keep
the Torah, and God will do the rest.

Although the God-is-the-king ideology shares the anarchist argument about the wrongfulness of subjugation, it is premised on God's ongoing
intervention in the political affairs of the community, hence the critical verse

"In those days there was no king in Israel; everyone did as he pleased" attains a sharper edge. It represents a voice within the book of Judges that is directed not only against the illusion of human goodwill in the state of nature but also against the argument that God is king. This internal biblical opposition to the rule of the judges declares that if the claim is made that God is king, then "in those days there was no king in Israel," not even God.

The alternative understanding of God's kingship is that the king is not a god. According to this understanding, God does not monopolize politics as his exclusive realm; instead, he sets limits on the claims that politics can make. The ascription of kingship to humans is not an act of deification; only the myth of kingship as an ahistorical institution rooted in the nature of things, only the claim that the king is a god, constitutes deification. When the king is not just a warrior, a legislator, or a judge but also the one who makes the Nile overflow and the sun rise—then the boundary between the human and the divine is crossed. God's kingship, according to this view, is manifest in the struggle against the transformation of the political into the cosmological and of the historical into the mythical.

The book of Samuel finally accepts the institution of kingship as long as the king does not sever his dependence upon God, as manifested in the prophet's subsequent critical stance (cf. 1 Sam. 12–15). But there is a further step in the biblical view of kingship, reflected in the royal theology of Psalm 89. Here the king is perceived as a mediator between the divine and the human, with an independent covenant with God. Indeed, some of the expressions in this psalm seem to cross the boundary, portraying the king as a divine being. The view that the king is not a god allows for the practice of mundane politics but aims to ensure that the political does not overstep its limits. The king has to fear God rather than become a god: "Thus he will not act haughtily towards his fellows or deviate from the commandment to the right or to the left" (Deut. 17:20).

Deification is the worst of political evils, and it is the constant temptation of the powerful. The claim that God is the king sets stricter limits on this evil than does the claim that the king is not a god: human kingship is described as a form of deification, and political subjection as a form of worship. The second claim is more lenient, maintaining that deification does not occur with the ascription of political titles but only with the ascription of nonpolitical attributes to political figures. Yet, paradoxically, the claim that God is the king is far more vulnerable to the dangers of deification than its lenient alternative. The institutional void created by the God-is-the-king ideology eventually will be filled by mediators who speak in God's name. Pure theocracy is doomed to deteriorate into priestly rule and prophetic claims. Since God is supposed to be the king, any political move will be absolutized by his human agents. The moderate view that the king is not a god, although it allows for political authority, affords better protection against deification. By suggesting that there is a human sphere of politics not monopolized by God, it allows room for human agents who make no claim to represent God's absolute will.

Moshe Halbertal

The Constitution of Monarchy

Laws Concerning the King—I
5. Deuteronomy 17:14–20

This text, which includes the Torah's only laws concerning kings, is a much discussed and disputed political statement. The critical interpretive dispute is about whether God is here permitting or commanding the appointment of a king. Our translation favors the "permitting" view, but the Hebrew words (at the point noted below) can be read differently. In its canonical setting this section of laws concerning the king is part of a larger group of what might be termed "constitutional" laws, most of which are featured in later chapters. The section immediately preceding (Deut. 17:8–13) is on the high court (C7), and those immediately following (18:1–9), on the priests and (18:9–22) the prophets (see CC4 and 5).

If, after you have entered the land that the Lord your God has assigned to you, and taken possession of it and settled in it, you decide, "I will set a king over me, as do all the nations about me," you shall be free to[1] set a king over yourself, one chosen by the Lord your God. Be sure to set as king over yourself one of your own people; you must not set a foreigner over you, one who is not your kinsman. Moreover, he shall not keep many horses or send people back to Egypt to add to his horses, since the Lord has warned you, "You must not go back that way again." And he shall not have many wives, lest his heart go astray; nor shall he amass silver and gold to excess.

When he is seated on his royal throne, he shall have a copy of this Torah written for him on a scroll by the levitical priests. Let it remain with him and let him read in it all his life, so that he may learn to revere the Lord his God, to observe faithfully every word of this Torah as well as these laws. Thus he will not act haughtily toward his fellows or deviate from the commandment[2] to the right or to the left, to the end that he and his descendants may reign long in the midst of Israel.

Contesting the Succession: Prophet and People
6. I Kings 11:1–4, 11–13, 26–32, 37–40, 43; 12:1–20, 26–30

In the previous selection the king is instructed to remain humble and abide by the law so that his rule and that of his dynasty will be preserved. Here we provide a historical-prophetic narration of the crisis of succession upon the death of David's son Solomon. The succession by Rehoboam to the Davidic throne apparently required confirmation by the people (cf. 2 Sam. 5:1–3). His loss of most of the realm followed politically from his folly in scorning their demands. But this folly was itself "brought about" by God in response to Solomon's sins, and the new king, Jeroboam, like Saul and David, was chosen by God's prophet.

1. The meaning of the Hebrew is ambiguous as to whether this is a permission or a commandment. The alternative translation, "Thou shalt in any wise set him king over thee," figures in §12.
2. New JPS: "instruction."

King Solomon loved many foreign women in addition to Pharaoh's daughter—Moabite, Ammonite, Edomite, Phoenician, and Hittite women, from
the nations of which the Lord had said to the Israelites, "None of you shall
join them and none of them shall join you, lest they turn your heart away to
follow their gods." Such Solomon clung to and loved. He had seven hundred
royal wives and three hundred concubines; and his wives turned his heart
away. . . .

And the Lord said to Solomon, "Because you are guilty of this—
you have not kept My covenant and the laws which I enjoined upon you—
I will tear the kingdom away from you and give it to one of your servants.
But, for the sake of your father David, I will not do it in your lifetime; I
will tear it away from your son. However, I will not tear away the whole
kingdom; I will give your son one tribe, for the sake of My servant David
and for the sake of Jerusalem which I have chosen." . . .

Jeroboam son of Nebat, an Ephraimite of Zeredah, the son of a
widow whose name was Zeruah, was in Solomon's service; he raised his hand
against the king. The circumstances under which he raised his hand against
the king were as follows: Solomon built the Millo and repaired the breach
of the city of his father, David. This Jeroboam was an able man, and when
Solomon saw that the young man was a capable worker, he appointed him
over all the forced labor of the House of Joseph.

During that time Jeroboam went out of Jerusalem and the prophet
Ahijah of Shiloh met him on the way. He had put on a new robe; and when
the two were alone in the open country, Ahijah took hold of the new robe
he was wearing and tore it into twelve pieces. "Take ten pieces," he said to
Jeroboam. "For thus said the Lord, the God of Israel: I am about to tear the
kingdom out of Solomon's hands, and I will give you ten tribes. But one
tribe shall remain his—for the sake of My servant David and for the sake of
Jerusalem, the city that I have chosen out of all the tribes of Israel. . . . But
you have been chosen by Me; reign wherever you wish, and you shall be
king over Israel. If you heed all that I command you, and walk in My ways,
and do what is right in My sight, keeping My laws and commandments as
My servant David did, then I will be with you and I will build for you a lasting dynasty as I did for David. I hereby give Israel to you; and I will chastise
David's descendants for that [sin], though not forever."

Solomon sought to put Jeroboam to death, but Jeroboam promptly fled to King Shishak of Egypt; and he remained in Egypt till the death of Solomon. . . .

Solomon slept with his fathers and was buried in the city of his father David; and his son Rehoboam succeeded him as king.

Rehoboam went to Shechem, for all Israel had come to Shechem to acclaim him as king. Jeroboam son of Nebat learned of it while he was still in Egypt; for Jeroboam had fled from King Solomon, and had settled in Egypt. They sent for him; and Jeroboam and all the assembly of Israel came and spoke to Rehoboam as follows: "Your father made our yoke heavy. Now lighten the harsh labor and the heavy yoke which your father laid on us, and we will serve you." He answered them, "Go away for three days and then come back to me." So the people went away. And the young men who had grown up with him answered, "Speak thus to the people who said to you, 'Your father made our yoke heavy, now you make it lighter for us.' Say to them, 'My little finger is thicker than my father's loins. My father imposed a heavy yoke on you, and I will add to your yoke; my father flogged you with whips, but I will flog you with scorpions.'"

Jeroboam and all the people came to Rehoboam on the third day, since the king had told them: "Come back on the third day." The king answered the people harshly, ignoring the advice that the elders had given him. He spoke to them in accordance with the advice of the young men, and said, "My father made your yoke heavy, but I will add to your yoke; my father flogged you with whips, but I will flog you with scorpions." (The king did not listen to the people; for the Lord had brought it about in order to fulfill the promise that the Lord had made through Ahijah the Shilonite to Jeroboam son of Nebat.) When all Israel saw that the king had not listened to them, the people answered the king:

> "We have no portion in David,
> No share in Jesse's son!
> To your tents, O Israel!
> Now look to your own House, O David."

So the Israelites returned to their homes. But Rehoboam continued to reign over the Israelites who lived in the towns of Judah.

King Rehoboam sent Adoram, who was in charge of the forced labor, but all Israel pelted him to death with stones. Thereupon King Rehoboam hurriedly mounted his chariot and fled to Jerusalem. Thus Israel revolted against the House of David, as is still the case. When all Israel heard that Jeroboam had returned, they sent messengers and summoned him to the assembly and made him king over all Israel. Only the tribe of Judah remained loyal to the House of David. . . .

Jeroboam said to himself, "Now the kingdom may well return to the House of David. If these people still go up to offer sacrifices at the House of the Lord in Jerusalem, the heart of these people will turn back to their master, King Rehoboam of Judah; they will kill me and go back to King Rehoboam of Judah." So the king took counsel and made two golden calves. He said to the people, "You have been going up to Jerusalem long enough. This is your god, O Israel, who brought you up from the land of Egypt!" He set up one in Bethel and placed the other in Dan. That proved to be a cause of guilt, for the people went to worship [the calf at Bethel and] the one at Dan.

Laws Concerning the King—II
7. Mishnah Sanhedrin, Chapter 2

This is the Rabbinic text most closely approaching constitutional law. It describes the relations between the basic institutions of the Israelite polity: the king, the high priest, and the seventy-one- member Sanhedrin, or high court (see CC4 and 7). By the time of the final redaction of the Mishnah, a century and a half had passed since the collapse of the Great Rebellion and an even longer time since the loss of Jewish sovereignty. Whether these laws reflect any historical reality—Hasmonean or other—remains unclear.

1. The high priest judges and is subject to judgment; he testifies, and testimony is heard against him. . . .

3. The king neither judges, nor is he subject to judgment; he neither testifies, nor is testimony heard against him. . . .

4. He leads forth to optional war, as approved by the court of seventy-one. He breaks through to make his highway, with no protest allowed; there is no fixed measure for the king's highway. [After a battle] the people all loot and lay down [their booty] before him, and he takes first choice.

5. "He shall not have many wives [lest his heart go astray]" (Deut. 17:17)—no more than eighteen. Rabbi Yehudah says: He may have many, as long as they do not lead his heart astray. Rabbi Shimon says: Even one [wife] is forbidden if she leads his heart astray; if so, to what effect is it written, "He shall not have many wives"?—[To exclude] even [women] like Abigail.[3]

6. "He shall not keep many horses" (Deut. 17:16): only those needed for his chariot. "Nor shall he amass silver and gold to excess" (Deut. 17:17): only as much as is needed for sustaining the army.

He must write for himself a Torah scroll. When he goes forth to war, he takes it forth with him; when returning, he brings it with him. When he sits in judgment, it is with him; when reclining [at meals], it is opposite him, as written, "Let it remain with him, and let him read in it all his life" (Deut. 17:19).

7. It is forbidden to ride on his horse, to sit on his throne, or to use his scepter. It is forbidden to see him when he is having his hair cut, or when he is naked or at the bathhouse; as written: "Set a king over yourself" (Deut. 17:15)—let his fear be upon you.

King Not Subject to Judgment: Compromise or Ideal?
8. JT Sanhedrin 20a; BT Sanhedrin 19a–b

The Jerusalem Talmud offers scriptural grounds for both aspects of the mishnaic exclusion of the king from judgment (mishnah 2:3 in the previous selection). The Jerusalem Talmud takes it to be fully appropriate that the king is subject only to God. In the Babylonian Talmud, by contrast, the king's exemption is radically reinterpreted: it re-

---

3. One of David's wives, noted for leading him away from evil deeds (see 1 Sam. 25).

flects no principle but merely an unhappy compromise determined by experience with autocratic monarchs. This experience is epitomized in a tale of confrontation between the Sanhedrin and a Hasmonean king.

JT Sanhedrin 20a

Does [the king] not judge? Is it not written, "And David executed justice and *tzedakah*[4] for all his people" (2 Sam. 8:15)?

Is this conceivable [that justice and *tzedakah* be executed simultaneously]? Rather, he would render a judgment, absolving the faultless and finding against the liable; then if the liable party were poor, he [David] would pay from his own assets. Thus he executed justice for one and *tzedakah* for the other. . . .

"Nor is he subject to judgment"—as implied by "A prayer of David . . . My judgment will come from You [i.e., King David invites God alone to judge him]" (Ps. 17:2).

BT Sanhedrin 19a–b

"The king neither judges, nor is he subject to judgment." . . . Rav Yosef said: This refers only to the kings of Israel.[5] Kings of the house of David, however, both judge and are subject to judgment. For it is written, "O House of David, thus said the Lord: Render just verdicts, morning by morning" (Jer. 21:12)—and if they are not subject to judgment, how can they judge others? For . . . Resh Lakish expounded [thus]: "Examine yourself and only then examine others!"

Why then are the kings of Israel not [subject to judgment]? Because of a certain event.

---

4. This biblical term derives from a root denoting "justice." In Rabbinic usage, however, it means "charity."

5. Here used as a generic term for non-Davidic monarchs, whose reign is nevertheless legitimate. Its initial reference was to the kings of the Northern Kingdom of Israel comprising the Ten Tribes, as distinct from the Southern Kingdom of Judea, where the Davidic dynasty ruled in Jerusalem. The Rabbis extended the term to include the Hasmonean dynasty. In the Bible, the "kings of Israel" are commonly evaluated negatively.

King Yannai's slave killed a person. Shimon b. Shatah said to [his colleagues] the sages: "Set your eyes upon him, and let us judge him." They sent him a message: "Your slave has killed a person." [Yannai] dispatched the slave [to appear] before them. They sent him a [further] message: "Come here yourself as well! [As written (Exod. 21:29)]: 'And its owner shall be admonished,' the Torah ordered that the owner should come and stand over his ox." [6]

He came and took a seat. Shimon b. Shatah said to him: "King Yannai, stand on your feet and hear the testimony against you; and it is not before us that you stand, but before Him who spoke and brought the world into being—as written, 'The two parties to the dispute shall stand before God'" (Deut. 19:17).

[Yannai] answered, "Not as you say, but as your colleagues say!" He turned to his right, and they pressed their faces to the ground; he turned to his left, and they pressed their faces to the ground. Then Shimon b. Shatah said to them: "You possess thoughts; let the Master of Thoughts come and take revenge upon you!" Immediately, [the angel] Gabriel came and knocked them to the ground, and they died.

At that point it was established that "the king neither judges, nor is he subject to judgment; he neither testifies, nor is testimony heard against him."

Commentary. A Monarchic Constitution?

The critical line in this sequence of texts is the Mishnah's dictum "The king neither judges, nor is he subject to judgment." Is this an acceptance of royal absolutism, or a piece of political realism, or a surrender to royal power? The Babylonian Talmud suggests the last, and I want to follow its argument and read this sequence of texts as the story of a failure to incorporate kingship within a constitutional structure.

The Deuteronomist makes the first attempt at incorporation: he has

---

6. Talmudic law takes this clause as requiring the owner's presence when testimony is heard regarding the viciousness of an animal (see BT Bava Kama 24a).

apparently had, or at least knows about, a bad experience with kingship, and, as a result, he aims to place the king firmly under the law. But his firmness is moral, not political. The king is told that he is no more than first among equals; he must not raise himself above his brethren. He must accept the instruction of the priests and, as a symbol of that acceptance, carry the book of the law with him and read it wherever he goes (note that more ordinary and sedentary Israelites are told to write the laws on the doorposts of their houses and teach them to their children). Limits are fixed on the king's marriages (dynastic alliances), his personal wealth, and his military strength. But all this is mere exhortation; no institutions or officials are described who can enforce the limits. In the discussion of judges and courts that immediately precedes our selection, the Deuteronomist says nothing that suggests their jurisdiction over the king. What he presents is little more than an ideal picture of a pious ruler.

By the time of the Babylonian Talmud, there is no Jewish king, but there remains a disagreeable memory of monarchy—which finds a twofold expression in the text. First, there is a new ideal picture, presented as an interpretation of the Mishnah. Now the king rules alongside and also with and through a high court, the Sanhedrin—the precise relation between the two isn't clear (something, perhaps, like the king-in-parliament in British constitutional history). The king (here the argument follows the Mishnah) is accorded the honor denied him in Deuteronomy, but he is also (here the Mishnah is "reread") placed within a set of institutional constraints. He participates in the work of the court, and he is subject to its judgments. But this subjection depends on his own agreement: the king is subject only if he subjects himself, which only Davidic kings are imagined to do.

Second, the Mishnah's dictum—he doesn't judge, he isn't judged—is now described as following from the sages' experience with a non-Davidic (in fact, Hasmonean) king. When such a king defies the court, as Yannai did and as others are expected to do, the ideal structure collapses; there is no restraint at all on a ruler who refuses to be restrained. Neither the rabbis of the Mishnah nor the rabbis of the Talmud imagine the Sanhedrin holding out against a tyrannical king. The Mishnah suggests that the Rabbis never aspired to hold out; the Jerusalem Talmud leaves the king to God's judgment; the Babylonian Talmud tells a tale of fearful withdrawal. What the rabbis have learned from history, on this last reading, is their own powerlessness in the face of the king—which may explain why many of them (see the midrashic texts below) were hostile to kingship. It is as if the Deuteronomist had written at the end of chapter 17 that because of Solomon's foreign marriages and his military buildup, the priests don't teach and the king doesn't read. The surrender is complete.

Insofar as the kingdom is the model state for most Jewish writers, and the king the model ruler, what this surrender amounts to is a withdrawal of the religious and legal authorities—priests, judges, and sages—from the political realm. Since the biblical elders and people make no appearance here at all, neither choosing nor even acclaiming kings and certainly not rebuking them, there are no effective limits on monarchic rule. Alternative authority structures are possible only when Israel is stateless. The central problem of Jewish political thinking is already evident here: none of these writers can describe a kingdom, that is, a state, in which there are independent political actors capable of controlling the king. Just as the king rules only when God is displaced, so priests, judges, and sages rule only when the king is displaced—when the people are living under foreign kings, as in Persian times, or in exile. The politics of the few (and later on of the many) is not constructed against the "one" but in his absence.

Michael Walzer

The King's Prerogatives
9. BT Sanhedrin 20b

*In the founding story of the monarchy, Samuel enumerates royal powers under the caption "the practice [*mishpat*] of the king." The Hebrew* mishpat *can also be rendered as "law"; on this reading, Samuel is proclaiming the law of kings. In the following talmudic text, a variety of positions are canvassed as to the grounds and legitimacy of this law.*

Rav Yehudah said, citing Shmu'el: All items mentioned in the section about the king [in the prophet Samuel's speech (1 Sam. 8:9–18)] are the king's prerogatives. Rav said: The section about the king was only pronounced in order to scare them.

This [dispute] corresponds to a tannaitic dispute:

Rabbi Yose says: All items mentioned in the section about the king are the king's prerogatives. Rabbi Yehudah says: The section was only pronounced in order to scare them.

Rabbi Yehudah also used to say: There were three commandments that Israel were obligated to fulfill once they had entered the land: appointing a king, exterminating the offspring of Amalek,[7] and building the temple.

Rabbi Nehorai says: The section was only pronounced in response to their complaints, as written, "And you shall say, I will set a king over me, as do all the nations about me" (Deut. 17:14).

Rabbi Eleazer b. Tzadok says: The wise men [elders] of that generation made a proper request, as written: "[All the elders of Israel assembled and came to Samuel . . . and they said to him,] . . . 'Appoint a king for us, to govern us'" (1 Sam. 8:4–5). But the *amme ha-aretz* amongst them spoke wrongly, as written, "that we may be like all the other nations" (1 Sam. 8:19–20).

Scope of the King's Prerogatives
10. Menachem Meiri, *Bet ha-Behirah,* Sanhedrin 20b

Meiri here comments on the preceding text, adopting and expounding the view of Shmu'el but also suggesting some legal limits on royal prerogative.

All [the items] that Samuel the prophet proclaimed to the nation in order to warn them when they asked him for a king are the king's prerogatives. It is written, "He will take your sons and appoint them as his charioteers"—this

7. Cf. Deut. 25:17–19.

implies that he may send [representatives] to every corner of his kingdom to select brave and competent men for waging his wars. Additionally, [such conscripts] run before him . . . and serve him. . . . He may also take craftsmen for his work and privately owned animals for his own needs, as written, "He will take your male and female slaves . . . and your asses, and put them to work for him."

However, he must give [to the original owners] their wages or their value. It is also permissible for him to marry or to take as a concubine anyone from among them as he pleases. He can also make some of them perfumers, cooks, and bakers, as written: "He will take your daughters to be perfumers, cooks, and bakers." He may also take from among those who are capable . . . overseers over his own [property]. They will be "chiefs of thousands and chiefs of fifties," depending on their capabilities. At a time of war, he can also take the produce of fields and vineyards, if they [the army] have nothing to eat, as written, "He will take your fields, vineyards, and olive groves and give them to his servants." However, he must evaluate their worth and reimburse [their owners]. He may also take a tithe from everything, as written "He will take a tenth of your seed and your vineyards . . . he will take a tenth of your flocks." He is also permitted to levy a tax for his needs and for waging his wars according to their capacity and the pressure of his needs, as written, "They shall be for you a tributary and shall serve you" (Deut. 20:11).[8] It is illegal to steal from him anything which he took, since he has a right to it. He also has a right to impose tariffs, and it is forbidden to smuggle.

A Code for Kings

11. Maimonides, MT Laws of Kings 2:5–6; 3:7–10; 4:1, 10; 5:3

The Code of Maimonides, Book Fourteen: The Book of Judges, translated by Abraham M. Hershman, Yale Judaica Series (New Haven: Yale University Press, 1949), pp. 211–15, 217.

Maimonides' "Laws of Kings and Their Wars" represent a unique feature of his code: unlike other codifiers, his Mishneh Torah *encompasses even those subjects of hala-*

8. Following Maimonides; see the next selection, 4:1.

khah *that "do not apply in present times." Hence the "Laws of Kings" is to this day the sole comprehensive treatise in Jewish law regarding the monarchy. The paucity of clear Rabbinic precedents in matters of monarchy and law leads Maimonides to draw heavily upon the biblical political history of Israel. An example is the story of Shimei the son of Gera in 1 Kings 2.*

Chapter 2

5. The king has his hair trimmed every day, pays due regard to his personal appearance, adorns himself with beautiful clothes—as it is written: "Thine eyes shall see the king in his beauty" (Isa. 33:17)—sits on his throne in his palace, sets his crown on his head. All the people come before him when he is disposed to see them, they stand in his presence, and bow down to the ground. Even the prophet stands in the presence of the king and bows down to the ground, as it is written: "Behold Nathan the prophet. And when he was come in before the king, he bowed down before the king with his face to the ground" (1 Kings 1:23).

The high priest, however, comes before the king only when he is disposed to do it; he does not stand in his presence, but the king stands before him, as it is said: "And he shall stand before Eleazar the priest" (Num. 27:21). Nevertheless, it is the duty of the high priest to give honor to the king, to ask him to be seated, to rise before him when the latter comes to see him. The king therefore shall not stand in his presence save when he asks him for directions given by means of the Urim.

So. too, it is incumbent upon the king to give honor to students of the Torah. When the members of the Sanhedrin and Sages of Israel visit him, he shall rise before them and seat them at his side. This is the way Jehoshaphat the King of Judah acted. When he saw even the disciple of a scholar, he rose from his throne, kissed him, called him "my teacher, my master." This humble attitude becomes the king in the privacy of his home only, when none but he and his servants are there. He may not act thus in public, he may not rise before any man, nor be soft of speech, nor call anyone but by his name, so that his fear be in the hearts of all.

6. Just as Scripture accords great honor to the king and bids all pay

him honor, so it bids him cultivate a humble and lowly spirit, as it is written: "And my heart is humbled within me" (Ps. 109:22). He must not exercise his authority in a supercilious manner, as it is said: "That his heart be not lifted up above his brethren" (Deut. 17:20). He should deal graciously and compassionately with the small and the great, conduct their affairs in their best interests, be wary of the honor of even the lowliest. When he addresses the public collectively, he shall use gentle language, as did David when he said: "Hear me, my brethren, and my people" (1 Chron. 28:2). It is also written, "If thou wilt be a servant unto this people this day . . . then they will be thy servants forever" (1 Kings 12:7). At all times, his conduct should be marked by a spirit of great humility. None was greater than Moses, our teacher; yet he said: "And what are we? Your murmurings are not against us" (Exod. 16:7). He should put up with the cumbrances, burdens, grumblings, and anger of the people as a nursing father puts up with a sucking child. The Bible styles the king "shepherd," [as it is written:] "To be shepherd over Jacob His People" (Ps. 78:71). The way in which a shepherd acts is explicitly stated in the prophetic text: "even as a shepherd that feedeth his flock, that gathereth the lambs in his arms, and carrieth them in his bosom and gently leadeth those that give suck" (Isa. 40:11).

Chapter 3

7. We have already stated that the kings of the House of David may be judged and testified against. But with respect to the kings of Israel,[9] the Rabbis enacted that they neither judge nor be judged, neither testify nor be testified against, because they are arrogant, and (if they be treated as commoners) the cause of religion [*dat*] would suffer.

8. The king is empowered to put to death anyone who rebels against him. Even if any of his subjects is ordered by him to go to a certain place and he does not go, or is ordered to stay home and fails to do so, he is culpable, and the king may, if he so decides, put him to death, as it is written: "Whosoever he be that shall rebel against thy commandment . . . shall be put to death" (Josh. 1:18).

9. See note 5 above.

So, too, if one reviles him, or taunts him, as did Shimei, the son of Gera, the king is empowered to condemn him to death. But the only mode of execution within his jurisdiction is decapitation with the sword.[10] To uphold his honor, the king is permitted to inflict the penalties of imprisonment and chastisement with whips. He may not, however, expropriate the property of an offender. If he does, he is guilty of robbery.

9. Whoever disobeys a royal decree because he is engaged in the performance of a religious command [*mitzvah*], even if it be a light command, is not liable, because (when there is a conflict) between the edict of the Master (God) and the edict of the servant (the king), the former takes precedence of the latter. It goes without saying that if the king issues an order annulling a religious precept [*mitzvah*], no heed is paid to it.

10. If a person kills another and there is no clear evidence, or if no warning has been given him,[11] or there is only one witness, or if one kills accidentally a person whom he hated, the king may, if the exigency of the hour demands it, put him to death in order to insure the stability of the social order [*letaken ha'olam*]. He may put to death many offenders in one day, hang them, and suffer them to be hanging for a long time so as to put fear in the hearts of others and break the power of the wicked.

Chapter 4

1. It is within the province of the king to levy taxes upon the people for his own needs or for war purposes. He fixes the customs duties, and it is forbidden to evade them. He may issue a decree that whoever dodges them shall be punished either by confiscation of his property or by death, as it is written: "And ye shall be his servants" (1 Sam. 8:17). Elsewhere it is said: "All the people found therein shall be tributary[12] unto thee, and shall serve thee" (Deut. 20:11). From these verses we infer that the king imposes taxes and fixes customs duties and that all the laws enacted by him with regard

10. As opposed to the four modes of capital punishment of the court; see Mishnah Sanhedrin 7:1.
11. See BT Sanhedrin 40b, cited and expounded by Gerondi in §16.
12. Hebrew *le-mas,* which also means "tax."

to these and like matters are valid, for it is his prerogative to exercise all the authority set forth in the section relating to the king.[13]

10. All the land he conquers belongs to him. He may give thereof to his servants and warriors as much as he wishes; he may keep thereof for himself as much as he wishes. In all these matters he is the final arbiter. But whatever he does should be done by him for the sake of Heaven. His sole aim and thought should be to uplift the true religion, to fill the world with righteousness, to break the arm of the wicked, and to fight the battles of the Lord. The prime reason for appointing a king was that he execute judgment and wage war, as it is written: "And that our king may judge us, and go out at our head and fight our battles" (1 Sam. 8:20).

Chapter 5

3. He may break through (private property) to make a road for himself, and none may protest against it. No limit can be prescribed for the king's road; he expropriates as much as is needed. He does not have to make detours because someone's vineyard or field (is in his way). He takes the straight route and attacks the enemy.

Critiques of Monarchy

Critique of the Request for a King
12. *Sifre Deuteronomy 156*

Sifre: A Tannaitic Commentary on the Book of Deuteronomy, translated by Reuven Hammer, Yale Judaica Series (New Haven: Yale University Press, 1986), p. 191.

The following midrashic statements develop a critique of monarchy by focusing on the first verse of the Deuteronomic section on kings. In contrast to God's pronouncement, taken above to reflect either commandment or permission, the focus here is the human initiative in seeking a king, which is portrayed in various negative ways.

13. I.e., 1 Sam. 8. Maimonides is quoting BT Sanhedrin 20b (§8).

"And shalt say: I will set a king over me" (Deut. 17:14): Rabbi Nehorai says: This is in disparagement of Israel, as it is said, "For they have not rejected thee, but they have rejected Me, that I should not be king over them" (1 Sam. 8:7). Rabbi Judah said: But is it not a positive commandment in the Torah itself that they should demand a king for themselves, as it is said, "Thou shalt in any wise set him king over thee" (Deut. 17:15)? Why then were they punished for doing so in the days of Samuel? Because they initiated it prematurely on their own.

"Like all the nations that are round about me" (Deut. 17:14): Rabbi Nehorai says: They demanded a king only so that he might lead them into idolatry, as it is said, "That we also may be like all the nations; and that our king may judge us, and go out at our head and fight our battles" (1 Sam. 8:20).

Monarchy as Folly and Sin

13. *Midrash Rabbah: Deuteronomy,* Shoftim 5:8, 9, 11

This text is from the Sephardic version of the midrash; for a printed Hebrew version, see *Midrash Debarim Rabbah,* edited by S. Lieberman (Jerusalem: Bamberger and Wahrmann, 1940).

8. *"If you say, I will set a king over me":* . . .

The Holy One said to Israel: My children, I endeavored that you be free of the monarchy [*malkhut*]. Where [is this derived] from? As written, "A wild ass used to the desert (Jer. 2:24)": just as the wild ass grows up in the wilderness, without fear of humanity, so I intended you to be without fear of monarchy. You, however, endeavored otherwise: "snuffing the wind in her eagerness" (Jer. 2:24)—"wind" signifying kingdoms [*malkhuyot*]. Where [is this derived] from? As written, "I saw the four winds of heaven," etc. (Dan. 7:2 ff).[14]

The Holy One said: Do you think I did not know that in the end

14. This verse introduces Daniel's vision of the four great beasts representing four great empires.

you will forsake Me? [In anticipation] I already instructed Moses, saying: "Seeing that in the end they will seek a king of flesh and blood, they should appoint one of their own, not a foreigner." Where [is this derived] from? From what we read in this section, "If you say . . . be sure to set as king over yourself one of your own people."

9. Another view, *"If you say, I will set a king over me"*: . . . "Impious man reigns from the people's folly" (Job 34:30). When kings arose over Israel and began to enslave them, the Holy One said: Was it not you who forsook Me to seek a king for yourselves?—as written, "I will set a king over me."

Another view, *"If you say, I will set a king over me"*: As Scripture says, "Put not your trust in the great," etc. (Ps. 146:3). . . . Whenever one relies upon flesh and blood, as he fails so does his word fail, as written, "In mortal man who cannot save" (Ps. 146:3). What is written next? "His breath departs; he returns to the dust; on that day his plans come to nothing" (Ps. 146:4). The Holy One said: Though they know that flesh and blood is nought, they abandon My glory and say: "Set a king over us." Why do you seek a king? By your life, in the end you will experience what befalls you under your kings, as written, "all their kings have fallen—none of them calls to me" (Hos. 7:7).

11. Another view, *"If you say, I will set a king over me"*: The rabbis say: The Holy One said, In this world you sought kings, and the kings arose and caused you to fall by the sword.—Saul caused them to fall on Mount Gilboa, as written, "the men of Israel fled before the Philistines and fell on Mount Gilboa" (1 Sam. 31:1); David brought upon them a plague, as written, "The Lord sent a pestilence upon Israel" (2 Sam. 24:15); Ahab caused them to suffer a drought, as written, "there will be no dew or rain" (1 Kings 17:1); Zedekiah caused the destruction of the Temple. When Israel saw what befell them because of their kings, they started screaming, "We do not seek a king, it is our first king that we seek!" as written, "For the Lord shall be our ruler, the Lord shall be our prince, the Lord shall be our king; he shall deliver us!" (Isa. 33:22). The Holy One replied: So shall I do. As written, "And the Lord shall be king over all the earth" (Zech. 14:9).

Republican and Theocratic Critiques

14. Isaac Abravanel, *Commentary on the Pentateuch*, Deuteronomy 17:14 (Premises)

Abravanel's classic critique of monarchy combines two distinct arguments, a combination that places it on the line, so to speak, between the Middle Ages and the Renaissance. Drawing on the Italian republican tradition, Abravanel argues generally that monarchy is not the best form of government. He then returns to the particular situation of the Jewish people and reiterates the biblical theocratic argument that all monarchic functions in Israel are ideally performed by God. Abravanel uses the word shofet *in the different senses of magistrate, judge, and Roman consul throughout. We have rendered it accordingly.*

First, we should establish whether a king is a . . . necessity, indispensable for a nation, or is he rather superfluous. The philosophers have considered him [necessary]: The king's function for . . . political society is similar to the relation of heart to body in an animal possessing a heart, or the relation of the First Cause to the entire universe. Insofar as these scholars hold society to require three things [that only monarchy provides]—

a) unified power, not shared;
b) permanence and the absence of change; and
c) absolute power,

their view concerning the indispensability of a king is surely wrong.

For it is not impossible that a nation should have many leaders who convene, unite, and reach a consensus; they can thus govern and administer justice. This refutes the first requirement. Then also, why cannot they have terms of office, extending for one year or for three, similar to the term of a hired worker [see Isa. 16:14]—or even for a shorter duration? When the turn of other magistrates comes to replace them, they will investigate the abuses of trust committed by the earlier [magistrates]; those found guilty will pay for their crimes. This refutes the second requirement.

Finally, why cannot their powers be limited and determined by divine laws or [human] nomoi? Reason suggests that [in a dispute] between the one and the many, the many should be heeded.[15] Furthermore, it is more likely that the one will commit a crime—as written, "The king's wrath is as the messenger of death" (Prov. 16:14)—than the many in concert, for when one of them strays, the others will protest. Additionally, since the rule [of many] is temporary and they will in the near future be held to account, the fear of other human beings will be upon them.

Indeed, why offer theoretical arguments? Experience outweighs inference! Look and see the countries that are governed by kings, and compare the several countries today governed by magistrates and temporary rulers chosen from among them, and God the King is with [the latter]. Theirs is an elected government within set limits; they rule the nation with a firm hand and lead it in wars [and] none can stand [against] them. . . .[16] Have you not heard of the great power [Rome] that ruled the entire world . . . while being governed by many excellent consuls serving temporary terms (even though it later declined [and became a] monarchy)? To this day, Venice, "the grand lady among nations and the princess among states" (Lam. 1:1), endures; and the republic [malkhut] of Florence is a splendor among the nations; and other states, great and small, have no king, but are rather ruled by governors elected for fixed terms. These states with elected [magistrates] experience no corruption or deceit, and no one there dares lift a finger to commit a crime. They conquer [other countries] through skill, perspicacity, and knowledge.

All this shows that a king is not necessary for a people, as is claimed by Maimonides. It is astonishing that the adherents of this false view liken the unity of the king, derived from popular consent, to the unity of the eternal, necessary, blessed First Cause. As for [the analogy] from animal physiology, men of science have written that there are [in fact] three principal organs that govern the body. . . .

A contrary proof should not be brought from the verse "When there is rebellion in the land, many are its princes" (Prov. 28:2)—since that

15. Literally, "the *halakhah* follows the many"—a citation of the halakhic principle of majority rule; cf. ¶22.
16. Hebrew obscure.

speaks of princes [i.e., nobles], not rulers or magistrates. [Anyway,] how can we deny what is obvious to all? If the rulers are good, it is better that there be many; and if they are wicked, it is more dangerous [if there is only one].

. . . [Now, when the people initially appointed] kings, [they] were appointed only as trustees, to serve the people; they have [instead] become lords, as though God had given the land and its fullness to them,[17] to be bequeathed to their sons and their grandsons forever like privately acquired property. Even this does not hold equally in all kingdoms, as in some the king's power is limited.

Second, even if we grant that the king is useful and necessary for a people in order to perfect political society and protect it, nevertheless, in regard to the Israelite people, this is not so: for them he is neither useful nor necessary. This is because kings are [presumed] necessary in a nation for three reasons: first, concerning wars, in order to rescue [the people] from their enemies and defend their land; second, in order to ordain the laws [*nomoi*] and lay down the doctrines needed for their perfection; and third, to administer punishment outside the law according to the needs of the hour. . . .

These three things are not necessary for the Israelite nation. They do not require [a king] for wars and for deliverance from their enemies, because Israel is delivered by God and He fights for them, as it is written, "O happy Israel! Who is like you, a people delivered by the Lord, your protecting Shield, your sword triumphant! Your enemies shall come cringing before you, and you shall tread on their backs" (Deut. 33:29). Besides, their judge goes forth and leads them in wars, as with Joshua, Gideon, Samuel, and the other judges.

They also do not require a king to lay down doctrines and laws, because "Moses charged us with the Torah" (Deut. 33:4). Moreover, God commanded us: "You shall not add anything [to what I commanded you]. . . . For what great nation is there that has a God so close at hand. . . . Or what great nation has laws and rules as perfect . . . ?" (Deut. 4:2, 7–8). And a king of Israel has no authority to innovate anything in the Torah nor to subtract from it, as written concerning him: "He will not deviate from the commandment to the right or to the left" (Deut. 17:20).

17. A bitter paraphrase of Ps. 24:1, "The earth is the Lord's and all that it holds."

Nor is a king required in Israel to punish [criminals] . . . in accordance with the needs of the hour, because God gave that authority to the Great Court, the Sanhedrin, as I explained [elsewhere]. Furthermore, God has informed us that if a judge who acts in accordance with . . . just law should acquit a wrongdoer, God Himself will punish the wicked person with His great judgment, as it is written, "Keep far from a false charge; do not charge death on those who are innocent and in the right, for I will not acquit the wrongdoer" (Exod. 23:7). This means, "I will punish him for anything for which you are unable to punish him legally."[18]

Thus, it has been explained that these three things—that is, delivering them through war, laying down laws and commandments, and determining occasional punishment outside the law—are all performed by God for His people. Therefore, God is their king, and they have no need for a [human] king for anything.

[Here Abravanel cites prooftexts from various biblical sources: Exod. 15:18–19, Isa. 33:22, and Ps. 24:7–8.]

From all this, it is apparent that even if we grant that a king is necessary for other nations, he is inappropriate for the Israelite nation. This is shown all the more clearly by our experience with the kings of Israel and of Judea, who were among those who rebelled against the light and turned the hearts of Israel astray [cf. 1 Kings 18:37]. This is well known regarding Jeroboam son of Nebat and all the rest of the kings of Israel, and most of the Judean kings, until on account of them "Judah has gone into exile" (Lam. 1:3). The opposite is evident regarding Israel's judges and prophets: they were all "capable men who fear God, trustworthy men" (Exod. 18:21). There was not one of the judges who strayed from God in order to worship other gods—the complete opposite of the kings: who of them avoided [worshiping other gods]? All of this proves that government by magistrates is good, whereas government by kings is bad, harmful, and extremely dangerous. . . .

On the basis of these two introductory comments, hearken to the true interpretation of the section concerning the king (Deut. 17:14–20) and the commandment therein. The verses "When you come to the land," etc.,

18. Following *Mekhilta*.

imply no commandment, as God did not command that they should say that nor ask for a king. Rather, it is a statement of what will occur in the future — what you will say after you arrive in the chosen land and conquer it, after all the wars and the parceling out of the land, referred to in the phrase "you shall possess it and dwell in it." [God is saying:] I know that you will be ungrateful, saying of your own initiative, 'I will set a king over me.' [This will] not be motivated by the necessity of wars with the nations nor conquest of the land, since it will have been conquered for you [by God]. The sole purpose will be in order to be like the nations who appointed kings over themselves. . . .

He then tells them that once this has come to pass, they may not appoint this king however they will, but rather [they must appoint] one whom God chooses from among their kinsmen. The true essence of the commandment consists in "You shall appoint a king . . . one of your own people" — not that He commands them to ask [for a king].

Monarchy Is Optional

15. Naphtali Tzvi Judah Berlin (Netziv), *Ha'amek Davar,* Deuteronomy 17:14

Writing in tsarist Russia in the late nineteenth century, Berlin's commentary here can be read as an echo of the new political ideologies prevalent in Europe. Berlin interprets the biblical command to appoint a king in line with the belief that the form of political authority should be determined by the needs and the will of the people.

"If you shall say, etc." — this does not refer literally to [their making such] an announcement; rather, it should be read as in "if you shall say I will eat meat . . ." (Deut. 12:20). This reading implies that there is no definite imperative to appoint a king, but only a permission, as in the case of eating meat. The Rabbis' teachings, however, show clearly that there is a commandment to appoint a king; why, then, is it written, "If you shall say" [implying mere permission]?

[The answer], it appears, is that there is a difference between government by monarchy and government by the people and their representatives. Some states cannot tolerate a monarchic regime, whereas others, without a monarch, would be like a ship without a captain. An issue like this cannot be decided by the binding force of a positive commandment. For matters of collective policy involve [dealing with] life-threatening situations in which positive commandments are overridden. Therefore, there can be no definite imperative to appoint a king, as long as the people have not consented to the monarchic yoke through seeing the surrounding nations being governed more adequately [by kings]. Only then is there a positive commandment upon the Sanhedrin to appoint a king. . . . It is for this reason that for three hundred years, while the tabernacle resided at Shilo, there was no king, [i.e.,] for lack of the people's consent.

"Like all the nations around me": This does not refer to their laws, for we are prohibited from abandoning the laws of the Torah—hence God's anger with Israel in the days of Samuel, when they said, "And our King shall judge us like all the nations . . ." (1 Sam. 8:20).

Neither does [the comparison to the nations] refer to matters of international warfare, for this too angered God, and he said to Samuel: "It is not you that they have rejected; it is Me they have rejected as their king" (1 Sam. 8:7). This means: They did not seek [to be like the nations] with regard to the laws—which would affect Samuel—but rather with regard to warfare. For throughout the period of the Judges they had been without a permanent overseer of national security,[19] having [to await] God's word through a Judge. They now wanted a king to oversee this, thus angering God.

The verse "like all the nations around me" therefore refers to the [form of] government. As I have explained, this is a matter in which people's opinions differ . . . ; hence there is a requirement of popular consent: "if you shall say." etc.

19. Literally, "necessities pertaining to international warfare."

The Realm of Torah and the Realm of Politics

Royal Law Complements Torah Law

16. Nissim Gerondi (Ran), *Derashot* 11

We have benefited from Leon A. Feldman's edition of the *Derashot* (Jerusalem: Shalem Institute, 1973).

Here is the most interesting medieval exposition of a theory of separation of powers. In this sermon Gerondi carries forward the mishnaic dictum that "the king neither judges, nor is he subject to judgment." He provides a justification for royal autonomy vis-à-vis the halakhah based on an argument s concerning the authority but also the limitations of divine law. The sermon may be read as an attempt to develop systematically the consequences of the legislative autonomy of the kahal (see C8). Gerondi was a leader of the Barcelona community. His views may also reflect the separation between royal and canon law in Christian Spain.

"You shall appoint magistrates and officers . . . and they shall judge the people by just law" (Deut. 16:18). . . . The plain meaning of the text is as follows. It is known that the human species needs magistrates to adjudicate among individuals, for otherwise "men would eat each other alive" (Avot 3:2), and humanity would be destroyed. Every nation needs some sort of political organization [*yishuv medini*] for this purpose, since— as the wise man put it—even "a gang of thieves will subscribe to justice among themselves."[20] Israel, like any other nation, needs this as well. Moreover, Israel needs it for another reason: to uphold the laws of the Torah and punish those who deserve flogging or capital punishment for disobeying these laws, even if their transgression in no way undermines political order. Clearly, these [purposes] give rise to two possible issues: first, the need to punish in keeping with true law; second, the need to punish so as to enhance political order [*tikkun seder medini*] and in accordance with the needs of the hour, even if the punishment is undeserved according to truly just law. God, may He be blessed, set these two issues apart, delegating them each to a separate agency:

[1] He commanded that magistrates be appointed to judge accord-

20. See Plato, *Republic*, 351c; and Halevi, *Kuzari* 2:48 (C2, §3).

ing to the truly just law, as it is written, "And they shall judge the people by just law." In other words, the verse tells us that He set forth the purpose of their appointment and the scope of their authority: they were appointed to judge the people according to a law that was in itself truly just and their jurisdiction is not to exceed that.

[2] But since political order cannot be fully established by these means alone, God provided further for its establishment by commanding [the appointment of] a king.

We may clarify this by considering one of the above-mentioned purposes. We read in the fifth chapter of tractate Sanhedrin: "Our Rabbis taught [The following questions are asked of a witness in a capital case]: Do you know him? . . . Did you warn him? Did he confirm your warning? Did he accept his liability to death? Did he commit the murder immediately?" etc. (BT Sanhedrin 40b). There can be no doubt that this is required by just law, for why should a man be put to death unless he was aware that he was committing a capital offence and [nevertheless] transgressed? Therefore it is requisite that he confirm and accept a warning, along with the other requirements mentioned there. This is the law, intrinsically and truly just, that is entrusted to the judges. However, punishing criminals in this way alone would completely undermine political order: murderers would multiply, having no fear of punishment.[21] That is why God ordered the appointment of a king for the sake of civilization. Thus, we read . . . , "When you come to the land . . . you may indeed set as a king over you . . ." (Deut. 17:14–15), which, according to the Rabbis' tradition, is the commandment to appoint a king. The king may impose a sentence as he deems necessary for political association [ha-kibbutz ha-medini], even when no warning has been given. The appointment of a king is equally essential for Israel and all nations requiring political order, but the appointment of magistrates is of particular importance in the case of Israel. So the text emphasizes: "And they shall judge the people by just law"—i.e., the appointment and jurisdiction of magistrates pertain to judging the people according to laws intrinsically truly just.

[Unlike] the nomoi of the nations of the world, the laws and com-

21. Alluding to Mishnah Makkot 1:10 (C23).

mandments of our Torah . . . include commandments that are ultimately not concerned with political order. Rather, their effect is to induce the appearance of the divine effluence within our nation and [to make it] cleave unto us. This may be either by means that are clear to us, such as sacrifices and other Temple activities, or by means unclear to us, such as the laws whose purpose has not been revealed [*hukkim*]. In any case, there can be no doubt that these laws, although far from rational comprehension, induced the divine effluence to cleave unto us. The causes of many natural phenomena are incomprehensible to us, yet their existence is verifiable, so it is certainly not strange that the causes of the divine effluence . . . should be incomprehensible. Our Holy Torah is unique among the nomoi of the nations, which reflect no such considerations and are instead concerned solely with enhancing the affairs of their society.

Therefore I maintain—and so one ought to believe—that while the *hukkim* are not relevant at all to the establishment of the political association . . . , the *mishpatim* are in fact crucial to it, and it is as if they serve both to bring down the divine effluence and to perfect our public affairs. But perhaps these [latter] laws are [also] addressed primarily to the more sublime matters rather than to the perfection of society, since our appointed king [has that task]. The purpose of the magistrates and the Sanhedrin, by contrast [to the king], was to judge the people in accordance with true and intrinsically just law, which will effect the cleaving of the Divine [*inyan elohi*] unto us, whether or not the ordering of the multitude's affairs has been perfected. That is why some of the laws and procedures of the [gentile] nations may be more effective in enhancing political order than some of the Torah's laws. This, however, does not leave us deficient, since any deficiency regarding political order was corrected by the king. Indeed, we have a great advantage over the nations: because the laws of the Torah are inherently just . . . , the divine effluence will be induced to cleave unto us. That is why the supreme magistrates were located in that place where the presence of the divine effluence was evident: I mean the assembly of the Sanhedrin[22] in the Chamber of Hewn Stones. . . .

22. Literally, "the Men of the Great Assembly"; Gerondi alludes to Mishnah Sanhedrin 11:2 (C7, §9).

In the same vein, the Rabbis said in the first chapter of tractate Shabbat: "A magistrate who judges truly, a judgement of truth, even one hour per day, is regarded as a partner in creation with God" (BT Shabbat 10a). . . . Just as, in creation, the divine effluence appeared at the mundane level—since it was the source of all being—so too a magistrate who judges truly draws down that effluence, whether or not his judgment perfects the order of the polity. Just as it is drawn down by the sacrificial rites . . . so too does it flow because of the Torah laws. Admittedly, for the sake of political order further enhancement is required, which is [the task of the king]. Thus, the judges were appointed to judge only according to the laws of the Torah, which are inherently just, . . . and the king was appointed to perfect the political order and [to meet] the needs of the hour.

Do not cite against my argument the passage in tractate Sanhedrin: "It has been taught: Rabbi Eli'ezer b. Jacob says: I have a tradition that a court may impose flagellation and [other] punishments not [warranted] by the Torah; not to transgress against the words of the Torah, but rather to make a hedge for the Torah" (BT Sanhedrin 46a).[23] This seems to imply that the court was appointed to render judgements as the times require. However, this is not the case: at a time when Israel had both Sanhedrin and king, the Sanhedrin's role was to judge the people according to just law only and not to order their affairs in any way beyond this, unless the king delegated his powers to them. However, when Israel has no monarchy, the magistrate holds both kinds of power, that of the judge and that of the king. . . .

This was Israel's sin in asking for a monarchy, which many earlier [scholars] have found problematic—since the people had been commanded to appoint a king. . . . I believe their sin consisted in wanting adjudication between persons to be mainly the charge of the monarch. We read: "All the elders of Israel assembled and came to Samuel at Ramah, and they said to him, 'You have grown old, and your sons have not followed your ways. Therefore appoint a king for us, to judge us like all other nations'" (1 Sam 8:4–5). . . . Israel was more interested in enhancing its political association. If they had asked for a king by saying simply "Appoint for us a king," or if they had sought a king for the sake of their military affairs, they would

23. See C24.

have committed no sin. In fact, it would have been a [virtuous act]. Their sin lay in saying "Appoint for us a king to *judge* us like all the nations." They wanted adjudication to be the charge of the monarchy, rather than of Torah judges. . . . That is why God told Samuel: "It is not you that they have rejected; it is Me they have rejected as their king" (8:7)—which is to say, they preferred to enhance their natural affairs rather than to bring the divine effluence down upon themselves. . . . For this Samuel reproved them afterwards, saying: "Now stand by and see the marvelous thing that the Lord will do before your eyes. It is the season of the wheat harvest. I will pray to the Lord and He will send thunder and rain" (12:16–17). This means: Know that you have erred in choosing something which, although it appears to you to be correct, [namely] the ordering of natural things, is not truly so. For one who cleaves to the Divine [*inyan elohi*] can alter natural things at will. "It is the season of the wheat harvest," which by way of natural things is not the right time for rain. Yet, by virtue of the Divine that cleaves unto me, I will call upon the Lord and change this, "and He will send thunder and rain."

Therefore, [Samuel continues,] it is more fitting for you to prefer that which induces the divine effluence amongst you—namely, [to prefer] adjudication by the magistrates, of whom it is written, "And they shall judge the people by just law"—over adjudication by the monarch wherein he decides according to his own will. For this is the difference between magistrate and king: the magistrate is more bound to the Torah's laws than is the king. That is why the king was admonished and commanded to keep a copy of the Torah by his side. . . . Since the king sees that he is not bound to Torah law as the judge is, he must be strongly admonished not to deviate from its commandments "to the right or to the left" [nor to] "act haughtily toward his fellows," in view of the great power God has given him. The magistrate, however, requires no such admonition, since his power is restricted by the scope of Torah law alone, as it is written, "And they shall judge the people by just law." He is admonished, . . . "You shall not deviate from justice."

. . . [Now] if the king annuls any commandment for the sake of addressing [the needs of] his time, he should have no intention of transgressing against the words of the Torah nor in any way removing the yoke of the fear of God. Rather, his intention should be "to observe faithfully every word of this Teaching as well as these laws." Anything he adds or takes away[24] must be done with the intention of furthering the observance of the Torah and its commandments. For example, in the case we have cited concerning the execution of a murderer without witnesses or warning, the king's intention must not be to demonstrate his power to the people by showing them that this too is under his domain. Rather, his intention should be to advance the realization of the commandment "You shall not murder" (Exod. 20:13) and prevent its disregard.

Since his power is mighty and induces arrogance, God admonishes [the king] not to "act haughtily toward his fellows" (Deut. 17:20). . . . It is well known that kingship is not a quality inherent in the king. It is rather granted to him by God, blessed be He, or by the people, for the purpose of perfecting the people, [not][25] for his personal enhancement. . . . King-ship is not inherent in the king, but an attribute conferred upon him for the strengthening of the whole. Therefore, the king should not see himself as the governor and lord of the people, but as a servant unto them for their benefit.

Commentary. The Price of Politics

Gerondi's statement on politics brings to a climax a long tradition that places politics alongside, indeed outside, divine law. This tradition can be traced from the biblical distinction between "matters of the Lord" and "matters of the king" (2 Chron. 19:11), through the mishnaic statement that "the king neither judges, nor is . . . subject to judgment" (Sanhedrin 2:3 [§7]), down to the broad range of legislative and executive powers allotted to the good men of the city by medieval halakhic authorities (¢8).

Writers in this tradition identify politics as a distinct realm of hu-man activity separate from halakhic decision making. Whatever the finer details of the constitutional directives in this chapter, they are all predicated

24. An ironic allusion is intended here to the very commandment which is overridden: "Neither add to it nor take away from it" (Deut. 13:1).
25. The text reads "or," evidently an error.

on a distinction between the king and his realm (politics) on the one hand and the courts of divine law and their realm (law) on the other. The tradition further assumes the king's capacity for prudence and, insofar as royal judgments are perceived to further justice, for morality too, independently of the directives of divine law: "The human species needs magistrates to adjudicate among its individuals for otherwise 'men would eat each other alive' (Avot 3:2), and humanity would be destroyed." All this in contradistinction to the arguments put forward by thinkers like Judah Halevi—who justified revealed law by questioning the adequacy of human moral judgment (C2, §3).

In short, this tradition can be characterized as a secularization of politics. Politics is recognized as a non-theocratic, this-worldly activity geared to the better ordering of human society (*tikkun medini, siddur medini*); and human beings are recognized as competent political agents. Both gentile and Jew are equal in their need for politics and their capacity for it: "Every nation needs some sort of political organization . . . Israel, like any other nation, needs this as well." So the comparison between Israel and "all other nations" (1 Sam. 8), which underlay the people's original request for monarchy, is a positive comparison: it describes and legitimizes what is necessary for human beings.

Gerondi's unique contribution to this secularizing tradition lies in the theoretical underpinning that he provides for it. Human politics is justified by means of a conception of the limits of divine law. The Torah, Gerondi argues, is so sensitive to the demands of absolute justice that it renders itself inapplicable to the real needs of the here and now—"the needs of the hour." Since, therefore, "political order cannot be fully established by [the Torah] alone, God provided further for its establishment by commanding [the appointment of] a king." Politics begins where divine law ends.

Moreover, Gerondi argues that "at a time when Israel had both Sanhedrin and king, the Sanhedrin's role was to judge the people according to just law [i.e., divine law] only and not to order their affairs in any way beyond this, unless the king delegated his powers to them." Gerondi has in mind the kind of powers described by Maimonides, according to which the king "may put to death many offenders in one day, hang them, and suffer them to [remain] hanging for a long time so as to put fear in the hearts of others

and break the power of the wicked" (Kings 3:10 [§11 above]). These prerogatives establish the king's pivotal political role. (Recall Locke's definition of
political power as the "right of making laws with penalties of death" [*Second
Treatise of Government,* chap. 1].) On Gerondi's view, the king's authority to
order society is more fundamental than that of the Sanhedrin, which is only
derivative.

But what is the price paid for this manner of vindicating politics?
A primary purpose of law is, no doubt, to order society; and a law deficient
in this matter, even if it is divine, needs remedial supplements. But law has
another function too, and that is to limit the arbitrariness of power. How,
then, is the king's power to be limited? Gerondi explains that the people's sin
at the time of Samuel consisted "in wanting adjudication between persons
to be mainly the charge of the monarch." But he fails to explain how exactly
the king and the Sanhedrin are to operate side by side given their overlap-
ping domains, or how the king's power can be limited given the precedence
accorded to his legal authority.

Even more troubling is the weight allotted to the argument from
necessity in Gerondi's legitimation of politics. What are the limits of the
necessary? Isn't this argument—a well-known rationalization of injustice—
dangerous? Without adequate answers to these questions, Gerondi might be
only a step away from a Machiavellian conception of politics as the duty to
do whatever is necessary to preserve the political order.

"When the safety of one's country wholly depends on the decision to be taken," Machiavelli argues, "no attention should be paid either to
justice or injustice, to kindness or cruelty, or to its being praiseworthy or
ignominious. On the contrary, every other consideration being set aside, the
alternative should be wholeheartedly adopted which will save the life and
preserve the freedom of one's country" (*Discourses* III:41, ed. Bernard Crick,
using the translation of Leslie J. Walker, with revisions by Brian Richardson).
Machiavelli's *Prince* can be read as an illustration of the kind of politics this
advice entails if we assume that the survival of the country really depends on
the prince and his policies and accept a Machiavellian conception of human
nature. Gerondi does not provide sufficient constraints on this kind of politics. Idealizing divine law does not seem to enable it to curb the claims of

necessity. Neither does his final admonition that "kingship is not inherent in the king, but an attribute conferred upon him for the strengthening of the whole. Therefore, the king should not see himself as the governor and lord of the people, but as a servant unto them for their benefit." The pious prince is, after all, nothing but a good servant holding the interests of the community and its pressing "needs of the hour" close to his heart. But do his good intentions guarantee that he will act well?

I am not arguing that Gerondi was a Machiavellian but rather trying to draw attention to the insufficiency of the constraints he provides while carving out the space he deems necessary for politics. It is important to notice, however, that theocratic politics does not fare much better. Spinoza's critique of theocracy alerts us to the fact that divine politics is always in need of human representatives. What can constrain a person who claims his policy is required by necessity—or commanded by God?

Better constitutional arrangements are needed than those described in this chapter. The main interest in establishing those arrangements is to preserve the integrity of divine law in face of the dangers of political power: the kings of Israel are not subject to judgment "because of a certain event" (BT Sanhedrin 19a, §8 above)—namely, the destruction of the Sanhedrin brought about by King Yannai. But if law is to restrain political power, it cannot remain outside the political realm. Therefore, if we accept Gerondi's firm conviction of the necessity of an autonomous leadership, we cannot escape the need for a full and independent royal law. This law must be firmly rooted in political life; it must determine the distribution of power in society and delineate the boundaries of necessity.

It is for this reason that Herzog (C10, §2) finds Gerondi's position unacceptable. Gerondi's arguments bequeath future rabbis a cruel dilemma: They may either reject the effort to create an independent royal law and thereby assume the risk—to society and to themselves—of dealing with tyrants like Yannai or they may espouse the distinction between civil and religious law, and further deepen it, while sacrificing the ideal of an all-encompassing divine law.

God's line in 1 Samuel "Heed their demands and appoint a king for them" suggests the inevitability of this sacrifice. The biblical story of the creation of the monarchy as Gerondi interprets it leads us to restate the dilemma: The central question of Jewish political theory should not be whether to choose a secular or a theocratic state but rather how to draw the line between the secular and the sacred. Acknowledging the role of the secular, however, involves setting limits to it in the form of constitutional law.

Menachem Lorberbaum

FOUR Priests

Introduction

In the Bible: Holy Priests

"A Kingdom of Priests"

1. Exodus 19:1–6

Consecration of Aaron

2. Exodus 28:1–2; 40:13–15

Day of Atonement—Priest as Intermediary

3. Leviticus 16

Royal Trespass in the Sanctuary

4. 2 Chronicles 26:16–21

"The Lord Is Their Portion"

5. Deuteronomy 18:1–5

Priest as Judge

6. Deuteronomy 17:8–13

Priest as Teacher

7. Deuteronomy 33:8, 10
   Commentary. Yair Lorberbaum, "The Place of the Priest"

Attacking Corrupt Priests

8. Malachi 2:1–9

Apolitical Priesthood

9. Baruch Spinoza, *Theological-Political Treatise,* Chapter 17

The Second Temple: Ruling Priests

The Splendor of the High Priest

10. *The Wisdom of Ben Sira* 45:6–26; 50:1–24

Introduction

Until modern times, theocracy was standardly listed as one of the possible political regimes or forms of government. But it was always an indeterminate form: Who actually ruled when God ruled? God can govern a human community only through intermediaries (this is one of the main points of Spinoza's critical reading of the biblical texts; see €1, §15, and below, §9): a single person or group or a number of different people who plausibly claim to have been chosen by him or to have access to his reason or will. In the biblical texts, as we saw in the last chapter, the most important political intermediaries of this sort were the *shoftim* (judges), whose intermittent rule, however, left a lot of room for the anarchic self-rule of the people. When God did not raise up saviors for Israel, his kingdom had no visible form of government at all, no established institutions, no authorized agents.

But there is another understanding of theocracy, and another group of Israelites stands poised to serve as political intermediaries, not in an intermittent but in a steady and routinized way: the priests. Their status is hereditary, carried in the male line, like that of kings. But they have a more obvious divine connection, deriving from their function rather than their blood, manifest in the performance of the all-important temple ritual that binds God to Israel and ensures his presence in Jerusalem. In any religion where priests play this kind of mediating role between God and humanity, humanity is likely to find itself ruled by its mediators. At least, priests will stake their claim, as in medieval Christianity, to theocratic legitimacy; whether the claim prevails will depend on the nature and strength of the lay opposition.

The biblical account of priestly tasks does not extend to ruling (as Spinoza makes clear in the selection below), although it does include teaching and interpreting the law, as well as providing oracles and legal decisions, an activity that is sometimes broadly described, sometimes limited to divine matters (as distinct from "the king's matters"; see 2 Chron. 19:11). It is prophets rather than priests who challenge and rebuke kings, defending both morality and religion; the priests seem to defend only their temple turf, as in the story of Uzziah and Azariah in Selection 4. But the prophets do not claim any kind of political office, whereas the priesthood is a centrally important office, coexisting with monarchy in what is usually, but not always, a subordinate position.

When Jews in Babylonia during the first exile imagined a constitutional regime for the promised restoration, they looked for a king and a high priest sitting side by side, their relative authority unclear. Zechariah 6 (not included here because the text is obscure and its meaning disputed) seems to describe an attempt at a double crowning of the two after the end of the exile, but the would-be king, the Davidic heir Zerubabel, has disappeared both from the text and from historical view: "Take silver and gold and make crowns," says the prophet. "Place [one] on the head of High Priest Joshua son of Jehozadak, and say to him, 'Thus said the Lord of Hosts. . . .'" There is no parallel instruction for placing the second crown on the head of the king; it has, as it were, fallen out of the text that has come down to us. But the prophecy that follows refers to king and priest together: "He shall build the Temple of the Lord and assume majesty, and he shall sit on his throne and rule. And there shall also be a priest seated on his throne [Septuagint: on his right hand], and harmonious understanding shall prevail between them" (Zech. 6:11–13).

In the absence of the king, harmonious understanding—never easy to achieve—was not necessary. Throughout the Second Temple period, Judea was effectively ruled by its high priests alone, with whatever counsel they required from the locally rich and famous—subject always, of course, to the various imperial governments. Indeed, it was imperialism that made priestly rule possible; the disappearance of Zerubbabel was probably Persian work. There never was a full restoration, no return of Davidic kings, and until the Hasmonean revolt there was nothing like political independence or recognized lay leadership—hence no political opposition could be mounted against Israel's experiment with priestly theocracy. Even after the Hasmoneans took the royal title, they retained the priestly office on which—since they could make no claim to Davidic descent—their legitimacy depended.

It doesn't appear that any of the priests ever sat down and wrote out a theoretical justification of the Second Temple regime. But Josephus, himself of a priestly family, provides us with a strongly favorable, if brief, account of it in its last days under the name "theocracy"—apparently the first use of the term. Almost three centuries earlier, sometime around 180 B.C.E., Simeon Ben Sira had painted a richly textured verbal portrait of the high priest of his own time, Simon the Just, son of Onias, in all his material and spiritual splendor: he is clearly conceived as a kind of king. Simon's is the culminating portrait in the section of Ben Sira's book that begins, "Let us now praise famous [or pious] men" (chaps. 44–50).

The priestly privileges and powers reflected in these texts from the biblical and Second Temple periods later became the subjects of Rabbinic criticism. Even before 70 C.E., the Pharisees had probably begun to question the ideas of priestly mediation and rule. Their arguments can be found in mishnaic and talmudic texts denying the Sadducean claim that the priests are the true custodians of the Torah. The contrasting views of priestly and rabbinic roles are represented here by the accounts of the Yom Kippur temple service in the biblical book of Leviticus and in Mishnah Yoma. In the first, the high priest stands by himself as mediator, representing the highest level of holiness possible for a human being. In the second, the high priest enacts the ritual only with the coaching, as it were, of a committee of sages. We can be sure of the priest's ritual purity and his proper performance of the service only if he is closely watched and admonished by legal experts. In the Israel of Mishnah Yoma, the learned rule over the holy, for only the learned know the rules of holiness.

Of course, it was the Romans, and not any group of Jewish reformers, who destroyed the Judaism of the priests. The Rabbis needed to worry only about the lingering prestige and status of the old priestly families. And once they had won their battle to establish law and legal interpretation as the central features of Jewish self-government, priestly theocracy ceased to be an issue in Jewish life. Although the claims of the Rabbis are sometimes characterized as theocratic, they have in fact a very different form. As we will see in Chapter 6, the Rabbis give a radically new account of what it means to teach God's law, an account in which study and argument play a far larger part than they ever did in the self-understanding of the priests.

In the Bible: Holy Priests

We begin with the preamble to the Sinai revelation as a backdrop for depicting the priestly functions in the Israelite polity. The verses describe the election of Israel as "a kingdom of priests." What precisely this means and how it might be squared with the further election of the men of a particular family as priests, described below, has been much debated. In Chapter 12 we reproduce the argument of Korah (Num. 16), who alludes to this text in his attack upon the priestly hierarchy.

"A Kingdom of Priests"
1. Exodus 19:1–6

On the third new moon after the Israelites had gone forth from the land of Egypt, on that very day, they entered the wilderness of Sinai. Having journeyed from Rephidim, they entered the wilderness of Sinai and encamped in the wilderness. Israel encamped there in front of the mountain, and Moses went up to God. The Lord called to him from the mountain, saying, "Thus shall you say to the house of Jacob and declare to the children of Israel: 'You have seen what I did to the Egyptians, how I bore you on eagles' wings and brought you to Me. Now then, if you will obey Me faithfully and keep My covenant, you shall be My treasured possession among all the peoples. Indeed, all the earth is Mine, but you shall be to Me a kingdom of priests and a holy nation.' These are the words that you shall speak to the children of Israel."

Consecration of Aaron
2. Exodus 28:1–2; 40:13–15

You shall bring forward your brother Aaron, with his sons, from among the Israelites, to serve Me as priests: Aaron, Nadab and Abihu, Eleazar and Ithamar, the sons of Aaron. Make sacral vestments for your brother Aaron, for dignity and adornment. . . .

Put the sacral vestments on Aaron, and anoint him and consecrate him, that he may serve Me as priest. Then bring his sons forward, put tunics on them, and anoint them as you have anointed their father, that they may serve Me as priests. This their anointing shall serve them for everlasting priesthood throughout the ages.

Day of Atonement—Priest as Intermediary
3. Leviticus 16

This chapter of Leviticus describes the Yom Kippur rituals, which epitomize the high priest's role in maintaining the relationship between God and Israel. Upon entering the holy of holies of the tent of meeting and later of the Temple building, the high priest achieves a unique intimacy with God; he then makes atonement for all the sins of the

people. A high point in the traditional Yom Kippur synagogue service is the liturgical
reenactment of this dramatic ritual.

The Lord spoke to Moses after the death of the two sons of Aaron who died when they drew too close to the presence of the Lord. The Lord said to Moses:

Tell your brother Aaron that he is not to come at will into the Shrine behind the curtain, in front of the cover that is upon the ark, lest he die; for I appear in the cloud over the cover. Thus only shall Aaron enter the Shrine: with a bull of the herd for a sin offering and a ram for a burnt offering. He shall be dressed in a sacral linen tunic, with linen breeches next to his flesh, and be girt with a linen sash, and he shall wear a linen turban. They are sacral vestments; he shall bathe his body in water and then put them on. And from the Israelite community he shall take two he-goats for a sin offering and a ram for a burnt offering.

Aaron is to offer his own bull of sin offering, to make expiation for himself and for his household. Aaron shall take the two he-goats and let them stand before the Lord at the entrance of the Tent of Meeting; and he shall place lots upon the two goats, one marked for the Lord and other marked for Azazel. Aaron shall bring forward the goat designated by lot for the Lord, which he is to offer as a sin offering, while the goat designated by lot for Azazel shall be left standing alive before the Lord, to make expiation with it and to send it off to the wilderness for Azazel.

Aaron shall then offer his bull of sin offering, to make expiation for himself and his household. He shall slaughter his bull of sin offering, and he shall take a panful of glowing coals scooped from the altar before the Lord, and two handfuls of finely ground aromatic incense, and bring this behind the curtain. He shall put the incense on the fire before the Lord, so that the cloud from the incense screens the cover that is over [the Ark of] the Pact, lest he die. He shall take some of the blood of the bull and sprinkle it with his fingers over the cover on the east side; and in front of the cover he shall sprinkle some of the blood with his fingers seven times. He shall then slaughter the people's goat of sin offering, bring its blood behind the curtain, and do with its blood as he has done with the blood of the bull; he shall sprinkle it over the cover and in front of the cover.

Thus he shall purge the Shrine of the uncleanness and transgression of the Israelites, whatever their sins; and he shall do the same for the Tent of Meeting, which abides with them in the midst of their uncleanness. When he goes in to make expiation in the shrine, nobody else shall be in the Tent of Meeting until he comes out.

When he has made expiation for himself and his household, and for the whole congregation of Israel, he shall go out to the altar that is before the Lord and purge it: he shall take some of the blood of the bull and of the goat and apply it to each of the horns of the altar; and the rest of the blood he shall sprinkle on it with his finger seven times. Thus he shall cleanse it of the uncleanness of the Israelites and consecrate it.

When he has finished purging the Shrine, the Tent of Meeting, and the altar, the live goat shall be brought forward. Aaron shall lay both his hands upon the head of the live goat and confess over it all the iniquities and transgressions of the Israelites, whatever their sins, putting them on the head of the goat; and it shall be sent off to the wilderness through a designated man. Thus the goat shall carry on it all their iniquities to an inaccessible region; and the goat shall be set free in the wilderness.

And Aaron shall go into the Tent of Meeting, take off the linen vestments that he put on when he entered the Shrine, and leave them there. He shall bathe his body in water in the holy precinct and put on his vestments; then he shall come out and offer his burnt offering and the burnt offering of the people, making expiation for himself and for the people. The fat of the sin offering he shall turn into smoke on the altar.

He who set the Azazel-goat free shall wash his clothes and bathe his body in water; after that he may reenter the camp.

The bull of sin offering and the goat of sin offering whose blood was brought in to purge the shrine shall be taken outside the camp; and their hides, flesh, and dung shall be consumed in fire. He who burned them shall wash his clothes and bathe his body in water; after that he may reenter the camp.

And this shall be to you a law for all time: In the seventh month, on the tenth day of the month, you shall practice self-denial;[1] and you shall

1. The Hebrew here refers primarily to fasting; cf. Isa. 58:3.

do no manner of work, neither the citizen nor the alien who resides among you. For on this day atonement shall be made for you to cleanse you of all your sins; you shall be clean before the Lord. It shall be a sabbath of complete rest for you, and you shall practice self-denial; it is a law for all time. The priest who has been anointed and ordained to serve as priest in place of his father shall make expiation. He shall put on the linen vestments, the sacral vestments. He shall purge the innermost Shrine; he shall purge the Tent of Meeting and the altar; and he shall make expiation for the priests and for all the people of the congregation.

This shall be to you a law for all time: to make atonement for the Israelites for all their sins once a year.

And Moses did as the Lord had commanded him.

Royal Trespass in the Sanctuary
4. 2 Chronicles 26:16–21

This is one of several biblical accounts of conflict between the king and the high priest. Note that the conflict is not over the political role of the priest but over the religious role of the king. The high priest is victorious on his own ground: Uzziah is afflicted with leprosy. Lepers were considered unclean and required to "dwell apart" (see Lev. 13:45–46).

When he [Uzziah] was strong, he grew so arrogant he acted corruptly; he trespassed against his God by entering the Temple of the Lord to offer incense on the incense altar. The priest Azariah, with eighty other brave priests of the Lord, followed him in and, confronting King Uzziah, said to him, "It is not for you, Uzziah, to offer incense to the Lord, but for the Aaronite priests, who have been consecrated, to offer incense. Get out of the sanctuary, for you have trespassed; there will be no glory in it for you from the Lord God." Uzziah, holding the censer and ready to burn incense, got angry; but as he got angry with the priests, leprosy broke out on his forehead in front of the priests in the House of the Lord beside the incense altar. When the chief priest Azariah and all the other priests looked at him, his forehead was leprous, so they rushed him out of there; he too made haste to get out, for the Lord had struck him with a plague. King Uzziah was a leper until the day of his death. He lived in isolated quarters as a leper, for he was cut off from the House of the Lord—while Jotham his son was in charge of the king's house and governed the people of the land.

"The Lord Is Their Portion"
5. Deuteronomy 18:1–5

The tribe of Levi was elected for special service to God. According to the classical priestly account (§2), only one Levite family, that of Aaron, was designated specifically for priesthood. The following verses seem to reflect a different tradition, one that accords priestly status to the entire tribe. Rabbinic accounts distinguish between priests proper— Aaron's descendants—and the Levites more generally, entrusted with auxiliary temple service.

The levitical priests, the whole tribe of Levi, shall have no territorial portion with Israel. They shall live only off the Lord's offerings by fire as their portion, and shall have no portion among their brother tribes: the Lord is their portion, as He promised them.

This then shall be the priests' due from the people: Everyone who offers a sacrifice, whether an ox or a sheep, must give the shoulder, the cheeks, and the stomach to the priest. You shall also give him the first fruits of your new grain and wine and oil, and the first shearing of your sheep. For the Lord your God has chosen him and his descendants, out of all your tribes, to be in attendance for service in the name of the Lord for all time.

Priest as Judge

6. Deuteronomy 17:8–13

This critical text, which directly precedes "the law of the king," describes the levitical priests, along with a "magistrate," whose source of authority is not given (possibly royal appointment), as Israel's judges. Deuteronomy 17 was later used by the Rabbis as a warrant for their own judicial powers.

If a case is too baffling for you to decide, be it a controversy over homicide, civil law, or assault—matters of dispute in your courts—you shall promptly repair to the place that the Lord your God will have chosen, and appear before the levitical priests, or the magistrate in charge at the time, and present your problem. When they have announced to you the verdict in the case, you shall carry out the verdict that is announced to you from that place that the Lord chose, observing scrupulously all their instructions to you. You shall act in accordance with the instructions given you and the ruling handed down to you; you must not deviate from the verdict that they announce to you either to the right or to the left. Should a man act presumptuously and disregard the priest charged with serving there the Lord your God, or the magistrate, that man shall die. Thus you will sweep out evil from Israel: all the people will hear and be afraid and will not act presumptuously again.

Priest as Teacher

7. Deuteronomy 33:8, 10

The following is an excerpt from Moses' blessing to the tribe of Levi, given just before his death. The priests' charge includes the divine oracle, the thummim *and* urim.

And to Levi he said:

> Let your Thummim and Urim
> Be with Your faithful one,

. . .

They shall teach Your laws to Jacob
And Your instructions to Israel.
They shall offer You incense to savor
And whole-offerings on Your altar.

Commentary. The Place of the Priest

Biblical accounts of the authority and function of the priests—and consequently of their standing relative to king, prophet, and judge—are not consistent with one another. Scholars who distinguish among the different sources and layers that underlie the redacted biblical text identify several conceptions of the priesthood. Israel Knohl, whose work forms the basis for the argument here (see *The Sanctuary of Silence* [1995]), has demonstrated that the source of the priests' authority and the scope of their activities according to the early Priestly School source differ substantially in other biblical sources, including the later Holiness School (which is closer to popular religious ideas) and the book of Deuteronomy. These differences are rooted in radically different views on God and his relationship to humanity and the world.

According to the Priestly School, God is transcendent and sublime; he resides high above the mundane realm, unconcerned with human beings and their universe. He does not oversee human or worldly affairs, nor does he punish or reward human actions. He transcends morality and politics. In short, the God of the Torah of the Priestly School plays no substantial role in the earthly realm.

The other biblical schools (particularly the authors of the Holiness Code) present opposing theological conceptions. Their God has anthropomorphic features: a human personality and even a humanlike form. He is involved in earthly events and profoundly concerned with human beings and their deeds.

These differing theological conceptions result in opposing visions of the sacramental realm and therefore in alternative accounts of the scope of priestly activity. According to the Priestly School, religious ritual emphasizes the inferior or, more precisely, the insignificant state of man in relation to the divine, the Holy Other. Consequently, the actual rituals are denied any of the practical functions ascribed to them in other biblical sources. Instead, their focus is exclusively on the encounter between a numinous God and the serving priest. One expression of this is the annual atonement ceremony described in Leviticus 16. According to the first twenty-eight verses of the chapter, which derive from the Priestly School source, the primary function of this ritual is the purification of the Temple. The significance of this early view of the atonement ritual is best revealed by contrast with other biblical sources (including verses 29–34 of the same chapter), where it is portrayed very differently: as a means of appeasing God and influencing his role in political, social, and economic affairs.

The theological conceptions of the Priestly School have a direct effect on its portrayal of the social and political status of the priest. Just as the God of the Priestly School is transcendent and removed from earthly affairs and certainly from state and society, so too are its priests, his servants, separated from these realms. Thus, the priest has no political, social, economic, or judicial function. He is confined to the sacral realm—the tabernacle or the Temple—and isolated from the social and political order. (He is involved in political conflicts only when they impinge directly upon the sacral realm; see 2 Chron. 19:10–11 and Lev. 5:20–26.) His activity is restricted to the sanctuary where he purifies himself so that he will be able to sustain the encounter with God.

This removal of the priestly sect from the affairs of the nation is further clarified through contrast with other biblical schools. For example, unlike the Priestly Torah, Deuteronomy grants the priests (as well as the Levites) substantial judicial authority and identifies them as the authoritative interpreters of the Torah. Consider also the difference between these biblical sources with regard to the functions of the holy ark and the *urim* and *thummim* oracle. According to some biblical passages, the holy ark is regularly carried onto the battlefield, evidently to aid in the war effort. In the Priestly Torah, however, the holy ark always remains in the sanctuary. Similarly, several biblical sources maintain that the priests counsel the nation through the use of the *urim* and *thummim* oracle (see, e.g., Judg. 20:27, 1 Sam. 22:10, 2 Sam. 5:19). In the Priestly Torah, these holy devices are carried by the priest only for ritual and for no other purposes (see Exod. 28:30; Knohl, p. 153 n. 122 and p. 164 n. 157).

The picture that emerges from the reconstruction of the early Priestly source in the Bible, therefore, is one of almost total separation between religion and state. Priestly concerns are confined to the Temple and its rituals; priests have almost no involvement in the state or society. The king, his officials, judges, and other authorities are charged with tending to political and social affairs, as well as to matters of ethics and law, without interference by the priests. Similarly, the policies administered by the political authorities have no relation to, and no effects within, the sacral realm.

The motivation for separating the secular from the sacred, society and state from divine worship, is religious and theological. It does not emerge from some unsuccessful effort to join together secular affairs and sacred ritual. Rather, it results from a tendency in religious thought that envisions God as transcendent and distant, elevated above human beings and society. Uncovering and revealing the hidden dimension of divinity necessitates a set of rituals isolated from all human concerns: social, political, economic, and even moral. God transcends reason, ethics, and society, and his rituals are, therefore, dissociated from all three. What results is—to apply a rabbinic term—"worship out of love," without anticipation of worldly reward.

This religious-theological intuition regarding God's nature and the nature of divine worship receives its clearest contemporary expression in the writings of Yeshayahu Leibowitz (see C2, §9). Leibowitz, too, perceives God as absolutely transcendent and his rituals as completely removed from any human dimension, rational, ethical, or national; he advocates a complete separation between religion and state. Their combination will ineluctably lead—in his opinion— to the debasement of religion and to idolatry.

In a paradoxical sense, the ideational nucleus of the early priestly theology has a certain attraction today. It consolidates a religion purified of human and earthly concerns. Consequently, it allows individual Jews to live religious lives within the social and political fabric without conflict and tension. Nonetheless, it is important to emphasize that the contemporary attraction to the priestly tradition is only to its central theological idea, because this tradition as a whole does not share, or leave room for, modern democratic sensibilities. Participation in the rituals performed in the "silent

sanctuary" is accessible only to the priests, whereas in the modern revival of
this idea, worship from love of God—sublime and indifferent, without any
anticipation of reward, and removed from any human concerns—is available
to all people.

Yair Lorberbaum

Attacking Corrupt Priests
8. Malachi 2:1–9

The last of the biblical prophets argues that the priestly covenant and the judicial authority of the priests are conditional on their just rulings.

And now, O Priests, this charge is for you: Unless you obey and unless you
lay it to heart, and do honor to My name—said the Lord of Hosts—I will
send a curse and turn your blessings into curses. (Indeed, I have turned them
into curses, because you do not lay it to heart.) I will put your seed under a
ban, and I will strew dung upon your faces, the dung of your festal sacrifices,
and you shall be carried out to its [heap].

Know, then, that I have sent this charge to you that My covenant
with Levi may endure—said the Lord of Hosts. I had with him a covenant of
life and well-being, which I gave to him, and of reverence, which he showed
Me. For he stood in awe of My name.

> Proper rulings were in his mouth,
> And nothing perverse was on his lips;
> He served Me with complete loyalty
> And held the many back from iniquity.
> For the lips of a priest guard knowledge,
> And men seek rulings from his mouth.
> For he is a messenger of the Lord of Hosts.

But you have turned away from that course: You have made the
many stumble through your rulings; you have corrupted the covenant of the

Levites—said the Lord of Hosts. And I, in turn, have made you despicable and vile in the eyes of all the people, because you disregard My ways and show partiality in your rulings.

Apolitical Priesthood

9. Baruch Spinoza, *Theological-Political Treatise,* Chapter 17

Tractatus Theologico-Politicus, translated by Samuel Shirley (Leiden: E. J. Brill, 1991), pp. 257–58.

Spinoza here provides his account of the only possible theocracy, which exists by virtue of the fragmentation of power after the death of Moses: theocracy is the work of many agents, including the people as a whole, all of whom can seek God's will. But no single person speaks directly with God and promulgates his laws as Moses had done; no single person issues commands. So the priests are custodians rather than rulers of God's realm.

The people were commanded to build a dwelling to serve as the palace of God, the state's supreme sovereign. This palace was to be built at the expense not of one man but of the entire people, so that the dwelling where God was to be consulted should belong to the nation as a whole. The Levites were chosen to be the courtiers and administrators of this palace of God, while Aaron, the brother of Moses, was chosen to be at their head, in second place, as it were, to God their king, to be succeeded by his sons by hereditary right. Therefore Aaron, as next to God, was the supreme interpreter of God's laws, giving the people the answers of the divine oracle and entreating God on the people's behalf. Now if, along with these functions, he had held the right of issuing commands, his position would have been that of an absolute monarch. But this right was denied him, and in general the whole tribe of Levi was so completely divested of civil rights that they did not have even a legal share of territory, like the other tribes, to provide them at least with a livelihood. Moses ordained that they should be maintained by the rest of the people, yet always be held in the highest honor by the common people as the only tribe dedicated to God.

[The text goes on to describe the powers of Joshua as military commander, of the various tribal councils, of the *shoftim,* and of the people as a whole.]

The Second Temple: Ruling Priests

The Splendor of the High Priest

10. *The Wisdom of Ben Sira 45:6–26; 50:1–24*

The Wisdom of Ben Sira, translated by Patrick W. Skehan, commentary by Alexander A. di Lella, The Anchor Bible 39 (Garden City, N.Y.: Doubleday, 1987), pp. 506–8, 546–48.

The Second Commonwealth was founded as a Jewish province in the Persian empire with the return of the exiles in the sixth century B.C.E. *Carrying an imperial license from Cyrus (cf. Ezra 1:1–4), the returnees rebuilt the Temple in Jerusalem and, led by Ezra the priest and Nehemiah the provincial governor, proceeded to establish a community around it. At the head of this community stood the high priest; the splendor of his figure is portrayed in this selection. The book of Ben Sira (dating from the early second century* B.C.E.*) is part of the Apocrypha, that is, the various books included in some Christian canons but not in the Hebrew Bible. Ben Sira continues the biblical tradition of "wisdom literature." Here the high priest is depicted among the exemplary "fathers of the world."*

(45) [God] raised up also, like Moses in holiness,
   Aaron his brother, of the tribe of Levi.
He made his office perpetual
   when he endowed him with its dignity;
He brought him to the fore in splendor
   and enveloped him in an aura of majesty.
He clothed him with sublime magnificence
   and adorned him with the glorious vestments:
Breeches and tunic and robe
   with pomegranates around the hem,
And a rustle of bells round about,
   through whose pleasing sound at each step

He would be heard within the sanctuary,
    and the families of his people would be remembered;
The sacred vestments of gold, of violet,
    and of crimson, wrought with embroidery;
The breastpiece for decision, the ephod and cincture
    with scarlet yarn, the work of the weaver;
Precious stones with seal engravings
    in golden settings, the work of the jeweler,
To commemorate in incised letters
    each of the tribes of Israel;
On his turban the diadem of gold—
    a frontlet engraved with the sacred inscription,
Majestic, glorious, renowned for splendor,
    a delight to the eyes, beauty supreme.
Before him no one was adorned with these,
    nor may they ever be worn by any
Except his sons and them alone,
    generation after generation, for all time.
His cereal offering is wholly burned
    as an established offering twice each day;
For Moses ordained him
    and anointed him with the holy oil,
In a lasting covenant with him
    and with his family, as permanent as the heavens,
That he should serve God in his priesthood
    and bless his people in his name.[2]
He chose him from all humankind
    to offer holocausts and choice offerings,
To burn sacrifices of sweet odor for a memorial,
    and to atone for the people of Israel.
He gave to him his laws,
    and authority to prescribe and to judge:

---

2. See Num. 6:22–27. This is one of the few priestly rituals that persist to this day in synagogue
services.

To teach the precepts to his people,
    and the norms to the descendants of Israel.
Strangers were inflamed against him,
    were jealous of him in the desert,
The followers of Dathan and Abiram,
    and the band of Korah in their defiance.[3]
But the Lord saw this and became angry;
    he destroyed them in his burning wrath.
He brought against them a miracle,
    and consumed them with his flaming fire.
Then he increased the glory of Aaron
    and bestowed upon him his inheritance:
The sacred offerings he allotted to him,
    with the showbread as his portion;
The oblations of the Lord are his food,
    a gift to him and his descendants.
But he holds none of the people's land,
    nor shares with them their heritage;
Rather, the Lord is his portion and inheritance
    in the midst of the Israelites.
Phinehas too, the son of Eleazar,
    was the courageous third of his line
When, zealous for the God of all,
    he met the crisis of his people
And, at the promptings of his noble heart,
    atoned for the people of Israel.[4]
Therefore on him again God conferred the right,
    in a covenant of friendship to provide for the sanctuary,
So that he and his descendants
    should possess the high priesthood forever.
For even his covenant with David
    the son of Jesse of the tribe of Judah,

3. See Num. 16; and ℂ12.
4. See Num. 25.

Was an individual heritage through one son alone,
   but the heritage of Aaron is for all his descendants.
So now bless the Lord
   who has crowned you with glory!
May he grant you wisdom of heart
   to govern his people in justice
Lest the benefits you confer should be forgotten,
   or the virtue of your rule, in future generations.

(50) Greatest among his kindred, the glory of his people,
   was Simeon the priest, son of Jochanan,
In whose time the house of God was renovated,
   in whose days the temple was reinforced.
In his time also the retaining wall was built
   for the residence precinct with its temple of the King.
In his day the reservoir was dug,
   the pool with a vastness like the sea's.
He took care for his people against brigands
   and strengthened his city against the enemy.
How splendid he was as he looked forth from the Tent,[5]
   as he came from the house of the veil!
Like a star shining among the clouds,
   like the full moon at the holy-day season;
Like the sun shining on the temple of the King,
   like the rainbow appearing in the cloudy sky;
Like the blossoms on the branches in springtime,
   like a lily by running waters;
Like the verdure of Lebanon in summer,
   like the blaze of incense at the sacrifice;
Like a vessel of beaten gold
   studded with an assortment of precious stones;
Like a luxuriant olive tree thick with fruit,
   a plant whose branches run with oil;

5. A poetic reference to the sanctuary deriving from the biblical tabernacle.

Wearing his splendid robes,
    and vested in sublime magnificence,
As he ascended the glorious altar
    and lent majesty to the court of the sanctuary.
When he received the sundered victims from his brother priests
    while he stood before the sacrificial hearth,
His sons ringed him about like a garland,
    like young cedars on Lebanon;
And like poplars by the brook they clustered around him,
    all the sons of Aaron in their dignity,
With the offerings to the Lord in their hands,
    in the presence of the whole assembly of Israel.
Once he had completed the service at the altar
    and arranged the sacrificial hearth for the Most High,
And had stretched forth his hand for the cup,
    to offer blood of the grape,
And poured it out at the foot of the altar,
    a sweet-smelling odor to God the Most High,
The sons of Aaron would sound a blast,
    the priests, on their trumpets of beaten metal;
A blast to resound mightily
    as a reminder before the Most High.
Then all the people with one accord
    would quickly fall prostrate to the ground
In adoration before the Most High,
    before the Holy One of Israel.
Then hymns would reecho,
    and over the throng sweet strains of praise resound.
All the people of the land would shout for joy,
    praying to the Merciful One,
As the high priest completed the service at the altar
    by presenting to God the sacrifice due;
Then coming down he would raise his hands
    over all the congregation of Israel;
The blessing of the Lord would be upon his lips,

the name of the Lord would be his glory.
Then again the people would lie prostrate,
     receiving the blessing from the Most High.
And now, bless the God of all,
     who has done stupendous things on earth;
Who makes humans grow from their mother's womb,
     and does with them according to his will!
May he grant you wisdom of heart,
     and may he abide among you as peace;
May his kindness toward Simeon be lasting;
     may he fulfill for him the covenant with Phinehas
So that it may be not abrogated for him
     or for his descendants while the heavens last.

High Priest and Prince
11. 1 Maccabees 14:25–49

The Anchor Bible: I Maccabees, translated with commentary by Jonathan A. Goldstein (Garden City, N.Y.: Doubleday, 1977), pp. 486–88.

The first book of Maccabees, also part of the Apocrypha, was written circa 100 B.C.E. in a quasi-biblical idiom and depicts the Maccabees as heirs to the long tradition of saviors of Israel. The Maccabean revolt was lead initially by Mattathias and his son Judah. The selection below describes the subsequent appointment of another son, Simon, as high priest and prince. It can be read as a parallel to the chapters in the biblical book of Samuel (see C3, §3) that describe the founding of the ancient Israelite monarchy. Here the founding of the Hasmonean dynasty of priestly rulers is documented.

When the People learned of these achievements, they said, "How shall we show gratitude to Simon and to his sons? He arose with his brothers and his family and fought off the enemies of Israel, and they gained freedom for our people!" They drew up a document on bronze tablets and set it up on stone slabs on Mount Zion. The following is a copy of the document:

On the eighteenth of Elul in the year 172, which is the year 3 under Simon, high priest and prince of God's People, at a great assembly of priests and people and chiefs of the nation and the elders of the land, the following was brought to our attention:

"Whereas: at a time when our land was repeatedly afflicted by wars, Simon son of Mattathias of the clan of Joarib and his brothers exposed themselves to danger and resisted their nation's foes, in order that their sanctuary might survive, and the Torah: they won great glory for their nation; Jonathan rallied his nation and became their high priest and then passed away; thereupon their enemies desired to invade their country in order to destroy it and violate their sanctuary; then Simon arose and fought for his nation and spent large sums of his own money, providing arms for the men of the army of his nation and paying their salaries; he fortified the towns of Judea, including Beth-Zur on the border of Judea, where previously there had been an enemy arsenal, stationing there a garrison of Jews; he also fortified Joppe by the sea and Gazara on the border of Azotus, previously inhabited by our enemies, settling Jews there; whatever was needed for removing impediments to pious Jewish life in those towns, he provided; observing Simon's fidelity and what he had accomplished and the glory which he proposed to bring upon his nation, the people appointed him their chief and high priest because of all these achievements of his and because of his righteousness and his uninterrupted fidelity to his nation, as he sought in every way to exalt his people; thereafter, during his time of leadership, he succeeded in expelling the gentiles from his people's land and in expelling the inhabitants of the City of David in Jerusalem, who had built themselves a citadel from which they used to go out and commit acts of defilement in the vicinity of the sanctuary and gravely impair its purity; Simon stationed in the citadel Jewish soldiers and fortified it for the sake of the safety of our country and our city; he built higher walls around Jerusalem; moreover, King Demetrius [the Second, ruler of Syria] in view of all this has confirmed him as high priest and admitted him to the ranks of his Friends and conferred great distinction upon him; indeed, he heard that the Romans had given the Jews the titles 'Friends and Allies (and Brothers)' and that they had treated Simon's ambassadors with honor—therefore, be it resolved by the Jews and the priests: that Simon be chief and high priest in perpetuity until a true prophet shall arise,[6] and that he be commander over them (and that he have charge of the sanctuary) so as to appoint on his own authority the officials responsible for services, for the countryside, for armaments, and for fortifications, and that he have charge of the sanctuary, and that all persons obey him, and that all contracts in our country be drawn up in his name, and that he wear purple robes and gold ornaments. No one of the people or of the priests shall have the power to annul any of these provisions or to oppose any of his future commands or to convoke a meeting in our country without his permission or to wear purple robes or use a gold brooch. Whoever acts contrary to these provisions or annuls any of them shall be subject to the penalty of death."

The entire people resolved to grant Simon the right to act according to these provisions. Simon accepted and agreed to serve as high priest and to be commander and prince of the nation of the Jews and of the priests and to preside over all. They ordered that this text be drawn up on bronze tablets and set up in the precinct of the sanctuary in a conspicuous place and that copies of the tablets be placed in the treasury so as to be available for Simon and his sons.

Theocracy

12. Josephus, *Contra Apion* II:164–67, 184–89, 193–94

Josephus, vol. I: *"The Life" and "Against Apion,"* translated by Louis H. Feldman, Loeb Classical Library (Cambridge: Harvard University Press, 1961), pp. 359, 367–69, 371.

A major focus of Josephus's writings is the defense of the Jewish religion against such Hellenistic critics as his contemporary the Egyptian grammarian Apion. Josephus here coins the term "theocracy" for the form of government practiced by the priest-rulers of Hasmonean descent.

(164–67) There is endless variety in the details of the customs and laws which prevail in the world at large. To give but a summary enumeration: some

---

6. This caveat seems to express a certain unease regarding the legitimacy of the Hasmonean monarchy.

peoples have entrusted the supreme political power to monarchies, others to oligarchies, yet others to the masses. Our lawgiver, however, was attracted by none of these forms of polity, but gave to his constitution the form of what—if a forced expression be permitted—may be termed a "theocracy," placing all sovereignty and authority in the hands of God. To Him he persuaded all to look, as the author of all blessings, both those which are common to all mankind, and those which they had won for themselves by prayer in the crises of their history. He convinced them that no single action, no secret thought, could be hid from Him. He represented Him as One, uncreated and immutable to all eternity; in beauty surpassing all mortal thought, made known to us by His power, although the nature of His real being passes knowledge.

(184–89) For us, with our conviction that the original institution of the Law was in accordance with the will of God, it would be rank impiety not to observe it. What could one alter in it? What more beautiful one could have been discovered? What improvement imported from elsewhere? Would you change the entire character of the constitution? Could there be a finer or more equitable polity than one which sets God at the head of the universe, which assigns the administration of its highest affairs to the whole body of priests, and entrusts to the supreme high-priest the direction of the other priests? These men, moreover, owed their original promotion by the legislator to their high office, not to any superiority in wealth or other accidental advantages. No; of all his companions, the men to whom he entrusted the ordering of divine worship as their first charge were those who were preeminently gifted with persuasive eloquence and discretion. But this charge further embraced a strict superintendence of the Law and of the pursuits of everyday life; for the appointed duties of the priests included general supervision, the trial of cases of litigation, and the punishment of condemned persons.

Could there be a more saintly government than that? Could God be more worthily honored than by such a scheme, under which religion is the end and aim of the training of the entire community, the priests are entrusted with the special charge of it, and the whole administration of the state resembles some sacred ceremony? Practices which, under the name of mysteries and rites of initiation, other nations are unable to observe for but a few days, we maintain with delight and unflinching determination all our lives.

(193–94) We have but one temple for the one God (for like ever loveth like), common to all as God is common to all. The priests are continually engaged in His worship, under the leadership of him who for the time is head of the line. With his colleagues he will sacrifice to God, safeguard the laws, adjudicate in cases of dispute, punish those convicted of crime. Any who disobey him will pay the penalty as for impiety towards God Himself.

Commentary. Flavius Josephus on Priesthood

Josephus, a priest by birth and a Pharisee by choice, was for the second half of his life a client of the Flavian emperors of Rome. Living among the gentiles, he wrote voluminously in Greek in defense of Judaism. He is the first of the writers in this section whose presentation is apologetic (in the theological sense of that term). He cannot vindicate the levitical priesthood simply with reference to Torah, for his intended audience rejects the authority of Torah. But this fact also frees him from the necessity of the most literal fidelity to Torah.

The very term "theocracy" (Greek *theokratia*), which Josephus either devised himself or borrowed from an unknown source (II:165), represents an attempt to subsume the Jewish tradition under a non-Jewish category. The synonymous Greek suffixes *-cratia* and *-archia,* preserved for us in such familiar words as "monarchy," "aristocracy," "oligarchy," and "democracy," denote political rule. Each term in which these suffixes figure identifies a regime (Greek *politeia* or *politeuma,* II:164), a comprehensive distribution of power and authority in a given society to the advantage of the designated group (in the terms listed above, the "one," the "best," the "few," the "people" or majority). As the character of a city is determined above all by its regime, so the regime furnishes the central principle of the classification of cities and therewith of classical political science. As elaborated by such writers as Herodotus, Thucydides, Plato, Aristotle, and Polybius, this understanding of political life was the common heritage of all whose minds were formed by Greek thought. It has no biblical counterpart. In expounding the levitical priesthood in such terms, then, Josephus assimilates it to the prevalent model of political authority among the educated gentiles of his time, a model which is this-worldly and rationalist.

This is the first of Josephus' paradoxes; others follow. Since every previous regime name had identified the human rulers of a given society (II:164), Josephus might have described the Jewish regime by inventing a term for the rule of priests. Instead he coins or borrows one denoting the rule of God, as if not men but God formed the "regime" whose institutional expression is the priesthood. While assimilating the priesthood to a model of human rule, he denies that in this case the ruler is human (165, 185)—and thereby denies that the priests rule.

As noted in the introduction to this chapter, theocracy is a problematic notion. Who really rules here? Given the ambiguity of Josephus's understanding, suspended as it is between Torah and Greek philosophy, this is an obvious difficulty for him, as it is for his intended readers, and for us.

In Josephus's presentation of priesthood (as in the preceding ones of Ben Sira and 1 Maccabees), no king clutters the political landscape. One way of approaching Josephus is therefore by seeing him as a "republican" whose praise of "theocracy," or rule by priests, is significant primarily for its implied rejection of monarchy. As such, he would foreshadow a much greater figure in the Jewish tradition, who is also its greatest republican, Isaac Abravanel (see C3, §14). Indeed, Abravanel follows Josephus's position when in his *Commentary* he rejects Maimonides and the predominant medieval tradition by interpreting the "law of the king" (Deut. 17:14) not as a divine injunction to establish a monarchy but merely as a "permission" to do so—with the strong implication that this outcome were best avoided (cf. Josephus, *Antiquities of the Jews* IV:223; also VI:36). Such an interpretation reconciles the passage in Deuteronomy with 1 Samuel—in effect interpreting the earlier passage in the light of the later—but is unpersuasive in its construction of the Hebrew of the Deuteronomic text. The question remains as to the positive content of Josephus's teaching: Can it be understood to imply an exaltation of republican self-government, of political life understood politically?

If we understand republicanism as the opposite of monarchy, Josephus's defense of Jewish "theocracy" appears in our passage (and elsewhere) as republican. If, however, republicanism is also understood (as both the classical Greek thinkers and we moderns have understood it) as incompatible with clericalism, Josephus's position will seem anomalous.

Already in the early fourteenth century, Marsilius of Padua—an Aristotelian who was nominally Christian but profoundly anticlerical—rejected the aristocratic tenor of Aristotelian republicanism because it played into the hands of the Catholic priesthood. He appealed from the political authority of the few, however conceived (including therefore the clergy), to the authority of the many (the laity). The work that he began was continued by Machiavelli and subsequently by adherents of the liberal anticlerical tradition (including, within Judaism, Moses Mendelssohn).

Not that Aristotle himself understood the argument for aristocracy as implying the rule of priests. He imagined priests as he knew them, not as rulers of the city but as its nonpartisan servants, officials of the pagan sacrificial cult, who invoked the favor of the gods on behalf of the regime of the city, whatever it happened to be. He regarded the priesthood as an appropriate sinecure for aged citizens of unblemished reputation (*Politics* 1329a, 27–34). As for which regime was best in general or for a particular society, this was a human rather than a divine question, regarding which priests could provide no special guidance.

Josephus, by contrast, defends the levitical regime as it seems it must be defended: as in accordance with the will of God. And yet, precisely because he defends it before philosophically educated gentiles, he must offer a universalist justification for institutions whose authority traditionally rested on divine revelation. Thus is he driven to elaborate a rationalist notion of conformity with the will of God, and an interpretation of the priestly regime as an aristocracy in Aristotle's sense. The virtue of the priests confirms that their rule is in accordance with God's will, and this virtue is manifest in terms fully intelligible to gentiles, which is to say, to reason. It is this regime's goodness in *political terms* that marks it as God's own (II:151–83; cf. especially the statement of principle at 163). Josephus's defense of priestly authority in our passage is of a piece with his immediately prior defense of the God of Israel as identical with, and the inspiration of, the God of the Greek philosophers (168).

Not the least of the questions that Josephus's treatment raises for Jewish readers is whether his claim that the priesthood constituted a regime accords with Torah. In the lifetime of Moses, it was not Aaron's authority that predominated; and the captains and judges whom Moses appointed (Exod. 18:13–24) were not priests. Deuteronomy 17:8–13 speaks not of priests alone but of priests and magistrates sharing ultimate authority to interpret the law. (Nor can we forget that Exodus 19:1–6 declares the entire people of Israel to be priestly.) The authority of Moses devolved on Joshua; and the judges prior to Eli were not priests—nor did the sons of Eli prove worthy of the mantle of their father (1 Sam. 2:12–36; cf. *Antiquities* V:338–40). And finally, there is the "law of the king" (Deut. 17:14), which we have already discussed.

In biblical times, then, the priest had to vie with magistrate and judge and later with king and prophet as arbiter of the law. Only in the postbiblical period did priests such as Simon the Just and the Hasmoneans assume supreme leadership in politics and war (and the Hasmoneans soon proclaimed themselves kings). Even in this period the interpretation of the law had largely passed out of the hands of the increasingly worldly, aristocratic, and hellenized priesthood into those of the Pharisees—who were mostly non-priests learned in the law. By the first century C.E., political authority was divided among the priests, the Jewish (non-priestly) aristocracy, a pro-Roman king, a Roman governor, and the Sanhedrin, composed primarily of the non-priestly sages. All these complexities we know from Josephus's own writings. The great rebellion and the Temple's destruction, in the aftermath of which Josephus is writing, not just qualified the authority of the priesthood but destroyed it forever (pending its messianic restoration).

Josephus offers, then, not only a deliberate idealization but a conscious simplification of the political situation as it had existed in biblical and postbiblical times. The crucial element of his simplification is to present us with a regime, a political arrangement in which supreme authority was not divided and contested but assigned to one particular class of society. Perhaps he aims at the presentation most impressive to gentile readers; perhaps he seeks also to provide a model for future generations (including future generations of priests) should the Jewish polity be restored.

The question remains whether we are to understand the priests as rulers. As Spinoza notes in the passage reprinted in this chapter, the right of legislation, the fundamental attribute of classical regimehood as of modern sovereignty, was never vested in the priests (or in any human hands). That is why Josephus can call the regime of Israel a theocracy: God rules by means of his law; priests merely interpret and administer it (II:185). Yet an ambiguity remains as to what Josephus understands as divine about this theocracy. In his version of 1 Samuel 8 (*Ant.* VI:36–39), the prophet—in reflections that Josephus has fabricated, but which find partial warrant in the rational and this-worldly character of Samuel's critique of kingship in the original—laments the people's request for a king because he (Samuel) is a partisan of aristocracy, the regime that is divine (*theian*) because it is the most beneficial for its subjects. In praising aristocracy as such as divine, the Josephan Samuel employs the term in a wholly rationalist sense. In our passage Josephus uses the same argument, among others, to establish that priestly rule was theocratic. At the very least he blurs the distinction between divine rule in the traditional Jewish sense and theocracy in the Greek philosophical sense as the rule of the most virtuous or reasonable men. The two traditions agree that only where the best human rulers apply the best law can we say that theocracy prevails. They diverge over whether the divine element in such rule is the Sinaitic revelation as interpreted by the devout or the unassisted reason of the most capable human beings.

Whatever Josephus's private thoughts, in our passage he tries to have it both ways—both ways as regards reason and revelation and both ways as regards the character of the priests. Inasmuch as his conception of Jewish law is implicitly a human one (Torah as the product of a supremely wise founder and an exemplary priestly class of interpreters), he implies a genuinely (and merely) political interpretation of Jewish life and thereby of the propriety of rational debate as to who in the community is best qualified to exercise ultimate authority. Explicitly, however, he defers to the tradition by limiting himself to the question of who is best qualified to exercise penultimate authority by interpreting and administering the word of God. This question he seeks to resolve with arguments drawn from pagan philosophy. For us he raises the broader question of whether the Jewish way of life can ever be adequately justified with arguments borrowed from the gentiles.

Clifford Orwin

From Priests to Sages

These three selections reflect the basic Pharisaic attitude toward the priesthood. The sages accepted the priests' role in the temple service but rejected their spiritual leadership. Learning and personal piety supplanted lineage as the basis for religious authority. The Mishnah's report of the service on the Day of Atonement probably derives from a tradition antedating the destruction of the Temple, and in re-creating the past it shifts continually between past and present tenses. It seems to reflect tensions between the Pharisees and the Sadducees; the latter, from whose ranks the high priests were mostly drawn, had their own traditions concerning the ritual.

"Do as We Tell You"

13. Mishnah Yoma, Chapter 1

1. Seven days before the Day of Atonement the high priest is removed from his home to the *Parhedrin* Chamber. Another priest is prepared to take his place, lest he become disqualified. . . .

2. All [these] seven days he sprinkles the blood and offers the incense and fixes the candles and places the head and leg [of the daily sacrifice on the altar]. On any other day, if he wishes to perform the offering, he may do so, for the high priest is first to offer a portion and first to take a portion.

3. Elders from among the elders of the *bet din* are placed at his disposal, and they read before him from the "order of the day" (Lev. 16). They say to him: "Sire, High Priest, read with your own mouth, lest you have forgotten or lest you have not studied." The day before the Day of Atonement, from morning, they stand him at the East Gate and have bulls, rams, and sheep pass before him, to familiarize and accustom him to the service.

4. All [these] seven days they do not deny him food or drink. The day before the Day of Atonement, from sundown,[7] they do not allow him to eat much, since food induces sleep.[8]

---

7. The Jewish calendrical day begins in the evening; this clause refers to the night before, twenty-four hours before the commencement of the holy day.
8. Should the high priest fall asleep, he might become defiled by a nocturnal emission.

5. The elders of the *bet din* placed him at the disposal of elders of the priesthood, who took him up to the loft of the *Avtinas* house. On taking their leave, they administered an oath to him, saying: "Sire, High Priest! We represent the *bet din,* and you represent us and the [entire] *bet din.* We administer this oath, [wherein you swear] by Him who caused His Name to dwell in this house [the Temple], [to the effect] that you will in no detail deviate from that which we have instructed you." He withdraws and weeps, and they withdraw and weep.

6. If he was a *hakham* [scholar], he expounds [the Torah]; if not, *talmide hakhamim* expound before him. If he is accustomed to read—he reads; if not—they read before him. What do they read from? From Job, Ezra and Chronicles. Zechariah b. Kevutal said: "Many times I read before him from Daniel."

7. If he tends to fall asleep, young priests snap their fingers before him, saying: "Sire, High Priest, take a turn standing up on the [marble] floor!" They thus occupy him until the time arrives for slaughtering [the morning sacrifice].

8. . . . By the time the crow called, the Temple court was filled with Israelites.

Rabbi Versus Priest
14. BT Yoma 71b

The emergent religious leadership of the Rabbis is represented here by Shemaiah and Avtalyon, the renowned teachers of Hillel and Shammai. In contradistinction to the priestly families with their superior lineage, the families of Shemaiah and Avtalyon were of gentile origin.

Our Rabbis taught: Once a certain high priest emerged from the Temple [at the end of the Day of Atonement service] and everyone followed him. When they saw Shemaiah and Avtalyon, they abandoned him and followed Shemaiah and Avtalyon. Finally, Shemaiah and Avtalyon came to take leave of the high priest. He said to them: "Welcome are the descendants of gentiles!" They answered: "Welcome are the descendants of gentiles, who act after the manner of Aaron [who loved peace and pursued it (Avot 1:12)]; and unwelcome is the descendant of Aaron, who does not act after the manner of Aaron."

Scholarship Versus Priesthood

15. Mishnah Horayot 3:6–8

The point of departure for this discussion is ceremonial precedence in matters of ritual. It moves on to rules of priority among claims for assistance. The high priest represents personal status based on lineage, dramatically contrasted with a mamzer *(bastard) scholar. (A fuller discussion of lineage and social hierarchy appears in C12.)*

6. Anything more frequent than some other thing takes precedence over that other; and anything more sanctified than some other thing takes precedence over that other. If the anointed [priest's] ox and the congregation's ox are waiting [to be offered], the anointed [priest's] ox takes precedence over the congregation's ox in all [details] of ritual performance.

   7. A man takes precedence over a woman for sustenance[9] and for the return of [his] lost property, whereas a woman takes precedence over a man for clothing and for rescue from captivity. If they are both subject to abuse, the man takes precedence.

   8. A priest takes precedence over a Levite, a Levite over an Israelite, an Israelite over a *mamzer,* a *mamzer* over a bondsman, a bondsman over a convert, a convert over a freed slave. When is this so? When they are all equal. But if a *mamzer* is a scholar [*talmid hakham*] and a high priest an ignoramus [*am ha-aretz*]—the *mamzer* scholar takes precedence over the ignorant high priest.

9. The word translated as "sustenance" can also be rendered "saving of life." See E. Rackman, "Priorities in the Right to Life," in *Tradition and Transition,* edited by J. Sacks (London: King's College Publications, 1986), 241–42.

Introduction

The Prophetic Calling

Prophecy as Political Challenge

God's Word: Truth, Falsehood, and Interpretation

Test of True Prophecy

9. Deuteronomy 18:9–22

The King's Prophets and the True Prophet

10. 1 Kings 22:2–38

Distinguishing True from False Prophecy

11. BT Sanhedrin 89a

Role of the Prophet and Criteria for Prophecy

12. Maimonides, MT Foundations of the Torah 7–8
    Commentary. Suzanne Last Stone, "Prophecy and Trust"

A Medieval Prophet: The Abulafia Controversy

Critique of Prophetic Claims

13. Solomon b. Abraham Adret (Rashba), *Responsa* 1:548

Defending His Own Claim to Prophecy

14. Abraham Abulafia, *Ve-Zot Lihudah*
    Commentary. Moshe Idel, "Can There Still Be Prophets?"

Introduction

Prophecy is surely the strangest and most complex of all the political-religious activities described in Jewish literature. It is a role enacted by figures as different as Moses, Deborah, Gideon, Samuel, Elijah, Jonah, Amos, Isaiah, and Ezekiel. Apart from the honorific title "prophet," what do these people have in common? And who are the "prophets" of Western political thought to whom they might be compared?

The literary prophets (whose speeches are collected in the biblical books from Amos to Malachi) are most readily recognizable to men and women familiar with political life in the West. Although the comparison is by no means exact, they are something like the social and moral critics who appear in classical, Christian, and contemporary secular settings: poets, preachers, publicists, intellectuals, and perhaps also demagogues, as Max Weber suggested in his *Ancient Judaism*. But the Jewish understanding of prophecy is considerably wider than this comparison suggests. For the prophet can also be a lawgiver (like Moses) or a judge (like Deborah and Samuel) or even a military leader (like Joshua and Gideon) or a king (like Saul).

These last figures are problematic; as warriors and rulers they appear mostly in the lowest "degree" of prophecy (according to Maimonides' ranking in *Guide* 2:45, not reprinted here), and their successors are excluded from the ranks altogether. After Solomon, the kings of Israel and Judah have no direct communication with God. In the days when God himself is said to have ruled Israel, the people he "raised up" were all of them charismatic and hence prophetic figures, who were granted a kind of divine intimacy: "The spirit of the Lord came upon him" (Judg. 14:6, referring to Samson). This period ends when the elders come to Samuel and demand a king who will "go out at our head and fight our battles." Charisma lingers in the young warriors chosen by God as Israel's first kings, although it seems a little surprising now: "Is Saul also among the prophets?" (1 Sam. 10:11). In fact, as we saw in Chapter 3, political power is at least potentially secular (concerned about what is autonomously determined to be prudent) from the moment the elders speak. Ruling and fighting are henceforth distinct from prophecy. David is the first of Israel's rulers to whom God sends prophets, who rebuke him for his sins. Samuel plays the same part for Saul, but no one plays this part for Samuel himself, or for any of the judges or for Moses or Joshua. These earlier figures combined the two roles that were separated in king and prophet. After the monarchy was established, prophets were raised up not to exercise power but to challenge the powerful.

But the relation between prophecy and power is still ambiguous. For Maimonides, the prophet takes the part of both philosopher and philosopher-king, providing the model of the ideal ruler: Moses is the only example. And yet the messiah himself, conceived as a warrior-king, David's rather than Moses' successor, does not seem to have prophetic powers, either in Maimonides' account or in more popular versions. Machiavelli's "prophet with a sword," his own activist version of an ideal ruler, is drawn in part (and rightly) from the Bible—Moses again provides the chief example—but this figure is never conceptualized in later Jewish literature. Among the Jews, from the time of the monarchy forward, prophecy is more closely tied to divine knowledge and critical judgment than to political office.

Solomon talks with God in 1 Kings 3, but what he asks for is wisdom, not prophetic power, and although these two are brought together by the sages, they are clearly separated in those biblical texts that date from or refer to the monarchic period. Kings are *challenged* by prophets (or at least by "true" prophets) and *counseled* by wise men. Wisdom is prudent, politic, worldly, and human; prophecy is radical, impolitic, utopian, and divine. Wisdom is at home in the royal court, prophecy in the desert and then in the streets and gates of the city and the temple courtyards. Rabbinic Judaism in some sense escapes this tension with its claim to be the joint heir of the wise and the prophets. But the escape is never complete, and we can see the rabbis defending themselves against the disruptive force of prophecy in the extraordinary confrontation of Adret (Rashba) and Abulafia in this chapter. The sages' critique of prophecy, which is crucial to their self-understanding, is included in Chapter 6.

What makes prophecy so dangerous is its divine origin. The prophet does not inherit his role, nor is he appointed by the king or ordained by the rabbis; he is called by God—like Moses at the burning bush. There is no official mediation or control. Prophets often report their own calling and describe its circumstances, for this is the crucial source of their authority; we reprint several of the texts here. Many of them describe the prophet's reluctance to heed God's call (see Exod. 3 and 4 for the classic case). There is no reason to think the reluctance feigned. When Moses says, "But, behold, [the people] will not believe me," he speaks the plain truth on behalf of himself and many of the prophets to come (Samuel is the most striking exception, instantly believed; see 1 Sam. 3:20). Once prophets are separated from political power, they find few friends among the powerful or, most of the time, among the people. Again and again, they are blamed for the dire messages they deliver and threatened with imprisonment and death, actually imprisoned (like Jeremiah), or killed (like Uriah, about whom we know nothing except what we are told in Jer. 26:20–23). And yet the divine call is inescapable, as Jonah learned; the prophet is seized by God, driven to speak his often menacing words. He is a political force beyond human control—and so he is a threat to every establishment, most clearly to the priests and kings of Israel and Judah, but also to the pharaoh in Egypt and the rulers of Nineveh.

Rulers who do not want to listen to God's prophets can always find someone else to listen to. The people want to hear "smooth words," says Isaiah (30:10), and there were plenty of prophets who were ready to provide them. The kings of Israel and Judah, who also wanted smooth words, found it easy to surround themselves with comforting and conformist prophets (like a modern ruler's academic advisers?) who regularly told them that they were doing well, whatever they were doing. The Bible makes it clear that from the moment the prophetic role was established, there was never a shortage of people to act it out.

Some way had to be found, then, to mark off the "true" prophets, critical and discomforting, from the "false" prophets, whose words were more likely to be welcomed. The arguments about true and false, in the Bible itself and in later literature, are very important: they address the question of trust in public life. Whom should we believe, whose advice and admonition should we heed, when many people, all talking at once, contend for the people's (and the king's) attention? The question continued to be debated long after "prophecy ceased in Israel," for it found no definitive answer—and who could know when God's call would be heard again? Moreover, there were always claimants to prophetic status, as Adret's text makes clear. So it will be useful to list five of the most interesting answers.

1. Deuteronomy suggests that only prophets whose prophecies come true are true prophets (Deut.18:22)—which is not very helpful at the moment of prophecy and leaves a lot of room for what we might think of as fortuitous or accidental fulfillment.

2. The sages (in Sanhedrin 89a) argue that only a prophet who speaks in his own voice can be trusted to speak for God. The contrast is with Ahab's four hundred prophets (1 Kings 22) who spoke their always smooth words in unison, "with one accord" [literally, "one mouth"]. Authenticity is a necessary, though not entirely sufficient, condition of true prophecy.

3. Maimonides claims that we can recognize the true prophet by his previously established reputation for wisdom and virtue. (Wisdom is here identified with philosophy, not only with prudence.) Whom else would God call but the wise and the virtuous? This is plausible enough in cases where we have prior knowledge of the prophet's character, although it is always possible that God sees wisdom and virtue where human eyes can't find it. But what are we to make of some obscure figure called from "following the flock," like Amos of Tekoa? What was Moses' reputation among the Hebrew slaves in Egypt when he first spoke to them? And what if God chooses to speak to humankind, as one of the Rabbis in Bava Batra suggests, through "children and fools"?

4. Another argument of Maimonides establishes only a negative criterion—necessary, again, but not sufficient to make the prophet fully trustworthy: he must not propose to change the laws of the Torah once these have been revealed. The aim here is to rule out charismatic antinomianism: "The law is thus and so, but I say unto you . . ."

5. Finally, there is the implicit argument of the prophetic books themselves, alluded to by Jeremiah in his denunciation of Hananiah: we know the true prophet by his courageous refusal to speak smoothly. He is a rough, unkempt, angry figure, the very embodiment of disruption (which is why Spinoza, defending secular political order, has no sympathy for him). The burden of proof, says Jeremiah, always rests on the prophet who "prophesieth of peace," for the truth about our collective future, given the way we live now, is likely to include "war and . . . evil and . . . pestilence" (Jer. 28:7–9).

It is a disturbing feature of these discussions, especially for modern readers, that they focus so narrowly on the standing of the prophets, their legitimacy, as it were, and not on the specific content of their messages. When the king's counselors, known by their worldly wisdom rather than their divine calling, give advice about this or that policy matter, they no doubt raise similar questions about trustworthiness (Absalom would have done well not to trust Hushai in 2 Sam. 17), but what they explicitly invite is a debate about the advice itself: Is this really what prudence requires in our present circumstances? The prophets, by contrast, do not invite a debate of that sort. Indeed, if they have actually been sent by God, there is no room for any debate at all. The only way to challenge them is to call their credentials into question, not the content of their prophecies.

Perhaps because of the profound impression left by the prophets on Jewish political thinking, their disappearance did not open the way for any explicit defense of worldly deliberation. But the sages call themselves wise and make room in the law for arguments about both prudence and principle. And they do everything they can to neutralize the disruptive force of prophecy. They are as bound as the prophets were to God's word, but they are its interpreters now, not its messengers. So claims about textual proofs replace claims about divine callings. Rabbinic interpretation replaces prophetic inspiration and turns out, as the chapters that follow will suggest, to be more accommodating (though never easily or entirely so) to political considerations.

The Prophetic Calling

The Kingdoms of Israel and Judea existed side by side, sometimes in cooperation, sometimes in rivalry, from the tenth century B.C.E. until their destruction at the hands of the Mesopotamian empires. Israel, the Northern Kingdom, was destroyed in the late eighth century; Judea in 586. This history provides the background for the activities and speeches of the classic literary prophets. Amos, though he was born in Judea, was active in the Kingdom of Israel in the decades preceding its demise. He prophesied in Bethel, one of the two main sanctuaries of the Northern Kingdom—and defended himself there against the charge that he was an interloper. Isaiah, a near contemporary, prophesied in Jerusalem, the Judean capital: his "call" reflects the Temple setting. A century and a half later, the prophet Jeremiah repeats the classic disclaimers of prophetic ambition (compare Exod. 3), but then provides an exalted account of prophetic fortitude.

The Calling—I
1. Amos 7:10–17

Amaziah, the priest of Bethel, sent this message to King Jeroboam of Israel: "Amos is conspiring against you within the House of Israel. The country cannot endure the things he is saying. For Amos has said 'Jeroboam shall die by the sword, and Israel shall be exiled from its soil.'"

Amaziah also said to Amos, "Seer, off with you to the land of Judah! Earn your living there, and do your prophesying there. But don't ever prophesy again at Bethel; for it is a king's sanctuary and a royal palace." Amos answered Amaziah: "I am not a prophet, and I am not a prophet's disciple. I am a cattle breeder and a tender of sycamore. But the Lord took me away from following the flock, and the Lord said to me, 'Go, prophesy to My people Israel.' And so, hear the word of the Lord. You say I must not prophesy about the House of Israel or preach about the House of Isaac; but this, I swear, is what the Lord said: Your wife shall play the harlot in the town, your sons and daughters shall fall by the sword, and your land shall be divided up with a measuring line. And you yourself shall die on unclean soil; for Israel shall be exiled from its soil."

The Calling—II
2. Isaiah 6

In the year that King Uzziah died, I beheld my Lord seated on a high and lofty throne; and the skirts of His robe filled the Temple. Seraphs stood in attendance on Him. Each of them had six wings: with two he covered his face, with two he covered his legs, and with two he would fly.

And one would call to the other,
"Holy, holy, holy!
The Lord of Hosts!
His presence fills all the earth!"

The doorposts would shake at the sound of the one who called, and the House kept filling with smoke. I cried,

"Woe is me; I am lost!
For I am a man of unclean lips.
And I live among a people
Of unclean lips;
Yet my own eyes have beheld
The King Lord of Hosts."

Then one of the seraphs flew over to me with a live coal, which he had taken from the altar with a pair of tongs. He touched it to my lips and declared,

"Now that this has touched your lips,
Your guilt shall depart
And your sin be purged away."

Then I heard the voice of my Lord saying, "Whom shall I send? Who will go for us?" And I said, "Here am I; send me." And He said, "Go say to that people:

" 'Hear, indeed, but do not understand;
See, indeed, but do not grasp.'
Dull that people's mind,
Stop its ears,
And seal its eyes —
Lest, seeing with its eyes
And hearing with its ears,
It also grasp with its mind,
And repent and save itself." [1]

I asked, "How long, my Lord?" And He replied:

"Till towns lie waste without inhabitants
And houses without people,
And the ground lies waste and desolate —

---

1. This can be understood either as a wish that the people not be allowed to repent and thereby escape their due punishment or, perhaps, as a bitter recognition that they are beyond remorse.

For the Lord will banish the population—
And deserted sites are many
In the midst of the land.

"But while a tenth part yet remains in it, it shall repent. It shall be ravaged like the terebinth and the oak, of which stumps are left even when they are felled: its stump shall be a holy seed."

The Calling—III

3. Jeremiah 1:1–10, 17–19

The words of Jeremiah son of Hilkiah, one of the priests at Anathoth in the territory of Benjamin. The word of the Lord came to him in the days of King Josiah son of Amon of Judah, in the thirteenth year of his reign, and throughout the days of King Jehoiakim son of Josiah of Judah, and until the end of the eleventh year of King Zedekiah son of Josiah of Judah, when Jerusalem went into exile in the fifth month.

The word of the Lord came to me:
Before I created you in the womb, I selected you;
Before you were born, I consecrated you;
I appointed you a prophet concerning the nations.
I replied:
Ah, Lord God!
I don't know how to speak,
For I am still a boy.
And the Lord said to me:
Do not say, "I am still a boy,"
But go wherever I send you
And speak whatever I command you.
Have no fear of them,
For I am with you to deliver you
—declares the Lord.

The Lord put out His hand and touched my mouth, and the Lord said to me: Herewith I put My words into your mouth.

> See, I appoint you this day
> Over nations and kingdoms:
> To uproot and to pull down,
> To destroy and to overthrow,
> To build and to plant.
>
> .   .   .
>
> So you, gird up your loins,
> Arise and speak to them
> All that I command you.
> Do not break down before them,
> Lest I break you before them.
> I make you this day
> A fortified city,
> And an iron pillar,
> And bronze walls,
> Against the whole land—
> Against Judah's kings and officers,
> And against its priests and citizens.
> They will attack you,
> But they shall not overcome you;
> For I am with you—declared the Lord—to save you.

Prophecy as Political Challenge

Naboth's Vineyard: Challenging the King
4. I Kings 21:1–20

Elijah is representative of those early prophets whose deeds are narrated in the historical books of the Bible (mainly Samuel and Kings). He is portrayed as the arch critic of King Ahab of Israel, who reigned in the first half of the ninth century B.C.E. Earlier chapters in 1 Kings tell of their confrontations over the worship of Baal, introduced by Ahab's foreign wife, Jezebel of Sidon. Here Ahab is defied by his subject Naboth, who refuses to part with his ancestral estate. The story reflects the legal situation in ancient Israel: the king does not own the land.

Naboth the Jezreelite owned a vineyard in Jezreel, adjoining the palace of King Ahab of Samaria. Ahab said to Naboth, "Give me your vineyard, so that I may have it as a vegetable garden, since it is right next to my palace. I will give you a better vineyard in exchange; or, if you prefer, I will pay you the price in money." But Naboth replied, "The Lord forbid that I should give up to you what I have inherited from my fathers!" Ahab went home dispirited and sullen because of the answer that Naboth the Jezreelite had given him: "I will not give up to you what I have inherited from my fathers!" He lay down on his bed and turned away his face, and he would not eat. His wife Jezebel came to him and asked him, "Why are you so dispirited that you won't eat?" So he told her, "I spoke to Naboth the Jezreelite, and proposed to him, 'Sell me your vineyard for money, or if you prefer, I'll give you another vineyard in exchange'; but he answered, 'I will not give my vineyard to you.'" His wife Jezebel said to him, "Now is the time to show yourself king over Israel. Rise and eat something, and be cheerful; I will get the vineyard of Naboth the Jezreelite for you."

So she wrote letters in Ahab's name and sealed them with his seal, and sent the letters to the elders and the nobles who lived in the same town with Naboth. In the letters she wrote as follows: "Proclaim a fast and seat Naboth at the front of the assembly. And seat two scoundrels opposite him, and let them testify against him: 'You have reviled God and king!' Then take him out and stone him to death."

His townsmen—the elders and nobles who lived in his town—did as Jezebel had instructed them, just as was written in the letters she had sent them: They proclaimed a fast and seated Naboth at the front of the assembly. Then the two scoundrels came and sat down opposite him; and the scoundrels testified against Naboth publicly as follows: "Naboth has reviled God and king." Then they took him outside the town and stoned him to death. Word was sent to Jezebel: "Naboth has been stoned to death." As soon as

Jezebel heard that Naboth had been stoned to death, she said to Ahab, "Go and take possession of the vineyard which Naboth the Jezreelite refused to sell you for money; for Naboth is no longer alive, he is dead." When Ahab heard that Naboth was dead, Ahab set out for the vineyard of Naboth the Jezreelite to take possession of it.

Then the word of the Lord came to Elijah the Tishbite: "Go down and confront King Ahab of Israel who [resides] in Samaria. He is now in Naboth's vineyard; he has gone down there to take possession of it. Say to him . . . 'Would you murder and take possession? Thus said the Lord: In the very place where the dogs lapped up Naboth's blood, the dogs will lap up your blood too.'"

And Ahab said to Elijah, "So you have found me, my enemy?" "Yes, I have found you," he replied. "Because you have committed yourself to doing what is evil in the sight of the Lord."

Jeremiah on Trial
5. Jeremiah 26

The sovereignty of the Judean kingdom was hostage to the shifting balance of power between the great empires of Mesopotamia and Egypt (cf. 2 Kings 23:29–25:7). Jeremiah's warnings of destruction should be seen in the context of his participation in the political debate over Judea's foreign policy and his explicit calls for Judea to accept the rule of the king of Babylon (cf. Jer. 27). Jeremiah has friends at court who protect him against his political enemies. This text reports an impromptu trial in the Temple courtyard. Note the appeal to the precedent of Micah, a rare instance of biblical cross-reference (see §7).

At the beginning of the reign of King Jehoiakim son of Josiah of Judah, this word came from the Lord:

Thus said the Lord: Stand in the court of the House of the Lord, and speak to [the men of] all the towns of Judah, who are coming to worship in the House of the Lord, all the words which I command you to speak to them. Do not omit anything. Perhaps they will listen and turn back, each from his evil way, that I may renounce the punishment I am planning to bring upon them for their wicked acts.

"Say to them: Thus said the Lord: If you do not obey Me, abiding by the Teaching that I have set before you, heeding the words of My servants the prophets whom I have been sending to you persistently—but you have not heeded—then I will make this House like Shiloh,[2] and I will make this city a curse for all the nations of earth."

The priests and prophets and all the people heard Jeremiah speaking these words in the House of the Lord. And when Jeremiah finished speaking all that the Lord had commanded him to speak to all the people, the priests and the prophets and all the people seized him, shouting, "You shall die! How dare you prophesy in the name of the Lord that this House shall become like Shiloh and this city be made desolate, without inhabitants?" And all the people crowded about Jeremiah in the House of the Lord.

When the officials of Judah heard about this, they went up from the king's palace to the House of the Lord and held a session at the entrance of the New Gate of the House of the Lord. The priests and prophets said to the officials and to all the people, "This man deserves the death penalty, for he has prophesied against this city, as you yourselves have heard."

Jeremiah said to the officials and to all the people, "It was the Lord who sent me to prophesy against this House and this city all the words you heard. Therefore mend your ways and your acts, and heed the Lord your God, that the Lord may renounce the punishment He has decreed for you. As for me, I am in your hands: do to me what seems good and right to you. But know that if you put me to death, you and this city and its inhabitants will be guilty of shedding the blood of an innocent man. For in truth the Lord has sent me to you, to speak all these words to you."

Then the officials and all the people said to the priests and prophets, "This man does not deserve the death penalty, for he spoke to us in the name of the Lord our God."

2. The first enduring religious center before the construction of Solomon's temple in Jerusalem; see 1 Sam. 2–4.

And some of the elders of the land arose and said to the entire as-
semblage of the people, "Micah the Morashtite, who prophesied in the days
of King Hezekiah of Judah, said to all the people of Judah: 'Thus said the
Lord of Hosts:

'Zion shall be plowed as a field,
Jerusalem shall become heaps of ruins
And the Temple Mount a shrine in the woods.'

"Did King Hezekiah of Judah, and all Judah, put him to death? Did
he not rather fear the Lord and implore the Lord, so that the Lord renounced
the punishment He had decreed against them? We are about to do great injury to ourselves!"

There was also a man prophesying in the name of the Lord, Uriah
son of Shemaiah from Kiriath-jearim, who prophesied against this city and
this land the same things as Jeremiah. King Jehoiakim and all his warriors
and all the officials heard about his address, and the king wanted to put him
to death. Uriah heard of this and fled in fear, and came to Egypt. But King
Jehoiakim sent men to Egypt, Elnathan son of Achbor and men with him to
Egypt. They took Uriah out of Egypt and brought him to King Jehoiakim,
who had him put to the sword and his body thrown into the burial place of
the common people. However, Ahikam son of Shaphan protected Jeremiah,
so that he was not handed over to the people for execution.

Attacking Ritual
6. Isaiah 1:10–20

*This is one of the classic examples of prophetic criticism, condemning ritual observance
when it is accompanied by injustice and oppression.*

Hear the word of the Lord,
You chieftains of Sodom;
Give ear to our God's instruction,

You folk of Gomorrah!

"What need have I of all your sacrifices?"

Says the Lord.

"I am sated with burnt offerings of rams,

And suet of fatlings,

And blood of bulls;

And I have no delight

In lambs and he-goats.

That you come to appear before Me—

Who asked that of you?

Trample My courts no more;

Bringing oblations is futile.

Incense is offensive to Me.

New Moon and sabbath,

Proclaiming of solemnities,

Assemblies with iniquity,

I cannot abide.

Your new moons and fixed seasons

Fill me with loathing;

They are become a burden to Me,

I cannot endure them.

And when you lift up your hands,

I will turn My eyes away from you;

Though you pray at length,

I will not listen.

Your hands are stained with blood[3]—

Wash yourselves clean;

Put your evil doings

Away from My sight.

Cease to do evil;

Learn to do good.

Devote yourselves to justice;

Aid the wronged.

---

3. New JPS: "crime."

Uphold the rights of the orphan;
Defend the cause of the widow.

"Come, let us reach an understanding—says the Lord.
Be your sins like crimson,
They can turn snow-white;
Be they red as dyed wool,
They can become like fleece."
If, then, you agree and give heed,
You will eat the good things of the earth;
But if you refuse and disobey,
You will be devoured [by] the sword.
For it was the Lord who spoke.

Denunciation of the Ruling Powers
7. Micah 3:9–12

Micah's prophecies, like those of his contemporary Isaiah, are a religious and social critique of Judea and Jerusalem. Unlike Isaiah, however, Micah envisages the total destruction of God's city and temple. It is to this effect that he is cited about a century and a half later during Jeremiah's trial (§5).

Hear this, you rulers of the House of Jacob,
You chiefs of the House of Israel,
Who detest justice
And make crooked all that is straight,
Who build Zion with blood,[4]
Jerusalem with iniquity!
Her rulers judge for gifts,
Her priests give rulings for a fee,

---

4. New JPS: "crime."

And her prophets divine for pay;
Yet they rely upon the Lord, saying,
"The Lord is in our midst;
No calamity shall overtake us."
Assuredly, because of you
Zion shall be plowed as a field,
And Jerusalem shall become heaps of ruins,
And the Temple Mount
A shrine in the woods.

Subversiveness of Prophecy

8. Baruch Spinoza, *Theological-Political Treatise,* Chapter 18

Tractatus Theologico-Politicus, translated by Samuel Shirley (Leiden: E. J. Brill, 1991), p. 274.

In this chapter of the Treatise *Spinoza analyzes the fall of the ancient Jewish state. He argues that prophecy, because it undermines civil order, was one of the causes of the fall. In his own political context, the subversive prophets are probably the sectarian opponents of the rulers of the Dutch republic.*

It is worthy of remark that the prophets, men of private station, in exercising their freedom to warn, to rebuke and to censure, succeeded in annoying men rather than reforming them, whereas men who were admonished or castigated by kings were more apt to turn from their ways. Indeed, even devout kings often found prophets intolerable because of their assumption of authority to decide what action was pious or impious, and even to berate the kings themselves if the latter had the hardihood to transact any business, public or private, against their judgement. King Asa, who according to Scripture was a pious ruler, consigned the prophet Hanani to prison (2 Chron. 16) for venturing to reproach him too freely in the matter of the treaty made with the king of Aramaea. There are other examples to show that such freedom brought religion more harm than good, not to mention that great civil wars also originated from the prophets' retention of so important a right.

Commentary. Prophetic Criticism and Its Targets

Spinoza's critique of prophecy reflects his commitment, almost as strong as Hobbes's, to political stability. He is certainly right to describe the prophets as disruptive. The texts from Jeremiah, Isaiah, and Micah are clear enough (and there are many other texts like these, especially from Amos). Speech of this sort undermines authority. It challenges the status quo and the people who benefit from it.

But these prophets are not agitators in the modern sense. They don't aim to create a political or social movement; they make no effort to organize their audience; they aren't looking for the response that Shakespeare's Marc Antony wins from the Roman crowd. On the other hand, they are also unlike modern social critics, who sit in their studies writing books and magazine articles and can hardly be imagined speaking in the streets.

The prophets are religious preachers, something like contemporary revivalists, and although they criticize the whole of society and hope for its moral transformation, their precise demand is for individual *teshuvah*—"repentance"; the literal meaning is "a turning back" to the laws of the covenant. What they want is that people repent of their sins (sometimes the emphasis is on idolatry, sometimes on injustice and oppression) and then turn, as it were, in place: each person is to enact the covenant in his or her sphere of activity. The goal is a series of turnings, not a change of political regime—although if princes and judges repent, the effect may be something like a change of regime. "Perhaps they will listen and turn back," says Jeremiah, "each from his evil way" (26:3).

The whole of Israelite society is indicted; some of the prophets imagine a divine lawsuit: God against Israel. But prophetic criticism is often much more specific, addressed explicitly to the rich and the powerful:

The Lord will bring this charge
Against the elders and officers of His people:
It is you who have ravaged the vineyard. (Isa. 3:14)

Or, in one of the texts that we have chosen for this chapter: "Hear this," says Micah, "you rulers of the House of Jacob" (3:9). Amos, Isaiah, and Jeremiah have been endlessly quoted in the long history of the political Left for their attacks on the upper classes, "who trample the heads of the poor/Into the dust of the ground" (Amos 2:7). But, again, none of the prophets takes aim at the political or social hierarchy, only at the individual men and women who occupy its high places; there is no prophetic program for a democratic politics or a classless society. All that the prophets demand—but how radical they make it sound!—is that the rich stop trampling the poor and that the powerful (judges, officials, kings) act forcefully to protect the weak.

Their criticism is mixed with threats—indeed, it is the threats that constitute the literal content of the prophecies. Disorder and riot are not what is prophesied here, nor social revolution, nor even the civil wars that Spinoza worried about; the prophets speak instead of divine anger and destruction. The fierceness of this anger is perhaps the most striking feature of many of the biblical texts. But what is less often noticed is its commonly unfocused character.

Elijah is an exception; he is almost as precise as we expect judges to be in delivering a sentence: Ahab and his dynasty, he says, will suffer God's anger. More often, however, the whole nation is threatened with destruction and exile—even when it is only the sins of the rich and powerful that figure in the texts. The rulers, the priests, and even the prophets take bribes and act unjustly, says Micah, and so "Zion shall be plowed as a field/And Jerusalem shall become heaps of ruins."

The popular hatred of prophets, described in the Jeremiah text, probably derives from lines like these—and it hardly seems entirely unwarranted. Why should the people as a whole suffer for the sins of the few? This question seems to have been asked at the time, for in a passage that echoes the story of Abraham at Sodom, Jeremiah tells his audience that they can

> Roam the streets of Jerusalem
> Search its squares,
> Look about and take note:
> You will not find a man,
> There is none who acts justly,
> Who seeks integrity—
> That I should pardon her. (5:1)

Still, the sins of ordinary people don't seem large enough to warrant the total destruction of the city. Perhaps the people are morally required to rise up against rich and powerful sinners, but, as I have said, nothing like that is ever urged upon them; even the halakhic requirement of "protest" (see ℂ17) is not asserted in the prophetic texts. So how can the punishment of the people be just?

Collective punishment is one of the critical issues of the biblical writings. It is both strongly affirmed and strongly denied. But the prophets whose texts are reprinted here seem to have no trouble with it—not at least as a truth about Israel's future (nor does it trouble them when they prophesy against the "nations"). And they are right in this important sense: nations do experience terrible calamities because of the conduct of their richest and most powerful members. It is odd, however, that these calamities should be described as punishments, and God as their agent. It is even odder that none of the prophets rejected Jeremiah's argument and took upon himself Abraham's role at Sodom.

Moses interceded for the people after the golden calf incident (which was not the sin of the few but of the many), and several of the literary prophets describe themselves playing the same role. But they ask for mercy, not for justice—as when Amos "beseeches" God (7:5): "By whom shall Jacob arise, for he is small?" They seem to accept what is not acceptable: that Zion plowed and Jerusalem in ruins represent a just response to oppression and corruption.

Their model is almost certainly the "idolatrous city" (see Deut. 13), where the sin is said to be general and the punishment is collective and total (some of the prophets, however, Amos and Micah above all, don't have much to say about idolatry). A major problem is passed over here: even if idolatry could be the sin of the whole people, great and small alike (but are the children also idolators?), oppression can't be—for there are always guiltless victims, oppressed men and women; there is always "the blood of the innocent" (Jer. 22:17). The prophets speak with extraordinary courage on behalf of the oppressed against the powers-that-be. But they don't speak, as Abraham did, against the Power-That-Is: "Will You sweep away the innocent along with the guilty?" (Gen. 18:23).

Michael Walzer

God's Word: Truth, Falsehood, and Interpretation

The following texts all deal with the problem of false prophecy. Deuteronomy represents the first effort to distinguish prophetic truth and falsehood. 1 Kings provides what became a paradigmatic case, frequently cited and discussed: Micaiah facing King Jehoshaphat of Judah and Ahab of Israel. In BT Sanhedrin we find an early effort to develop a systematic distinction, while Maimonides, drawing freely on the Bible and the Rabbis, works out a comprehensive legal and philosophical account of prophecy.

Test of True Prophecy
9. Deuteronomy 18:9–22

When you enter the land that the Lord your God is giving you, you shall not learn to imitate the abhorrent practices of those nations. Let no one be found among you who consigns his son or daughter to the fire, or who is an augur, a soothsayer, a diviner, a sorcerer, one who casts spells, or one who consults ghosts or familiar spirits, or one who inquires of the dead. For anyone who does such things is abhorrent to the Lord, and it is because of these abhorrent things that the Lord your God is dispossessing them before you. You must be wholehearted with the Lord your God. Those nations that you are about to dispossess do indeed resort to soothsayers and augurs; to you, however, the Lord your God has not assigned the like.

The Lord your God will raise up for you a prophet from among your own people, like myself [Moses]; him you shall heed. This is just what you asked of the Lord your God at Horeb, on the day of the Assembly, saying, "Let me not hear the voice of the Lord my God any longer or see this wondrous fire any more, lest I die." Whereupon the Lord said to me, "They have done well in speaking thus. I will raise up a prophet for them from among their own people, like yourself: I will put my words in his mouth and he will speak to them all that I command him; and if anybody fails to heed the words he speaks in My name, I myself will call him to account. But any prophet who presumes to speak in My name a word[5] that I did not command him to utter, or who speaks in the name of other gods—that prophet shall die." And should you ask yourselves, "How can we know that the word was not spoken by the Lord?"—if the prophet speaks in the name of the Lord and the word does not come true, that word was not spoken by the Lord; the prophet has uttered it presumptuously: do not stand in dread of him.

The King's Prophets and the True Prophet
10. 1 Kings 22:2–38

In the third year, King Jehoshaphat of Judah came to visit the king of Israel. The king of Israel said to his courtiers, "You know that Ramoth-gilead belongs to us, and yet we do nothing to recover it from the hands of the king of Aram." And he said to Jehoshaphat, "Will you come with me to battle at Ramoth-gilead?" Jehoshaphat answered the king of Israel, "I will do what you do; my troops shall be your troops, my horses shall be your horses." But Jehoshaphat said further to the king of Israel, "Please, first inquire of the Lord."

So the king of Israel gathered the prophets, about four hundred men, and asked them, "Shall I march upon Ramoth-gilead for battle, or shall I not?" "March," they said, "and the Lord will deliver [it] into Your Majesty's hands." Then Jehoshaphat asked, "Isn't there another prophet of the Lord here through whom we can inquire?" And the king of Israel answered Jehoshaphat, "There is one more man through whom we can inquire of the Lord; but I hate him, because he never prophesies anything good for me, but only misfortune—Micaiah son of Imlah." But King Jehoshaphat said, "Don't say that, Your Majesty." So the king of Israel summoned an officer and said, "Bring Micaiah son of Imlah at once."

The king of Israel and King Jehoshaphat of Judah were seated on their thrones, arrayed in their robes, on the threshing floor at the entrance

5. New JPS here and below: "oracle."

of the gate of Samaria; and all the prophets were prophesying before them. Zedekiah son of Kenaanah had provided himself with iron horns; and he said, "Thus said the Lord: With these you shall gore the Arameans till you make an end of them." And all the other prophets were prophesying similarly, "March upon Ramoth-gilead and triumph! The Lord will deliver it into Your Majesty's hands."

The messenger who had gone to summon Micaiah said to him: "Look, the words of the prophets are with one accord [literally, "one mouth"] favorable to the king. Let your word be like that of the rest of them; speak a favorable word." "As the Lord lives," Micaiah answered, "I will speak only what the Lord tells me." When he came before the king, the king said to him, "Micaiah, shall we march upon Ramoth-gilead for battle, or shall we not?" He answered him, "March and triumph! The Lord will deliver [it] into your Majesty's hands." The king said to him, "How many times must I adjure you to tell me nothing but the truth in the name of the Lord?" Then he said, "I saw all Israel scattered over the hills like sheep without a shepherd; and the Lord said, 'These have no master; let everyone return to his home in safety.' " "Didn't I tell you," said the king of Israel to Jehoshaphat, "that he would not prophesy good fortune for me, but only misfortune?" But [Micaiah] said "I call upon you to hear the word of the Lord! I saw the Lord seated upon His throne, with all the host of heaven standing in attendance to the right and to the left of Him. The Lord asked, 'Who will entice Ahab so that he will march and fall at Ramoth-gilead?' The one said thus and another said thus, until a certain spirit came forward and stood before the Lord and said, 'I will entice him.' 'How?' the Lord asked him. And he replied, 'I will go out and be a lying spirit in the mouth of all his prophets.' Then He said, 'You will entice and you will prevail. Go out and do it.' So the Lord has put a lying spirit in the mouth of all these prophets of yours; for the Lord has decreed disaster upon you."

Thereupon Zedekiah son of Kenaanah stepped up and struck Micaiah on the cheek, and demanded, "Which way did the spirit of the Lord pass from me to speak with you?" And Micaiah replied, "You'll find out on the day when you try to hide in the innermost room." Then the king of Israel said, "Take Micaiah and turn him over to Amon, the city's governor, and to Prince Joash, and say, 'The king's orders are: Put this fellow in prison, and let his fare be scant bread and scant water until I come home safe.'" To which Micaiah retorted, "If you ever come home safe, the Lord has not spoken through me." He said further, "Listen, all you peoples!"

So the king of Israel and King Jehoshaphat of Judah marched upon Ramoth-gilead. The king of Israel said to Jehoshaphat, "Disguise yourself and go into the battle; but you, wear your robes." So the king of Israel went into the battle disguised. Now the king of Aram had instructed his thirty-two chariot officers: "Don't attack anyone, small or great, except the king of Israel." So when the chariot officers saw Jehoshaphat, whom they took for the king of Israel, they turned upon him to attack him, and Jehoshaphat cried out. And when the chariot officers became aware that he was not the king of Israel, they turned back from pursuing him. Then a man drew his bow at random and he hit the king of Israel between the plates of the armor; and he said to his charioteer, "Turn the horses around and get me behind the lines; I'm wounded." The battle raged all day long, and the king remained propped up in the chariot facing Aram; the blood from the wound ran down into the hollow of the chariot, and at dusk he died. As the sun was going down, a shout went through the army: "Every man to his own town! Every man to his own district."

So the king died and was brought to Samaria. They buried the king in Samaria, and they flushed out the chariot at the pool of Samaria. Thus the dogs lapped up his blood and the whores bathed [in it], in accordance with the word that the Lord had spoken.

Distinguishing True from False Prophecy
11. BT Sanhedrin 89a

Our rabbis taught: Three are put to death by a human court, while three [others are subject to] death by heaven.

One who prophesies that which he did not hear, or that which was not said to him, or who prophesies in the name of an idol, is put to death by a human court.

One who holds back [literally, "represses"] his prophecy, or one who disregards the words of a prophet, or a prophet who transgresses against his own words, is [subject to] death by heaven.

From where does [all] this derive? Rav Yehudah said, quoting Rav: Scripture says, "But any prophet who presumes to speak in My name" (Deut. 18:20)—this refers to one who prophesies that which he did not hear; "that I did not command *him,*"—implying, "but that I did command his fellow"— this refers to one who prophesies that which was not said to him. And he "who speaks in the name of other gods"—this refers to one who prophesies in the name of an idol. [Regarding these three] it is written, "that prophet shall die."

One who holds back his prophecy, or one who disregards the words of a prophet, or one who transgresses against his own words, is [subject to] death by heaven—as written, "if anybody fails to heed the words he speaks in My name" (Deut. 18:19), which can also be rendered, "fails to make heard." "I myself will call him to account"—by heaven.

"One who prophesies that which he did not hear"—such as Zedekiah son of Kenaanah. . . . [But] what could he have done? The [lying] spirit was misleading him![6] . . . —He ought to have scrutinized [the matter] in light of what Rabbi Yitzhak said. For Rabbi Yitzhak said: One message may come to several prophets, yet no two prophets convey their messages in the same way. [For example,] Obadiah (1:3) said, "Your arrogant heart has seduced you," while Jeremiah (49:16) said, "Your horrible nature has seduced you, your arrogant heart." [In the case of] these [four hundred prophets], however, since they were all speaking identically, it could be concluded that their speech is worthless.—But perhaps he did not know the teaching of Rabbi Yitzhak?—Jehoshaphat was present, and he told them.[7] As written, "Then Jehoshaphat asked, 'Isn't there another prophet of the Lord here?'" (1 Kings 22:7)—[The king of Israel] asked him: "Aren't all these here?" Jehoshaphat answered: "Thus runs a tradition I hold from my grandfather's house: 'One message may come to several prophets, yet no two prophets convey their messages in the same way.'"

"One who prophesies that which was not said to him"—such as Ha-

6. See §10.
7. The Rabbis standardly depict righteous Davidic kings as great scholars.

naniah ben Azzur. Jeremiah stood in the upper marketplace and proclaimed, "Thus said the Lord of Hosts: I am going to break the bow of Elam" (Jer. 49:35). Hananiah, on his own, reasoned a fortiori: If with regard to Elam, who merely came to assist Babylon, God said, "I am going to break the bow of Elam"—how much more so the Babylonians themselves! So he came to the lower marketplace and proclaimed, "Thus said the Lord of Hosts . . . I am going to break the yoke of the king of Babylon" (Jer. 28:2).

     Rav Papa said to Abaye: That was not said to his fellow [prophet] either!—He answered: Since it is legitimate to reason a fortiori, it is as though it [the implication] had been said; yet to him it was not said.

Role of the Prophet and Criteria for Prophecy

12. Maimonides, MT Foundations of the Torah 7–8

Translated by Bernard Septimus, forthcoming in the Yale Judaica Series (Yale University Press).

The Jewish tradition includes many accounts of prophecy, reflecting a wide range of spiritual orientations; many do not share Maimonides' rationalistic portrayal. Within the halakhic tradition, however, the chapters in Maimonides' code regarding prophecy were especially influential. His discussion has a twofold purpose. On the one hand, he presents (true) prophecy as a perennial religious ideal, and on the other hand, he highlights the unique truth of Mosaic prophecy. The latter is of crucial political significance because it establishes the eternal authority of the Torah.

     Chapter 7

     1. One of the foundations of religion is to know that God causes prophecy in humans. But prophecy comes into effect only in a sage [*hakham*], possessed of great wisdom, a champion in [regulating] his moral qualities—never mastered by his nonrational part, but ever, by his reason, mastering it—[and] possessed of a most ample and sound intellect. When a person, brimming with all these qualities [and] sound of body, enters Pardes [i.e., the

study of philosophy],[8] becomes absorbed in its great and wondrous topics (having an intellect fit to understand and apprehend [them]), progressively sanctifies himself, forsakes the ways of the crowd who walk in temporal darkness, continually girds himself and trains his soul to have no thought whatever of any idle matter nor of temporal vanities and wiles, but whose mind is ever turned upward, fixed below the Throne [i.e., God in His sublimity] in contemplation of those holy and pure Forms, and he reflects upon the full wisdom of the Holy One, blessed be He, [evident in everything] from the First Form to Earth's center, and discerns thereby His grandeur—straightaway the Holy Spirit rests upon him. And when the spirit rests upon him, his soul partakes of the angelic rank called *Ishim* [i.e., the Active Intellect], he is transformed, and understands, rationally, that he is no longer as he was, but has rather been elevated above the rank of other wise persons, as it is said with regard to Saul: "And you shall prophesy[9] with them and be turned into another person" (1 Sam. 10:6).

2. Prophets are of diverse ranks. Just as in [the realm of] wisdom, one sage can be greater than his fellow, so too in [the realm of] prophecy, [one] prophet [can be] greater than [another] prophet. But all perceive the prophetic vision nowise but in a dream, [i.e.,] a night-vision, or, during the day, after being overcome by a trance, as it is said: "I make Myself known to him in a [daytime] vision [or] speak to him in a dream" (Num. 12:6). [The experience of] all of them, when prophesying, [is that] their limbs tremble, [their] bodily force is enfeebled, and their [ordinary] mental images are disrupted, leaving the mind free to comprehend what it sees, as it is said, regarding Abraham, "And behold a great, dark fear fell over him" (Gen. 15:12), and as it is said regarding Daniel: "For my radiant appearance was fearfully changed, and I retained no strength" (Dan. 10:8).

3. The things communicated to a prophet in a prophetic vision are done so in figurative mode: and straightaway the interpretation of the figure is impressed upon his mind in [that] prophetic vision, so that he understands

---

8. The term *pardes* (literally, "grove"), etymologically linked to "paradise," appears in Rabbinic accounts of the search for esoteric knowledge (cf. BT Hagigah 14b). Maimonides identifies this with philosophy; cf. MT Foundations of the Torah 4:13.

9. To prophesy, on this understanding of the verse and in Maimonides' usage in this chapter generally, is to experience a prophetic state, not to issue prophetic pronouncements.

what it signifies. For example: the ladder that Jacob, our father, saw, with angels ascending and descending it (Gen. 28:12), which was a figure for the [foreign] empires and subjugation [of Israel]. Other examples: the "living creatures" seen by Ezekiel (Ezek. 1:5), the boiling pot and almond rod seen by Jeremiah (Jer. 1:13, 11), the scroll seen by Ezekiel (Ezek. 2:9), and the *efa* [measure] seen by Zechariah (Zech. 5:6). So too the other prophets. Sometimes they say [both] the figure and its interpretation, as in the instances mentioned above; sometimes they say only the interpretation; and sometimes they say only the figure, without interpretation, as in some of the words of Ezekiel and Zechariah. But all of them prophesy in figure and symbolic mode.

4. None of the prophets prophesy at will. They rather focus their minds, remain joyful and glad of heart, and withdraw [into inner concentration]. For prophecy rests [upon the prophet] neither in a state of sadness nor in a state of lassitude, but in a state of joy. That is why "the sons of the prophets" have "before them harp and timbrel, pipe and lyre" (1 Sam. 10:5) as they seek prophecy. . . .

5. Those who seek to prophesy are the ones called "sons of the prophets." Though they focus their minds, the *Shekhinah* [i.e., the prophetic spirit] may or may not come to rest upon them.

6. All of the above constitute the prophetic mode for all prophets, early and late, save Moses, our master and master of all prophets. How does the prophecy of Moses differ from [that of] all other prophets? All [other] prophets [prophesy] in a dream or vision [state], whereas Moses, our master, [prophesied] awake and erect, as it is said: "And when Moses went into the Tent of Meeting to speak to Him, he heard the Voice" (Num. 7:89). All [other] prophets [prophesy] through the intermediacy of an angel, which is why they perceive what they do in figure and symbol; [whereas] Moses, our master, [prophesied] without the intermediacy of an angel, as it is said, "With him I speak mouth to mouth" (Num. 12:8); and it is said, "And the Lord spoke to Moses face to face" (Exod. 33:11). It is further said, "And he perceives the [true] form of the Lord" (Num. 12:8), which is to say that there is no figure; he rather perceives the matter as it truly is without symbol, without figure. This is what the Torah [means when it] testifies concerning him, "Through a [mental] vision without symbols" (Num. 12:8)—[namely]

that he prophesies not in symbol, but in [a rational] perception that discerns the matter as it truly is. All [other] prophets dissolve in fear and terror [when prophesying]. Not so Moses, our master. That is what Scripture [means when it] says [that God spoke to Moses] "As a man speaks to his fellow" (Exod. 33:11): just as a person is not terrified to hear his friend's words, so did Moses' mind have the strength to comprehend the prophetic words, while standing his ground intact. All [other] prophets cannot prophesy at will. Not so Moses, our master: whenever he wished, the Holy Spirit would invest him, and prophecy rest upon him. He had no need to focus his mind and to ready himself for it, for he was ever focused and readied, like the ministering angels. He could therefore prophesy at any time, as it is said: "Stand by and I will hear what the Lord commands concerning you" (Num. 9:8). Of this, God [Himself] assured him, as it is said: "Go and say to them: 'Return to your tents'; but you abide here with Me" (Deut. 5:27–28). From this you learn that all [other] prophets, when the prophetic state departs [them], return to their "tent" namely, the totality of bodily needs, [being then] like the rest of the populace. They do not, therefore, withdraw from their wives. But Moses did not return to his original "tent": he, therefore, withdrew forever from marital relations and the like; his mind was knit to the Eternal Source; the splendor never departed him; the skin of his face was radiant; he was sanctified like the angels.

7. The prophecy that a prophet experiences may be his alone, [its purpose being] to expand his mind and augment his intellect so that he comprehends what he had not, of those great matters [mentioned in paragraph 1]. He may, on the other hand, be charged with a mission to one of the nations of the earth or to the inhabitants of a city or a kingdom to enlighten them, to apprise them of what they should do, or to prohibit them from their evil deeds. When charged with a mission, he is given an evidential sign so that the people know that God has truly sent him. But not just anybody who produces an evidential sign is believed to be a prophet. Rather: [if] someone was previously known to us to be worthy of prophecy, by reason of his wisdom and deeds, wherein he has surpassed all his contemporaries and [if] he has followed in the paths [prerequisite for] prophecy, its sanctity and its temperance, and he then comes forward, produces an evidential sign, and says that God has sent him, we are commanded to heed him, as it is said: "To him

shall you hearken" (Deut. 18:15). Now it is possible that such a person will produce an evidential sign though not a prophet, that "sign" being deceptive, and yet we are commanded to heed him: because he is a great person, a sage, and worthy of prophecy, we accept his presumptive condition; for that is what we were commanded [to do]. [It is much] as we were commanded to decide legal cases on the testimony of two proper witnesses, though it is possible that they have testified falsely, because they are, to our knowledge, fit, [and so] we presume their fitness. Of these things and the like it is said: "The hidden things belong to the Lord our God, while the apparent things belong to us and to our children, etc." (Deut. 29:28). And it is said: "Man [perforce] sees what meets the eye, whereas the Lord sees the heart" (1 Sam. 16:7).

Chapter 8

1. Now, as for Moses, our master [who was himself the source of the previously mentioned command]: Israel did not believe in him on account of the signs that he produced. For whoever believes on the basis of signs [necessarily] entertains doubts, since a sign can be produced by secret art and sorcery. Whatever signs Moses performed in the wilderness were performed, rather, to meet some exigency, not to validate [his] prophecy: we needed sustenance, so he brought down the manna for us; when [Israel] thirsted, he split the rock for them; when Korah's company denied him, the earth swallowed them; and similarly [with] all the other signs [performed in the wilderness]. Whence, then, [Israel's] belief in him? [It derived] from the gathering at Mount Sinai: for our eyes saw, not some stranger, and our ears heard, not some other, the fire, the thunder, the torches, [and how Moses] approached the thick darkness, and the Voice was speaking to him, and we heard: "Moses, Moses, go and tell them such-and-such." Thus does [Scripture] say: "The Lord spoke to you face to face" (Deut. 5:4). And it is said: "Not with our fathers did the Lord make this covenant [but with us]" (Deut. 5:3). How do you know that doubt-free validation of [Moses'] prophecy rests exclusively on the gathering at Mount Sinai? For it is said, "Lo, I am coming to you in a thick cloud, that the people may hear when I speak with you,

and may also believe in you for ever" (Exod. 19:9). It follows that before this, they had not believed in him with a perdurable trust, but with a trust that remained susceptible to suspicion and second thoughts.

2. . . . All Israel bears witness to Moses after the gathering at Mount Sinai; he need produce no sign for them. This is [the import of] what the Holy One, blessed be He, told him at the beginning of his prophetic mission. When [God] gave him the signs to produce in Egypt, and told him, "They will hearken to your voice" (Exod. 3:18), Moses, our master, knowing that one who believes on the basis of signs entertains doubt, harbors suspicions, and has second thoughts, attempted to extricate himself from the mission, saying, "But behold they will not believe me" (Exod. 4:1), until the Holy One, blessed be He, informed him that "these signs will be [necessary] only until they leave Egypt; but once they leave, and stand at this mountain, whatever suspicion they harbor about you will vanish; for here I will give you a sign through which they will know that I really did send you from the first; no suspicion will remain in their hearts." This is what Scripture [means when it] says: "And this shall be the sign for you, that I have sent you: when you have brought forth the people out of Egypt, you shall serve God upon this mountain" (Exod. 3:12). One can therefore say of every post-Mosaic prophet that we believe in him not just on his sign—which would lead us to say, "As long as he performs a sign, we will heed whatever he says"—but rather on the commandment that Moses laid down for us in the Torah, which says: Should he give you a sign, "heed him" (Deut. 18:15). Just as he commanded us to decide legal cases on the testimony of two witnesses, even though we do not know [with certainty] whether their testimony is true or false, so too we are commanded to heed this prophet, whether his sign be true or [unbeknownst to us] the product of sorcery and secret art.

3. Therefore, should a prophet arise, produce great evidential signs, and seek to contradict the prophecy of Moses, our master, we pay him no heed: we know, with certainty, that those signs were [performed] by secret art and sorcery. For the prophecy of Moses, our master, is not [believed] on the basis of signs, that we should measure the signs of the one against the signs of the other. We, rather, witnessed it with our own eyes, and heard it with our own ears, just as he did. This may be compared to witnesses who tell a person who saw something with his own eyes that it was not as he, in

fact, saw. [That person] will pay them no heed, but rather know, with certainty, that they are false witnesses. That is why the Torah said that should the "evidential sign come to pass . . . do not heed the words of that prophet" (Deut. 13:3–4). For that [alleged prophet] comes to you with an evidential sign in order to deny what you have seen with your own eyes! Since we believe [prophets] not on the basis of signs, but because of the commandment [to do so] laid down by Moses, how could we possibly accept, on the basis of a sign, someone who comes to deny the Mosaic prophecy, that we saw and heard?

Commentary. Prophecy and Trust

We are obliged to "heed" the prophet on penalty of "death by heaven." But how does one know that the prophet is not a pretender or a victim of his own delusion? All political communities face a version of this question: How does one distinguish between the dangerous zealot, the misguided idealist, and the authentic visionary, each claiming exclusive knowledge of the truth? Who among such individuals deserves our trust?

Deuteronomy remits the prophet to the judgment of history. "If the word does not come true, that word was not spoken by the Lord." But this test is of no use at the critical juncture when action is required. Kings, for example, must choose immediately between competing prophecies. Whom should they trust—the four hundred who speak in unison or Micaiah, the lone dissenter? Zedekiah, who repeats the message of the prophetic band, sincerely believes in his prophecy. Should he suppress it, risking "death by heaven," or utter it, risking execution if it fails to materialize?

The sages' resolution of this case is motivated, not by the practical dilemma of the kings, but by the moral dilemma of the judiciary. How can the court punish someone who speaks sincerely? Zedekiah's fault was in failing to "scrutinize [the matter]" in light of Rabbi Yitzhak's tradition: "One message may come to several prophets, yet no two prophets convey their messages in the same way." As the four hundred spoke identically, Zedekiah should have realized that their prophecy was "worthless."

This text is enigmatic. Why, in the sages' view, must a genuine prophet deliver his message in distinctive language? Does this bear on the truth of a prophet's claim that he received a message from God? Does the test identify qualities of mind or character necessary for the prophet to fulfill his mission?

It is tempting to argue, as our editors imply in their introduction, that the sages are affirming the value of individualism, a quality critical for the fulfillment of the prophet's mission. In political life, the individualist, who is true to his own ideals and not those of society, can be trusted to stand up to the reigning powers or the masses. Like the nonconforming Micaiah, who calls the king to account before the kingdom of God, the prophet who speaks in his own voice announces that his words are impelled by God alone and so can be trusted to represent God's will. The contrast, our editors tell us, is with the "always smooth words [spoken] in unison" of the king's minions.

But the sages do not read the contest of the prophets as a political battle between the individualist who "speaks truth to power" and the appeasers allied with the royal court. They focus on the reported source of Zedekiah and the band's prophecy: a lying spirit sent by God to lure the king to his death. This reading is compatible with the text, which does not identify the political affiliation of the four hundred prophets, and daring in its acknowledgment that false prophecy may be erroneous rather than deliberate, induced by God to further the divine plan of history.

The larger legal discussion of the sages also centers on the source and form of the prophet's utterance, not his character or political role. According to the sages, the anonymous *baraita* cited to open the talmudic discussion ("Our rabbis taught . . .") identifies three types of false prophets: one who delivers a message not heard from God, one who delivers a message sent by God to another prophet, and one who speaks in the name of idols. The sages offer examples of each category, culled from the literary record. In this context, Rabbi Yitzhak's tradition — that prophets may receive the same message yet express it differently — is cited by the sages not only to justify Zedekiah's punishment but also to clarify how the literary record comports with the *baraita*'s categories. The case of the four hundred falls within the first category because a single message is expressed identically by prophets speaking in unison. But a prophecy that appears to cite a prior prophecy, with variation in wording — as in the case of Obadiah and Jeremiah — may be genuine, rather than an instance of the second category. Obadiah and Jeremiah received the same message, yet each expressed it distinctively.

But the sages do not explain why they accept Rabbi Yitzhak's test as not merely descriptive of the literary record but normative: binding on the prophet himself. Nor do the sages specify how distinctive the prophet's speech must be. The cited example (Obadiah and Jeremiah) exhibits only minor variation in language. It is even unclear whether the sages thought that the specific wording of the message was the work of the prophet or of God. Certainly, a prophetic vision must be interpreted. But is a prophet's choice of language and metaphor conscious and free or, as Maimonides puts it, an interpretation "straightaway impressed" upon the prophet's mind?

How, then, might the sages explain why a genuine prophecy must bear the stamp of individual expression? Possibly, Rabbi Yitzhak's tradition conforms with the sages' views about the irreducible singularity of true prophetic revelation. In contrast to the lying spirit, which places words directly in the mouths of the prophets, God does not speak *through* a prophet, but *to* a prophet, who inevitably brings his individuality to bear on the content of the revelation. As Maimonides points out, the prophets varied in their prophetic capacities. Just as a picture will be perceived differently by each viewer, depending on her perspective, the prophetic vision will be perceived differently given the life experience and talents of the individual prophet. If so, each prophet's formulation of the same message must vary.

A simpler explanation of Rabbi Yitzhak's test, less evocative but closer to the Rabbinic legal tradition, is that individual speech is given to the prophet (or required of him) as an external sign of his trustworthiness. In assessing the credibility of speakers, the law recognizes the evidentiary significance of individual human speech. Witnesses who testify in identical language are disqualified because of the suspicion that they colluded and invented their testimony, even though they may be telling the truth. Rabbi Yitzhak's tradition, one rabbinic commentator points out (Samuel Eli'ezer Edels, Maharsha), applies this evidentiary criterion to prophecy. Only a message conveyed in distinctive language is exempt from the suspicion of plagiarism or collusive invention. Zedekiah should have "scrutinized" the band's prophecy and disqualified it, as does the judge who "scrutinizes" the testimony of witnesses.

Maimonides also understands prophecy as analogous to judicial testimony and subject to similar legal requirements. The prophet is a witness testifying that he has received a message from God. None of the conventional signs of the prophet's truthfulness will satisfy the rational person, yet, as with a judicial witness, judgments about the credibility of the prophet must be made. Israel is obligated to trust the prophet who brings signs because Mosaic law so stipulates. The command to "heed" the prophet is comparable to the presumption of truthfulness extended to two competent witnesses.

Thus, prophecy, like every other human experience, is analyzed within the framework of the *halakhah*'s legal categories and ultimately is tamed by them. The sages focus on Zedekiah's obligation to question the source of his prophecy. He must examine his experience, no matter how powerful, in light of accepted criteria of trustworthiness. Must the prophet also scrutinize the substance of his message in light of the standards of the law? Maimonides points to the community's obligation to disregard a prophecy that annuls Mosaic law. Indeed, by distinguishing Mosaic prophecy, which we know to be true, having publicly witnessed its communication, from all other prophecies, which are open to doubt, Maimonides effectively safeguards the law from the revolutionary potential of later claims to revelation. Prophecy, which is subject to doubt, logically must be subordinate to Mosaic law, which is certain. Maimonides further defuses the unruly force of prophecy by turning, unlike the sages here, to the prophet's internal qualities of mind and character. By treating the prophet as a self-witness, Maimonides is able to assert that, as with judicial witnesses, the presumption of trustworthiness extends only to those who are competent—who are possible prophets. For Maimonides, it is the wise and righteous who are "worthy of prophecy." He thus virtually collapses the once distinct categories of prophet and sage.

Maimonides, however, is forthrightly responding to the critical questions Who deserves our trust when the truth is unverifiable? What qualities of mind and character and degree of loyalty to existing institutions should those to whom we grant authority over our actions possess? The individual, no matter how charismatic or heroic, whose claim to authority is based on private access to a revelatory vision does not justify his claim in terms of argument, institutional authority, or the accumulated learning of the past. By contrast, the sage, who frames his arguments within the accepted structures of the law, has the capacity to persuade and to transmit the inherited tradition over the generations. The tradition may be enlarged through the discovery of new solutions pre-existing in it, but the tradition will not be transcended. Those who yearn for more radical transformation must be willing to accept the price: the creation of a new political community.

Suzanne Last Stone

A Medieval Prophet: The Abulafia Controversy

In 1290, in Sicily, Abraham Abulafia, the author of several prophetic tracts and mystical works, announced the onset of the messianic era. Abulafia's opponents turned for help to Solomon b. Abraham Adret of Barcelona (Rashba), whose specific letters regarding Abulafia are now lost. In the responsum we reprint here, Adret addresses the general phenomenon of prophetic pretensions in his own time with critical reserve. He first discusses the case of Rabbi Nissim of Avila, who claimed prophetic powers, and then strongly condemns Abulafia's "imagined and false words." Adret was himself a leading kabbalist, and his opposition to Abulafia stems in part from a rejection of the latter's version of mystical doctrine. Following Adret's letter, we present a section from Abulafia's subsequent defense, Ve-Zot Lihudah.

Critique of Prophetic Claims
13. Solomon b. Abraham Adret (Rashba), *Responsa* 1:548

We have benefited here from the collection of Adret's responsa edited by H. Z. Dimitrovsky, *Teshuvot Harashba* (Jerusalem: Mossad ha-Rav Kook, 1990); see 1:34.

This is what I wrote to the communities who inquired concerning the prophet of Avila:

Reports alarm us. They secretly relate matters inaccessible to mind and intellect, leaving us confounded.

I have examined your important letter. Even before it had reached us, a man arrived carrying a letter from Rabbi Abraham the Scribe, the father of that person, Rabbi Nissim [the prophet of Avila], relating his experiences. And it said that it has been four years since "the spirit of the Lord began to move him" (Judg. 13:25). [This occurred] sometimes while he was awake and other times while he was dreaming. An angel spoke to him, revealed his name, and wrote for him a book—twenty-three measures of paper in length—which he named *The Wonders of Wisdom*. He further began to write a lengthy commentary on every word [of the book], and the commentary for a page of the book was two measures in length. He [Rabbi Abraham the Scribe] also sent me a précis of fifty chapters. I took an extremely skeptical view of these matters. . . .

Some such cases I have seen and heard [myself]. One of them was that scoundrel, may the name of the wicked rot, that Abraham [Abulafia] who claimed to be a prophet and messiah in Sicily. With his lies he seduced some Jews; had I not shut the door against him—with God's mercy, through my letters and the letters of the holy communities—he would have quickly consummated what he had begun. [For he spoke] with an abundance of imagined and false words which to a fool seem lofty wisdom. He would think about them for a few days with the diligence that he generally employed. And he took scriptural verses and the words of the Sages concerning numerology, mixing them with a few true things taken from the books of wisdom.

Now, you say (with some of the people who claimed to have known him initially) that he [Rabbi Nissim] was a well-known ignoramus, who had not [studied] continuously with any person, and did not understand [the opinions] of any person, nor of any book of wisdom. If this is true, our suspicion [of forgery] is untenable. However, it is also impossible that he is a prophet or that an angel of God spoke to him, taught him, and wrote a book for him. I cannot believe or entertain this notion, for several reasons.

First, because our Rabbis of blessed memory, the masters of true wisdom, have already taught us that prophecy only dwells in someone who is wise, wealthy, and courageous [see BT Nedarim 38a]. [Thus the possibility] that a person might go to sleep with no wisdom and arise at dawn a prophet among us is hardly credible. Our Rabbis of blessed memory have clearly instructed us that this is wrong. Admittedly, I do not assert conclusively that no [divine] word or commandment ever came to any person unless he fulfilled these three conditions. For we have the cases of Laban, Abimelech, Gideon, and Manoah and his wife, of whom they [the sages], peace be unto them, said: "Manoah was an ignoramus [*am ha-aretz*]" (BT Ber. 61a). But all these were only temporary, to address a [particular] need or for a miraculous effect. . . .

Moreover, our generation is not worthy of [prophecy]. Even of the students of Hillel the Elder, who achieved a supreme holiness and were of great wisdom and piety, it has been said: They were worthy of having the *shekhinah* dwell among them like Moses our master, but their generation was unworthy. Could it be that the generation of Hillel and his pious students was unworthy and this, our generation, is worthy?

. . . Moreover, it is contrary to the tradition [*kabbalah*] we have received from the true sages[10] [stating] that [the spirit of] prophecy does not dwell outside of the Land [of Israel]. How can we believe in something that contradicts the knowledge of the sages of Israel received from the prophets? . . . But what I find particularly distressing and frightening is that a man unwise and ill-read, who was never trained by any *hakham*—if [we are to believe] the reports as they are—could write systematically about such exalted matters. I find this immensely incongruous, and my heart is caught between these [opposite propositions]. Searching for some cause for this phenomenon, I say that there are numerous differences in human nature and in the natural dispositions of the human imagination. There are infinite accidents[11] attached to them, whether essentially or incidentally. There have been many people in the past with a powerful imagination whether by birth or by virtue of some later development. They have true visions and the wise call them *kahin* [Arabic: visionary]. I have heard that some such powers are temporary and subsequently cease.

10. Among Nahmanides and Adret's circle of kabbalists "the true path" denoted the authentic esoteric tradition. Thus, Adret's choice of terms in this sentence, including his use of the word *kabbalah*, suggests a polemic against Abulafia's mystical pretensions.
11. In the Aristotelian sense of a nonsubstantive quality.

[At this point Adret relates stories of other such visionaries and how the communities dealt with them.]

Finally [I must say that] my mind and the minds of such wise men as you are perplexed by this matter. We have striven to comprehend and have not succeeded—providing that the testimonies that he has not studied and has not been trained by a *hakham* are true. Following this perplexity, I say this matter needs considerable investigation, an investigation of this man by the wise and by men of knowledge concerning his soundness of mind, his actions and practices from earlier times to the present. For prophecy and the holy spirit only dwell upon a worthy and pious person who has achieved the moral and intellectual virtues, just like the true prophets. This investigation would necessarily uncover the root of the matter or [at least] some of it. He must be tested to see if all his prophecies come true,[12] or whether there occurs some inaccuracy—even a hairbreadth's [miss]. Even [if there is no inaccuracy], it would remain doubtful. . . .

Israel, inheritors of the true religion, the children of Jacob, man of truth whose seed is all true, prefer enduring the yoke of exile and whatever befalls them [in exile] to believing this matter. And not before they investigate it thoroughly—investigation following investigation—so as to remove any doubt from what they hear or what they may perceive to be a sign or miracle. . . . [So too in] the case of Moses and Israel. They were exhausted by hard labor [in Egypt], and Moses was commanded to proclaim [their redemption]. Even so he argued: "They will not believe me . . ." (Exod. 4:1).

This is a true sign to our people, the People of the Lord, not to be seduced but to ascertain the truth through a complete and thorough investigation. And . . . the God of truth will show us a true sign by a true prophet, Elijah the prophet of blessed memory whose coming He truthfully promised us, as is written, "Lo, I will send the prophet Elijah to you before the coming of the awesome, fearful day of the Lord" (Mal. 3:23).

12. See Deut. 18:9–22 (§9).

Defending His Own Claim to Prophecy

14. Abraham Abulafia, *Ve-Zot Lihudah*

Auswahl Kabbalistischen Mystik, edited by A. Jellinek (Leipzig, 1853), vol. 1, pp. 18–19. The text is in Hebrew.

I wrote this . . . letter to make known to you, my brothers, that Rabbi Solomon ben Abraham ben Adret's view regarding me—or the information he received—is vain and foolish. Proof of this is the fact that I, thank God, have followed the proper course of studies. I have studied Scripture and grammar sufficiently, and composed grammar textbooks; anyone who masters them would be considered, nowadays, an accomplished grammarian. I have studied Talmud: judicial reasoning and rulings, from two teachers, gaining knowledge of a fair share of the *mitzvot.* I have studied midrash, *aggadah,* and *baraitot* to a medial level. I have studied logic, natural science, and mathematics—though not in depth. I have studied divine science according to the method of the philosophers. I have also studied some medicine. . . . I have studied *The Guide of the Perplexed,* which is truly a guide of astounding profundity—including its esoteric [teachings]. In addition, [I have studied] the *Malmad* [*ha-Talmidim,* by Jacob Anatoli] and the *Book of Beliefs [and Opinions]* by Rabbi Saadiah and the book *Duties of the Heart* by Rabbi Bahya.

All these, with the addition of the wise works of Abraham ibn Ezra, moved me and led me to seek the secret of the *sefirot,* the [divine] names and the ways of the [divine] Seal. All the aforementioned studies did not—prior to my attaining knowledge—lead me to the grandeur of prophecy but rather to glory in [my] wisdom. Now, it has already been stated that "a wise man should not glory in his wisdom" (Jer. 9:22). However, when I attained the [divine] names and unraveled the knots of the seals, the Lord of all was revealed to me. He revealed to me His secret and informed me of the end of the exile and the beginning of redemption. . . . He then compelled me to assume the grandeur of prophecy, leading me to discourse of the sciences [wisdom], and to write wondrous, novel praises [of God] and beautiful poetry.

Commentary. Can There Still Be Prophets?

This controversy between Abraham Abulafia and Solomon Adret is one of many such incidents in Abulafia's exceptionally adventurous life. His career can be presented as a long series of clashes between his claims as a prophet and messiah and the Jewish and non-Jewish reactions to these claims. Perhaps the most extraordinary example is his desperate attempt to meet the pope (in August 1280 on the eve of the Jewish New Year). Abulafia was warned of the danger of his attempt, arrested when he persisted, kept in custody for two weeks, but then set free. Most of Abulafia's "prophetically" inspired writings have unfortunately been lost. But his commentary on these works, written in Sicily, has survived. It is mainly from this text that we learn about Abulafia's far-reaching claims. One of his prophetic works was called *Sefer ha-Haftarah,* because he instructed that it be read during the Sabbath service directly after the portion from the Pentateuch—just like a canonical prophetic book.

Abulafia's messianic and apocalyptic messages were intended to awaken the Jews, but not only them. Thus, for example, he writes that God has sent him to convey "the words of the Living God to the Jews, who are circumcised in their flesh but uncircumcised in their heart." However, Abulafia claims that the Jews, to whom he was especially sent and for whose sake he has provided his revelation, have not paid due attention to the "form of his coming"—they have pronounced regarding him and his God "words that should not be said." Then, he adds that "God has commanded him to speak to the gentiles, those of uncircumcised heart and uncircumcised flesh, in his name. And he has done so, and he spoke to them and they believed in the message of the Lord. But they did not return to God because they relied on their sword and bow, and God has hardened their uncircumcised and impure hearts."

This is a very precious testimony of the propagandistic activities of Abulafia. But even the dissemination of an eschatological-kabbalistic message to Jews alone would have sufficed to suggest a turning of ecstatic Kabbalah to external affairs, a radical change in kabbalistic "politics" from esotericism to exotericism. Prior to Abulafia, the main thrust of the kabbalists in Spain was esoteric, but the ecstatic kabbalist, who identified his ultimate goal as the attainment of a redemptive experience, sought a wider audience.

Toward the end of his life, Abulafia was involved in the bitter controversy with Solomon Adret of Barcelona that is reprinted here. This heretofore neglected controversy was apparently precipitated by a fierce assault on Abulafia's messianic and prophetic claims, mounted by Adret in a letter to the Jews of Palermo. The letter testifies to Abulafia's influence, for Adret seems to view him as a dangerous threat on two levels: as a propagandist for his peculiar type of ecstatic Kabbalah and as a (false) prophet and messiah. But Adret's fiery argument is focused on the issue of prophecy. In Abulafia's response, he distanced himself from the theosophical Kabbalah, and even more from its specific formulation as found in Nahmanides' (and thus Adret's) school: that the ten *sefirot* constitute the very essence of the divine. Abulafia contends that this is a view worse than the Christian trinitarian belief, since it assumes even greater plurality in the divine realm.

As for his own prophetic role, I assume that Abulafia's claim in his *Commentary on the Pentateuch,* that prophecy originated outside the Land of Israel, is a response to a now lost argument by Adret, similar to the claim made here against the prophet of Avila, that Abulafia cannot be a true prophet because he prophesies in Sicily. Against this, Abulafia claims that the real Land of Israel is the inner, spiritual one.

Adret, a member of the primary elite—an author who had a firm position as a halakhic figure and as a leader of his community—attempted to obliterate the "pernicious" impact of the emergence of prophecy in his lifetime. Abulafia, who belonged to what I propose to call the secondary elite—an intellectual whose main field was not halakhic scholarship and who was not a prominent figure in communal life—strongly believed that prophecy was not an experience of the past, closed to postbiblical Judaism. He not only claimed to be a prophet himself, in exactly the way Maimonides defined this religious experience, but also proposed precise techniques to achieve prophecy, devoting many of his voluminous books to developing those techniques.

The Adret-Abulafia controversy is apparently one of the main reasons for the bitter tone we detect in Abulafia's later writings, where rabbinic figures of his generation are sharply criticized along with their version of theosophic Kabbalah. According to Abulafia, these rabbis ignored true spirituality, which focuses on the centrality of the divine name as the main path to an ecstatic experience of a salvific nature.

Abulafia's assumption that prophecy is, in principle, still available in the present, and the techniques he provided to achieve it, remained part of Jewish culture. The numerous manuscripts in which the most important books of Abulafia are extant, the fact that they were studied by major figures in the history of Kabbalah, such as Moshe Cordovero and Hayyim Vital, and that the controversy between him and Rashba was not forgotten—all bear testimony to the centrality of the continued belief in the possibility of achieving prophecy. Indeed, its traces can be detected in at least two major moments in the history of Jewish mysticism—Sabbateanism and Hasidism—when Rashba's responsa were quoted and discussed.

It is reasonable to assume that the concern with the attainment of prophecy remained an ideal in mystical forms of Judaism, as shown by Hayyim Vital's influential book *Sha'arei Kedushah,* and in the prophetic claims of Nathan of Gaza in Sabbateanism. Even in late eighteenth-century Hasidism we find testimony on the possibility of attaining a self-induced prophecy in a manner very reminiscent of Abulafia's technique. Rabbi Aharon ha-Kohen of Apta argues that

> it is impossible, by and large, to prophesy suddenly, without a certain preparation and holiness, but if the person who wants to prepare himself for prophecy sanctifies and purifies himself; concentrates mentally and utterly separates himself from the delights of this world; serves the sages, [including] his Rabbi, the prophet (and the disciples that follow the way of prophecy are called the sons of the prophets); and when his Rabbi, [who is] the prophet, understands that this disciple is already prepared for [the state of] prophecy, then his Rabbi imparts to him the . . . recitations of the holy names, which are the keys to the supernal gate. (*Or ha-Ganuz la-Tzaddikim* [1800], 46ab)

The later confrontations between prophetic charisma and halakhic authority in Judaism draw upon the arguments found in the earlier debate between the ecstatic and the theosophical-theurgical Kabbalah. The "sublime" promises and the immanent "dangers" of these views are features of the ongoing struggle between the forces of stability and dynamism that combine in creating the tension and then the vitality that makes possible the survival of religions. Perhaps religious establishments of one sort or another can survive for a while in the absence of this struggle (this is always the claim of the primary elite)—but not a vivid faith, a profound spiritual engagement, on the part of large numbers of men and women.

Moshe Idel

six

Rabbis and Sages

Introduction

Custodians of the Law

Judicial Authority

1. Deuteronomy 17:8–13

Chain of Tradition

2. Mishnah Avot 1:1

The Oral Law: From Sinai to the Talmud

3. Maimonides, Introduction to the *Mishneh Torah*

Beyond Prophecy

Decline of Prophecy

4. Tosefta Sotah 13:3–4

A Hakham Is Superior to a Prophet

5. BT Bava Batra 12a–b

The Hakham's Advantage

6. Joseph ibn Migash, *Novellae on Bava Batra* 12a–b

The Hakham's Prophetic Powers

7. Nahmanides, *Novellae on Bava Batra* 12a

The Teachings of Scribes Are More Beloved Than Scripture

8. *Midrash Rabbah: Song of Songs* 1:2

Moses in Akiva's Academy

9. BT Menahot 29b

Modern Concerns: Halakhic Innovation and Rabbinic Authority

Introduction

Knowledge has always been one of the central warrants for political rule—or, at least, for the claim to rule. Plato's argument on behalf of philosophers is the classic example. As it suggests, the claim is not often successful: the Republic is an entirely imaginary polis. School learning and professional expertise more often position people as advisers or counselors than as actual rulers—thus the role of "wise men" in the biblical histories and the book of Proverbs. China's mandarin bureaucrats are perhaps the great exception here; they actually ruled the country, although they were formally subordinate to an emperor who, since he held the "mandate of heaven," did not have to pass the civil service examinations. In the West, kings sometimes claimed special insight into the "mysteries of state," but they ruled by virtue of their birth, not their knowledge, and they chose their officials from an aristocracy that rarely prized school learning.

The kings of Israel and Judah were much like other kings: they did not inherit Solomon's wisdom (nor was Solomon the ideal ruler in the popular imagination; that place was filled by David, remembered mostly as a young warrior and singer of songs). Israel's priests are identified in the Bible as carriers of Torah, but in the post-exilic commonwealth they ruled chiefly by virtue of their role in the Temple service, not by virtue of their political or religious knowledge. The Hasmoneans fought their way to the throne. In the Sanhedrin, priests and sages sat together, but their relative power is unclear to us today. It was the loss of independence, second exile, and dispersion that ultimately led to the ascendancy of the learned.

After 70 C.E., Israel no longer possessed a geographical center in Jerusalem or an institutional center in the royal court or the Temple. It became a text-centered society, focused on the Torah, bound by its covenant to a set of laws. After several centuries of confusion and conflict, it was effectively, but never monolithically, ruled by a fellowship of legal scholars (*hakhamim,* sages), trained in the rabbinic academies. The subject of their training was the text—first its meaning, then its application under ideal conditions (as if the Temple still stood and the king ruled), and then its application in the world as it actually was and in the conditions of Israel's exile. So the sages ruled both in imagination and in fact, as philosophers and as judges.

But why were these particular people the authorized interpreters of the authoritative texts? There is no historical moment when the texts were delivered to them, like the law to Moses; nor were the sages called by God, as the prophets were. Historical and biographical legitimation is replaced now by a special kind of genealogy. First described in Mishnah Avot, this genealogy is constituted as a chain of succession extending backward from the sages to Sinai, connecting them with Moses and the prophets, who had what the sages so clearly did not have: a direct, unmediated experience of divinity (priests and kings are omitted from the chain).

The genealogical argument can be read as implying two rather different positions. The first of these suggests that interpretive authority is handed down from Moses to his successors, each generation recognizing, as it were, the generation that comes next and conferring legitimacy on its version of the Torah. The second position suggests that the Torah itself is handed down from one generation to another, but this is a Torah understood to include its own interpretations, the written and Oral Law together, revealed to Moses and passed on in its entirety. This latter view represents a very strong version of the standard defense of tradition—stressing continuity, denying the reality of revision and innovation. But on both these views, the carriers of the tradition today are authorized by its original recipients.

In fact, the sages prove their authority by their knowledge: they know the texts and they know the hermeneutical rules through which the texts are interpreted. These two together give them access to the word of God, but since this is indirect access, seemingly less than the prophets had, the sages continually compare themselves to the prophets and worry about their relative standing. Sometimes they claim that prophecy has ceased in Israel and that they are its legitimate heirs—that their knowledge of God's word is the only possible knowledge available in the exilic world. Sometimes they claim to be prophet-like, responding to a "voice from heaven." And sometimes they claim that their readings of the texts are superior to prophetic disclosure—at least with regard to *halakhah* and the work of the courts, and perhaps more generally. The argument about the relative merits of prophets and rabbis is an ongoing one, reflecting in some writers an entirely understandable insecurity and in others an extraordinary self-confidence. In this century, the argument is best represented by the text reprinted here from Abraham Isaac Kook.

The authority of the sages makes their own texts similarly authoritative. Henceforth, interpretation and commentary are the central genres of Jewish legal and political literature. These are at first the products of academic discussion, preserved through memory. But the written form they took much later was probably fixed early on in the mind's eye: the text surrounded by, enclosed within, its commentaries. The commentaries never entirely supersede the original texts, though the originals seem sometimes to survive only in quotable bits and pieces, sentences and phrases used as "proofs" by commentators and judges. But the authority of Scripture, and then of the Talmud, can never be replaced. There is a pragmatic explanation for this textual foundationalism: the ongoing interpretive enterprise would cease to make sense, the judicial applications would lose their legitimacy, without the "proofs." But pragmatism would never have sufficed to sustain the authority of the original texts without religious faith—in Scripture as the word of God and in the Talmud as the revealed or genealogically authorized interpretation and application of that word.

For this reason, it is always possible to return to the originals, quoting God, so to speak, against the rabbis. This is what the Karaites do: they oppose the whole interpretive tradition in the name of biblical literalism. Their relation to the rabbis is like that of Protestant reformers to the Catholic doctors of medieval and early modern times.

The Karaites survived for centuries as an alternative Jewish community, challenging the *halakhah* of the rabbis, who expended much energy in both literary and political responses. Judah Halevi's *Kuzari* provides the greatest and most enduring literary response, and we reprint excerpts from it in this and the next chapter. The arguments are familiar because they arise within every interpretive tradition. The Karaites ask why God's word is not sufficient unto itself, available to any conscientious reader (this is the Jewish equivalent of Luther's "priesthood of all believers": every man his own rabbi). The Rabbanites respond that the word is not self-evident; the Karaites are themselves interpreters, but what they produce is a chaos of interpretations — in contrast to the coherent and stable rabbinic tradition, continuous with Moses and the prophets.

Karaite writers were certainly correct to argue that rabbinic Judaism is as much innovation as continuation. That, indeed, is the strength of an interpretive tradition: it adapts, more or less readily, to changing political and social realities. But this adaptive process raises hard questions. How strong are the constraints of the original texts? How far can an interpreter move from their plain meaning (*peshat*)? How much can an interpreter do, right now, and how openly? When and how do interpreters of the law become legislators in their own right? The answer to the last of these questions is probably: *Never in their own right,* for the original text says *lo tosif* (do not add [to the law]), and the rabbis must claim to be bound by the text. Insofar as the interpreters revise by elaboration and addition, the interpretation is always open to challenge. When the rabbis act against the law in an emergency, responding to "the needs of the hour," aren't they replacing it with something new? When they "build a fence around the law," aren't they adding to it?

Halevi claims that so long as the needs are met and the fences are built *by the sages,* that is, by scholars committed to the tradition and always acting in fidelity to its principles, these questions don't apply; *lo tosif* is a prohibition only for the multitude (and therefore, of course, for the Karaites). Maimonides takes the prohibition to apply also to the rabbis, but what it prohibits, he argues, is only change in the Torah; it poses no bar to rabbinic legislation so long as this legislation doesn't claim to be "from Sinai." The rabbis can do what they think necessary so long as they leave the public face of divine law intact. A standard distinction between God's law and the rulings of the rabbis underlies the Maimonidean argument: the latter can always be changed, though there are significant restraints on the process; the former is in principle unchangeable, though always subject to interpretation.

The closest analogy to these kinds of arguments is the role of lawyers and judges in a country like the United States, with a written and much revered constitution. Americans are constantly engaged in debates that closely resemble those that have characterized Jewish legal and political history—about texts, intentions, meanings, interpretations. And these debates lead to comparable worries about legal maneuvers and manipulations . . . and usurpations. Consider Justice Holmes's famous claim that the law is what the judges say it is. A rabbinic maxim provides a rough equivalent: *Ha-kol lefi re'ut eine bet din* (Everything depends upon the judgment of the court). But like most American judges, the rabbis are eager to deny that they ever change the law. Perhaps it makes a difference that for them the law is divine. Still, the rabbis in their courts are hardly less authoritative than Holmes's judges in theirs. How else can a foundational text serve the needs of an ongoing community except through judicial interpretations that are also de facto revisions? And who can provide these interpretations except the learned?

When the learned disagree, disputes among them are settled by majority vote. The story of Akhnai's oven in Bava Metzia suggests that the crucial alternative to this political procedure is to invite divine intervention—and the Rabbis are as uneasy about that as they are about prophecy. Rabbi Eli'ezer's claim to be seconded by God carries no weight once the law is in the hands of its human interpreters. In much the same way, the intentions of the American founders are routinely overridden in constitutional law—and would be overridden even if the founders themselves miraculously appeared before the Supreme Court. Collective wisdom effectively replaces both revelation and legislative intention. But this is the collective wisdom of specialists, not of ordinary people.

We offer Hillel's *prosbul* as the classic example of Rabbinic innovation—for a biblical law is here effectively canceled. This was done, Hillel would certainly have said, with due respect for the spirit and purpose of the law, in order to meet changing circumstances. The talmudic discussion of Hillel's ruling reveals the sages' ambiguous mix of uneasiness and confidence with regard to this sort of legislative or near-legislative activity. Their arguments cover the whole range of possibilities, characteristically without any attempt by the editor at resolution. Hillel has repealed a Torah law; no, only a ruling of the rabbis. He has acted for all times and places; no, only for his own time. What he has done should be repealed; no, it should be confirmed. There are not many cases where such an open innovation is so openly debated. Few of the Rabbis were prepared to claim for themselves the authority of Hillel. Most often, they preferred the mode of innovation through interpretation, exemplified here by Akiva (see §9). There is a great deal of quiet or concealed boldness in the history of halakhic decision making even in post-talmudic times, particularly in the early years of the *kahal*. The rabbis of the autonomous communities of premodern times could not imitate Moses or speak like the prophets, but a good many of them walked in Hillel's or Akiva's footsteps. Their successors were often more cautious.

Centuries later, under pressure from reformers and *maskilim* ("enlighteners"), caution had hardened into a rigidly conservative dogmatism —nicely reflected in Moses Sofer's famous dictum "Anything new is everywhere forbidden by the Torah." It is important to recognize that the reformers, at least initially, did not challenge rabbinic authority. We reprint here a characteristic text by one of the leading Russian *maskilim,* Moses Leib Lilienblum, who is the first of our authors to distinguish the *maskil* from the rabbi and so to suggest the emergence within Jewish life of the lay intellectual. Writers like Josephus and Philo may provide earlier examples, but from talmudic times until the nineteenth century, any recognized scholar of *halakhah* or Kabbalah, even if he also studied philosophy, was called a rabbi. Despite their traditional learning, the *maskilim* represent something new. Lilienblum is prepared to accept the authority of the rabbis, but only if they deal creatively with the mounting difficulties of Jewish life in central and eastern Europe—and only if they do this together with enlightened intellectuals like himself. Reform rabbis in Germany tried to meet this demand (see the David Einhorn text in the next chapter), but Sofer's maxim is the more typical response of the European rabbinate. In the East, Sephardi rabbis, who never had to confront either enlightenment or reform, were much more flexible in responding to the problems of their own communities. Hayyim David Halevi, a twentieth-century Israeli rabbi working in this tradition, actually identifies rabbinic authority with the right and obligation to innovate in *halakhah:* his argument would have gratified Lilienblum. Later *maskilim* in Russia, laymen all and increasingly impatient with the rabbis, asserted their own authority and that of secular knowledge more generally.

A very different challenge to the "orthodox" rabbinate grew out of the traditions and practices of Jewish mysticism (in which many rabbis were themselves fully engaged). We cannot provide here a historical account of the emergence of the hasidic movement and its charismatic leader, the *tzaddik.* It is perhaps useful to imagine the *tzaddik* as the near-perfect opposite of the *maskil*—a mystic rather than a rationalist, a wonder-worker rather than a worldly pragmatist. But the *tzaddik,* like the *maskil,* is also engaged with, and opposed to, the rabbis of the talmudic academies. And his is the immanent threat to the culture of halakhic interpretation, for Hasidism is a development wholly within traditional Judaism, while the chief enlighteners, from Mendelssohn on, drew sustenance from outside.

The *tzaddik* is a rabbi with a difference—not so much a man of learning as a mystical adept, a "master of the name," who provides magical services as well as spiritual advice (but only rarely legal rulings) and inspires ecstatic awe in his followers. Hasidic Judaism seems less text-centered than person-centered: "I did not go to the Maggid [of Miedzyrec]," said one of his disciples, "in order to hear Torah from him, but to see how he unlaces his felt shoes." The reasons for the awe are suggested by Elimelekh of Lyzhansk in his classic account of tzaddikism, from which we have taken central segments.

Our last selection, by Eliyahu Dessler, a twentieth-century scholar influenced by Hasidism, suggests that the deference to the person of the *tzaddik* can take a more intellectual form and can be incorporated into rabbinic doctrine. Here, too, the tradition of interpretive argument is effectively given up. Rabbinic authority and legal learning are personally embodied rather than demonstrated in the ongoing discussions of the academy and the *bet din.* Dessler describes a version of rabbinic authority—now the dominant version in ultraorthodox circles—that seems intended to reject a priori all possible arguments for enlightened secularism or religious reform.

We take up the argument about arguments in the next chapter, which forms a kind of pair with this one. The question of rabbinic authority and the question of permissible disagreement are closely related. What distinguishes them is simply this: the first deals with the prerogatives and powers of the rabbis generally, the second with the right of dissent and the possibilities of pluralism both within and beyond the rabbinic community.

Custodians of the Law

Judicial Authority

1. Deuteronomy 17:8–13

These verses establish a central institution for interpreting the law, whose officials are priests and some kind of magistrate (shofet). The Rabbis viewed themselves as the heirs of this institution, hence this selection is pivotal for subsequent discussions of the authority of the Oral Law and its rabbinic proponents (cf. C4, §6).

If a case is too baffling for you to decide, be it a controversy over homicide, civil law, or assault—matters of dispute in your courts—you shall promptly repair to the place that the Lord your God will have chosen, and appear before the levitical priests, or the magistrate in charge at the time, and present your problem. When they have announced to you the verdict in the cases, you shall carry out the verdict that is announced to you from that place that the Lord chose, observing scrupulously all their instructions to you. You shall act in accordance with the instructions given you and the ruling handed down to you; you must not deviate from the verdict that they announce to you either to the right or to the left. Should a man act presumptuously and disregard the priest charged with serving there the Lord your God, or the magistrate, that man shall die. Thus you will sweep out evil from Israel: all the people will hear and be afraid and will not act presumptuously again.

Chain of Tradition
2. Mishnah Avot 1:1

This is the opening statement of tractate Avot, *"The Fathers," which consists of ethi-cal aphorisms by many of the key figures of the Rabbinic tradition. The first mishnah depicts these teachers of the Oral Law—and by extension the Mishnah itself—as the authentic carriers of the Torah. The omission of priests from this account of the chain of tradition lends it a polemical edge, presumably directed against other Second Common-wealth parties such as the Sadducees or Essenes. The subsequent aphorisms (continuing with the formula "A and B received from them") proceed in chronological order through the traditions of Hillel's descendants and the students of Yohanan ben Zakkai.*

Moses received Torah from Sinai and passed it on to Joshua, and Joshua to the elders, and the elders to the prophets, and the prophets passed it on to the Men of the Great Assembly [*anshe knesset ha-gedolah*].

The Oral Law: From Sinai to the Talmud
3. Maimonides, Introduction to the *Mishneh Torah*

Translated by Bernard Septimus, forthcoming in the Yale Judaica Series (Yale University Press).

Maimonides' great legal work, the Mishneh Torah, *aims to codify talmudic law. In the introduction, Maimonides sets forth his own historical account of talmudic and rabbinic authority.*

All the commandments given to Moses at Sinai were given along with their explanations, as it is said, "and I will give you the tablets of stone, the *torah* and the *mitzvah*"[1] (Exod. 24:12): *torah* refers to the Written Torah—while *mitzvah* refers to its explanation. [Moses] commanded us to carry out the *torah* in accordance with the *mitzvah*. This *mitzvah* is what goes by the name "Oral Torah."

1. New JPS: "teachings and commandments".

Moses, our master, wrote down the entire *torah* before he died in his own hand and gave a scroll to each tribe. One additional scroll, he deposited in the Ark to serve as a witness [to the true text], as it is said: "Take this scroll of the *torah,* and place it along the [inner] side of the ark of the covenant of the Lord your God that it may be there for a witness . . ." (Deut 31:26).

But the *mitzvah,* which is the explanation of the *torah,* he did not write down; he rather commanded it [orally] to the elders, Joshua and all the rest of Israel, as it is said: "Everything which I commanded you, that you shall observe to do; do not add to it or diminish from it" (Deut. 13:1) — which is why it is called the Oral Torah.

[Maimonides here enumerates the leading sages over the generations.]

All the above-mentioned sages were the great men of [their] generations. Some were academy heads; some were exilarchs; some were members of the Great Sanhedrin. Together with them, in each generation, were thousands and tens of thousands [of others] who heard [the tradition] from them and with them. Ravina and Rav Ashi were the last of the sages of the Talmud. It was Rav Ashi who compiled the Babylonian Talmud in the land of Shin'ar [Babylonia], some one hundred years after Rabbi Yohanan compiled the Jerusalem Talmud.

The purpose of the two Talmuds is [to provide] explanation of the words of the Mishnah; explication of its profundities; and the innovations introduced in all the various courts from the days of Our Saintly Master through the compilation of the Talmud. From the two Talmuds, the Tosefta, Sifra, Sifrei and the [other] supplements [to the Mishnah] — from all these [sources] emerge what is prohibited and what permitted, what is impure and what pure, what is liable and what exempt, what is fit and what unfit, as transmitted in direct succession from Moses, [who received it] from [God at] Sinai.

From these [sources] also emerge the measures that the sages and prophets of each generation decreed to make a hedge round the Torah, in accordance with [the charge] they heard on the authority of Moses, who — in explaining [the verse] "you shall preserve my charge" (Lev. 18:30) — said: "Establish a safeguard for my charge." In addition, there emerge from [these

sources] the customs and ordinances, ordained or practiced in each generation, as the court of that generation saw fit. For it is forbidden to deviate
from them, as it is said, "You shall not deviate from anything they tell you,
to the right or to the left" (Deut. 17:11).

In addition, legal judgments, [once] obscure, that were not received
[on tradition] from Moses. [Rather] the Great Court of a particular generation deliberated on them, using the canons whereby the Torah is expounded,
and its elders [then] decided them, concluding that the law is such and such.
All such [rulings made] from the days of Moses up until his own, Rav Ashi
compiled in the Talmud. The sages of the Mishnah compiled other works
to interpret the words of the Torah. . . . Other sages, after them, compiled
collections of midrashim. All [of these works] were compiled prior to the
Babylonian Talmud.

Thus, Ravina, Rav Ashi, and their colleagues were the last of Israel's
great sages who transmitted the Oral Torah, who issued decrees, ordained
ordinances, and instituted customs, and whose decrees, ordinances and customs gained acceptance among all [the people of] Israel, wherever they
dwelt.

After [the term of] the court of Rav Ashi, who compiled and completed the Talmud in the days of his son, Israel was scattered still further,
through all the lands of the earth, reaching the ends [of the inhabited world]
and its remote regions. [Armed] conflict increased in the world and travel
routes were disrupted by marauding troops. Study of the Torah diminished;
and Israel no longer gathered to study at their academies by the thousands
and tens of thousands as they had in times past.

Rather, individuals, the remnants whom the Lord called, would
gather in every city and province, engage in [study of the] Torah, reflect upon
all the compilations of the sages, and discern, from them, what course [the
principles] of legal judgment [mandate].

Of all the post-talmudic courts that arose in the various provinces
and established decrees, ordinances, or customs for the inhabitants of its
province or [a group of] provinces, there was none whose enactments gained
the acceptance of all Israel, because their settlements were scattered, travel
routes were disrupted, and the provincial court in question consisted of
[mere] individuals [lacking ecumenical authority], whereas the Great Court

of Seventy [wherein such authority did reside] had been defunct for many years prior to the compilation of the Talmud.

Therefore, the inhabitants of one province are not compelled to follow the custom of another province; nor is one court told to uphold a decree that another court enacted in its province. Similarly, if one of the Geonim taught that [on a certain issue] the course [mandated by the principles] of legal judgment is such and such and it becomes clear to another, subsequent court that such is not, in fact, the course [mandated by the principles] of legal judgment inscribed in the Talmud, one heeds not the earlier [authority] but the one to whose view reason inclines, be he the earlier or the later. The above applies [only] to inferences, decrees, ordinances, and customs introduced after the compilation of the Talmud; but whatever is included in the Babylonian Talmud, the whole House of Israel is duty-bound to follow. Every city and province is compelled to follow all customs followed by the sages of the Talmud, to uphold their decrees and to follow their ordinances.

For all the aforementioned things included in the Talmud have been accepted by all Israel. Moreover, the sages who established [those] ordinances, decrees, or customs, or who drew [those] inferences and taught that the law is such and such, were the entirety or majority of the sages of Israel, and the ones who heard the tradition on the rudiments of the entire Torah [i.e., the 613 commandments] in direct transmission extending back to Moses.

Beyond Prophecy

Decline of Prophecy
4. Tosefta Sotah 13:3–4

This chapter of the Tosefta is part of a narrative of catastrophes connected with the decline of the Second Commonwealth. One of the chief among them is the end of prophetic inspiration. All that remains are echoes, and reports of outstanding individuals who should have attained prophecy, or perhaps did attain it just before death.

3. When the last of the prophets died—Haggai, Zechariah, and Malachi— the holy spirit ceased in Israel. Even so, they [i.e., the celestial powers] would inform them by a *bat kol*. Once, the *hakhamim* [sages] assembled upstairs in the house of Guria in Jericho. A *bat kol* called out to them: "There is one among you worthy of [being inspired by] the holy spirit, but his generation does not merit it." They set their eyes upon Hillel the Elder. After he died they said [in eulogy]: "O humble one, O pious one, disciple of Ezra."

4. Yet again, they were seated in Yavneh and heard a *bat kol* saying: "There is one among you worthy of [being inspired by] the holy spirit, but his generation does not merit it." They set their eyes upon Shmu'el ha-Katan. At his death they said [in eulogy]: "O humble one, O pious one, disciple of Hillel the Elder." Indeed, at his death he proclaimed: "Shimon and Ishmael unto execution; the rest of their colleagues unto the sword; the rest of the people unto plunder; and great catastrophes will then follow."

A Hakham Is Superior to a Prophet

5. BT Bava Batra 12a–b

This is perhaps the most explicit Rabbinic juxtaposition of scholarship and prophecy, and includes the radical proclamation "a hakham *is superior to a prophet." The precise relationship between the two and the nature of this superiority are expounded by the medieval commentators ibn Migash and Nahmanides in the selections that follow.*

Rabbi Avdimi of Haifa said: Since the day the Temple was destroyed, prophecy was lost to the prophets and given to the *hakhamim.*

But are the *hakhamim* not themselves prophets?[2] He means to say: Although prophecy was lost to the prophets, it was not lost to the *hakhamim.*

Amemar added: Indeed, a *hakham* is superior to a prophet, as writ-

---

2. This (somewhat mysterious) question is explained by Rashi thus: Were none of the prophets sages? Why then does the text seem to imply that sages gained access to prophecy only after the destruction of the Temple?

ten, "And a prophet has the heart of wisdom" (Ps. 90:12). — Who is compared to whom? Surely, the lesser is compared to the greater!

Abaye said: This can be proven from instances where a great man states something and [then] an identical statement is quoted from another great man. Said Rava: What proof is this? Perhaps they simply both have the same mindset![3] Rather, said Rava, it can be proven from instances where a great man states something and [then] an identical statement is quoted from Rabbi Akiva ben Yosef!

Said Rav Ashi: What proof is this? Perhaps they simply both have the same mindset in this matter! Rather, said Rav Ashi, it can be proven from instances where a great man states something and [then] an identical statement is quoted from a tradition given to Moses at Sinai. But perhaps it is [a coincidence], like a blind person [stumbling] upon the right passage?[4] — Well, but does he not offer a reason?

The Hakham's Advantage

6. Joseph ibn Migash, *Novellae on Bava Batra* 12a–b

The Talmud leaves unexplained its assertion of the scholar's superiority over the prophet. Writing in twelfth-century Spain, ibn Migash provides a straightforward explanation in terms of the scholar's independence: Human understanding does not need prophetic revelation.

"Amemar added: Indeed, a *hakham* is superior to a prophet, etc. . . . Said Rav Ashi, it can be proven from instances where a great man states something and [then] an identical statement is quoted from a tradition given to Moses at Sinai" — even though this individual had never heard that statement previously!

---

3. Literally, "both are of the same constellation."
4. Literally, "shaft" — i.e., he finds by sheer luck the shaft leading down from one level to another in a house.

A *hakham* is thus superior to a prophet: for a prophet only relates that which he heard and that which was placed in his mouth to repeat, while a *hakham* relates a tradition given to Moses at Sinai, even though he had never heard it [from anyone]!

The Hakham's Prophetic Powers
7. Nahmanides, *Novellae on Bava Batra* 12a

Nahmanides' interpretive concern is different from ibn Migash's. He contrasts the juxta-position of prophet and scholar with another talmudic statement that posits wisdom as a precondition for prophecy. Nahmanides' solution involves a rejection of Rashi's asser-tion that there are prophets who are not scholars. Instead, he suggests a close affinity between scholarship and prophecy as modes of divine inspiration.

The talmudic statement "Since the day the Temple was destroyed . . . al-though prophecy was lost to the prophets, it was not lost to the *hakhamim*" was explained by Rashi: "Lost to those prophets who were not *hakhamim*." Against this, one may cite a statement in Nedarim (BT Nedarim 38a): "God causes His *shekhinah* to dwell only on someone who is wise [*hakham*], strong and wealthy" [implying that *all* prophets are necessarily sages].

Some answer that [the statement] "God causes His *shekhinah* to dwell only on someone who is wise" [refers only] to a continuous state of prophecy. In the case of prophecy for [conveying] a message, such as that of Jonah (the son of Amitai), which is [merely] temporary, the *shekhinah* may indeed dwell even on the pious, though they are not *hakhamim*.[5] . . .

[However,] I am not satisfied [with this answer]. Rather, the Tal-mud [here in Bava Batra] means to say that although the prophecy of the prophets—by means of image and vision—was lost, the prophecy of the sages—by means of the intellect—was not lost. Rather, they know the truth from the holy spirit which [dwells] within them.

---

5. The order of these sentences in the printed edition is corrupt.

The Teachings of Scribes Are More Beloved Than Scripture
8. *Midrash Rabbah: Song of Songs* 1:2

The following selections depict the teachings of the Rabbis (here called Scribes)—the Oral Law—as superior not only to the teachings of the prophets but even to the Torah itself, God's Written Law. This midrash begins with a prooftext from the Song of Songs, understood as celebrating the love between God and Israel; "mouth" alludes to the Oral Law.

Shimon b. Abba said in the name of Rabbi Yohanan: The teachings of the Scribes are as cherished as the teachings of the [written] Torah. What is the proof? "And your mouth like choicest wine" (Song of Sol. 7:10).

[Several] scholars said in the name of Rabbi Yohanan: The teachings of the Scribes are more cherished than those of the Torah. . . .

Rabbi Abba b. Kahana in the name of Rabbi Yehudah b. Pazzi derived this from this [mishnah]:

Rabbi Tarfon said: I was once on the road, and I reclined to recite [the *shema*] following the words of Bet Shammai[6] and endangered my person in a confrontation with brigands. [They said to him: You deserved to forfeit your person, for you transgressed the words of Bet Hillel.] (Mishnah Berakhot 1:3)

[Here] you see: Had he not recited the *shema* at all, he would only have transgressed a positive commandment [from the Torah],[7] whereas having recited it [but, by reclining, having transgressed against the words of Bet Hillel,] he forfeited his life. This shows that the teachings of the Scribes are more cherished than those of the Torah.

Rabbi Hanina b. Rabbi Adda said in the name of Rabbi Tanhum b. Aha: They also carry more weight than the teachings of the Torah and the prophets. . . . They [the prophets and scribes] are like two agents whom a

---

6. Bet Shammai hold that one must recline for the evening recitation of the *shema* (and stand erect for the morning recitation), while Bet Hillel oppose taking a special posture for the *shema*. The law generally follows Bet Hillel (see C7, §16).

7. A violation of a positive commandment carries no fixed punishment.

king sent to a province. With regard to one he wrote: If he shows you my signature and seal, trust him, but otherwise do not trust him. With regard to the other he wrote: Even if he does not show you my signature and seal, trust him. Thus of the teachings of prophecy it is written, "If there appears among you a prophet . . . and he gives you a sign or a portent" (Deut. 13:2), but of the teachings of the Scribes it is written, "You shall act in accordance with the instructions given you and the ruling handed down to you; you must not deviate from the verdict that they announce to you either to the right or to the left" (Deut. 17:11).

Moses in Akiva's Academy
9. BT Menahot 29b

This story explores the relation between the Written and Oral Laws in terms of an encounter between Moses and Akiva, their respective representatives. Among the Rabbis, Akiva's hermeneutics were distinguished by his bold departure from the semantics of the biblical text. His midrashic expositions, which often rely on a single letter, are represented here—somewhat hyperbolically—as focusing on the decorative coronets of the letters in the handwritten Torah scroll, and even on these coronets' individual horns.

Rav Yehudah said, citing Rav: When Moses ascended to heaven [to receive the Torah] he found the Holy One sitting and fashioning coronets for the letters. He said to Him: "Master of the world, who requires you [to do this]?" He replied: "There is a person who will come to be after many generations, called Akiva b. Yosef; he will one day expound heaps upon heaps of laws from each and every horn." He said before Him: "Master of the world, show him to me." He replied: "Turn around." He turned around and [found himself] behind the eighth row [in the talmudic academy—behind the regular students]. Moses did not understand the discussion and was dazed. When [Akiva] came to a certain point, his students asked him "Whence do you know this?" He replied, "[This is] a law [given] to Moses from Sinai." Then Moses was calmed.

He turned back and stepped before the Holy One and said before

Him: "Master of the world, you have such a man, yet give the Torah through me?" He replied: "Be still, that is how it entered my mind."

Then he said before Him: "Master of the world, you have shown me his Torah; show me his reward." He said: "Turn around." He turned around and saw Akiva's flesh being weighed in a butcher shop.[8] He said before Him: "Master of the world, such Torah and such a reward?" He replied: "Be still, that is how it entered my mind."

Torah Is "Not in Heaven"

10. BT Bava Metzia 59b

This is the famous story of Akhnai's oven. In a dispute over a detail of the laws of purity, Rabbi Eli'ezer found himself in the minority, as was often the case. This occasioned a confrontation over the criteria for deciding the law, in which Rabbi Yehoshua boldly affirmed the independence of rabbinic interpretation from divine intervention. In support he adduces the biblical statement that the Torah is "not in heaven" (Deut. 30:12 [C1, §3]), which in its biblical context signifies something quite different.

On that day, Rabbi Eli'ezer presented all the proofs in the world, but [the other Rabbis] did not accept them.

[Rabbi Eli'ezer] said: "If the law is as I say, then this carob tree will prove it." The carob jumped a hundred cubits. (Some say: four hundred cubits.) They said: "One does not prove anything from a tree." Rabbi Eli'ezer then said: "If the law is as I say, then this aqueduct will prove it." The [water in the] aqueduct began to flow upstream. They said: "One does not prove anything from an aqueduct." Rabbi Eli'ezer said: "If the law is as I say, then the walls of the academy will prove it." The walls began to fall. Rabbi Yehoshua reprimanded [the walls]: "If scholars argue a point of law, what business is it of yours?" To show respect for Rabbi Yehoshua, they did not fall further; and to show respect for Rabbi Eli'ezer, they did not straighten up; and

---

8. A reference to Akiva's martyrdom: "His flesh was ripped off with iron combs" (BT Berakhot 61a [C11]).

so they are still leaning. Then Rabbi Eli'ezer said: "If the law is as I say, it shall be proven from heaven." A *bat kol* pronounced: "What have you against Rabbi Eli'ezer? The law is always as he says." Rabbi Yehoshua then stood up and said: "It is not in heaven" (Deut. 30:12). What does this mean? Rabbi Yirmiyah said: "As the Torah has been given from Mount Sinai, we take no heed of a *bat kol*—for at Mount Sinai You have already written in the Torah [that we should] 'follow the majority.' "[9]

[Some time later,] Rabbi Natan met Elijah [the prophet]. He asked him: "What did the Holy One do at that moment?" Elijah replied: "God smiled and said: 'My children have defeated me, my children have defeated me.' "

It is related that on that day the rabbis collected everything that Rabbi Eli'ezer had pronounced pure and burned it in a fire. Then they voted on him and placed him under the ban.

. . . [Rabbi Eli'ezer] tore his clothes and took off his shoes and sat down on the ground. Tears fell from his eyes; then the world was afflicted: one third of the olives, one third of the wheat, one third of the barley. . . . It is said: "There was great woe that day, for every spot toward which Rabbi Eli'ezer directed his eyes was burned."

Furthermore, Rabban Gamaliel [head of the academy] was in a ship; a great wave threatened to sink him. He said: "I suppose this is on account of Rabbi Eli'ezer." He stood up and said: "Master of the world, it is manifest and known to you that I have not done this for my honor nor for the honor of my father's house, but for Your honor, so that controversies should not abound in Israel." Then the sea ceased to rage.

Commentary. Expanding the Covenant

This well-known aggadic story is in many ways a key to understanding the distinctive nature of Rabbinic Judaism. After failing to convince the sages through rational argument, Rabbi Eli'ezer invokes supernatu-

9. Rabbi Yirmiyah is actually citing a phrase midrashically severed from the context of a verse whose plain meaning is, in fact, an admonition not to "follow the majority" in perverting justice (Exod. 23:2). The verb may also be translated as "to side" or "to favor"; see C22.

ral phenomena to persuade his colleagues of the truth of his position. Seeing that they still are not swayed by these miraculous hints of divine support, Rabbi Eli'ezer seeks what he considers the "knockout blow" by appealing directly to God for confirmation. But Rabbi Yehoshua insists that "It is not in heaven," and God only smiles at this "defeat" by His "children."

While this midrash can be interpreted in a variety of ways, by all accounts it expresses the clear preference for orderly procedures of legal adjudication over nonrational intrusions of miracles and heavenly voices in the academies of Torah study. Supernatural interventions undermine the centrality of rational debate in the understanding and elaboration of the law.

Apart from the social and institutional reasons that can be adduced to justify the rejection of the supernatural in legal decision making, there is another issue involved here: the nature of covenantal religion or, more specifically, the related ideas of divine revelation and human responsibility.

God's "defeat" signifies a divine form of self-limitation that allows the human partners to the covenant to assume responsibility for developing the content of revelation. The midrashic use of "It is not in heaven" captures the sense of intellectual competence characteristic of talmudic scholars, who are confident in their right and ability to apply the Word of God without the need for prophecy or divine intervention. Extra-rational forms of persuasion (as defined within the intellectual tradition of rabbinic Judaism)—for example, the signs and wonders in our text—are both unnecessary and invalid in legal argument.

Another midrashic text expresses this idea by referring to the period following the death of Moses as a time when the role of prophets and the appeal to revelation became irrelevant. "Rav Yehudah reported in the name of Shmu'el: Three thousand traditional laws were forgotten during the period of mourning for Moses. They said to Joshua: 'Ask.' He replied: 'It is not in heaven.'" After describing several cases where Phinehas and Joshua tried in vain to recover the lost laws by appealing directly to God, the Talmud quotes Rabbi Abbuha, who said: "Otniel, the son of Kenaz, restored [these forgotten teachings] by means of his dialectics" (BT Temurah 16a).

In other words, human beings can rely on legal analysis to compensate for the absence of God's active involvement in deciphering the meaning of the Torah. What this metaphysical notion of divine withdrawal means is that students of the law must exercise intellectual initiative and creativity to complete the process that began with revelation. When the heirs of Moses feel sufficiently confident to interpret what they received from their prophets, when students of the law are not overwhelmed by their teachers and do not simply repeat their teachings verbatim, when the content of revelation becomes a living and expanding corpus of law and commentary, only then does the covenantal community emerge as God's mature partner.

But to appreciate the full implications of this divine "defeat," we must adopt a larger theological perspective and distinguish between the biblical account of God's relationship to Israel and the Rabbis' rethinking of this relationship in light of their own historical experience.

The biblical drama is dominated by the active presence of God. History and politics are shaped throughout by a God who is directly involved in the destiny and daily life of His people. By means of prophets and miracles, God's presence is felt in concrete and palpable ways. When Moses, for example, encounters problematic applications of the law, the text describes him turning to God for instructions (e.g., Num. 27:1–11). God is never "defeated" in the Bible. He controls the text as he controls the history of Israel and the nations. Here the religious situation involves total dependency on Him as the protagonist of the biblical story.

When the Talmud announces that "It is not in heaven," human beings replace God and take responsibility for applying the law without need of further revelation. The signs and wonders of our text serve the ironic purpose of providing an occasion for the Rabbis to admonish God. To paraphrase the midrash, God is told politely: "Please stay out of this discussion. Your presence here is inappropriate. You gave us the Torah, but we must now apply it in our own lives according to our own understanding. And"—this point is crucial for grasping the religious phenomenology of Rabbinic thought— "we are not going to try to intuit Your thoughts about what is right. We have to make sense of the law in particular situations through our own practical reasoning."

In the Bible, the community is called upon to choose between "life and death," between "good and evil" (Deut. 30:15). Revelation provides a law for the community but leaves responsibility for fulfilling the law in the hands of the community itself.

In the Rabbinic tradition, covenantal consciousness gains a new dimension: Israel is called upon not only to fulfill the law but also to define and expand its content. This radically new understanding of the covenantal relationship with God points toward a theological framework where the human partners, in the form of scribes and talmudic scholars, become major figures determining the spiritual destiny of the community. The scholar, whose authority derives from his intellectual competence, is raised to unprecedented heights, above even the prophet, whose authority depends upon the miraculous signs of God.

There is another way of looking at the implications of this text. One of the crucial theological concerns of the Rabbinic period was how to understand the idea of divine power. The Exodus drama—the total defeat of the pharaoh, the public triumph of Israel over its enemies—could no longer serve as the paradigm for understanding Israel's exile and powerlessness. Titus and the Roman army were visibly victorious. Contemporary pharaohs were not being defeated. History did not elicit spontaneous songs of praise to God as a "man of war" (Exod. 15:3) who defeats His enemies in order to become known as the lord of history.

The difference between past and present is poignantly expressed in the contrast between Moses' defiant confrontations with the pharaoh and Yohanan ben Zakkai's meeting with Titus to plead for the privilege of building a religious center in Yavneh for the surviving remnant of Jews (cf. BT Gittin 56a). In Rabbinic history, the visible signs of God's triumphal power are gone.

To make sense of the notions of a living God and divine election and to rebut suggestions that God had broken the covenant and abandoned Israel, God's power had to be understood in ways that could explain Israel's powerlessness, vulnerability, and humiliation. A revision of traditional theology began with a new reading of the language of divine power. "Who is as mighty as God?" (Exod. 15:11), the line sung when Israel crossed the sea, is midrashically taken to mean "Who is as silent as God?" "Who is like You, O Lord, among the mighty [elim]?" (Exod. 15:11)—"Who is like You among the dumb ones [ilmim]; who is like You that beholds the humiliation of his children and keeps silent?" (Mekhilta, Shirah 8).

This is another version of "It is not in heaven." Now God's historical silence and distance are interpreted so as not to entail feelings of debilitating guilt and unworthiness. On the contrary, the sense of God's love is intensified by shifting attention away from the material conditions of history toward Torah as the main framework that mediates His love for Israel. The absence of miracles in Israel's history is not taken to imply divine anger or rejection. It is as if God's historical distance is an invitation to His covenantal partner to take the initiative in the development of the Torah. The Rabbis respond to the diminishing signs of God's visible power by seizing that initiative and utilizing the study of Torah to mediate His living presence.

But it is important to qualify this account of the Rabbinic transformation of Jewish religious consciousness by pointing out that although the need for prophecy and miracle was greatly neutralized with respect to the law and its study, the need for miraculous divine intervention remained a vital component of the hope for historical change and national renewal. Despite the assertive boldness of the Rabbinic tradition of learning, classically represented in the oven of Akhnai story, exilic spirituality continued to be characterized by a passive, prayerful longing for a new messianic intervention in history to heal the overwhelming injuries of exile and statelessness. Jewish political liberation and national restoration were still perceived in terms of the biblical paradigm of divine power.

In contrast to this traditional attitude, modern secular Zionism created historical conditions in which Jewish national existence could be renewed without waiting for supernatural intervention. In terms of the conceptual approach to the covenantal idea discussed above, the Zionist revolution can be seen as having opened up yet another dimension of Jewish life to the spirit of rabbinic confidence and initiative, liberating the community from the prevalent attitude of helpless dependency.

On this view, the state of Israel is not a sign of the messianic unfolding of Jewish religious eschatology but rather part of a process that began at Sinai when Israel agreed to build its religious life in response to God's self-limiting covenant. The diminishing presence of God as the visible, triumphant victor in history was met in the Rabbinic tradition with a new and vital sense of covenantal *intellectual* responsibility: that is the subject of this chapter. Analogously, the distance and silence of God experienced in the modern period can be an impetus to a new appreciation of Israel's *political* responsibility — extending the rabbinic sense of human adequacy beyond the areas to which it was restricted in the past. Here is a further implication of the Rabbis' courageous insistence that "It is not in heaven."

David Hartman

Excluding Prophecy from the Halakhic Process

11. Maimonides, MT Foundations of the Torah 9:1–4

Translated by Bernard Septimus, forthcoming in the Yale Judaica Series (Yale University Press).

As we have already seen, Maimonides grounds the authority of the Torah in the unique prophecy of Moses (℃5, §12). Therefore, no subsequent prophet can make law. Maimonides here excludes prophets from any participation in the legal process, turning Rabbi Yehoshua's pronouncement "It is not in heaven" into a constitutional principle.

Chapter 9

1. It is a point [made] clear[ly] and explicit[ly] in the Torah that the latter is legislation that endures for ever and all eternity: it is subject to neither alteration, nor diminution, nor addition. For it is said: "Everything which I command you, that you shall observe to do, do not add to it or diminish from it" (Deut. 13:1). And it is said: "But those things that are revealed belong to us and to our children forever, that we may do all the words of this Torah forever" (Deut. 29:28). Likewise it is said: "It is a statute forever, throughout your generations" (Lev. 23:14). Moreover, it is said, "It is not in heaven" (Deut. 30:12): you thus learn that henceforth no prophet is authorized to innovate anything.

Therefore, should any man arise, Israelite or gentile, produce an evidential sign, and claim that God sent him to add a commandment, detract a commandment, or give to any of the commandments an explanation that we did not hear from Moses, or should he claim that the commandments given to Israel are not eternal and for all generations but were rather provisional commandments, he is a false prophet; for he seeks to deny the prophecy of Moses. He is executed by strangulation, because he presumed to speak in the name of the Lord, what he did not command him (Deut. 18:20). For He, blessed be His name, commanded Moses that this legislation be "ours and our children's forever" (Deut. 29:28); and "God is not man, that he should lie" (Num. 23:19).

2. Why then is it said in the Torah, "I will raise up for them a prophet like you from among their brethren, and I will put my words in his mouth, and he shall speak to them all that I command him?" (Deut. 18:18). [This prophet] comes not to found a religion but to exhort concerning the Torah's teaching and to warn the populace against violating it, as the last of [the prophets] said: "Remember the Torah of Moses, My servant" (Malachi 3:22).

So, too, if he issues commands to us on discretionary matters, like "Go to such and such a place" or "Don't go," "Do battle today" or "Don't," "Build this wall" or "Don't build it," we are commanded to heed him. Whoever transgresses his words is liable to death at the hands of heaven, for it is said: "And whoever will not give heed to My words which he shall speak in My name, I Myself will require it of him" (Deut. 18:19). Likewise, a prophet who transgresses his own words or who suppresses his prophecy is liable to death at the hands of heaven. Regarding [all] three it is said: "I Myself will require it of him" (Deut. 18:19).

3. So, too, if a prophet, known to us to be a prophet, should tell us to transgress any of the commandments in the Torah, or many commandments, minor or grave, temporarily—we are commanded to obey him. We have the following on tradition from the ancient sages: "Should a prophet tell you, 'Transgress the words of the Torah,' as Elijah did on Mount Carmel, obey him in all things, save idolatry."

This, with the proviso that the [transgression] be temporary (as in the case of Elijah on Mount Carmel, who sacrificed a burnt offering outside [the Temple precincts] although Jerusalem had [already] been chosen and anyone sacrificing outside [its Temple] was liable to excision [karet]). Because the person in question is a prophet, we are commanded to obey him, and this, too, comes under [the commandment] "You shall heed him" (Deut. 18:15).

Had they asked Elijah, "Shall we then abrogate the [prohibition] inscribed in the Torah 'that you not offer your burnt offerings at every place that you see'" (Deut. 12:13)? he would have responded: "No: one who sacrifices outside [the Temple precincts] remains ever liable to excision, as Moses commanded; but I, today, will sacrifice outside [the Temple precincts], in accordance with the word of the Lord, in order to controvert the prophets of Ba'al."

4. If, after this fashion, any of the prophets command [us] to transgress temporarily, we are commanded to heed them. But should they say that the [law] has been permanently abrogated, they are executed by strangulation, for the Torah has said: "Ours and our children's forever" (Deut. 29:28). Similarly, should [a prophet] abrogate anything that we have learned on tradition, or say, on any legal issue, that God instructed him that its determination is thus and such, or that the authoritative decision follows so-and-so, he is a false prophet and is to be put to death by strangulation, even if he produced a sign; for he seeks to contradict the Torah, which has said: "It is not in Heaven" (Deut. 30:12). But on a temporary basis, one obeys him in everything.

A Modern Synthesis

12. Abraham Isaac Kook, "A *Hakham* Is Superior to a Prophet"

Orot (Jerusalem: Mossad Harav Kook, 1963; Hebrew), pp. 120–21.

We conclude the section "Beyond Prophecy" with this short historiosophic essay—first published in 1914—in which Kook contrasts prophetic vision with legal attention to detail and describes their ultimate synthesis. Combining aspects of the positions of Maimonides and Nahmanides, he portrays a reemergence of Mosaic prophecy in an impending messianic age.

Poets and rhetoricians are characteristically adept at describing the general splendor of life, all its especially beautiful aspects, those which encompass mighty streams and abundant vitality. They are also able to expose the general ugliness of life's perversions and to protest vigorously against them. However, penetrating the details of particular causes, [determining] how to set life on a solid foundation, preserving it from even the slightest perversion — which would eventually cause it to run aground and be ruined — all these are not within the competence of enthused and vigorous imaginative power. Rather, they lie within the province of analytic wisdom [*hokhmah*]. Here begins the work of physicians, economists, engineers, judges, and all those engaged in practical wisdom.

On a higher plane: Prophecy beheld the perverse stream of idolatry in Israel and powerfully protested against it. [Prophecy also beheld] the blissful splendor of the one Lord, [Israel's] God, portraying its full beauty and magnificence. [It beheld too] the corruption of various [forms of] moral lawlessness: the oppression of the poor, the exploitation of the needy, murder, adultery, violence, and theft. [Prophecy] became infused with the spirit of God to deliver and [provide] remedy through lofty, holy oration.

. . . Hidden from the prophetic, visionary eye are [the workings of] all the practical *mitzvot* with the meticulous precision of their detailed laws. When these are observed and studied, become familiar and beloved, their concealed, inner bliss will eventually be revealed. The divine, pure life-stream will dispel with its might the darkness of idolatry so it may never rise again. [Prophecy also cannot discern] how the gradual neglect that devalues actions and their many branches and details, initiates a process of ruin and destroys the vessels that can receive the exalted spirit,[10] whereby the inclination of the human heart — that misleading imagination magnificently adorned [but] filled with poisonous dust inside — grows in and of itself. All this was not accessible to prophecy, that is, to prophecy through a dim glass.[11]

True, it is accessible to the prophecy of Moses, which was prophecy through a clear glass, [delivered] "mouth to mouth" (Num. 12:8), [and] which alone could perceive both the power of generalities and the precision of particulars. But there has never arisen another like him, [as it is written:] "Never again did there arise another prophet like Moses, whom the Lord singled out,

---

10. Kook here alludes to the Lurianic myth of creation; see G. Scholem, *Major Trends in Jewish Mysticism* (New York: Schocken, 1946), pp. 260–68.
11. The reference is to all the prophets except Moses. Cf. BT Yevamot 49b: "All the prophets looked through a dim glass, but Moses looked through a clear glass."

face to face" (Deut. 34:10). It was thus necessary to assign to the prophets the task of generalities, and to the *hakhamim* the task of particulars. "A *hakham* is superior to a prophet" (BT Bava Batra 12a): that which prophecy did not accomplish with its fiery arsenal—namely, to purge Israel of idolatry and to uproot the worst degradations of oppression, violence and robbery, murder, sexual corruption, and the pursuit of bribes—the *hakhamim* accomplished through the expansion of Torah, by raising up many students and by constant review of particular rules and their applications. "'The eternal paths lead to Him' (Hab. 3:6). Do not read 'paths' [*halikhot*] but 'laws' [*halakhot*]" (BT Niddah 73a).

In the course of time, the work of the *hakhamim* superseded the work of the prophets, and prophecy ceased. A long time having passed, the generalities began to wane; they were swallowed up in details and disappeared from sight. Therefore, at the End of Days, when the light of prophecy will revive . . . [as it is written,] "I shall pour out My spirit on all flesh" (Joel 3:1), then the loathing of particulars will abound. "The wisdom of Scribes will decay. And those who live on the boundary"—that is, the *hakhamim* who set boundaries in their teachings—"will wander from city to city, finding no favor" (BT Sanhedrin 97a).[12]

Finally, the sparks of emerging prophetic light will be revealed, not as unripe fruit but as "first fruits," filled with vitality and life. And [prophecy] will recognize in general the greatness of the works of wisdom, and with true humility will exclaim: "A *hakham* is superior to a prophet." "Faithfulness and truth meet; justice and wellbeing kiss. Truth springs up from the earth; justice looks down from heaven. The Lord also bestows His bounty; our land yields its produce" (Ps. 85:11–13). And the soul of Moses shall again appear in the world.

12. This talmudic phrase—along with the entire apocalyptic description in which it is set—is opaque, and there is great variation in its reading. Kook transposes two clauses from the original and interpolates his own account.

Authority of the Oral Law

Rabbinic Legislation: "You Must Not Deviate"
13. BT Shabbat 23a

The Hanukkah festival is not considered de'orayta—*that is, it does not derive from the written Torah. The lighting of the Hanukkah candles is ordained by the Rabbis; it is* derabbanan. *Should the performance nevertheless be viewed as an act commanded by God?*

Rav Hiyya b. Ashi said, citing Rav: When lighting the Hanukkah candle, one should pronounce a blessing. . . . What blessing? "[Blessed are You, O Lord our God, king of the universe,] who has sanctified us with His commandments, and commanded us to light the Hanukkah candles."

But where did He command us? Rav Ivya said: This is [derived] from "you must not deviate" (Deut. 17:11; see above, §1). Rav Nehemiah said: "Ask your father, he will inform you; Your elders, they will tell you" (Deut. 32:7).

Revising the Law by Midrash
14. BT Makkot 22a–b

*The scope of rabbinic authority is not exhausted by the power to enact secondary legislation (*derabbanan*). This selection both illustrates and celebrates rabbinic power to revise scriptural law itself through the (re)interpretive tools of midrash.*

Mishnah: How many lashes are administered? Forty less one [i.e, thirty-nine], as written, ". . . by number. Forty [stripes he may give him]" [13] (Deut. 25:2–3)—a number leading up to forty. Rabbi Yehudah says: He is given a full forty lashes. . . .

13. Old JPS; in the New JPS the syntax of the original Hebrew is altered.

Gemara: What is the reason [for this reading]? If it had been written "forty by number," then I would say: a count of forty. Now that it is written "by number forty"—[this means] a count that leads up to forty.

Said Rava: How foolish are all those people, who rise before a Torah scroll but fail to rise before a great man [i.e., a scholar]! For in the Torah scroll it is written "forty," and the rabbis came along and subtracted one.

"Hillel Enacted the Prosbul"
15. BT Gittin 36a–b

The background for this selection is the law of debt remission every seventh year, connected to the (partly utopian) biblical system of social justice described in Leviticus and Deuteronomy (see C20). In the face of the practical pressures of economic life, Hillel devised the prosbul *(a Greek word of uncertain meaning) to circumvent the biblical injunction. Legally, the* prosbul *works by consigning the debt to the court, for debts already in the process of collection by a court were not subject to remission. Despite this technical justification, the Talmud voices dissatisfaction over the Rabbinic uprooting of biblical laws. The discussion here introduces the maxim that the court has the power to expropriate, to which we return in subsequent chapters.*

Hillel enacted [*tikken*] the *prosbul* on account of *tikkun olam* (Mishnah Gittin 4:3); the Mishnah (Shvi'it 10:3–4) reads: [A debt secured by] a *prosbul* is not remitted. This is one of the things enacted by Hillel the Elder. He saw that the people refused to make loans to each other, thus transgressing against that which is written in the Torah: "Beware lest you harbor the base thought 'The seventh year, the year of remission, is approaching,' so that you are mean to your needy brother and give him nothing" (Deut. 15:9). So he arose and enacted the *prosbul*.

The text of a *prosbul* runs thus: "I, X, hereby consign to you, the judges at location Y, any debt owed me by Z, [so that I] may collect it at any time I see fit." And the judges or witnesses sign below.

But is such a thing possible, that according to the Torah [*de'orayta*] the seventh year effects remission, yet Hillel enacted that there be no remission?

Said Abaye: [*Prosbul* applies] only to the seventh year in these times, following the view of Rabbi [Judah the Prince, who holds that according to basic Torah law, debt remission does not apply under conditions of incomplete sovereignty]. . . . It was the rabbis who enacted that there should nevertheless be remission, to preserve the seventh year; then when Hillel saw that the people refused to make loans to each other, he arose and enacted the *prosbul*.

But is such a thing possible, that according to the Torah [*de'orayta*] the seventh year [in "these times"] brings no remission, yet the rabbis enacted that there be remission [*Rashi:* and thus the borrower becomes a robber]? Said Abaye: This is [merely an instance of] "hold back and do not act"[14] [i.e., there is no active breach of a prohibition].

Rava said: The court has the power to expropriate.

[*Rashi:* [This relates even to] the position which holds that [even] in these days, the seventh year effects remission of debts *de'orayta*—yet Hillel enacted that it should not; . . . yet there is no difficulty, since [intervention] in monetary matters [*mamon*] does not constitute "uprooting something from the Torah," as long as it is a case of [building] a fence; for in monetary matters, the court has the power to expropriate.]

For Rabbi Yitzhak said: Whence [do we know] that the court has the power to expropriate? As written, "[a proclamation was issued in Judah and Jerusalem that all who had returned from the exile should assemble in Jerusalem] and that anyone who did not come in three days would, by decision of the officers and elders, have his property confiscated and himself excluded from the congregation of the returning exiles" (Ezra 10:7–8). Rabbi Eleazar said, [This derives] from "These are the portions bequeathed by lot to the tribes of Israel by the priest Eleazar, Joshua son of Nun, and the leaders of ancestral houses [literally, "fathers"]" (Josh. 19:51). What is this connection between "leaders" and "fathers"? It tells us [that] just as fathers [can] bequeath

---

14. This complex distinction between actively and passively "uprooting something from Torah law" is the subject of the talmudic discussion in BT Yevamot 89a–90b.

to their sons whatever they wish, so too [can] leaders bequeath to the people whatever they wish.

The question was raised: When Hillel enacted the *prosbul,* was it for his generation that he enacted it—or perhaps for future generations as well? The implications concern [the possibility] of annulling it. Should you say that he enacted it for his generation, we can annul it, whereas if you say that he enacted it for future generations as well, then "A court cannot annul the ruling of a fellow court unless it excels it in wisdom and in number" (Mishnah Eduyot 1:5 [C7, S2]).

What [is the answer]? Come and hear this saying of Shmu'el: "A *prosbul* can be written only by the court of Sura or by the court of Neharde'a." [15] Now if you suppose that he enacted [it] for future generations as well, let it be written by any court!—Perhaps, when Hillel enacted it for future generations, [this extended] not to any court, [but only] to a court like his own, such as [that of] Rav Ami and Rav Assi, who have the power of expropriation.

Come and hear this saying of Shmu'el: "This *prosbul* is a judicial insult; if I have the power, I will annul it."—Annul it? But "A court cannot annul the ruling of a fellow court unless it excels it in wisdom and in number!"—He means to say: If I had more power than Hillel, I would annul it.

Rav Nahman, however, said: "I would confirm it."—Confirm it? But it is firmly in place! He means to say: I would make a pronouncement regarding it, so that even without being written, it will be as though it had been written.

Commentary. The Oral Law: Celebrating Radical Reinterpretation

Respect for the Torah is traditionally shown by rising before the scroll—the only concrete object of reverence in synagogues to this day. Rava wryly complains that the same measure of respect is not shown toward Torah scholars: "How foolish are all those people, who rise before a Torah scroll but fail to rise before a great man [i.e., a scholar]!" But why, precisely, does Rava believe that scholars should be revered just like the book they have mastered?

15. Sites of the two great academies in Babylonia.

The scroll itself is revered as an embodiment of the sublime Torah, God's word. Does Rava perceive the scholar in a similar light? Surely he cannot mean simply that Torah's holiness (or its wisdom, or whatever other qualities make it worthy of reverence) resides also in the scholar. For surely no scholar can possess the Torah's qualities to the full degree that they are present in the Torah itself. If people refuse to equate the partial with the full presence, that hardly justifies calling them "foolish."

What Rava seems to believe, then, is that the scholar is in some sense *superior* to the Torah, a superiority reflected in the feat of midrashic reinterpretation: "For in the Torah scroll it is written 'forty,' and the rabbis came along and subtracted one." Clearly, this midrash is not cited as a unique occurrence, but rather as a fine example of halakhic midrash as it operates throughout the law. The implied superiority of scholar over scroll—of midrash over the text's plain meaning—can be understood in two very different ways: one in terms of value, the other in terms of authority.

Superiority of value would mean that the midrashic rendition of the law is better than the original—better, that is, for the people subject to the law, because their punishment is reduced, or perhaps better for the law itself, because the harshness of its justice is tempered by a touch of mercy. To be sure, the improvement here is rather minimal. The significance of reducing the number of stripes from forty to thirty-nine lies not in the (minuscule) difference in physical suffering, but in the symbolic message of underlying compassion. Corporal punishment is delivered not with a vengeance but with restraint.

If this understanding has some plausibility, it derives less from Rava's specific example here—the symbolic sparing of one stripe—than from other Rabbinic sources. Alongside the clause upon which Rava is commenting, the same chapter of the Mishnah includes several other clauses that appear to promote compassion toward the sinner and reduce the severity of corporal punishment. Similarly, and even more significantly, the Rabbis virtually abolished capital punishment. Rava can be taken, then, as pointing to the numerical reduction as representing a broad midrashic remaking of biblical law.

If Rava's dictum is put in theological terms, it attains a striking boldness. People ought to show greater respect to the Rabbis, because the Rabbis' law is better than that originally given by God! This elevated conception of the midrashic enterprise, which may well have been shared by many of the classical sages, certainly calls for some explanation. Perhaps nothing less than such boldness could support fidelity to Torah in the face of the powerful critique—expressed saliently in Paul's epistles—that fulfilling the demands of God's law is incompatible with human weakness. Living "under the law" in its plain meaning, with its harsh condemnation of any willful sinner, may indeed be untenable. If Torah law was not to be superseded, its punitive stance had to be corrected to accommodate human frailty.

I offer this suggestion in lieu of a proper theological account—a difficult-to-meet desideratum, in which the project of improving God's law would have to be squared with the notion of an all-wise and benevolent God. If this seems too daunting, let us consider the alternative understanding of Rava's statement, focusing not on the value of midrashic law but on Rabbinic authority. Such a focus involves a subtly different sense of standing before the Torah: here, it is not so much an expression of reverence as an acknowledgment of authority. People rise before the Torah scroll to declare their allegiance to its commands; and they are fools not to recognize the superior authority of the Rabbis, who have the final word in determining *halakhah*.

This interpretation fits well with the discussion about the blessing before lighting a Hanukkah candle. There, no one doubts that a commitment to *halakhah* implies a duty to observe Rabbinic decrees. But however great the Rabbis' authority, there is some hesitation with regard to the religious status of observing their decrees: Can their decrees truthfully be called something that "God commanded"? And the answer is that yes, in a sense it is God's command to observe even laws that are *derabbanan* (ordained by the Rabbis)—without blurring the distinction between such laws and God's own commands, the laws that are *de'orayta*.

But if Rava's main purpose is to exalt the Rabbis' authority over that of *de'orayta* law, how are we to understand the talmudic perplexity over Hillel's enactment of *prosbul?* Why does the Talmud ask, "Is such a thing possible, that according to the Torah [*de'orayta*] . . . , yet Hillel enacted that . . ."?

Perhaps, indeed, not all the sages shared Rava's celebration of Rabbinic power. It is noteworthy that according to Abaye, Rava's contemporary, an enactment like Hillel's *prosbul* is restricted to alterations of Rabbinic laws. Rava himself, not surprisingly, is prepared to go much further, allowing for outright Rabbinic abrogation of the biblical law of debt remission: "The court has the power to expropriate."

Even this power, however, appears to be restricted to "[intervention] in monetary matters [*mamon*]," which—as Rashi explains—"does not constitute 'uprooting something from the Torah.'" This implies that the Torah's criminal or ritual law, by contrast, would not be subject to similar Rabbinic abrogation or circumvention. And even with regard to the *prosbul* itself, the ensuing talmudic discussion reveals great unease. Why is the *prosbul* depicted as so problematic, rather than as a fine instance of Rabbinic improvement (or at least authority) over the given biblical law?

The answer may lie in Shmu'el's pejorative description of the *prosbul* as a "judicial insult." According to the mishnah, Hillel sought a remedy for a difficult situation: continued upholding of the law of remission was producing unacceptable results. But he did not act to change (or reinterpret) the law. Instead, he arranged to harness the court's power to circumvent it: that is the "insult." Hillel's enactment may indeed encourage extension of credit to the needy and work for the general benefit of mostly everyone. But even if it truly promotes the great end of *tikkun olam,* this is achieved through an objectionable legal mechanism.

The *prosbul* is problematic, then, because it fails to employ the full Rabbinic power of midrash. In some sense, admittedly, it does rely on the midrashic exclusion of notes of credit consigned to the court from the law of remission. In fact, several traditional commentators suggest—citing the *Sifre* to Deuteronomy 15:3 (*piska* 113)—that this midrashic innovation and Hillel's institution of the *prosbul* are one and the same. But the talmudic discussion here clearly views the two halakhic moves as distinct, and directs its criticism not to the midrashic reinterpretation, but to Hillel's abrogation of Torah law.

The insufficiently clear boundary here between midrash and enactment may be due to the nascent condition of midrash in Hillel's time. Subsequently, the full flowering of reinterpretation as the chief mode of halakhic creativity heralded the supremacy of the Oral Law over the written Torah. Radical reinterpretation characterizes midrashic treatment of the biblical text and then in turn the treatment of the Mishnah by talmudic *amora'im* and of the Talmud by authors of responsa and codes. True, explicit enactments by rabbis—and later by community leaders—continue to be promulgated beside (and sometimes even against) Torah law. Such enactments are prone to continued scrutiny and restriction, as exemplified in the talmudic discussion of *prosbul*. But in assessing the true scope of Rabbinic authority, we must not allow such discussions to eclipse the central importance and value of midrashic creativity, celebrated by Rava.

Noam J. Zohar

Medieval Arguments: Karaites and Rabbanites

Karaite Critique of Midrashic Innovation

16. Elijah Basyatchi, *Adderet Eliyahu* I:33–35

Karaite Anthology, edited by Leon Nemoy, Yale Judaica Series (New Haven: Yale University Press, 1952), pp. 249–50.

Basyatchi was one of the greatest Karaite legal scholars, the author of a code that became standard in much the same way as the Shulhan Arukh, *which it preceded by about fifty years (Basyatchi worked on it from 1460 to 1490). Like any rabbinic text, his* Aderet *accumulated commentaries, yet Basyatchi maintained the distinctiveness of Karaite "tradition."*

33. . . . There are, however, other ordinances in the observance of which we have been raised since the days of our fathers, and their fathers before them, and which are a matter of custom with us. They are not recorded in the Law and have become as second nature with us; nevertheless, they flow in a sense from the intent of prophetic utterances. Such ordinances are called by scholars "the burden of inheritance" or "tradition"; for example, the slaughtering of animals, which must be performed by means of a slaughtering knife and by proper cutting of the prescribed parts of the body. . . .

34. The learned Rabbi Tobiah states that he who says that there are traditions which have no support in Scripture does so merely because of his

insufficient comprehension of the particular ordinance. That is why scholars have said that all ordinances are valid, whether written in Scripture or derived by way of analogy or transmitted by tradition; and they have said also, "The observance of Scripture rests on three things: the written texts, analogy, and the 'burden of inheritance.'"

35. Karaite tradition, however, is not like the tradition believed in by the Rabbanites, since the latter add to and subtract from Scripture and say that tradition overcomes the written biblical text, notwithstanding that Scripture says expressly: "Ye shall not add unto the word which I command you" (Deut. 4:2). If their intention be merely to interpret the prophetic utterances, it is not seemly for them to say that tradition overcomes the written biblical text. For example, with regard to the ordinance "Forty stripes may he give him" (Deut. 25:3), they say that the meaning is forty less one (§14). . . . Karaite tradition, on the other hand, is such as is acknowledged by all Israel, and it does not stand up against that which is recorded in the writ of divine truth; and our scholars have said that every tradition which does not stand up against Scripture, does not add to what is stated in Scripture, is acknowledged by all Israel, and has indirect support in Scripture, is to be called genuine tradition, and we must accept it. They said further that most of the Mishnah and the Talmud comprises genuine utterances of our forefathers, and Rabbi Nissi ben Noah has said that our people are obligated to study the Mishnah and the Talmud.

"Neither Add to It" Applies Only to the Multitude

17. Judah Halevi, *The Kuzari* 3:39–41

Translated by Lawrence Berman and Barry S. Kogan, forthcoming in the Yale Judaica Series (Yale University Press).

In its final form, The Kuzari is presented as a defense of Judaism against its religious opponents and philosophical rivals. However, the book's core, preserved in its third part, was originally conceived as a polemical work against Karaism. Halevi defends the Rabbis' power to depart from Scripture by reconceiving their teachings in terms of prophetic inspiration.

(3:39) The sage said: Truly, our [entire] religious Law is bound to the "law given to Moses from Sinai" or "the place which the Lord shall choose" (Deut. 17:8, 10), "for instruction shall come forth from Zion and the word of the Lord from Jerusalem" (Isa. 2:3) in the presence of judges, officials, priests, and [members of] the Sanhedrin. We are ordered to obey the authorized judge in every generation, just as [Scripture] says: ". . . [And appear] before the . . . judge in charge at that time, and present your problem. When they have announced to you the verdict in the case, you shall carry out the verdict that is announced to you from the place that the Lord chose, observing scrupulously all their instructions to you" (Deut. 17:9–10). Then [it adds]: "Should a man act presumptuously and disregard the priest," etc., . . . "that man shall die. Thus you will sweep out evil from your midst" (Deut. 17:12). [Scripture] associates disobeying the priest and the judge with the very greatest crimes when it says, "Thus you will sweep out evil from your midst" (Deut. 17:7), and it follows with [this explanation]: "All the people will hear and be afraid and will not act presumptuously again" (Deut. 17:13), [that is,] as long as the proper ordering of the [sacred] service, the Sanhedrin, and the other groups through which the proper ordering [of the community at large] is perfected, continues. Moreover, the divine order will undoubtedly be attached to them, either [directly] through prophecy or [indirectly] through support and inspiration, just as it was during the [period of] the Second Temple.

For people such as these, conniving and collusion are [just] not possible. That is why the commandment [to read from] the Scroll of Esther and [to observe] Purim as well as the commandment [to observe] Hanukkah became obligatory, and also [why] we were permitted to say [in the appropriate blessings recited before fulfilling these obligations], ". . . And who has commanded us to read the Scroll [of Esther] and to kindle the light of Hanukkah" (cf. §13). . . . If they were [merely] customs that arose after the exile, they surely would not have been designated as "statutory," and it would not have been necessary for us [to recite] a blessing [in connection with them]. Rather, they would have been called [in each case] an ordinance or a custom. . . .

(3:40) The Khazar said: How can this be reconciled with [the commandment that says,] "Neither add to it nor take away from it" (Deut. 13:1)?

(3:41) The sage said: This was said only to the multitude so that they would not engage in intellectual speculation, make arbitrary judgments, and lay down [religious] laws for themselves as the Karaites have done. Moreover, it encourages them to accept [the instructions that came] from the prophets after Moses, peace be upon him, and from the priests, and from the judges too, just as [Scripture] says with regard to the prophet: "I will raise up a prophet for them," etc., . . . "and he will speak to them all that I command him" (Deut. 18:18). With regard to the priests and the judges it also said that their rulings should be obeyed. Thus, the statement "You shall not add anything to what I command you or take anything away from it" (Deut. 4:2) has come to mean: all that I have commanded you through Moses and also all that I have commanded you through "a prophet from among your own people" (Deut. 18:15), in keeping with the conditions that establish [who is fit] for prophecy, or all that the priests and the judges have agreed upon "from the place which the Lord shall choose," for they are indeed supported by the divine presence. It is inconceivable for them to have colluded on something that is contrary to the religious Law because of their great numbers. And it is also inconceivable to ascribe a faulty opinion to them because of their vast [store of] knowledge, which is [partly] inherited, [partly] innate, and [partly] acquired [by their own investigations], because they [themselves] reported that the [members of the] Sanhedrin were obligated to acquire [knowledge of] all the sciences, and especially [because] prophecy or what substitutes for it, such as a heavenly voice and other such things, rarely abandoned them.

"Neither Add to It" Applies to Rabbinic Legislation

18. Maimonides, MT Laws of Rebels 1:1–2; 2:1, 9

The Code of Maimonides, Book Fourteen: The Book of Judges, translated by Abraham M. Hershman, Yale Judaica Series (New Haven: Yale University Press, 1949), pp. 138–40, 142.

In his account of rabbinic authority, Maimonides upholds the distinction between law and prophecy on the one hand (§11) and the authority of the Oral Law on the other. He views the bulk of the Oral Law as a product of the institutional responsibility of the Sanhedrin to interpret and implement Torah law and only a minimal portion as the result of a direct ongoing tradition from Sinai.

Chapter 1

1. The Great Sanhedrin of Jerusalem is the root of the Oral Law. The members thereof are the pillars of instruction; out of them go forth statutes and judgments to all Israel. Scripture bids us repose confidence in them, as it is said, "According to the law which they shall teach thee" (Deut. 17:11). This is a positive command. Whoever believes in Moses, our teacher, and his Law is bound to follow their guidance in the practice of religion and to lean upon them.

2. Whoever does not act in accordance with their instruction transgresses a negative commandment, as it is said, "Thou shalt not turn aside from the sentence which they declare unto thee, to the right hand, nor to the left" (Deut. 17:11). . . . Whether the direction given by them is with regard to matters that they learned by tradition—matters that form the contents of the Oral Law—or with regard to rulings deduced by any of the hermeneutical rules by which the Torah is interpreted—rulings which they approved—or with regard to measures devised by them to serve as a fence about the Law—measures designed to meet the needs of the times . . . : with regard to any of these three categories, obedience to the direction given to them is a positive command. . . .

Chapter 2

1. If the Great Sanhedrin, by employing one of the hermeneutical principles, deduced a ruling which in its judgment was in consonance with the Law and rendered a decision to that effect, and a later [High] Court finds a reason for setting aside the ruling, it may do so and act in accordance with its own opinion, as it is said, "And unto the judge that shall be in those days" (Deut. 17:9), that is, we are bound to follow the directions of the court of our own generation.

9. Since the court is authorized to issue decrees prohibiting what is permitted and the prohibition is binding upon succeeding generations; and since it is empowered to permit provisionally what is forbidden in Scripture, how are we to understand the scriptural injunction "Thou shalt not add thereto, nor diminish from it" (Deut. 13:1)? [It is to be understood as an ad-

monition] not to add to the precepts of the Torah, nor to take any precept away from it, that is, not to impart to any regulation [evolved in the course of time] the character of an old, established law, as though it were a command embodied in the Written or the Oral Law. To elucidate this point: The Bible says: "Thou shalt not seethe a kid in its mother's milk" (Exod. 23:19). We have it on tradition that this verse prohibits the cooking or eating of flesh with milk, be it the flesh of a domestic animal or of a beast of chase; that the flesh of fowl with milk is permitted by biblical law. Should the court permit the flesh of a beast of chase with milk, it would be taking away [from the commands of the Torah]. On the other hand, should it forbid the flesh of fowl [with milk] on the ground that the prohibition in the text extends to [the cooking or eating of the flesh of] fowl with milk, it would add [to the commands of the Torah].

What the court should say, is: "By the law of Scripture, flesh of fowl [with milk] is permitted, but we forbid it." It is imperative that we inform the people that the prohibition has been decreed in order to obviate harmful results that might otherwise ensue. For some people would argue thus: flesh of fowl [with milk] is permitted because it is not expressly forbidden in the text; it follows therefore that the flesh of a beast of chase [with milk] is likewise permitted, since it is not expressly stated in the text. Others would contend that even the flesh of a domestic animal is permitted [with milk] except that of a goat; still others might assert that even the flesh of a goat may be eaten with the milk of a cow or of a sheep, because the text states "its mother's milk," that is, milk of its own kind; still others might [go so far as to] say that the flesh of a goat may be eaten even with the milk of a goat, provided that the milk is not that of its own mother, because the text reads "*its* mother's." Therefore, we forbid all flesh with milk, even the flesh of fowl. In this way, the court does not make any addition [to the precepts], but is only making a fence to the Torah. This applies to similar regulations.

Critique of Rabbinic Authority

19. Leone Modena (attrib.), *Kol Sakhal,* Second Essay, Chapter 5

Talya Fishman, *Shaking the Pillars of Exile: "Voice of a Fool," an Early Modern Jewish Critique of Rabbinic Culture* (Stanford: Stanford University Press, 1997), pp. 112–14.

Kol Sakhal, *"Voice of a Fool," comes from an anonymous manuscript first published in 1852 but written, according to modern scholars, by Leone Modena in the early seventeenth century. Modena also wrote, or began to write, a refutation of the* Kol Sakhal, *but only a few pages have been found. Assuming his authorship, his intentions are perplexing. Perhaps he was expressing his own views, and the refutation is merely self-protection (for the views are, as he says, heretical). But none of his other books even hint at such unconventional ideas. Perhaps he was expressing views current in the Italian Jewish community (or more widely, among returning* conversos, *for example), which he thought needed to be refuted. But if so, the arguments are presented with remarkable force. In either case, the radical critique of rabbinic authority developed here is worth reprinting. Modena's critique echoes Karaite claims, but also goes beyond them, and is virtually unprecedented in Jewish literature; it anticipates Voltaire's critique of "priestcraft" a century and a half later.*

Among the things that you ought to know is that all these matters relating to the commandments and details that the Pharisees continued to create from the time of the Great Assembly onward were not initially [designed] in order that the entire population fulfill them obligatorily, with the violator considered a heretic and judged like a violator of matters of Torah, as became widespread after the Destruction. Rather [Pharisaic practice was intended] as a way of consecrating oneself with respect to what is permitted and [as] a life of separateness, in the manner of the monastic sects among today's Christians who are even more stringent than they were. They thought that the commandments would be fulfilled in their most proper manner through these deeds. Note that this is why they were called "Pharisees" [*Perushim*]. That is, their custom was to be stringent in separatism [*perishut*], set apart from the masses of the people of Israel.

And even when the Pharisees became more powerful than the other sects during the time of the Second Temple kings, they did not judge and punish violators of these ordinances of theirs. But little by little, those who accepted them . . . went on progressively strengthening everything like the statutes of the Torah itself, until it *too* was called "Torah"—"Oral Torah." And they said that everything was received, either from Sinai or from the prophets.

However, after our city was destroyed and our Temple laid waste and Israel was exiled from its land during the days of the *tanna'im* . . . those sages and early leaders should have established for the exiled a new order and almost a new Torah, though on the foundation of the Torah of Moses, to follow in the Exile. For the priesthood and sacrifices, purity and impurity, and certain laws dependent upon the land were nullified [i.e., were no longer practicable], and there was no Sanhedrin, and they were transformed from a kingdom to [a people under] enslavement.

But where they should have eased and lightened the load of the de-tails of the commandments—without ever deviating from their principles, however—it would, in any event, have been fitting for them [the leaders] to interpret and explain [them] in such a manner that they [the Jews] would be able to survive in the lands of their enemies, both in finding a livelihood and also in not being hated and oppressed by them. [And the Jewish leaders ought] to have thought about our being in Exile and that it is difficult to perform the details of the commandments and that perhaps Israel's condition could change for the worse and [for it] to be dispersed even more widely, as happened for our sins. They did the exact opposite, taking for themselves whatever had been practiced as a manner of separatism by the Pharisees, as I have told you. And they added to these over and over. They are all bad stat-utes to drain the financial resources of Israel and to sadden their lives and render them odious and despised in the places to which they go. For they [the rabbis] then had no way of lording it over the people without this. And [they did] not [encourage them] to investigate any knowledge that would raise them above their fellows aside from the [Oral Law]. For they were all required to consult them [the rabbis] regarding the details of the command-ments. They therefore did not commit them to writing, giving the reason, "Things that are oral may not be committed to writing," in order that they [the masses of Jews] would have need for them [the rabbis] at all times, and would honor and revere them.

Were it not for the fact that when our Saintly Master [R. Judah the

Prince] arrived and saw that the masses already comported themselves under the yoke of these stringencies and inventions—and he was already wealthy and wise and a patriarch—he wished to put an end to this once and for all. He collected all that had been created up until then and wrote it in one code— these are the *Mishnayyot* in six Orders—in order that a reader might hasten through it and that Israel need not need its leaders every minute. Nor would they [the leaders] continue to add commandments and ordinances and details without end.

However, they shortly found room to return to their former strength; for how [else] would the sages and Patriarchs lord it over their generation if there were no innovation and casuistry . . . ? [So] they said that one could not derive legal instruction from the Mishnah, for the matters are obscure and require interpretation.

They persisted in doing to the Mishnah what they had done to the Torah, to the point that the Talmud was compiled of the wisdom of people who had grown up in the Valley of Shin'ar in Babylonia, devoid of civility and political know-how, who did not recognize the firmament, but only what was suspended over their heads above. . . .

And they established the entire Talmud, which, in truth, is Babel-ish and babbled and a hodgepodge of straw and hay and wheat. As they themselves said, "'You have set me down in dark places': This is the Babylonian Talmud" (BT Sanhedrin 24a).

And those who came after it did to it what they [their predecessors] had done to the Mishnah, via the writings of the *geonim,* the Tosafot, [and the talmudic commentaries]. . . .

Modern Concerns: Halakhic Innovation and Rabbinic Authority

Critique of Halakhic Atrophy

20. Moses Leib Lilienblum, *Orhot ha-Talmud,* Appendix

Complete Works of Moshe Leib Lilienblum (Cracow, 1910–13; Hebrew), vol. 2, pp. 37–39, 49–51.

Written in 1868, this is a representative text of the last years of the Russian haskalah *(enlightenment). By the 1870s, Lilienblum was a socialist, and by the 1880s a Zionist, but here he still defends a moderate* haskalah *position, demanding a reform of Jewish life led by the rabbis and based on interpretation of the Talmud.*

Latter-day [rabbis] have come to regard the Talmud just as the talmudic sages regarded the Torah of Moses! Just as they derived many laws from every little horn of the Torah's letters [see §9], so too today's codifiers have derived and created many laws from each word in the Talmud. Yet they differ, for the talmudic sages knew well that the legislator had not intended to encrypt within his words a host of laws, but rather that *time and common sense* were the causes of the new laws—the words of Scripture merely furnishing a prop [*asmakhta*] for their rulings. Not so the latter-day codifiers! They believed wholeheartedly that any innovation by an advanced student and any word that emerged from the mouths of the talmudic sages were revealed to Moses at Sinai. They similarly imagined that the talmudic sages hid a host of laws beneath the surface of their casuistic discussions and statements. From these [discussions] they thus derived new laws that would never have occurred to the talmudic sages, laws that contravene both the spirit of the age and common sense!

If only these codifiers had attended to the *methodology of the Talmud;* if only they had realized that the Talmud is more a guide to halakhic adjudication than a halakhic code; if only they had not forgotten that one does not derive [laws] from aggadic passages and that regarding rabbinic law one should be lenient;[16] if only they had chosen wisdom as did our sages prior to Rabbi Jacob Pollack and Rabbi Isaac Luria, the disseminators of casuistry and Kabbalah; if only they had not attributed to every word and to all the casuistries of the Talmud a holiness like that of the Torah of Moses! Then they would not have created new laws for us each day, nor established them as eternal laws for Israel, like a burdensome stone that injures all who carry it. They would recognize that God alone gives laws; without a prophet among us, we cannot, after the compilation of the Talmud, create new laws, saying "This is God's will!"—for who has shared His counsel? Indeed, even a prophet, except for Moses, the man of God, cannot add laws; how much less so one who, through his casuistry, brings about obscurity and creates

---

16. See Maimonides, MT Laws of Rebels 1:5.

darkness, confounding the laws of *shema* with the laws concerning a goring ox . . . and the like! When the talmudic sages, may their memory be blessed, added laws, this [involved] solely *received* laws and interpretations, and decrees and ordinances that simply preserve God's Torah in accordance with the [contingencies of their] place and time! . . .

The entire Talmud, except for a few ancient laws and received interpretations . . . is the *work of wise people* who understood the spirit and manner of human beings and the precious value of the days they live here on earth. With great wisdom, they infused a living spirit into the Torah of God, lest it be like a frozen monument, unmoved by any strong wind or whirling storm. By delving into [the Torah], they found devices for explicating it in a discerning and intelligent manner, lest it become an obstruction in our life's course; they eloquently steer it where the *spirit of life* desires, while detracting nothing from it. Therefore, their memory is blessed by all who are upright and understand their actions.

Those, however, who are so wise in their own opinion and deride the Talmud, [thereby] proclaim their own foolishness and ignorance of [the Talmud's] methodology; they understand the Talmud no better than those who believe that everything [in it] was revealed to Moses at Sinai. Both these [groups] are wholly ignorant of its methodology! . . .

The Talmud is an anthology of disparate opinions. Now, since individual opinions differ—as [the Talmudic sages] themselves stated, (BT Berakhot 58a; Sanhedrin 38a)—it includes conflicting opinions in the area of belief as well as in *halakhah*. . . . Yet there is one thing, dear reader, on which we find agreement among all the *tanna'im* and *amora'im:* namely, that any ordinance or decree whose grounds have disappeared can be annulled; and that each court has the authority to depart from its predecessors' rulings (subject to the conditions I define [elsewhere]), and that their every statement was asserted in accordance with the [contingencies of their] place and time! . . .

Look here, our rabbis! We come before you in the name of truth, in the name of the Talmud, and in the name of the noble men of our people, the shepherds of Israel. . . . In their name, we demand that you convene and— in the company of intellectuals [*maskilim*] who understand the Torah, who are faithful in spirit and knowledgeable about the times—give us a pure and perfected *Shulhan Arukh,* a table [*shulhan*] free of all dross and false vanities, a *Shulhan Arukh* that will not counsel us thus: "We should not lift our heads and look up during prayer, so that the angels do not mock us" (*Magen Abraham* [on *Shulhan Arukh,* Orah Hayyim] 95:1). . . . A *Shulhan Arukh* that will not encumber us with rules . . . devoid of both Torah and wisdom! . . . A *Shulhan Arukh* that will not introduce out of thin air laws that are not mentioned in the Talmud, such as the observance of self-affliction during the first eight days of the fifth month—the Talmudic sages did not command this![17] Is it not painfully ludicrous that the sages who witnessed the desolation of our Holy Temple and the exile from our land established only a few rites of mournful remembrance, yet more than a thousand years later, many [rites of] remembrance were added, without an ancient foundation! A *Shulhan Arukh* that will distinguish between law and pious supererogation! A *Shulhan Arukh* that will not burden us with faulty laws and unfounded stringencies. . . . A *Shulhan Arukh* that will prohibit *only that which is [truly] prohibited* and will not decree harsh and evil enactments that separate us from humanity and from the universe, and will allow us to stride confidently; one founded exclusively on the *spirit of the Talmud!* . . .

For too long you, our rabbis, have sat with folded arms. You should not be silent. It is time for initiative, a time to act for our religion and people. A time to remove the disgrace cast upon ourselves and upon the Talmud by our enemies, who have turned the Talmud into a stumbling block in our path, claiming that "it increases lazy and worthless people in Israel; it elevates the honor of the person who studies it, so that he can subjugate the masses; it increases animosity between the Jew and the people in whose land he resides; it gives cunning to the devious!" We know that, in all these things, the "sin of Jacob" (Micah 1:5) lies not in the Talmud, but in the serpentine scholarship, both heartless and proud, that has been our undoing! It is a time to reprove the people so that they [will come to] love work and enjoy the labor of their own hands. This follows the statement of Raba to his students:

17. The ninth day of Av, the fifth month, was from biblical times a fast day commemorating the destruction of the Temple in Jerusalem. According to the Mishnah (Ta'anit 4:7), certain customs of mourning are observed from the Shabbat preceding the fast. Under later practice, as reflected in the *Shulhan Arukh,* these customs are observed from the first day of the month.

"I would ask you not to appear before me during *Nisan* [the month of harvest] and *Tishre* [the month of grape and olive pressing] so as to avoid being concerned with provisions the year long" (BT Berakhot 35b). [It is] time to remove pride from the hearts of Torah scholars, for we are prohibited from making the Torah a crown for self-aggrandizement (Avot 4:5)! It is time to teach the sons of Judah to increase peace between those of different and disparate religions, just as the Talmud commands [us] to increase peace even with idolaters (BT Berakhot 17a) — how much more so with the peoples who are our neighbors [today]! It is time to place in their hearts the understanding that the commandments relating to man and his fellow man are far more valuable than those relating to man and God (BT Yoma 85a; BT Bava Batra 88b), and that it is prohibited to deceive even an idolater (BT Hullin 94a). Machinations for illicit gain are abhorrent to God! It is a time to perform great deeds on our behalf, to raise our dignity and to cause us to succeed in our endeavors. A wise person should not be silent at a time like this!

"Anything New Is Forbidden"
21. Moses Sofer, *Responsa Hatam Sofer,* Orah Hayyim 1:28

Written in 1830, this is the most clearly argued of a number of responsa in which Sofer articulates what became the central principle of the orthodox — soon to be "ultraorthodox" — response to haskalah *and reform: "Anything new is everywhere forbidden by the Torah." Sofer boldly imparts an entirely new meaning to these words taken from Mishnah Orla 3:9, where they refer simply to the Torah's prohibition on consuming the new crop before the requisite sacrifice is offered (see Lev. 23:9–14). The word "everywhere," which in the original refers to all locations, assumes, in Sofer's polemic, the emphatic meaning of "under all circumstances."*

You wrote regarding the old synagogue, which the members of the holy community took down, erecting a new, larger building to give glory to our God's house. Now they wish to place the *bimah* [dais] for the Torah reading at the front of the synagogue, near the holy Ark, rather than in the center, where it had always been. They argue that this would be more aesthetic and provide greater space in the synagogue, as compared to having it in the center. Your question is, whether it is acceptable to make this change or not.

Answer: . . . You write correctly that Maimonides (MT Prayer 11:3) explicitly rules that the *bimah* should be built in the center of the synagogue, so that everyone may hear equally [well], and the same was written in *Tur* (Orah Hayyim 150) . . . [and thus] "anyone seeking a change is at a disadvantage." It is true that [Joseph Karo in his] *Kesef Mishneh* wrote in defense of people in some places in [Sephardi] lands who built their *bimah* at the front of the synagogue. He explains that they held that the [rule of placing it in the center] applied only in ancient times, when the people were numerous and could hear the reader's voice only from the center. In small communities, with few people, they can, however, hear . . . [the reading] from a *bimah* at the front.

[As for] the grounds for requiring the *bimah* to be in the center, . . . I suggest the following reason: Since we view the *bimah* . . . as the equivalent of the altar . . . , and the inner altar in the Temple, before the holy Ark, was placed in the center of the house, exactly between the lamp and the table, . . . the *bimah* too should be placed in the center of the synagogue, so as to render it as similar as possible to the Temple; and there should be no change in our microtemple.

Even the defense offered by *Kesef Mishneh* for [the practice of Sephardi] communities—that does not apply to us. For our forefathers who built this synagogue placed it in the center, which shows that such was their preference, so that all the people may hear. Thank God, the community has not been diminished; on the contrary, it has grown. Therefore, even had [the synagogue] originally been built [with the *bimah*] at the front because they were few, they would now certainly be required to build it in the center. In any event, God forbid that there should be a change from the way it has been.

Moreover, it seems to me that even *Kesef Mishneh*'s argument regarding those [other] communities applies only to building a new synagogue in a place where there had never been one. But as they are building to replace an old synagogue, there should be no change. . . . Even though "additions can be made to the city [of Jerusalem] and to the temple courts" (Mishnah

Sanhedrin 1:5), and consequently things will change, nevertheless there will not be a change of placement between north and south, or any move . . . away from the center. For the Second Temple was larger than the First Temple, yet there was no change in the array of the [holy] utensils: the altar, the lamp, and the table were not moved away from the center. Even though, in proportion to the size of the building, the center will now be in a different place from the center of the old synagogue, nevertheless this new synagogue also merits having its *bimah* in its center. . . . The principle is, Anything new is everywhere forbidden by the Torah. . . . Your honor will surely protest powerfully [against this change] and erect the sanctuary properly, and the people too will be in peace.

The Need for Halakhic "Innovations"

22. Hayyim David Halevi, *Aseh Lekha Rav* 7:54

Aseh Lekha Rav (Tel Aviv, 1986; Hebrew), volume 7 section 54, pp. 234–38.

The development of halakhah *among Ashkenazi communities over the past two centuries was dominated by the cultural debate over* haskalah *and reform. Sephardi halakhists, in contrast, were not party to this debate, and their attitude toward questions of legal innovation is markedly free of both traditionalist and reform tendencies. Halevi, who was Sephardi chief rabbi of Tel Aviv, argues here that innovation is the life of* halakhah.

I acknowledge Your Honor's letter, written in response to my essay . . . in which I concluded that "there is a clear need to seek solutions in the spirit of the sources and in utter faithfulness to them, and introduce halakhic innovations." Your Honor expresses wonder: Are we permitted to depart even a hair's breadth from the *halakhah* as written and received? What is the meaning of "innovating" halakhic rulings—for if they exactly conform to the *Shulhan Arukh,* they constitute no innovation whatever, while if they do not conform, what permission have we . . . , etc.?

    . . . All this is indeed completely true, just as Your Honor writes:

that we may not depart even a hair's breadth from the *halakhah*. But I do not agree that . . . innovations in the spirit of the *halakhah,* as written and received, and in utter faithfulness to it, constitute deviation—even if these innovations change, in a particular instance, the *halakhah* as written. . . .

The term *halakhah* derives from the root *h.l.kh.* [to go]. It signifies something that extends from early on until the end, that is to say, that which is received and transmitted in Israel from Sinai down to the present. . . .

Now we must ask: Since it is abundantly clear that no law or ordinance can persist for long owing to the changing circumstances of life, a law that was good for its own time is no longer suitable after a generation or more, and requires correction [*tikkun*] or change or the like. How is it, then, that the holy Torah gave us just and righteous laws and ordinances thousands of years ago, and we continue to observe them to this day, and will indeed continue unto the last generation? How did it come to pass that the very same laws were good for their own time and are good up to this very day? Of course, God who gave us the Torah . . . sees unto the last generation; yet ours is the duty to understand "How is it done?"

Now, this [continuity] was possible only because permission was granted to the *hakhamim* of Israel in every generation to introduce halakhic innovations in accordance with changes of time and circumstance. Only thus was it made possible for Torah to persist in Israel. . . .

What, then, did the Rabbis mean when they said: "This teaches that the Holy One revealed to Moses all details specified in the Torah, and all details specified by the scribes, and all that the scribes would eventually innovate" (BT Megillah 19b; JT Peah 17a)? Certainly the meaning is not literally that He taught [Moses] all of the Torah that would . . . be innovated [from the generation of Sinai] until the last generation in order that he should teach it to Israel. For, if so, what would there be left to innovate? Rather, it is as explained by [Rabbi Yom Tov Lipmann Heller] author of *Tosafot Yom Tov* (in the introduction to his commentary on the Mishnah), [that God merely revealed to Moses this body of knowledge but did not give it to him to teach to Israel]. Now let us understand, To what . . . purpose did God reveal to Moses everything that a qualified student would eventually innovate, seeing that he was not to teach it to Israel?

We must presume that Moses reported this to Israel (namely, that all that a qualified student would eventually innovate had been revealed to him), for, otherwise, knowledge of that fact could not have reached us. Surely this was in order to indicate to Israel the permission granted them to "innovate" in every generation, and that innovation is part of the *halakhah* given to Moses, our Master.

Whoever thinks that the *halakhah* is frozen, and that we may not deviate from it right or left, errs greatly. On the contrary, there is no flexibility like that of the *halakhah*. . . . Only by virtue of this flexibility were the Jewish people, relying on numerous and useful innovations introduced by the *hakhamim* of Israel, each in his generation, able to walk in the path of Torah and its commandments for thousands of years. If the *hakhamim* of our [own] generation will have the courage to introduce halakhic innovations true to Torah, with utter faithfulness to the body of Torah as written and received, then the *halakhah* will continue to be the path of the Jewish people unto the last generation.

The Power of the Tzaddik
23. Elimelekh of Lyzhansk, *Noam Elimelekh,* Va'ethanan, s.v. *hayom*

The expanding power of the hasidic movement at the end of the eighteenth century affected not only religious ideals and practice but also Jewish communal life. The movement created a revolutionary form of communal authority around charismatic leaders, tzaddikim. *Elimelekh of Lyzhansk played the leading role in developing the doctrine of the* tzaddik. *In contrast to the rabbi, whose authority depends on his knowledge of the law, the* tzaddik *gains his authority by virtue of his intermediary role between the divine and material worlds.*

"We have seen this day that man may live though God has spoken to him" (Deut. 5:21). It then says: "If we hear the voice of the Lord our God any longer, we shall die" (5:22). These two verses contradict each other. . . .

Let us first expound this verse in Psalms: "I had taken you for gods [*elohim*], sons of the Most High, all of you; but you shall die as men do" (82:6–

7). We have already indicated many times that the *tzaddik* is called man of God, as it is written, "Moses, the man of God" (Deut. 33:1). For the *tzaddik* is the master of the judgments [*dinim*]. They are in his hands. He may channel them however he wishes [so as] to subdue and mellow them. The *tzaddik* is the judge, for judges are called *elohim*. . . . He may thus annul all judgments and all decrees against Israel. Therefore the *tzaddik* is called man of God, that is, master of *elohim*.

Thus the Talmud states: The Holy One decrees and the *tzaddik* annuls. As it is written: "You will decree and it will be fulfilled" (Job 22:28).

But how does this [verse] prove that the *tzaddik* may annul the judgments and decrees that the Holy One decrees? Isn't the meaning of the verse that when the *tzaddik* decrees, the Holy One fulfills? Following our exposition above, it all fits well. When the *tzaddik* judges below and decrees, there is no judgment above, they [the judgments above] are annulled of themselves.

However, it must still be understood whence is it that the *tzaddik* may heal the sick [person] by means of his prayer and bring him vitality, so that a man shall live. For the *tzaddik*'s vitality is not eternal but rather an accident; how then can an accidental object give life? God . . . who lives and exists eternally, whose vitality is His essence, may give life to accidental man, but not so man [himself], whose vitality is not essential. However, this [fact, that the *tzaddik* can heal] is only so because the *tzaddik* cleaves [*middabbek*] unto God, and therefore his vitality cleaves unto eternal and essential life — thereby rendering the *tzaddik*'s vitality eternal and essential too, for they have been united into one substance. Therefore the *tzaddik* has the power in his hand to bring vitality to the sick.

Now, should you say, why doesn't the *tzaddik* live and exist forever? This is impossible. For the *tzaddik* is not always in a state of *devekut*. Sometimes he ceases cleaving [to God]. For the worlds are thus created: attaining and not attaining. That is to say, the *tzaddik* must always go from level to level. And when he wishes to ascend to a higher and more elevated level, he must [first] descend and go down a bit and then ascend. . . . And when the time comes that he must go "in the way of all the earth" to the world of truth, and he is disconnected from his *devekut,* then he will go and "be gathered to his kin." Indeed, it was God's wish that we would all cleave unto Him. Therefore, the first two commandments were heard directly from God. For

"I am" is a positive command and "You shall not" is a negative command pertaining to divinity and *devekut*. God Himself therefore proclaimed [these commandments] to us so that we should cleave unto Him, to eternal life.

This is, then, the meaning of [the verse] "I had taken you for Gods [*elohim*]." . . . You should thereby cleave unto eternal life. "But you shall die as men do"—that is, when you disconnect from *devekut*. This too is the meaning of the verse "While you, who held fast [*devekim*] to the Lord your God, are alive today" (Deut. 4:4). The word "today" is seemingly redundant. But according to the [text] above it is understood: when you cleave unto God, each and every one of you, you are alive by cleaving unto God . . . unto eternal life. But this is only "today." On each and every day you must return and cleave unto Him as explained above, because it is impossible to be in continuous *devekut*. Thus Israel said, "We have seen this day that man may live though God has spoken to him"—which is to say, with man, [God converses with man as men] converse with each other: God speaks and decrees and the *tzaddik* decrees and annuls. Even if death has been, God forbid, decreed for a man, the *tzaddik* can bring vitality to him. . . .

Da'at Torah: Extending Rabbinic Authority

24. Eliyahu Eliezer Dessler, *Mikhtav me-Eliyahu*

Mikhtav me-Eliyahu (Tel Aviv: Committee for the Publication of the Writings of Rabbi E. E. Dessler, 1955; Hebrew), vol. 1, pp. 59, 75–77. A full English translation of these texts can be found in Dessler, *Strive for Truth!* (Jerusalem and New York: Feldheim, 1978), vol. 1, pp. 176–78, 217–23.

The founding of the orthodox, anti-Zionist Agudat Yisrael party in the early twentieth century created a framework for the periodic gathering of leading scholars in the form of a "council of sages." This council evolved as the main forum for deciding matters of policy for the party and its followers. The terms da'at torah, *"the Torah view," and its attendant* emunat hakhamim, *"faith in the sages," conceptualized the authority claims of these leading scholars in many areas of policy that traditionally were not subject to halakhic jurisdiction. Dessler was a leading exponent of these ideas; his account of the status of the sage may reflect the influence of hasidic conceptions of the* tzaddik. *The first passage in the following text offers a theory of* emunat hakhamim; *the second is a letter admonishing the recipient for lacking requisite faith.*

Torah of Truth

What shall the blind man do when he must tread an unfamiliar path? He takes one who sees as his guide, or at least, at every turn, asks those who see.

So too has God in His lovingkindness provided us with guides, our sages, the scholars of Torah. For anyone who contemplates their teachings perceives their clarity of vision regarding their own psychological constitution and that of humans generally, and regarding the path that a person ought to follow for his own good.

. . . This shows us the essence of *emunat hakhamim.*

Whoever wills to have faith in them can benefit from their clear vision, and they become his eyes. Their teachings can provide us with right guidance in our view of the world and the governance of our actions. Moreover, insofar as we become their disciples and strive to comprehend their modes of thought, our mind too is rightly guided. Therefore, the great ones of our time whose vocation is to continue as loyal disciples in the sages' modes of thought achieve this [sense of] rightness to the utmost degree. Thus, their opinions—whether instructions lacking an explicit source or even counsel on worldly matters—are clear and true "like an oracle sought from God" (2 Sam. 16:23), as is evident to us even in our time.

A Letter on *Emunat Hakhamim*

From his honor's words I see that he holds that all the great scholars of Israel, whose deeds are for the sake of heaven, together with the intellectual giants and mighty ones of righteousness, . . . could err completely. God forbid! . . .

Whoever witnessed their assemblies . . . was certain that he beheld the divine presence [*shekhinah*] in their acts, and that the holy spirit hovered in their gathering. . . .

The Rabbis have instructed us to obey the teachings of the *hak-hamim,* even if they say of left that it is right, rather than determine—God forbid—that "they are certainly mistaken, since I, the tiny one, clearly perceives their mistake." Instead, [one should say.] "My perception is insignificant, like the dirt of the earth, in relation to the clarity of their wisdom and their divine support." . . . This is *da'at torah* defined by faith in the sages. . . .

The failure to acknowledge our insignificance in relation to our sages—this is the root of all sin and the cause of all calamity—may God spare us. All one's merits are not equal to the root of all [good], namely, faith in the sages.

Commentary. Rabbinic Authority and Modernity

The modern era has been marked by the rise of radical criticism directed at all forms of traditional authority, not least traditional religious authority. In the Jewish community such criticism has been directed primarily against the authority of traditional Jewish law and of the rabbis as its guardians and interpreters. The five texts under consideration (§§20–24) treat of two separate but, as I will indicate later, interrelated issues of rabbinic authority: (1) the authority of rabbis to innovate, adjust, or make changes in the *halakhah* to meet what many believed to be the needs of the modern era—and the limits of that authority; and (2) the authority of rabbis as spiritual, charismatic leaders uniquely qualified to guide all aspects of the life of the individual Jew and, beyond that, to be the exclusive setters of public policy for all issues confronting the Jewish community, even, and perhaps especially, issues not strictly halakhic in nature. All these texts, in varying and sometimes conflicting ways seek to maintain and even bolster rabbinic authority in the light of and as a response to the modern challenges directed at it.

The first three texts treat the first issue described above. Lilienblum and Halevi, despite significant differences, argue that the rabbi has both the authority and the duty to innovate within, and perhaps even change, the *halakhah* to meet the changing circumstances of the modern era. Moses Sofer, to the contrary, argues that all changes in traditional Jewish practice, *even changes that do not violate formal halakhic dicta,* are forbidden precisely because they are innovations. Rabbis, as guardians of the *halakhah,* and more broadly of traditional Jewish practice and the traditional way of life grounded in that practice, cannot countenance such change.

The Lilienblum text differs from all four others in two important and interrelated respects. First, Lilienblum was not a rabbi but a layman. Second, this text is the only one of the five to criticize contemporary rabbis for what Lilienblum saw as their inadequate and, indeed, counterproductive response to the challenges of the modern era. Despite this rather sharp criticism, Lilienblum is supportive of rabbinic authority, for, so he believed, only if the rabbis accepted his advice would they be able to maintain their authority and, beyond that, the authority of a refined and renewed Jewish law.

Lilienblum wrote this text while he was still a proponent of moderate Jewish enlightenment (*haskalah*). He urges contemporary rabbis to return to the methodology of the Talmud, which "infused a living spirit into the Torah" by interpreting Jewish law in "accordance with the [contingencies] of place and time." He criticizes the *Shulhan Arukh* and its defenders, who "burden us with unfounded stringencies" and "enactments that separate us from humanity and the universe." Jewish law needs to be made more lenient to foster greater integration of the Jews within the societies in which they lived. Particularly striking, Lilienblum argues that these changes should not be undertaken by the rabbis alone, but only together with "intellectuals [*maskilim*] who understand the Torah," intellectuals, that is, like Lilienblum himself.

From a critical-historical point of view one may argue that Lilienblum's distinction between the methodology of the Talmud and the *Shulhan Arukh* is overdrawn. He was certainly naive in assuming that his harshly phrased demands would elicit a positive response from the rabbis to whom he addressed his call. Perhaps most significantly, Lilienblum erred in assuming that the crisis of authority of traditional Jewish law could be resolved by making particular adjustments in that law, however justified such adjustments might be in themselves. For example, whatever might be said in favor of observing the days of semi-mourning before Tishah be-Av only from the previous Sabbath and not from the beginning of the month, would changes like that strengthen the Jewish community's adherence to the law? Perhaps not surprisingly, soon after he wrote the work from which this text is excerpted, Lilienblum moved in the direction of greater radicalism, adopting a more positivist and materialist position and dismissing the issue of halakhic reform as beside the point.

The twentieth-century Sephardic scholar Hayyim David Halevi, unlike Lilienblum, criticizes neither the *Shulhan Arukh* nor (except by implication) contemporary rabbis. Moreover, whereas Lilienblum argues that the *halakhah* became frozen sometime after the redaction of the Talmud and that it is the task of contemporary rabbis to "unfreeze" it, Halevi insists that the "*hakhamim* of Israel each in their generation" introduced "numerous and useful innovations."

Halevi, however, is in broad agreement with Lilienblum concerning the need to revise *halakhah* "in accordance with the changes of time and circumstance." Perhaps to distinguish himself from liberal rabbis, he is quick to reject the slightest "deviation" from *halakhah*. But, for him, "halakhic innovations in the spirit of the *halakhah*" do not "constitute deviation," even if—as he goes on to state in an exceptionally bold statement for an unimpeachably Orthodox rabbi—"these innovations change, in a particular instance, the *halakhah* as written."

Halevi's essay contrasts sharply with the text by Moses Sofer, the leading figure in the orthodox struggle against reform. In this responsum, as in several others, Sofer makes use of the epigram "Anything new is . . . forbidden by the Torah." But exactly what does this mean?

Sofer discusses here the permissibility of building a synagogue with the *bimah* (dais) in the front rather than in the center "as it has always been." He concedes that there is no strict halakhic requirement to place the *bimah* in the center of the synagogue and, moreover, that at least one noted medieval authority defended the decision of some synagogues to place the *bimah* in the front. But, he concludes, given the accepted current practice, to build a synagogue with the *bimah* in front constitutes an innovation, and as such, it is forbidden.

Though Sofer does not say so, part of his rationale for banning this change may have been the fact that those who advocated moving the *bimah* to the front did so, among other reasons, to make synagogue architecture conform to contemporary non-Jewish aesthetic standards. Thus, for Halevi halakhic innovations in response to "changes in time and circumstance" are the call of the hour, but for Sofer such innovations are halakhically forbidden precisely because they respond positively to "changes of time and circumstance." As the leaders of the traditional Jewish community, the rabbis are to insulate the community from such change. Sofer intuitively felt that all changes in traditional Jewish practice aimed at meeting non-Jewish norms, even if they did not violate the *halakhah,* would lead to acculturation, and that it is a small step from acculturation to assimilation. For Sofer, the opportunities for greater participation by Jews in the general society, opened up by emancipation and enlightenment, threatened the very foundations of traditional Jewish existence.

The last two texts treat the second issue described above, namely, the claims made on behalf of the broad, extra-halakhic, charismatic authority of the rabbinic scholar. Selection 23, in a certain sense, is a digression. For Elimelekh of Lyzhansk, one of the early hasidic rabbis, speaks here about the unique, all-inclusive, almost divine authority, not of the traditional scholar —the communal rabbi (*mara de-atra*) or head of a talmudic academy (*rosh yeshivah*)—but of the *tzaddik.* The *tzaddik* is the "master of the [divine] judgments" and is thereby endowed with superhuman powers; for example, he can heal the sick by canceling the divine decree of death issued against them. Even more, as one contemporary scholar of Hasidism notes, "the main innovation of . . . Hasidism is its firm belief that the proper service of God is possible only via the intermediation of the *tzaddik*" (Joseph Dan, "Rabbi Israel of Ruzhin," *Jewish Studies* [1997]). But what is significant for our story is that in the twentieth century some of the charismatic authority attributed to the *tzakkik* was extended to leading rabbinic scholars, the "great ones of Israel" (*gedolei yisrael*), in particular to the heads of yeshivas. This leads us to our final text.

The Dessler text is a response, written after World War II, to a criticism leveled against the "great scholars of our generation" for not encouraging *aliyah* (immigration to the Land of Israel) on the part of European Jews during the interwar period. Had they done so, the critic argues, the lives of thousands and perhaps tens of thousands of Jews might have been saved. Rather than responding to the substance of the criticism, Dessler simply denies that these great scholars could have erred, for certainly "the holy spirit rested in their assembly." What is called for is not criticism but *emunat hak-hamim,* "faith in the sages," the acknowledgment that "my seeing is null and void in relation to the clarity of their intellect." Here Dessler introduces the notion of *da'at torah* (the Torah view; in the Ashkenazi pronunciation of its leading advocates, *da'as torah*), the claim that the "great ones of Israel" are qualified to express the authoritative Torah view on all matters of public policy and that their views are beyond criticism. As one contemporary *haredi* (ultraorthodox) spokesman argues, "The great ones of Israel possess a special endowment to penetrate objective reality . . . and apply the pertinent halakhic principles. This is a form of *ruah ha-kodesh* [the holy spirit] bordering, if only remotely, on the periphery of prophecy." From this premise the following conclusion is derived: "The great ones of Israel ought to be the final and sole arbiters on all aspects of communal policy."

One key factor in the rise of the ideology of *da'at torah* has been, ironically, the manifold modern challenges to the authority of the rabbinic tradition, for these challenges have led many of the rabbinic exponents of the tradition to make far-reaching claims on its behalf and, even more important, on their own behalf as its authorized interpreters. Also, the breakdown of traditional Jewish communal structures and the concomitant weakening of the power of communal rabbis and lay religious leaders have resulted in the emergence of the yeshiva heads, with their Torah scholarship and personal charisma, on center stage. The concept of *da'at torah* serves as well as a weapon in the hands of the antimodern *haredim* to delegitimate modern Orthodoxy. The *haredim* thus argue that the "great ones" who possess *da'at torah* are precisely the nonmodernist Torah scholars, whose views are "pure" Torah, uncorrupted by the modern world. Above all, the ideology of *da'at torah,* with its extreme reading of *emunat hakhamim,* is perhaps the central element in the ethic of submission that characterizes the antimodern, *haredi* worldview.

In sum, both the claim that "anything new is forbidden by the Torah" and the notion of *da'at torah* are expressions of a rejectionist Orthodoxy that, at best, is highly suspicious of the modern world. It is not surprising, then, that both are ardently affirmed by the contemporary *haredi* community. Conversely, those Jews, like myself, who believe in the legitimacy of halakhic innovation, who are willing to respond positively to the challenges of modernity, grant the modern world some measure of value. Precisely because we are both modern and halakhic we seek to balance autonomy and authority, independence and submission. We find this balance in the process of reasoned *pesak* (juridical ruling), which allows for criticism and debate within a revealed framework. Consequently, we oppose the anti-modern notion of *da'at torah,* whose entire purpose is to suppress discussion by demanding an *akedah* of the intellect in which one submits to the superior wisdom of the "great one."

Lawrence Kaplan

SEVEN Controversy and Dissent

Introduction

Majority and Minority

Interpretive Pluralism
1. *Midrash Psalms* 12

Preserving Minority Opinions to Rely On
2. Mishnah Eduyot 1:4–5

Preserving Minority Opinions to Refute
3. Tosefta Eduyot 1:4

A Recalcitrant Scholar
4. Mishnah Eduyot 5:6–7

The Individual: Knowledge and Responsibility

Erroneous Ruling
5. Mishnah Horayot 1:1

A Discerning Student
6. BT Horayot 2b

"Only If They Say Right Is Right"
7. JT Horayot 45d

Against Conformity
8. Asher b. Yehi'el (Rosh), Tosafot ha-Rosh, Horayot 2a, s.v. *horu*

The Rebellious Elder: Institutional Authority

The Rebellious Elder and the High Court
9. Mishnah Sanhedrin 11:2–4

307

Introduction

Sectarianism is the mark of Jewish life in the last centuries of the Second Temple period. But we know very little about what it felt like to be a Pharisee, Sadducee, Qumran sectary, or early Jewish-Christian. How did members of these parties/schools/sects understand themselves and one another? Probably they each saw their own way as the only right way; they are unlikely to have been tolerant in the modern liberal style. But the existence of the Judean commonwealth and the Temple (even for groups that withdrew from its services) held these groups together more or less, whatever they said or thought about one another. No fully developed understanding of heresy or apostasy is apparent at this stage of Jewish history, although what we might think of as experimental accusations of one or the other probably played a role in party and sectarian conflict. The destruction of the Temple brought about the first efforts to define some sort of theological and legal orthodoxy. The Christians were the first Jewish heretics. Later on, the Karaites achieved a similar status, though they are in some respects heirs to the Sadducees, who were once part of mainstream Israel.

Exile and dispersion pressed Jewish writers toward definition — What was it exactly that held these scattered men and women together? — even as it deprived the Jews of the political power to enforce any particular definition. The sages of the talmudic period mostly left the enforcement of theological orthodoxy to God (some of them seem to have favored self-help or private zealotry; we take this up in CC15 and 16), saying only that anyone who did not believe that, for example, the Torah was revealed at Sinai "had no share in the world to come." The number of obligatory propositions was small, and Maimonides' attempt to expand it met with resistance. Moses Mendelssohn was probably wrong to argue that Judaism was a religion without dogmas, but the idea of a creed played a far smaller role in Jewish than in Christian religious life. If groups like the Karaites were excluded not only from the world to come but also from the Jewish community in this world, it was more likely because of their rejection of rabbinic *halakhah* than for any heretical beliefs.

Theological pluralism probably existed in all the major exilic communities, but since it only rarely posed political problems, we do not deal with it here. What was politically problematic was disagreement about the law. From the time of the Talmud until the emancipation, Jewish identity was defined most significantly by halakhic commitment. But the *halakhah* itself was defined, as we have seen, by rabbinic argument and majority vote — and across the diaspora, in different times and places, majorities decided differently. How were these differences understood and accommodated? What

were their limits? How did legal authority work in the absence of a central-
ized legal system? These are the questions that we mean to address in this
chapter.

For ordinary Jews, the *halakhah,* however it was decided, was simply
the law, enforced by the local *bet din* (court), with whatever coercive power
it was permitted to wield. The Karaites aside, no significant religious movement advocated a rejection of halakhic authority (until the nineteenth-
century Reform movement) or defended any sort of passive resistance or
conscientious objection. Dissent and disagreement were common only in
the Jewish elite; the rabbis argued mostly among themselves.

The range of permissible argument was determined in part by the
looseness of exilic authority structures. It was hard to repress disagreement
locally, and the autonomy of the *kahal* and the mobility of Jewish scholars
made it impossible to achieve anything remotely resembling diaspora-wide
conformity. But there is another reason for the legal "liberalism" of the rabbis (relative at least to the Christian and Muslim societies in which they
lived), which has to do with their understanding of textual and interpretive
authority.

The text was divinely revealed and hence absolute. But interpretation was a human activity ("It is not in heaven"), fallible, inconclusive,
ongoing. Some of the sages looked back to an interpretive golden age, when
all the interpreters agreed with one another; it was sin or ignorance, they
said, that brought disagreement (see BT Sanhedrin 88b). But the relish with
which disagreement was pursued, and the honor accorded the pursuit, suggests that another view was dominant: to engage in these inconclusive discussions was a very good thing to do. It was necessary in any case, because
no ecclesiastical office or social institution provided a platform for divinely
sanctioned and hence conclusive interpretations or decrees; no human being
(prophecy having ceased) could speak in God's name. When a conclusion
was required, the rabbis voted. But the majorities thus formed were shaped
by the previous argument; they were the products of what must have been
regarded as *legitimate* disagreement.

Was disagreement still legitimate after the majority had ruled? What
was the status of minority views? Could the argument be resumed, the majority challenged, even overturned? Though posed in a different idiom, these

questions were argued by the sages from very early on—and answered in a way that kept all arguments, including these, alive and ongoing. Minority views were preserved (as they are today in the recorded decisions of American courts), and decisions could always be changed, so long as the new majority, as we saw in the last chapter, was wiser or larger than the old one (and these criteria were also subject to interpretation). What governs and constrains the ongoing arguments is the mutual respect of the sages. The much-told stories of the rival schools of Hillel and Shammai serve to illustrate and legitimate this mutuality—and may well have been fashioned for just these purposes. If such great and learned men could disagree so sharply and yet accommodate one another, then surely no later disagreement about points of law should be allowed to divide the Congregation of Israel.

But there did have to be some sort of obedience rule: no legal or political system can function if the law is always in dispute among the judges. In the Jewish tradition, this rule is provided by the doctrine of the "rebellious elder." In its talmudic formulation, the rule is very firm, but its firmness depends on a highly idealized version of the legal system; in practice, adapted to the realities of the exile, the rule is very weak.

In tractate Sanhedrin, the sages imagine a fully articulated hierarchy of courts and an improbably rigorous system of procedural justice. Disputed rulings are appealed from one court to the next, until a decision is rendered by the Sanhedrin itself, conceived as the supreme court of ancient Israel, meeting in the sacred precincts of the Temple. A rebellious elder is one who, subsequent to this final appeal, rules against the Sanhedrin in his local *bet din*. His rebellion lies in his ruling; he is free to expound his dissenting view, even to teach it to his students, but not to make it the decree of his court. He is intellectually independent but judicially subordinate.

The story in Mishnah Eduyot about Akaviah b. Mahallalel suggests what is probably an alternative view. (Many scholars believe that it reflects an earlier view, worked out before but not necessarily rescinded by the more liberal doctrine of the rebellious elder, hence our placement of the text.) Akaviah was put under a ban—excommunicated, not condemned to death—for failing to retract an opinion; judicial ruling is clearly not at issue here, only legal interpretation and teaching. One of the Rabbis disputed the ban, suggesting that the disagreement of a truly good and learned man should be respected, but according to our text, the ban was in fact enforced. Note that Akaviah's goodness was not a matter of his private conscience, nor of his kindness or humility, but only of his steadfast commitment to a "tradition." Pluralism among the Rabbis was focused less on individuals than on schools—and, later on, as we will see, on courts and districts. At the same time, there was a lot of disagreement about these matters, often among individual scholars, as the Akaviah story makes clear. This is true even with regard to the doctrine of the rebellious elder, although the text in Sanhedrin seems plain enough.

We don't know whether there really were such rebels, but they certainly inhabited the Jewish imagination—testimony to the liveliness of rabbinic debates. It appears that some of the sages believed, against tractate Sanhedrin (or, again, before it reached its final form), that rebellion was sometimes morally or legally required. Imagine that the highest court made a ruling on this or that topic and then, sometime later, recognized that this ruling was mistaken, and ruled again. Ordinary Jews who had acted in accordance with the first ruling would be exonerated by their obedience to the court, but what about "elders," sages, who knew the first ruling to be wrong? They are culpable for their *obedience*. At least with regard to their own actions, they should have done what they believed to be right. Should they also have ruled, according to their own convictions, for others? JT Horayot might be taken to demand such "rebellious" rulings, as if the elder says: Surely I cannot tell the people who come to my *bet din* that right is left! But the argument in the *Sifre* and later in Nahmanides' commentary on Deuteronomy 17 is that everyone must defer to the superior wisdom of the higher court—or, more pragmatically, that everyone must obey for the sake of social order.

Horayot provides a hint of justified disobedience (which doesn't appear, however, in the fully developed doctrine of Sanhedrin), but there is nothing in that text like the sixteenth- and seventeenth-century Protestant argument that the "lesser magistrates" had a right, and perhaps even a duty, to nullify the religiously incorrect decisions of their superiors. Nor does the *Sifre* or Nahmanides argue for anything that could be called a "Catholic" alternative. The issue never arose in practice because there were no established hierarchical superiors, no bishops or pope whose authority had to be accepted or subverted. Hence no full-scale theoretical resolution was ever reached.

The commitment of tractate Sanhedrin to hierarchy and discipline, while it may have played a part in sustaining Jewish unity, doesn't describe the actual conditions of life in exile. We get a sense of the adjustments that exile required in BT Yevamot 14, where, all hierarchy gone, the sages acknowledge first that different courts in different cities might reach and enforce different rulings and then that different courts in the same city might also disagree—without any of their elders being "rebellious." Now the elders seem bound only by their own courts. What made this a viable system was the fact that all the courts were disagreeing about the same texts, reading and commenting on the same commentaries, working within a common tradition that they were able to describe, whatever divergent customs and practices it allowed, as singular in character.

The simultaneous reality of divergence and unity is something of a mystery today. On the one hand, there existed among the sages an acceptance of interpretive freedom and a recognition of its pluralizing effects. A bright student, they say, could give forty-nine reasons for deciding a point of law one way and forty-nine reasons for deciding it the opposite way—and this sort of thing was never seen within the Jewish tradition as mere sophistry. God's word really was open-textured, available for study, discussion, disagreement, even a kind of intellectual play. Talmudic arguments most often end inconclusively, for when there was no need to conclude, the sages preferred not to, so that the next generation could resume the argument without prejudice. All this would seem to require what tractate Sanhedrin provided: a tight and clear procedure for reaching conclusions when they were needed. But that system probably never existed in reality.

And yet the *halakhah* was more or less the same across the diaspora, disagreements were successfully contained for many centuries, and the fear of "many Torahs" was never realized—not, at least, until modern times. (Even mysticism did not produce a *halakhah* of its own, for many of the mystics were also legal scholars of an entirely conventional sort: another mystery.) The sociological explanation for this remarkable achievement probably lies in the nature of the rabbinic elite, its small size, common language, and shared texts and references. But the intellectual explanation must lie in the traditional understanding of the Torah itself, which was regarded as absolute and eternal and, at the same time, many-sided and adaptable.

This radical dualism was resisted by the greatest of the medieval rabbis, Maimonides, whose *Mishneh Torah* was aimed precisely at ending all the arguments. Maimonides probably hoped that Jewish scholars would study philosophy rather than *halakhah*. What sorts of debates he thought that study would involve is not clear; in any event, his own philosophical work provoked an extraordinarily intense controversy about whether philosophy should be studied at all. But controversy was not Maimonides' purpose, certainly not with regard to the law. His great legal code was something new in Jewish literature, for it presented the Oral Law in what was meant to be definitive form, without the prooftexts, disagreements, and alternative views that marked the Talmud itself and all the commentaries and compilations that followed upon it. Students of the law, Maimonides boasted, would henceforth need no other book. But the tradition took its revenge: not only are there other books, but the *Mishneh Torah* is now printed together with its own critical (and supportive) commentaries. Indeed, Maimonides shares the page with his severest critic, Rabad (who was also an important kabbalist); we reprint here a classic exchange between the two. It is Rabad who represents the common rabbinic view that prooftexts, reasons, and alternative positions must be included in all legal codes. This assertion is not defended at any length, but the defense would presumably go something like this: Argument about the law is the essential activity of a learned Jew, so there will never be a definitive account or an end to the writing of lawbooks. Every code, then, must contain the materials necessary to its own supersession.

This acceptance of argument and disagreement, at least among the rabbis, was severely tested in the modern period, first by the hasidic movement and then by enlightenment (*haskalah*) and Reform. In the fierce controversy between the Hasidim and their opponents (*mitnagdim,* "those who are against"), both groups referred themselves to the texts we have reprinted here. It was the Hasidim who defended the old pluralism—see Elimelekh's invocation of the maxim "These and those are the words of the living God" (BT Eruvin 13b)—while the *mitnagdim* defended an equally old authoritarianism, invoking the maxim about "right and left." Hasidism was a movement with strong and enduring centrifugal tendencies, producing numerous dynasties and sects. It has to be said, however, that pluralism found no place in any of these; hasidic doctrine encouraged a radical dependence on the ruling *tzaddik*. The opponents of Hasidism were anti-pluralists from the beginning. Hostile to popular mysticism, they worried about multiplying sects and spreading superstition. Their own mysticism was esoteric and elitist; for ordinary Jews, they urged only piety and halakhic observance, and in their communities they tolerated no deviation at all.

In the later controversies between Orthodoxy and Reform, it was the reformers who first argued for pluralism and—because they were strongly influenced by Mendelssohn and other German *maskilim*—toleration. David Einhorn's use of the "rebellious elder" texts nicely represents their position. By the late nineteenth century, the orthodox were a minority in most German communities, so they also were forced to defend a kind of pluralism, though not the traditional kind. Their intellectual leaders, Samson Raphael Hirsch the most important among them, could not repeat maxims like "These and those . . ." or talk about rebellious elders, because they denied the very permissibility of a reformed Judaism (as in the case of the Karaites, the denial focused on halakhic, not theological, issues). They argued with the reformers on various public occasions, but they were not prepared to legitimize the argument. Instead, they claimed the right of voluntary association, hence also the right of separation from the community, which liberal society guarantees but which has no clear place in the Jewish tradition (although there were separate Sephardi and Ashkenazi congregations in many Jewish communities after the Spanish expulsion of 1492). They separated, as Hirsch insists, for the sake of their own emphatically singular view of Judaism; they sacrificed unity to live in accordance with religious truth. Of course, they then had to recognize the right of the reformers to associate in the same way for the sake of their understanding of the truth. But, so Hirsch says, theirs is no longer a Jewish association. They are like the Karaites; they exist outside the bounds of Jewish life, and presumably can exist freely only in the conditions of exile, protected by gentile rulers.

Majority and Minority

Interpretive Pluralism
1. *Midrash Psalms 12*

In this midrash, the psalmist's praise for the "purity" of God's words is taken to refer to the multifaceted character of Torah. This appreciation of hermeneutic complexity reflects the positive recognition given to controversy in Rabbinic traditions. In Selection 10, Rabbi Yose maintains an alternative view: that controversy is caused by a decline of Torah.

"The words of the Lord are pure words, silver purged in an earthen crucible, refined sevenfold" (Ps. 12:7). Rabbi Yannai said: The clauses of the Torah were not given as clear-cut [edicts]. Rather, concerning each clause that the Holy One imparted to Moses, He would impart forty-nine [1] reasons to [rule] "pure" and forty-nine reasons to [rule] "impure."

[Moses] said before Him: Master of the Universe, how long? Let us clarify the matter!

He answered: "Follow the majority!" (Exod. 23:2; cf. ₡6, ſ10 above). If the majority rule "impure," it is impure; if the majority rule "pure," it is pure.

*After the destruction of Jerusalem in the Great Rebellion (70 C.E.), scholars reconvened in Yavneh under the leadership of Yohanan ben Zakkai. One of the first steps they took was to assemble the existing oral traditions by accepting testimonies (*eduyot*) from the scholars present. These traditions later formed the foundation for Judah the Prince's compilation of the Mishnah, the core document of Rabbinic Judaism. The Mishnah does not document a monolithic tradition, but is primarily a record of controversies, including many opinions that clearly did not prevail. The following selections should be read as the Rabbis' own reflections upon the multivocal character of their project. The*

---

1. The midrashic interpretation of "sevenfold" is seven times seven.

first text, Eduyot 1:4, refers to the preservation of the views of Shammai and Hillel in
a case in which a third view prevailed.

Preserving Minority Opinions to Rely On
2. Mishnah Eduyot 1:4–5

[4] And why are the opinions of [both] Shammai and Hillel recorded in vain? So as to teach generations to come that a person should not
hold fast to his opinion, for the fathers of the world did not hold fast to their
opinions.

[5] And, since the *halakhah* follows the majority, why are the opinions of the individual recorded along with the majority's? So that if a [future]
court leans to the opinion of the individual, it can rely upon him, for a court
cannot annul the ruling of a fellow court unless it excels it in wisdom and
in number. If it excels in wisdom but not in number, in number but not in
wisdom, it cannot annul the [earlier court's] opinion. . . .

Preserving Minority Opinions to Refute
3. Tosefta Eduyot 1:4

The *halakhah* forever follows the opinions of the majority. The opinions of the individual were recorded along with those of the majority [so as]
to be annulled.

Rabbi Yehudah says: The opinions of the individual were recorded
among those of the majority because an hour [may come when] they are
needed and they will be relied upon.

And the sages say: The opinions of the individual were recorded
among those of the majority so that, in a discussion of purity and impurity,
a disputant who maintains [that something is] "impure" according to the
opinion of Rabbi Eli'ezer may be told: "Your tradition is according to [the
minority opinion of] Rabbi Eli'ezer" (℄6, §10).

A Recalcitrant Scholar

4. Mishnah Eduyot 5:6–7

When assembling the various traditions at Yavneh, numerous disagreements emerged. The Mishnah cited above assumes that the majority prevails; but this selection tells of an early scholar who refused to renounce his opinions. Interestingly, he too is reported as endorsing his own version of the maxim: Follow the majority.

[6] Akaviah ben Mahallalel testified to four opinions.

They said to him: Retract the four opinions you held and we will appoint you Head of the Court in Israel.

He said to them: I prefer being called a fool all my life and not being considered a wicked man before God for a moment. So it should not be said, "He retracted [his opinion] for the sake of office." . . . He maintained: A woman convert or a freed bondswoman is not made to drink [the water of bitterness given to the adulteress wife (Num. 5:11–29)].

The sages say: They are made to drink.

They said to him: There was a case in Jerusalem of a freed bondswoman named Karkamit, who was made to drink by Shemaiah and Avtalyon.

He said to them: It was for show [*dugma*] that they made her drink.[2] Whereupon they put him under the ban, and he died banished, and the court stoned his coffin.[3]

Rabbi Yehudah said: God forbid that Akaviah was banned! For the gates of the Temple were never closed to a man of Israel with Akaviah's stature in wisdom and piety. And who was it [then] that was banned? Eleazar ben Hanokh, who questioned [the sages' teachings on] the purity of hands. And when he died the court sent a stone to be placed on his coffin. . . .

[7] At the time of [Akaviah's] death he said to his son: My son, retract those four opinions I maintained.

2. "I.e., they merely pretended to give her the real bitter waters; another opinion: they performed the act on one who was, like themselves [Shemaiah and Avtalyon, who were converts], a descendant of gentiles." Marcus Jastrow, *A Dictionary of the Targumim, the Talmud Babli and Yerushalmi, and the Midrashic Literature,* (New York: Pardes, 1950), s.v. *dugma*.
3. A token of excommunication.

He said to him: And why didn't you retract them?

He answered: I received my tradition from a majority and they received their tradition from a majority; I held fast to my tradition and they held fast to their tradition. But you have received [both] from an individual and from a majority; it is better to relinquish the opinion of the individual and adopt the majority opinion.

He said to him: Father, commend me to your colleagues.

He answered: I will not commend you.

He said: Have you found unrighteousness in me?

He answered: No, but it is your deeds that will join you to them and your deeds that will alienate you from them.

The Individual: Knowledge and Responsibility

Erroneous Ruling

5. Mishnah Horayot 1:1

According to scriptural law (Lev. 4), an inadvertent transgressor must bring a sacrificial "sin offering"; the Rabbis emphasize that this does not apply to intentional transgressions, which entail punishment instead. Scripture ordains a specific offering for a collective sin, where a "matter escapes the notice of the congregation" (4:13). According to the Rabbis, this refers to a case in which the community followed an erroneous ruling of the high court. The court then brings a collective sin offering, and individuals who acted in obedience to the court (who are "dependent upon" it) are exempt. But what about individuals who know the law and who don't (need to) rely on the court: are they also exempt?

If the court ruled to transgress any one of the *mitzvot* mentioned in the Torah, and an individual proceeded to act in error accordingly, whether they acted and he acted along with them, or they acted and he followed them, or they did not act and only he acted, he is exempt [from an individual's sin offering], because he was dependent upon the court.

If the court ruled and one of its members, or a student worthy of ruling, knew they had erred but proceeded to act accordingly, whether they acted and he acted along with them, or they acted and he followed them, or they did not act and only he acted, he is liable [for an individual's sin offering], because he was not dependent upon the court.[4]

This is the rule: Whoever is self-dependent [in his decisions] is liable, and whoever is dependent upon the court is exempt.

A Discerning Student

6. BT Horayot 2b

The text has been amended according to the Munich MS.

"Or a student worthy of ruling." Like whom?

Rava said: Like Shimon ben Azzai and Shimon ben Zoma.[5]

Said Abaye to him: Is this a case of inadvertent transgression?

[Rava retorted:] According to your argument, [how can you explain] the following *baraita*:

["And if an individual from among the populace unwittingly incurs guilt by doing any of the things which by the Lord's commandments ought not to be done . . ." (Lev. 4:27):][6] An individual acting on his own is liable; [acting] according to the court's ruling, he is exempt. How so? If the court ruled that [forbidden] suet was permitted and one of its members, or a student sitting before them worthy of ruling, like Shimon ben Azzai, knew they had erred—is it possible that such a one should be exempt? Thus Scripture teaches us: "an individual" acting on his own is liable; [acting] according to the court's ruling, he is exempt.

4. I.e., he must atone for doing that which he knew was wrong.
5. Both are scholars who are not referred to by the title Rabbi: they are described elsewhere as "discussants before the sages" (BT Sanhedrin 17b).
6. This is the opening verse of the portion dealing with individual sin-offerings.

Is this a case of inadvertent transgression? Rather, you must say that he knew it was forbidden, but he erred in [assuming] it a *mitzvah* to adhere to the words of the sages [*hakhamim*]. I too can say that he knew it was forbidden, but he erred in [assuming] it a *mitzvah* to adhere to the words of the sages.

"Only If They Say Right Is Right"

7. JT Horayot 45d

Rabbi Imi said in the name of Rabbi Shimon b. Lakish: The mishnah refers to a case like [one in which] Shimon ben Azzai sits before them.

What is the case? If he is knowledgeable about the whole Torah and ignorant of that particular matter, he is not a "Shimon ben Azzai," and if he knows that particular matter but is ignorant of the whole Torah, he is a "Shimon ben Azzai" for that particular matter!

Rather, the case is of one who is knowledgeable about the whole Torah and that particular matter but who errs in thinking that the Torah said: "Follow them, follow them."

But if he errs in thinking that the Torah said, "Follow them, follow them," he is not a Shimon ben Azzai!

This is addressed by the *baraita:* Can it be the case that if they [the court] say to you that right is left and left is right, you should obey them? Scripture therefore teaches us "to the right or to the left" (Deut. 17:11)—that they say to you, right is right and left is left.[7]

---

7. Apparently, the advanced student's error is deemed plausible since it is along the lines of the *baraita*'s initial suggestion (indeed, the same suggestion is endorsed in §12). Therefore, he is not considered an intentional transgressor and stands on roughly the same footing as a layperson who errs through simple ignorance; they both are to bring the sin offering stipulated for an inadvertent transgressor. (A layperson whose error stems from depending on the court's wrongful ruling brings no offering at all.)

Against Conformity
8. Asher b. Yehi'el (Rosh), Tosafot ha-Rosh, Horayot 2a, s.v. *horu*

Rosh, the great fourteenth-century codifier, carries the Talmud's logic to a radical conclusion: Individual opinions in general entail personal responsibility.

"If the court ruled and one of its members, or a student worthy of ruling, knew they had erred . . . he is liable [for a sin offering], because he was not dependent on the court."

The text's order here signifies "not only this, but even that": Not only if one of the members of the Sanhedrin itself knew they had erred—in which case the ruling was not conferred unanimously—is he liable, but even one of the students sitting below them as discussants and worthy of ruling is liable. [Indeed,] not only if he is worthy of ruling, but even if he is "knowledgeable but not capable of analysis"[8] and in light of his studies perceives that the court has erred, is he liable. For anyone whose opinion differs from that of the court is dependent upon his own mind [i.e., decides for himself].

The Rebellious Elder: Institutional Authority

The Rebellious Elder and the High Court
9. Mishnah Sanhedrin 11:2–4

The following mishnah is part of the Rabbinic criminal code, which elaborates biblical stipulations for capital punishment. As with many other items in the code, there is some doubt regarding the extent to which its norms and procedures ever prevailed in practice. Still, these formulations serve as a classic statement about authority in halakhah. *Their background is the biblical law concerning an individual who defies the central judicial*

---

8. Rosh derives this expanded definition from the Talmud (Horayot 2b), where individual liability is extended both to a student who is "knowledgeable but not capable of analysis" and to one "capable of analysis but not knowledgeable."

authority (Deut. 17:8–13 [C6, §1]). According to the Rabbis, "rebellion" against the high court is not a capital offense for just anyone, only for a qualified "elder" (rabbinic judge). This mishnah describes the procedure leading up to the individual's condemnation. If an elder, in disagreement with his local peers, continues to contest their position, they all go to Jerusalem, and the dispute then works its way through the hierarchy of central courts at the Temple.

An elder who rebels against the court [is liable to death by strangulation]. As written, "If a case is too baffling for you to decide," etc. (Deut. 17:8).

There were three courts [in Jerusalem]. One sits[9] at the entrance to the Temple Mount, one sits at the entrance to the Temple courtyard, and one sits in the Hall of Hewn Stones. They [the elder and his peers] first come to the court at the entrance to the Temple Mount.

He says: "Thus have I expounded, and thus have my colleagues expounded; thus have I argued, and thus have my colleagues argued." If the court has received a tradition [on the disputed matter], they inform them. If not, these and those come to the court at the entrance to the Temple courtyard, and he says: "Thus have I expounded, and thus have my colleagues expounded; thus have I argued, and thus have my colleagues argued." If the court has received a tradition, they inform them. If not, these and those come to the Great Court in the Hall of Hewn Stones, from which instruction [Torah] goes forth to Israel. As written, "from that place which the Lord chose" (Deut. 17:10).

When he returns to his town, if he teaches and argues as he had been arguing, he is not liable. If he renders a ruling for action, he is liable, as written, "Should a man act presumptuously" (Deut. 17:12): he is not liable unless he renders a ruling for action.[10]

A student who renders a ruling for action is not liable; thus the

9. The shift to the present tense is typical of Rabbinic discourses of this sort, vividly transporting readers to a past reality.
10. And what if, in addition to teaching his views, he also acts on them, without issuing rulings for others? The mishnah seems (almost intentionally) to leave this issue open; it is touched upon in the last lines of §10.

severity of his [deed] works in his favor [i.e., he rules without authority *and* wrongly, yet is not punished because his ruling carries no weight].

Defining the Elder's Rebellion
10. BT Sanhedrin 87a–88b

The first section of the talmudic discussion below records fundamental differences among the tanna'im *regarding the type of legal dispute to which the "rebellious elder" punishment applies. At stake is the nature of the culpable rebellion: Is it against the core laws of the Torah itself, against the authority of the rabbis (here called "scribes") as the Torah's interpreters, or against the rabbis' own authority as legislators?*

Our rabbis taught: A rebellious elder is liable only if [his ruling concerns] a matter for which an intentional transgression entails *karet,* and an inadvertent transgression entails a sin offering; this is the view of Rabbi Meir. Rabbi Yehudah says: A matter founded in the words of Scripture and interpreted in the words of the scribes. Rabbi Shimon says: Even a subtle detail specified by the scribes. . . .

Rav Kahana said: If he argues from tradition and they argue from tradition, he is not put to death. If he argues "This is my view" and they argue "This is our view," he is not put to death. And certainly if he argues from tradition and they argue "This is our view," he is not put to death. He is only put to death when he argues "This is my view" and they argue from tradition. This is proven by the fact that they did not put Akaviah ben Mahallalel to death (§4).

Rabbi Eleazar, however, said: Even if he argues from tradition and they argue "This is our view," he is put to death—so that controversies do not abound in Israel. Now should you wonder, Why did they not put Akaviah ben Mahallalel to death? it was because he did not render a ruling for action.

The Mishnah reads: "Thus have I expounded, and thus have my colleagues expounded; thus have I argued, and thus have my colleagues argued."

Does this not [include] the case where he argues from tradition and they argue "This is our view"?

No, it [may refer to a case where] he argues "This is my view" and they argue from tradition.

Come and hear that which Rabbi Yoshiyah said: Three things were told to me by Ze'ira the Jerusalemite:[11]

> A husband who forgives with regard to his warning—
> he can forgive.
> A rebellious son whose parents wish to forgive him—
> they can forgive.
> A rebellious elder whom the court wish to forgive—
> they can forgive.

When I came to my colleagues in the South, they concurred with the [first] two—but not regarding a rebellious elder, so that controversies do not abound in Israel.

Indeed, this retort is irrefutable.

It was taught: Said Rabbi Yose, At first, controversies did not abound in Israel. Instead, the court of seventy-one sits in the Hall of Hewn Stones; and two [other] courts, of twenty-three each, sit—one at the entrance to the Temple Mount, and one at the entrance to the Temple courtyard. Other courts of twenty-three sit in every town of Israel. If a question arises, [the disputants] inquire of the court in their town. If the court received a tradition, they inform them. If not, they go to a neighboring court. If the court received a tradition, they inform them. If not, they go to the court at the entrance to the Temple Mount, and he [the elder contesting the majority view in his local court] says: "Thus have I expounded, and thus have my colleagues expounded; thus have I argued, and thus have my colleagues argued." If the court has received a tradition, they inform them. If not, these and those come to the court at the entrance to the Temple courtyard, and he says: "Thus have I expounded, and thus have my colleagues expounded;

---

11. The offenses enumerated are against honor, and forgiving entails the waiving of claims of authority by the offended party. For the husband's "warning" and its consequences, see MT Laws of Wayward Woman, chap. 1; for the rebellious son, see Deut. 21:18–22 and our ¢18.

thus have I argued, and thus have my colleagues argued." If the court has received a tradition, they inform them. If not, these and those come to the Hall of Hewn Stones, where [the court] sits from the morning sacrifice until the afternoon sacrifice. . . . The question is presented before them. If the court has received a tradition, they inform them. If not, they take a vote. If the majority votes "impure," they declare it impure; if the majority votes "pure," they declare it pure. When students of Shammai and Hillel, insufficiently schooled, abounded, controversies abounded in Israel, and the Torah became like two Torahs.

Our rabbis taught: He is not liable unless he acts on his ruling, or else renders a ruling to others and they act on his ruling.

Distinction Between Heresy and "Rebellion"

11. Maimonides, MT Laws of Rebels 3:1–4

The Code of Maimonides, Book Fourteen: The Book of Judges, translated by Abraham M. Hershman, Yale Judaica Series (New Haven: Yale University Press, 1949), pp. 143–44.

Maimonides here distinguishes between rebellion against the rulings of a particular authority and a heretical denial of the authority of the Oral Law itself. He goes on to distinguish between the initial instigators of the heresy, on the one hand, and descendants raised in their views, on the other.

1. He who repudiates the oral law is not to be identified with the rebellious elder spoken of in Scripture but is classed with the epicureans [whom any person has a right to put to death].[12]

2. As soon as it is made public that he has repudiated the oral law, he is cast into the pit and is not rescued from it. He is placed on a par with heretics, epicureans, those who deny the divine origin of Scripture, informers, and apostates—all of whom are ruled out of the community of Israel. No witnesses or previous warnings or judges are required. Whoever puts any of them to death fulfills a great precept, for he removes a stumbling block.

12. These issues are discussed in the context of apostasy in C15.

3. This applies only to one who repudiates the oral law as a result of his reasoned opinion and conclusion, who walks light-mindedly in the stubbornness of his heart, denying first the oral law, as did Zadok and Boethus[13] and all who went astray. But their children and grandchildren, who, misguided by their parents, were raised among the Karaites and trained in their views, are like a child taken captive by gentiles[14] and raised in their religion, whose status is that of an *anoos* [one who abjures the Jewish religion under duress], who, although he later learns that he is a Jew, meets Jews, observes them practice their religion, is nevertheless to be regarded as an *anoos,* since he was reared in the erroneous ways of his fathers. Thus it is with those who adhere to the practices of their Karaite parents. Therefore efforts should be made to bring them back in repentance, to draw them near by friendly relations, so that they may return to the strength-giving source, i.e., the Torah.

4. The rebellious elder of whom the Bible speaks is one of the wise men of Israel who is at home in traditional lore, functions as judge, imparts instruction in the Torah, as do all the wise men of Israel, but is in disagreement with the [High] Court with regard to a question of law, refuses to change his view, persists in differing with them, gives a practical ruling which runs counter to that given by them. The Torah condemns him to death, and if he confesses before his execution, he has a portion in the world to come. Though both he and the members of the [High Court] base their respective decisions either on reason or on tradition, the Torah pays regard to their view. Even if they are willing to forgo the honor due to them and let him go unpunished, it is not within their competence to do so, "in order that controversies do not abound in Israel."[15]

Commentary. Living Dangerously

According to the sources before us, as codified by Maimonides, once the guilt of a rebellious elder is established, the only question left for

---

13. Traditionally portrayed as the founders of the Sadducee sect.
14. YJS: "them"; amended according to the *Mishneh Torah,* Rome 1480.
15. Paraphrasing BT Sanhedrin 88b, the previous selection. YJS: "strife may not increase in Israel."

the high court is that of pardon. Favoring the approach of Rabbi Yoshiyah over that of Ze'ira (see §10), Maimonides rules that the defiant elder's high court colleagues are powerless to forgive him even if they feel that he no longer poses a threat. If the appropriate conditions of rebellion are met, the death penalty is compulsory.

But in the wake of such a trial, the court might wish to exercise its discretion in quite a different way, of which Maimonides makes no mention—and, seemingly, neither do the tannaitic and amoraic texts he was working from. After finding an elder guilty of knowingly issuing an independent and defiant ruling, the court, sufficiently perplexed by the elder's arguments, might see fit to rethink its own position. And as a result, the court might decide not merely to forgive their rebellious colleague, but actually to endorse his view. This possibility is not to be confused with cases in which a suspect rebel succeeds in proving that the case brought against him was misconstrued and that he had ruled on a matter to which no former ruling or tradition in fact applied. In the hypothetical case I want to consider, all agree that the rebel's ruling had been issued in defiance of a known high court opinion. What happened was that in the course of his trial he managed to convince the court that the ruling in question should be reconsidered.

This possibility is not discussed in the texts before us, and to the best of my knowledge it is nowhere raised in connection with the rebellious elder. Had it been raised, the argument could, in principle, have gone either way. The fact that the high court ended up endorsing the learned rebel's opinion and revising the law, some might say, does not change the fact that he knowingly defied the court in the first place. Therefore, regardless of the court's praise for the quality of his reasoning and its subsequent ruling in his favor, the elder should have been executed for urging others to break what even he admits was the law at the time. Mutiny is mutiny.

Elsewhere in talmudic literature, however, one can detect other voices. The first mishnah of Horayot (§5) clearly urges people well versed in the law not to follow the courts blindly. "Students worthy of ruling" are held personally responsible for their actions regardless of the court's rulings. If they believe a particular ruling to be mistaken, they are obliged to defy it and act as they see fit. On such a view, court rulings play an importantly different role for these students than they do for laity. Unlike the latter, the former are encouraged not to rely automatically on the courts but to follow their own conscience. And if students are expected to behave in this manner, the argument might go, all the more so elders of standing.

The line between defying the courts in the manner valorized in Horayot and doing so in the manner deemed high treason in Sanhedrin is customarily drawn between acting for oneself and ruling for others. For the learned, ruling is considered mutiny; acting for oneself is bravely doing the right thing. But this distinction is at best a formality. As far as mutiny is concerned, it makes little sense to distinguish between a sage of standing issuing a defiant halakhic verdict by announcing it verbally and his laying down the law in similar defiance by setting a personal example. In religious societies, "follow the leader" is more than a children's game. The difference between the attitudes of Horayot and Sanhedrin, it seems to me, has to do less with the formal aspects of dissent and more with who is eventually found to have been right. Horayot, I suggest, is about cases in which the learned dissenter's criticism of the court's ruling is deemed valid, whereas Sanhedrin is about cases in which the criticism is considered groundless.

Read together, might not these two texts allow the court to reconsider its own ruling and exonerate a rebellious elder on the grounds that he was right? But I am moving a little too quickly. Deliberating the fate of a rebel who convinces the high court to rethink the halakhic issue he contested presupposes the liberty of the court to overturn rulings associated with such levels of defiance. Again, I am not speaking of cases in which the court's understanding of the law in question was proven mistaken, but of cases in which the elder convinces the court that the law itself is contestable. On this, more basic question, I believe, the texts before us remain divided. The extreme view—according to which the court is granted the authority only to supplement, but never to amend, the *halakhah*—is voiced clearly in texts originating from the Tosefta. In the *baraita* cited in BT Sanhedrin (Tosefta Sanhedrin 7:1) before us, Rabbi Yose argues that the court system is wholly bound by received tradition. At every level—including that of the high court in session in the Hall of Hewn Stones—the same formula is repeated: "If the court has received a tradition [on the matter in hand], they inform [the parties]." Only in the absence of authentic precedents does the high court have the authority to issue a ruling of its own. Faced with an existing tradition, asserts the *baraita,* the court is powerless to rule differently and, consequently, is powerless ever to grant a rebellious elder his point.

What is to count as "received tradition"? Tosefta Eduyot 1:4 (§3) implies that the body of law to which all courts are committed consists not only of the established traditions but also of all former high court decisions. Ruling against Rabbi Yehudah's minority opinion, the redactor of the Tosefta has "the sages" claiming that rejected minority opinions remain on record in order to ensure that they remain rejected—that the rulings issued by the high court are never reversed! The "tradition," the body of law that the court system is powerless to change, comprises the entire body of existing *halakhah.* The Tosefta thus espouses what we might term a "traditionalist" position, holding that it is legally impossible for anyone to talk a high court into reconsidering an existing ruling.

The mishnaic parallels to these two texts tell a very different story, however. In Mishnah Eduyot the minority and majority opinions regarding the future role of minority opinions are dramatically reversed. Now "the sages" rule that minority opinions, contrary to Rabbi Yehudah's minority view, remain on record in case a future court wishes to use them to overturn a former decision. Unlike the Tosefta, the Mishnah speaks explicitly of halakhic change and of the possibility of a later high court annulling the rulings of a former one. Bearing this in mind, we can see that the slight difference between the Mishnah's and Tosefta's descriptions of the court system becomes highly significant. According to the Tosefta, the entire court system remains at all times bound by received tradition, whereas the Mishnah's wording suggests that the high court is not bound. At every other level, license to rule is granted by the Mishnah only "if the court has received a tradition [on the disputed matter]." But when talking of "the Great Court in the Hall of the Hewn Stones," this formula is conspicuously dropped, strongly implying, contrary to the Tosefta, that this court is allowed not merely to supplement but actually to amend the existing law.

Read together, Mishnah Eduyot, Horayot, and Sanhedrin paint an interesting picture of a society run by a judicial system headed by a high court that has the power to reconsider and revise the law as it sees fit, but which is kept in check by a learned elite charged to defy the courts whenever they feel them to be in error. There is no absolute authority: the *halakhah,* granted permanence by traditionalists, is considered revisable; the court system, whose rulings, according to traditionalists, are immune to future revision, is perpetually open to objection by critics; and the critics, in turn, are in constant danger of being declared rebellious. All involved are obliged to live dangerously. On such a reading, the high court is perhaps powerless to forgive a rebellious elder, but it would have the right to grant him his freedom by granting him his point.

Finally, according to the "traditionalist" viewpoint of the Tosefta, rebellion means to rebel against a *halakhah* to which all involved are wholly bound. It follows that, in principle, an entire Sanhedrin could be deemed a "rebellious elder" if it knowingly voted against an appropriately weighty halakhic ruling. According to the "antitraditionalist" approach of the Mishnah, the high court's discretion is not limited to legal lacunae, and it can, therefore, never be accused of rebelling against what it is at liberty to change anyway!

This meta-halakhic disagreement is fundamental. It is nowhere decided "officially," and when acknowledged, it is treated—as the introduction to this chapter implies—as yet another example of talmudic polyphony. But whether or not the halakhic system is in principle revisable is a question that communities governed by such a system cannot afford to avoid. Unfortunately, the traditionalist approach is endorsed by virtually all orthodox communities today. To bring about halakhic change, halakhists have for generations been required to show that their new position fits more exactly with the tradition. Change is resisted altogether or, at best, achieved surreptitiously. Since traditionalism deems the very notion of a faulty or morally inappropriate *halakhah* incoherent, it renders the system impossibly inflexible in times of significant cultural, social, and political change. The most profound change of this kind undergone by Jews since the composition of the Mishnah and Tosefta has been the establishment of the state of Israel, where halakhic traditionalism is proving to be an enormous liability. There is no way in which even the most basic civil liberties can be accommodated within the traditionalist system adhered to by all Israeli orthodoxy, which therefore finds itself on a collision course with the state envisioned by political Zionism. The Mishnah's antitraditionalism is an authentic alternative meta-halakhic position. Its revival, I believe, is essential for all those who are committed to the texts discussed in this book and who wish to partake in the great political opportunity offered by modern Zionism.

Menachem Fisch

This midrash, reproduced in Rashi's commentary on the Torah, is often cited in support of unquestioning obedience to rabbinic authority. A theoretical defense of such obedience, and therefore an argument against the import of the Horayot texts above (especially the line of interpretation developed radically by Rosh), is provided by Nahmanides in the next selection.

"Even If They Say Right Is Left"
12. *Sifre Deuteronomy* 154

"To the right or to the left" (Deut. 17:11). Even if they tell you that right is left and left right, obey them.

Justifying Conformity
13. Nahmanides, *Commentary on the Torah*, Deuteronomy 17:11

"To the right or to the left." "Even if he says to you that right is left and left is right"—these are Rashi's words. The meaning of the matter is that even if you think in your heart that they are mistaken, and even if the matter is as obvious to you as the difference you discern between your right and left, you are to follow their command. And do not say: How can I eat this real suet? or How can I kill this innocent man? Rather you should say: I have thus been commanded by the Master who issued the commandments that I should act in all His commandments in accordance with whatever I am instructed by those stationed before Him in the place He has chosen. It is on the basis of their understanding of its meaning that He has given me the Torah—even if they err. . . .

This *mitzvah* relates to a very great need. For the Torah was given to us in writing, and it is known that opinions will not concur regarding newly arisen matters. As a result, controversies will abound, and the Torah will become several Torahs.[16] Scripture has thus determined the law: that we listen to whatever the high court stationed before God in the place He has chosen says concerning the exposition of the Torah, regardless of whether they have a tradition of exposition leading back—witness by witness—to Moses from God, or whether they decree the matter by deriving it from the meaning of the Torah or its intention. For it is on the basis of their understanding that He has given them the Torah, even if in your eyes it seems that they are confounding right and left. And how much more so is it incumbent upon you to think that they are expositing the right as right, for the spirit of the Name is upon the servants of His sanctuary: "He does not abandon His faithful ones, they are preserved forever" (Ps. 37:28) from error and pitfall. The *Sifre*'s words: "Even if they tell you that right is left and left right, obey them."

Living with Disagreement

The following texts focus on a special subset of the many disputes between the schools of Shammai and Hillel. Each school's positions here entail the endorsement of marriages that are, according to the other school, strictly forbidden, the offspring being viewed as mamzerim. *The divergent teachings, if reflected in practice, would seem to require the adherents of each school to avoid marrying those of the other, producing an irrevocable split. The legal background for the first case is "levirate marriage": if a man dies childless, his brother (the levir) is obligated to marry the widow (Deut. 25:5–10). The particular matter at hand involves cases where the levirate obligation is dissolved because*

---

16. Paraphrasing BT Sanhedrin 88b (§10).

the marriage is barred (e.g., the surviving brother is already married to the widow's sister). But what if the deceased has another wife as well? According to Bet Shammai, the levirate obligation holds for the other widow (the "co-wife"); according to Bet Hillel, the levirate link is completely dissolved, leaving in place the general prohibition on a woman marrying her husband's brother.

Accommodating Disagreements—I

14. Mishnah Yevamot 1:4

Bet Shammai permit co-wives to marry the brothers, while Bet Hillel forbid them to. . . .

Even though these forbid while those permit, . . . Bet Shammai did not avoid taking wives from Bet Hillel, nor Bet Hillel from Bet Shammai.

[Despite] all the items of purity and impurity, which these declared pure while those declared them impure, they did not avoid relying on each other in producing pure foods.[17]

"Love Truth and Peace"

15. Tosefta Yevamot 1:10–11

The Tosefta here adds several other disputes in marital law, all sharing the crucial and disturbing characteristic of marriages endorsed by one school and prohibited by the other. It also furnishes a richer discussion of the remarkable "They did not avoid. . . ."

Even though Bet Shammai and Bet Hillel disagreed regarding co-wives and sisters, an uncertain marriage, an old *get* (writ of divorce), betrothal with a *perutah,* and the case of a man who divorced his wife and then shared a

---

17. Lending each other, e.g., cooking utensils.

room with her at an inn—Bet Shammai did not avoid taking wives from Bet Hillel, nor Bet Hillel from Bet Shammai. Instead, they acted with truth and peace between them, as written, "Love truth and peace" (Zech. 8:19).[18] Even though these forbid while those permit, they did not avoid relying on each other in producing pure foods. Thus they fulfilled that which is written, "Every man's path is pure in his eyes, while the Lord appraises hearts" (Prov. 21:2).

Rabbi Shimon says: They did not avoid the unknown, but did avoid known [cases].[19]

Halakhah Follows Bet Hillel
16. BT Eruvin 13b

After the destruction of the Second Temple, the Rabbinic community generally adopted the teachings of the school of Hillel; still, the many disputes between the two schools were faithfully preserved in the Mishnah. Here is the talmudic account of how the great dispute came to be resolved. Although the text speaks directly of only three intense years, relating perhaps to a particular argument, the resolution is understood to apply across the board. Thus the Talmud consistently holds that "the words of Bet Shammai have no force in the face of [contrary positions on the part of] Bet Hillel" (e.g., BT Yevamot 9a).

Rabbi Aba, citing Shmu'el, said: For three years, Bet Shammai and Bet Hillel disagreed.

These said: The law should be according to us, while those said: The law should be according to us.

---

18. New JPS: "love honesty and integrity."
19. Literally, "They did not avoid the doubtful but did avoid the certain." The suggestion is that they would not avoid marrying adherents of the other school because of a general concern over divergent practices; yet they did avoid individuals definitely known to have descended from marriages allowed by the other school but unacceptable by their own rules.

[Then] a *bat kol* was pronounced: "These and those are the words of the living God;[20] and the law is according to Bet Hillel."

But since these and those are the words of the living God, why was it granted to Bet Hillel that the law be established according to them? Because they were tolerant and meek, and related[21] both their own words and Bet Shammai's words. Moreover, they placed Bet Shammai's words before their own. This teaches you that whoever humbles himself is exalted by the Holy One, while whoever exalts himself is humbled by the Holy One.

Controversies That Endure

17. Mishnah Avot 5:17

The particular disputes between the two schools, like those between Hillel and Shammai themselves, were eventually decided. At the same time, these controversies became a model for disagreement and coexistence. The Mishnah here, somewhat paradoxically, promises that the best controversies are eternal.

Every controversy which is for the sake of heaven will endure; but one which is not for the sake of heaven will not endure.

What is a controversy for the sake of heaven? The controversy of Hillel and Shammai. And one not for the sake of heaven? The controversy of Korah and his company (Num. 16).

Accommodating Disagreements—II

18. BT Yevamot 14a

Given the critical nature of the controversies between the schools, the Talmud is led to explore how in fact they lived together without dividing into separate factions. Our text

---

20. The Hebrew syntax allows also for an alternative translation: "the living words of God."
21. The Hebrew word (*shonim*), from the same root as *mishnah*, denotes both studying and teaching: they made the words of Bet Shammai part of their standard text.

contemplates the situation both before and after the pronouncement of the bat kol *in favor of Bet Hillel (§16).*

Rav says, "Bet Shammai did not act on their opinions," whereas Shmu'el says, "They certainly did!"

When was this? If it was prior to the *bat kol,* then what is the reason for holding that "they did not"? If, however, it was after the *bat kol,* what is the reason for holding that "they did"?

If you wish, I can say it was prior to the *bat kol;* and if you wish, I can say it was after the *bat kol.*

If you wish, I can say it was prior to the *bat kol,* assuming that Bet Hillel constituted a majority. Those who hold that "they did not"—well, Bet Hillel were a majority. Those who hold that "they did" [can] explain: We follow the majority only when both sides are equal; here, however, Bet Shammai were more astute.

If you wish, I can say it was after the *bat kol.* Those who hold that "they did not"—well, the *bat kol* had been pronounced! While those who hold that "they did" follow Rabbi Yehoshua, who said, "We take no heed of a *bat kol*" (BT Bava Metzia 59b [℃6, §10]).

Regarding those who hold that "they did," we might cite the verse "You shall not cut yourself up" (Deut 14:1), [midrashically interpreted to mean] "You shall not become divided into factions."

Said Abaye: "You shall not become divided" only applies to two courts in the same town, one ruling according to Bet Shammai and the other ruling according to Bet Hillel. With two courts in two [separate] towns, there is no problem.

Rava retorted: But Bet Shammai and Bet Hillel are like two courts in the same town!

Rava therefore said: "You shall not become divided" only applies to a [split] court in one town, with one faction ruling according to Bet Shammai and another faction ruling according to Bet Hillel. With two [separate] courts in the same town, there is no problem. . . .

Come and hear: "Even though these forbid while those permit, . . . Bet Shammai did not avoid taking wives from Bet Hillel, nor Bet Hillel from

Bet Shammai." If we suppose they did not [act on their opinions], it is clear why they did not avoid [taking wives]. But if we suppose they did [act on their opinions], why did they not avoid [taking wives]? . . . [The offspring] would be *mamzerim!* . . . Does this not prove that they did not [act on their opinions]?

No, they informed [each other of mutually problematic cases] and refrained from marriage.

Commentary. Interpretive Pluralism

The Western liberal tradition prizes debate and disagreement, and the sages, for all their emphasis on authority and obedience, at points manifest some of liberalism's spirit. It is true that, according to some sources, legal controversies result from a sad historical circumstance, a calamitous break in the chain of authoritative transmission caused by human failings (BT Sotah 47b; Sanhedrin 88b; Tosefta Hagigah 2:9). But the texts now before us show a more representative, positive view of *mahloket* (controversy, dispute, disagreement). Midrash Psalms 12 suggests that disputes arose from design, not misfortune: God deliberately made the *halakhah* open to differing interpretations and rulings, personally supplying Moses with forty-nine possible reasons on each side, so that the *halakhah* would not be cut and dried. For the most part, the sages greeted well-intentioned halakhic controversy with enthusiasm, encouragement, and appreciation. "Every controversy that is for the sake of heaven will endure" (Avot 5:17).

Various possible reasons for the sages' attitude spring to mind: a recognition of the vitality and richness that controversy generates in a community; a Mill-like conviction that the clash of opposites yields truth; a desire to show the human intellect to be central in the halakhic process; and a sense that controversy serves to make the Torah great and glorious (*le-hagdil torah u-le-ha'adirah*) by assuring *halakhah* a prominent place in the intellectual life of the community. Notice, however, that the tradition's esteem for disagreement is not limited to periods when sages are trying to decide the law. Rather, even after the dust has settled and one side's view has been declared normative, we find a remarkable respect for earlier minority viewpoints and for arguments that did not carry the halakhic day.

I do not refer here merely to the recording of rejected opinions—dissenting rulings along with their attendant reasonings. That practice makes good judicial and religious sense. For one thing, as the mishnah Eduyot 1:5 points out, some later courts will have the power to overturn an earlier court's decision, but only if they can cite a previous minority. (A contrasting view, in Eduyot 1:6, is that the minority opinion is recorded so it can be quashed should it ever be revived under the guise of an authentic tradition.) Also, a line of argument rejected in one context might prove serviceable or significant in others (see Rashi to BT Ketubot 57a). Minority opinions may be adopted in exigent circumstances; or they sometimes might enter into such decision-making procedures as "double doubt" (sefek sefeka), whereby a combination of disputed or undetermined factors may be assembled to justify a lenient ruling.

Keeping a record of debate and dissent makes each accepted view more understandable. It also inspires an ethic of discussion, encouraging later scholars to defend their own opinions on all subjects. And in any case, must the only aim of Torah study be to determine the practical halakhah? Can its goal not be as well to develop legal analysis and theory, for which purpose a full record is necessary?

The preservation of rejected minority opinions is, then, eminently reasonable. By studying Talmud and not riveting attention only on apodictic codes, Jews keep alive debates that long ago reached closure, revealing a conviction that reasoning on all sides should be preserved for posterity. (To be sure, many sectarian views are not preserved by the Talmud.) What is striking and even perplexing, however, is how far the Rabbis' respect for dissenting views goes. Talmudic sources push so hard to legitimate such views that they place them on a par with the accepted one as regards legal cogency—and perhaps even as regards truth.

A radical path to valuing minority opinion is paved by our sources' interpretive pluralism. As is often noted, legal reasoning is not a deductive science. But sometimes the Talmud gives the discomfiting impression that halakhic give-and-take resembles the relativistic philosophizing of the ancient Sophists. A trained dialectician can defend any position on any issue (in forty-nine ways!)—and to qualify for the Sanhedrin a judge must be able to find reasons for declaring "pure" a rodent that we all know not to be so (BT Sanhedrin 17a). If modern liberalism takes its pluralistic cue from skepticism and epistemological underdetermination, the Talmud takes its cue from a radically permissive epistemology.

The Talmud does not stop at interpretive pluralism; it courts an extravagant metaphysical pluralism, according to which all halakhic opinions of sages who join the debate are true, even though they contradict one another. The heavenly voice proclaims that "these and those," that is, both sides of the Bet Hillel–Bet Shammai *mahloket,* are "the words of the living God." What kind of God says contradictory things? Furthermore, if both teachings are true, wherein lies the superiority of the view that is eventually accepted? The heavenly voice's declaration that "the *halakhah* follows Bet Hillel" seems arbitrary and mysterious.

One could retort—and many have—that the *elu va-elu* ("these and those") principle affirms merely the *partial* validity of the rejected view, for example, its applicability in other circumstances. Alternatively, "these and those are the words of the living God" may mean that a *measure* of inspiration is behind both views, or that both views grow out of divinely licensed methods—not that neither view is truer than the other. But our difficulties are not over. According to the Eruvin passage, the reason that Bet Hillel's views merited being accepted over Bet Shammai's is not that Bet Hillel's were logically more penetrating—in that respect, as we know from BT Yevamot 14a, Bet Shammai's were superior. The reasons are, rather, that the sages of Bet Hillel were tolerant and forbearing and that they were deferential to Bet Shammai—expounding the latter's views before their own. Evidently, a rejected view may reflect greater legal acumen and cogency than the accepted one! The Talmud's explanations for Bet Hillel's prevalence call to mind the ad hominem arguments catalogued in textbooks among logical fallacies. What does a jurist's moral probity have to do with the legal standing of his views?

Actual halakhic decision making employs such formal criteria as majority rule and consistency with sources, rather than heavenly voices or considerations of virtue. Bet Hillel's humility is invoked as a theodicy, not as a description of how the law came to be decided. Still, the notion that nice sages finish first conveys an important moral point: not simply that God likes modesty, nor that He points modest people in the direction of truth, but that a *natural link* exists between moral virtue and legal credibility (and perhaps between legal credibility and the ability to muster a majority).

A good procedure in legal reasoning is one that takes account of the opposition. If legal reasoning can be marshaled in favor of either side, then the fact that you can present a line of argument to establish your own view does not yet show that you are right. You must take account of the other side's view, either by refuting it or by integrating its valuable part into your own logic. And the greater respect you accord your opponent—the greater humility you possess—the more likely you are to assimilate what the other side is saying. Bet Hillel, we presume (this is not explicitly stated), either found flaws in Bet Shammai's logic or else incorporated whatever was correct in it. That Bet Shammai was sharper in presenting their own position does not offset the superior truth-conduciveness of Bet Hillel's procedure and temperament. Again, that Bet Hillel reversed themselves more often than Bet Shammai did (Eduyot 1:12–13) indicates not that Bet Hillel's logic can't be trusted but, to the contrary, that ultimately it is more dependable. The world knows many brilliant scientists whose personal arrogance renders them obstinate, incapable of backing down or revising their beliefs. Openness and self-criticism promote truth. Moral virtue and epistemic virtue go hand in hand (see also BT Hagigah 3b). It seems to follow that later authorities, because they are cognizant of earlier views, are more reliable than earlier ones. This dovetails with the principle that "the *halakhah* follows the later view," although this principle is not an across-the-board rule (for example, it doesn't permit rejection of talmudic rulings).

Admittedly, the context in which Bet Shammai's superior analytical ability is mentioned suggests that this ability *is* conducive to discovering truth. For those impressed by this point, we can explain in yet another way why Bet Hillel's moral character led to their arguments being accepted. Bet Hillel's practice of taking account of "the other" shows greater appreciation than Bet Shammai evinced for the importance of controversy and of the *elu va-elu* principle. Bet Hillel is more committed to the process of discussion, and that commitment makes their views more representative, even symbolic, of a well-functioning halakhic process than Bet Shammai's.

The limits of the Talmud's pluralism may be tested by pondering its treatment of the following question: Are those who hold opinion X entitled to live in accordance with their own principles when they deal with people who hold opinion Y? In our texts a central question is whether followers of Bet Shammai and Bet Hillel could marry each other when such marriages might be prohibited by the principles of one or the other school. (Some unions would even produce *mamzerim*.) Preserving personal integrity in these cases means segregating oneself from the other group, thereby threatening communal unity. Deuteronomy 14:1, as read by the sages, cautions against fragmenting the Torah. Should each side continue to abide by its principles in these circumstances?

If we adopt a broad interpretive pluralism, we should expect that neither side would be giving up much in the way of truth by accepting the other side's more lenient rulings. Now, the Mishnah states that followers of Bet Hillel and Bet Shammai did marry each other. Further, Tosefta Yevamot 1:10, invoking Proverbs 21:2, implies that God accepts opposing practices so long as the adherents of each practice are sincere; when interacting with an adversary, one may therefore rely on the other's view. Other sources, however, clearly decline to view Bet Hillel and Bet Shammai's acceptance of intermarriages as an outgrowth of interpretive pluralism. When the Tosefta invokes Zechariah 8:19, "Love truth and peace," it implies that for Bet Hillel, truth was valuable, but not as valuable as peace.

A particularly important nonpluralist thesis advanced in the talmudic discussion is that followers of Bet Hillel and Bet Shammai married each other only because—thanks to a mutual policy of "full disclosure"—they had prior assurance that the husbands- or wives-to-be were not prohibited to them on their own principles. This is a pleasing ode to mutual trust and to the possibility that peace can be achieved without compromise; but simultaneously it bespeaks a firm and principled commitment that allows no leniency in problematic cases. Thus, it is not that the stringent view must compromise its principles to accommodate the permissive view, but that the latter must accommodate the former and ensure that proponents of stringency will not have to compromise their principles.

The tension between peace and integrity is felt acutely today. There is passionate debate over whether one denomination of Judaism should recognize conversions and marriages conducted according to another's more lenient standards. Who should accommodate whom? Complicating the issue is the fact that the principles enunciated in the Talmud are meant to apply to legitimately formed positions, and the definition of legitimacy is itself contested. The basis of pluralism and hence its bounds are themselves understood in plural ways. With mutual respect eroding, the practical problem of negotiating social life in the midst of divergent understandings is perhaps even more pressing than seeking a single understanding.

David Shatz

Medieval Arguments: The Value of Uniformity

Controversy as Decline
19. *The Epistle of Sherira Gaon*

This epistle was written in 987 to the community of Kairouan in North Africa in response to queries about the Oral Law arising from a controversy with Karaites. Sherira's account of "how the Mishnah was written" gained wide acceptance among Rabbanites. His basic argument follows the line already advanced by Saadiah, of assigning the main body of the oral tradition to the Sinai revelation. In this selection from the opening pages of the epistle, Sherira attributes the emergence of controversies to a decline of Rabbinic tradition following the destruction of the Temple (he elaborates the position of Rabbi Yose in §10). His argument starts from the fact that the sages mentioned by name in the Mishnah are by and large from the post-destruction era, which might seem to indicate that the Oral Law was not taught by earlier sages.

With respect to your query, "Why did the ancients leave most [of the Torah's elaboration] to the later [sages]?" No, the ancients did not leave it to them. Rather, it was the teachings of the ancients that the later [sages] all transmitted, and it was their explications that they conveyed. . . .

It was thus: The names of the ancients were not preserved . . . be-

cause there were no controversies among them. Rather, all explications of
the Torah were clearly known to them. The Talmud too was clearly known
to them, as were all discussions and subtleties deriving from their teachings
regarding each and every matter. For in [BT Bava Batra 134a the Talmud
states that Rabbi Yohanan ben Zakkai knew] "the discussions of Abaye and
Rava"—which shows that even the discussions of Abaye and Rava [in the
fourth century C.E.] did not originate with them but were all known by the
ancients.

While the Temple stood, each one of the eminent ones would explicate to his students in his own words the Torah, the Mishnah, and the Talmud, teaching his students in whatever fashion he chose. Wisdom abounded,
and they were not troubled by other matters; it was only the single issue of
"the laying on of hands" (cf. Tosefta Hagigah 2:8) that was [disputed] among
them. . . .

When the Temple was destroyed, and they moved on to Betar, and
[then] Betar too was destroyed, the sages were thoroughly dispersed. By reason of the disorders and persecutions and troubles that occurred in those
times, the students were insufficiently schooled and controversies abounded.

Karaite Critique of the Oral Law

20. Salmon ben Jeroham, *Book of the Wars of the Lord,* Cantos I–II

Karaite Anthology, translated and edited by Leon Nemoy, Yale Judaica Series (New Haven:
Yale University Press, 1952), pp. 73–78.

This fiercely polemical critique of Saadiah's arguments for the validity of the Rabbanite
oral tradition was written sometime in the 930s, possibly in Jerusalem, while Saadiah
was still alive and Salmon a very young man. Saadiah adduced the talmudic explana-
tion that the Oral Law was put into writing out of necessity so that it should not be
forgotten, despite the original principle that "written words may not be conveyed orally,
and oral words may not be conveyed in writing" (BT Gittin 60b).

Canto I

12   We believe firmly that the written Law
  Was in truth given to Israel by the right hand of the
   Almighty
  According to the testimony of the whole congregation of
   the Lily [Israel],
  Who are scattered in every land.

13   All of them, believers as well as unbelievers,
  Divided as they are by language and tongue,
  All Israel, from the east to the westernmost ends of the
   world,
   Testify to the sanctity of the written Law, all of them,
    the little and the great.

14   This testimony has become firmly established in their midst
  By their united and universal consent, without challenge.
  Likewise, the signs and miracles which the Dweller of the
   heavenly abode has wrought
   Are written therein and are explained for them who wish
    to understand.

15   Selah! They remember the splitting asunder of the Red Sea
  And they do not deny the words spoken by the
   Almighty on Mount Sinai;
  And with their mouths they sing of the glory of the Law
   and of the other miracles.
  Israel and all other nations speak of this as one.

16   Now if Israel and Judah are both united
  Concerning the validity of the oral Law, which is, as they
   [the Rabbanites] say, perfect,
  Let them offer their testimony, and let their voices be
   heard;
   If not, then the Fayyumite's [Saadiah Gaon's] words are
    void and his tongue has been silenced.

Canto II

2   I have looked again into the six divisions of the Mishnah,
          And behold, they represent the words of modern men.
      There are no majestic signs and miracles in them,
          And they lack the formula "And the Lord spoke unto
      Moses and unto Aaron."

3   I therefore put them aside, and I said, There is no true Law
              in them,
          For the Law is set forth in a different manner,
      In a majestic display of prophets, of signs, and of miracles;
          Yet all this majestic beauty we do not see in the whole
              Mishnah.

.   .   .

6   I have turned again to my first argument,
          To fortify it with truth and uprightness, without
              falsehood,
      And with might and power, like the power of Samson
          However, the best answer of the tongue is from the
              Lord.

7   I have set the six divisions of the Mishnah before me,
          And I looked at them carefully with mine eyes.
      And I saw that they are very contradictory in content,
          This one Mishnaic scholar declares a thing to be
              forbidden to the people of Israel, while that one
              declares it to be permitted.

8   My thoughts therefore answer me,
          And most of my reflections declare unto me,
      That there is in it no Law of logic,
          Nor the Law of Moses the Wise.

9   I said, Perhaps one of the two did not know the right way,
          Wherefore he did not know how to reason it out with
              his companion;
      Perhaps the truth lies with his companion;

Let me look into his words; perchance I will find relief
    from my perplexity.

10   But instead I found there other men—
    Sometimes they say, "Others say,"
    While anon the scholars issue a decision,
        Agreeing neither with the one nor with the other, but
        contradicting both.

11   Had I been among them—I say, had I been among them—
        I should not have accepted the words of these "others"
        and "scholars."
    Rather would I have weighed the word of the Lord with
        them,
        And I would have judged accordingly every word which
        they had contrived.

12   Gird thyself with thy strength and hearken, and step up
        to me
        And let the scholars of my congregation of Israel judge
        between us,
    And let them place our words upon the scales,
        So that I may walk in truth upon the road of my life's
        course.

13   Know that there is no difference in learning between them
        and me.
        When they say, "Rabbi So-and-so said thus-and-so,"
    I answer and say, I, too, am the learned So-and-so.
        Thine escape has been cut off by this argument, else
        answer me, if thou canst.

14   His [Saadiah's] heart is overlaid with stupidity as with fat,
        and I know well what he says and speaks,
        As he has set it forth in his written scroll;
    Therefore will I turn my face toward him and do battle
        with him,
        And I will shake his loins and strike down his sword.

15   He has written that the six divisions of the Mishnah are as
        authoritative as the Law of Moses,

And that they wrote it down so that it would not be
forgotten.
I shall answer him concerning this, for I will not be silent,
Lest the blackguard think that he had uttered an
unanswerable argument.

16   He who remembers forgotten things and knows what is
hidden,
Had He deemed it proper to have them skillfully written
down
In order that they might not be forgotten upon earth,
He would have ordered His servant Moses to inscribe
them, with might and power, in a book.

17   If it is proper for men like us,
Who have none of the holy spirit in us,
To turn the oral Law into a written Law, by writing it
down,
Why would it not be right for us to turn the written
Law into a Law preserved only in our mouths?

18   Hearken unto me and I will speak further:
If thou shouldst say, "This took place in the days of the
Prophets and in the days of Ezra,"
Why is there no mention in it of these Prophets
In the same manner as the names of the Prophets are
recorded throughout Scripture?

19   Be silent, and I will teach thee wisdom
If it be thy desire to learn wisdom.
It is written: "The Law of the Lord is perfect" (Ps. 19:8).
What profit be there for us, then, in the written
Mishnah?

20   Moreover, if the Talmud originated with our master Moses,
What profit is there for us in "another view,"
And what can a third and a fourth view teach us,
When they tell us first that the interpretation of this
problem in law is thus-and-so, and then proceed to
explain it with "another view"?

21   The truth stands upon one view only,

For this is so in the wisdom of all mankind,

And right counsel cannot be based upon two contradictory
things.

Now in this one thing he has fallen down and cannot
stand up:

22   If the Talmud is composed of the words of prophets,

Why are contradictory views found in it?

Now it is evident that this view of Saadiah's is foolishness,
and the words of fools.

So testify all mankind.

Against Karaism: The True Torah Is One

21. Judah Halevi, *The Kuzari* 3:35–38

Translated by Lawrence Berman and Barry S. Kogan, forthcoming in the Yale Judaica Series
(Yale University Press).

Halevi's polemical defense of the veracity of the oral tradition is based upon a bold por-
trayal of rabbinic Judaism as essentially uniform. In The Kuzari *he nowhere takes note*
of the phenomenon of rabbinic controversy. Instead, Halevi argues that the very reading
of the Torah necessitates a singular and detailed tradition even for its vocalization and
punctuation, and certainly for its legal explication.

(3:35) . . . Have you heard, O King of the Khazars, about [any] treatise of the
Karaites on [any]thing pertaining to what I have mentioned [that is] clearly
traceable to its original authorities, widely accepted, tied to tradition, [and]
not in dispute among them, with respect to *massoret* [the commonly accepted
traditional text of Scripture], or vocalization, or musical accents, or forbidden and permitted things, or legal rulings?

(3:36) The Khazar said: I have neither seen them nor heard about
them, but I do see them making a diligent effort.

(3:37) The sage said: This relates to what I told you about engaging
in intellectual speculation and arbitrary judgment [3:23]. Those who engage

in intellectual speculation about worship pertaining to the work of heaven (Jer. 7:18; 44:17) exert themselves [far] more than someone who does the work of YHWH that he is commanded [to do]. For the latter have found rest in their acceptance of [authoritative] tradition on faith, and their souls have come to be at ease, like someone who goes about freely within the city, so that they don't have to be on the alert for any challenge, while the former are like someone who goes about on foot in the desert, who doesn't know what he will meet up with. Therefore, he is armed, alert for battle, schooled in combat [and] accustomed to it. So don't be surprised by what you see of their resoluteness, and don't be caught off guard by whatever laxity you see on the part of those subject to [authoritative] tradition—I mean, [of course,] the Rabbanites. The former sought out a fortress in which they might be secure, while the latter are asleep, lying quietly on their bedding, in an ancient, [well-]fortified city.

(3:38) The Khazar said: Everything you have said follows logically, because the religious Law was intent on there being one Torah and one judgment [for all]. But, in keeping with their [different ways of] reasoning the commandments will multiply [so as to be] in accord with the [individual] reasoning of each one of them. Yes, [and what is more,] the individual will not even remain [faithful] to a single revealed law because some new opinion becomes "obvious" to him every day, as his knowledge increases. Moreover, he will [inevitably] meet someone who refutes [his opinion] with [some] argument so that it becomes necessary for him to change with [his] change of opinion. And so, if we find them agreeing, let us recognize that they are accepting on faith [either] an individual or a group that came before them.

But then we must take issue with their agreement and say to them: "How did you come to agree about such and such a commandment when [someone's individual] opinion might [equally well] tip the scales in favor of many [other] ways of [understanding] the speech of God?" Now, if they say that Anan or Benjamin or Saul or someone else used to believe this, they make themselves vulnerable to the argument that they ought to accept on faith the [authoritative] tradition of those who are older and even more worthy [of being obeyed than these men are] in connection with accepting tradition—I mean the sages, because they are [comprised of entire] groups, while these [others] are [merely] individuals. Also, the reasoning of the sages is clearly linked by a chain of authorities to what has been handed down by the prophets, while [what has been handed down by] those [others] is nothing more than mere reasoning. [Beyond this,] the sages are in agreement, while those people differ with one another. [Again,] the sayings of the sages are [ultimately taken] "from the place that YHWH . . . will choose" (Deut. 17:10), and [for that reason,] even if one of their rulings derived from nothing more than mere reasoning, it would certainly have to be accepted [in any case], while [the legal rulings of] those others are not like that.

Commentary. Pluralism and Singularity

The most curious feature of the argument between the Karaites, represented here by Salmon ben Jeroham, and the Rabbanites, represented by Judah Halevi, is that the two sides agree in their theological or metaphysical commitment to a singular truth; they also agree in their practical (though always unacknowledged) accommodation with pluralism. Salmon and Halevi each charge their opponents with this accommodation—and each of them is right. Neither side denied God's oneness; the argument had to do with the nature of the Torah. One God revealed one Torah, but this was a revelation in words, written or spoken, and these words had to be understood. What is given must also be received. And reception means reading, studying, interpreting; it is a social process.

According to the Karaites, so Halevi says, this process has the form of a series of individual acts. One by one, each person confronts the Torah and "speculates" on its meaning, with the result that he "will not even remain [faithful] to a single revealed Law because some new opinion will become clear to him every day as his knowledge increases. Moreover, he will [inevitably] meet someone who refutes him with some argument so that it becomes necessary for him to change." According to the Rabbanites, Salmon says, the process of understanding is collective and authoritative; it takes place in schools; it is the work of scholars; it gives rise to a tradition that incorporates and preserves scholarly disagreement; its character is reflected in the common phrases of the Rabbis—"others say" and "another view."

These are both good descriptions; Halevi and Salmon have grasped, each for the other, what a social process is and why, in the absence of coercive power, it never reaches a definitive end. If there were no disagreements, the rabbinic schools would have no ongoing purpose. Similarly, if one Karaite "speculation" were to achieve the status of final truth, there would be no need for individual confrontations with the text.

But Halevi thinks that the "new opinions" of the Karaites are a sign of inconstancy and falsehood. And Salmon thinks that the second, third, and fourth views of the Rabbis are necessarily abominations: "The truth stands upon one view only." This common commitment to singularity derives in part from a common anxiety. How can the Jewish people survive in the diaspora if their internal disagreements are acknowledged and validated? Many opinions will make for many legal codes and divergent practices. This is certainly a possible consequence of interpretive pluralism—as we can see from the later proliferation of Protestant sects within Christianity. But it is also possible that the anxiety is misplaced.

First of all, its urgency is unclear, for both Karaites and Rabbanites managed to sustain strong communities for many years despite the disagreements that arose within each group. A variety of political mechanisms— majority rule the most obvious—can turn the plurality of opinions into a singular law. And second, active disagreement and even sectarianism may well be signs of religious vitality. This is what they signaled among the Jews of the later Second Temple period (among Protestants, too, in the sixteenth and seventeenth centuries). Halevi points to the zealotry of Karaite sectaries and contrasts it with the complacency of people on his own side. For him, this is a sign of Karaite nervousness and uncertainty and of Rabbanite assurance; those with a secure tradition are at ease in their faith. But they are not entirely at ease, as Halevi's book proves. The liveliness of Karaite opposition was a great intellectual stimulus to rabbinic Judaism.

The theological or metaphysical argument is harder to deal with in a brief commentary. But it is important at least to notice the historical coexistence of principled singularity and practical pluralism. Revelation may be singular in character, the Bible may be a unified book (though it doesn't read that way), but human engagement with this oneness is always, necessarily, a pluralizing and differentiating process. Individuals and groups come to the one text with their different experiences, interests, and questions; and they come away with different readings. It follows that any successful tradition of interpretation will incorporate difference, as the Karaites said of the Talmud, and change over time, as the Rabbanites said of Karaite doctrine. Whenever difference is repressed and change is blocked, the tradition dies.

So the practices that Salmon and Halevi chose to ridicule are in fact signs of strength. Why wasn't it possible for them to see this? It is sometimes argued that pluralism can't be "seen," that is, recognized and valued, because it is only the by-product of a search for the one true doctrine. What holds the interpreters to their task is the conviction that they are reading God's will *rightly*. If it isn't possible to do that, why bother to study the texts or work within the tradition?

We don't know whether the talmudic sages who argued the second, third, and fourth views believed that they were right in this strong sense. But the editors who preserved the different views, and the generations of students who studied them, must have had a looser understanding of their enterprise. Perhaps they thought about God what Walt Whitman thought about himself: "I am large; I contain multitudes." (Compare the God of Midrash Psalms, who provides forty-nine arguments for each of two contradictory positions.) Or perhaps they accepted the argument of another midrash: "Behold it says: 'A dream carries much implication' (Eccles. 5:2). Now by using the method of *kal vahomer* [a fortiori], we reason: If the contents of dreams which have no effect may yield a multitude of interpretations, how much more then should the important contents of the Torah imply many interpretations in every verse" (Midrash Hagadol Bereshith). This argument for one Torah and many interpretations might be the product of epistomological skepticism. Though there is in principle one true interpretation, we can never know which one it is. But the midrash in fact suggests something different: that aspects of the (one) truth are reflected in the diverse interpretations. This is not to say that every reading of a text is of equal value; knowledge increases, as Halevi says, and arguments are refuted; the normal standards of coherence and consistency apply; a rough hierarchy of legal and moral principles governs the particular cases. There are better and worse accounts of the law. But the diversity itself, and the debates it provokes, serves significantly to enhance our understanding. Surely this view provides a stronger defense of Karaite individualism and Rabbanite traditionalism *as they actually were* than do Salmon's and Halevi's claims to uphold a one-and-only-one view of moral and legal truth.

Michael Walzer

A Code Omitting Argumentation

22. Maimonides, Introduction to the *Mishneh Torah*

Translated by Bernard Septimus, forthcoming in the Yale Judaica Series (Yale University Press).

After describing the tradition of Oral Law and the breakdown of central halakhic au-thority (C6, §3), Maimonides addresses the unsatisfactory situation in halakhic juris-prudence that led him to compose the Mishneh Torah. In contrast to the Talmud, which is a compendium of legal reasoning and argumentation, the Mishneh Torah *provides a systematic and univocal codification of halakhah. Perhaps Maimonides aspired to serve, through his work, the unifying function of the high court of old.*

Nowadays, troubles proliferate, one hard by the next, and the times oppress all. The wisdom of our wise is perished and the discernment of our discern-ing is lost. Thus it is that the commentaries, responsa, and rule-collections compiled by the Geonim [post-talmudic authorities] and considered by them to be plainly put, have turned difficult in our days: none but a small few understand their meanings properly. It goes without saying then [that few understand] the Talmud itself, Babylonian and Palestinian, Sifra, Sifrei, and the supplementary *baraytot.* For they require a capacious mind, a wise spirit, and a long time. Only then can one discern from them the correct course concerning the forbidden and permitted and the Torah's other legal cate-gories [e.g., impure and pure, liable and exempt, fit and unfit].

For this reason, I, Moses, son of Rabbi Maimon, the Sephardi, roused myself, put my reliance in the [Divine] Source, blessed be He, pon-dered all of these books, and resolved to compile what emerges from all of these works regarding the prohibited and permitted, the impure and pure, as well as the Torah's other legal categories, all in clear language and economical style, so that the Oral Torah, in its entirety, can be ordered in everyone's mouth, free of dialectical thrust and parry, without one [authority] saying this, and another, that. Rather: words that are clear, accessible, and authoritative according to the [final] ruling that emerges from all the compilations and commentaries that we have from the days of Our Saintly Master [Judah the Prince] to the present.

So that all of the rules, in the [various bodies of] law [that, respectively, explicate] each of the commandments and each of the enactments instituted by the sages and prophets, be manifest to small and great [alike]. In sum: in order that, a person need no other work whatever, on any of the laws of Israel; that this compilation, rather, encompass the entire Oral Torah, along with the ordinances, customs, and decrees established from the days of Moses, our master, until the compilation of the Talmud, as interpreted for us by the Geonim in all the works that they composed after the Talmud. I have therefore entitled this work Mishneh Torah [Companion to Scripture]:[22] For a person can first read the Written Torah and then read this [work] and know the entire Oral Torah from it, without having to read another intervening volume.

Insisting on Argumentation

23. Abraham b. David of Posquieres (Rabad), Glosses to MT: Introduction

Isadore Twersky, *Introduction to the Code of Maimonides (Mishneh Torah),* Yale Judaica Series (New Haven: Yale University Press, 1980), p. 103 n. 10.

Maimonides' code quickly became a focus for numerous glosses, commentaries, and controversies. The earliest set of critical glosses were those of Rabad (an older contemporary of Maimonides), which soon attained classical status alongside the code itself. In this

---

22. "*Mishneh torah*" is a biblical phrase (Deut. 17:18), translated in context (New JPS) as "a *copy* of this teaching." The phrase, used in Rabbinic times to denote the fifth book of Moses, is the equivalent of the Greek *Deuteronomy.* Here the YJS offers "companion"; an alternative translation might be "restatement."

gloss to Maimonides' introduction, Rabad criticizes the pretentiousness of Maimonides'
method.

He intended to improve but did not improve, for he forsook the way of all
the authors who preceded him. They always adduced proof for their statements and cited the proper authority for each statement; this was very useful,
for sometimes the judge would be inclined to forbid or permit something,
and his proof would be based on some other authority. Had he known that
there was a greater authority who interpreted the law differently, he might
have retracted. Now, however, I do not know why I should reverse my tradition or corroborative views because of the compendium of this author. If
the one who differs with me is greater than I, fine; and if I am greater than
he, why should I annul my opinion in deference to his? Moreover, there are
matters concerning which the Geonim disagree and this author has selected
the opinion of one and incorporated it in his compendium. Why should I
rely upon his choice when it is not acceptable to me, and I do not know
whether the contending authority is competent to differ or not? It can only
be that "an overbearing spirit is in him" (Dan. 6:4).

Modern Disputes: The Problem of Authority

Banning Hasidism

24. The Brody Proclamation of 1772

Zmir Aritzim, reprinted in M. Wilensky, *Hasidim and Mitnagdim* (Jerusalem: Bialik Institute, 1970; Hebrew), vol. 1, pp. 44–49.

This is one of the earliest calls to ban the budding hasidic movement. Deeply rooted
in mystical traditions, the movement inspired the wide adoption of kabbalistic prac-
tices. Specifically, this involved supplanting the traditional Ashkenazi prayerbook with
that of Isaac Luria (Ari)—formerly used exclusively by a scholarly and pietistic elite.
The esoteric prayers of such elites were conducted in the shtibel, *a small prayer room,*
located beside their special study hall, the kloyz. *Hasidism proposed to transform this*
esotericism into common practice.

A Public Proclamation made here at our Glorious Community of Brody, may God protect it, on the 20th of Sivan 5532 [= 1772], during the fair when all congregate

Listen, O holy community. With your permission, the honored notables, rulers, leaders, together with the well-known selectmen of the county, have unanimously ordered that the following be proclaimed:

Whereas it has been reported throughout the camp of the Hebrews that by reason of our great sins the [sinful practice] has been rekindled, in the midst of our people, of sects and groups detaching themselves from the unified and just community, adopting new practices and evil laws. They throw off the yoke of Torah and prefer license.

. . . They build themselves [separate] altars to set themselves apart from the holy community, making their own special *minyanim,* not praying with the community in the synagogues or study halls appointed for the public. They also alter the phrases coined by the sages, the great codifiers [who determined] the entire liturgical order in these lands. They also blaspheme and mock the messengers of God [i.e., the recognized scholars], and let pass the [prescribed] time for the recital of the *shema* and for prayer, deliberately altering the formulas that are customary in these lands, having been established by the great ones of old, from which there is no way to depart, whether right or left. It has now been discovered that these criminals in their very persons — their evil is immeasurable — remove the yoke and abandon eternal life; [they gather] in groups and gangs, chanting all day long. They deride the entire oral Torah, saying: learn only Kabbalah. They pray out of the prayerbook of the holy man of God, Ari of blessed memory, thereby surely "cutting the branches."[23] . . .

For some time now these evildoers have been around . . . and there is room for concern lest . . . , God forbid, the divine name become desecrated amongst the nations; lest [the gentiles] say that our Torah is, God forbid, like two Torahs; so that we become, God forbid, a laughingstock amongst the nations. How long shall these people be a snare to the House of Israel? Arise in righteousness to the aid of the Lord among the warriors! Anyone who has the fear of God in his heart should wholeheartedly take the initiative in this

---

23. The kabbalistic term for destructive misuse of mystical knowledge; cf. BT Hagigah 14b.

matter, to act zealously for the Lord of Hosts, for the honor of His great and awesome name. . . . [And act] to secure the breach, to repulse these evil men in any location where they or their influence prevails, for certainly there is some trace of heresy and apostasy [among them]. How much longer shall this wicked community [persist], who contrive . . . new practices unknown to our fathers? . . .

Therefore the holy community has decreed by the great and awesome *herem* . . . by all the sanctions and curses written in the Torah . . . : That, from this day onward, it is strictly forbidden for any one of the synagogues or fixed *minyanim* in our community . . . to alter—God forbid—anything of our customary formula of Ashkenazi prayer. Certainly, none may dare pray out of the prayerbook of the godly Ari of blessed memory, or of the other kabbalists, whose secrets were never attained by these sinful men. Also it is forbidden for any individual to pray other than according to the Ashkenazi liturgy, which we received from the ancient great of the world—except for the remnants named by God, those who pray within the first *shtibel* by the side of the *kloyz* of our congregation. With regard to them, it is crystal clear that these persons . . . are full of the exoteric Torah—Talmud and codes— and are also established scholars of the esoteric Kabbalah. They have for years been praying out of the prayerbook of Ari of blessed memory, which practice they have followed in the presence of rabbis advanced in age, the . . . great ones of our community, who never protested against this. For these [individuals], from a young age, were well known in [their] piety, and their main studies concerned the exoteric Torah, Talmud, and codes. They know their Master and have true intentions. [They] are permitted to pray, as has been their practice, out of the prayerbook of God's holy one, Ari of blessed memory—and none besides them. And outside of the *shtibel,* it cannot even be suggested that any *minyan* alter the formula of Ashkenazi prayer by even one letter; they have no business whatever with esoteric matters, nor [may they adopt] Sephardi customs, but rather [must adhere to] the customs of this land alone. Any alteration from the custom of our fathers is strictly forbidden. (The exception mentioned above applies only to men over thirty years of age, but those less than thirty are strictly forbidden from joining the . . . *shtibel.*) . . .

There is a stern admonition upon all members of our community and those under our authority: . . . they are strictly forbidden from deviating from anything said above, on pain of incurring the punishments of the great and awesome bans. . . .

Now, it is true that our community lacks power to enact a decree upon other communities of Israel. . . . We only make a plea, for the honor of the blessed God, the Holy One of Israel, that all communities act zealously for the Lord of Hosts; we are all alike sons of one father, the living God. . . .

Defending Hasidic Practice

25. Elimelekh of Lyzhansk, From the "Holy Epistle"

Reprinted in M. Wilensky, *Hasidim and Mitnagdim* (Jerusalem: Bialik Institute, 1970; Hebrew), vol. 1, pp. 169–72.

This retort by Elimelekh of Lyzhansk to the sort of accusations leveled against the Hasidim in the Brody proclamation is cited in a letter written by his son Eli'ezer (c. 1780) to one of his hasidim. Elimelekh criticizes the argument that prayer according to Ari's prayerbook is the exclusive right of an esoteric elite. He depicts instead an inclusive religious community spiritually transformed by connecting itself to a charismatic tzaddik.

I asked my master, my father and teacher, to tell me the reason for [our] altering the prayer formulae, and he answered me thus:

Has not *Bet Yosef* [Joseph Karo], chief among the codifiers, set down these formulae? Then Rema [Moses Isserles], also chief among codifiers, examined and tested and set down the entire [liturgical] order properly for all of Israel. He realized that in [the Sephardi] formula there is great light, of which the world is not worthy,[24] and established for us the Ashkenazi formula, which is commonly good for people like us. As for those *tzaddikim* who have cleansed themselves from all filth and who adhere to the highest standard—surely he did not mean this to apply [to them], barring them

---

24. Following the Rabbinic midrash that tells of a primordial great light of which, God decided, the world was unworthy. And so He concealed it for the present; it was to be enjoyed by the righteous in the future; cf. *Midrash Rabbah: Genesis* 3:6. "World" here may, however, mean "the common folk."

from employing in their prayer that formula codified by *Bet Yosef.* "These and those are the words of the living God" (BT Eruvin 13b [§16]).

Should you wonder: Are there not many people who are not at that high level I have described, yet who employ [the Sephardi] formula, and attach themselves to the sublime *hasidim,* being also called *"hasidim"*? I tell you, in the Song upon the Sea it is written: "They had faith in the Lord and in His servant Moses" (Exod. 14:31). Now what concern is it to us that Israel had faith in Moses? By the same token, God [later] promised him, "They will have faith in you ever after" (Exod. 19:9)—what concern was it to Moses? Was it his desire that Israel should have faith in him? Certainly he desired only that they should have faith in God!

In fact, the holy Torah imparts to us here a great matter, namely, that it was necessary for them to have faith in Moses. For God's purpose, in taking us out of Egypt, was that we should receive the Torah; for this, it was necessary to be refined like silver sevenfold. That was the purpose of all those events, the parting of the Red Sea and all the other miracles. Moses our master, may he rest in peace, sanctified himself until he attained the level of prophecy, ascended to heaven, and brought down the Torah to Israel. Now all of Israel were certainly not able to be, all of them, at the level that Moses [attained], so that they might receive the Torah in accordance with the level of prophecy. Still, since they had faith in Moses and connected themselves to him, he brought upon them a holy spirit; it was as if they too were at that level, and through this they were all able to receive the Torah, through uniting and connecting with Moses.

The parallel is clear.

Authority Transcending Reason

26. Nahman of Bretzlav, *Likute Moharan,* 123, 66:1, 34:4, 64:2–4

While legitimizing a new source of absolute religious authority (see C6, §23), the doctrine of the tzaddik *also made for a unique form of pluralism. In the first three of the sections reproduced here, Rabbi Nahman describes the depth of connection between the hasid and his* tzaddik, *but also the transfer of "rulership" from God to Israel and even to every individual. In the fourth section, he offers an account of the positive value of controversy.*

(123) The principle and foundation of everything is that one connect oneself to the *tzaddik* of that generation and receive his instructions in every single matter, whether small or great, and not to deviate from his instructions — God forbid — right or left; as our rabbis of blessed memory said, "Even if he tells you that right is left," etc. (*Sifre Deut.* 154 [§12]). One must renounce all manner of wisdom, annulling one's mind as if one had no reason except that which he receives from the *tzaddik,* the rabbi of that generation. As long as a person retains any independent reason, he lacks perfection and is not connected to the *tzaddik.*

Israel, at the time of receiving the Torah, possessed great wisdom. For they [had been] worshipers of contemporary idols, a mistake that had flowed from great wisdom and investigations, as is well known. Had Israel not renounced that wisdom, they would not have received the Torah. [Rather,] they could have denied everything, and everything that Moses our master performed on their behalf would have been to no avail; even all the awesome signs and miracles that he performed before their eyes would have been of no avail to them. Indeed, nowadays too, there are heretics whose denial comes from their foolish and mistaken wisdom. Israel, the holy people, however, saw the truth and renounced wisdom, and had faith in the Lord and in His servant Moses (Exod. 14:31), and thereby received the Torah.

(66:1) . . . The disciple ought to experience all the ascents and descents of the *tzaddik,* if he is truly and properly connected [to him], just like branches of a tree. For the branches experience all ascents and descents in [the condition of] the tree. Thus in summer they grow and show vitality, since the tree draws its vitality from its roots through its ducts. . . . Therefore, in winter when the moisture dries up, as the ducts constrict, the branches too constrict. That is the reason why the leaves then fall off; and the opposite [takes place] in summer. Now, with one who is connected to the *tzaddik* it is the same: that is, he experiences all the ascents and descents of the *tzaddik.*

(34:4) Within every single individual of Israel there is a quality of *tzaddik*-ruler, . . . as it is written, "Your people are all righteous [*tzaddikim*]" (Isa. 60:21). This too is the meaning of "Israel, His rule[rs]" (Ps. 114:2).[25] [This verse is to be interpreted in light of the statement attributed to God:] "Who rules me? A *tzaddik*" (BT Moed Katan 16b). For within every individual Israelite there is a precious thing, a point which none of his fellows possesses . . . . This quality, which he possesses more than any fellow, influences, enlightens, and awakens his fellow's heart; his fellow ought to receive the awakening of that quality from him, as it is written, "And they receive one from another" (*Targum* to Isa. 6:3).

For prior to the giving of the Torah, rulership was in the hands of God, may He be Blessed, but following the giving of the Torah He gave rulership into the hands of all Israel, each individual according to his [particular] quality. For the letters of the Torah are embodiments of God's will, since God's will is that the commandments should be [just] so. For example, [with regard] to the commandment on phylacteries, His will was that there be four sections, housed in leather and not in silver, for such is His will. Hence His will is embodied in the entire Torah; thus, now that the Torah has been given into our hands, God's will too is given into our hands. We rule, as it were, in that His will is determined by our will, in line with "Israel, His rule[rs]" mentioned above.

A central idea of Lurianic Kabbalah is that of tzimtzum, *or withdrawal. A precondition for creation was God's withdrawal, providing a vacuum—a "vacant space"— within which the world could be brought into existence. Rabbi Nahman points out that contemplation of the world therefore leads to an inescapable paradox: God is both all-present and absent. Ordinary Jews retain their faith by avoiding the contemplation of this paradox, which must lead to heresy—except for a* tzaddik *like Moses, whose contemplation of the vacant space involves a silence beyond words. Nahman employs this doctrine in offering a positive account of the controversies among* hakhamim: *their "departure from one another" produces the selfsame quality of "vacant space," crucial for creation.*

25. A midrashic reversal of the verse's plain meaning, that Israel became God's dominion.

(64:2–4) Those who investigate [the paradox of God's presence and absence] fall into several perplexities and quandaries, which in truth do not constitute any [kind of] wisdom; there is basically nothing to these quandaries. Yet, since human reason cannot resolve them, they have the appearance of wisdom and of [genuine] quandaries. In truth, it is impossible to resolve these quandaries, because these heretical quandaries derive from the vacant space, wherein God is, as it were, absent. . . . If one had been able to find God, may He be blessed, there too—then it would not have been vacant. . . . There is no retort to this heresy, since it derives from the vacant space, from which God, as it were, withdrew Himself.

Only Israel, through faith, transcends all wisdom, even this heresy which derives from the vacant space, as they believe in God without any investigation or wisdom. . . . Certainly, one should avoid and escape this kind of heresy, neither contemplating nor [even] glancing at its arguments. Otherwise, one will, God forbid, surely become submerged in it. . . .

If there is a great *tzaddik* with the quality of Moses, he is, on the contrary, obliged to contemplate these words of heresy, even though it is impossible to resolve them, as stated above. Nevertheless, through contemplation, he lifts out several souls who fell and became submerged in that heresy. For the perplexities and quandaries of this heresy, which derives from the vacant space, have the quality of silence, since no reason or letters are applicable for resolving them. [This is] because creation was by means of words, as it is written, "By the word of the Lord the heavens were made" (Ps. 33:6), and words contain wisdom. . . . But in the vacant space, which surrounds all worlds, . . . there are no words . . . and thus the perplexities deriving from it have the quality of silence.

Thus, concerning Moses, when he asked with regard to the death of Rabbi Akiva, "Such Torah and such a reward?" he received the reply: "Be silent, that is how it entered my mind [literally, "rose in my thought"]" (BT Menahot 29b [C6, §9]). That is [to say], you must be silent and not ask for a reply or a resolution for this quandary, for thus has it risen in thought, which is above words. Therefore, you must be silent with respect to this question, as it has the quality of "risen in my thought," for there are no words to resolve it. Similarly, these quandaries and perplexities that derive from the vacant space, from which both words and reason are absent, have the quality of silence; one must simply have faith and silence there. Hence, no one should enter into contemplation of these words of heresy and perplexities except for a *tzaddik* like Moses, who has the quality of silence. He was called "slow of speech" (Exod. 4:10), signifying the quality of silence which is above words. . . .

You should know that controversy has the quality of creating the world. For the beginning of creation was by means of the vacant space, as explained above, since otherwise all would be Infinity, and there would be no room for creating the world. Therefore He withdrew the light to the sides, providing the vacant space, within which He created all that was created . . . through words. The same applies to controversies. For if all the sages [*hakhamim*] were of one [mind], there would be no room for creating the world. It is only by virtue of their controversies, in which they depart from one another, each taking himself to one side, that a quality of vacant space is provided between them. . . . For all the words each of them speaks are all for the sake of creating the world, which they effect within the vacant space between them. For the *talmide hakhamim* create everything through their words . . . but they must be careful not to speak too much. . . .

Limiting Traditional Authority

27. David Einhorn, Responsum on Free Inquiry and Rabbinic Office

In W. Gunther Plaut, *The Rise of Reform Judaism: A Sourcebook of Its European Origins* (New York: World Union for Progressive Judaism, 1963), pp. 119–22. The German source is *Rabbinische Gutachten über die Verträglichkeit der freien Forschung mit dem Rabbineramte,* 2 vols. (Breslau, 1842–43), vol. I, p. 125 ff.

In 1838, Abraham Geiger, a leading figure in the emerging historical-critical study of Judaism, was appointed assistant rabbi of Breslau. The appointment of Geiger, who a year earlier had called the first convention of Reform rabbis, met with opposition led by Shlomo Tiktin, rabbi of the community. The community board turned to several other rabbis, mostly of the younger generation, seeking support for the appointment. This selection is from the response by David Einhorn, one of the more radical reform voices.

Question: Does a rabbi forfeit his right to occupy his post when he departs in some respects from biblical interpretations and traditionally valid rules of the Talmud, and if so, under what conditions?

Answer: Departure from the Talmud in respect to the exegesis of biblical passages and the validity of traditional laws results in inability to occupy a rabbinic post if the following three conditions exist together:

a. The rejected talmudic interpretation and the disputed traditional law must concern a tradition which in the Talmud is described and recognized by everyone as genuine and undoubted (Maimonides, in his introduction to the Mishnah, enumerates such traditional interpretations);

b. . . . Such departure is not sufficiently motivated by changed conditions of time and place; and

c. It is not merely expressed as an opinion, but is meant to be practically applied either by the person advocating such departure or by others.

Ad a. Every adherent of talmudic Judaism is obligated to observe all those ordinances which, even though they lack every biblical basis, are listed by the Talmud as having been handed down by tradition and which as such are disputed by no one. The practice of these laws, which have come down to us from the Men of the Great [Assembly], makes a Jew a "Talmud Jew," and this is the chief distinction between him and the Karaites, who recognize the biblical word exclusively and do not want to hear of any tradition, whatever its name. However, this category of laws forms and completes the whole circle within which the faithful Israelite concedes authority to the Talmud. There is no legal foundation whatever for a further extension of this authority to ordinances lying outside this circle, to subjective exegesis, and to those laws the traditional character of which is a matter of dispute between the Talmudists themselves. Therefore, one cannot deny the name Jew nor his fitness for the rabbinic post to one who objects to the kind of authoritarianism which would make Judaism an unreplenished swamp and condemn it to eternal stagnation. We cannot, we must not, ascribe such infallibility and apotheosis to the Talmud. We believe in its validity, but at the same time we must reject its deification and say to it: Israel believes you but not in you; you are the channel of the divine but not divinity itself!

"But," it is said, quoting Maimonides as an authority, "after the codification of the Talmud, Israel sanctioned and accepted all its views, expositions, and ordinances!" (Introduction to the MT [C6, §3]). Where are the documents of so solemn a vow, which was to bind all future descendants? How is it possible that so important an event is never mentioned in the Talmud and is not, as at the conclusion of the Book of Esther, documented as a memorial for all time? But suppose, indeed, that our forefathers had pledged themselves and all their descendants to accept the Talmud with everything it contained, how could such a pledge, the existence of which is seen as the reason for the immutability of the Talmud, result in a binding obligation for us? Quite aside from the fact that such a conclusion would be in contradiction to all the laws of normal reason—and especially so in religious matters—it is, in any case, a fundamental rule of talmudic Judaism that no father can burden his minor child with a vow against the latter's will. And, even if the child has agreed to it during his minority, once he reaches his majority he is no longer under any obligation to fulfill such a vow. (Of course the obligation to fulfill a divine command needs no intermediary justification; it follows directly from our relationship to God, and is not dependent on any voluntary agreement. This is stressed so that what was said above should not lead to dangerous conclusions regarding Deut. 29:14 [see C1, §3].)

Maimonides, in his introduction to the Mishnah, already acknowledges as genuine tradition only that about which there is no difference of opinion in the Talmud. . . .

Ad b. Unfitness to occupy the rabbinic post cannot be caused by a divergence from ceremonial laws, if such divergence is not just frivolous tampering with the sacred, but rather is founded in the spirit of Judaism and represents a pressing demand of its natural development. Of course, such divergence must have nothing in common with mere fashion or convenience or with forced application of an un-Jewish view to Jewish matters, or reflect merely a subjective attitude or a kind of general antipathy to the status quo. It must be the product of profound, honest, and unprejudiced research in the sacred documents, of pious sincerity, of a glowing enthusiasm for God's work, and, finally, of mature advice from several God-intoxicated men who are experts and whose judgment has carefully weighed the causes and consequences of the matter. Such procedure, far from being objectionable, is highly commendable, and it was often followed in both talmudic and post-talmudic times. The well-known ordinances issued by Rabbenu Gershom [Me'or ha-Golah] amply show that the conclusion of the Talmud could not limit the development of Judaism in accordance with the needs of the times.

But suppose even that the divergence of a rabbi would occur relative to a ceremonial law which until now was recognized as indisputably divine, and for the elimination of which changed conditions could offer no reason; and suppose the divergence is founded solely on the conviction, obtained through scientific research, that the law is not of divine origin. If the rabbi does not transgress the bounds of theory and gives it practical expression in neither his private nor his professional life, how then could he lose the right to occupy his post? As a Jew in general, and as a rabbi specifically, he is indeed obligated and duty-bound to observe and practice strictly all biblical and genuinely traditional laws. But when did Judaism ever ban and damn a mere expression of opinion which runs counter to the status quo? When did it ever declare as unfit for rabbinic office someone who took such a position, and even brand him with the name of *kofer* [denier of the principles of faith]? Genuine Judaism, which, despite Maimonides, knows of no binding dogmas, looks at deeds, not opinions. Now, if, in addition, I live fired by love for my sacred religion; if without surcease I search and seek for truth in the books of life, but have the misfortune to gain an opinion which differs from the status quo; if, driven by noble zeal, I at once express this opinion without fear and hesitation for the honorable and pious sake of my faith — if I just *express* this, I belong . . . to the category of thieves and murderers! Worse, I am said to have no share in that divine possession for the sake of which I loathe all falsehood and hypocrisy, and am to forgo all community with the house of Jacob, which I at least try to cleanse of dirt and refuse! Is such tyranny the preachment of Torah, which makes *knowledge* a duty and which calls itself Israel's wisdom and reason in the eyes of all nations?

But listen to the judgement of the Talmud itself in this matter! In BT Sanhedrin 86b and 88b (§10) it says: The [rebellious elder] becomes guilty only if he either practices his divergent opinion or by *direct teaching* attempts to lead others to do so, but not if he only holds to a point of view. Furthermore (in BT Sanhedrin 88a), Akaviah ben Mahallalel could not be held to account for his opinions which differed from those of the sages, "because he did not teach in order that his interpretation might be practiced." From this it is abundantly clear that Maimonides, when he speaks of the teacher who decries the traditional interpretation, refers exclusively to one who not only denies tradition as such (which is the distinction between [heretic] and [rebel]), but who also gives practical expression to his heretical teaching.

Justifying Orthodox Secession

28. Samson Raphael Hirsch, "Open Letter to Rabbi S. B. Bamberger"

Samson Raphael Hirsch, *The Collected Writings,* edited by Elliot Bondi and David Bechofer, translated by Paul Forchheimer and Gertrude Hirschler (New York and Jerusalem: Feldheim, 1990), vol. 6, pp. 201–6.

As the Reform movement spread and took over many of the Jewish communities in Germany, its orthodox opponents split over the issue of their own continuing membership in the community. In 1876 the Prussian Landtag *recognized the right of individuals to leave their churches. Hirsch, a leading voice in the call to secede, had supported the bill, requesting the parliament that Jews be permitted to leave their local community "for reasons of conscience." The bill paved the way for some orthodox Jews to secede, in response to Hirsch's claim that otherwise their taxes would make them, in effect, participants in illicit practices. Still, the majority of traditional German Jews opposed secession. We reproduce here Hirsch's arguments in the course of a heated public exchange with his equally orthodox contemporary, Seligmann Baer Bamberger, district rabbi of Würzburg. Bamberger opposed secession provided that the taxes collected from the orthodox members would be earmarked for supporting separate, orthodox religious services. Hirsch rejects this arrangement, arguing that failure to secede is tantamount to legitimizing heresy.*

In your statement you report that, according to information received by you, the trustees of the Frankfurt Reform community were now prepared to meet the requirements of those Orthodox members who will not secede from the community. You report that the trustees will do this by committing funds from the community for the establishment of religious institutions required by the Orthodox. In addition, institutions would be under Orthodox administration and supervision, and the Orthodox members would not have to contribute any funds to the ritual facilities of Reform.

You thereupon state that full guarantees must be provided for the implementation of these concessions and that, if these guarantees really materialize, secession from the Reform community could no longer be described as mandatory.

You obviously assume that the Reform community with all its facilities that violate religious law, its doctrine, and its administrative staff will continue to exist. The community as such will not satisfy the requirements of God and His holy Law any more than it has done hitherto; in other words, the community will continue to be Reform. . . .

Thus, according to your statement, an Orthodox Jew is permitted to remain a member of the Reform community without any qualms of conscience as long as the institutions required for his religious needs are supplied within and by the Reform community and as long as he does not have to make any contributions to the Reform institutions.

Dear Rabbi! Voluntary membership in a religious community of necessity implies the espousal of the principle to which that religious community subscribes. Everything that this community does in matters of religion is done with the consent of every single member who is and remains a member of the community of his own free will. A community consists only of the sum total of all its members, and whatever is done, is done in the name of all. That is a truth that all arguments and mental reservations in the world cannot alter even by a hair's breadth. An Orthodox Jew who remains a member of the Reform community, even though he can and does have the use of all the religious institutions he needs elsewhere, remains a member of that Reform community only for the sake of being a member. He thereby makes it clear beyond question that his personal religious conscience approves of the idea that Jews may create and support, for use by non-Orthodox Jews, Reform institutions that violate religious law. This is true even if he does not make any payments towards these Reform institutions, and has his own special institutions within that same community. Indeed, by remaining a member of the Reform community, he participates in the creation and maintenance of Reform institutions by Jews, and he helps commit funds from the community (in whose control he shares as long as he does not secede from the community) for these Reform institutions. The assets of the community are the joint property of all its members, to be used for the needs of the community. They can be used only with the direct or indirect approval of each individual member, and you are aware, dear Rabbi, that according to our *halakhah*, it is mandatory to give ear to the objection of even one person if the law is on his side.

It is difficult to believe that you were fully aware of the implications of your statement. Your statement sets forth, in unequivocal terms, that Reform has full legitimacy in the eyes of the Orthodox, as long as it tolerates the existence of Orthodoxy at its side and accords it proper consideration. In other words, the Orthodox conscience can accept the existence, before the One sole God and His one sole Law, of two kinds of Judaism, each co-equal with the other—the one with the Torah and the other against the Torah, all depending on the views of the individual. In your view, even the most extreme Reform community is "kashered" if its members maintain "kosher" institutions.

In the eyes of Jewish orthodoxy, to just what kind of Reform would your statement—surely without clear thought and intention on your part—accord legitimacy? If you consult our legal codes to learn the attitude which we must take toward Reform, under what name or category would you classify the religious system to which the Reform community in this city subscribes? How would you classify a community that, as a matter of principle, has stricken from its prayer book every reference to the person of the messiah, to the ingathering of exiles, to the restoration of the temple, to the temple's sacrificial service past and future, and that has eliminated the land and the covenant and the kingdom of the House of David from the grace after meals? What name would you give to a system whose pulpit and school preach and teach that the *mitzvot* of the Torah and its laws are outdated, and that applies this principle also in the shaping of its other institutions? What would you call the belief system which this community professes in its worship, its pulpit, its school, and its other institutions? Into what category would our codes of law class such a system? Can it be anything else but the most blatant heresy [*minut ve-apikorsut*]? (For reasons which, with your permission, I will explain further on, I am deliberately using terms that describe the system rather than individuals that adhere to it.)

Now, our codes of law command us to keep a much greater distance
from heresy than even from idolatry. We are commanded to stay much further away from contact with Jewish elements that are opposed in principle
to Jewish law and truth than from dealings with idolatrous paganism. For
only in the case of the former are we told "keep yourself far away from her"
(Prov. 5:8) and "all who go to her cannot return" (Prov. 2:19; BT Avodah
Zarah 17a). I need only mention Rabbi Tarphon's maxim that, in order to
save your life, you may take shelter in a house of idolatry but not in a house
of heretics [minin]. "Even if I am pursued by a killer or chased by a snake, I
will enter a house of idolatry, but will not enter the houses of these [here-
tics]. For the latter know, and [yet] deny, while the former do not know,
and [hence] deny" (BT Shabbat 116a). And Rabbi Ishmael let his nephew die
rather than allow him to be treated by a heretic [min], although he would
have considered it permissible for him to seek treatment from an idolator
(BT Avodah Zarah 27b). The explanation for this ruling is that "heresy is
different because it entices and might lead one to follow it"—contact with
Jews who are opposed in principle to Jewish law and truth is far more likely
to lead a Jew astray than dealing with outright idolatry. Consequently, it is
clear beyond question that anything forbidden to us with regard to idolatry
is forbidden even more emphatically with regard to heresy.

One must be careful to avoid creating even the appearance of association with idolatry, or the impression that one approves of it or speaks
of it in terms of praise. One who accepts an invitation to a feast arranged
by an idolater transgresses the commandment "You must not make a covenant," etc., "and you will eat of their sacrifices" (Exod. 34:15), even if he eats
only kosher food there and is served by members of his own household (BT
Avodah Zarah 8a). Even if my life is in danger, I am forbidden to say that
I am an idolater; the most that I can do in such a situation is to create an
impression, without actually saying so, that I am an idolater (*Shulhan Arukh,
Yoreh De'ah* 157:2).

Knowing all this, could an Orthodox Jew deliberately permit himself to be numbered as a member of a community of heresy, from which we
are commanded to keep even further away than from dealings with idolatry? Could there be a worse desecration of God's Name, a more flagrant
empowering of heretics than this? . . .

To this day it is considered obligatory to separate ourselves completely from the Karaites, this despite the fact that the defection of the Karaites from legitimate Judaism was by far not as great or as drastic as the contrast between modern Reform and Torah-true Judaism. After all, the Karaites denied only the Oral Law. They loyally and steadfastly affirmed the eternal binding force of the Divine laws and did not reject any of the other principles of faith. Today's Reform, on the other hand, categorically denies the eternal binding force of the Divine laws. In its liturgy, the Reform movement has rejected truths that are proclaimed by the Word of God in scripture and are part and parcel of the basic verities and principles of Judaism.

It is my most profound and earnest belief that only a separation such as had been made possible, thank God, by the Law of July 28, 1876, can bring healing also in our day for the diseased conditions that have prevailed among German Jewry for more than half a century. Anyone who is sincere in his adherence to religious truth, to whom anything religious is not just a jumble of meaningless forms that can be muddled at will, must give his support to such a separation. One who would attempt to hold up secession is delaying our spiritual redemption.

Commentary. Authority, Tradition, and Community

It is noteworthy that David Einhorn, premier architect of Reform Judaism, relies so heavily upon warrants drawn from the classical rabbinic texts in constructing his argument. His stance reflects a nonsectarian reform, anxious to affirm its traditional ties. Einhorn insists that he is a "faithful Israelite" who "concedes authority to the Talmud," and despite the claims of Orthodox spokesmen like Hirsch, he specifically distinguishes his approach from that of the Karaites. Indeed, he carefully employs a distinction between the "Talmud Jew" and the Karaite to advance the cause of the Reform rabbinate and its program of innovation. After all, the Talmud Jew rejects the doctrine of *sola scriptura;* the Bible alone is not authoritative. Instead, the rabbis, embedded in the tradition, give free reign to their legal imagination. Einhorn cites the Mishnah Commentary of Maimonides and the *takkanot* of Rabbenu Gershom, as well as the classic talmudic passages concerning Akaviah ben Mehallalel and the argument about the rebellious elder, to affirm the right of each rabbi to interpret biblical texts and rabbinic teachings according to his own conscience.

But Einhorn also maintains that there is a limit to the practical application of such freedom. This theoretical stance is vital to the argument he is constructing, for it provides him with a powerful rhetorical weapon against his Orthodox opponents. Thus Einhorn "concedes" that rabbinic laws and interpretations cannot be challenged by later generations of rabbis whenever (1) they are universally recognized as genuine and undoubted, (2) all authorities agree that they are legally binding (not mere opinions), and (3) "changed conditions of time and place" do not provide "sufficient" grounds to legitimate dissent or change. When a statute or ruling fulfills all these conditions, it is indeed eternal, and alternate rulings cannot be issued.

However, given the argument Einhorn has constructed, it is difficult to imagine such an absolute ruling and therefore virtually impossible to conceive of an infringement of authority in the halakhic system. If it is true that Judaism possesses no binding dogma, what grounds could be offered for asserting that conditions of "time and place" had not changed "sufficiently" to allow for change and dissent? Any such judgment would be tenuous at best. Little wonder, then, that Einhorn holds rabbinic tradition to permit "the development of Judaism in accordance with the needs of the time."

The burden of proof in every instance falls upon those who would forbid rather than those who would promote change. In the final analysis, "everything depends upon the judgment of the rabbinic court" (*Bet Yosef,* Yoreh De'ah 268). The only genuine question remaining—one left unanswered by Einhorn—is how a rule of recognition might be established that would allow the community to determine who the "God-intoxicated . . . experts" are in whom legitimate authority is vested. That aside, tradition has been interpreted to support the cause of reform. Einhorn subtly ensconces the case for reform within a heritage of Jewish intertextuality, and his argument is of enduring import precisely because it testifies to a reform that sees itself as part of the historic community of rabbinic Judaism.

Nevertheless, Einhorn's case is not built upon the texts of rabbinic Judaism alone. Throughout his essay, he speaks of the "natural development" that marks Judaism, and he champions the discipline of academic research,

Wissenschaft des Judentums, as the means whereby the divine origin of Jewish laws and teachings can be determined. In so doing, Einhorn indicates that his arguments derive from a nineteenth-century German worldview as much as they do from traditional rabbinic values. As a Reform rabbi writing in 1841, Einhorn may well have taken the only path open to him—drawing upon both traditional warrants and modern approaches—to support his position. In the final analysis, however, it is clear that he has transformed the argument, and moved it from the self-referential realm of rabbinic prooftexts to the rather different world of academic research. The cause of reform ultimately depends upon the fruits of modern scholarship. Rabbinic prooftexts alone are not decisive and are, at best, of secondary importance.

So the Einhorn essay foreshadows a Reform Judaism that would soon depart from the classical rabbinic canon. History, not legal precedent, will soon sanction the actions of reform. Einhorn constructs a novel justification for rabbinic authority: the academic study of Jewish history and texts. Contemporary liberal Jews, in analyzing the approach that Einhorn has adopted, must argue that such an approach is Jewishly legitimate on the grounds that the new methodology—fully informed as it is by historical consciousness—conforms to what we know to be true about the developmental nature of religious realities, which are always embedded in particular times and places.

Hirsch clearly understood this shift in the grounds of legitimation, and he condemned the new foundation that men such as Einhorn had constructed for Jewish law. Such an approach, to the degree that it purported to be based upon rabbinic prooftexts, was, in Hirsch's view, completely disingenuous. History was decisive in the stance the reformers adopted, and the rabbinic prooftexts they adduced only disguised and obscured their true intent. So furious was Hirsch at their departure from what he saw as the received basis for Jewish law and authority that he demanded the creation of a separate institutional structure, apart from the traditional *kahal,* to house the orthodox community. Analyzing Hirsch's position, one hears echoes of the famous words of Saadiah Gaon almost a millennium earlier, when, in his *Book of Beliefs and Opinions,* he asserted: "Our nation is a nation only by virtue of its teachings [*torot*]" (3:7).

But the specific view of community that informs Hirsch in this instance derives also from the transformations that the modern world had wrought in the ideal of community. As Ferdinand Tönnies argued, the history of the West has been marked by a move from the face-to-face relationships of the premodern *Gemeinschaft* to the rationally ordered and bureaucratically dominated patterns of an impersonal *Gesellschaft* (Tönnies, *Fundamental Concepts in Sociology,* 1940). In this transition, traditional frameworks for community have been challenged and a distinction between public and private spheres has arisen. Religion has been consigned to the private realm and a society created in which the institutional structures that formerly supported and sustained religious organizations have shifted from the community as a whole to much smaller groups of committed individuals. Individuals are now able to choose freely among collectivities that promote specific ideologies and practices, and these collectivities then mediate between their members and the pluralistic world outside.

This insight is crucial for an appreciation of the argument put forward by Hirsch. The traditional *kahal* and its institutions were significantly altered as the Jews moved from a corporate political structure into the congregational patterns of association that mark religious life in the modern West. How to create a new structure appropriate to the Jewish community's institutional needs — this was the challenge confronting all segments of the German-Jewish religious world in the nineteenth century.

For Hirsch and the proponents of separatist Orthodoxy, the traditional notion that common descent provided a sufficient ground for the maintenance of a unified Jewish community no longer obtained. Instead, Hirsch viewed Judaism in terms that were almost exclusively based on religious dogma. It is therefore hardly surprising that he and his supporters put forth an ideal of community in keeping with a modern congregational model of committed individuals set apart from the Jewish polity as a whole. To support or even to be members of a community that would countenance the possibility of heretical reform was in his view halakhically forbidden. And so Hirsch ruled that secession from the *Einheitsgemeinde* (united community) was obligatory in any place where it was possible. Otherwise, orthodox Jews would be guilty of transgressing the prohibition against aiding and abetting heresy.

Many orthodox Jews dissented from this posture in Hirsch's own day, and many Jews, orthodox and non-orthodox alike, would disagree with Hirsch today. They do not believe that participation in the general Jewish community logically entails an affirmation of the religious views upheld by all community-supported institutions. There are strong grounds for such a view. First, one can argue that membership in the general community does not derive in any way from voluntary consent. Rather, it springs from the idea that all Jews are members of one body. In instances where the unified community is willing to support a variety of institutions, and to allow them to be supervised by members of specific denominations, the concept of *klal yisrael* (the community of Israel) allows for, even requires, a unified community. In the nineteenth century, no less a personage than Seligmann Baer Bamberger adopted this position, and others such as Abraham Geiger concurred. It remains a viable position today.

Second, the classical rabbinic notion of *arevut* (mutual responsibility) also dictates that a Jew not secede from the general community even when institutions holding views deemed hostile or incorrect are supported by communal funds. This principle, based on BT Sanhedrin 27b, holds that *kol yisrael arevin zeh ba-zeh* (all Israelites are responsible for one another). It demands that Jews follow the example of the talmudic sage Shimon ben Shatah, who refused to secede from a Sanhedrin dominated by Sadducees, despite the danger that their teachings might lead fellow Jews astray (*Megillat Ta'anit,* chap. 10-Tevet). Instead, Jews must participate in the life of the general community to bring Jews with whom they disagree closer to the Torah as they understand it.

Finally, if Jews are tied to the community by powerful bonds of kinship and responsibility, how can secession be required whenever the community appropriates funds to an institution that a particular member finds objectionable? It is difficult to imagine that all the individual members of any community — even a religious community — would approve every budgetary appropriation. Not even Hirsch suggested that orthodox Jews should refuse to pay taxes to the German government on the grounds that tax money was employed to finance the teaching of biblical criticism in German universities. Participation in a polity need not entail approval of all that the polity does, and a commitment to community, for all the reasons cited above, might well be accorded primacy over the discomfort that individuals feel with specific issues. At the very least, the elasticity of rabbinic tradition permits a greater degree of religious latitude than Hirsch would allow in matters of faith and dogma. And the polyvocal nature of Jewish law, as well as the sense of peoplehood that has always marked Judaism, are sufficiently central to support the view that secession from the community is not required under the conditions that Hirsch describes.

David Ellenson

Introduction

Talmudic Foundations

Justifying the *Kahal*'s Authority: Early Ashkenaz

Restricting the *Kahal*'s Authority: Early Spain

Introduction

Nowhere in the Bible, and only marginally in the Talmud (in the brief passages with which we open this chapter), are any claims made on behalf of what are today called "lay leaders," ordinary members of the community selected by their fellow members to take charge of communal affairs. The biblical elders play a role something like this, but the exact contours of that role are never formulated, never even discussed, in the Bible itself. We don't know how the elders were chosen or what exactly they did or what claims they made. They are not among the political leaders recognized in any of the biblical or talmudic "constitutional" texts—where leadership apparently requires a religious justification. So kings are selected by God and designated by prophets, or they are the male heirs of people so selected and designated. The priesthood is hereditary within a divinely chosen family. Prophets respond to a divine call. The appointment of judges and magistrates is commanded by God. Sages and rabbis devote themselves to the study of sacred texts and derive their authority from their knowledge of God's word. What role can there be for lay leaders in a religious community like Israel? And yet the medieval *kahal* was governed primarily by a leadership of "selectmen" (*berurim*), "the good men of the town," whose authority came from below, not from above; from the community, not from God.

We will describe the *kahal* in Volume III as the Jewish polis and investigate its governmental structure and everyday activities. Here we are concerned only with the authority and legitimacy of its leaders. Their role is not entirely without precedent: we might imagine them as the heirs of Israel's kings, considered now as the secular rulers requested in 1 Samuel 8 (C3, §3) to meet the biblical equivalent of "the needs of the hour." Or perhaps they are the heirs of the counselors who advised the king as to what the needs of the hour were—although counselors have no clear representative role in the biblical texts. It is secular wisdom that makes good counsel—experience rather than revelation or the study of revealed texts. Or perhaps the lay leaders of the *kahal* are the heirs of the exilarch, who ruled the Babylonian community in all secular matters and mediated its relations with foreign rulers. Only Solomon Adret (Rashba), in the texts that follow, actually invokes precedents of this sort, but his is one of the most important defenses of the "good men."

Such people appear in every political culture; they sometimes co-operate with and sometimes compete with the religious authorities—and sometimes replace them entirely. Among the Jews, or at least in Jewish litera-ture, the competition is muted, for most of the texts come from rabbis. The sole exception in this chapter are the Livorno ordinances, which, not surpris-ingly, take a radically expansive view of lay authority. The rest of the material reflects the rabbis' acceptance and legitimation of the rule of the "good men," but also their worries about it, protests against it, and efforts to impose limits upon it—not only for the sake of the rabbis' own authority but also for the sake of religious law as they understand it and in defense of their (differ-ent) conceptions of justice. So they sometimes appear in these texts as the guardians of individual rights against the threat of majority tyranny—see, for example, the responsa of Meir Abulafia and Meir of Rothenburg below. And, sometimes, when the leaders of the *kahal* were wealthy and powerful men, rabbinic opposition took on a populist tone, as in Jacob Sasportas's let-ter protesting the Livorno ordinances. (We take up the struggles of Jewish oligarchs and plebeians in €22.)

What was the basis of lay legitimacy? The texts that we have are mostly flat statements that individuals must obey this ruling or pay that levy even though its source is not the *bet din* (court) but only their neighbors in the courtyard, the members of their guild, or the inhabitants of their town. The authority of these people and the leaders they choose stands alongside that of the rabbis, with whom they share political and legal space, and it overrides the claims of the individual, at least for some purposes. What we find in the responsa literature is a sustained effort to fix the boundaries of this authority and define its purposes.

But where does the authority itself come from? Consent theory should provide the answer to this question, and often does, but it is not sys-tematically elaborated. There is no clear doctrine, no theory of lay legitimacy like that suggested, for example, by the much repeated (non-Jewish) medi-eval maxim "What touches all should be decided by all." This suggests at least a proto-democratic politics which gives to the people (or their representatives) authority to decide all matters that have a palpable impact on their lives—chiefly matters of taxation and welfare. No medieval writer would have thought that the maxim extended to the high politics of war and peace.

Some rabbis write as if they accepted a maxim like this one—with a similar exception, not for high politics, but for religion: the laws of Sabbath observance, for example, "touch" every Jew but are not available for lay determination. In fact the unarticulated rabbinic doctrine seems somewhat different. It hangs on the idea of worldly necessity, as in the talmudic example of the town's gates and locks. The talmudic principle seems to be that what everyone needs, everyone must pay for—and those who pay are likely to decide, and are apparently entitled to decide, how the needs should be met (see especially §2).

Still, it is not easy to say how this entitlement was understood. It appears that the members, or the leading members, of the *kahal* took on certain functions and provided together for their common needs, and local rabbinic authorities accepted their de facto authority. It is unlikely that the rabbis withdrew in principle as well as in practice, though they did recognize that on these sorts of issues, relating first of all to physical security, law and order, and the punishment of criminals, Torah law was not a useful political model. It was ideal law, and it was meant for ideal conditions; it tended to ignore the actual circumstances of everyday life. The Adret responsum is clearest on this point, which we have already seen argued by a later representative of the Barcelona school, a student of one of Adret's students, Nissim Gerondi (℄3, §16). If the *kahal* followed Torah law, it would march to ruin. But the rabbis, granting this, might still provide political guidance, drawing on other parts of the tradition or on their own wisdom—and sometimes, again, they do so. Perhaps the best account of their position is that learning defers to everyday experience and actual lay engagement, though without surrendering its own claims. So the *berurim* are entrusted by the citizens to do whatever is necessary, and the rabbinic authorities confirm the trust, subject to limits that they set or try to set case by case.

These limits are much debated. Most often, they are given a personal form: if there is an *adam hashuv* (an important or prominent person, which usually means a scholar or leading rabbi) in the town, then the lay leaders can only act subject to his agreement. This is the argument of BT Bava Batra 9a, repeated again and again in the responsa and commentaries (by Maimonides, Mizrahi, and Sasportas in this chapter) but by no means universally accepted. It was explicitly rejected, for example, by Isaac bar Sheshet Perfet (Rivash), writing in fourteenth-century Spain, who limits the talmudic precedent to guilds and other secondary associations; the community as a whole has an unquestioned right, he insists, to act on its own behalf—as if it were sovereign for certain common purposes.

The *kahal* might also be constrained institutionally, by a court of sages. In fact, the argument of the Babylonian Gaon, as transmitted to the early European and North African communities, was that only a duly constituted religious court (*bet din*), operating in accordance with its classic procedures, could exercise authority over other Jews. In Babylonia, apparently, local communities of artisans and merchants made no more extensive claims to rule themselves than those reported in our talmudic texts; the only recognized lay leader was the exilarch. But in Europe, local communities had seized the initiative and were already ruling themselves, and soon important European sages recognized the *kahal* itself as a kind of court, with authority equal to, and even local precedence over, any out-of-town *bet din,* at least for certain common purposes.

Finally, the *kahal* might be constrained in policy terms (this is implied by "the needs of the hour," since the phrase is meant to be restrictive: it doesn't in principle extend, though it was often in practice extended, to the needs of every hour). The standard distinction, expounded at length in the next chapter, is between *mamona* and *isura,* which we can briefly define, pending the discussion there, as civil and economic matters, on the one hand, and religious matters, on the other. But this leaves the criminal law—which is where the doctrinal argument for lay leadership probably got started— hanging in the air, without a clear category of its own. *Mamona* and *isura* overlap in all sorts of ways: questions raised under one heading are regularly answered in ways that implicate the other. But, in theory at least, the *kahal*'s leaders deal independently only with *mamona*. Unlike the Congregation of Israel, the *kahal*'s government exists for practical and material purposes and is limited by those purposes (but who draws the line and prevents trespasses?).

In time, these purposes were extended; the *kahal,* after all, was a political success, an effective adaptation to the conditions of the exile, and success commonly brings expansion. The "good men" grew more self-confident and more ambitious, and local rabbis, or some of them, accepted their wider prerogatives. In the responsa of Perfet, for example, the authority granted the *kahal* extends even to regulations that impinge on marriage practices, which are standardly *isura*—although the author is obviously made nervous by his own boldness and retreats a bit at the end. As we will see, this was one of the most contested areas of the law, particularly with reference to the authority of gentile rulers (see C9). It wasn't much easier, sometimes it was harder, for rabbis to make concessions to Jewish rulers.

Clearly, there were conflicts in the medieval communities (and earlier, and later on, too) between secular and religious, lay and rabbinic authority. Clearly, also, the rabbis themselves were on both sides of the conflict. This tension in rabbinic argument, well represented in the texts in this chapter, reflects the realities of Jewish politics—which are not in this case very different from the realities of non-Jewish politics. Officially, as it were, the sages in Bava Batra (or some of them) claim that the "good men" rule only when there is no "prominent person" or resident sage. In fact, most often sages rule only when there is no strongly established lay authority. The case is similar to that for medieval Catholicism, where pope and priests could not withstand powerful and determined kings. Where the *kahal* is strong, it chooses the sages to whom it regularly turns for advice (much as Israelite kings choose their counselors and even their prophets). This is the thrust of Meiri's commentary on Bava Batra. The *adam hashuv* has almost become, in passages like this one, the town rabbi—interviewed and hired by a committee of laymen. So long as political argument among the Jews took the form of legal interpretation, rabbis retained significant authority, whatever institutional arrangements prevailed. Some of them, however, used this authority to defend a version of lay self-government, which could as yet have no lay defenders.

It is only at the end of the nineteenth and the beginning of the twentieth centuries that the "good men" found a defender who was one of themselves. Simon Dubnow, who appears in Volume III, is the secular theorist of communal autonomy and lay leadership. His own historical focus is on the federated *kehillot* of Poland and Lithuania in early modern times

(1551–1764), where elected laymen ruled—with the same partial exception for "prominent persons" that is argued for in the medieval texts. Only "great authorities," writes Dubnow, "far-famed [for] talmudic erudition, were able to assert their influence in all departments of communal life." But Dubnow's theory evoked a world that no longer existed, for in the aftermath of emancipation, the communal structures of European Jewry collapsed, leaving only voluntary associations that were run but no longer ruled by laymen. It was Dubnow's political rivals, the Zionists, who claimed, rightly it appears, that the rule of "good men" (and women) now required a Jewish state. Their arguments about authority and legitimacy appear in €10.

Talmudic Foundations

Taxation for Public Works
1. Mishnah Bava Batra 1:5

The following two selections document the construction of the public domain and the first steps toward a code of public law. In the Mishnah, the public's authority over individuals is restricted to public works related to security. The collective that wields this authority ("they compel him"), can include not only the "townspeople" but also the group of neighbors who live in several buildings opening onto a shared courtyard.

They compel him [to share] in [the cost of] building an antechamber and door for the courtyard. Rabban Shimon b. Gamaliel says: Not every courtyard requires an antechamber. They compel him [to share] in [the cost of] building a wall and gates for the town and [buying] a bolt for the gates. Rabban Shimon b. Gamaliel says: Not every town requires a wall. How long shall one reside in a town to be considered a townsman? Twelve months. If, however, one acquires a residence there, one is considered a townsman immediately.

Laws of the Town

2. Tosefta Bava Metzia, 11:8, 16–17, 23–25, 27, 29, 31–37

The Tosefta, for the most part, closely follows the clauses of the Mishnah; sometimes, however, its discussions develop independently. In these passages from the Tosefta the Mishnah's specific concern with security is set in a much broader framework that aims to define the relation between the public and the private domains—hence the references to the "conditions" attached to Joshua's apportioning of the Land of Israel to the Israelite tribes and clans. The conditions (which have no biblical foundation) are enumerated in BT Bava Kama 80b; they are presented as the terms of the original division of the land and hence as norms and entitlements for all future owners of property.

8. A person may take manure out and pile it in the public domain near his door to use as fertilizer. He may not, however, store it [there]. If another comes along and is harmed, he is liable. Rabbi Yehudah says: In the season of taking out manure, a person may take his manure out and pile it in the public domain near his door, to be trodden upon by human and animal feet for thirty days—for on that condition did Joshua apportion the Land to Israel.

16. Residents of an alley can compel one another not to locate among them a tailor, a tanner, or the practitioner of any particular trade. They cannot [however] compel a neighbor [who is himself a tradesman]. Rabban Shimon b. Gamaliel says: They can compel a neighbor too.

17. One who owns a house in another courtyard can be bound by the residents of that courtyard to participate with them in making a door, a lock, and a key for the courtyard; regarding all other things, they cannot compel him. If he resides with them in the courtyard, they can bind him to everything. One who has a house in another town can be bound by the townspeople to participate with them in digging cisterns, hollows, and caverns[1] and in fixing the [ritual] baths and the aqueduct. Regarding all other things, they cannot compel him. If he resides with them in the town, they can bind him to everything.

1. All these are part of the water supply system.

23. Townspeople can compel each other to build a synagogue and to purchase scrolls of the Torah and the prophets for themselves. Townspeople are authorized to stipulate regarding prices, measures, and the pay of laborers. Townspeople are authorized to pronounce, "Anyone seen at X's shall pay thus and so";[2] "Anyone seen [dealing with] the authorities [*malkhut*] shall pay thus and so"; "Anyone whose cow grazes amid the seedlings shall pay thus and so."[3] And they are authorized to enforce their decree.

24. The wool dealers and dyers are authorized to pronounce, "Any merchandise that comes into town—we shall all be partners in [handling] it."

25. The bakers are authorized to make an arrangement among themselves. The ass drivers are authorized to pronounce, "Anyone whose ass dies, we shall furnish him with another ass." If it died through negligence, they are not obligated to furnish him with [another] ass; if not through negligence, they must furnish it. If he said, "Give me [the money] and I will buy it for myself," they [need] not accept this; rather, they buy it and give it to him.

27. One who was a bath attendant, a barber, or a baker serving the public who, come the holiday, wishes to retire to his home, there being none other but him [to provide the service], they can prevent him, unless he furnishes a replacement. If he had stipulated with them at court, or if they mistreated him, he is free.

29. If one digs a cistern for the public, one may draw [water] to drink or draw [water] to take home. But he should not draw [water] to provide or to sell in the marketplace.

31. If one makes caverns[4] for the public, one may wash his face, hands, and feet in them. If his hands or feet are soiled with clay or excrement, it is forbidden. In a cistern or hollow, it is in any case forbidden.[5]

32. One who enters a bathhouse may heat the cold water and cool the hot water. He may wash his hair with natron or urine, even though he

---

2. S. Lieberman, in his commentary to the Tosefta., suggests that "X" might have been a collaborator with the Roman government.

3. In all these clauses, we have followed the Erfurt MS; the Vienna MS, generally preferred by Lieberman, offers more complex and somewhat obscure possibilities.

4. The "cavern" here is a covered pool that collects the waters of a small spring.

5. Because these have no source of running water.

creates a nuisance to those who come after him—for on that condition did Joshua apportion the Land to Israel.

33. [In the case of] a spring belonging to townspeople: [If a choice must be made in a case of] themselves versus others, they take precedence over others. Others versus their [i.e., the townspeople's] livestock, others' lives take precedence over their livestock. Rabbi Yose says: Their livestock takes precedence over others' lives.

34. Their livestock versus others' livestock, their livestock takes precedence over others' livestock.

35. Others versus their [i.e., the townspeople's] laundry, others' lives take precedence over their wash. Rabbi Yose says: Their laundry takes precedence over others' lives.

36. Their laundry versus others' laundry, their laundry takes precedence over others' laundry.

37. Others' livestock versus their laundry, others' livestock takes precedence over their laundry. Their irrigation versus others' livestock, their irrigation takes precedence over others' livestock. And they all come to a final reckoning.

Guilds, Townspeople, and the "Prominent Person"

3. BT Bava Batra 9a

Discussing the validity of an agreement among butchers, the Talmud here cites the principle that "they may enforce their decree," which in the Tosefta above (clause 23) refers to townspeople.

Certain butchers made a mutual agreement that anyone who slaughters on another's day will have his hide [i.e., that of the slaughtered animal] ripped. One of them went ahead and slaughtered on another's day, and they ripped his hide. The case came before Rava, and he ordered them to repay him.

Against this, Rav Yemar b. Shlamia cited: "And they may enforce their decree." Rava offered no reply. Said Rav Papa: He appropriately offered no reply. That applies only where there is no prominent person [*adam hashuv*]; where there is a prominent person, they cannot unilaterally make decrees.

Selling the Synagogue
4. Mishnah Megillah 3:1; BT Megillah 26a–b; JT Megillah 74a

These selections introduce the "good men of the town" as custodians of public assets. The mishnah defines limitations upon the sale of publicly owned sacred objects, from the town plaza (sometimes used for public prayers) to the Torah scroll in the synagogue. The talmudic discussions then address the issue of the agents authorized to act on the public's behalf.

Mishnah Megillah 3:1

The townspeople who sold the town plaza may use the funds to buy a synagogue. [If they sold] a synagogue, they may buy an ark; if an ark, wrappings [for holy scrolls]; if wrappings, they may buy books [of Scripture]; if books, they may buy a Torah scroll. But if they sold a Torah scroll, they may not buy books; if books, they may not buy wrappings; if wrappings, they may not buy an ark; if an ark, they may not buy a synagogue; if a synagogue, they may not buy a plaza. The same applies even to a surplus.

A publicly owned [sacred] object may not be sold into private ownership, since its sanctity is thereby diminished; thus holds Rabbi Yehudah. They said to him: If so, it would also be forbidden to sell from a large town to a small one!

BT Megillah 26a–b

Rabbi Shmu'el b. Nahmani said, citing Rabbi Yonatan: This applies only to a synagogue in a small town. A synagogue in a city, however, to which [people] come from all over, may not be sold, since it is public property.

Said Rav Ashi: [Regarding] the synagogue of Mata Mahsia, even though [people] come to it from all over, since they come under my auspices, if I wish, I may sell it. . . .

Rava said: [The mishnah's prohibition] applies only when the sale was not executed by the seven good men of the town in the presence of the townspeople. If, however, the sale was [so] executed . . . the funds may be used even to drink beer.

JT Megillah 74a

Three of the synagogue [members] are equal to the [entire] synagogue; seven of the townspeople are equal to the [entire] town.

What is the case? If they accepted [these three or seven] over themselves—even one [should suffice]! If they did not accept [them] upon themselves—even many [should not suffice]!

Rather, the case is one in which [the scope of their authority] was not specified.[6]

Justifying the Kahal's Authority: Early Ashkenaz

Communal Power to Expropriate

5. Gershom b. Judah Me'or ha-Golah, *Responsa of Zarfat and Luthir* 97

Responsa of Zarfat and Luthir, edited by J. Muller (Vienna, 1881; reprinted, Jerusalem, 1967; Hebrew), pp. 54–55; emended at points according to the version in Mordechai, Bava Metzia 257.

This responsum relates to a case of a foundered ship carrying the property of Jewish merchants. Some of the property was recovered by local gentiles, who sold it to other Jews. The responsum addresses a claim by Re'uven, one of the merchants, against Shimon, who had come into possession of some of the lost property. According to talmudic law, Shimon was within his legal rights. Gershom upholds the authority of a communal decree to the contrary, extending to the kahal *the rabbinic court's power to expropriate.*

---

6. I.e., a body of three or seven individuals was appointed for overseeing collective affairs, but the terms of appointment did not specifically authorize the sale of such public assets as holy objects.

The communities gathered there strove to recover the losses of their brethren. They decreed by way of oath and vow that anyone who comes to possess anything lost from that ship must return it to its owner—following the custom of most Jewish communities regarding anyone who suffers a loss, whether by theft or otherwise. Namely, a [legal] remedy[7] is provided for him, one ordaining that anyone who comes to possess a particular lost object must return it to its owner. [Now, what is the law] in the case of Shimon, who refuses to return it to Re'uven, claiming that he has obtained it legally, since "it is permissible [for the finder of] an article lost through the flooding of the river [to keep the article]" (BT Bava Metzia 22b)?

Answer: . . . Even if Re'uven despaired [of finding the lost object], nevertheless, since the *kahal* present there decreed that anyone who obtained anything lost from that ship must return it to the owner, Shimon must return the money to Re'uven, even though according to the Torah he legally obtained it, since "the court has power to expropriate" (BT Gittin 36b [C6, §15]). . . . One might reply that the statement "The court has power to expropriate" applies only to a prominent court such as that of Shammai or Hillel, and that courts today do not [possess this power]. But this is not true, for . . . "Jepthah in his generation is like Samuel in his generation: whoever is appointed as leader [*parnas*] of the community is as a prince among princes."[8] Therefore, the decree of the communities is valid and their ruling is binding, and Shimon cannot disobey their decree.

Communal Authority

6. Yehudah b. Meir Hakohen and Eli'ezer b. Yittzhak Hakohen, *Kolbo* 142

Emended at points according to the version in *Meged Yerahim* 1, pp. 8–10; both versions reprinted in Haym Soloveitchick, *The Use of Responsa as Historical Sources* (Jerusalem: Zalman Shazar Center, 1990; Hebrew), pp. 93–94.

This eleventh-century responsum was requested by the communal leaders of Troyes, on the Seine River, from two of Gershom's students. It describes a dispute that ultimately

---

7. *Takkanah:* although this term usually refers to an ordinance, in this case it seems to mean "remedy."

8. Paraphrasing BT Rosh Hashanah 25b: Each generation must obey its leaders even if they are far inferior to those of previous generations.

produced a split in the Troyes community. The majority sought affirmation of their right
to impose decrees upon a dissenting minority. In a description of the dispute, the leaders
of the majority identify themselves as "the kahal," *implying the schismatic character*
of their opponents.

Question: Re'uven came to the synagogue and complained: "O Holy *Kahal!*
Shimon's gentile maidservant came to my house yesterday, and reviled and
cursed me. You all know that she is a habitual vilifier and has done so to you
all." The entire *kahal* responded: "Indeed, so it is." One man said that she hit
him with a stick; another said that she called his wife a harlot; and a third,
that she called him a cuckold. Thereupon Re'uven stated: "Given the fact
that she is a habitual transgressor, I implore you to decree that for half a year
she derive no benefit from any Jew; perhaps she will [thus] learn her lesson.
And if you empower me to do so, I will pronounce the decree myself." They
empowered him, and he pronounced the specified decree. Shimon alone,
however, protested against the decree and stated that he would never abide
by it. The decree, [he argued,] was not binding, because it was pronounced
by a person hostile to him. The entire *kahal* replied: "His pronouncement was
made solely on our behalf; the decree was not pronounced merely because
of him but because [of her abuse] of several members of the community."
Shimon then declared: "We are not bound by the decree, because many of
those who participated in its pronouncement are friendly to our adversaries
and hostile to us." The entire *kahal* replied: "Far be it from us to pronounce a
decree because of our friendliness toward one man; for as we love him, so do
we love all Israel—'the remnant of Israel shall not do iniquity' (Zeph. 3:13)."

   We [the *kahal*] cautioned Shimon and his followers on several occasions against such excessive willfulness, but they disregarded us. When our
kahal saw this, we separated from them. But the entire *kahal* feared that Shimon and his friends, living so near the synagogue, would remove the Torah
scrolls and other public articles, and that no one would be able to stop them
from taking these articles. . . .

   May our teachers instruct us [on the following]: May the townspeople enact decrees [binding] a minority of *kahal* members? [Do they have
the right] to coerce the minority, force them to participate in communal
enactments, and restrain them from withdrawing from the community? Is

Shimon justified in his argument? For if Shimon is correct, every man or woman who so desires will free himself or herself from authority by putting forth similar claims.

Further instruct us: May townspeople bind by oath people of another town and thereby coerce them in their own town even though they are several miles away, and the respective towns are independent? Or may [the people from the neighboring town] claim: "We will do [as we please] and you do as you [please]. We ignore your decrees and oaths."

Further instruct us: We are a small *kahal*. The humble members among us have always abided by the leadership of our eminent members, never protesting against our ordinances. Rather, they have always followed our decrees. Now, when we are about to enact a decree, must we ask each individual member whether or not he is in agreement with us? In the event that we did not ask, and a certain individual kept silent and did not protest, could he then claim that the decree had not been enacted with his consent, even though he did not protest either at the time of the enactment of the decree or subsequently? Instruct us in detail, on all these matters.

Answer: This is our opinion, assuming [the accuracy of] the content of the query: All Israelites are obligated to coerce and compel one another to live in accordance with truth, justice, God's laws and His precepts. This principle is expressed in the Pentateuch, the Prophets, and the Writings. In the Pentateuch: . . . "You shall appoint magistrates and officials" (Deut. 16:18); in the Prophets: "[When the Lord raised up judges for them] the Lord would be with the judge" (Judg. 2:18); in the Writings: "I censured them, cursed them, [flogged them, tore out their hair, and adjured them by God]" (Neh. 13:25). . . .

Therefore, if the *kahal* agrees together to enact decrees forming a fence around the Torah, an individual may not exclude himself from the collective and cancel the pronouncement of the many by saying that he did not agree to the enactment. The individual, being a minority, is himself canceled [out]; whereas the many are authorized to bind by oath, to decree, to place under a ban, expropriate his property, and enact any [such] decree.

We find support for this in a number of sources in the Torah. Whence [the rule] that one cannot exclude himself from the collective? As it is written: "[I make this covenant] . . . not with you alone, but both with those who are standing here with us this day [before the Lord our God and with those who are not with us here this day]. Perchance there is among you some man or woman, [or some clan or tribe, whose heart is even now turning away from the Lord our God]. . . . When such a one hears the words of these sanctions, [he may fancy himself immune, thinking, 'I shall be safe, though I follow my own willful heart.' . . . The Lord will never forgive him]" (Deut. 29:13–19). . . .

Whence is it that an individual may not cancel a ban enacted by the majority? . . . Note that Rabbi Eli'ezer did not challenge the authority of his colleagues when they placed him under a ban, but conducted himself as [a person legally] banned. Thus we read: "On that day the rabbis collected everything that Rabbi Eli'ezer had pronounced pure and burned it [in a fire. Then they voted on him and placed him under the ban. [Rabbi Eli'ezer] tore his clothes and took off his shoes and sat down on the ground]" (BT Bava Metzia 59b [C6, §10]). Thus, if Rabbi Eli'ezer—who was an outstanding *hakham* [and] his views were even supported by a voice from Heaven—submitted to his colleagues . . . , an ordinary man must surely act similarly.

Whence is it that [a community is empowered] to expropriate property?

[The authors quote Ezra 10:8 and the talmudic discussion of this verse and others; see C6, §15.]

An individual, therefore, cannot exclude himself from the communal collective.

Moreover, the inability of the individual to cancel decrees, or to exclude himself from such decrees, is not limited to matters requiring a fence around the Torah, but even extends to such optional matters [*reshut*] as taxes and other *takkanot* that the *kahal* enacts for itself. Thus we read: "Townspeople are authorized to stipulate regarding prices, measures, and the pay of laborers. . . . And they are authorized to enforce their decree" (BT Bava Batra 8b). Therefore, no one should ever entertain such an idea.

Now concerning your forcing Shimon to discharge his servant: If it is as you say that the *kahal* agreed to it, they are authorized to do so. For a person is not permitted to harbor a habitual public nuisance in his house. . . . If, however, Shimon's version of the story is the correct one—that, as we have heard, she is not habitually vicious, and that the *kahal* did not reach an agreement in the matter, but that Shimon's enemies alone enacted the decree . . . we do not think that Shimon should be forced to discharge his servant. . . . But, if the *kahal* did agree, Shimon cannot disqualify them on grounds of hostility or conflict. For [hostility] disqualifies [someone] only from [serving as a judge in] court.

[Concerning communal autonomy:] . . . If the decree that they are enacting deals with the needs of their locality, such as taxation, weights, measures, and wages—certainly, in all such matters townspeople may compel only [their own members]. As it is said, "Townspeople are authorized"— the people of that town, not the people of another town. If, however, God forbid, the inhabitants of another town transgressed the Torah or the law, or decided a point of law not in accordance with *halakhah,* the inhabitants of another town might coerce them, and even pronounce the *herem* [ban] against them, in order to force them to mend their ways. The inhabitants of the former town may not say to the latter: "We will do [as we please] and you do as you [please]." For all Israel are commanded to compel them. . . .

You write that in your place the humble were accustomed to obey the eminent and never protested against them. It is right that the humble obey the eminent in whatever they decree upon them. This is so not only if they failed to protest, but . . . even if they protested vigorously . . . , for the eminent are more numerous than the humble. Should you say that [in your community] the humble were more numerous than the eminent, and that the former refused to obey the latter—if they [the humble] were silent, showed no disapproval, and did not protest at the time the decree was enacted, they can no longer [do so now]. Although the humble are more numerous than the eminent, it is right that they obey their elders. . . . Happy is the generation whose humble obey the eminent[9] . . . , as we see in the case of Rehoboam the son of King Solomon (1 Kings 12 [C3, §6). May the Almighty consent to our efforts for truth and peaceful justice.

9. Cf. BT Rosh Hashanah 25b.

Obedience to the Kahal Is a Mitzvah

7. Rashi, *Responsa* 247

The number refers to the Elfenbein edition of Rashi's responsa. Following Haym Solo-
veitchick's analysis in *The Use of Responsa as Historical Sources* (Jerusalem: Zalman Shazar
Center, 1990), pp. 112–19, we have preferred the version reprinted in S. D. Luzzato, *Ozar
Nehmad* (Hebrew), vol. 2, pp. 178–79.

*In this case, an individual who evidently recognized the community's authority sought
to escape it by buttressing his recalcitrant position with the power of an oath. He expected the religious duty to fulfill one's oaths to override communal authority (see Lev.
19:12). Rashi retorts by equating communal enactments with Torah law. Already the
Mishnah has established that an oath to abrogate a mitzvah has no force; it is a "vain
oath," a transgression of the commandment "You shall not take in vain the name of
the Lord your God" (Exod. 20:7). Individuals are bound to fulfill the commandments
by a prior oath taken at Sinai (see Mishnah Shevu'ot 3:6, and C1, §12).*

You asked about one who heard that the community were planning to enact
a decree against him and quickly took a preemptive oath not to obey their
decree. Must he abide by their decree, or does it have no effect because of
his oath?

      In my view, an oath to transgress communal proclamations consti-
tutes a "vain oath." If he was forewarned, he is immediately liable to be lashed
in accordance with scriptural law [*de'orayta*]. He went to great lengths to no
avail and is not freed from the communal decree—provided the decree was
lawful—even though his oath preceded their decree. For he has sworn to
abrogate a *mitzvah*, to depart from the laws of Israel[10] and not be subject to
their jurisdiction. The Mishnah reads: ". . . If one swears to abrogate a *mitzvah*—an oath not to build a *sukkah*, or not to perform *lulav*, or not to put on
phylacteries, this constitutes a vain oath for which . . . one is liable for lash-
ings" (Shevu'ot 3:8). Since he has taken an oath to transgress the Torah, he
has thereby sworn the impossible, for he is already under oath from Mount

10. The term *hukkei Yisrael* here can cover both the laws of the Torah and the communal enactments.

Sinai with regard to both positive and negative [commandments]. . . . The oath of the ancients precedes his own. . . .

Restricting the Kahal's Authority: Early Spain

Decisions Are Made by the Court

8. Anonymous Gaonite Responsum, *Responsa Geonica* (Assaf) 26

Simha Assaf, *Responsa Geonica* (Jerusalem: Mekize Nirdamim, 1942; Arabic and Hebrew), sec. 26, pp. 106–8. Our translation deviates from Assaf's Hebrew in light of our understanding of the Arabic original. This translation benefits from the expertise of Zvi Zohar.

The practice of interrupting the synagogue Sabbath services evolved in early medieval times as a mechanism for mobilizing public support in defense of an aggrieved individual. Queried about its legitimacy, the Gaon (head of the Babylonian academy) responds that "in Iraq this is unknown." What he questions, however, is not only this particular practice but the entire shift of authority from the court to the kahal.

You asked: Is it permissible for an Israelite to halt the Sabbath prayer services in order to exact his due from his adversary, or to compel [someone] to appear with him in court after the Sabbath? Instruct us . . . what the law is in this matter.

The answer is this. Provided the defendant is an Israelite, if the plaintiff [has pursued him] for some time, or seeks to raise support against him, it is permissible. However, if [the plaintiff] obstinately continues to obstruct the service, he may not do so. He must be dissuaded and the service proceed.

But in Iraq this is unknown: [It is not] for the community to determine rights and liabilities; rather, this is the court's responsibility. And it is incumbent on the community to follow the court's finding of liability [and enforce it], whether by means of warning or *herem*. Likewise, in every town in which there is an appointed judge to determine rights and liabilities, the plaintiff should turn to him alone, not to the community.

Restricting Authority to Annul Property Rights
9. Meir Halevi Abulafia (Ramah), *Responsa 285*

*Here is a responsum, written in the first half of the thirteenth century by the lead-
ing scholar of the Jewish community in Toledo, concerning the case of an individual
who wanted to operate a furnace in a residential courtyard. Normally, this would have
been deemed an impermissible nuisance, but the community as a whole had agreed to
allow it. There was, however, one neighbor who objected to the furnace. Abulafia was
asked, "Can he bar it or not?" The responsum begins with a detailed discussion of
the legitimate uses of residential areas and then goes on to argue for the inviolability of
individual rights.*

Whenever he is [legally] required to remove [the nuisance], even though all
others have conceded to it except for one neighbor who is harmed, that one
may bar it. For no person can concede to harm on behalf of another.

Now, [regarding] the analogy you draw from the case of a synagogue . . . which may be sold by the seven good men of the town in the presence of the townspeople, what resemblance does it bear? [The synagogue]
was originally consecrated for public use. And it was consecrated under the
auspices of the seven good men of the town for the sake of anything they
would see fit. But in this case, who authorized the seven good men of the
town to concede to harm on behalf of this individual?

Furthermore, all individuals stand equal in regard to the synagogue,
for they all have a share in it. When they originally became partners, they
did so subject to the understanding that [the partnership would be governed]
according to the majority of partners. But in this case, the seven good men
of the town and the majority of townspeople are not harmed by the smoke.
How then can one who is not harmed concede to harm on behalf of this
individual who is harmed?

Nor is there any resemblance to the rule that "the court has power to
expropriate." That too is not an arbitrary expropriation of individual property by the court. [The rule] applies only in a case where the property owner
has [alternatives available] that will save him from expropriation. If he does

not act accordingly, he then . . . brings the loss upon himself. But in this case, what other recourse does this individual have?

Therefore, [in the case of] an individual wishing to operate an oven or furnace adjacent to his fellow's property: If the smoke reaches [his fellow] only by an uncommon wind, he cannot be barred at all. But if smoke reaches him by a common wind—even if there is public property in between [the oven and the private residence], even if the entire community has conceded except for this individual who is harmed, and even if the smoke is infrequent—he can bar it.

Developed Doctrines of the Kahal

Against the Tyranny of the Majority

10. Meir b. Baruch of Rothenburg (Maharam), *Responsa* (Prague) 968

The text here is based on *Responsa of Maharam b. Baruch,* edited by M. Bloch (Budapest, 1895; Hebrew), with some corrections from other manuscripts, for which we thank Simha Emanuel.

Among the classical defenders of communal authority we find also a certain apprehension about its potential abuse by a local majority. Rothenburg's critique here of majority tyranny in the kahal *addresses the authority of the greater number and their chosen leaders. Both the details of the case (involving a dispute between a majority of the community and one of its leading members) and the import of Rothenburg's ruling are somewhat opaque. At one point he seems to require unanimous consent for all communal decrees and appointments (a position often attributed to Jacob Tam), but his main concern is clearly to protect individual members (or is it only "great men"?) against unilateral impositions by the majority.*

Regarding townspeople who got together—some or most of them—and appointed one chief, not by unanimous consent: they seek to lord it over the others unlawfully, to impose the tax and [to dictate] all religious and civil affairs at their will. . . .

They are not masters in this, for they are not authorized to institute new [arrangements] without unanimous consent. Now, the talmudic statement [that] "they are authorized to enforce their decree" (BT Bava Batra 8b) means: unanimously. . . . They are authorized to impose a penalty upon someone who initially accepted the enactment and subsequently transgressed it. They are authorized to exact the specific penalty they [all the members of the community] initially "confirmed and accepted"[11] upon themselves. Alternatively, the seven good men of the town who were initially selected with the unanimous consent of the townspeople to oversee their civil affairs and to impose penalties—they too are authorized to enforce their decree.

The like of these, however, who set themselves up as kings, cannot [act] unilaterally against a great man.

[Rothenburg cites here the talmudic discussion regarding the "prominent person": §3.]

Thus, even a stipulation made among themselves is invalid because they acted without the consent of the prominent person in their town. Even more so, they cannot act unilaterally to enforce their enactment upon a great man.[12]

[Their position] is completely untenable, since this R. Meir Cohen agrees to share with them in whatever levy they have to pay from all their possessions, whether by *herem* or by selecting tax assessors through mutual agreement.[13]

If, despite all this, you do not heed him [but] again seize his possessions through the gentiles or on your own, he is authorized to rescue his property by any available means. He may even enter another's house to retrieve his property, [and] even have recourse to the gentiles. . . .

Therefore, desist from any further such evil deeds. If you heed and obey, we will [in future] treat your words with respect.

Peace, Meir b. Baruch.

---

11. Alluding to the talmudic understanding of Esther 9:27; see BT Shabbat 88a (C1, §8).
12. The use of a different term ("great man" as opposed to the talmudic "prominent person") reflects the sense of the argument. It is not that this R. Meir Cohen had the status of an *adam hashuv* (the "R." likely denotes not "Rabbi" but merely a common honorific), but that this is a case of illegitimate legislation similar to one in which the views of a "prominent person" are overridden.
13. These are the two accepted modes of assessment: (a) personal declarations by oath, on pain of *herem,* or (b) the judgment of a mutually agreed-upon committee.

Legislative Authority and Autonomy
11. Solomon b. Abraham Adret (Rashba), *Responsa* 3:393, 3:411

These two responsa, written in Barcelona in the late thirteenth or early fourteenth cen-
tury, suggest the fully developed doctrine of rule by the kahal's *majority. In the first,*
the text of the question has not been preserved. What is at issue is the scope of the
"appointees'" authority, as indicated by the question in a similar case (4:311): "The
kahal *agreed to appoint us to eliminate sins, and we have taken an oath to so do. And*
the charter of the mandate states that we are authorized by the [gentile] government
to impose penalties, whether corporal or fiscal, as we see fit." Can such authority be
defended? Adret's response affirms the broad powers implied in the language of the char-
ter: "The whole principle informing your appointment was that you should judge as
you see fit, just as it is written in the letter of mandate you mentioned. This is deemed
a straightforward matter both by us and in all places where similar stipulations were
enacted." In the first case below, the appointees evidently asked Adret whether their
court could accept testimony from witnesses disqualified by talmudic law.

The next responsum begins by discussing the authority of one community
over another. Adret's argument leads, however, to a critical and more fundamental issue:
How can anybody rule over anybody else without gaining specific consent to every de-
cree and every enactment? How is legitimate government possible in the absence of
unanimity?

Responsum 3:393

If the appointees [*berurim*] find the witnesses trustworthy, they are
permitted to impose monetary fines or corporal punishment as they see [fit].
Society [*olam,* literally, "the world"] is thereby sustained. For if you were
to restrict everything to the laws stipulated in the Torah and punish only
in accordance with the Torah's penal [code] in cases of assault and the like,
the world would be destroyed [*ha-olam harev*], because we would require two
witnesses and [prior] warning. The Rabbis have already said that "Jerusalem

was destroyed only because they restricted their judgments to Torah law" (BT Bava Metzia 30b).[14] How much more so outside the Land [of Israel], where there is no Torah authority to impose penalties, and the unscrupulous will "breach the fence of the world," and the world will become desolate. Already the Rabbis of blessed memory have imposed fines for assault (Bava Kama, chap. 3) even though these constitute penalties that may not be imposed in Babylon [i.e., abroad], as stated there. Nevertheless, such cases are everywhere brought to justice . . . in order to restrain the current generation.

[Adret goes on to cite the talmudic precedents for extralegal punishment; see C24.]

Therefore, the appointees who acted thus, if they saw it to be the need of the hour to impose penalties, whether fiscal or corporal, for the perfection of the polity [*tikkun ha-medinah*] and for the needs of the hour, have acted lawfully. How much more so where they have royal authorization [by the non-Jewish king]. . . . The appointees [*berurim*] must [however] carefully consider the matter and act [only] after taking counsel, and their intentions should at all times be for the sake of heaven.

Responsum 3:411

You asked about our custom in regard to various taxes: Do we include the surrounding towns in our enactments and *herem*s without consulting them, or does each locale impose a *herem* independently, or do the wealthy members of those localities come to our city to participate in [decreeing] our enactments? You also requested that I relate my opinion with reasons and proofs.

You initially [inquired as to] the custom and concluded [by inquiring] about the law.

Concerning our customs: Know that we [in Barcelona] and the *kahal* of Villafranca and the *kahal* of Tarragona and of Montblanc share a common fund and purse for the payment of various taxes and [other] govern-

---

14. This is a revolutionary interpretation of the talmudic source. The Talmud contrasts *din,* "law," with *lifnim mishurat ha-din,* which means going beyond the law in the sense of supererogation. Adret instead employs the text to sanction the infringement of *din.*

ment impositions. Whenever we wish to revise the enactments concerning
the assessment [of tax liability] or the submission of records and declaration
of capital assets as required by our master the king, we never impose decrees
upon the [other *kehillot*] even though we are the many and the capital city for
all matters. If we acted without their counsel, they would not obey us. With
their consent, we sometimes send people to them, and at other times representatives [*berurim*] come to us. However, if they do not heed us regarding
either of these [arrangements], we compel them by the force of the government either to come to us or to make enactments or [impose] a *herem* in their
locality identical to ours. However, in other localities, the capital community [*kehillah*] will sometimes decree enactments regarding its neighboring
towns and villages and include them regardless of their consent. Concerning
all these matters, localities are divided in custom.

[Rule by consent] has always been our practice, and our common
custom; it is certainly what the law [prescribes]!

For what right [*zekhut*] or authority does one *kahal* have over another, or indeed the individual over the many,[15] in cases of monetary law,
customs, or enactments—except in a few well-defined instances?—For example, when the high court decrees the enactment of a custom or prohibition (and it is something that the public can endure), e.g. [the prohibition
on consuming gentile] bread, wine, and cooked food.[16] . . .

Or [when, for example,] the king [decrees], as in the case of the
herem of Saul by which Jonathan incurred the death penalty, even though he
did not know or hear [of it].[17] For anything the king enacts in the council
of Israel[18] is valid and [considered] acceptable to everyone.

It is also written: "And anyone who did not come in three days
would . . . have his property confiscated" (Ezra 10:8). So too with regard to
a *herem* imposed by the *nasi* or the exilarch. . . .

So too are the decrees or enactments of the majority of the *kahal*
regarding the needs of the community [*kehillah*]. Since the majority enacted

15. The logic of this clause is obscure.
16. See BT Avodah Zara 36a–b; MT Laws of Rebels 2:5–6.
17. 1 Sam. 14; see, too, Nahmanides' discussion in ¶23.
18. *Si'at yisrael;* this term does not appear in the Bible or in the Talmud; Adret here, too, is
following Nahmanides.

it, even against the will of individuals, it is valid. Providing it was [really] the majority that acted and that the majority of the public can endure it. . . . For in each and every public, individuals are considered to be under the rule of the many and must pay heed to them in all their affairs. They [the minority] stand to the people of their city as all Israel stands to the high court or the king. [This holds] whether they are present or not [at the time of enactment]. Even their descendants . . . are obligated to follow the enactments and *herem*s that their ancestors placed on themselves. . . . This was the case in the acceptance of the Torah, as well as such Rabbinic enactments as [the reading of the] *megillah* and [the observance of] Hanukkah. Even if the ancestors [merely] observed a fixed custom, [it is treated as] a tacit oath [and] the descendants must follow it. . . . Whoever breaches these [principles] is like one who breaches the fence of the Torah, for the ancestors are the roots of the descendants. Therefore, "an individual placed under a ban by his own town is thereby under ban for other towns, but an individual placed under a ban by another town is not under ban for his own town" (BT Mo'ed Katan 16a).

The same applies to enactments by the eminent of Israel, when they [believe the enactments necessary for] social order [*takkanah la-olam*]. . . . Furthermore, the high court can coerce and place a *herem* on a defendant so that he will come and be judged before them, even though he is not a local inhabitant. . . . How much more so may a court compel a local defendant to be judged before them against his will . . . ?

These are the instances where I believe that it is possible to compel others to conform. However, in other matters, when the people of one town want to impose their will on the people of another town, I cannot see how they have the authority when they [the other townspeople] do not consent. Nor may they impose a *herem* or forcibly tax them. [The inhabitants of the second town] are not subjects . . . in such matters, unless [the inhabitants of the first town] . . . impose a *herem* or enforce [the law] in order to prevent [religious] transgressions. This is certainly permissible, proper, and necessary [if it is done] to prevent transgressions. . . .

Enhancing Communal Powers
12. Isaac b. Sheshet Perfet (Rivash), *Responsa* 399

In talmudic law, marriage is a private transaction, sanctioned by religious law. In its standard form, matrimony is enacted by the transfer of a symbolic sum of money or item of value from the man to the woman; this is called "betrothal." Various medieval communities sought to regulate marriage and bring it under public control. Such regulation required dealing with, and partially transforming, the private and religious character of the transaction. The transformation is effected by using the community's power to expropriate, thereby declaring the betrothal money ownerless. In confirming the authority of the kahal, *first over private property and then in the realm of marriage, Perfet considerably extends the medieval doctrine of public law.*

Question: The *kahal* enacted a preventive ordinance prohibiting any man from betrothing a woman unless the community officers are informed and present, and [only] in the presence of ten people. If anyone transgresses and betroths otherwise, the betrothal will be null and void. The *kahal* at this time [of enactment] expropriates in advance the money or item of value that he would use for betrothal. [His ownership of] the money will be null and void, and the betrothal will be annulled, and the woman can remarry without a *get* [writ of divorce]. . . .

You question whether the *kahal* is empowered to expropriate private property, especially that of minors who are unable to consent to the ordinance. And how much more [difficult is the case of] the property of those yet unborn or of newly arrived residents! For even if the town's rabbi and elder endorses the ordinance, the [townspeople] are not empowered to annul a betrothal [which is a prerogative of prominent rabbis]. . . . However, the *hakhamim* of today are considered laymen and have no power to expropriate private property,[19] and certainly not to annul a betrothal that was performed in accordance with Torah law. Now, the statement "Jepthah

19. See C6, §15.

in his generation is like Samuel in his generation" (BT Rosh Hashanah 25b) refers to ruling within Torah law but not to abrogating it. . . .

Answer: According to Torah law, the townspeople may enact ordinances, preventive laws, and regulations—and impose penalties upon all transgressors.

We read in tractate Bava Batra: "Townspeople are authorized to stipulate regarding prices, measures, and the pay of laborers, and they are authorized to enforce their decree" (8b). Rashi explains it, "to punish a transgressor of their decree beyond the provisions of Torah law."

Furthermore, their power is not confined to these matters; rather, they are empowered to enact any ordinance that they consider proper and to punish a transgressor. . . . Thus the Tosefta adds: "Townspeople are authorized to pronounce, 'Anyone seen at X's shall pay thus and so'; 'Anyone seen [dealing with] the authorities shall pay thus and so'; 'Anyone whose cow grazes amid the seedlings shall pay thus and so' " (§2).

This power is not only granted to the townspeople; the members of a particular trade may also stipulate among themselves in matters pertaining to their trade and [they may] punish transgressors. For with respect to their trade they are comparable to townspeople. This is stated in the Talmud regarding the butchers who made a mutual agreement that anyone who slaughters on another's day will have his hide [i.e., that of the slaughtered animal] ripped (§3). . . .

However, regarding the [subsequent] proviso, "That applies only where there is no prominent person [*adam hashuv*]; where there is a prominent person, they cannot unilaterally make decrees" . . . , it seems that this applies only in the case of a trade: wherever there is a prominent person and they act without endorsement, they are not comparable to townspeople and lack the power to stipulate save as contracting individuals. But townspeople can always stipulate and do not require endorsement by a local prominent person. . . . Rather, whatever the majority of the *kahal* and the leaders tending to public affairs enact is valid.

. . . Minors too when they come of age are subject to the enactment. Otherwise, the townspeople . . . would have to renew their ordinances daily on account of the minors who come of age every day—which is absurd.

Rather, the townspeople as a whole are subject to the decree, including those born subsequently. . . .

Similarly, newly arrived residents are considered townspeople and are obligated to follow their ordinances. It is as if, upon arrival, they explicitly accept all the town's ordinances—unless they plan to go back [elsewhere]. Indeed, any practice forbidden to them by the custom of their [original] town is [now] permitted to them if this town's custom permits it, provided they do not intend to return.[20] . . . If this applies to ritual matters [isur], it certainly applies to monetary matters [mamon]. . . .

However, a question can be posed. The Talmud says in tractate Gittin (36b [C6, §15]) in regard to prosbul: "Perhaps, when Hillel enacted [it] for future generations, [this extended] not to any court [but only] to a court like his own, such as [that of] Rav Ami and Rav Assi, who have the power of expropriation"—but not to other courts. Consequently, not all courts are able to expropriate money!

Even if we accept this, it poses no difficulty to the case at hand. For this [restriction] applies [only] to cases like prosbul [whose very function is to] expropriate private property against the law by means of the prosbul. However, wherever the townspeople act [to enforce] their ordinances within their town, they are equal to, even greater than, the court of Rav Ami and Rav Assi.

Moreover, Rabbenu Tam commented that the requirement is not specifically for a court equal to that of Rav Ami and Rav Assi, but for a court that is the most senior in its location: "Jepthah in his generation is like Samuel in his generation" (BT Rosh Hashanah 25b). . . . The established court of every town has power to expropriate; how much more so the kahal!

[Perfet goes on to cite the talmudic source for the court's power of expropriation (C6, §15), Maimonides' codification of the court's extralegal powers, and the talmudic dictum regarding the court's special punitive powers (C24). He concludes:]

The kahal is thus empowered to expropriate the money of anyone who transgresses its ordinances. Now, it has enacted that the money [used for] a betrothal performed without the community officers being in-

20. Rivash here cites the talmudic discussion of local customs in BT Hullin 18b.

formed and present be reappropriated prior to his giving it to the woman. The money therefore ceases to be the rightful property of either the man or the woman, and the betrothal is void. . . .

This is my view on this issue as a matter of law [*la-halakhah*]. But with regard to actual implementation, I would consider being stringent and would not rely on my stated opinion, owing to the gravity of the issue [at hand, i.e.,] to release her without a *get*—unless [doing so was] endorsed by all the [leading] scholars [*hakhamim*] of the various provinces.

A Contested Communal Enactment: Two Theories of Consent
13. Elijah Mizrahi (Re'em), *Responsa 57*

Elijah Mizrahi was in effect the chief rabbi of the various Jewish communities in Constantinople during the first quarter of the sixteenth century. His teacher and predecessor Moses Capsali, settling a long-standing dispute, had ruled that Rabbanites are forbidden to teach Talmud to the Karaites. Mizrahi, however, as is reflected in the case below, was a lifelong opponent of efforts to isolate the Karaites.

Concerning the *herem* [imposed as follows]: Some of the members of the congregations in Constantinople assembled with some of the good men of the town in the Poli congregation's synagogue to impose a *herem*—to wit, to prohibit teaching to the Karaites any subject whatsoever: Bible, Mishnah, Talmud, *halakhah, aggadah,* literal exegesis of the Bible, kabbalistic exegesis of the Bible. Also any science written by the Greek philosophers,[21] whether logic, physics, metaphysics, arithmetic, algebra, astronomy, music, or ethics. [The prohibition extends to] any aspect of these sciences, whether by way of instructing, questioning, debating, or reading [texts], even teaching the *alef-bet* [alphabet].

[The good men] sent for . . . the chief rabbi of all the congregations

---

21. The printed edition adds: "May their name and memory be blotted out." This comment is not added to other references to the Greek philosophers below and seems inauthentic.

in order to impose the said *herem*. However, he[22] refused to do this because he argued: "There is no right to bar someone from matters permitted to him. And it is well known that these sciences were authored by the Greek philosophers through their own wisdom and investigations. Anyone may teach them to Christians, Muslims, Karaites, or any other nationality at will, and there is no prohibition involved. How can you, then, impose this *herem?*"

When he saw that they were taking no heed, he put them off till the morning. The promoters of the *herem* sensed that the rabbi's intention was to procrastinate, so they went ahead and imposed a *herem* among themselves to assemble in the morning to execute their plan, specifying also that no one be permitted to reconsider, even if the opposite view gained wide support.

When the teachers heard this, they cried out to them: "Why do you multiply prohibitions concerning matters permitted to us [as practiced by] our forefathers and fathers down to the present time? For these sciences were authored by the Greek philosophers . . . and from the day they were composed to the present day they have been taught from nation to nation: from Christians to Jews, from Jews to Christians, from Muslims to Jews, from Jews to Muslims, from Christians to Muslims, from Muslims to Christians. Several of [our] most distinguished ancient scholars would teach Karaites, Christians, and Muslims in order to earn an honest livelihood without having to demean themselves in other occupations. No criticism or opposition was voiced against them. Now then, what is our crime or sin that you have come against us with the sword of this *herem* to destroy our livelihood while we are blameless?"

Some of the teachers . . . went to the chief rabbi of all the congregations of the city of Constantinople and cried out in complaint. He answered them: "Their intentions are not good. They certainly have no power to bar anyone from matters permitted to him. Return now to your homes, and I will duly proceed to dissuade them from their plan."

While they were talking, some of the good men promoting this *herem* arrived, having heard that the teachers had gone there to complain. They quarreled, with much shouting. The promoters of the *herem* left, greatly

---

22. Mizrahi is referring to himself in the third person.

angered, and summoned wicked . . . men with clubs in their hands to strike
anyone who [tried to] protest against those gathering at the Poli synagogue
to impose the *herem*.

In the morning, the teachers summoned a great gathering of people
of the [various] congregations, the good men, and the elders of the town, at
the synagogue of the congregation of Ziton. They invited the chief rabbi in
order to annul the plan of the gathering promoting this *herem*.

He [the rabbi] came there. When they began to [make their com-
plaint], messengers came from the other gathering to say [to the rabbi]: "Why
do you not come with us to the Poli synagogue, to the first gathering?" . . .
The rabbi replied: "Because I saw that . . . men of low character whose every
thought is evil . . . had joined with you. And they intend to have their way
whether it is right or wrong!"

They pleaded passionately that he go with them, but he refused to
go. They then sent him an additional message: "If you come along, you will
fare well; however, if you do not, take heed that the entire gathering . . . has
already agreed to appoint another rabbi in your place to lead and rule them."

When the rabbi heard this, he rose and went along with them.
Some of the elders followed him. Now the thugs wielding their clubs were
standing at the entrance of the Poli synagogue to see who dared oppose them.
They spread word among the crowd, saying: "Any outsider to our plan who
encroaches the 'Tent of Meeting' imposing the *herem* shall be put to death!"[23]
So the teachers . . . could not enter the "Tent of Meeting" to speak and defend
themselves.

The rabbi saw that none of the teachers were present. Furthermore,
no one present was prepared to speak against the *herem* for fear of the thugs.
In any case, the gathering had already, on the previous day, imposed a *herem*
among themselves to be united in promoting this *herem* . . . . Consequently,
he was silent and said nothing, either on behalf [of the proposal] or against
it. And the people contending against the teachers rose, ascended to the holy
ark, took out the Torah scrolls, and loudly imposed the *herem* as they had
planned.

23. They are alluding to the verse "Any outsider who encroached was to be put to death" (Num.
3:38), which refers to the Tent of Meeting.

[Mizrahi here engages in an extensive legal analysis of the workings of *herem,* of the proper policy regarding Karaites, and of the community's powers of legislation. The latter discussion concludes as follows:]

Thus, we have explained to you the dispute between the rabbis concerning the interpretation of the *baraita* "[Townspeople] are authorized to enforce their decree" (BT Bava Batra 8b). Maimonides, Rabbenu Tam,[24] [and others] all maintain that [this text] refers to a stipulation that they had first endorsed unanimously, and that some of them had then retracted, wishing to transgress. It is then that [the townspeople] are authorized to punish anyone who transgresses. However, regarding dissenters who never endorsed the stipulation—whether individuals or a group—the townspeople have no authority to punish them, for they never endorsed the stipulation at all. On the other hand, Rashi, Rashba, [and others] maintain that [the text] refers even to a stipulation that was not endorsed unanimously but only by a portion of the townspeople. Since the majority of the townspeople and all the good men of the town endorsed it, they may compel the dissenting minority. They may impose upon them any penalty they see fit, whether a monetary fine, *herem,* or censure, should they transgress the stipulation. For the good men of the town have, with regard to their town, the status of "the great men of the generation." . . .

[Mizrahi now goes on to argue that the *herem* against the teachers is invalid on each of these views.]

Authority was granted to the high court in Jerusalem to enact decrees and ordinances and establish customs. This derives from the verse "In accordance with the instructions given you" (Deut. 17:11), which refers to the decrees, ordinances, and customs concerning which they instructed the public in order to strengthen religion and order society [*letakken ha-olam*]. The first group of scholars maintain that this authority was given to none but one court in each generation—namely, that court whose position is similar to that of the high court in Jerusalem. . . .

How then could [such powers be claimed by] any scholar in any town, even if he is unparalleled in his region or country? Certainly the good men of the town, who are neither scholars nor leaders, cannot compel any-

24. See headnote to §10.

one [to abide by] their stipulations despite his having been one of those who protested. . . . Accordingly, they interpret the *baraita* as referring only to a stipulation that they first endorsed unanimously, without any compulsion. If then [some of them] retracted, [the townspeople] are authorized to impose penalties upon the transgressors. . . .

The second group of scholars [point to the reason that the same] authority was granted to the high court in Jerusalem and to the courts of subsequent generations . . . even though they are not equal. This is because all the people of the generation assent to [their court's leadership] concerning decrees, ordinances, and customs. . . .

Therefore, the great men of the town[25] also [possess this authority]. This is so because all the townspeople look to them in matters of order-ing [*tikkun*] the town. . . . It is as if they appointed them with the express mandate that whatever they do be done. Even though this was not stated explicitly, it is manifest that they all assent to whatever is done. Even though some of them cry out [in protest] against those decrees and ordinances, this is no different from parties stipulating consensually and then recanting.

According to this second view, the *baraita* "[Townspeople] are au-thorized . . ." need not be interpreted as referring [exclusively] to stipulations adopted through unanimous consent. Rather, it can [refer to] a case where some seek to coerce others who are protesting against a stipulation adopted by the good men of the town. For the good men of the town are fully equal to the great men of the generation. . . .

We thus rule: This *herem* imposed by the gathering at the Poli syna-gogue that Rabbanites should not teach Karaites any science whatsoever au-thored by the wise men of the nations is completely invalid save for those who assented. . . .

Concerning those who . . . protested in the streets and marketplaces, it is patently clear that no *herem* or vow exists. For several reasons: First, they did not assent to it nor agree to it at all. And according to the scholars of the first group [mentioned above] . . . the great men of the town . . . cannot enact any decree or ordinance for their townspeople, except for those who

25. *Gedolei ha-ir:* this alternative to "the good men of the town" is employed a number of times by Mizrahi in this responsum; it is probably meant to reflect the parallel he draws with *gedolei ha-dor,* "the great men of the generation."

consent. But as for those who did not consent, they cannot coerce them by any form of coercion, whether a fine, *herem*, or censure, even if all the great men and all the [rest of the] people of the town jointly consent. This is so even if these great men are the town leaders who govern all its affairs. . . .

Second, this *herem* was not imposed with the consent of the chief rabbi of all the congregations by whose word all the enactments and customs of the town are established and who is appointed over them [to conduct] all their affairs. On the contrary, he protested against . . . this *herem*. On three occasions he addressed them to dissuade them from their plan . . . but they were unwilling to listen. Instead, they . . . threatened him to induce his consent, because they were possessed by fiery anger and wrath and intended to have their way whether it was right or wrong!

Consequently, it is evident that the *herem* has no force whatsoever over those who did not consent to it. For these people have no authority to enact any ordinances or decrees without the consent of the chief rabbi, since they are all subordinate to him. [This is true] both according to the first and according to the second group of scholars. . . . On all views, wherever there is a chief rabbi and yet they acted against his position . . . , the *herem* has no validity whatsoever for those who did not agree to it. Whoever mistakenly thinks otherwise errs in a manner that even schoolchildren do not err!

. . . Third, this *herem* was not [in any case] enacted by a majority of the townspeople, nor by all the good men of the town. For the opposite gathering at the Ziton congregation's synagogue . . . was more numerous. Besides, the good men and the scholars of the town were also divided over this into two camps. . . .

Finally, this *herem* was not imposed for the sake of heaven nor for the purpose of *tikkun olam*. Ordinarily, *herem* or censure is imposed for the sake of *tikkun olam* and to strengthen and sustain religion. But this *herem* was imposed out of jealousy and hatred. Some begrudged the teachers the respect they were receiving from the Karaites. Others hated the Karaites themselves because of the interest that they collected [from members of the Jewish community], as all usurers are hated. . . . Their gathering was thus motivated by vengefulness. Were it not for their jealousy and hatred they would not have engaged in this initiative. Everyone knows and recognizes this! . . . Can anyone [then] entertain the notion that this *herem* could be considered valid?

Commentary. Emerging Democratic Ideas

   The novelty of the *kahal* as a political entity is reflected in the response of the anonymous Gaon (§8) to a query about the right to protest
some supposed injustice by interrupting the Shabbat service: "But in Iraq
this is unknown: [It is not] for the community to determine rights and liabilities; rather, this is the court's responsibility." To the Gaon—head of the
traditional hierarchy of religious courts—the notion of turning to "the community" appears totally misplaced. Do the people who sent this query not
have a rabbinic judge? They surely ought to, and "the claimant should address
him alone, not the community."

   Actually, the practice of disrupting the service was widespread, and
it nicely illustrates the birth of the *kahal* as a political institution. To establish
and maintain a synagogue and the Torah scrolls for public readings on Shabbat—that is one of the very few functions assigned to "the townspeople" in
tannaitic law. Now a claimant is permitted to disrupt this ritual, spoiling the
holiness of Shabbat with arguments about money. The *kahal* is told, in effect:
You cannot proceed with your functions as a ritual community without first
addressing issues of injustice in your midst.

   But why should defendants feel obligated to accept the community
at large as an arbiter of their case? And, as the *kahal* expands its legal purview
from the enforcement of existing law to the creation of new law, the question expands as well: Why should anyone deem himself (or herself) bound
by its authority?

   This is no idle question. Indeed, Maharam's argument seems to
imply a rejection in principle of any coercion except where it serves to enforce prior consent. And it is worth noting that according to certain traditions, Rabbenu Tam persistently denied communal authority altogether.
Against such doubts, medieval authors offer various justifications for the
kahal's authority. Most striking, perhaps, is Rashi's position, for *without any
argumentation* he simply ascribes to communal decrees the same force as Torah
law: each individual "is already under oath from Mount Sinai" to obey. Communal decrees and God's commandments are conflated under the caption
"the laws of Israel," indicating perhaps that allegiance to the collective is the
Grundnorm for both.

   An explicit collectivist account is offered by Rashba and Rivash.
Rashba holds that "individuals are considered to be under the rule of the

many and must pay heed to them in all their affairs"; likewise, later generations are bound by earlier decrees, "for the ancestors are the roots of the descendants." Rivash emphasizes the connection between these two points: all these obligations are not incurred individually, but rather "the townspeople as a whole are subject to the decree, including those born subsequently." The subjection of individuals to the collective is not derived from Torah; on the contrary, Rivash explains, it is a necessary precondition for the commitment to Torah itself.

This account of the foundation of communal authority hits bedrock here. Subjection of individuals to their community "just is," as part of the natural order of things; nothing more need or can be said. It may well be doubted whether such a naturalistic account is satisfactory on the theoretical level; other rabbinic authors—notably, in the selections before us here, Elijah Mizrahi—clearly sought alternative justifications. But the problem is not only one of theory; such a blanket grant of power to the majority is bound to conflict with what is right and just. This conflict is described in one of the questions posed by the community of Troyes, where the traditional authority of the "great ones" was questioned by the more numerous "humble ones." The responding scholars seem unsure here: Ought not the humble obey the great, despite the fact that the elite are fewer in number?

More emphatically, Ramah insists that the community cannot grant permission for an economic enterprise that produces a nuisance harming even a single individual. Ramah resists an expansion of the communal power to expropriate, and defends individual rights in terms of inviolable property rights, reminiscent of contemporary critiques of "Takings": "Who authorized the seven good men of the town to agree to harm on behalf of this individual?" The individualism of this rhetorical question seems diametrically opposed to the collectivist stance of Rashba and Rivash. Yet, despite an explicit commitment to curtailing the powers of the *kahal,* Ramah does not offer any institutional barrier to the excessive exercise of such powers. It is simply hoped that the *kahal* will bow to the religious authority of respondents like Ramah, and that the latter will faithfully protect the rights of minorities and individuals. Insofar as local authorities were prepared to be overruled by responsa from rabbis of great prestige, recourse to such rabbis functioned rather like modern judicial review.

Rivash himself also cites an alternative account of communal authority, one cast in more nearly normative (rather than naturalistic) terms. The townspeople have powers analogous to those of a court [*bet din*]: "Wherever the townspeople act [to enforce] their ordinances within their town, they are equal to, even greater than, the court." This analogy is in fact implicit already in the eleventh-century Ashkenazi responsum (§6), for example, where the talmudic prooftext for the power of the *court* to expropriate is cited in support of a similar power vested in the *kahal*.

But why should the (majority of the) people, or their selected *parnasim,* have powers like those of a court? Some of the authors here may have assumed a functional reply: whoever carries out the functions of leadership must be accorded the powers necessary for fulfilling those functions. Mizrahi, however, offers an analytic explanation, which looks to the source of the powers of the high court itself. The authority of local leaders, supported by popular majority, is analogous to the national authority of the Sanhedrin because both are equally based on the (tacit) consent of the governed.

The notion of consent had figured also in earlier sources, for example, in Rashba's emphasis on the requirement of representation from the minor communities. Here, however, it is presented as the underlying justification for any form of political authority. Thus, Mizrahi's treatise amounts in effect to a theoretical endorsement of the democratic principle of government by consent.

The major weakness of Mizrahi's position, and of the tradition that it represents, is the gap between theory and practice. More precisely, the problem is that the actual workings of the *kahal* lag behind the abstract theory that is said to justify them. In principle, government draws its powers from popular consent, and the authority of laws depends on their acceptance by the majority. In reality, there may be several synagogues, rival gatherings — and at times even "wicked men with clubs" producing a false appearance of consent.

This weakness bears a structural similarity to the problem noted above with regard to the tension between majority rule and the requirements of justice. In principle, the townspeople may not use their power to disenfranchise an individual, but there is no systematic definition of the realm of protected rights. In practice, however, there is some guarantee of procedural (if not substantive) protection. First, this comes through the negative mechanism of "interrupting the service": a license to interfere with the *kahal*'s normal functions. Then, on some views at least, there is also the requirement of consent by the *adam hashuv,* the "prominent person." If the *adam hashuv* acts as rabbi, his function is analogous to judicial review; if as chief *parnas,* "community leader," his power to prevent a law from taking effect resembles the power of executive veto.

With regard to government by consent, however, there is a marked deficiency of worked-out procedures. It is almost as though the emergent democratic ideas are put forward as retroactive justifications for existing communal institutions. The commitment to popular consent often does produce—as in the responsum by Mizrahi—a check on the exercise of brute force. But it does not produce an extensive refurbishing of the *kahal*'s political structures.

In sum, it may be said that the medieval *kahal* bequeaths to us—on some accounts, at least—a principle of democracy, but not an established heritage of democratic institutions.

Noam J. Zohar

The Kahal *and the Rabbi*

The "Prominent Hakham"

14. Maimonides, MT Laws of Sales 14:9–11

For reasons of linguistic consistency this translation is ours rather than that of the Yale Judaica Series.

Maimonides' codification of the legislative and coercive powers of tradesmen and townspeople shows his preference for rabbinic over lay authority. In his rendering of the talmudic story of the butchers' agreement (§3), he replaces the vague talmudic term "prominent person" with the clearer "prominent scholar" (hakham)—whose task is to guide the polity to excellence.

9. The townspeople are authorized to fix the price of anything they choose, even of meat or bread. They may stipulate among themselves that whoever violates [their decree] will be punished in this or that manner.

10. Tradesmen are similarly authorized to decide among themselves that no one may operate on another's day . . . and that whoever violates the stipulation will be punished. . . .

11. All this applies in a city [*medinah*] without a prominent *hakham* to order civic affairs and to bring about excellence in the activities of its inhabitants. If, however, it has a prominent *hakham,* their stipulation has no effect whatever . . . unless he had joined in it and it was done under the *hakham*'s auspices. Anyone who imposes a loss [upon a purported violator] of a stipulation not [adopted] under the *hakham*'s auspices must pay compensation.

The Scope of the Prominent Person's Authority
15. Shimon b. Tzemah Duran, *Tashbetz* 4:1:15

In the previous selection Maimonides casts his "prominent hakham*" in the role of civic leader. Even so, Perfet (§12), commenting on Maimonides and relying on the immediate context (§14, clause 10), had restricted the hakham's authority to rules made by tradesmen. Against this, Duran, who succeeded Perfet as chief rabbi of Algiers in 1408, argues here for an expanded conception of the prominent person's role.*

Maimonides amplified here, saying, "A prominent *hakham* to order civic affairs [and to bring about excellence in the activities of its inhabitants]." [By this] he means to say that the *hakham* must be appointed for these [matters]. If, however, there is among them an *adam hashuv* who is not appointed over their affairs, their ordinance takes effect even without him. . . . Rivash comments that ordinances of the townspeople [are valid] in any case without the *adam hashuv.* He supports this from the text of Maimonides, who only mentions this requirement of *adam hashuv* in the context of [ordinances passed by] tradesmen.

In my humble opinion, however, it seems that with respect to ordinances of the townspeople as well, if there is among them an *adam hashuv* appointed over all their affairs, their ordinance is not valid [literally, "is no ordinance"] without him. No punishment may be imposed for [the breach of] anything enacted without him, since they have already accepted him over themselves, [that is, accepted] that all their acts be subject to his review, so they cannot act without him. And regarding the support [Rivash] brought from the text of Maimonides . . . it can be argued that Maimonides merely followed the Talmud, where this requirement is adduced in the context of the case of the two butchers—and that case simply happened as it did [i.e., with an ordinance of tradesmen which, nevertheless, applies to townspeople as well].

The Rabbi as a Communal Employee
16. Menachem Meiri, *Bet ha-Behirah*, Bava Batra 8b

Much of the ongoing controversy among medieval commentators regarding the extent of the prominent person's authority evolved around the interpretation of Maimonides' code. Meiri's comments on the talmudic discussion (§3), are influenced here (as often is the case) by Maimonides' formulation. Yet he describes the hakham, *or rabbi, as a mere employee of the town.*

It has already been stated that tradesmen are authorized—without approval of the town—to stipulate among themselves that no one may operate on another's day, and to impose a specified penalty upon violators. Nevertheless, as stated below [in the talmudic text], this applies only in a town without a prominent *hakham* to order civic activities. If, however, it has a prominent *hakham,* they may not punish or impose loss except under the *hakham*'s auspices; anyone who so punishes [a violator] must repay. However, this applies only to a *hakham* who is a governing officer [*parnas*] appointed to inspect the town's activities and correct wrongs. But other scholars have no [standing] in such matters. . . .

Some maintain that this applies even to [stipulations of] the towns-people as a whole. That is, if there is a *hakham* thus appointed, their stipulations are null without his approval. So have most commentators maintained. This, however, does not appear to me to be correct except in regard to individuals of the town, such as members of one or several trades. However, regarding the town as a whole, it seems to me that they may stipulate without his approval, seeing that they can cancel his appointment.

Commentary. Who Should Rule?

Should political power be exercised by those who are most expert at ruling or by those who are most affected by the rulings? The question is posed less philosophically but more vividly in BT Bava Batra 9a by the example of some butchers who mutually agree to fine any fellow butcher in the town who slaughters an animal on another's designated day. They fine a fellow butcher who violates their agreement. Although the butchers are certainly more affected by the agreement than is Rava, the resident rabbi, and although they have given prior consent to the agreement, Rava overrules them. So much is his authority in such matters taken for granted that he offers no reply to the challenge of a colleague that "they [the butchers] may enforce their decree." Rav Papa simply says in Rava's defense, "He appropriately offered no reply."

Perhaps Rava refuses to reply because the butchers themselves did not seek his advice. But the text at least suggests that, had they come to him, he could have overruled them in a similarly authoritative fashion, without providing reasons for his decision. The implicit argument would be that the butchers lack the relevant knowledge to rule themselves. They are bound by a body of divinely ordained law whose dictates require expert interpretation. Offering them reasons would be a significant concession to the claim that they are capable of interpreting the law and therefore of ruling themselves. They could then offer rebuttals, and were the rebuttals reasonable, perhaps even more reasonable than the expert's reasoning, they would call into question the expert's presumed expertise. Instead of a series of arguments that might demonstrate the wisdom of Rava's decision to overrule the butchers' mutual agreement, Bava Batra simply declares that ordinary people may govern themselves only when experts allow them to do so. The presumption of expert rule seems to be at least as deeply rooted here as the presumption of democratic rule is in our own times—so much so that a mutual agreement among butchers that extends only over their own trade is considered a "unilateral" decree, unless a "prominent person," a learned man (women need not apply), is unavailable to rule.

Nonetheless, in the absence of such a person, the townspeople and tradesmen are authorized to make decisions and to rule among themselves. In Maimonides' view, this concession seems to be one of necessity, not morality. He seems to think that without a recognized sage, it isn't possible "to bring about excellence in the activities of [a town's] inhabitants." In the sage's absence, rule among mediocrities might as well be mutual. But this mutuality receives no positive recommendation. And why should it be recommended when the presumption is that excellence in ruling requires expert knowledge of a divinely revealed law that can be acquired only through a lifetime of intense study?

One reason for mutual rule might be that the townspeople considered as a collective self-governing group are in fact experts in ruling themselves because together they know their collective interests better than a resident rabbi, even a prominent resident rabbi. No one makes this argument (or, for that matter, the contrary argument), but Perfet strains to interpret Maimonides' explicit prohibition on the butchers' self-rule as permitting townspeople (but not tradesmen) to rule themselves. "Whatever the majority of the *kahal* and the leaders tending to public affairs enact is valid," he claims. Perfet's interpretation of Maimonides is unpersuasive as an interpretation, but the more democratic position that he takes on town rule has the useful effect of pushing his respondents to defend expert rule on more democratic grounds.

In response to Perfet, Shimon Duran offers the outlines of an argument for expert rule from consent, the very same basis that would seem to support the townspeople's self-rule. Why are the townspeople's ordinances not valid without the sanction of the "prominent person"? Not simply because he is wise or expert in the laws, but also because "they have already accepted him over themselves, [that is, accepted] that all their acts be subject to his approval." Acceptance by the people: this reply suggests that the expert's right to rule is not, and cannot be, taken for granted. The people could conceivably respond: We have not accepted your rule; it has been forced upon us. Or they could agree that they have indeed consented to the rule of this particular prominent person.

But, critics of consent will argue, can the townspeople really agree? If they have no alternative but to accept the rule of the resident rabbi, then the argument from consent is a fiction to support the rule of experts—though perhaps a convenient fiction in a time when incipiently democratic arguments have begun to surface. Meiri's comment on Bava Batra 8b suggests that consent to expert rule was not simply a fiction, and therefore that there is more to consent theory than its critics admit. Meiri argues that when and only when a wise man is a governing officer of the town are his views authoritative for the tradespeople. "Other scholars have no [standing] in such matters." Why? Surely they may be as expert as the governing officer whom the townspeople have appointed. But the fact is that they were not appointed by the townspeople. The townspeople did not consent to any wise person's rule or even to the wisest person's rule. They consented to be ruled by a particular governing officer, and presumably a majority could have decided otherwise. Or so Meiri's commentary suggests.

But Meiri does not stop with this credible defense of the medieval equivalent of judicial review. He takes another, far more radical step, going beyond the idea of binding consent to expert rule. Since the town appoints the wise man, the townspeople, presumably acting as a group, can "stipulate without his approval, since they can cancel his appointment." This claim seems to be the equivalent of saying that since the people appoint judges, who are authorized to engage in judicial review, and since they can cancel the judges' appointments, it follows that the people can rule without judicial approval. Judicial review over democratic decisions may or may not be a good way for a people with democratic commitments to govern themselves. But appointing experts and consenting to their review and then overruling them whenever a majority disagrees with their decisions is probably worse than doing without experts as governing officers altogether.

Let us give up the presumption that the people are incapable of ruling themselves. They may still think themselves better off being governed in some realms by expert authority. In that case, the giving of reasons for obeying or disobeying authoritative experts becomes critical to reaching a defensible decision as to who should rule, in what realms, with what degree of legitimacy. Yet reason giving is precisely what is missing in these discussions.

Amy Gutmann

Dispute over Separation of Civil and Religious Law

17. Ordinances of the Livorno Community with Letters and a Critical Circular by Jacob Sasportas

The ordinances are from the Livorno community archives, at the Ben Zvi Library in Jerusalem, pp. 110 and 55–58, respectively; the letters and the circular are from Isaiah Tishby, "Iggrot R. Ya'akov Sasportas Neged Parnase Livorno," *Kobez Al Jad* (Jerusalem) 4, no. 14 (1946), 148–52. We thank the library and its librarians for their permission and aid in photocopying these pages, and we thank Yosef Kaplan and Judith Preminger for assisting in the translation. Much of the information in the headnote comes from Alfredo S. Toaf, "The Controversy Between R. Sasportas and the Jewish Community in Leghorn (1681)," *Sefunot* 9 (1964; Hebrew), 169–91.

The Jewish community of Livorno, founded in 1593, was granted judicial autonomy by Ferdinand Medici, Grand Duke of Tuscany. The community was administered by the "Senhores del Mahamad," a council of "appointees" led by a committee of "the Dozen Senhores"—prominent and powerful individuals. Every Jew had the right to request judgment by Torah law, although legal findings by rabbinical scholars were, formally at least, only advisory. In reality, many matters were judged under non-talmudic laws and procedures. Drawing upon the accepted rule that "the custom of the merchants" sometimes supplants talmudic law (in fixing, for instance, the mode of concluding a sale), the committee acted to define a wide range of issues that would be excluded altogether from din torah. *This gave rise to opposition, led by Rabbi Jacob Sasportas, who had come to Livorno in 1676. Sasportas lived in the city for only a short period and subsequently led the campaign by correspondence from Marseilles and Amsterdam. We reproduce here two documents from the Livorno community archive:*

a. Ordinance LXIX from 1670, which sets procedural limits to access to din torah

b. Excerpts from the subsequent ordinance (unnumbered and undated), which excludes many matters from din torah *and was the cause for Sasportas's campaign*

Finally, we print excerpts from two letters written by Sasportas to the hakhamim *in Livorno and from his critical circular, written in 1681. The several passages are combined to present the main line of Sasportas's critique.*

Ordinance LXIX

The 23d of March 1670

The Senhores do Mahamad, having seen and experienced the obstructions that result . . . when one of the parties evil-mindedly demands *din torah* after the arguments have already been presented in commercial disputes; and having convened in consultation with the Dozen Senhores, describing to them these obstructions; they have, to remedy this, ordained

That any litigant requesting *din torah* must demand this at the first or second session of the trial. If he fails to do this, it shall not be granted to him. . . . And they ordered that this ordinance be written in the ledger of the *kahal.*

An Unnumbered, Undated Ordinance

Having recognized that in the past, great altercations have repeatedly arisen in the court of the Senhores, the *parnasim,* in matters of jurisdiction, on account of the difference between our customs and Jewish law (on the one hand) and the civil law, municipal laws, trade regulations, and the special privileges granted to our nation by his [highness the Grand Duke] in his blessed estates (on the other hand), as a result of which the losing party seeks revision, causing additional, excessive expenses—in order to remove these obstacles and, as far as possible, produce a remedy; With the authority conceded to us by the law, and granted by our Sages, and the privileges given us by our Prince, to enact *takkanot* [*"tecanot"*], that is, to issue decrees [when] in competent quorum; [now] with the consensus of said quorum, the following *takkanot* are decided and ordained . . . , all with the purpose of protecting our nation, preventing discord, and alleviating the [situation of] the litigant parties. . . .

2. The *yeshivah* [assembly of talmudic scholars] shall not respond in writing, qua *yeshivah,* to any query [*she'elah*]', whether presented from outside or from within the city, in any financial matter, save with the consent of the Senhores, the *parnasim.*

3. Considering that many suits and disputes that pertain to civil and commercial [matters] are delayed, causing great expenses, because the parties at various points demand judgment strictly by the *din,* without regard for commercial practice or for the customs of the city or the state, whose decisions and ordinances do not always conform strictly to the *din;* and believing that this disparity might cause unjust rulings with respect to transactions whose principles were formed civilly and commercially—in order to remove these obstacles as well as others, it is determined, ordained, and declared that:

Each and every transaction declared hereby to pertain to the jurisdiction of the Senhores, the *parnasim,* or their agents . . . shall adhere to commercial custom or the regulations of the marketplace, to which we assent and approve as if they were expressly decided in *din torah,* without need for any further grounds. They must be carried out, confirmed, and [followed in the] rulings of the Senhores del Ma'amad. . . .

It is also declared and ordained that [regarding] all cases, suits, and disputes that pertain to divine or spiritual law [as] enumerated below and similar [matters], the *parnasim* . . . , arbiters and empowered judges alike, shall be required—even without the parties so demanding—to decide and rule according to Jewish laws and customs. They are therefore permitted to refer these cases to Senhores *hakhamim* as they choose, so that they shall render their opinion and the ruling shall then be promulgated by the Senhores del Mahamad, judges, or arbiters.

Issues pertaining to din torah

marriage contracts (in accordance with the enactments)
beliefs, *gittin* [writs of divorce]

entitlements [to ritual roles] (in accordance with the enactments)
kashrut [propriety], *mashkantot* [mortgages], [and] usury
spiritual matters pertaining to divine law, wills, donations

Issues pertaining to the Senhores del Mahamad

commerce over sea and land
buying and selling of merchandise, jewels
pledges, liens — on land or sea
insurance, securities, deeds and commercial contracts
brokering and provisioning, finances, deposits
loans . . .
confidences and bankruptcy
companies, compromises
[family] preferences in [financial] shares

Letters and a Critical Circular by Jacob Sasportas

[Letter from Marseilles]

My own eyes have witnessed the outlandish decrees like a malig-
nant scab, which were enacted by those who cast off the yoke of the kingdom
of heaven. In an attempt at apology, they wrote to the men of the *ma'amad*
[in Amsterdam], claiming that—having observed the procrastination in *din
torah*—they enacted that all monetary cases will be judged as they see fit by
the custom of the merchants, except for donations, bequests, *ketubot* [mar-
riage contracts] and *gittin*. And even if the litigants agree to be judged according to *din torah,* they will be refused.

Woe to the ears that hear this and the eyes that see this! For of what
use is this apology? Rather, . . . their sin has become an extreme crime and
a rebellion, since both reason and the law[26] stand in opposition to them.
Who has seen or heard the like of this, namely, that if both parties accept
upon themselves two laypersons as judges, this is not binding? [Surely this
would not be accepted] by human reason, nor by any of the legal systems of

26. The Hebrew word here is *dat,* which may refer particularly to religious law.

428   The Good Men of the Town

the nations, even the king's law! Should not the priestly woman be treated as well as the innkeeper,[27] the mistress as well as the maidservant? Is divine law to be considered inferior to lay law, and the reasoning of Torah scholars incapable of distinguishing between what [should be] determined by human reason and judged according to the custom of the merchants and what is [properly] determined by divine law? . . . [Instead,] they [the Livorno leaders] employ the false claim that, having observed the procrastination that occurs in [obtaining] a ruling from the *hakhamim,* they have wisely devised their [own] enactment. But it is exactly the opposite! On the contrary, in judgment by laypersons we observe procrastination. [Even in] a simple judgment, where the law is straightforward and the case [itself] . . . should not involve a great time period . . . , days and years pass, expenses accumulate, and litigants multiply. As for a case that confounds them, they explore it through investigations . . . that follow the [literal] meaning of words rather than their sense. They turn light into darkness and darkness into light. They produce nothing in good order, yet attribute defects to that which is well ordered! . . .

[Letter from Amsterdam]

If they argue that they judge according to the custom of the merchants, and "the custom of the merchants is Torah," then there was no need for their proclamation, whose language annuls *din torah!* . . . In any case, the custom of the merchants is Torah only for issues relating to acquisitions, but in regard to laws concerning pledges, credit, and the requirement of taking an oath . . . the custom of the merchants [has no authority]. However, the complete truth is that their aspiration and desire is to cast away . . . and dismiss anything that bespeaks the honor of the *hakhamim,* to deprive them of all authority and lower them to the dust to be trampled upon by the laity. In this way they [seek to] cast off the kingdom of heaven. . . .

[Critical Circular from Amsterdam]

Indeed, the original rule was diametrically opposite: if one party, at the outset, requested *din torah,* the other would perforce have to comply.

27. A mishnaic idiom (Yevamot 16:7) commonly employed to demand that holy persons or institutions be accorded at least as much reverence as that accorded to their mundane counterparts.

[Now], however, the people's masters, who wield the whip, have reversed the rule. It is true that, even initially, judgment by the *hakhamim* was vulnerable, dependent on the will and whim of the *parnasim,* who could inscrutably confirm the judgment or annul it. Still, this did not constitute such a flagrant disgrace as this new abuse does, for the former was implicit, whereas the latter is explicit. . . .

If the [enactment] had been endorsed by the *kahal,* in accordance with accepted practice, I would have kept silent, so as not to insult their honor. They [the Livorno leaders], however, seized power for themselves through their wealth and might, finding favor by transferring silver. When a seat becomes vacant, they obtain from the lord of the land writs of appointment to a place among the Twelve—whether [they are] worthy or unworthy. Money reigns supreme, the deficient [man] gains an appointment and is deemed a[n appropriate] "replacement." Virtually all of them are thus [appointed].

. . . They revoked the initial enactment without the consent of the whole people or a majority thereof. [Such consent would be required] not just for this outlandish decree—which destroys [entire] worlds by canceling the *din torah* upon which the world stands—but even in matters involving advantage to one and disadvantage to another. [Indeed], according to most *poskim,* even matters of making a fence require endorsement by the *kahal.* Certainly this enactment should be utterly ignored. . .

Even if they claim that the *kahal*'s representatives joined in this rebellion and went along with them, they are not empowered to act against our holy Torah. . . . Let no one suggest . . . that God's people might erect an *asherah* [28] or a statue . . . , for upright people of Israel are not suspected of such deeds.

---

28. An allusion to Deut. 16:21–22, and to the midrashic comment: "Whoever appoints an unworthy judge—it is as though he has planted an *asherah* [a tree connected to idolatrous practices]" (BT Sanhedrin 7b).

NINE The Gentile State

Introduction

Legitimacy of Non-Jewish Authority

Modern Disputes: Civil and Religious Law

Introduction

Exile and diaspora forced the Jews to confront a new and unprecedented political issue: the legitimacy of non-Jewish kings, states, and laws. We have already seen how questions of legitimacy were discussed when the authority of Jewish institutions or particular Jewish claimants—kings, priests, prophets, rabbis—was in dispute. Arguments were historical, textual, and practical, but they were shaped and ordered by a religious understanding, and they were incorporated within a legal system that had its ultimate source in divine revelation. In a formal sense, non-Jewish legitimacy was treated in the same way. Jeremiah's injunction to the Babylonian exiles to "seek the peace of the city to which I have exiled you and pray to the Lord in its behalf; for in the peace thereof you shall have peace" (29:7) provided simultaneously a divine command, a biblical precedent, and a practical argument for recognizing and accepting gentile authority. The argument was incorporated into Jewish law by the early Babylonian *amora* Shmu'el, who ruled that "the law of the kingdom is law," *dina de-malkhuta dina.* Later rabbis made this a legal maxim, thus providing a halakhic reason for obeying non-halakhic laws—and for acknowledging the legitimacy, not only the power, of non-Jewish rulers.

But this formal recognition of the king's law was thus far with-

out substantive legal or moral grounds. Jeremiah's reason was merely prudential, and Shmu'el, who gives no reason at all for his ruling, may well
have had nothing else in mind. Certainly it was a common view of exilic
Jews that their submission to gentile rulers, the political quietism urged by
Jeremiah, was nothing more than a pragmatic recognition of brute force.
Everyday submission concealed both anger and resentment—and hope for a
future messianic overturn. But that was never the whole story. Submission
also gave rise to what might be called a theory of submission. For maxims
like Shmu'el's are not by themselves either intellectually satisfying or finally
persuasive; they don't answer the inevitable questions. Why is the *dina de-
malkhuta,* the law of the kingdom, law? What do the terms of the maxim
mean? Is every "law" equally legitimate? How far does the maxim extend?
If Jeremiah's reasons are accepted, are there any limits on peace seeking and
accommodation? *Dina de-malkhuta* might differ from, even contradict, the
Torah of Moses and the rulings of the Rabbis: was it *dina*—law—even then?
How can the authority of the king be reconciled with the authority of the
one and only King?

Responding to these questions, Jewish judges, sages, and philosophers produced arguments about legitimacy that were essentially secular in
character. The limits of gentile authority were fixed, of course, by whatever was taken to be central and crucial in *halakhah,* but obedience within
those limits was justified, and disobedience permitted, for reasons internal
to the sphere of the "kingdom." And the reasons canvassed in Jewish legal
writings were essentially the same as those canvassed in non-Jewish political
theory. Indeed, *dina de-malkhuta* made political theorists out of writers who
(Maimonides being virtually the only exception) had little idea of and were
hardly attracted to the theoretical enterprise. Divine right, popular consent,
customary usage, feudal land law—all these play a part in rabbinic responsa
and legal commentaries. We provide a range of examples, most of them from
Ashkenaz, from the eleventh to the thirteenth centuries, when the public
law of the *kahal* was first debated.

Consent is the doctrine most likely to be invoked; of all the available doctrines, it was, as we have seen, the one most familiar to Jewish writers,
the one that resonated most with their own understanding of how law—
even divine law, all the more so human law—became obligatory. (Recall
the arguments about the covenant in C1 and about the "good men" in C8.)

But this deep justification dealt only with authority in general—the gentile kingdom, the king, and the king's or the kingdom's law; particular royal enactments don't seem to have required consent. Before the rabbis were prepared to call them binding, they did, however, have to be at least minimally just. Or, in a striking anticipation of modern arguments, it had to be possible to claim that they had been tacitly accepted or to imagine some sort of hypothetical consent—which is to say that had they been asked, reasonable human beings would have accepted the enactments. One or the other of these possibilities seems to be implied by the second of Hayyim Or Zaru'a's two responsa excerpted below, though the argument is made in a more traditional idiom.

Minimal justice was all that most Jewish writers required, or, perhaps better, all that they expected, of non-Jewish rulers. This meant two things. First, the content of the laws had to be made explicit (the amount of the required taxes, say, known in advance). Second, the application of the laws had to be universal (the same taxes collected from all the king's subjects). Law, in other words, could not be either arbitrary or discriminatory. In fact, Jewish writers typically believed that these requirements were analytic to the concept of law: arbitrary and discriminatory enactments or practices were not law at all, hence not covered by the maxim *dina de-malkhuta dina*. The practical distinction is between taxation and robbery; it is elaborated most systematically, as usual, by Maimonides.

Taxation is the standard example not only because it was the most common practical issue but also because it suggested the range of issues to which the maxim was meant to apply. The economic life of the diaspora communities was legitimately regulated by non-Jewish authorities, but not the religious life. Exactly how and exactly where this line should be drawn were questions of ongoing dispute. This is the form in which Jews debated what was called in the non-Jewish world the relations of church and state. The problem is anticipated, though hardly dealt with, in the biblical account of King Jehoshaphat's courts: "See, Amariah the chief priest is over you in all matters concerning the Lord, and Zebadiah . . . is the commander of the house of Judah in all matters concerning the king" (2 Chron. 19:11).

When the rabbis came to map the two jurisdictions, they adopted a more practical terminology: they distinguished between *mamona,* civil and economic matters, where *dina de-malkhuta* was legitimately dominant even over Torah law, and *isura,* literally, "forbidden," that is, religious matters, where the Torah could not be superseded. We may read this as a more or less straightforward distinction between secular and religious regulation, *mamona* representing but not necessarily exhausting the secular interest. Jews were to accommodate themselves (when they had no choice) to gentile rule in the secular realm, but in the religious realm accommodation was impossible; they were to resist, if necessary, even to the point of martyrdom.

Whatever its difficulties, this distinction was easier to draw when Jews lived within their own semiautonomous communities (though even there it was sometimes contentious, as when the authority of the "good men" vis-à-vis the rabbis was being worked out). But the rise of the modern state, and the emancipation of the Jews within it, brought an enormous expansion of the "king's matters" and of the secular interest, far beyond anything the old categories could accommodate. Eighteenth- and nineteenth-century rabbis, for example, disagreed fiercely over the obligatory character of military service: was this a question of *mamona* because time, like money, could legitimately be taxed, or of *isura* because soldiers often were unable to observe religious prohibitions? Similar debates arose over civil marriage and divorce, for marriage was at once a religiously sanctioned union and (because of dowries and inheritances) an economic contract. But even rabbis who held that the whole of marriage law, the financial aspects included, were *isura* had to find a way to acknowledge the legitimacy of secular authority: the responsum of Akiva Eiger suggests both the difficulties and the inevitable resolution. Reform rabbis like Samuel Holdheim (but he was one of the most radical) were ready for a more wholehearted embrace of the secular state; they pushed *dina de-malkhuta* far beyond its medieval limits.

Once these matters were broached and various doctrines elaborated, it was inevitable that someone would ask whether Shmu'el's maxim also applied to Israelite kings and to a Jewish state. Might a self-governing community of Jews find in *dina de-malkhuta dina* a principle of legitimation for non-halakhic law? Most Jewish writers were uncomfortable with the idea, for it suggested a division within the Jewish community much sharper than any that had been recognized in biblical or talmudic times (both Amariah and Zebadiah, priest and commander, most of them would have said, were bound by the *halakhah*). But the idea was plausible enough, if not in the case of a Davidic king, the future messiah, then in the case of any other Jewish ruler. Just as Gerondi found in the biblical idea of kingship an opening to explore the meaning of politics (see €3, §16), so other writers might find in the exilic acknowledgment of gentile law an opening to explore the meaning of Jewish as well as gentile secularism. In fact, there wasn't much eagerness for exploration—not, at least, until the emergence of a Jewish state in 1948. Writers within the tradition were likely to regard Shmu'el's maxim as an involuntary and prudential concession, to be rescinded as soon as possible, while writers outside the tradition regarded it as largely superfluous, since they had already conceded virtually everything to state authority. In fact, however, this Babylonian Shmu'el, with regard to non-Jewish kings, like the biblical Samuel with regard to Jewish kings, began an important and not yet finished argument about religion and the state. We return to it in the next chapter.

Legitimacy of Non-Jewish Authority

Dina de-Malkhuta Dina

1. BT Bava Kama 113a–b

This talmudic discussion introduces the principle "the law of the kingdom is law" (dina de-malkhuta dina). Paradoxically, the starting point for the discussion is a statement that places tax collecting on a par with robbery. This may reflect the ambiguity of the Rabbinic stance vis-à-vis the practical power of gentile rulers. The Rabbis then labor to define the parameters of legitimate taxfarming and government takings.

"[In the face of demands by] those who threaten to kill or to confiscate, or by tax collectors, it is permissible to vow that one's crop is *terumah* [the priests' portion] or the king's property, even though it is neither *terumah* nor the king's property."[1]

---

1. This is a citation from Mishnah Nedarim 3:4.

"[O]r by tax collectors"—but did not Shmu'el say, "The law of the kingdom is law"? Said Rav Hinnena b. Kahana, citing Shmu'el: This [permission to lie] refers to [the case of] a tax collector who is subject to no limit [i.e., one who is granted license to collect as much as he can]. Rabbi Yannai's school says: This refers to a tax collector acting on his own [*Rashi:* One not appointed by the king].[2]

. . . To return to Shmu'el's statement, "The law of the kingdom is law." Said Rava: This can be proven from the fact that [state officials] cut down palm trees to build bridges, and we cross upon them.[3] Abaye said to him: But perhaps that is because the [trees'] owners forsake them! He answered: If the law of the kingdom were not law, why should they forsake them? [*Tosafot:* They ought rather to sue anyone who crosses!]

But do the officials not [in fact] deviate from the king's decree? For the king decrees, "Go forth and cut [trees] from all groves," whereas they go and cut from one grove!—The king's representative is like the king, and he is not required to exert himself. It is [the tree owners] who caused their own loss, for they ought to have collected [money] from all [the] owners and made payment [for timber from one location]. . . .

Said Rava: One townsman may be made answerable on account of another. This applies only to the land tax or poll tax of the current year, but [not to that of] the past year, [because] once the king has been satisfied, it is past.

Divine Right Argument

2. Anonymous Gaonite Responsum, *Responsa Geonica* (Assaf) 13

Simha Assaf, *Responsa Geonica* (Jerusalem: Mekize Nirdamim, 1942; Hebrew), sec. 13, p. 75.

The divine right argument of this Gaonic text derives its special flavor from its prooftext (Neh. 9:37). In the Bible, this is a passage of lamentation; it concludes a grim account

---

2. A third answer, proposed by Rav Ashi, identifies the tax collector as a non-Jew; this gives rise to a discussion about the wrongfulness of robbing a non-Jew. We take up this issue in €16.

3. Rava's point is that unless state takings are considered legitimate it would be wrong to use bridges constructed by the government from privately owned trees.

of Persian rule with the line *"and we are in great distress."* Yet, the Gaon implies, what God has willed is normative, even if he willed it *"on account of our sins."*

. . . This is the import of Shmu'el's dictum [*dina de-malkhuta dina*]: that just as God established the rule of the kingdoms in His world, He also subjected people's property to the rule [of these kingdoms] according to their will. [This applies] even to Israel, as written: "[On account of our sins, [the Land of Israel] yields its abundant crops to kings whom you have set over us]. They rule over our bodies and our beasts as they please" (Neh. 9:37).

The next five selections trace the development of arguments concerning dina de-malkhuta dina *within one school of thought, that of the tosafists of the twelfth and thirteenth centuries, whose starting point here (as is often the case) is Rashi's commentary to the Talmud. Rashi's grandson Rashbam studied with his grandfather, and Selection 4 is from his commentary on tractate Bava Batra, portions of which were used to complete the commentary that Rashi left unfinished at his death in 1105. Rashbam's younger brother, Jacob Tam (§5), was too young to study with Rashi, but he was the central figure of the school. Eli'ezer b. Samuel of Metz was Tam's student and one of the teachers of "Avi ha-Ezri" (Eli'ezer b. Yoel Halevi), who in turn taught Isaac Or Zaru'a, named for his magnum opus (from which we take §6); Hayyim Or Zaru'a (§7) was Isaac's son. We end with a selection from Meir of Rothenburg (§8), the leading figure of the tosafist school in the thirteenth century.*

Validity of Gentile Civil Law
3. Rashi, BT Gittin 9b

Talmud: All legal documents made in non-Jewish courts, even if their signatories are non-Jews, are valid, except writs of divorce.

Rashi: "Are valid": Even though the parties are Jews, because the law of the kingdom is law. "Except writs of divorce": [Non-Jews] are not [deemed effective agents for] severing [a *halakhic* marriage], because they are not party to [halakhic] matrimonial law. Noahides were, however, commanded to institute justice [4] [therefore all other legal transactions are valid].

Argument from Consent

4. Samuel b. Meir (Rashbam), BT Bava Batra 54b, s.v. *veha-amar*

All taxes, rates, and rules of kings' law commonly established in their kingdoms are law, for all subjects of a kingdom willingly accept the king's laws and statutes. Therefore they are perfectly valid law. . . .

Enlisting the Court's Power to Expropriate

5. Jacob b. Meir Tam, *Responsa of the Tosafists* 12

Responsa of the Tosaphists, edited by Irving A. Agus (New York: Talpioth, Yeshiva University, 1954; Hebrew), responsum 12.

Dina de-malkhuta dina applies only to gentiles, but Israelite kings and the kings of David's House are subject to judgment, as set forth in tractate Sanhedrin (℃3, §§7–8); they may not steal, that is to say, [take private property] wrongfully. Even according to those who hold that "whatever is mentioned in the section about the king is the king's prerogative" (BT Sanhedrin 20b [℃3, §9]), nothing further may be implied beyond the items explicitly mentioned—[namely:] "He will seize your choice fields, vineyards, and olive groves and give them to his courtiers" (1 Sam. 8:14), [i.e.,] to those who wage his wars. But he may not take them for himself to increase his wealth or to make himself a vegetable garden.[5] . . .

Dina de-malkhuta dina applies, however, even to wrongful acts, [such as] cutting down palm trees. This is wrongful and refers only [i.e. is permitted only] to gentile kings.

4. The seven Noahide commandments are discussed in ℃16.
5. Alluding to the story of King Ahab's seizure of Nabot's vineyard, ℃5, §4.

. . . [Still,] Shmu'el himself. who formulated [the principle] *dina de-malkhuta dina,* qualified it, [excluding] "a tax collector who is subject to no limit," . . . thus implying that there are restrictions on *dina de-malkhuta.* For example, a tax collector subject to no limit [is excluded] even though the king appointed him, as in the case at hand. This is because *dina de-malkhuta dina* applies only to governmental [*malkhut*] functions, such as taxing within a limit, [constructing] bridges, [etc.].

The principle is this: Not any legal innovation introduced by any king is law, but rather only the law of the kingdom [*malkhuta*] as practiced by their ancients. For [our] sages have nullified property [rights] to accord with the practice of the kingdom, just as they nullified [property rights] . . . on account of *tikkun olam* and the ways of peace [*darkhei shalom*].

Feudal Argument

6. Isaac Or Zaru'a, *Or Zaru'a,* Bava Kama 447

Our Rabbi "Avi ha-Ezri," of blessed memory, wrote: "There are those who maintain that *dina de-malkhuta dina* applies only to land, while others say that it applies to other financial matters as well"—he did not decide [between them]. And Rabbi Eli'ezer b. Samuel, of blessed memory, of Metz, commenting on BT tractate Nedarim (28a), wrote: "My teacher says that *dina de-malkhuta dina* applies only when the king decrees equally for all his subjects, but if he issues special [decrees] for one province, his law is not law." . . .

Regarding the case of a king of Israel, we do not say his law is law. Thus we read in tractate Sanhedrin, "The section about the king was only pronounced in order to scare them" (20b [C3, §9])—whatever is mentioned there is [in fact] forbidden to him. Even according to the opinion that "whatever is mentioned in the section about the king is the king's prerogative," this is limited to the items mentioned.

And it is my opinion that [the gentile king's] law is law only in regard to land and legal matters dependent upon land—for example, where he pronounces that no person may pass through his land without paying the tariffs. . . . Similarly the poll tax, where he pronounces, "No one may reside in my land unless he pays a certain sum." This is the reason that his laws are law: because the land is his and no one has permission to pass through it except in accordance with his command. But if he levies a tax on a kingdom that is not his, which he conquered abroad, . . . or upon a person who has no interest in [the king's] land, the king has no business robbing him.

The law of Israelite kings, however, is not law, because the Land of Israel was given to each and every Israelite, and it is not the king's. But in the case of the other nations, it is their law that the entire land belongs to the king. The same applies in a case where all the commoners stipulate that a man may benefit from their land only in accordance with their rules—their law is law.

The point of Shmu'el's teaching is that the entire land is the king's. Accordingly, we read in BT Bava Kama: "They cut down palm trees to build bridges" (113b)—since the trees and the land belong to [the king].

Hypothetical Consent

7. Hayyim Or Zaru'a, *Responsa* 80, 206

(80) One member of the *kahal* was granted a separate tax arrangement by the official. I responded as follows:

If they did not hear of this [arrangement] directly from the ruler, but only from the official, it is void. . . . If they heard the order directly from the ruler, [then] if this was after the collective levy—even if prior to the individual distribution of the tax burden—it seems that [the member of the *kahal*] is already obligated [to the *kahal*], because it is the custom of all the communities [*kehillot*] that if an individual leaves town after hearing of a tax decree, he must [still] participate in payment with the *kahal*. . . .

When the king decrees the tax, declaring, "Give me such and such," from that moment on, every individual is obligated to give a certain share of his property. And if afterwards the king wants to make alterations, subtracting from one and adding to the other, this is not "the law of the kingdom." As Rashbam, of blessed memory, explained: "[It is because] all subjects of the kingdom willingly accept the king's laws and statutes [that] they are perfectly valid law." [The subjects] did not, however, accept that [the king] should determine the distribution of the tax, but rather that each individual should give according to his means, because this has been his [the king's] practice and that of his predecessors throughout time. And if he now wishes to say, "Take from this person such and such, or completely exempt him [from the tax]"—this is not law. . . . Furthermore, it seems to me that even if this individual did not ask the king for a separate arrangement, but rather the king did this [on his own], even before decreeing the [collective] tax, saying, "X shall give me a certain sum, and you [the community] shall give me a certain sum," thereby preferentially reducing the burden of this individual—for if he had participated with the community as he originally would have, his share of the burden would have been greater—the king has no authority to grant a separate arrangement: for this is not the law of the kingdom. The subjects accepted upon themselves the laws of the king . . . only in accordance with his practice and that of his predecessors. But if he [the king] wishes to alter [the practice] and treat individuals separately, and it is clear that he does this only in order to change the distribution while the total sum of the tax remains the same—he does not have this authority, for this is not the law of the kingdom. . . .

(206) . . . People commonly hold that any property that has not been brought into the kingdom is not taxable, because [it] has not been subjected to the king's rule . . . and that therefore an individual newly arriving in the kingdom may offer the king [thus]: "I will pay you a specific sum and be exempt from paying taxes with the community." It seems, however, that this is wrong. For the law of the kingdom is that all those who live in a town shall together share the burden of the taxes. Now [this new person] wishes to alter this law, which would increase the burden of the others. For if he would [be taxed] along with them, his share would be greater than that which he would now give the king. The subjects of his kingdom did not accept this upon themselves, because this is not a fair law, and is not law. . . .

Criticizing the King's Edicts

8. Meir b. Baruch of Rothenburg (Maharam), *Responsa* (Prague) 943

Responsa of Maharam b. Baruch, edited by M. Bloch (Budapest, 1895; Hebrew).

This responsum mirrors the precarious relationship between many Jewish communities and the local gentile rulers. It is possibly related to an early attempt by Emperor Rudolph I to bring the Jewish communities under the direct control of the crown. Eventually, the emperor tried to confiscate Jewish property by claiming absolute subjection of person and property to his will. Rothenburg led the opposition to the emperor's attempts; the culminating act of resistance was a mass exodus to Italy (1286). Captured in Lombardy and handed over to the emperor, he refused to be ransomed and ultimately died in prison.

The case here involves a more specific issue. Its background is the talmudic permission to make one member of the community answerable on account of taxes due from another (see §1); the second member must then reimburse the payer. May the king, then, rightly confiscate money from the kahal *in order to enforce any claims he has against an individual Jew?*

As to your question [regarding a case in which] the king contrived against the *kahal* to make them answerable for Re'uven, who had failed to appear by an appointed date, and took money from them.

Since Re'uven affirms that they had not made guarantees for him, he need not reimburse them. For it is unlawful to seize [the property of] one Jew on account of another, as is stated in the Jerusalem Talmud . . . and in our [Babylonian] Talmud as well: "One townsman may be made answerable on account of another. This applies only to the land tax or poll tax of the current year" etc. (§1). The reason is that [with respect to the tax], the law of the kingdom is law in such matters; but to make one answerable on account of another for a [totally] different matter—that is not "law of the kingdom" but rather "robbery of the kingdom" and is not lawful.

Tacit Consent

9. Maimonides, MT Laws of Robbery and Lost Property 5:9–18

The Code of Maimonides, Book Eleven: The Book of Torts, trans. H Klein, Yale Judaica Series (Yale University Press, 1954), pp. 108–10.

Here, as often in the Mishneh Torah, *Maimonides' codification of talmudic law involves not only the weaving together of diverse strands but also an effort to define central terms and concepts. In the course of his treatment of* dina de-malkhuta, *Maimonides addresses the questions What counts as "law"? and Who counts as "king"?*

9. When persons are presumed to be robbers and all their property is presumably obtained by robbery, because they are robbers by occupation, such as tax collectors and bandits, it is forbidden to benefit from them since the presumption is that their occupation involves robbery. . . .

10. If tax collectors take away [some]one's coat and give him another instead, or if they take away his ass and give him another instead, he may keep the one given him because this is regarded as a transaction of sale and the presumption is that the owner has already abandoned hope of recovery. Nor does the recipient know for certain that it is property obtained by robbery. But if he is a conscientiously pious person who is particularly strict with himself, he should return it to its original owner.

11. This rule, namely that a tax collector is regarded as a brigand, applies only if the collector is a heathen, or is self-appointed, or was appointed by the king but is not required to collect a fixed amount[6] and may take what he likes and leave what he likes. But if the king fixes a tax of, say, a third or a quarter [of a *denar*], or another fixed sum, and appoints to collect it on his behalf an Israelite known to be a trustworthy person who would not add to what was ordered by the king, this collector is not presumed to be a robber, for the king's decree has the force of law. Moreover, if one avoids paying such a tax, he is a transgressor, for he steals the king's property, whether the king be a heathen or an Israelite.

12. The same rule applies to cases where a king imposes as a tax on

6. Maimonides' phrase here is the same as that translated above (§1) as "subject to no limit."

the citizenry, or on each person individually, a fixed annual amount, or imposes a fixed amount on each field, or decrees that if one breaks a specified law, he shall forfeit all his property to the palace, or decrees that if one is found in a field at harvest time, he shall pay the tax due on it whether he is the owner of the field or not, or makes some similar regulation. None of these cases is deemed robbery, nor is an Israelite who collects these levies on behalf of the king presumed to be a thief; rather he may well be a worthy person, provided only that he does not add, alter, or take anything for himself.

13. Similarly, if a king becomes angry with one of his servants or ministers among his subjects and confiscates his field or his courtyard, this is not deemed robbery and one is permitted to benefit from it. If one buys it from the king, he becomes its owner and the original owner cannot take it away from him. For the law of all kings permits them to confiscate all the property of those ministers with whom they are displeased, and the king has therefore canceled the owner's original right to it, so that the courtyard or field in question is regarded as ownerless, and if one buys it from the king, he becomes its lawful owner. But if a king takes the courtyard or field of one of the citizens, contrary to the laws he has promulgated, he is deemed a robber, and the original owner may recover it from anyone who buys it from the king.

14. The general rule is: any law promulgated by the king to apply to everyone and not to one person alone is not deemed robbery. But whatever he takes from one particular person only, not in accordance with a law known to everyone but [rather] by doing violence to this person, is deemed robbery. Consequently, when the king's treasurers or officers sell fields for the fixed tax due on such fields, their sale is valid. But the tax imposed on each individual may not be collected except from the person himself, and so, if they sell his field to recover the poll tax, it is not a legal sale unless the king's law permits such action.

15. If the king's law provides that if one fails to pay the tax on his field the field shall belong to whoever pays the tax, and the owner of the field runs away because of the tax, and another comes and pays the king the tax due on it and consumes its produce, this is not deemed robbery; rather, he may consume the produce and pay the tax until the owner returns. For, as we have explained, the king's law is binding.

16. Similarly, if a king decrees that whoever pays the fixed tax due from any individual may compel the one delinquent to work for him, and then an Israelite comes and pays the tax due from some other impoverished Israelite, he may make him work more than would be usual, for the king's law is binding. But he must not make him work like a slave.

17. If a king cuts down trees belonging to a private individual and makes them into a bridge, it may be crossed. Similarly, if he demolishes houses and makes from the material a road or a wall, one is permitted to benefit from it. The same rule applies in all similar cases, for the king's law is binding.

18. All the above rules apply only to a king whose coins circulate in the localities concerned, for then the inhabitants of the country have accepted him and definitely regard him as their master and themselves as his servants. But if his coins do not circulate in the localities in question, he is regarded as a robber who uses force, and as a troop of armed bandits, whose laws are not binding. Moreover, such a king and all his servants are deemed robbers in every respect.

Limiting the Scope of Dina de-Malkhuta
10. Menachem Meiri, *Bet ha-Behirah,* Bava Kama 113b

Meiri links the discussion of dina de-malkhuta *to the talmudic discussion about the legitimate powers of the monarchy within the Israelite polity. In both settings the monarchy is, therefore, subject to the same restrictions, determined by the proper scope of sovereignty (contrast Jacob Tam's responsum, §5, written about two centuries earlier).*

All we have said concerning the law of the kingdom—that it is a perfectly valid law—pertains to laws the king has legislated either for his [own] benefit or for the benefit of his estate. Even if he legislates that each individual should give him a certain amount each year, or that he should take a certain portion of everyone's trade, or imposes a toll upon anyone who does a particular thing, or anything of the like, even though it goes against our laws, it is law. It is forbidden to steal from [the king] or transgress his ordinances. For this is proper for him qua sovereign, [exactly as in] the statement about Israelite kings, "Whatever is mentioned in the section about the king is the king's prerogative" (BT Sanhedrin 20b [ℭ3, §9]). Accordingly, [Shmu'el] said "the law of the kingdom [*malkhuta*]"—that is, the laws proper for him *qua* sovereign [*malkhut*]—and did not say "the law of the king."

But anything that he introduces arbitrarily, and the laws that the nations maintain according to the teachings of their books or the laws [*nomoi*] of their ancient sages, which oppose our laws, are not included. For if they were, all the laws of Israel would be canceled. Thus, in the earlier generations, when the gentiles would adjudicate [suits about] money on the evidence of one witness, [if there arose a case where] a gentile sued an Israelite and called another Israelite as a witness, he [the witness] was forbidden to testify unless he knew that another Israelite could join him [as a second witness], for otherwise he would be causing [suits about] money to be adjudicated on the evidence of one witness. [But] if he knew another could join him, he had to testify and would be blessed. . . .

Commentary. Consent Theory in *Dina de-Malkhuta Dina*

Doctrines of consent play a central role in many theories of justice. Their appeal derives from the moral intuitions that they introduce to political discourse. Beginning with the basic intuition that individuals cannot be held responsible unless they are free to choose, the argument often proceeds to the strong claim that individuals are only obligated when they have freely chosen. Applying these arguments to the polity leads us to imagine individual citizens prior to the existing distribution of power as capable of consenting or not. We are invited to examine critically the existing distribution of power and determine political and social arrangements to which the citizens could or would or did actually agree.

Given the long history of ideas of consent in the Jewish tradition (see ℭ1), it is not surprising to find medieval scholars invoking versions of it in their deliberations concerning political legitimacy. Nor were such arguments foreign to the medieval context; medieval Christian thinkers regularly appealed to the maxim that "what touches all should be decided by all." Against the background of a feudal or authoritarian monarchy, consent theory had an obvious radical potential. To what degree were rabbis aware of the critical possibilities of consent theory?

The general form of the argument is put forward by Rashbam. All customary royal enactments, he argues, are legally binding, "for all the subjects of a kingdom willingly accept the king's laws and statutes." It is this voluntary acceptance of the king's law that renders it "perfectly valid law."

Consider first the conclusion of Rashbam's argument, that the king's law is "perfectly valid." This may be addressed to Jews who feel that they have no part at all in a gentile polity; although they must concede to its dictates, they need not acknowledge its authority. Rashbam is arguing against this position, claiming that the gentile kingdom is entirely legitimate. But what is the reach of this claim? Does the king's law directly bind Jews as subjects of the kingdom, the maxim *dina de-malkhuta dina* merely recognizing this obligation? Or are Jewish residents only indirectly subjects of the king, bound only by the halakhic maxim that constitutes their obligation? These questions touch upon a fundamental concern: Can Jewish law concede dual citizenship to its subjects?

Rashbam remains unclear about this point. His grandfather Rashi had already held that contracts made in heathen courts are valid because "the Noahides were commanded to institute justice"—which implies an essential continuity between Jewish and non-Jewish law. Rashi circumvents the problem of duality, but at the price of breaking down the barrier between these two legal systems.

Let us return to the first part of Rashbam's statement. Since he provides for no explicit consensual process, he defends an essentially passive consent (in contrast, for example, to later social contract theory, which seeks active popular consent in creating government). Kings simply assume power. Their legitimacy is determined ex post facto, over the course of time, by the degree to which people actually abide by their laws.

But given the tacit character of consent, can it serve as a constraint upon the king? Are there any moral or political limits to his rule that we can know prior to an actual rebellion?

Rashbam hints at a possible constraint when he refers to "commonly established" royal enactments. Rabbis consulted on a specific enactment would be required, he suggests, to determine whether it is in fact a customary law of the kingdom. But this is a very limited solution. Laws are made all the time, and Rashbam does not tell us how long we would have to wait to validate new legislation.

Maimonides too presents a theory of tacit consent, but addresses the question of constraint in a different way. He provides an objective criterion for assessing consent; the maxim applies "only to a king whose coins circulate in the localities concerned, for then the inhabitants of the country have accepted him." But what exactly does the inhabitants' recognition indicate? One may argue that dealing in the king's money reflects acceptance of his authority to mint coins. But is it perhaps only a recognition of his economic reliability by participants in the market? The connection with political legitimacy remains unclear.

According to Maimonides, consent indicates that the inhabitants of the country "regard [the king] as their master and themselves as his servants." Consent is given to the fundamental relation of ruling and being ruled. Rashbam's theory of consent restricted it to those laws which have been accepted (i.e., become customary). Maimonides' formulation lacks this restriction, because consent is given to monarchic activity as such, including the right to promulgate law.

The critical limit on the king's power is that his laws must live up to the minimal analytic requirements of all law: "Any law promulgated by the king to apply to everyone and not to one person alone is not deemed robbery." But how much of a limit is this? In *The Guide of the Perplexed,* Maimonides defines justice as "the granting to everyone who has a right to something, that which he has a right to, and giving to every being that which corresponds to his merits" (3:53). The expectations of *dina de-malkhuta* clearly fall short of this.

Maimonides probably believed that there exists a wide middle ground between just and unjust law, between law and robbery, where distinctions may be drawn between the minimum formal qualities of law and the substantive demands of justice. Perhaps he was simply looking for a practical criterion by which a community in exile could distinguish between legitimate and illegitimate decrees.

Both Rashbam and Maimonides could be interpreted as presuming that political rule is legitimate unless proven otherwise by a clear act of rejection. The main difference between them lies in the scope of laws validated by this presumption. Rashbam holds a restrictive view that only established customs reflect the presumption, while Maimonides allows for new laws as well. Hayyim Or Zaru'a takes a stronger position concerning consent by turning it into an active measure of valid legislation in the rabbi's hand.

Contrary to Isaac Or Zaru'a, who provided a feudal justification for *dina de-malkhuta dina,* basing it on land ownership, his son Hayyim Or Zaru'a follows Rashbam. He does not, however, restrict "customary" to past rulings. In the course of his argument he moves from a contrast between old and new enactments to a contrast between different kinds of law. There is the accepted (customary) law, and there is unjust law: "The law of the kingdom [for example] is that all those who live together in a city will share the burden of the taxes." Hence this king, who wishes to lessen the burden of a favored individual at the expense of the others is acting unjustly. "The subjects . . . did not accept this upon themselves, because this is not a fair law, *and is not law.*"

Hayyim Or Zaru'a is not engaged in a historical description; rather he reconstructs the kinds of decrees that would hypothetically be consented to: this is how he determines the validity of the new decree. An unjust and unfair law, he argues, would not have received the consent of the subjects and is therefore not binding. Consent is no longer assumed but made into a critical tool that can determine the validity of specific laws issued by the king.

Hypothetical consent of this sort involves several assumptions:

1. The consent of the subjects is a necessary component of political legitimacy.

2. Particular enactments of the ruler should be judged according to a principle of consent.

3. In the absence of actual consent it is possible to construct a hypothetical argument about what the subjects would indeed agree to.

4. Substantive assumptions about what constitutes a fair or just law can guide us in constructing this hypothetical argument.

Isolating these assumptions enables us to locate particular concerns that remain unattended—especially the relations among the several assumptions. Maimonides, as we have already seen, accepted a version of the first assumption concerning the general need for consent, but gave a different criterion for judging particular royal enactments. But even if we accept a strong version of assumption 2, we can still ask whether hypothetical consent can take the place of actual consent. What is the basis for attributing this hypothetical construction to the living subjects of the kingdom? Hayyim Or Zaru'a suggests that a priori substantive claims of justice inform us of the subjects' will, but if he is already equipped with substantive claims concerning what is just and fair, isn't talk about consent redundant?

Examining these different positions, we are led to conclude that although consent theory has radical implications, the results of its deployment by medieval rabbis were not far-reaching. Rather, consent operates alongside the assumed legitimacy of the king as a limiting principle upon his power. It is true that Rashbam sounds as though he is taking a stronger position, but he remains silent about actual practice. Hayyim Or Zaru'a provides an example of the scrutiny of practice by a creative *posek,* but the full possibilities of consent probably cannot be explored within the framework of a legal ruling. The power of responsa literature relative to talmudic novellae is that its point of departure is reality rather than the text. But a more developed political theory is needed to take this reality into account within a framework that allows for sustained critical arguments.

Menachem Lorberbaum

Modern Disputes: Civil and Religious Law

Civil and Religious Divorce—I

11. Ishmael of Modena, "The Answers to the Twelve Questions of the Emperor Napoleon," 2

Judah Rosenthal, "The Answers to the Twelve Questions of the Emperor Napoleon by R. Ishmael of Modena, Italy" (Hebrew), *Talpioth* 4, nos. 3–4 (1949), 569–72.

On May 30, 1806, Napoleon decreed that a Jewish assembly be convened to help deter-
mine the status of Jews as citizens of France. He posed twelve questions to the Jewish
dignitaries. One of the senior invitees, Rabbi Ishmael of Modena, was unable to at-
tend and responded in writing. The text below is part of his response to the second
question: "Without pronunciation of divorce by a gentile [i.e., civil] court, is a get
valid, even though this would violate the French codes?" Rabbi Ishmael strives to offer
a justification, in terms of Jewish divorce law, for the implicit requirement of a civil
divorce.

According to our legal principles, we are obliged to bow our heads to all laws of the kingdom of our sovereign. For Shmu'el said, *dina de-malkhuta dina.* And all the *poskim* have written that as long as the laws of the kingdom do not contradict Torah law, we must abide by them. Therefore, concerning the issue at hand, we are obligated to follow the laws of the kingdom just as we do the laws of our holy Torah, for they are both together good.

Hence, where Torah law requires a man to divorce his wife, he must first go to the gentile courts and do whatever is necessary to obtain a civil divorce, and then go to the local rabbi and give a *get* to his wife in accordance with our holy Torah. [The case is the same] in marriage, where the bride and groom go together to the gentile court to inform them that they are getting married, committing themselves to the powerful bond of matrimony, and the court registers it in an official document which ratifies the marriage in accordance with civil law. They then proceed to perform a marriage cere-mony according to the Torah's marriage laws with *kiddushin* and a *huppah* and all the benedictions. We must follow the same procedure regarding divorce and comply with both civil law and Torah law.

And because we must abide by the kingdom's laws, providing they do not contradict Torah law, any rational person will see that if one gives a *get* to his wife before he obtains a civil divorce from the gentile court ac-cording to the laws of the kingdom, the *get* is void. [Since] the *get* does not completely sever the relationship between them, it is clearly void. As stated repeatedly in the Talmud, explicating the verse "Let him write her a bill of di-vorce" (Deut. 24:1), "An instrument divorcing [literally, "severing between"] them" (BT Gittin 21b): unless it completely severs, it is not a *get*. The Talmud states (Gittin 83b) that if a man stipulates, "Here is your *get*, on condition that you never drink wine"—this is not considered "severing," for this *get* does not sever the relationship between them. . . . How much more so is this *get* [without civil registration] void! For even though he gave her the *get*, the woman cannot marry another on account of the king's decree.

Civil and Religious Divorce—II
12. Akiva Eiger, *Responsa* (second edition) 83

Napoleon sought to establish the exclusivity of civil procedures for marriage and divorce. In central Europe, however, although marriage and divorce were made subject to the state's jurisdiction, they were executed through the religious ceremonies of each denomination, followed by civil registration—hence, paradoxically, the same talmudic rule that served as the legal solution in Selection 11 is now the source of the difficulty: If no get *is valid unless it effects complete severance, does not the requirement of civil recognition undermine the* halakhic *soundness of Jewish divorces?*

To my esteemed friend the great rabbi and head of the court of the holy community of Berlin, Rabbi Meir Weil, may his light shine.

Your honor's letter arrived today. [You write] of your misgivings concerning your local custom that whenever the *bet din* arranges a divorce, they inform the couple as follows: "Know that concerning laws of *mamona*, e.g., conjugal inheritance and similar matters, all is as before [i.e., your relationship still holds], until such time as a civil divorce is obtained from the non-Jewish courts."

This is certainly a very difficult matter. The following can however be argued.

Many authorities maintain that *dina de-malkhuta dina* does not apply to the laws of inheritance. . . . Maimonides' position concerning laws of inheritance is that they are "not subject to change, and a condition qualifying [an inheritance] is not valid" (MT Laws of Inheritance 6:1), because Scripture says, "And it shall be unto the children of Israel a statute of judgment [*hok*]" (Num. 27:11), making this an immutable law. Matters of inheritance are therefore not included in the rule that stipulations [against the law] concerning monetary matters [*mamon*] are valid. Accordingly, we must say that although *dina de-malkhuta dina* applies to *mamon,* this is because [*mamon*] may be relinquished. An individual has the power to stipulate and forgo his right. But in this case, which Scripture deemed a *hok,* in no way can it be changed, and it is like a matter of *isura.*

Even according to those authorities who maintain that *dina de-malkhuta dina* applies to all matters [including inheritance], it seems to me that the king's law [*hok ha-melekh*] certainly does not declare that a *get* does not sever [the relationship] for matters of inheritance, [so that] the former wife is [still] his kin and the former husband her inheritor. Rather, it is as if the king's law says, "This nonrelated man, X, who is not her husband, shall inherit from her."

Concerning the fact that finalizing the *get* depends upon the civil divorce, [this is not an impediment to the severance of the relationship because] it is like a separate stipulation to the effect that, so long as the civil divorce is not obtained, he will have the right to her inheritance. But it does not mean that he is still her husband for these matters; rather, it is the case that by the laws of the kingdom he retains rights in his wife's property akin to those of a husband . . . even though he is not related to her.

This will be legally sufficient to establish that although he generally retains his right by virtue of the law of the kingdom [*dina de-malkhuta*], this does not disqualify the divorce. But to state explicitly to the couple "Know that concerning all matters of *mamona* the rights are as before" is like stipulating [that a *get* severs the relationship] "except for inheritance" [and that invalidates the *get*] . . . unless he explicitly says: "I give this *get* without any qualification and it severs [the relationship] for all matters, and I have no rights in your property as a husband. It is only due to the law of the king that even though you are no longer my wife for any matter, I am granted the rights a husband has concerning his wife's property." [He must say this,] or the *bet din* should thoroughly explain it to them. And the matter still needs reflection.

Expanding the Scope of Dina de-Malkhuta

13. Samuel Holdheim, *On the Autonomy of the Rabbis*

Über die Autonomie der Rabbinen und das Princip der jüdischen Ehe (Schwerin, 1843), pp. 5–
19, 56–62. This text was translated by Almuth Lessing. We are also grateful to Andreas
Gotzmann, Yosef Schwartz, and Michael Silber for sharing their expertise with us.

*Holdheim, a leading figure of the second generation of Reform rabbis in Germany,
strongly supported abolishing the legal autonomy of the Jewish community as a necessary condition for full civil integration. In his view, the Rabbinic dictum* dina de-
malkhuta dina *was a first step, albeit a partial one, on the way to this integration. Full
emancipation would require a sharp distinction between the civil and religious aspects
of Judaism. As an exemplary instance of this distinction, Holdheim cites the Prussian
edict of 1812, which retained the religious ceremonies for Jewish weddings and divorces
but excluded marriage entirely from rabbinic jurisdiction.*

(pp. 5–19) Subjecting private relations among Jews to the law and the protection of the state is the first, but also the most effective, step toward their
civil and spiritual emancipation. This alone has transformed the Oriental into
a native European, the Jew who partly obeyed a law [he regarded as] foreign while carrying all the burdens of his own [law] into a native [citizen],
a full participant in the state's highest good, its legal system. This closer affiliation of the Jews with the state and its law necessarily produced a greater
engagement with the state's well-being [and] a more lively interest in the
further development of legislation fitting this enlightened century. Similarly
the feeling, the pleasant feeling, of greater community with the other citizens was necessarily created. It is of considerable importance here that Jews
will no longer have to fear defamation by a modern Haman [saying,] "There
is a certain people, scattered and dispersed among the other peoples in all the
provinces of your realm, whose laws are different from those of any other
people and who do not obey the king's laws; and it is not in Your Majesty's
interest to tolerate them" (Esther 3:8). . . .

The cancellation of the autonomy of the Jews was very fruitful not
only in moral terms, but also for their intellectual education. As soon as the
Jewish subject and his private legal affairs came under state law, knowledge

thereof became more essential than before, partly as duty and partly as necessity. The advantage in personally getting to know relevant legal clauses [which now govern his] close and frequent relations with his fellow believers is obvious enough. The necessity of knowing the local language now seemed more urgent than ever. [A parent,] out of his own lack of knowledge, often had to be helped by his children. Not quite an exclusively moral incentive, but still a powerful impulse was now given for educating the young beyond the narrow borders of Hebrew and religious[7] instruction. Trivial occasions often cause important results, and this was also the case here. The closer connection to state law facilitated a closer connection with the state and its language—and then its customs and all its intellectual and moral goods.

. . . The present legal condition of the Jews, [namely,] that their relations among themselves are subject to civil law, . . . is a true blessing and is crucial for any other civil and religious progress. For this we cannot be thankful enough to the wise state authorities. It has also been recognized as such by every Israelite who is aware of his position in civil society; and there probably is hardly anyone who would like to exchange this legal status for the former autonomy of the rabbis. Also, all state authorities, who have a humane attitude toward legislation concerning the Jews and the improvement of their civil status, have begun the work of refinement and improvement with the cancellation of Jewish autonomy and jurisdiction. In all of Germany, where the legal status of Jews has created a map with many nuances, I know of no land (except Altona, and the Jews there really are not to be envied for this privilege) where the autonomy of the rabbis is permitted by state law.

Although in most European states the rabbis' autonomy and jurisdiction, with all their consequences, have been canceled, many governments have felt the need to take into account denominational differences and religious considerations that might be closely connected with private law and [therefore to] establish certain special laws. . . . A need was felt to sacrifice consistency for [the sake of] higher considerations. Again, the Prussian edict of March 11, 1812, deserves to be mentioned here as exemplary, and the rigor

7. Our translation uses "religious" and "religion" for several different German terms which may be variously rendered as "religion," "confession," "faith," and so on.

with which it implements the higher principles of law, attests to the high position occupied by legislation in that period of general intellectual flowering. It states (section 20): "Private law concerning the Jews is to be dealt with according to the same laws that apply to other Prussian citizens." [And further] (section 21): "Exceptions are hereby made concerning such procedures and transactions, which are necessarily tied to special legal clauses and forms due to differences in religious concepts and worship." . . . There is no legal state that is excepted from this rule. Only procedures and transactions, but not legal states [in themselves], can possibly be tied to special legal clauses and forms because of the difference in religious concepts and forms. And here we recognize the spirit of the legislator, who separates religion from law as two different spheres. The cancellation of Jewish autonomy and jurisdiction thus proclaims a true principle: Religion deals with belief and customs; the state deals with the law. Religion has to watch over the former, and the state over the latter. This also [means] that the law cannot be subject to religion. . . .

(pp. 56–62) The Jew lives with the Jews of his fatherland in a double, religious and civil, community; [and] with the Christians of his fatherland and with the Jews of another fatherland in only one—with the former only in a civil and with the latter only in a religious community. The religious community is based on the identity of religious convictions, that is, the perceptions of God and the revelation of God's will to mankind. However deeply divided in space and by secular and worldly concerns, [its members] feel deeply united by a shared, lofty view of the divine. The civil community is based on the common interests of the state in which both [Jews and Christians] live, on their participation in its well-being and destiny. One may separate Jews in their private relations among themselves from general state law and subject them to a foreign law; one may exclude them from the higher laws of the fatherland, from owning property, from lower and higher civil service, and so on; one may even exempt them from the duty of defending their fatherland. But one will never succeed in making them completely indifferent to the interests of the country in which they live, nor in totally excluding them from community with their brother-citizens as long as this country remains the base of their worldly existence, i.e., as long as they are not expelled [from it]. If their fatherland is destroyed by war, Jews have to fear no less for their lives and property; they thus have an interest in peace. If a bad year destroys the harvest, Jews are truly not the last ones to experience general misery; they thus have a lively interest in their fatherland's prosperity. And is there any fortune or misfortune in their fatherland whose repercussions the Jews would not feel? In these cases the reality of their sympathies with their brother-citizens and the illusion of civil community with foreign Jews become apparent. Jews will always feel the common civil misfortune of their brother-citizens, not the undisturbed good fortune of their brother-believers abroad. If in such cases Jews receive help from foreign fellow believers, this is not owing to the civil but only to the religious community. Whatever similarity in civil law or other national relations Jews from different countries may share, this definitely does not bind them closer than they already are by virtue of their religious ties. Equally they are not distanced from each other by even one hair's breadth once they have acknowledged just how purely unreal all [their] national relations are. In modern times this truth has often been confirmed. Jews in countries where they are recognized as equal citizens [still] feel related—through the sole bond of religion—to Jews in countries where they continue to be oppressed by the chains of the Middle Ages. [This is true] no less than [it was] during the times when the bonds of religious community were strengthened by common oppression.

That the rabbinic age after the destruction of the Jewish state endowed the religious community with so many national elements can be explained [in part] by the fact that the Jews were not lucky enough, after the destruction, to find a fatherland that would accept and include them. . . . The Palestinian Jews of the Roman empire were regarded and treated by the Romans as conquered and enslaved subjects, but their political institutions were left intact so long as they didn't endanger the state. After the destruction of the state, rabbinical Judaism could (except for minor interruptions caused by rebellions) develop more peacefully than before, with judicature an important part of it. The Babylonian [Jews] were also subjected in all worldly relations to the exilarch, and depended in all religious matters on the Palestinian [sages]. . . .

After the condition of the Jews improved under the protection of the Persian king Schabur (Saper), the teacher Shmu'el in Nahardea (having returned from Tiberias) implemented—in agreement with the Exilarch Mar Ukva—the following principle: that in [matters of] civil law, state law must be respected.[8] The Rabbis thus felt pressed to study Persian civil law and to align it with the Mishnah. This historical fact shows that no religious scruples prevented the rabbis of old from adopting the civil law of another country and that they surely would have done so earlier, and more radically, if the countries in which they lived had not stopped them by force and alienated them from the [common] interest. Thus it was not the Jews who wanted to create for themselves an artificial nationality after the destruction of their national existence, but the states [of the exile] that forced a kind of nationality upon them—separating them from the state organism as a distinct political corporation and forcing them into an unnatural and awkward position. We, who now very well recognize our position in the state, which is entirely compatible with our religious conscience, have to protest solemnly against every enforced nationality that is not the nationality of the fatherland. Judaism—apart from its arrangements for the ancient Jewish regime— has given no directions for any other regime and thus relates only to the religious aspects of man. . . . And since [Judaism] is of a divine, eternal, and absolute nature, it must be realizable under all conditions and circumstances, and [it must] guarantee the Israelites those higher goods of life which are promised [them] by their divine nature. Because it allows and has to allow the Israelite to live in different states, this also has to be morally possible for him—that is, his religion has to permit him without any exceptions to fulfill all civil obligations of the state, which are the moral conditions upon which he is accepted into the state. It is impossible to argue in religious terms for a nationality other than [that of] this state—consisting, for example, in a separate autonomy or something like that—since that would cancel whatever has already been permitted.

After what has been said so far, one can neither argue [in the name] of the obligation of the Jew toward Jewish law as such nor question the admissibility—according to Jewish religious or ritual law—of fulfilling civil obligations. Concerning law and its jurisdiction, as well as the civil obedience of the Jew in his fatherland, religion refrains from all special rules and obligates him only generally to justice, loyalty, and obedience.

8. Clearly, this is Holdheim's rendition of Shmu'el's dictum *dina de-malkhuta dina*.

Commentary. Judaism and the Secular State

Ishmael begins his response to Napoleon's query with an invocation of the familiar consensus that "as long as the laws of the kingdom do not contradict Torah law, we must abide by them." To Ishmael, evidently, no such contradiction exists. He is satisfied that "concerning the issue at hand," both the laws of the Torah and the laws of the kingdom are good (and presumably, therefore, consistent). Thus we are obligated to follow the laws of the kingdom.

What exactly is the "issue at hand?" That is hard to fix precisely, because Ishmael goes somewhat beyond the narrow confines of Napoleon's question. At the very least, the issue includes whether a kingdom can require civil marriage and divorce in addition to what is explicitly required by *halakhah,* and without which the halakhic regulations are insufficient to make a marriage or divorce valid. Since Ishmael finds no impediment to applying *dina de-malkhuta dina* to this issue, he concludes that if a kingdom requires a civil divorce before a rabbinic *get,* or requires civil registration before a Jewish wedding ceremony, these laws must be followed.

So the answer to Napoleon's specific question looks straightforward: In lands governed by French law, a *get* would be invalid without the prior civil divorce mandated by the French codes. But Ishmael seems to think that this conclusion doesn't follow as straightforwardly as it at first appears, for he goes on to provide further halakhic support for his view. According to *halakhah,* a *get* must completely sever the relationship between husband and wife. On account of the king's decree, however, without a civil divorce a married woman cannot marry another man. Thus a *get* without a civil divorce fails to satisfy the halakhic conditions for a *get* and is therefore void. To reach Ishmael's conclusion we need to attribute a twofold legal power to *dina de-malkhuta dina.* First, the maxim establishes that the king's law is binding; in addition, it licenses us to use this law as a premise in further halakhic reasoning. It is only because it can be used in the second way that Ishmael can arrive at his conclusion that a *get* is invalid in the circumstances Napoleon imagines.

Eiger utterly rejects Ishmael's conclusion that if the king's law requires a civil divorce, then any *get* that is not accompanied by such a divorce is invalid. He also rejects Ishmael's reasoning, insisting that "the king's law certainly does not declare that a *get* does not sever [the relationship]." What lies behind this dramatic difference?

It is hard to tell, because Eiger focuses on the issue of conjugal inheritance and gives us no inkling of whether he views a woman who has received a *get* without a civil divorce as halakhically free to marry another man. What we do know is this: Eiger has produced an ingenious way to accommodate the king's law without giving this law the power to change the halakhic conditions for a *get*. The king's law, he maintains, rather than keeping in force one aspect of the marriage—namely, inheritance (which would have the effect of invalidating the *get*)—simply brings into existence a new "inheritance bond" between two formerly married people. How far can Eiger's ingenuity be pushed? Can it provide a systematic way to accommodate the king's law without letting it penetrate into the heart of the *halakhah?* If so, then the difference between Ishmael and Eiger may be over whether *dina de-malkhuta dina* has the twofold power that, according to our interpretation, Ishmael attributes to it. This would have the ironic consequence that Eiger's solution is more far-reaching, though Ishmael's is, after a fashion, more radical.

In any case, the terms "far-reaching" and "radical" are relative, as the selection from Holdheim amply demonstrates. In his book *On the Autonomy of the Rabbis and the Basis of Jewish Marriage,* Holdheim, no less than Ishmael and Eiger, is concerned with the relationship between Jewish marriage (and divorce) and civil law. But his approach is breathtakingly different. He rejects outright what to Ishmael and Eiger must have seemed a self-evident axiom, that Judaism is a halakhic system. In its stead, Holdheim pronounces his own axiom: Judaism is a religion. (One is reminded of the nineteenth-century revolution in geometry engendered by giving up Euclid's axiom of parallels.)

Holdheim acknowledges that Judaism was once embodied in a legal system with an elaborate array of laws governing countless aspects of human relationships. But—and here he echoes Spinoza—by Scripture's own lights, these laws were meant to apply only in the specific political conditions of ancient Israel's national theocracy. Of course, he acknowledges that "the rabbinic age after the destruction of the Jewish state endowed the religious community with . . . many national elements," but this is to "be explained [in part] by the fact that the Jews were not lucky enough, after the destruction, to find a fatherland that would accept and include them." In an enlightened state like Holdheim's, the true nature of Judaism as a "religious community" "based on the identity of religious convictions" and embodying a "shared, lofty view of the divine" can emerge. So conceived, Judaism "relates only to the religious aspects of man . . . and is of a divine, eternal, and absolute nature." Even more specifically, it is constituted by its monotheistic vision of God and its ethics, as grasped by the "higher"—indeed, (to Holdheim) almost messianic—"consciousness" of Holdheim's age.

Holdheim's conception of Judaism enables him to know a priori that Jewish marriage and divorce are utterly subservient to civil law. Indeed, he knows a priori that there are *no* Jewish legal limits to what the secular state can demand of Jews as a price for their full participation in civil society. Were the state to deny Jews the right to circumcise, for example, Holdheim would have no religious reason—nor any (philosophically grounded) desire—to object, however much he might criticize the ban on the grounds of religious freedom. We can only imagine what counsel Ishmael or Eiger would offer in the face of such a legislative restriction. But, whatever it would be, it certainly could not emerge from an extension of the reasoning they so deftly employ to deal with civil marriage and divorce.

Holdheim's radical view of Judaism is helpful for the way it dramatizes the inevitable interplay between one's self-definition as a Jew and one's willingness to accommodate the modern secular state. As a proposed self-definition, Holdheim's view had little appeal in its own day. And it has none today, in an age of ethnic and national sensibility. No Jewish community that hopes to survive can offer up all its ceremonies and practices, or its national and ethnic character, on the altar of an allegedly enlightened secular state. That said, there is every bit as little appeal in forms of Jewish self-definition at the opposite extreme of Holdheim's religious universalism—ones, for example, whose strenuous particularism would limit Jewish authenticity to life in a Jewish state, be it secular or theocratic, or to a sectarian life utterly on the margins of a diaspora society.

Countless views inhabit the space between these extremes. Perhaps the most prominent and controversial endorses Jewish life in the diaspora (and presumably accepts *dina de-malkhuta*) while insisting that Israel, as a Jewish state, must be governed by a religious law whose authoritative interpretation is in the hands of a clerical establishment. Holdheim's conception of Judaism as a pure religion whose civil and, at least potentially, ceremonial legislation is a historical relic would render such a view nonsensical. This assessment is no doubt grounded in a flawed conception of Judaism. But fifty years of even the severely circumscribed "jurisdiction of the rabbis" in contemporary Israel, and the consequent mixture of religion and politics that has corrupted both, provides more than enough reason to share Holdheim's antipathy toward every manifestation of theocracy.

The willingness of committed Jews to accommodate the secular state (wherever its territory) depends on more than their Jewish self-definition. It depends as well on the political and legal shape of the state. America's constitutional guarantees of nonestablishment and free exercise of religion leave little room, given any reasonable mode of Jewish self-definition, for principled objection to American democracy. Perhaps the same cannot be said for French democracy, where a more stringent separation of church and state comes at the price of restricting free exercise in public places. But even if American democracy is immune from principled objection, accommodation will not always be easy.

Interpreting the free exercise clause of the American Constitution can be no less challenging than defining oneself as a Jew. The day may yet come when circumcision, because it seems barbaric to a majority of Supreme Court justices, is deemed no more worthy of protection by the First Amendment than polygamy is today. Civil disobedience may then become the Jewish order of the day.

Jonathan W. Malino

Introduction

Legal and Political Continuity

Religious Significance of the State

A Jewish and Democratic State

"A Jewish and Democratic State"

10. Laws of the State of Israel: Foundations of Law, and Basic Law: Human Dignity and Liberty

A Liberal Secular Position

11. Aharon Barak, "The Constitutional Revolution: Protected Basic Rights"

A National-Religious Position

12. Menachem Elon, "Constitution by Legislation: The Values of a Jewish and Democratic State in Light of the Basic Law: Human Dignity and Personal Freedom"

A Secular Interpretation of Jewish Values

13. Haim Cohn, "The Values of a Jewish and Democratic State: Examining the Basic Law: Human Dignity and Liberty"
Commentary. Joseph Raz, "Against the Idea of a Jewish State"
Commentary. Sanford Levinson, "A Multicultural Jewish State?"
Commentary. Yael Tamir, "A Jewish Democratic State"

Introduction

The creation of the state of Israel in 1948 was largely the work of secular nationalists. They aimed at a condition they called "normality," which is to say, a state and society "like all the nations." And they also claimed to address, in the only practical and effective way allowed in the modern world, "the needs of the hour." The Jews were driven by necessity to seek normality: that was the central argument of political Zionism. Zionist legitimacy, then, had a twofold foundation. It derived, first, from the specific crisis of diaspora Jewry in an age of nationalism and dictatorship; and it derived, second, from the standard contemporary doctrines of self-determination and "normal" sovereignty. Neither of these derivations was in any sense problematic for secular writers.

At the same time, the struggle for statehood and specifically for statehood in *eretz yisrael* inevitably generated a larger hope—not for normality but for the most abnormal of all conditions: redemption. This hope could take both secular and religious forms, drawing directly or indirectly on traditional discussions of messianic politics. We will take up these discussions in C29. But it is important to note here that contemporary understandings of the authority of the state of Israel are largely determined by the ideological-theological views of those writers who address the question. Does the state actually serve the needs of the hour in the same way that "normal" states do? Or does it have a larger purpose? And how are those needs best served or that purpose best expressed?

Secular writers begin with an affirmative answer to the first of these questions (which does not preclude an affirmative answer to the second) and then go on to fashion a state ideology in modern democratic and nationalist terms. Religious understandings of the state start from the same affirmation but move on differently, assimilating modern Israel's rulers and officials to earlier, non-messianic authorities, well known from Jewish history. These authorities are basically of three sorts, each of which has already been discussed in the preceding chapters: the non-Davidic kings of Israel, "the good men of the town," and the gentile rulers of the lands of the exile. Each of these was, as we have seen, religiously sanctioned but conceived in functional terms. They dealt with the "king's matters" (foreign affairs and criminal law) or with questions of *mamona* (civil and fiscal law)—which were subject to religious regulation in principle but were conceded in practice, at least some of the time, to secular authority. Or they dealt with problems of social order or with crises or emergencies that were acknowledged by some, though not all, writers to lie beyond religious control entirely. The kings and communal magistrates who, in theory or in fact, took charge of these routine but often critical matters provide three models for a restored Jewish state.

The strongest reassertion of the (non-Davidic) king-of-Israel model comes from Abraham Isaac Kook—somewhat surprisingly, perhaps, since he views the future state (he wrote before its establishment) in explicitly messianic terms. But he also had an acute sense of the mundane instrumentalities of religious aspiration, and he thought that the secular leaders of the *yishuv* (the Jewish population in Palestine before 1948) and of the Zionist movement, whatever their self-understanding and ideological intention, served to advance the long-term redemptive process—hence his choice of Israelite kings over exilic or gentile rulers as precedents for modern Zionism. Like those kings, the Zionists ruled or hoped to rule *in the land,* and they claimed to rule in the interests of the nation as a whole. Through the medium of the nation, Kook argued, they have become the legitimate and authoritative heirs of the kings of ancient Israel.

This appeal to the royal model is deeply troubling to Isaac Herzog, who sees in it the halakhic argument of Nissim Gerondi (Ran; see ₵3): that the king (and hence the prime minister) can act outside the laws of the Torah for the sake of social order (*tikkun olam*). Herzog represents a more conventional orthodox position; he disagrees with Gerondi in principle and shudders to think of such a "king" in power in a Jewish state. Unwilling to make messianic claims for this state and even more unwilling to relinquish the claims of *halakhah,* he seeks to establish a privileged position for Jewish law and for the rabbinic courts (though he already expects little more than a "small corner" in the new Israeli regime), and he emphatically rejects the idea that the "laws of the king" could possibly constitute (or, by analogy, justify) an independent legal system.

The arguments that start from the maxim *dina de-malkhuta dina* or that build on the experience of the "good men" have a similar form. They have secularizing implications (of exactly the sort that worried Herzog), which are resisted by religious writers, though with little hope of success. For these two models also suggest a realm of mundane concerns that is not, or not necessarily, or not entirely, governed by halakhic authority, within which Jewish lay leaders or gentile kings elaborate a second legal system. The rule of gentile kings may seem an odd model for a Jewish state (although the applicability of *dina de-malkhuta* to Israelite kings was discussed, as we have seen, in the Middle Ages). Certainly, secular Zionists would have preferred to be compared to the Hasmoneans, say, or even to medieval *berurim* rather than to rulers like Pedro II, Charles V, or Napoleon Bonaparte. But from a certain orthodox perspective, once it was clear that Israel would not be a halakhic state, *dina de-malkhuta* was probably the most satisfactory way of recognizing its legitimacy. Although that model seems symbolically unappealing, it was a legal device of great usefulness, for it gave the sanction of *halakhah* to the new state while preserving the autonomy of the halakhic system as a whole.

To reject all these models is to reject the state itself, which does not, after all, conform to the traditional religious belief that the restoration of Jewish statehood would be and could only be the (literal and direct) work of the messiah. The kingdom that he establishes will presumably replicate David's, but it won't require the legitimation of precedent: the messiah will bear, so to speak, God's own writ. On this view, there can't be an end to the exile, there can't be a truly Jewish state in *eretz yisrael* that isn't messianic; the existing state of Israel therefore represents a usurpation of divine authority; it has no *halakhic* legitimacy at all, not even the legitimacy that gentile states can claim. It is far worse than the gentile states, with which the Jews have made a lawful peace; it is a satanic creation, the work of heretics who oppose all the laws of the Torah. This latter view is represented here by Yerahmiel Domb (and in C29 by Yoel Teitelbaum); it is defended today by only a tiny minority of Jews in Israel and the diaspora, but it obviously has some resonance with traditional understandings of exile and redemption.

Even for those who work within one or another of the three models, there is plenty of room for different views of the Jewish state's authority and of the authority of Jewish law in the state. We include here two different religious arguments, the first from Kook, whose messianic hopes led him to grant religious value even to the secular politics of the Zionist pioneers, the second from Isaac Breuer, who could not imagine a Jewish community of any sort that was not governed by Torah law. The strongest secular position is taken by Yeshayahu Leibowitz: the Jewish state meets worldly needs exactly like all the gentile states, and its authority is of exactly the same kind. This is the inner logic of *dina de-malkhuta,* although Leibowitz invokes Hobbes rather than the rabbis and so denies any religious authorization of the state. The law of the Israeli *"malkhuta"* is law only because no other law can guarantee physical security, which is the state's first and most essential purpose. Religious purposes, by contrast, must be served elsewhere, beyond the reach of state officials.

But such a radical separation of state and religion, though it can be grounded in the tradition, is not common within it. David Ben-Gurion, who knew the tradition well, explains why this is the case and defends a certain sort of pluralism as a necessary substitute for separation. In the background of his argument, signaled by his use of the term "general will," lurks the Rousseauian idea of a single civil religion of patriotism and citizenship. Other nations have this kind of ideological unity, Ben-Gurion suggests; but as a result of the long Jewish experience of statelessness and exile it does not yet exist in the new state.

Among contemporary religious writers, there is considerable reluctance to concede that a Jewish state can really be like all the others. Shouldn't it enact and maintain at least some of the traditional religious prohibitions (as the kings of Israel and the "good men of the town" presumably did)? Shouldn't it recognize and enforce (some) rulings of the *bet din?* Or, alternatively, shouldn't it live up to the Deuteronomic and prophetic teachings about justice—as even secular Zionists hoped it would? And doesn't its legitimacy depend upon its readiness to do one or another of these things?

In the public life of the new state, these questions have been addressed most often and most interestingly by the judges of the Supreme Court. Working from "basic laws" (Israel's only constitutional, or semi-constitutional, documents) that assert both the Jewishness of the state and its democratic character, and that also legislate its commitment to principles of human "dignity," the judges have been forced to ask what these terms mean and how they relate to one another. With regard to the first of them, there is obviously a wide range of possibilities. Both prophetic and rabbinic Judaism are historical-cultural artifacts that can be disassembled, as it were, and adapted for contemporary use by judges variously committed to their authority. Two prominent religious jurists, Moshe Silberg and Menachem Elon, for example, have carved out of *halakhah* a body of law they call *mishpat ivri* (Hebrew law)—*halakhah* without its theological references or its ritual codes—and proposed that this secularized version of the Jewish legal tradition be incorporated, whenever opportunities arise, into Israeli civil and criminal law. They think of the sages and rabbis as their own legal predecessors. Haim Cohn would draw upon the whole of Jewish history, with as great an emphasis on biblical texts as on *halakhah* or *mishpat ivri,* and with a more selective eye in both cases. Traditional Jewish law can be a valuable source for Israeli jurisprudence, as long as one remembers that the former's grounding in divine authority is incompatible with the latter's commitment to democracy. Cohn thus provides a strategy of interpretation that results in an actual list of principles that are, he claims, both Jewish and democratic. Aharon Barak argues for a much greater independence from the tradition. For him, the idea of democracy provides a crucial criterion with which to confront biblical and rabbinic texts. Only those aspects of the Jewish tradition (but presumably also aspects of other religious and legal traditions) that pass the democratic test can be used in judicial decision making.

The authority of the state is as radically secular for Barak as it is for Leibowitz, although Barak is more Lockean than Hobbist in his argumentative style, relying on the consent of the citizens (not all of whom are Jewish) rather than on a generalized fear of external aggression or internal disorder as the foundation of his secularism. The religious significance of the state for some of its citizens is not, in his view, a subject for judicial reflection. Barak is a liberal committed not only to the separation of synagogue and state but also to the separation of theology and jurisprudence. His more traditionalist opponents in the legal community are not all that differently committed (since they presumably believe in their own authority, which derives from a secular state), but they insist that *halakhah* or the secularized *mishpat ivri* ought to be a more ready, or a more obligatory, reference for Israeli judges than Turkish or British or American law, all of which have figured in the Supreme Court's decisions. The disagreement, then, is about the legal culture of the new state: How large a presence should this specifically Jewish tradition have in the world of its lawyers and judges? And this question is likely to depend, as we have already said, on the answer to other questions: What does it mean to call Israel a Jewish state? Is a Jewish state "like the other [democratic] states"? Or does it have some larger purpose? It is worth noting again, however, that the three judges represented here, although they disagree about the authority of Jewish law, agree in practice that they, rather than the rabbis (who, sitting in their own religious courts, presumably have a different view of secular jurisdiction), will finally answer all these questions.

Because of the resonance of their answers with contemporary political theory, we have tripled our commentaries on the Israeli judges, concluding this first volume with three different arguments about the authority and legitimacy of a "Jewish and democratic state."

Legal and Political Continuity

"Laws of Kings" Express the Nation's Sovereignty

1. Abraham Isaac Kook, *Mishpat Cohen* 144

Mishpat Cohen (Jerusalem: Mossad Harav Kook, 1985; Hebrew), pp. 237–38.

In this responsum, written in the 1920s, Kook interprets the ongoing political signifi-
cance of the monarchic tradition for the modern nation-state. Evidently drawing on the
position of his teacher Naphtali Tzvi Judah Berlin (Netziv [C3, §15]), he suggests a
distinction between the specific institution of monarchy, on the one hand, and its basis
in national sovereignty, on the other. Reasserting Jewish political sovereignty does not
depend, then, upon restoration of the monarchy.

. . . All general matters affecting the nation, and any enactments [*tikkun*]
of temporary measures to make a fence against those who act unjustly—all
these are part of the laws of kings. In all such matters the king is authorized
to act as he sees fit, even when it does not pertain to his well-being or honor
but to the well-being and honor of Israel. As [Maimonides] wrote: "If a person kills another and there is no clear evidence . . . the king can, if the need
of the hour demands it, kill him in order to ensure the stability of the social
order [*le-takken ha-olam*] and to break the power of the wicked" (Laws of
Kings 3:10 [C3, §11]). The powers [granted by] the laws of kings thus extend
far beyond the scope of the king's [personal] honor or privileges. . . .

Furthermore, since the laws of kings extend to the general affairs
of the nation, it would seem that in the absence of a king the prerogatives
of these laws revert to the nation as a whole. In particular, it seems that any
ruler who arises[1] in Israel has the status of king with regard to certain of
the laws of kings, especially those that pertain to governing the nation.[2] . . .
Whoever governs the nation may exercise [the powers enumerated in] the
laws of kings, which [meet] all the nation's necessities, as required by the
[needs of the] hour and for social stability. . . .

This is supported by Maimonides' statement "The exilarchs of Baby-

1. The noun (lit., "judge") and verb together are taken from the biblical book of Judges, which
repeatedly tells of God "raising up" Israel's leaders.
2. Lit., "the Whole."

lon stand in the place of the king. They exercise authority over Israel everywhere, etc." (MT Laws of Sanhedrin 4:13). [This applies] a fortiori to the
leaders consented to by the nation while [the nation resides] in its own land
and [exercises] self-rule. Whoever is appointed to govern the people, on
whatever level, [has this authority. Admittedly,] those appointed primarily
to disseminate Torah, such as the descendants of Hillel who did not [hold a]
"scepter" but were [only] "legislators" (as is evident from BT Sanhedrin 5a),
do not stand in the place of the king, and have only the authority of a court.
But concerning those who were originally appointed to their positions for
the nation's general government, including its mundane aspects—like the
Hasmonean kings or the *nesi'im*—they are obviously at least the equals of the
exilarchs of Babylon. . . . When a ruler is appointed to govern the nation in
all its needs in regal fashion, with the consent of the people and the court,
he certainly stands in the place of the king. . . .

Israel as a Jewish State: Jewish Law
2. Isaac Halevi Herzog, "Toward a Jewish State"

Betzomet Hatorah Vehamedinah, edited by Y. Shaviv (Jerusalem: Tzomet, 1991; Hebrew), pp.
3–9.

Besides his rabbinic training, Herzog had general legal training, which made him unique
among leading rabbinic authorities, able to appreciate the intricacies of modern con-
stitutional law. In this essay, written in July 1948, two months after the declaration
of Israel's independence, Herzog asks whether the new state will maintain the his-
toric Jewish commitment to Torah—and to the Jewish legal tradition. In examining the
halakhic acceptability of the state's legal system he criticizes Nissim Gerondi's (Ran's)
constitutional theory (€3, §16).

The State of Israel has confronted us with difficult problems calling for investigation and clarification by Torah scholars. I was among the enthusiasts
for the idea of creating a Jewish state even though I knew that among the
great men of Torah, lovers of Israel, as I am, there were those who feared [its]
creation. They would have been satisfied with free immigration [to Pales-

tine]. But I had the clear and acute recognition that the latter would depend on the former: free immigration will not be realized in the absence of a sovereign state, besides which I had come to the conclusion that the State of Israel is a vital necessity not only for the salvation of hundreds of thousands of our brothers, remnants of the hellish [holocaust] in Europe, but also for the relief and deliverance of our brothers in the lands of Islam where religious zealotry reigns. The opinion had become firm in my mind that this is an urgent and inherent need of Judaism itself.

. . . If the state had been created even fifty years ago, there would also have been certain problems, but not of the dimensions and level of difficulty [we face today]. At that time, the majority of the people of Israel observed Torah and *mitzvot*. Today, to our great consternation, this is not the situation. The main problems . . . are:

> a. Securing the observance of our holy Shabbat at least in public. . . .
>
> b. Securing public *kashrut,* insofar as this is within the competence of the central government and municipal or local administrations.
>
> c. [Securing] Torah law.
>
> d. Securing marriage and divorce according to the law of Moses and Israel.

For the time being I will limit myself to the question of Torah law. Of course, it would not occur to a truly religious Jew that the Jewish State would abandon "the source of living waters"—our Holy Torah—"to dig wells" and [adopt the] laws of another people.[3] For this would be a terrible upheaval internally, and a horrific desecration of [God's] Name externally. It would be equivalent to divorcing, God forbid, the Torah of Israel. We had imagined that immediately after the declaration of the state, those responsible for these matters would consult with the Torah authority in the land in order to determine what to do according to the Law. Although it is common practice in conquered lands that the formerly existing law is left to continue temporarily so as not to disrupt commercial life, . . . this applies

---

3. Following Jer. 2:13 and the traditional representation of the Torah as water.

[only] to the gentiles, who have no law that is part of their religion. But this is not the case with us. It is a very grave matter to sustain even briefly a law that does not accord with the Torah—not to mention an alien law imposed by the [British] Mandate government, even apart from the substance of the existing law, which is a patchwork of British [and] Turkish law.

Even if the existing law were . . . wonderful, it would still be unacceptable from a national, and especially a religious, point of view. This is gentile law! National pride should have barred the path of such wholesale assimilation. The sages have already vociferously denounced adjudication in front of gentile courts even if they rule according to our laws.[4] . . . In my opinion this is a thousand times worse than any Jewish individual, individuals, or community going to gentile courts—that the people of Israel in their own land rule in accordance with foreign laws! "Is there no God in Israel?" (2 Kings 1:3).

. . . In the days when many imagined the idea of founding an independent and sovereign [*malkhutit*] Jewish state to be a vision unrealizable before the coming of our righteous messiah, I aspired to create a powerful movement among us whose purpose would be to influence the future legislative council to include in the constitution a basic clause stipulating that the law of the state will be Torah law. Knowing well that . . . if we follow the rule of the [Torah] as it is written, we will encounter grave difficulties concerning [halakhically] disqualified judges and witnesses—so too concerning the law itself, e.g., women witnesses[5]—I began seeking solutions by way of general consent.[6] And while I was still busy investigating and contriving [to construct solutions], the great events occurred [and overtook me], and with the help of God the state of Israel became established as an actual reality. And now when I see the indifference [toward the law], my hands are weakened and my mind is skeptical. For even if we should find solutions and arrangements, and receive the consent of most of the great men of Torah, would we still be able to gain a majority for including that basic clause in the constitution? And if not, why all this work?

4. See Maimonides, MT Laws of Sanhedrin 26:7; we take up these issues in €24.
5. See the discussion of gender roles in €13.
6. Presumably, Herzog refers to halakhic innovation by means of communal consent.

. . . But this is a fundamental point. Religious Judaism should exert all possible efforts that under all circumstances, there should remain in the Jewish state a corner for our holy Torah, i.e., that the right be given to any Jew sued before a secular court in property [disputes] to say: I wish to appear in a *bet din* of the rabbinate. A time will be clearly established for his appearance before the court, after which the court will be empowered to hear the case in his absence . . . [and] there will be a supreme court of appeals[7] of the chief rabbinate in Jerusalem, the holy city. . . . So too . . . we will demand that there be no [way of] appealing the rulings of the rabbinic *bet din* before the state supreme court, the great majority of whose members would, with all due respect, be complete laymen with regard to erudition in Hoshen Mishpat.

. . . With respect to my efforts to solve the problem of bringing Torah law into correspondence with a democratic Jewish state, I anticipate puzzlement: Why all this effort? One of the later medieval authorities, Rabbenu Nissim [Gerondi] of blessed memory, has already provided the solution. In his *Derashot,* sermon 11, Ran presumes that there are two kinds of law in Israel, the law of Torah and the law of the state, or royal law [in a monarchy]. According to the laws of the Torah, a criminal would rarely be punished and a murderer would easily go free. There exist similar difficulties with regard to monetary laws because of the laws of testimony. [So] royal law serves to complete Torah law.

I do not know if the author of the *Derashot* was indeed Rabbenu Nissim Gerondi of blessed memory, one of the greatest of our rabbis . . . after the sealing of the Talmud.[8] In any case, he was one of the great [scholars] of the [past] generations. Accepting his opinion certainly would greatly relieve us. But I see grave difficulties in [doing so]. After the [1937 report of the] Peel Commission, when we were faced by the partition plan and the founding of a Jewish State, I corresponded with the great Rabbi Hayyim Ozer Grodzinsky, suggesting ways to overcome the difficulties confronting

---

7. Herzog is here conceding a point to his secular opponents. Traditionally the halakhic legal hierarchy does not include a court of appeals. In the great debate concerning the status of halakhic courts in the 1920s, the British mandate forced legal reform by linking the formation of officially recognized halakhic courts to the founding of a court of appeals.

8. The attribution is no longer doubted.

us in the matter of public appointments of gentiles who are not party to the covenant. The law of the Torah stipulates that all appointments shall be only of "one from among thy brethren" (Deut. 17:15). In his reply he alluded to the above-mentioned sermon of Ran of blessed memory.

[Following are excerpts from Rabbi Grodzinsky's letter:[9] In regard to furnishing a constitution for the rule of Torah in the Hebrew state: regarding [civil] law, this is truly a difficult matter in need of much reflection. My initial thought is perhaps to arrange matters so that the judges in cases of property disputes [*mamonot*] between two Israelites would be rabbis whose summons and judgment would be recognized by law. Cases between a Jew and a non-Jew would be adjudicated according to the general [non-Jewish] law. Concerning theft and robbery and criminal law in general, it appears to follow from the responsum [*sic*] of Ran that there was a separate [system of] royal law alongside the *bet din* administering Torah law. For it would truly impair the order of the polity [*takkanat ha-medinah*] if a thief would be exempted [from further punishment] by paying double.[10] . . . You must necessarily concede that in such cases one must enact ordinances for the polity [*takkanot ha-medinah*]. This is like the matter of a court that "may impose flagellation and [other] punishments [not warranted by the Torah]" (BT Sanhedrin 46a).[11]]

I replied that in my view this is not an acceptable solution, but received no further response. I maintain my position that it is inconceivable that the laws of the Torah should allow for two parallel authorities—like the courts of law and the courts of equity, the latter stemming from the authority of royal law, that operated in the past in England. . . . According to [Torah law], there is no basis for this assumption of the double or parallel jurisdiction of two authorities. All we have is the ruling that the king executes a murderer even when he is released by the *bet din*. This is not to say that in all cases where a court releases an intentional murderer for technical reasons, the king executes him. . . . The situation according to the *halakhah* is

9. From Issac Herzog, *Constitution and Law in a Jewish State According to the Halacha*, edited by I. Warhaftig (Jerusalem: Mossad Harav Kook, 1989; Hebrew), p. 31 n. 19.
10. The biblical penalty for theft: "But if what he stole . . . is found alive in his possession, he shall pay double" (Exod. 22:3).
11. On the emergency powers of the courts, see ₡23.

as follows: Capital cases are within the authority and competence of the Sanhedrin (i.e., a small Sanhedrin, a *bet din* of twenty-three ordained [judges]).
But even after the Sanhedrin released the defendant, the king had the authority to execute him for the sake of *tikkun olam* and the need of the hour.
But this does not mean that the monarchy in Israel had its own distinct constitution not in accordance with the Torah, following which kings would
judge, appoint judges, and accept testimony. It only means that in the case of
a murderer the matter is given over to the discretion of the king, according
to his assessment of the moral condition of the people. And if there are very
few murderers and there is no danger that their acquittal will "cause murderers to multiply" (Mishnah Makkot 1:10), the king should make no use of
this [power] at all.

Dina de-Malkhuta, "the Good Men of the Town," and the State

3. Ovadyah Haddayah, "Does *Dina de-Malkhuta Dina* Apply to the State
of Israel?"

Hatorah Vehamedinah, 9 (1958), 36–44.

Ovadyah Haddayah, who was a member of the Supreme Rabbinic Court in Jerusalem,
emphasizes the halakhic legitimacy of representative government. Haddayah's argument
draws upon the classic discussions of dina de-malkhuta *and of the self-government*
of the kahal. *He makes special use of Moses Sofer's argument (incorporated into the*
discussion below) justifying dina de-malkhuta *in terms of the consent of the governed.*

This question can be divided into two parts:

A. Does the principle *dina de-malkhuta dina* apply to all
types of kings, Israelite and gentile alike, or is there a distinction to
be made between them?

B. Does it apply only to a state ruled by a king who legislates laws and promulgates statutes—[so that] no one can act without his authority—or does it apply also to a state that does not have
a king but a president? Does it apply where the authority to legis-

late laws and statutes is in the hands of a house of representatives which promulgates laws as it sees fit for the good of the state and its inhabitants? Are these equal to a kingdom? . . .

A. . . . [Gerondi] quotes the Tosafot, who maintain that *dina de-malkhuta dina* applies only to a gentile king because the land is his, etc.[12] . . . Maimonides, however, among others, clearly disagrees with this. In chapter 5 of the Laws of Robbery and Lost Property, he explicitly rules [that a tax evader "is a transgressor, for he steals the king's property] whether the king be a heathen or an Israelite" (C9, §9). Both the *Tur* and the *Shulhan Arukh* have ruled similarly. . . . As to the proper legal holding, it is clear that we follow solely the position of Maimonides, endorsed also by the *Tur* and the *Shulhan Arukh*. They unequivocally state that there is no distinction between gentile and Israelite kings. Regarding the authority of both we equally apply [the principle] *dina de-malkhuta dina*. [We hold thus,] against the Tosafot and Ran, because we have a general rule that in cases of legal disagreement between the interpreters of the Talmud and the codifiers we follow the codifiers; for the latter write for the sake of guiding practice, whereas the former write for the sake of exposition, not in making a ruling.

Furthermore, Hatam Sofer argues:

[Haddayah here presents an abstract of the following argument developed by Moses Sofer in his responsa (*Hatam Sofer*, Hoshen Mishpat 44): Regarding the principle *dina de-malkhuta dina*, Rashbam writes, "All taxes, rates, and rules of kings' law commonly established in their kingdoms are law, for all subjects of a kingdom willingly accept the king's laws and statutes. Therefore they are perfectly valid law" (C9, §4). . . . Therefore, no distinction should be made between a gentile king and a Jewish king. For even regarding a Jewish king who does not own the land—since it was apportioned [by Joshua] to the tribes—they still willingly accept all his laws and statutes, which constitutes a complete waiver. All this, however, is only when he does not contravene an explicit statement of the Torah. But when he contravenes an explicit statement of the Torah, then even a gentile king is not to be

---

12. In his commentary to BT Nedarim 28a, Gerondi cites the position of the tosafist Isaac Or Zaru'a, given in C9, §6.

obeyed—how much less so a Jewish king! . . . This applies not only to civil law regulating interpersonal affairs . . . but even to taxes and tariffs, where we also say that the citizens willingly waive [their rights]. Thus the law of a Jewish king is law too.

[Ran (Nedarim 28a), however, writes: "The tosafists have written that *dina de-malkhuta dina* applies only to a gentile king, because the land is his and he can say to them, 'If you do not obey my decree, I will expel you from the land.' Not so, however, with regard to Jewish kings, for the Land of Israel is owned jointly by all Israelites." . . . Nevertheless it seems to me that he [Ran]disagrees only with respect to taxes and tariffs if they are imposed without consent. Here he holds that since we cannot impute tacit consent to the citizens, [the taxes are thus valid] only by virtue of his [the king's] being master of the land. This entails, then, a distinction between Jewish and gentile kings. But concerning laws and statutes . . . , Ran agrees that the reason [for their validity] is consent, and no distinction should be made between Jewish and gentile kings.]

B. . . . There are no grounds for a distinction between a crowned king and a minister or governor who has no crown: *dina de-malkhuta dina* applies to all. Therefore the same [maxim] applies also to a . . . legislature whose members are not crowned as royalty. They have the status of a king, and we apply to them [the principle of] *dina de-malkhuta dina*. This follows a fortiori, because they were elected by the people, and they were elected to promulgate laws and statutes as they see fit for the good of the state. For even the taxes they impose upon the citizens are for their own good, because without taxes a state cannot exist, and every citizen of the state wishes the state to exist.

. . . In the ordinances of a town three conditions must obtain: (a) that the "good men of the town" must initially be selected by the *kahal;* (b) that issues must be decided by all the good men with the approval of the town's official rabbi; and (c) that the ordinances be for the good of the *kahal,* not that some benefit at the expense of others. . . .

Therefore we must say in the case at hand, of a house of representatives, that if all these conditions are met, it is certainly equivalent to the "good men of the town." They too were initially chosen by the *kahal* since they were elected by all the citizens for the express purpose of making laws and statutes and imposing taxes as in any other state. The condition that none benefit at the expense of others is also met. Since . . . the taxes are [imposed] upon all residents [equally], each according to his income and profits, no one benefits at the expense of another. But it seems that the condition that this legislation should meet the approval of the "town's rabbi" is missing in this case, for they never consult him. Since, however, the town's rabbi is also among the voters, it is as if he had already initially concurred in whatever they do for the good of the town, so long as it does not contravene Torah law. Even regarding the principle *dina de-malkhuta dina,* it is explicitly stated that it applies only when it does not contravene Torah law. It applies only with regard to issues of *mamona* [where *dina de-malkhuta dina* resembles] the rule that the court has the power to expropriate—provided again that it does not involve benefiting some at the expense of others. Furthermore I say, in line with the explanation provided above, that our house of representatives has a status equal to that of a king, and nowhere is it required that a Jewish king consult the town's rabbi.

Religious Significance of the State

Against the Rule of Priests

4. Theodore Herzl, "Theocracy"

The Jewish State (New York: American Zionist Emergency Council, 1946), pp. 146–47.

In 1896, Herzl published his proposed solution to the "Jewish question," Der Juden-staat (best rendered as "The State of the Jews"), which soon became the manifesto of the Zionist movement. Herzl envisioned a secular aristocratic republic and anticipated later confrontations regarding the "Jewish" character of the state.

Shall we end by having a theocracy? No, indeed. Faith unites us, knowledge gives us freedom. We shall therefore prevent any theocratic tendencies from coming to the fore on the part of our priesthood. We shall keep our priests within the confines of their temples in the same way as we shall keep our professional army within the confines of their barracks. Army and priesthood shall receive honors high as their valuable functions deserve. But they must not interfere in the administration of the State which confers distinction upon them, else they will conjure up difficulties without and within.

Every man will be as free and undisturbed in his faith or his disbelief as he is in his nationality. And if it should occur that men of other creeds and different nationalities come to live amongst us, we should accord them honorable protection and equality before the law.

The State of Israel as the Foundation of God's Throne

5. Abraham Isaac Kook, *Orot ha-Kodesh,* The Morality of Holiness 136

Orot ha-Kodesh, edited by David Cohen (Jerusalem: Mossad Harav Kook, 1964; Hebrew), vol. 2, p. 191.

Kook refers to the state of Israel by name decades before its creation. He adopts kabbalistic symbolism to construct his political theology, combining it with the Hegelian notion of the state as the supreme concretization of the Spirit.

The state is not the supreme happiness of man. This [denial is true] of an ordinary state that amounts to no more than a large insurance company, where the myriad ideas that are the crown of human vitality remain hovering above, not touching it.

[But] this is not the case regarding a state that is ideal in its foundation, in whose being is engraved the . . . ideal content that is, truly, the greatest happiness of the individual. This state is truly supreme in the scale of happiness, and this state is our state, the state of Israel, the foundation of God's throne in the world.[13] Its entire aim is that "God be one and His name one" (Zech. 14:9). For this is, truly, the supreme happiness.

Of course, this sublime happiness is in need of extended elaboration so as to shine in [these] days of darkness. But it does not on that account fail to be the supreme happiness.

---

13. The ninth and tenth *sefirot* (divine emanations) are *yesod* (foundation) and *malkhut* (kingship).

The Negative Significance of the State: Zionism Is Heresy

6. Yerahmiel Domb, "Judaism and Zionism"

Et Nisayon (Jerusalem, 1972; Hebrew), pp. 4–5, 10–11.

Domb's vehement attack on Zionism is an example of the ultraorthodox rejection of the Jewish return to statehood and involvement in this-worldly politics. Domb invokes the critiques of monarchy (see C3) that respond to the people's wish to have a king "like all the nations." He thus rejects the Zionist hope for normalcy and denies the legitimacy of the state of Israel.

The heresy [*kefirah*] [14] of Zionism is greater than any that preceded it, [greater than that] of the various heretical sects that arose from time to time. The Sadducees denied the Rabbinic traditions from Mount Sinai but did not deny the entirety of our holy Torah. On the contrary, they were committed to their cause unto death. . . . The Karaites too did not deny the entirety of our holy Torah. So too all other heretical sects. . . . In no other time was there a sect in Israel that totally denied the holy Torah, whose heresy extended to its full scope and [reached down] to its roots, as does this Zionism standing before us. [Zionism] does not merely deny some part of our Torah, or some detail of our faith, but uproots everything. Furthermore, it is no longer a motivating force of some part of Israel but asserts its domination over all Israel, in all its locations, throughout the diaspora.

    The total and deep heresy is that of Zionism in itself, which is more vile than any of the acts of the Zionists. The Zionists desecrate the holy Sabbath and transgress the entire Torah, but there are other sinners too who desecrate the holy Sabbath and commit transgressions. The conquest of the land, which derives specifically from Zionism—and in the course of which the Zionists committed severe transgressions— . . . is but the actualization and result of their will and ideas. . . . Zionism in itself, even before it succeeded in bringing about the establishment of the state and its attendant deeds, and before the Zionists became desecrators of the holy Sabbath and sinners, this Zionism that consists in nothing more than the aspiration that

14. The literal meaning of this Hebrew word is "denial"; the cognate verb *kafar* is translated as "deny" below.

Israel should have a state and a place of refuge in the Land of Israel— . . . this Zionist aspiration is founded on denial of all of the thirteen principles.[15] [It is] a general and fundamental heresy. Zionism in itself negates all faith in the holiness of Torah and in the holiness of Israel, in the coming of the Messiah and in the resurrection of the dead, in [divine] reward and punishment, and in all divine things granted us by God.

Zionism denies everything. [It denies] the entire idea of election, whereby God chose us from among all peoples, and the entire idea of exile on account of our sins, and of redemption by God through our righteous Messiah. Zionism—which means, that we should have a state, freedom, and independence—may appear to go against no explicit commandment . . . , and can even be made to seem attractive through various devious [arguments] and confusions, and through justifications appealing to particular circumstances. This Zionism is the [most] terrible heresy. The Zionist heresy [minut] . . . consists in a basic opposition to the entire system of faith, to all principles of our holy Torah on the theoretical [level], leading to desecration of the Torah in practice as well. . . .

It might be argued: What transgression is there in that Jews should live in the Land of Israel? What sin is it that they should relocate from the lands of the gentiles to our holy land? What evil is there in that there should be Jewish villages or cities [in the Land of Israel]; and that when the Arabs want to expel them it is necessary to establish a state in order to protect their lives? Thus argue those who observe certain of the practical mitzvot, who are at present known as religious (or "Torah") Zionists. . . . They are drawn by the superficial and the convenient, [drawn] to follow their emotions and the popular trend, by the power of Satan embodied in that trend— by the deceptive reality of temporary success, by this-worldly allures and lusts. They adhere to all the ways that lead, directly or indirectly, to the ultimate and absolute evil that has in recent times come to have almost complete dominion.

15. The "thirteen principles of faith" were formulated and explicated by Maimonides in his commentary to the Mishnah (introduction to the tenth chapter of tractate Sanhedrin). They never gained universal endorsement, but come closest to an accepted formulation of Judaism's articles of faith (see C15).

In truth, there is no halakhic issue of settling the Land of Israel at stake here, nor any [true] desire to observe any of the obligations that apply there . . . , nor anything with any trace of holiness . . . . What is at stake is the basic foundation of Judaism and the Torah in their entirety. . . . For this act of obtaining a settlement and a state in the Land of Israel implies our total destruction: it is no mere physical act. The great, basic question is: Are we—God forbid—a nation like all the nations of the world? Do we succeed and fail according to the same causes by which they succeed and fail? Are we in essence the same as the French, or English, or Russian nations, subject to the same order as they? [Will] the same faults that caused them failure and humiliation—such as military weakness, an enemy's good plan, dispersal of [their own] forces—bring particular failures to us too? And [will] the same efforts and assets that brought advantage and success to the English or the French bring success and benefit to us as well? [Is it true that] progress and acquisition of knowledge in science and economics, which have improved the economic situation of other nations of the world, will bring us the self-same [improvement]? Will organizing a fighting force [of the sort] that has provided security to other nations of the world provide for us, too, security and strength in the land, national honor and respect in the world, reten-tion of power and a secure future? Or are we something different from all other nations of the world, a chosen people whom God has elected from amongst all peoples, to be governed by manifest divine providence, under the divine order of the Torah's commandments and warnings of reward and punishment, exile and redemption . . . ?

Divine Sovereignty: A Jewish State Requires Torah Law

7. Isaac Breuer, "Judaism and National Home"

Concepts of Judaism, edited by Jacob S. Levinger (Jerusalem: Israel Universities Press, 1974), pp. 89–92. The essay excerpted here was translated in 1946 by Jacob Bar-Or (Brener) for the Anglo-American Committee of Inquiry.

Breuer was trained as a lawyer, and his argument here on God's sovereignty, and the state's, reflects the European legal theory of his time. The following text, presented to

the Anglo-American Commission of Inquiry on Palestine in 1946, was part of his effort
to shape and define the opposition of the Agudat Yisrael party to the secular Zionist
movement.

From the everlasting creation by God there follows for Judaism the conclusion that the world, after the completion of creation, continues to be guided by God, and is hence a *theocracy*. As universal as is the creation of God, so universal is His *political rule* over the nations of mankind, and over the creation which has been entrusted to them. God is not merely "Father" of His creation, but also "King" of his nations. . . .

In Judaism, such qualitative oneness of God makes any other kind of *sovereignty* insufferable. God is the only sovereign, in nature as well as in the life of man as an individual or as a national unit. God is the sole source of the laws of nature, of the rules for the individual conduct of man, and of the laws of nations. There is nowhere any room for sovereign autonomy in the face of the oneness of God. There is no distinction on principle between the laws of nature, the rules of individual conduct, and the rules of law. It is merely that the former are addressed to unfree beings and, therefore, find ready realization at all times, while the two latter must be absorbed by the will of free man and be followed by the actions of free man.

From the qualitative oneness of God there follows, therefore, the idea of nation and state of Judaism. The nation, according to Holy Writ, is born of the family. But the family is already a society regulated by divine law. God allocates to the families now developing into nations their land, in order that they may, in such a land, continue and complete, as societies of the law of God, their part in the creative work of God. To Judaism, therefore, the nation is a legal entity, based on the family and constituted with a view to a particular territory, whose law is none other than the law of God. Just because the nation is in essence a legal entity, it cannot do without territory, in which God-the-King's will, as revealed to it, is the sovereign law of the land. The nation as a community of divine law can never accept anything as supreme except the will of God if it is to develop fully. Since only the will of God is valid for the nation, it requires that territory in which God alone is sovereign. The nation may be formed, perhaps, on desert ground, where no foreign will rules. But national life in the multiplicity of its activities can only develop on national territory.

Nation and national territory are united by the law of God into the *state.* The state is not the source of law, but wholly and completely subject to the law of God. The state is the first servant of the law. Its supreme task is the realization of divine law. The nation as a community of the law precedes the state in both terms and time, and it is never merged in it. As opposed to the nation, the state, like the territory, has a mere function—a vital and altogether indispensable one, but always a function. Just as the territory affords the possibility in space of unrestricted and all-embracing expansion under the rule of divine law, so it is the state which is to protect such expansion from internal and external disturbance. *The community of the law remains in existence also within the state,* at all times prepared to oppose and, indeed, to fight the state, should it abuse the power entrusted to it, in any manner contrary to its ordained function; at all times prepared, too, to resume its desert existence, should the state succumb to the abuse of its function and draw the national territory to its ruin.

Just as phenomena existing mutually side by side in natural space are governed by the divine law of nature, so too humanity existing mutually side by side in history is governed by divine law. The destiny intended for mankind was that it should subject itself freely to the revealed law of God and that it should regulate its relations according to such a law. Mankind has been ailing because of the usurped autonomy of nations and the rebellious sovereignty of states. The problem of history is, for Judaism, a *problem of law.* As long as states insist on claiming sovereignty as theirs and every state takes the law upon itself both internally and externally, there can be neither social peace nor international peace. The anarchy of mankind shows itself in continuously recurring historical catastrophes, foretold with tremendous insistence by all prophets, to which only the law of God can put an end.

For Judaism the idea of the law is wholly transcendental. Law is not made by the nation, but law makes the nation. Man may find the road to *God* by himself and with his own powers by perceiving the miracles of heaven and earth. The *law of God* must be revealed to the nation. In the national experience of this revelation absolute nationalism vanishes into nothingness, and there appears that relative nationalism for which the revealed law is the sole supreme value, and service to such law becomes the life-destiny of a nation.

. . . The religion of the nation is nothing else but law. Religion exists for that nation which does not set up the law for itself but takes the law from the mouth of God. It desires not merely to establish itself in idolatrous self-worship but, accepting the law of God, is prepared to subject itself unstintingly to the divine will. It is ready to reject sovereignty and conceive of its land as the land of God and of its state as the servant of divine law.

A "national" God!—never! The God of heaven and earth, the king of all nations—that is the God of Judaism, and he remained so even when he showed mercy to those who had been wickedly enslaved in the land of Egypt and led them into freedom, to the mount of the law, to the land of the law.

What of "national" religion? What is there in the confession of belief in the God of heaven and earth, the confession of belief in the King of *all* nations, that it should be nationally limited? The religion of Judaism is surely not national, but for Judaism the nation is *"religious."* The nation has not created "religion," but "religion" the nation. To Judaism, God is not . . . only dispenser of ethics but also dispenser of law. And because such a law, in its all-embracing totality, can realize itself only in national life, and because its claim to rule can satisfy itself only in national life, and because its claim to rule can satisfy itself only on national territory, therefore nation and law are essential and indispensable parts of Judaism.

Separating Religion and State

8. Yeshayahu Leibowitz, "The Religious Significance of the State of Israel"

Judaism, Human Values, and the Jewish State, edited by Eliezer Goldman, translated by Eliezer Goldman et al. (Cambridge: Harvard University Press, 1992), pp. 214–19.

This text is taken from a talk delivered in 1975 at a meeting of the Movement for a Judaism of Torah, founded by religiously observant intellectuals who sought to work for the spiritual influence of Torah in Israeli society. Leibowitz's unnamed opponents at this meeting probably held opinions close to those of Kook in Selection 5, or, more generally, the view expressed in the special prayer included in the Shabbat liturgy which refers to the state of Israel as "the dawn of our redemption."

I wish to introduce myself at the outset as one who hasn't been at all disappointed by the state of Israel. For me, the state of Israel has fulfilled all the hopes I had for it ever since my early youth. Of course, it is very difficult for a seventy-year-old man vividly to envision himself as he was in his youth. But it seems to me that ever since I reached maturity and became a Zionist, Zionism meant for me the endeavor to liberate Jews from being ruled by the Gentiles. The state of Israel completely satisfies the demand for freedom from domination by others. . . . In opposition to one of the earlier speakers here, I believe that no state whatsoever, in the past, present, or any foreseeable future, in any society, in any era, in any culture, including the Jewish culture, ever was or will ever be anything but a secular institution. The function of the state is essentially secular. It is not service of God. Whenever the Jews had a state, the history of that state was that of a continuous struggle between religion and the political leadership. Even when the state was established in the name of Torah, for the sake of Torah, as the outcome of struggle for the Torah—I have in mind the Hasmonaean state— the sixty years of that state's existence witnessed a constant struggle between the bearers of the Torah and the secular regime. This struggle is logically and factually inevitable. Religion, that is, man's recognition of his duty to serve God, cannot be integrated with the machinery of government. The political organization, necessary as a condition of survival, merely sets the ground for the struggle for religion, which is by its very nature an eternal struggle that will never end in victory.

Some twenty years ago I had a lengthy conversation with Ben-Gurion, whose attitude toward Judaism is well known to you, about the problem of religion and the state. He said to me: "I understand very well why you demand the separation of religion from the state. You want the Jewish religion to be reinstated as an independent factor with which the political authority will have to contend. Therefore I shall never agree to the separa-

tion of state and religion. I want the state to hold religion under its control."
The official representatives of Jewish religion are resigned to this state of
affairs; even worse, they count on being "kept" by the secular government.

The state, as such, has no religious value. No state ever had. Political
achievements, conquests, victories—none of these are religiously significant.
Who "restored the border of Israel from the entering of Hamath to the sea
of the Aravah," and "recovered Damascus and Hamath which had belonged
to Judah in Israel" (2 Kings 14:25, 28)? Who was the greatest of warriors and
conquerors among the Israelites? "The King Yerov'am the son of Joash," who
"did that which was evil in the sight of God and departed not from all the
sins of Yerov'am the son of Nebat" (14:24). What was the religious significance of these enormous conquests about which we know only from two
verses of the Book of Kings? From the empirical religious point of view,
from the standpoint of the religious tradition, from the mark that these deeds
left upon religious consciousness—it was nil. Our Sages of blessed memory
found some merit in Yerov'am in that he did not harm the prophet (Amos)
who said: "Yerov'am shall die by the sword and Israel shall surely be led captive out of their own land" (Amos 7:11). This is what counts in his favor,
whereas the tremendous events summed up in these two verses left no mark
in the religious consciousness of Israel.

I contend that it is not by accident that no festival or holiday com-
memorates the conquest of the Land of Israel by Joshua, the son of Nun, and
that no festival or holiday marks the conquest of Jerusalem by King David.
We do have the holiday of Hanukkah, in memory of a civil war between the
Jews who observed the Torah and the Hellenized Jews.

Theologically speaking, as a man of faith, and without special reference to the state of Israel, I emphatically deny that a state might have any
intrinsic value at all. Moreover, beyond any considerations of theology or
of faith, but by general axiological criteria, a state is not a *value*. A state is
needed in order to fulfill two needs. The first is the individual's need for survival, "for were it not for fear of the political ruler men would swallow one
another alive" (Mishnah Avot 3:2). "The impulse of man's heart is evil from
his youth" (Gen. 8:21). Unlike Robinson Crusoe on his island, human beings
in society cannot coexist unless a regime and government is imposed upon
them, or they impose it on themselves. What that Sage said aphoristically

was repeated in systematic fashion some one thousand and five hundred years later by one of the greatest social and political thinkers, Thomas Hobbes.

The state's role in assuring a nation's survival is far more problematic than its function of safeguarding the existence of the individual. We shall not, however, delve too deeply into the matter but will recognize both needs as legitimate. . . .

Regarding the state as an intrinsic value is the essence of fascism. If this is true in general, it is all the more true when the values of "the Judaism of Torah" are attached to it. The state certainly has its place in the Halakhah, because the Halakhah concerns itself with mundane matters. It deals with man as flesh and blood, with his food and drink, with his copulation, his work, and so on. Political reality as a value is not accorded much prominence in Judaism. We saw how the exploits of the greatest victor and conqueror are buried in two verses in 2 Kings! Those who are not well versed in the Hebrew Bible are not aware of them even if they are religiously committed Jews.

I cannot ascribe religious significance to our having regained political independence. From the pronouncements of colleagues who preceded me in this evening's debate one might infer that they "hear the words of God and see the vision of the Almighty" (Num. 24:4); that in historical events they discern "the finger of God" and the final cause of the overflow descending from the upper to the lower world. I have no reliable source for knowledge of the divine intentions and do not detect in the occurrences of the lower world any religious significance, unless they incorporate an intention in the lower world aimed at the upper world; in other words—insofar as human beings act for the sake of Heaven. Apart from this, history has no religious meaning. History belongs to the course of the world and it is this course which constitutes divine providence. Every historical event is an instance of divine providence, so no particular event has greater religious significance than others. The selective invocation of the "finger of God" regarding what is convenient or desirable is comparable to the use of the concept of "holiness," which is so often abused for national-political purposes. When the holiness of the Temple Mount is imputed to its being "God's estate," I ask: is not any plot of land equally the "estate of God"? After all, "the earth is God's and the fullness thereof"! (Ps. 24:1, a verse religious Jews repeat four

times a week). The ingathering of exiles in itself is not yet a religious phenomenon; see the verse "but when you entered, you defiled my land, and
made my heritage an abomination" (Jer. 2:7). Yet this consideration does
not deter certain rabbis from the Sabbatean announcement of "the dawn of
redemption."

Mamlakhtiyut: Statehood Requires Tolerance

9. David Ben-Gurion, "The Eternity of Israel"

The Government Yearbook (Jerusalem, 1954; Hebrew), pp. 14–23.

*This essay by Israel's first prime minister is an early reflection on the conflicts within
Israeli society and a defense of* mamlakhtiyut, *a central theme of Ben-Gurion's ideology. The word suggests a civic consciousness or public spiritedness grounded in the
commitment of citizens to the state.* Mamlakhtiyut *here implies a call for all Israel's
parties and groups, religious and secular, to acknowledge each other's legitimacy and
accommodate each other's interests.*

Never in Jewish history has the unity of [the people of] Israel been revealed
in a fuller or more perfect manner than in the Declaration of Independence
of our state in our times. The Sinai covenant, according to the tradition, required holding "the mountain over them like an [overturned] tub" (C1, §8).
And when Moses was merely delayed in descending from the mountain, the
people gathered with Aaron at their head and made the golden calf. And
after all the tribes had come to David in Hebron to appoint him as leader
over all Israel . . . the rebellion of Absalom broke out. And after Joab and
Abishai, sons of Zeruiah, and Ittai the Gittite, suppressed the family rebellion
and restored the kingship to David, a more severe rebellion spread, the rebellion of Sheba, the son of Bichri, a Benjamite—which led, after the death
of Solomon, to a split between Judea and Israel. Only a few [of the Jewish
exiles in Babylonia] emigrated with Ezra and Nehemiah to the Land of Israel,
about fifty thousand (including some seven thousand male slaves and maid-
servants), and those who returned encountered opposition by "the people of

the land" who had not been exiled. In the days of the Second Temple, quarrels proliferated between the Sadducees and the Pharisees and between the Hasmonean brothers themselves, and prior to the destruction, between the moderates and the zealot rebels. The rebels too fought among themselves no less than they fought the Romans. . . . Nor did quarrels and conflicts cease in Israel during the exile.

On the eve of the establishment of the state, the Jewish *yishuv* in the Land was perhaps the most divided and fragmented of all the Jewish settlements in the world. In no other land could one find such a conglomeration of different ethnic groups, cultures, organizations and parties, beliefs and opinions, shifting ideologies and international orientations, conflicting economic and social interests, as in the *yishuv*—[which was] as a result of the ingathering of the exiles, the center of all the divisions and splits in Israel. With the wondrous occurrence of . . . independence, it was as if all the divisions were overcome. Representatives of all the parties in Israel signed the Declaration—from the Communists, who had forever fought against the Zionist enterprise as reactionary, bourgeois, chauvinistic, and counterrevolutionary, to Agudat Yisrael, which had perceived as apostasy any attempt to bring about the redemption of Israel through natural means. . . .

However, it was not only these two extremes that . . . overcame their prolonged and bitter opposition to the state of Israel. The representatives of Shomer Hatzair, who for over twenty years had maintained that a binational state was the only means to realize the Zionist goal . . . participated in the signing. . . . [And] representatives of the Revisionists, who had vehemently fought against a state based on partition, also signed the Declaration.

The only obstacle . . . was the last paragraph [of the Declaration] referring to "trust in the Rock of Israel." Some radical intellectuals considered these words an apostasy against atheism; on the other side were ultra-orthodox extremists who perceived the failure to add "and its Redeemer" . . . as an apostasy against fundamental dogma. Nevertheless, everyone signed after negotiations. And not only the parties in Israel but the Jewish people throughout the world were united on that day in their joy and pride over the establishment of the state. It is difficult to assess which of the two miracles was greater—the miracle of independence or the miracle of unity. . . .

However, these two miracles were conjoined only on that wondrous day. The state was established; there then began a bitter and protracted military struggle for its survival, which has not yet been decided and will not end in the near future. This struggle, along with the effort to gather in all the exiles and to cultivate the desert, requires . . . a united Jewish people no less than did the declaration of the state. Yet the unity that glowed on the day of the Declaration soon vanished. The transition from *yishuv* to state did not diminish the internal divisions and splits; on the contrary, they increased and were exacerbated . . . by the very events that opened a new period in Jewish history: (1) the establishment of a sovereign [*mamlakhtit*] framework and (2) the beginning of the ingathering of the exiles.

A state cannot exist without government, coercion, and majority rule (unless it is a despotic totalitarian state). But a state cannot exist only through [these three things]; it draws its vitality, power, and integrity from the general will of the people, from their shared historical imperatives, from their mutual responsibility and internal unity. . . . This applies to every state; it applies even more to the state of Israel, which is not only a state of its inhabitants and for its inhabitants. It is not a state with a developed country and an established economy. . . . The people residing within it are only the nucleus of the people for whom it was established. Most of its area is desolate and waste, requiring development. Its economy is only in its infancy. All its neighbors are scheming to destroy it. Great world powers are unsympathetic to it. The tasks of absorption, development, and security that fall upon this state cannot be accomplished solely by the coercive power of government. Without an extended and continuous effort . . . supported by the entire people, the ingathering of the exiles will be impossible, the cultivation of the desert will not be accomplished, and security will not be established. This effort requires consolidating the people's powers and activating its general will.

. . . The divergence of commitments and beliefs regarding issues of religion requires both religious and secular citizens . . . to respect the feelings and perceptions of the other side and to relate to each other not only with tolerance but also with respect and mutual trust. Each side may simply desire that everyone be like it; indeed, in a totalitarian regime this is achieved through inquisitorial methods or through dictatorship. Israel is a democratic state. And its existence cannot be contemplated without a democratic rule that is founded upon the liberty and free choice of its inhabitants. There are religious Jews who believe sincerely that the day will come when God will purify the hearts of the people and every Jew will believe and be God-fearing like them. And there are secular Jews who are certain that time will achieve what the intellect has not and . . . everyone will be like them. [But] no one knows when such a wondrous unity of belief within Judaism will come to pass. The state must act within an existing reality that may endure for years, while these very years are critical . . . for the fate of the people and the future of the state. We must take heed of the differences of opinion in the spiritual realm. It is particularly here that the differences are radical because they touch the deepest roots from which both sides are nurtured. Both sides are certain that they are faithful to the sources and roots of Judaism as they understand them. There is no objective Supreme Court to decide between them, nor would either accept its judgment even if there were such a court. They both must live together and build together the nation and the state, without one imposing its opinions on the other.

The Declaration of Independence, also signed by representatives [of all the religious parties], includes a proclamation of "freedom of religion and conscience." This principle is intended to secure full opportunity for the most observant Jew to live according to his religious belief, and [also] for every other Jew to live according to his own way. The state, under all coalitions to date, has undertaken to provide for the communal religious needs of its inhabitants and to prevent any coercion in religious matters. This wise and fair arrangement should have appeased all sides and was in fact accepted by them. However, formulating an abstract principle is one thing; implementing it in practice is another—especially when . . . the mutual respect, trust, and tolerance of a united nation is lacking.

. . . The gravity of the problem is grounded not only in the division between parties but in the conflict between two different conceptions of Judaism and between two opposing programs for shaping the character of the Jewish people and of the state of Israel:

a. Faith in "Torah from heaven," strict adherence to the *Shulhan Arukh* and to practices considered traditions from Sinai, and a desire (overt or concealed) to impose the laws of the Torah—as interpreted by the Council of Distinguished Scholars of the Agudah or the rabbinical leaders of the Mizrachi—upon the state and all its citizens by force of state [*mamlakhti*] law

      b. Belief in freedom of conscience and in the liberty of each person to think, speak, and act as he sees fit, provided that he does not harm the rights of another or of the state

Those who demand freedom of conscience and of religion . . . include not only freethinking [secularists] who perceive any imposition [of Torah law] as an assault upon their conscience but also many traditional and religious persons who themselves adhere to the *Shulhan Arukh* and carefully observe all traditional norms. Nevertheless, they view the transformation of religion into a political tool and the attempt to impose religious practice by state power as morally damaging to the state and as a perversion of the spirit of Judaism. They are opposed to political parties based on religion, which they view as detrimental to popular respect for religion. They view the politicization of the rabbinate and the mixing of divine and human relations with . . . factional maneuvers as unwholesome to both religion and state. Many simply . . . desire that the state restrict itself to relations "between man and his fellows."[16]

The religious debate in Israel is further complicated by the particular nature of the Jewish religion. The problem of religion in Israel does not resemble the problem of church and state in Christian countries. The Jewish religion is fundamentally different from the Christian religion. It is not satisfied with abstract dogmas but is grounded in positive and negative commandments that encompass the full span of human life from birth to death, leaving no neutral ground free of religious concern. Furthermore, the Jewish religion is a national religion and has absorbed within it the entire heritage of the Jewish people from its inception to the present. The national and religious aspects are not easily separated.

The blending of [these two] is not a novelty in our history. . . . In

---

16. As opposed to the relations "between man and God"—see the traditional distinction in Mishnah Yoma 8:9.

our earliest literature, the origin of our people [is twice described]: first, the common descent from the line of Abraham and the sons of Israel [the line of Jacob]; second, the covenant made between God and His servant Moses and the people: "The Lord our God made a covenant with us at Horeb. It was not with our fathers that the Lord made this covenant, but with us, the living, every one of us who is here today" (Deut. 5:2–3).

The . . . separation of church and state adopted in the United States did not result from antireligious arguments, but, on the contrary, from a deep attachment to religion and a desire to assure for every citizen complete religious freedom. [But] this comfortable arrangement, even were it adopted in Israel, would not solve the problem. Jewish holidays have a dual meaning: both religious–cosmic and historical–national. . . . A Jew need not be observant in order to appreciate the great value of the observance of the Sabbath and the holidays as days of rest and as commemorations that lend Jewish color and historical continuity to our public life. Passover, Pentecost, and Tabernacles too have both historical and national-religious meaning. . . .

The religious parties—for religious and other reasons—cannot rest content with the national and social aspects of the Sabbath and the holidays. . . . Anyone committed to [the idea of] a religious party—a political party being first and foremost an instrument for power—is [thereby] committed, wittingly or not, to establishing religion in the state.

[Ben-Gurion goes on to describe the legal arrangements established under the Ottomans, sustained during the British mandate, and subsequently adopted by the state of Israel. Under these arrangements, marriage and divorce, and certain other matters of family law, are regulated by Jewish, Muslim, and Christian religious courts.—Eds.]

In the state of Israel, two opposite objections to this arrangement are advanced. Some object to granting state [*mamlakhti*] authority to the rabbinate and to imposing its yoke on [Jewish] citizens who disavow the rabbis and their authority and have no interest in their rulings. Others object to restraining the rabbis by state law and subjecting them to sovereign [*mamlakhti*] authority. Still others welcome state-ordained rabbinic jurisdiction—indeed, they seek to expand it as far as possible. At the same time, they seek to free the rabbinate from its subjection to the state and its legislative institutions, placing the rabbinate above the state and its institutions.

The existing arrangement is the product of compromise. And as is common with compromises, it does not satisfy everyone. This compromise was accepted to prevent a religious war—a war for religion and a war against religion that would seriously obstruct the integration of the exiles, . . . the first of the state's priorities. The compromise can endure only if people with opposing outlooks regarding religion and spiritual matters are able to demonstrate mutual tolerance and respect by virtue of Jewish solidarity. [Granting] official [*mamlakhti*] status to the rabbinate in a state committed to freedom of conscience and religion, which contains both religious parties seeking the rule of religion and traditionalists who oppose such rule, as well as a large free-thinking [secular] public, creates a dangerous minefield. Such a status is possible [only] if those interested in its existence accept voluntarily and faithfully the authority [of the state] and the limitations it entails. Benefits are accompanied by burdens; state authority entails restrictions. The rabbinate must not overstep the bounds . . . set by the state, and may not intervene in matters outside the jurisdiction determined by law. Unless the rabbinate accepts the yoke of the state and its laws without qualification, it cannot morally obligate citizens who entirely disavow rabbinic authority.

Human conscience, whether religious or moral . . . is far more powerful than law. But those who act on their conscience in opposition to state law must accept all the consequences of their actions, including the punishments whereby the state defends its authority. . . . In any event, they are not entitled to request from the state authority to impose their will upon others against their own consciences.

The capacity for compromise is an essential condition for the existence of any community. . . . How much more so is this capacity required in the state of Israel! There is no need to precipitate decisions that might be severely obstructive to the integration of the exiles and to . . . political [*mamlakhti*] cooperation. [Of course,] not all debates nor all decisions can or should be avoided. No abstract rules can distinguish the areas for [clear-cut] decision from the areas for compromise. Yet it is certain that there is no necessity at present to reach decisions in matters of opinion and faith, in which we shall long continue to be divided. History has a sequence, and one must distinguish between the primary and the tangential, between the permanent and the temporary. An uncompromising confrontation on the status of religion in the state . . . has the potential to explode the nation. In the best case, it will delay the process of internal consolidation, which is the essential requirement . . . for the existence of the state.

Commentary. Hobbes and Rousseau in Israel

During the 1980s a well-known professor at the Hebrew University remarked that for the foreseeable future Israel could not expect to produce philosophers of the first rank because the leisure that philosophical reflection requires was unavailable amid the continuing crises of Israeli social and political life. Yet in Israel a famous public intellectual such as Yeshayahu Leibowitz could, in a political forum, casually connect his conception of the state to that of the political theorist Thomas Hobbes. And Israel's first prime minister, David Ben-Gurion could, on behalf of his conception of *mamlakhtiyut,* invoke Rousseau's "general will." Perhaps the truth was more nearly the reverse of what the professor proclaimed: in Israel, philosophy so flourishes that even in addressing the needs of the hour prominent intellectuals and public figures could not express their political opinions without reference to the history of philosophy. Or perhaps there is a third and more precise alternative: that people who must think and speak on the run may invoke the names of famous philosophers or philosophical notions to dramatize a critical point that bears a limited, but nevertheless instructive, connection to the philosopher or notion invoked.

But passing reference or dramatic allusion may obscure important complexities. Indeed, despite the appeal to Hobbes, Leibowitz was, in decisive respects, not a Hobbist. And, notwithstanding his invocation of the general will, Ben-Gurion was, in crucial ways, no Rousseauian. My purpose in saying this is not to accuse either one of committing malpractice as a political theorist. Rather, what I wish to suggest is the need on our part to engage in political theory to make sense of their arguments. When this is done, and the arguments behind the allusions are brought into focus, we can see that Leibowitz and Ben-Gurion do not, in effect, offer us a stark choice between Hobbes and Rousseau. Instead, the juxtaposition of their opinions invites us to connect a point about the purpose of the state that Leibowitz had in mind when he declared a philosophical alliance with Hobbes to a claim about the preconditions of the state that Ben-Gurion sought to vindicate in terms of the general will.

Leibowitz's immediate objective is to oppose religious Zionists who ascribe a religious significance to the state of Israel. Like Hobbes, Leibowitz rejects the view that the goal of the state is perfection or redemption and argues instead that the state of Israel, like all states, was properly established for the sake of peace and security and nothing more. But this view does not a Hobbist make. For Hobbes reaches his conclusion about the limited goal of the state by a distinctive line of reasoning that Leibowitz does not follow. Unlike Hobbes, whose conclusions about the state are rooted not only in his materialist metaphysics but also in his account of the restless passions that rule human conduct, Leibowitz derives the state's limited role in part from reflections about the dignity of the individual and in part from reflections on the exalted meaning of "service of God." But perhaps the most fundamental difference is this: whereas in *Leviathan* Hobbes famously argues that civil peace requires the elimination of private judgments about right and wrong, Leibowitz's fame in Israel rests, in significant measure, on his outspoken and unrelenting moral criticism of state policy pursued by the duly elected Israeli government in the administration of the West Bank and Gaza Strip. Thus, Leibowitz's Hobbes-like demand that the authority of the state be restricted to matters of peace and security and his extremely un-Hobbesian public opposition to the Israeli exercise of state authority spring from the same source: devotion to the Torah and a severe moral conscience.

In referring to Rousseau's general will, Ben-Gurion's principal aim is to identify one of the crucial preconditions for democracy in Israel. Like Rousseau, Ben-Gurion understood that political societies will not prosper or endure if they are not grounded in shared beliefs, practices, and purposes. And with Rousseau, Ben-Gurion believed that religion is a vital element in politics. But in contrast to Rousseau, for whom the general will signifies the logic of legitimacy, a formula by which the laws issuing from a popular assembly can legitimately bind each member of the state, Ben-Gurion invoked the general will to denote a particular people's passionate attachment to its common descent and common destiny. And there is an important difference between Rousseau's civil religion and the civil purposes to which Ben-Gurion sought to put the Jewish religious tradition. Rousseau's civil religion, which stands opposed to private religious belief, supplies the defect of particularistic revealed religions by teaching "sentiments of solidarity" and the duties of patriotism and citizenship. In contrast, Ben-Gurion's *mamlakhtiyut* blurs the distinction between private and civil religion in the effort to derive "mutual respect, trust, and tolerance"—qualities of mind and heart that would enable secular and religious Jews, despite "radical" differences of opinion, to cooperate in maintaining the state—from Jewish religious sources.

Ben-Gurion knew that the quest for mutual accommodation involved considerable costs from the perspective of "radical intellectuals" as well as from that of "ultraorthodox extremists." And he understood that the outcome of such a quest was not predetermined. By the very use of the term *mamlakhtiyut,* he implied that the private sphere could not be counted on to produce the requisite public spirit, and that therefore the cause of democracy in Israel required the state to play a major role in teaching citizens how to share the common good of freedom. In advising the contending factions in Israel that in a free and democratic society "benefits are accompanied by burdens," Ben-Gurion saw in Israel in the early 1950s what thoughtful participants on both sides of the American debate about liberalism and communitarianism in the 1990s came to recognize: the question for liberal democracies is not whether to protect rights or foster responsibility, but how to strike the elusive balance between them.

But perhaps Ben-Gurion's *mamlakhtiyut* suppresses certain fundamental issues that are brought into focus by Rousseau's radical formulations. When the general will, following Rousseau, is understood as the articulation of a logic of legitimacy and not as an appeal to common descent and destiny, then the problem of how members of Israel's non-Jewish minorities can view the laws of the state as a reflection of their good emerges as a crucial issue for democracy in Israel. And when civil religion is understood in opposition to particular revealed religions and as an institution to be promoted for distinctly secular political purposes, then certain dangers spring into view, dangers to democracy and to Judaism that stem from enlisting the Jewish tradition on behalf of state purposes. For it is reasonable to suppose that the Jewish tradition cannot be a vital source of political education for all Israel's citizens, especially its Arab minority; and that in making use of resources within Judaism for public purposes well-meaning democrats run the risk of distorting or debasing Judaism by turning it into a tool of the state.

In the *Ethics,* Aristotle emphasizes the importance of seeking the appropriate degree of precision in each kind of inquiry. In a highly charged public forum in which observant Jews debate the religious significance of the state of Israel, a reference to Hobbes may carry connotations not present to the minds of Hobbes's seventeenth-century readers and may lack specifications of prime importance to twentieth-century scholarly interpreters. In a state document written by the prime minister in the aftermath of a daring war for independence and in the face of numerous daunting political challenges, an invocation of the general will may, in addressing the needs of the hour, slight the needs of scholarly exactitude. In the effort to understand precisely what figures such as Leibowitz and Ben-Gurion argued, we must not ascribe to them a precision in speaking and writing foreign to the demands of their speeches and publications.

One reward is that unseen connections come into focus. Even if Leibowitz were correct that peace and security and nothing more ought to be the goal of the Israeli state, Ben-Gurion's analysis suggests that the state would at its peril neglect the resources within the Jewish tradition that might enable its gloriously and excruciatingly diverse citizenry to pursue peace and maintain security. And even if Ben-Gurion were correct that in Israel those resources must also be marshaled to foster a democratic disposition and the virtues of freedom, Leibowitz's stern voice transmits Hobbes's warning that the passions stirred by religion pose a perennial threat precisely to the goods of peace and security that liberal democracy affirms.

Peter Berkowitz

A Jewish and Democratic State

"A Jewish and Democratic State"

10. Laws of the State of Israel: Foundations of Law, and Basic Law: Human Dignity and Liberty

Laws of the State of Israel (official English translation), 1980, p. 181; *Sefer ha-Chukkim* (Laws of the State of Israel), 1996 (Hebrew), p. 150.

The Declaration of Independence of the state of Israel promises to ensure the basic rights of all its citizens. Israel does not have a complete constitution or bill of rights. It has a body of basic laws adopted over a period of several decades that are ultimately meant to combine in a constitution. These laws have an overriding regulative status vis-à-vis ordinary laws, and it is here that Israeli judges turn for legally binding statements about the values of the state and the rights of its citizens. One such basic law is presented here, along with another law aimed at guiding legal interpretation. These are followed by three articles from leading Supreme Court justices, published shortly after the passing of the Basic Law on Human Dignity and Liberty. These articles attempt to determine the contours of future judicial interpretations. The articles do not have the specificity of an actual decision in a case; they have instead the power of ideological statements written with an eye to future applications.

Foundations of Law, 5740–1980

1. Where the court, faced with a legal question requiring decision, finds no answer to it in statute law or case law or by analogy, it shall decide it in the light of the principles of freedom, justice, equity, and peace of Israel's heritage.

Basic Law: Human Dignity and Liberty, 5752–1992, 5754–1994

1. Basic human rights in Israel are founded upon recognition of the value of human beings, of the sanctity of their lives and of their being free. They will be respected in the spirit of the principles included in the declaration establishing the state of Israel.

1a. The purpose of this basic law is to protect human dignity and liberty so as to anchor in a basic law the values of the state of Israel as a Jewish and democratic state.

A Liberal Secular Position

11. Aharon Barak, "The Constitutional Revolution: Protected Basic Rights"

Mishpat Umimshal/Law and Government in Israel, 1 (1992; Hebrew), 30–31.

Chief Justice Barak has played a key role in the move away from legal formalism and toward liberal judicial activism in the Israeli Supreme Court. This is an example of a liberal interpretation of the first clause of the Basic Law: Human Dignity and Liberty.

What is a "Jewish state" and what is the relation between the phrase "Jewish state" and the phrase "democratic state"? Are there foundational values inferred from Israel's being a Jewish state which would not be inferred from Israel's being a democratic state? Can contradictory values be inferred from the Jewish versus the democratic character of the state?

These questions will no doubt be examined in the future by the courts. In my opinion, the phrase "Jewish and democratic" does not contain two contradictory elements but rather consonance and harmony. The content of the phrase "Jewish state" will be determined according to the degree of abstraction imparted to it. In my opinion, this phrase should be understood at a high level of abstraction—which would unite all members of the society, revealing what they hold in common. The level of abstraction must be so elevated so that it will coincide with the democratic character of the state.

Indeed, the state is Jewish not in the halakhic sense, but in the sense that Jews have the right of *aliyah* [immigration], and that their national culture is the culture of the state (expressed, for example, in the language and in the days of rest). The foundational values of Judaism are the foundational values of the state. I mean the values of love of mankind, the sanctity of life, social justice, "doing what is good and right,"[17] the protection of human dignity, the rule of law over the legislature, etc.—the values Judaism has bequeathed to the world at large. The appeal to such values is on a universal level of abstraction corresponding to the democratic character of the state. Therefore, one must not identify the values of the state of Israel as a Jewish state with *mishpat ivri*. One should not forget that there is in Israel a substantial non-Jewish minority. Indeed, the values of the state of Israel as a Jewish state are those universal values common to the members of a democratic society, which have grown out of Jewish tradition and history. Alongside are those values of the state of Israel which grow out of the democratic nature of the state. The merger and concurrence between these two will forge the values of the state of Israel.

A National-Religious Position

12. Menachem Elon, "Constitution by Legislation: The Values of a Jewish and Democratic State in Light of the Basic Law: Human Dignity and Personal Freedom"

Tel Aviv University Law Review, 17 (1993; Hebrew), 663–68.

Justice Elon's disagreements with Justice Barak serve to delineate the argument between liberal secularism and modern orthodoxy in Israeli culture. Elon's argument here implicitly addresses Barak's position. Elon too seeks a consensual meaning for "Jewish" and "democratic," but he finds it in the operative consensus of the Knesset. He views the traditional body of Jewish law as the specific source of the Jewish values that the legislator has in mind. In comparison to Barak, Elon lends a particular content to the Jewish component of the law of the Foundations of Law.

It is well known that in its interpretation of a legal phrase the court must also take into account the purpose of the legislation and the legislative history

---

17. Deut. 12:28. In contemporary legal use, following the Rabbinic tradition, the phrase commonly denotes equity.

so as to explicate the words of the law. . . . In this basic law, the legislator has done us the service . . . of clearly stating—insofar as this is possible in legal phraseology—the purpose of these basic statutes: namely, to establish the values of the state of Israel as a *Jewish and democratic state*. This double-valued purpose . . . is but one; each illuminates the other and each complements the other, and they are thus unified in our hands. Therefore, the terms "human dignity" and "liberty," and all the statutes of this basic law, will be interpreted as serving to accomplish this double-valued purpose.

. . . Prior to the passing of the Basic Law on Human Dignity and Liberty, Israeli judges were not obligated to expound this double-valued purpose. Court rulings had only attended to expounding the term *democratic* state, and had discussed at length, and delved into the meaning of, democratic values. . . . In contrast, the great majority of Israeli judges have not attended to the values of the state of Israel as a *Jewish* state while interpreting basic rights. . . .

What are the values of the state of Israel as a Jewish state? How are we to discover them and by what measure? We have already cited the chairperson of the Constitution, Law, and Justice Committee [Member of Knesset Lynn, who spoke] . . . in the Knesset about the importance of reaching "a broad consensus of all the parties of the Knesset" for the said legislation. Later in that speech, MK Lynn also made reference to the meaning imparted by the legislator to the concept of the values of the state of Israel as a *Jewish* state:

> . . . We were aware of the fact that we could not pass a basic law establishing the values of the state of Israel as a Jewish and democratic state, without reaching a broad consensus of all the parties of the Knesset. . . . The law begins with a ceremonious declaration, proclaiming that it is intended to protect human dignity and liberty so as to anchor in law the values of the state of Israel as a Jewish and democratic state. The law thus stipulates in its first clause that we hold ourselves committed to the values of Israel's heritage and Jewish heritage. . . . The law defines several fundamental individual liberties none of which stands in contradiction to Israel's heritage or to the full range of values prevalent and accepted today in the state of Israel by all the house parties.

. . . In this context I wish to recall what I have repeatedly stated concerning the manner in which we should consult the sources of Israel's heritage in accordance with the law of the Foundations of Law (1980):

> . . . It is well known that the world of Jewish thought through-out its generations is, like the world of the *halakhah* itself, . . . filled with differing opinions and contradictory positions. Opposing liti-gants would have no difficulty culling grounds for their arguments and opinions from the labyrinth of the sources. That is the situation in each and every issue, and so it is regarding the issues of free-dom of opinion and freedom of speech and other issues we will discuss below. It is clear, and goes without saying, that all the posi-tions together contribute to deepening and enriching the world of Jewish thought in its different periods of time. The scholar seeking knowledge must distinguish between words pronounced for a par-ticular time and place and those pronounced for all time, between accepted opinions and exceptions, and make other similar distinc-tions of meaning. From this rich and great treasure the scholar must draw [wisdom] to address the needs of his generation and time.

I presume that the judges of Israel will not all see eye to eye regarding the in-terpretation of the concept "the values of the state of Israel as a *Jewish* state," just as the judges of Israel do not always see eye to eye regarding the interpre-tation of the concept "the values of the state of Israel as a *democratic* state." . . . The plurality of different opinions and positions is an honor to a thoughtful society. . . . All the more so in our young state, which is deeply pondering its path and its social and spiritual culture. It is also the manner of judges to ponder over the exposition and meaning of basic values and overarching principles. Hence, it is entirely possible that the concept "the values of the state of Israel as a *Jewish* state" would be interpreted in accordance with one or another understanding of the heritage of Israel. . . . Only he need do no more than repeatedly emphasize that just as the concept of a *democratic* state is to be interpreted by *studying* the *"halakhot"* of democracy [as practiced] in the enlightened democracies, so too ought the concept of a *Jewish* state be interpreted by *studying* the Jewish sources at the heart of Judaism and *engaging* them.

A Secular Interpretation of Jewish Values

13. Haim Cohn, "The Values of a Jewish and Democratic State: Examining the Basic Law: Human Dignity and Liberty"

Hapraklit Jubilee Book, edited by M. Deutch (Jerusalem: Hebrew Bar Association, 1993; Hebrew), pp. 35–45.

Like Elon, Cohn seeks to give positive content to the Jewish values of the state. Unlike Elon, however, he draws on the Declaration of Independence rather than Jewish law to enumerate these values.

. . . The values and foundational principles [of the law] are intermeshed: A legislator or judge who determines these principles is articulating the values aspired to or existing in the life of the state.

And this is what the legislator did in the law of the Foundations of Law (1980). This law stipulates: "Where the court, faced with a legal question requiring decision, finds no answer . . . it shall decide it in the light of the principles of freedom, justice, equity, and peace of Israel's heritage." . . . The principles of liberty, justice, equity, and peace are, as every one agrees, democratic values; and when they grow out of the heritage of Israel, they are Jewish values. It thus follows that the values of the state of Israel as a Jewish and democratic state must include liberty, justice, equity, and peace as present in the heritage of Israel, although they are not exhausted by them. This is not only a reasonable exposition of the Basic Law [Human Dignity and Liberty], it is also a reasonable exposition of the law of the Foundations of Law. The legislator certainly did not intend to provide room for principles that do not faithfully reflect the values of the state.

Trying now to enumerate the values of the state of Israel as defined in the legislation and in the Declaration of Independence, we arrive at something like this long list:

1. Human dignity
2. Human liberty
3. Jewish *aliyah* and the ingathering of exiles
4. Developing the land for the prosperity of all its inhabitants
5. Equal rights to all citizens without regard to any differences of religion, race, or gender

6. Justice

7. Peace

8. Freedom of religion

9. Freedom of conscience

10. Freedom of speech

11. Freedom of education

12. Freedom of culture

13. The culture of Israel, the heritage of Israel

14. The vision of the prophets of Israel

15. The achievements of science

16. Labor, art, pioneering

17. Tolerance

18. Mutual help

19. Love of mankind

20. Equity

. . . The Basic Law declares the values of the state of Israel to be *Jewish and democratic.* The greatness of this law inheres in the mutual abode created by the legislator, uniting Judaism and democracy as a pair. Not that he makes the effort to clarify for himself and for the people what the Jewishness of the state or its democratic quality is, and what they share or hold in common. All this he leaves to the interpreters. . . .

An initial interpretive problem arises concerning the conjunctive "and" in "Jewish and democratic." It could be interpreted as setting "Jewish" and "democratic" apart as if there were two creatures set loose in the state with nothing in common. . . . According to this interpretation, it is incumbent upon the judge—or the legislator—to choose a Jewish value or a democratic value as the issue at hand demands. He would at one time have to prefer one and reject the other, and at another time, the opposite. He could at most contrive an ad hoc mixture of elements of both values when the matter at hand permits it and justifies it.

I cannot accept this kind of interpretation. To me, a "Jewish and democratic state" is not a state in which Judaism and democracy are engaged

in constant dispute and obstinate competition, whether political or ideological. For that we would not need a Basic Law. We may presume that the
legislator did not intend the perpetuation of evil but rather the advancement
of good. The conjunctive "and" must be interpreted as combining Judaism
and democracy into one supreme value—Judaism that is democratic and a
democracy that is Jewish—as if Judaism and democracy were one: "each illuminates the other and each complements the other, and they are thus unified
in our hands."[18] This is a true innovation and constitutes real progress: The
interpreter's task is to impart the supreme framing value with normative
legal content conforming to Judaism and democracy together.

    . . . In the eyes of the religious members of the legislature a "Jewish
state" should perhaps aspire to be a halakhic state; maybe this is the reason
they gave [the state] this name and predicate in the Basic Law. Maybe the
secular MK's [Members of Knesset], or some of them, agreed to this name
and predicate simply owing to political considerations and not from any connection to Judaism. These matters do not add or detract from the objective
interpretation of the terms. Similarly, it makes no difference if one would
hold the possible position that the state is "Jewish" only insofar as it is the
state of the Jewish people.

    . . . The distinction (made by Ben-Gurion) between a state gov-
erned by law and a halakhic state is parallel in common parlance to the distinction between a democracy and a theocracy. Even if you were to say that
a true or pure "Jewish" state ought to be a halakhic state—a position I am
far from maintaining—a "Jewish and democratic" state cannot be a halakhic
state—not because the norms of *halakhah* are necessarily undemocratic, but
because the whole system is antidemocratic. With respect to a specific norm,
the state can be a law-abiding state and a halakhic state at one and the same
time. This is the case when the halakhic norm is authorized as law by legal
democratic procedure. But a democratic legislator would betray his charge
were he to adopt the *halakhah* as such. The result would be—perhaps in the
eyes of an individual who abides by the *mitzvot*—a Jewish state, but it would
certainly be an undemocratic state, and the state is not meant to be Jewish
unless it is democratic. In other words, the Jewishness of the state cannot

18. Cohen is quoting Elon (§12).

be halakhic or religious; it must be a Judaism sanctioned by the values of democracy.

Commentary. Against the Idea of a Jewish State

A state is home to its people, to its inhabitants. Some states are good, even though none is so good that it cannot be bettered; some are bad. They have no value in themselves. Their value depends on their being good homes for their inhabitants (and on other factors as well). Can Israel be a good state, can it be a (good) home for its inhabitants, while its constitution declares it a Jewish state? This is the question that Aharon Barak is confronting in his exposition (§11). He does not state it as such, for as a judge he uses an interpretive method. He asks himself: Is there a way of interpreting the law that is consistent with Israel being a good state? He is committed to giving an affirmative answer even if in order to do so he has to empty the law of all or much of its content. Interpreting statutes out of their meaning is the judicial way of neutralizing immoral or unjust laws. His answer to my question is: Yes, Israel can be both a Jewish state and a good state, provided we understand by a Jewish state a state that embraces the values which Judaism gave the world, namely, "the love of mankind, the sanctity of life, social justice, equity, protecting human dignity, the rule of law over the legislature, etc."

Notice that in the same sense France too can be a Jewish state. It too can embrace the values that Judaism gave to the world, namely, the love of mankind, the sanctity of life, social justice, equity, protecting human dignity, the rule of law over the legislature, etc. Indeed, it may well be said that in that sense no state can be a morally good state unless it is a Jewish state.

Some may regard this as a reductio ad absurdum of Barak's interpretation of the law. But that would be a mistake. It would disregard the fact that courts have the power to interpret a morally unacceptable law out of existence. I do not mean that they have the power to do so whenever they find some moral blemish in the law. But they have it when the law is morally unacceptable, as the Israeli Basic Law: Human Dignity and Liberty, 1992, 1994, is. To show that it is morally unacceptable one has to show that an interpretation that does not expunge its content renders it immoral.

That is more than one can do in a brief commentary. Instead I will mention and dismiss as morally unacceptable three possible interpretations, and then comment briefly on a more reasonable fourth interpretation.

The law may be interpreted to mean that the Jewish religion should have special privileges in Israel, perhaps that Judaism be a state religion. Alternatively it may give people who are Jewish special standing in the state, endow them with rights that other inhabitants do not have (to a certain extent this happens in Israel owing to other laws, and even more so owing to governmental practices). I will take it for granted that given the character of Israel's population, a large proportion of which is secular or avows other religions, and a large proportion of which is not Jewish, both these interpretations render the law morally unacceptable. Some of the reasons for this will become clear later in my comments.

A third interpretation says that Israel is to be a Jewish state in that it should uphold values that are uniquely Jewish, that is, values which—unlike the universal values Barak refers to—are not universal values of mankind but specifically Jewish values. Barak's comments imply an awareness of the difficulties with the idea of special Jewish values. Morality is universal, and so are values generally. Ethnic or national values are the false values of national self-aggrandizement and chauvinism.

But often what are mentioned as special values are but particular instances of universal values. This brings us to the fourth interpretation, which I want to dwell on. It regards the Jewishness of the state as consisting in its dedication to implementing universal values, as Barak would have it, but to implementing them in the form they took in Jewish history. According to this interpretation of the notion of a Jewish state, the state would apply the universal principles of justice and morality, just as Barak says; but whenever their implementation could take different forms, the Jewish state would implement them where possible in the forms they were given in Jewish communities in the past.

Does this interpretation make the law morally acceptable? It is necessary and inevitable that the pursuit of universal values takes local forms. To give an example, think of the political virtues of democracy and social justice, inasmuch as they involve protecting inhabitants from poverty and deprivation. If we think of but four Western democracies—Germany, France, Britain, and the United States—we find a vivid illustration of how democracy can be implemented in a variety of ways. The democratic institutions of these countries differ in many respects: the relations between the executive and the legislature, the constitutional roles of the courts, the electoral systems, and more. None of them is perfect, but improvement in each should proceed from within the constitutional practices established in it, rather than by rejecting them in favor of alien institutions. Similar differences exist in the institutions that implement social justice. For example, methods of providing healthcare in Canada, Britain, France, and Germany (the United States falls far short of the minimum required to be a good candidate here) vary widely, but all of them are capable of being improved within the confines of the basic institutional principles they are based on.

So could not Israel, as a state, implement universal values in the ways and forms familiar from Jewish traditions without being immoral? Not so. The examples show the rationality of a state relying on its own traditions and practices, or the traditions and practices of its population. If doing that would make Israel into a Jewish state, then in the same sense the United States is an American state, Britain a British state, and so on. We cannot but wonder why Britain can be a British state without a law that declares it to be so. The reason is that following established traditions to give effect to universal values in one's country is simply the rational and the moral thing to do. It does not require a special law to decree that that should be done. It is the course that any rational legislature will almost automatically pursue and that the courts will follow in matters entrusted to them. That is why all the morally decent countries of the world have the character they have and follow the traditions of their people without the need to declare "I am a Danish state," "I am a Norwegian state," and so on. They are that by being morally decent.

But the natural way of understanding the resort to Jewish ways of implementing universal values is different from the above. It is not an appeal to the practices and institutions that grew in Israel over the years. It appeals to the traditions of the Jewish people throughout their history. Israel, according to this interpretation, is a new and exceptional state built on immigration from different Jewish communities whose traditions can be revived on the soil of Israel only with deliberate effort. Understood in this way, the fourth interpretation, too, renders the law morally unacceptable.

There is no value in preserving traditions as an end in itself. Many people have a sentimental attachment to the traditions of their ancestors and wish to see them preserved. Others rebel against them in whole or in part. That is the way human civilizations evolve. No, my earlier remarks about the rationality of implementing universal traditions in ways that are sensitive to local traditions have nothing to do with nostalgic preservation. They have nothing to do with reviving Jewish institutions of the time of the Second Temple, or from eighteenth-century Poland, or fourteenth-century Spain. They relate to the rationality of keeping to existing institutions as they evolved in the life of the population of Israel while striving to improve them in a way consonant with their basic character, rather than overhauling their foundations in favor of models derived from other countries.

So, as Barak sees, only an interpretation that expunges the law's content avoids making it morally unacceptable. Israel should live by universal values, implementing them in accordance with its own traditions and practices and those of its population. This morally acceptable interpretation does not regard the law as giving a special importance or role to the ancient traditions of Jewish communities. It is important to remember in this context that in Israel not only is the interpretation of the traditions of the Jewish people controversial, as Justice Elon points out, but the very desirability of resorting to the traditions is controversial. By and large, that recourse is rejected by Israeli Palestinians and by those who still adhere to the original ideals of the Zionist movement, whose goal was normalization and whose adherents found inspiration in the best European ideas of the time. That tradition found its most inspiring expression in Herzl's *Altneuland* and in the writings of Borochov and other social Zionists.

This interpretation of the law makes it redundant: it merely states the obvious. But does it render it harmless? It does render it as harmless as judicial interpretation can, but the law is still one that some of us would rather not have. One reason for that is that as it stands, the law invites misinterpretation. You may say that every law is open to misinterpretation, so that cannot be an argument against having the law. But not every law has to be denuded of content or made redundant to avoid all other interpretations, while in this case all interpretations make the law morally unacceptable. Moreover, the effort to denude the law of content is itself damaging. The courts must do that to avoid a morally unacceptable interpretation. But it is better, much better, to avoid the need to do that, especially since in the process it is difficult to avoid some intellectual dishonesty or untruths, such as the preposterous claims made by Barak regarding the contribution of Judaism to the moral enlightenment of the world.

It is time, however, to turn to the main objection to the law that we are discussing, an objection that is not overcome by interpreting it out of all content,—for even then it remains a symbolic presence, and its symbolic meaning makes it impossible for the state to be home to a large proportion of its people: those who are not Jewish. For Israel to be my home I must be able to say that this is my state, and if I am not Jewish, then unless I suffer from false consciousness, a Jewish state cannot be my state. It cannot be my state not because I—a non-Jew—do not want to have it as my state. I cannot have it as my state because it declares that it is not mine. Its being a Jewish state, the state of the Jews, is official. For many in Israel this means that Israel is the state of the Jews wherever they are. Some non-Israeli Jews value that knowledge. They like to feel that the state of Israel is their state, that it is more theirs than it is the state of its non-Jewish inhabitants. But even if we disregard that aspect of the question, the problem is still with us. So long as Israel defines itself as a Jewish state, it cannot be home to those of its people who are not Jewish. Indeed, so long as that is the case, they are not really its people.

"The people of Israel are the Israeli Jews. It also has, unfortunately, a large non-Jewish population. Of course, they should be treated humanely, and their rights should be respected. They are not to blame that they are not living in their proper countries, just as French Jews should not be blamed for the fact that the circumstances of their lives make them live in France. They are a tolerated minority."

Such "enlightened" attitudes are indeed to be found in France, and in other countries, just as they are to be found in Israel. Some French people regard their country as French and regard French Jews as a tolerated minority. Most French Jews resent this. In most Western countries such attitudes are rejected by the governments, which insist that they have no second-class citizens. Morally speaking, a state is the home of all its inhabitants, and none are second-class; none of them belong to tolerated minorities. The law of most Western countries is consistent with this view. So far as I know, Israel and Germany are the only ones that define themselves as the state of an ethnic group, a definition which is symbolic but which in both countries has practical consequences. In both of them this blemish on their law cultivates racism, hatred, and the inability of part of their population to regard themselves as equal citizens in their homeland.

Joseph Raz

Commentary. A Multicultural Jewish State?

Judicial opinions are rhetorical performances. Those who write them must inevitably be concerned with the likely responses of their intended audiences. The actual litigants compose one such audience, although, as a matter of fact, particularly as one moves from the trial to the appellate level, the more important audience consists of persons observing the case from a distance. These range from lawyers seeking guidance for future cases to citizens concerned about the general sociopolitical issues raised by a given case. These audiences will be receptive to different rhetorics. The lawyer may want careful parsing of traditional legal materials and tend to ignore extraneous commentary as mere window dressing. The lay audience, on the other hand, may want reassurance about the character of the society in which they live; what the lawyer dismisses as irrelevant may, for the laity, be treated as constitutive of the society itself.

Although the issue of multiple audiences will arise in any society that is divided between professionals and laity, it is especially acute in what we have learned to call "multicultural" societies. Almost by definition, such societies are composed of a number of significantly different subpopulations. Even if they all speak, in some literal sense, the same language—although in Israel that surely is not the case—they will nonetheless resonate to different possible sentences within that language. What will be appealing to one part of the population will not simply be different from what appeals to another. Instead, the different rhetorics are likely to be "oppositional": what will sound like music to some ears will sound like chalk across the blackboard to others—quite independent, incidentally, of the decision reached. To win for the "wrong" reasons or by reference to the wrong rhetoric may significantly diminish any joy attached to the victory itself, perhaps by underscoring its precariousness.

So what should one expect from judges in the de facto multicultural state of Israel? Were Israel in fact *not* multicultural—were it a homogeneous country of religiously observant Jews with shared notions of what observance required—it is hard to believe that the rhetorical practices of its judges would excite much interest, save in the most detached academic sense. Once one concedes, however, the multicultural nature of the actual society, then one must ask whether judges, when writing their decisions, ought to adopt the most "neutral," because most universalist, rhetoric possible. Or, alternatively, should they actively attempt to insert more particularist references to explicitly "Jewish" law or what the law of the Foundations of Law calls "the principles of freedom, justice, equity, and peace of Israel's heritage"? (We must put to one side the extremely important question of whether there is any singular "Israel[i] heritage" that could generate determinate principles in regard to such abstractions as "freedom, justice, equity, and peace.")

I am disinclined to offer an abstract, theoretical response. My own political preferences are in line with a version of liberalism that, as much as possible, avoids religious language in the "public square," including the courts. But there are many who disagree, and it is difficult, especially if one is a pragmatist, to explain why *these* citizens must necessarily bear the cost of being marginalized so that liberals feel no discomfort when reading judicial opinions. And "marginalization" or "alienation" may be the least of it; at some point one might be concerned about even more basic questions of legitimation, loyalty, and, at the extreme, insurrection.

The American Supreme Court justice Oliver Wendell Holmes once said that "general propositions do not decide concrete cases," and it is especially difficult to believe that one theoretical proposition should be dispositive as to societies as different as the United States, France, Israel, and Italy, to name only four that are well within the "Western" tradition. The practical issue is this: To assert, dogmatically, that judges ought never refer to specifically Jewish sources is to say at the same time that judges must deprive themselves of any advantages, relative to important audiences within Israeli society, attached to such references. After all, it is at least thinkable that some of the bystanders might find more persuasive (as well as more generally legitimate) opinions that invoke Rashi or contemporary halakhic decisors, whereas they would turn away from opinions (and perhaps the courts themselves) reaching similar results but failing to discuss any such references. No judge should be expected to engage in such self-denial, especially if the perceived legitimation costs are high. Although analytic jurisprudes may properly separate law from the rest of the social order, no one concerned with the actual operation of a legal system can afford to do so, and judicial rhetoric must always absorb the myths and symbols of the wider society.

To the extent, then, that a significant portion of Israel's population takes halakhic arguments seriously, one might well expect crafty judges to weave such arguments into their own opinions, whether or not the judges themselves are sufficiently observant to regard them as dispositive reasons. The same may be said, perhaps, of arguments drawn from "Israel's heritage," an ill-disguised euphemism for "the history of the Jewish people." Even secular Jews, after all, might well find appealing the kind of apologetics associated with writers like Abba Eban or, in this collection, Aharon Barak, who heroically attempt, with whatever degree of plausibility, to identify that heritage with the most attractive features of Western liberalism.

So what is the problem? The answer, of course, is that Israel is *not*, sociologically speaking, an exclusively Jewish state, even if we ignore the bitter cleavages within the Jewish population. It contains a significant and, demographers would suggest, increasing Arab population, some of it Muslim, some Christian (and some, undoubtedly, secular), all united in the view that *halakhah* is not *their* law, the history of the Jewish people not *their* history. For the judiciary to look only to Jewish materials when "the court, faced with a legal question requiring decision, finds no answer to it in statute law or case law or by analogy" is guaranteed to cause insult, to reinforce the sense of marginalization and alienation that cannot possibly be good for the future of the state of Israel.

Perhaps one should learn from the changing norms of American judges. It was once quite common for them to refer to the United States as a "Christian country" or to offer the specific teachings of Christianity as support for some legal proposition or other. This has been replaced with the evocation of a "Judeo-Christian" tradition that, whatever its historical provenance, is clearly designed to recognize the demise of the Christian hegemony of an earlier era and to announce the symbolic integration of Jews as core members of American society. (One is curious about the future of this rhetoric as the American people come to include an increasing number of Muslims. Will we see references to the "Abrahamic" traditions? This would not resolve any questions presented by the immigration, especially from Southeast Asia, of persons who are outside any religious tradition identified with the "holy land" of Israel.)

If it is unrealistic, and perhaps even impolitic, to expect Israeli judges to adopt a relentlessly secular rhetoric, it may still be feasible to ask that greater attention be paid to the multicultural nature of "Israel's heritage" and then to pay due rhetorical respect, say, to the teachings of Islam and Christianity, especially when particular legal controversies involve issues likely to be important to *all* Israelis. If, as one suspects is often the case, these teachings do not in fact conflict, it is hard to see what the costs would be of such broadened reference. Committed secularists might object, although this would not be very important unless the actual results of the decisions were offensive as well. Perhaps more important would be the objection of ardent Zionists, who might see any approving reference to the teachings of the Quran, say, as the equivalent of waving the white flag of surrender in regard to the classic vision of a hegemonically "Jewish" state. This is only to underscore that the ostensibly theoretical debate about sources of law for the Israeli judge is deeply linked with the far more fundamental conflict, within both Israeli-Jewish society and the wider community of self-conscious Jews, about the contemporary relevance of classical Zionism, with its linkage to the nineteenth-century flourishing of organic nationalism and the critique of liberal universalism.

But it is hard to say what classical Zionism, which was mostly a secular politics, would say about this subject. Its protagonists would presumably expect the judges of a Zionist state to refer to the historical experiences of the Jewish people and perhaps even to some secularized version of *hala-khah*—like Elon's *mishpat ivri*—although this latter expectation, especially, might well be qualified by modernist commitments to democracy, freedom, justice, and so on. But even if this is a legitimate starting point in a state with an 80 percent Jewish majority, it cannot be the stopping point, for there is also the remaining 20 percent who must also be considered. And other legal resources are available that derive from both religious and political traditions. Indeed, Israeli courts have regularly referred to the teachings of British and even Ottoman law, and several justices, including Haim Cohn and Aharon Barak, have made good use of American materials. One might expect (and wish) for suitable use of Muslim and Christian sources as well, whether for reasons of rhetorical legitimation or the substantive wisdom found in them. Of course, all of these sources are contested and require interpretation—exactly like Jewish law. Might one suggest that this rich salmagundi of materials will produce a specifically Israeli tradition to refer to: the record of the courts' own readings (and, inevitably, misreadings) of both Jewish and non-Jewish sources?

Sanford Levinson

Commentary. A Jewish Democratic State

Israel defines itself as a Jewish democratic state. This dual nature is, for some, a source of moral and political discomfort. It violates, so it is argued, a basic democratic principle: that of cultural-national neutrality. I question this claim and argue that the ideal of cultural neutrality is both theoretically inconsistent and politically unrealistic. No actual state can be free of all particularist features, so each state should democratically determine the particular set of characteristics it chooses to endorse—and Jewishness is as legitimate a form of particularism as any.

Democratic theory is in no way committed to the ideal of neutrality. This ideal has been introduced to political theory in conjunction with a particular type of liberalism that requires state institutions to take upon themselves only coordinating and mediating roles and refrain from adopting perfectionist or symbolic ones. By narrowing the range of issues in which the state intervenes, liberal neutrality places the state at an equal distance from all its citizens, reassuring them all that the state will treat them with equal concern and respect.

This ideal of state neutrality misconstrues the role of culture in public life. Trying to restrict culture to the private sphere, it empties the state of its symbolic role. The result is a state that can serve all its citizens impartially but cannot be a home to any of them. A home is not an institution, not even a fair and efficient one, but a place to which one is tied emotionally, which reflects one's history, memories, fears, and hopes. A home cannot have merely universal features; it must always be embedded in the particular.

So here is the source of the tension: if Israel is a home to the Jewish people, its non-Jewish citizens will feel estranged from it. Must it then shed its particularist nature, be a state like all others? Israel should indeed aspire to normality. But every state must operate within a cultural-historical context; it must have an official language(s), a flag, an anthem, public holidays, and public celebrations. It must build monuments, print money and stamps, adopt a historical narrative and a vision of the future. As feminists and members of national and racial minorities discovered long ago, the idea that a state can be void of any cultural, historical, or linguistic affiliation is a misleading illusion—which is not only naive but also oppressive.

It is therefore one of Israel's advantages that it openly declares its cultural national bias. This allows those who are harmed by this bias—mainly its Palestinian citizens, but also other non-Jews—to explain the source of their grievances. Must a just democratic state do more than acknowledge these grievances?

Democratic life constantly produces losers, and loss is always a source of discontent. The modern conception of democracy is, in many ways, majoritarian. It assumes that all citizens must be allowed to participate in an open democratic process, and then the majority wins. There are obvious limits to majoritarianism. The majority should not use its power to oppress the minority or violate its rights. But when is the fact that the minority's preferences and interests are not accepted a matter of oppression or violation of basic rights, and when is it simply a fair but painful defeat?

One might argue that oppression occurs when members of a certain group become permanent losers. But in the democratic game, members of many groups are permanent losers: vegetarians, opera lovers, individuals with eccentric or expensive tastes, commonly fail to convince others to support their demands. Do members of all these groups deserve special protection? If they do, what is left of the idea of majoritarian decision making? Nowadays it is common to answer this question by drawing a distinction between identity-providing affiliations and all others. Individuals, it is assumed, can endure different kinds of losses, but not ones relating to their identity.

But the politics of identity does not require the naive illusion that politics could be emptied of cultural, national, or religious content or that particularist features could be restricted to the private sphere; it does not phrase its argument in terms of cultural neutrality. On the contrary, it takes for granted the symbolic, emotional aspects of politics and structures its aims in accordance with them.

Once a politics of identity allows different groups to come out of hiding and occupy public space, all groups, majority and minorities alike, openly compete to imprint state institutions with their particular features. Even if the competition is perfectly fair, the minority's success must be less than that of the majority. A politics that recognizes identity thus cannot solve the problem of marginalization. Is the imbalance between the majority and the minorities unfair? Does it violate democratic principles? I daresay not. Democratic states must treat all citizens equally, but they cannot, nor should they, equalize the influence of the majority and a minority.

It follows that Israel can be a Jewish democratic state as long as this dual nature expresses the preferences of the majority of its citizens. Its non-Jewish citizens must be given a due place in public life, but this will not redeem their sense of estrangement. The Palestinian citizens of Israel are bound to feel excluded. Like women in the army and secular Jews in religious neighborhoods, they will always feel the unease of those who do not fit the reigning social and cultural norms. This feeling of alienation will not disappear even if Palestinian citizens come to be treated with respect, their rights guaranteed, their participation assured, and their fair share of social services secured. The only way for them to feel included is to give up those identifying features that set them apart and to assimilate into the majority. A few choose this way, but for most Palestinians, as for most diaspora Jews, it is not a viable option. They do not wish to surrender their identity. This decision has a price that cannot be avoided.

Like other states Israel cannot avoid adopting a set of particularist features. By majoritarian means it has decided that Judaism will be its reigning culture—though other cultures can play a secondary role. There is then no reason why Israel should not establish the cultural preferences of its citizens by law, as it establishes by law their economic or distributive preferences. Yet Israel ought not adopt a law that would prevent future majorities from changing the character of the state in accordance with their preferences. This implies that the present election law banning political parties that question the Jewish nature of the state is antidemocratic and should therefore be repealed.

Israel can retain its Jewish character only so long as Jewishness enjoys democratic support. Hence democratic values take precedence over Jewish ones. The two descriptions of the state, Jewish and democratic, thus play different roles: the former's role is mainly interpretative; it translates the universal into local terms. The latter sets the universal foundations and marks the boundaries of acceptable interpretations. As a result, democratic interpretations of Judaism will take precedence over nondemocratic ones. This is well exemplified by the law of the "Foundations of Law," which states that the court ought to rule "in the light of the principles of freedom, justice, equity, and peace of Israel's heritage." The decision to specify which of the many values found in Israel's heritage is to be adopted by the court is meant to assure that Israel will draw from its heritage a political morality that fits democratic values and attitudes.

The priority given to democratic values in the legal sphere is rarely admitted, and the tension between Judaism and democracy is ignored or veiled. One way to veil the tension is to claim that at some abstract level, Judaism and democracy coincide. Justice Aharon Barak is the main advocate of this approach. The content of the phrase "Jewish state," he argues, "should be understood at a high level of abstraction which would unite all members of the society, revealing what they hold in common. The level of abstraction must be so elevated so that it will coincide with the democratic character of the state." Barak's position reflects a presumption dominant among liberal philosophers that at the core of all reasonable doctrines lies a set of shared values. The way to resolve conflicts between such doctrines is to elevate the discussion to as high a level of abstraction as possible. The work of abstraction, John Rawls argues, "is a way of continuing public discussion when shared understandings of lesser generality have broken down. We should be prepared to find that the deeper the conflict, the higher the level of abstraction to which we must ascend to get a clear and uncluttered view of its roots" (*Political Liberalism,* 1996, p. 46).

Is it true that raising issues to a higher level of abstraction will solve the conflicts surrounding them? Consider some examples. The most crucial political question of all is the source of authority. For Judaism, as for any other religion, the source of authority is divine; for democracy it is human. At what level of abstraction can this disagreement be resolved? As it is inconceivable that a political system could leave the question of authority open, and as it is quite clear that Israel has chosen the democratic approach, the role played by "Jewish" and "democratic" in the definition of the state should be reevaluated. We do not have two competing descriptions; rather, the Jewishness of the state is limited by its democratic nature.

Can other, less fundamental tensions between Judaism and democracy be resolved by means of abstraction? Think about the legitimacy of abortions, the right of women to serve in religious courts, issues concerning euthanasia, the right to commit suicide, or the right to waive one's rights. None of these issues can be resolved by raising the level of abstraction.

While individuals with different fundamental commitments may agree on how to act, we suspect that they reach this conclusion for very different reasons. If we examine these reasons, we will be faced with a deeper controversy than the one we began with. If we raise the debate to a higher level of abstraction, we will reach metaphysical issues concerning the existence of God and the role he plays in our world, which are impossible to settle. Rawls and Barak are misled by their own theories, which exclude a priori all those interpretations that do not share the humanitarian democratic perspective. Given that exclusion, abstraction must logically lead to agreement. Actual political life, however, does not mimic such theories. The participants are more diverse, and not all of them share reasonable or democratic presuppositions. Under such circumstances, abstraction might intensify conflict rather than reduce it.

Are Judaism and democracy doomed to be in permanent conflict? The answer is probably yes. But there are ways of ameliorating such conflicts, not by means of abstraction but by concrete compromises based on specific patterns of behavior. This was Ben-Gurion's approach. It is not necessary at present, he argued, "to reach decisions in matters of opinion and faith, in which we shall long continue to be divided." Ben-Gurion was seeking a compromise, even though he knew that compromises are, by nature, transient and untidy. But he understood that although compromises may be flimsily grounded, they are politically more desirable and more just than many tidy, abstract solutions.

Israel can be a Jewish and democratic state if its citizens aspire that it be one, and if Judaism and democracy concur on a wide enough range of practices to allow such a state to function. At present, both conditions are fulfilled. As for the future, Israel will be able to retain its Jewish identity only if it maintains a Jewish majority and is able to inspire among its Jewish citizens democratic modes of behavior.

Yael Tamir

Glossary of Names

The place-names in parentheses indicate where the person was born and died, when that is known, or where the person resided for the major part of his life.

Abraham b. David of Posquieres; Rabad—(Provence, c. 1125–98), talmudic scholar. Born in Narbonne, Rabad moved to Posquieres, where he established a yeshivah that became a center for the study of Talmud in Provence. His works include commentaries on talmudic literature, responsa, homiletic discourses, and critical glosses (*hassagot*) on famous works of rabbinic literature, including Maimonides' *Mishneh Torah,* for which he became known as *ba'al ha-hassagot* (master of the glosses).

Abravanel, Isaac b. Judah—(Lisbon–Venice, 1437–1508), statesman, philosopher, and biblical exegete. Born into one of the leading Portuguese Jewish families, Abravanel was an important figure in the court of King Alfonso V and, later, in Spain, in the court of Isabel and Ferdinand. He chose exile over conversion and left Spain in 1492, living subsequently in a number of Italian cities. He is best known for his biblical commentaries and for three books on messianism.

Abulafia, Abraham b. Samuel—(Spain–Sicily–?, 1240–after 1291), kabbalist, founder of the school of Prophetic and Practical Kabbalah. Abulafia believed that, given the correct mystical doctrines and practices, prophecy was possible even in the exile. In Sicily, in 1290, he prophesied the beginning of the messianic era, and many Jews, believing him, prepared to leave for Palestine. He was opposed by the most prominent rabbinical authority of the time, Solomon b. Abraham Adret (see entry), who accused him of being a false prophet. The controversy resulted in a ban on Abulafia that forced him to flee from Sicily to a tiny island near Malta. He defended his Kabbalah against Adret in his letter *Ve-Zot li-Yehudah.*

Abulafia, Meir; Ramah—(Spain, 1170?–1244), talmudist and poet. Abulafia was actively involved in the Toledo *kahal,* for which he promulgated important *takkanot*. He worked in various literary genres, among them *halakhah* and Hebrew poetry, and participated in contemporary religious disputes, e.g., the debate over Maimonides' view of resurrection.

Adret, Solomon b. Abraham; Rashba—(Barcelona, c. 1235–c. 1310), Spanish rabbi, communal leader, halakhic authority, and kabbalist. Adret, a disciple of Nahmanides (see entry), was one of the central figures in the development of what may be called the "constitutional law" of the *kahal*. He wrote commentaries on the Talmud and other halakhic books, but he is probably best known for his thousands of responsa, many of which deal with communal matters—most importantly, the authority of the *berurim* and rabbinic courts.

Agudat Yisrael—lit., Association of Israel; world Jewish movement and political party, founded in Katowitz, Poland, in 1912, in opposition to Reform and to Zionism. Agudat Yisrael seeks to preserve orthodoxy by adherence to *halakhah* as the governing principle for both private and public Jewish life.

Albo, Joseph—(Spain, d. 1444), philosopher and preacher. Albo is the author of *Sefer ha-Ikkarim* (Book of Principles), a treatise on the articles of faith that also deals extensively with the philosophy of law. Albo was a disciple of Hisdai Crescas and the student and colleague of Nissim Gerondi (see entry). He was influenced by both Arabic and Christian writers, including Thomas Aquinas.

Ari. *See* Luria, Isaac b. Solomon

Asher b. Yehiel; Rosh (also known as Asheri)—(Germany–Spain, c. 1250–1327), rabbi and halakhist. Asher was born into an Askkenazi pietist family. In Worms he studied under Meir b. Baruch of Rothenburg (see entry), who appointed him a member of the city's *bet din*. After the imprisonment of Meir, Asher was probably the leading figure of German Jewry. But, fearing to suffer Meir's fate, he left with his family for Spain, settling finally in Toledo, where he accepted the position of rabbi. He promoted the methodology of the tosafists in Spain and tried to establish Ashkenazic *minhag* (customs) there. Among his writings are *Piskei haRosh,* a collection and codification of previous halakhic decisions and commentaries, and about one thousand surviving responsa. His son Jacob was the author of the *Tur.*

Ashi—(Babylonia, c. 335–427/28 C.E.), prominent *amora*. Ashi studied under Rava and Rav Papa, among others; after the latter's death (371/72) and until his own, he headed the yeshivah of Sura. With the cooperation of his older contemporary Ravina (see entry), Ashi began editing the Babylonian Talmud, a task continued by later *amora'im,* particularly Ravina II b. Huna (see Ravina entry).

Ashkenaz—Germany.

Ashkenazi—a Jew from Ashkenaz; later, from central and eastern Europe. Contrasted with Sephardi, a Jew from Spain; by extension, a Jew from the Orient. Ashkenaz and Sepharad designate two distinct halakhic traditions within Judaism from the Middle Ages on.

Avtalyon—colleague of Shemaiah. *See also* Shemaiah and Avtalyon

Barak, Aharon—(Lithuania–Israel, 1936–), Israeli jurist. Born in Kovno, Barak emigrated to Israel in 1947. He studied law at the Hebrew University, where he became a professor (1974). Later (1975) he was appointed attorney general. In 1978 Barak was nominated as a justice of the Supreme Court and in 1995 became its chief justice. He is perhaps the leading defender in Israel of an American-style "judicial review."

Basyatchi, Elijah b. Moses—(Constantinople, 15th and 16th centuries), the most important Karaite scholar of his time, regarded as "the final decider." His code of law, *Adderet Eliyahu,* became the Karaite equivalent of the Rabbanite *Shulhan Arukh.*

Ben-Gurion, David—(Russia–Israel, 1886–1973), Israeli statesman, first prime minister, and defense minister. Ben-Gurion was the dominant figure in the labor movement in Palestine and, as head of the Jewish Agency, played a leading role in the struggle for Israel's independence. Although he was committed to the socialist parties of the *yishuv,* he stressed the ideal of *mamlakhtiyut* ("stateness" or political consciousness, civic spirit) in an attempt to bring together the Jewish community's disparate groups and factions, religious and secular, within one political framework.

Ben Sira, Simeon b. Jesus—(Palestine, 2d century B.C.E.), Hebrew aphorist, author of *The Wisdom of Ben Sira* (Ecclesiasticus). The book (probably completed around 180 B.C.E.) is written in the style of biblical wisdom literature, but it is less focused on the royal court and more sympathetic to the priesthood. *The Wisdom of Ben Sira* was preserved as a whole in the Christian Bible (Apocrypha), but many sections of the original Hebrew are extant; a few verses are quoted in early Rabbinic sources.

Bergman, Samuel Hugo—(Prague–Jerusalem, 1883–1975), philosopher. During his student days at Prague, Bergman met Martin Buber (see entry), who had a lasting influence on his work. After emigrating to Palestine in 1920, he became the first director of the National Library and, afterwards, in 1928, a philosophy professor at the Hebrew University. He was a founding member of Berit Shalom (a movement supporting a Jewish-Arab binational state). Bergman's main intellectual interests were in the philosophy of science and religion.

Berlin, Naphtali Tzvi Judah; Netziv—(Poland/Russia, 1817–93), rabbi and *rosh yeshivah*. Berlin headed the famous yeshivah at Volozhin for some forty years, transforming it into a spiritual center for east European Jewry. He joined the Hibbat Zion movement and urged observant Jews to support the settlement of Palestine. His work includes important commentaries on the Torah as well as on extratalmudic Rabbinic texts.

Bet Hillel. *See* Hillel the Elder

Bet Shammai. *See* Hillel the Elder

Boethus—founder (?) of a religious and political party that existed in the last centuries of the Second Temple period (1st century B.C.E.–1st century C.E.), evidently a branch of the Sadducees (see entry).

Breuer, Isaac—(Hungary–Israel, 1883–1946), orthodox spokesman and thinker. Breuer was one of the intellectual leaders of Agudat Yisrael, first in Hungary, then (after 1936) in Palestine, where he helped to organize the Po'alei Agudat Yisrael (an ultraorthodox socialist party), of which he became the president. He was the grandson of Samson (b.) Raphael Hirsch (see entry), whose heritage he sought to preserve and pass on. Though initially opposed to Zionism, he came to see in it the hand of Providence.

Buber, Martin — (Austria–Israel, 1878–1965), philosopher, theologian, and biblical critic. Born in Vienna, Buber studied in German universities, finishing his education in Berlin, where Georg Simmel was among his teachers. He was active in the early Zionist movement. Buber began his Jewish studies as a scholar of Hasidism, and he developed his own theological position, first articulated in *I and Thou* (1923), alongside his interpretations of hasidic writings. He defended a "philosophy of dialogue," which also found expression in socialist politics and, after he emigrated to Palestine (1938), in his leadership of Berit Shalom (see Bergman entry). Together with Franz Rosenzweig, he translated the Bible into German, producing also a series of books interpreting biblical texts — the most important of these is the *Kingship of God* (1932).

Cohen, Hermann — (Germany, 1842–1918), German philosopher. Cohen began his studies at the Jewish Theological Seminary in Breslau, then studied philosophy at the University of Berlin and became a leading figure of the Marburg school of neo-Kantianism. He developed a liberal interpretation of Judaism that emphasized monotheism and morality, but remained himself traditionally observant and was critical of Reform Judaism. Cohen worked out an interpretation of Jewish law that was consistent with Kantian moral philosophy. He rejected Zionism as a betrayal of the universal messianic ideal.

Cohn, Haim — (Germany–Israel, 1911–), Israeli jurist. Cohn was born in Lübeck and settled in Palestine in 1930. He studied at Abraham Isaac Kook's yeshivah (Merkaz ha-Rav) in Jerusalem (see Kook entry), then returned to Germany to study law. He was Israel's attorney general from 1950 to 1952 and again from 1953 to 1960, and the legal and judicial system of the new state owes much to his work. In 1960 he was appointed a justice of the Supreme Court, where he was one of the leading defenders of liberalism in both religious and civic affairs.

Dessler, Eliyahu Eliezer—(Russia–Israel, 1891–1954), a leading figure of the Musar movement (founded by Rabbi Yisrael of Salant, who emphasized moral perfection over traditional learning). After serving as a director of a center for advanced Talmud study in Gateshead, England (1941–46), Dessler accepted an invitation to become the spiritual director of Ponevezh yeshivah in Bene-Berak, Israel. He brought elements of Kabbalah and Hasidism into his Musar ideology.

Domb, Yerahmiel Israel Isaac—(Poland–England, 1917–), anti-Zionist spokesman. Born in Lodz to a hasidic family, Domb studied in his youth at a yeshivah in Lublin. During World War II he fled to London and developed close contacts with the Satmar leader, Yoel Teitelbaum. From the early 1950s, Domb was one of the main ideologists of the Neturei Karta (Guards of the City), the most radical anti-Zionist branch of ultraorthodox Jewry. He published numerous pamphlets and articles; among his books are *Et Nisayon* (1972) and *Ha'atakot* (1980).

Duran, Shimon b. Zemah; Tashbetz—(Majorca–Algiers, 1361–1444), halakhic authority, religious philosopher, and physician. In his youth in Palma, Duran studied Talmud and *halakhah* as well as medicine. After the persecutions of 1391 he left for Algiers and became a member of Perfet's (see entry) *bet din*. Duran served on a commission appointed by the Algiers community to deal with questions of matrimonial status and was the chief author of its ordinances, observed in North Africa for hundreds of years. He succeeded Perfet as chief rabbi of Algiers and was considered the supreme halakhic authority of his generation. He is mostly known for his responsa.

Eiger, Akiva b. Moses—(Germany, 1761–1837), rabbi, communal leader, opponent of Reform. In 1814 Eiger became the rabbi of Posen, where he established a large yeshivah. He played a major role in shaping the earliest orthodox response to the Reform movement. He was the father-in-law of Moses Sofer (see entry).

Einhorn, David—(Germany–U.S.A., 1809–79), rabbi and reformer. Einhorn received a rabbinical education and also studied philosophy in various German universities. In 1838 he was nominated as rabbi of Wellhausen but was rejected by the government because of his liberal views. After serving in several other Reform congregations—among them Mecklenburg-Schwerin, where he succeeded Samuel Holdheim (see entry)—he left for the United States. From 1866 he was the rabbi of Congregation Adath Israel, New York. Einhorn was one the leading advocates of radical reform. Among his works is the prayer book *Olat Tamid* (written in German), which was the basis for the first *Union Prayer Book*.

Eli'ezer b. Yittzhak Hakohen (of Worms)—(Germany, 11th century), scholar. Born in Worms, Eli'ezer moved to Mainz and studied under Gershom Me'or ha-Golah and Judah b. Meir Hakohen (see entries). After Gershom's death he headed the yeshivah in Mainz. Only fragments of his writings have survived, preserved in the books of Rashi's school (see Rashi entry).

Elimelekh of Lyzhansk—(Galicia, 1717–87), *tzaddik* of the third generation of Hasidism. Elimelekh was a disciple of Dov Baer, the Maggid of Mezhirech, and the leading theoretician of "practical tzaddikism"—which held that the *tzaddik* was not solely a spiritual figure but a leader in all spheres of life, acting out in his own life a dialectical tension between *devekut* (bonding with God) and the practical work of communal service. Apparently unable to endure this tension, Elimelekh withdrew from the community in his last years.

Elon, Menachem—(Germany–Israel, 1923–), Israeli jurist. Born in Düsseldorf, Elon emigrated to Palestine in 1935. From 1966 he taught Jewish law at the Hebrew University. In 1973 he published a three-volume account of *mishpat ivri* (English translation, 1994), designed to make possible the integration of halakhic concepts and decisions into the Israeli legal system. He was appointed to Israel's Supreme Court in 1977.

Essenes—a religious sect in the last half of the Second Temple period (2d century B.C.E.–end of the 1st century C.E.) that made its first appearance sometime after the Hasmonean revolt (167–160 B.C.E.). Though the matter is disputed, the Qumran sect, whose members lived a communal life and emphasized strict observance of the purity laws, was probably Essene. The discovery of the Dead Sea scrolls shed new light on the sect's practices and beliefs.

Gerondi, Nissim b. Reuben; Ran — (Spain, 1310–75?), talmudist and halakhic authority, physician in the royal court. Born in Gerona, he later moved to Barcelona, where he played a leading role in communal affairs and headed a yeshivah. Among his disciples were Isaac b. Sheshet Perfet (see entry) and Hasdai Crescas. Gerondi's main works are his Novellae on the Talmud (in which he followed the tradition of Nahmanides and Adret; see entries), a commentary on Isaac Alfasi's *halakhot,* and *Derashot ha-Ran,* twelve sermons or public lectures, one of them devoted to kingship.

Gershom b. Judah Me'or ha-Golah — (Germany, c. 960–1028), one of the first talmudic scholars in Ashkenaz. Probably born in Metz, he later headed a yeshivah in Mainz; among his pupils were the teachers of Rashi (see entry), who summed up Gershom's reputation: "Rabbenu Gershom . . . who enlightened the eyes of the exile [*me'or ha-golah*], and upon whom we all depend." Gershom is known in later literature as the author of many *takkanot;* both the ban on bigamy and the prohibition of the divorce of a wife against her will are attributed to him.

Grodzinski, Hayyim Ozer — (Lithuania, 1863–1940), talmudic scholar and leader of Lithuanian Orthodoxy. Grodzinski was present at the founding of Agudat Yisrael in 1912 and later served on its Council of Sages. A strong opponent of Zionism, of the Reform movement, and of secular education, he defended the traditional way of life of the Lithuanian *yeshivot* and small towns.

Haddayah, Ovadyah — (Syria–Israel, 1893–1969), rabbi. Born in Aleppo, Haddayah was brought to Jerusalem in 1898 and studied at Yeshivat Porat Yosef, where (from 1923) he taught Talmud and Kabbalah. Haddayah later refounded the kabbalist yeshivah Kehal Hasidim Bet El in Jerusalem. He was a member of the *bet din* of the Jerusalem Sephardi community and from 1951 served as the chairman of the rabbinical high court of appeals.

Halevi, Judah. *See* Judah b. Samuel Halevi

Herzl, Theodore (Binyamin Ze'ev) — (Hungary–Austria, 1860–1904), founder
of political Zionism. As a young man, Herzl studied law, but dedicated himself to literature and playwriting. Witnessing the Drey-
fuss trial in Paris (1894), he concluded that the only solution to the
"Jewish question" was a Jewish state. His manifesto *Der Judenstaat*
(The State of the Jews) was published in 1896, and the remaining
years of his life were wholly devoted to Zionist advocacy and organization. In Basel, in 1897, he convened the first Zionist Congress
and founded the World Zionist Organization.

Herzog, Isaac — (Poland–Israel, 1888–1959), rabbinic scholar, chief rabbi of
Israel. Born in Poland, Herzog moved to Ireland and served as rabbi
in Belfast and Dublin. In 1936 he went to Palestine, succeeding
Abraham Isaac Kook (see entry) as chief rabbi. A fervent Zionist,
Herzog founded the Mizrachi Federation of Great Britain and Ireland. In Israel he sought to meet the challenges posed to the halakhic tradition by the conditions of political sovereignty. Herzog was
responsible for the enactment of important *takkanot* in matters of
personal status.

Hillel the Elder — (Babylonia–Palestine, end of 1st century B.C.E.–1st century
C.E.), probably the most prominent sage of Second Temple Judaism. A native of Babylonia, Hillel spent his early days in Jerusalem,
joining the circle of Shemaiah and Avtalyon (see entry); he and his
rival Shammai succeeded them as leaders of the Pharisees. A school
of disciples, Bet Hillel (opposed by Bet Shammai until the destruction of the Temple) and a rabbinic dynasty descended from him.
Though still debated among the later sages, the views of Bet Hillel
were decisive in shaping the *halakhah* of the Talmud. A number of
Hillel's *takkanot* were probably adopted during his lifetime, among
them the *prosbul*.

Hirsch, Samson (b.) Raphael — (Germany, 1808–88), rabbi, leader of nineteenth-century German Orthodoxy. Born in Hamburg, Hirsch
studied Talmud with his father and history and philosophy at the
University of Bonn. In 1851 he was nominated as rabbi of the first
separatist Orthodox congregation, Adass Jeshurun, in Frankfurt,

where he served until his death. Hirsch's key doctrinal commitment is to the concept of *Torah im derekh eretz* ("Torah with worldly
occupation," i.e., secular education—based on Mishnah Avot 2:2).
On this concept he built a religious ideology and an educational
system, the two intended as answers to the multiple challenges of
the Reform movement and modernity. His main works are *Iggerot
Tzafon* (Letters from the North), *Horeb,* and a commentary on the
Torah.

Holdheim, Samuel—(Germany, 1806–60), a leading Reform rabbi in Germany. Born into a strict religious family, Holdheim received a traditional Jewish education. After serving as a rabbi in Frankfurt (on
the Oder), he moved to Berlin (1847), where he introduced far-
reaching ritual reforms. He distinguished the religious and ethical
content of Judaism, which is binding for all time, from its political-
national content, which can be revised (or discarded). Jews, he argued, are politically bound only by the laws of the state in which
they live.

Horeb—Mount Sinai.

Ibn Migash, Joseph b. Meir Ha-Levi—(North Africa–Spain, 1077–1141), talmudic scholar. Ibn Migash studied under Isaac Alfasi and succeeded
him as head of the yeshivah in Lucena, Spain, occupying this position until his death. Maimon, Maimonides' father, may have been
one of his pupils, and Maimonides occasionally relies upon his
views. Ibn Migash had a significant impact on the study of Talmud
in Spain and Provence, but very little of his work has survived.

Isaac b. Moses of Vienna: Isaac Or Zaru'a—(Bohemia–Germany, c. 1180–c.
1250), halakhic authority. Isaac is usually referred to by the title of
his halakhic compendium, *Or Zaru'a.* Because of its great length,
the book had only a limited circulation. But it was frequently
quoted in secondary sources and in this way had an impact on later
scholars. *Or Zaru'a* is a valuable collection of halakhic rulings and
customary practices from the High Middle Ages (see also headnote
to C9, §3).

Isaac Or Zaru'a. *See* Isaac b. Moses of Vienna

Ishmael b. Abraham Isaac Hakohen of Modena — (Italy, 1723–1811), rabbi and halakhic authority. Ishmael of Modena was among the rabbis formally asked by Napoleon, in May 1806, to respond to twelve questions concerning the status of Jews as citizens of France. Although Ishmael was not sympathetic to the Jewish enlightenment, his writings and rulings reflect an effort to narrow the gap between the demands of the new secular politics and the requirements of the legal tradition.

Josephus Flavius (Joseph b. Mattathias) — (Palestine–Rome, c. 38–after 100 C.E.), general, historian, apologist; writer in the Jewish-Hellenistic tradition. Josephus was born in Jerusalem into a priestly family related to the Hasmonean dynasty. At the beginning of the rebellion in 66 C.E., he was appointed commander of the Galilee, but when the war in the north was almost lost, he went over to the Roman side — in what seems to have been an act of treachery toward his comrades — becoming an adviser to Titus and Vespasian. After the war, Josephus moved to Rome, where he wrote (in Greek) a history of the rebellion and an account of the history, culture, and religion of the Jewish people (*Antiquities*). In this work, and also in his response to critics of Judaism, *Against Apion,* he appears as a defender of his people, arguing for the spiritual value and practical utility of their religion and its ethical superiority to Hellenism.

Judah b. Meir Hakohen — (Germany, 11th century), rabbi and halakhic authority. Judah was a disciple of Gershom Me'or ha-Golah. About forty of his responsa were preserved among the responsa of his teacher. His book, *Sefer ha-Dinim* (Book of the Laws), and his other responsa are no longer extant.

Judah b. Samuel Halevi — (Spain–Palestine[?], before 1075–1141), Hebrew poet and philosopher. Born in Toledo, after years of studying and traveling he settled in southern Spain, where he worked as a physician. Around 1140 Halevi decided to emigrate to *eretz yisrael,* a decision that reflected a lifetime's yearning, expressed in both his religious-philosophical and poetic writings. Halevi's philosophy is contained in his famous book, *The Kuzari* (finished c. 1140), which is subtitled "The Book of Refutation and Proof on Behalf of the Despised Religion." *The Kuzari* is both an argument against the Karaites (see entry) and a critique of efforts to provide a fully rationalist account of Judaism. His philosophy emphasized the bond between God and Israel, to be fully realized only in *eretz yisrael.*

Judah the Prince (ha-Nasi)—(Palestine, second half of the 2d and beginning of the 3d century C.E.), patriarch of Judea and redactor of the Mishnah. Judah, referred to simply as "Rabbi," was the son of Rabban Simeon b. Gamaliel and a direct descendant of Hillel (see entry). His erudition, judgment, and political skill in dealing with the Roman authorities raised the patriarchate to its highest point of effectiveness and authority. His main achievement was the editorial organization of existing laws (and legal disputes) in the Mishnah.

Karaites—Jewish sect originating in eighth-century Babylonia, with possible Sadducee or Essene origins (see entries). Its doctrine is characterized primarily by a critique of rabbinic interpretation, a denial of the Oral Law, and a defense of scriptural literalism. (The term *kara'im* comes from *benei mikra,* "children of the Bible.") Karaite criticism forced the advocates of rabbinic Judaism (Rabbanites) to respond defensively but also to reconsider and elaborate their own views. Among those who rose to the challenge were Saadiah Gaon and Judah Halevi (see entries).

Kook, Abraham Isaac—(Latvia–Palestine, 1865–1935), rabbi, kabbalist, and philosopher. In 1904 Kook emigrated to Palestine, where he served as rabbi of Jaffa, then of Jerusalem; in 1921 he was elected the first Ashkenazi chief rabbi of Palestine. Kook developed a unique view of the dialectical role of Zionism in Jewish history, holding that the return to Palestine, though initiated by secular (even antireligious) Jews, had redemptive significance. He called for a spiritual renewal of Judaism as the necessary completion of the political renewal sought by the Zionist movement.

Leibowitz, Yeshayahu—(Latvia–Israel, 1903–94), scientist, philosopher, social critic. Leibowitz was born in Riga and studied chemistry, medicine, and philosophy. In 1935 he joined the Hebrew University, where he taught organic biochemistry and neurophysiology. Leibowitz's religious writings argue for an absolute duty to serve God. Religious Jews must accept the yoke of *halakhah* for its own sake (*lishmah*), rejecting all other ends, including physical or spiritual perfection or the improvement of society. In the first years of the state of Israel, Leibowitz hoped that national independence would stimulate innovative halakhic legislation to meet the challenges of statehood. When these hopes were frustrated, he became an advocate of the radical separation of religion from the state.

Lilienblum, Moses Leib—(Lithuania, 1843–1910), Hebrew writer, social critic, and political journalist. Born near Kovno, Lilienblum was one of the leaders of the east European *Haskalah,* and then, toward the end of his life, of the Zionist movement Hibbat Zion. At the age of twenty-five he published important articles in the weekly *Ha-Melitz* arguing for religious reform. Lilienblum also called for the liberation of women, defended individual freedom, and criticized Jewish communal leaders. In 1874–81, he turned to socialism; his famous article "Mishnat Elisha ben Avuyah" is one of the earliest Jewish calls for a revaluation of physical labor.

Loew, Judah b. Bezalel; Maharal—(Prague, c. 1525–1609), rabbi, talmudist, kabbalist, and moralist. A scholar of both Jewish and secular studies (particularly mathematics), Loew is a transitional figure between medieval and early modern intellectual life. In his voluminous works in the fields of ethics and theology he interprets Rabbinic *aggadah* in light of his mystical philosophy. He wrote extensively on the relationship between God and Israel, on the mediating role of the Torah, and on the moral-political meaning of the Jewish exile.

Luria, Isaac b. Solomon—(Palestine, 1534–72), kabbalist, referred to as Ha-Ari ("the Lion," acronym of "the divine Rabbi Isaac"). Luria is the most innovative kabbalist of the period following the expulsion of the Jews from Spain. Born in Jerusalem and raised in Egypt, he settled in Safed in 1569, gathering students around him. His followers believed that he was infused by the holy spirit and that the prophet Elijah spoke to him of hidden things. Some of his teachings suggest that he thought himself to be "the Messiah, the son of Joseph." Luria's time in Safed was brief; he died in an epidemic only three years after his arrival. The overabundance of his thoughts, so it is said, prevented him from writing them down. His oral teachings were gathered and variously systematized by his disciples, primarily by Hayyim Vital.

Maharal. *See* Loew, Judah b. Bezalel

Maharam. *See* Meir b. Baruch of Rothenburg

Maimonides, Moses; Moses b. Maimon; Rambam—(Spain–Egypt, 1135–1204), rabbi, codifier, philosopher, and physician; the most prominent Jewish thinker in the post-talmudic era. Born in Córdoba, Maimonides wandered with his family through North Africa; they settled in Cairo, where he later headed the Jewish community. Maimonides' first important work was his Commentary to the Mishnah completed at age thirty-three. His greatest achievements were the halakhic code *Mishneh Torah* (1180) and the philosophical treatise *The Guide of the Perplexed* (1190). The *Mishneh Torah,* written in Hebrew, systematically organizes the whole of Jewish law. The *Guide,* written in Arabic, was designed for readers whose faith had been undermined by philosophical criticism. The book aimed to harmonize philosophy and Judaism, thus enabling a renewed, but also a refined, religious faith. Although his philosophical views were the subject of fierce opposition, his influence on the development of Judaism was enormous.

Meir b. Baruch of Rothenburg; Maharam—(Germany, c. 1215–93), tosafist, halakhic authority, communal leader. Meir was born in Worms and died in prison after an eight-year incarceration ordered by the emperor Rudolph. He played a critical role in establishing the public law of the German communities. We have more than a thousand of his responsa, most of them dealing with matters of *mamona:* business transactions, real estate, inheritance, partnerships, community property, and taxation. He greatly influenced later codifiers, particularly Jacob b. Asher, author of the *Tur* (see Asher entry), whose father was Meir's student (see also headnote to C9, §8).

Meiri, Menachem b. Solomon—(Provence, 1249–1316), rabbi and commentator on the Talmud. Meiri is best known for his interpretive summary of the Talmud, *Bet ha-Behirah,* which untypically includes halakhic conclusions. He was a follower of Maimonides, both in philosophical bent and in *halakhah;* like him, he engaged in secular and scientific studies. He was apparently in touch with Christian scholars and was one of the earliest advocates of tolerance toward gentile society.

Mendelssohn, Moses—(Germany, 1729–86), enlightenment philosopher and Jewish thinker. Born in Dassau, Mendelssohn became a central figure in the European intelligentsia; among his friends was the dramatist Gotthold Ephraim Lessing. Responding to German critics of the Jewish religion, he dedicated himself to the defense of Judaism and German Jews, arguing for the separation of religion and state and urging equal rights for Jewish citizens. Within the Jewish community, he insisted upon the obligatory status of religious law in the modern world. His main works are *Jerusalem* (1783) and a German translation of the Pentateuch with the *Biur* (interpretation).

Mizrachi—religious Zionist movement, founded in 1902 as a religious faction in the World Zionist Organization.

Mizrahi, Elijah—(Constantinople, c. 1450–1526), the most prominent rabbi in the Ottoman empire of his time. Mizrahi played a leading role in the Jewish community of Constantinople, headed a yeshivah where both Talmud and secular subjects were taught, and gave halakhic decisions on many different matters. He was actively involved in the absorption of exiles from Spain and Portugal. As a writer, he is chiefly known for his supercommentary to Rashi's commentary on the Torah.

Nahman (b. Simhah) of Bratzlav—(Medzibezh–Uman, 1772–1810), hasidic *tzaddik,* the founder the Bratzlav sect. Nahman was a direct descendant of Israel Ba'al Shem Tov, the founder of Hasidism. After a visit to Palestine (1798), he settled in Bratzlav, where he developed a circle of disciples and followers. He was a controversial figure, accused of being a Sabbatean and a Frankist. His personality was difficult, his teachings paradoxical; he demanded from his adherents complete loyalty and faith. Nahman perceived himself as a messiah, hence he could have no successor as the *tzaddik* of his sect. Among his works (all of them transcribed by his close disciple Nathan Sternhartz) are *Likute Moharan* and *Sipure Ma'asiyot*.

Nahmanides, Moses b. Nahman; Ramban — (Spain–Palestine, 1194–1270), rabbi, prominent talmudist, kabbalist, and biblical commentator; also a poet and physician. Born in Gerona, Nahmanides was the chief rabbi of Catalonia and the most influential Jewish figure of his generation. In 1263 he was forced by the king to participate in a public disputation in Barcelona with the apostate Pablo Christiani — which ended in a rare Jewish victory. Toward the end of his life he emigrated to Palestine. Many leading halakhists of the next generation, including Solomon b. Abraham Adret (see entry), were his students. His works include interpretations of the Talmud, halakhic monographs — e.g., *Mishpat ha-Herem* (Laws Concerning Bans) — responsa, sermons, and letters. He also wrote a classic commentary on the Torah that incorporates kabbalistic readings of the text.

Perfet, Isaac b. Sheshet; Rivash — (Spain–North Africa, 1326–1408), rabbi and halakhic authority. Perfet was born and studied in Barcelona — under, among others, Nissim Gerondi (see entry) — where he acted unofficially as rabbi. Later he moved to Saragossa; driven from there by the anti-Jewish riots of 1391, he went eventually to Algiers. Perfet is best known for his responsa, which influenced subsequent *halakhah* — including Karo's *Shulhan Arukh*.

Pharisees — Hebrew *perushim,* "the separated ones"; a religious and political party or sect during the Hasmonean period (167–37 B.C.E. The Pharisees argued (against the Sadducees; see entry) for the validity of the Oral Law and the authority of the sages. Their doctrine and traditions were followed by the *tanna'im*.

Qumran — site of the community that composed or collected the Dead Sea scrolls.

Rabad. *See* Abraham b. David of Posquieres

Rabbenu Tam. *See* Tam, Jacob b. Meir

Ramah. *See* Abulafia, Meir

Ran, ha-Ran. *See* Gerondi, Nissim b. Reuben

Rashba. *See* Adret, Solomon b. Abraham

Rashbam. *See* Samuel b. Meir

Rashi; Solomon b. Isaac—(France, 1040–1105), the most prominent Jewish exegete of both the Bible and the Talmud. Born in Troyes, where he lived all his life, his reputation extended throughout the Jewish world. Rashi interpreted the Talmud line by line, opening the text to a much wider audience than ever before. His work gained such authority and popularity that almost all printed editions of the Talmud include it. No less influential is Rashi's biblical commentary, which follows Scripture line by line and interprets it according to both the *peshat* (literal meaning) and the midrashic understanding. Beside being the ultimate exegete, Rashi was also a halakhic authority; some of his rulings are scattered in his talmudic commentaries, and some appear in his responsa.

Ravina—abbr. of Rav Avina, Babylon, a name shared by several Babylonian *amora'im*. The two most prominent are Ravina I (d. 422), a disciple of Rava and a student and colleague of Rav Ashi; and Ravina II b. Huna (d. 499), probably a nephew of Ravina I, who served as judge in Babylonia. According to tradition, Ravina and Rav Ashi mark the closure of the talmudic era. It is not entirely clear which Ravina is meant.

Rivash. *See* Perfet, Isaac b. Sheshet

Rosh. *See* Asher b. Yeheil

Saadiah (b. Joseph) Gaon; Saadiah al-Fayyumi—(Egypt–Babylonia, 882–942), talmudist, halakhic authority, philosopher, grammarian, and leader of Babylonian Jewry in the gaonic era. Born in Fayyum, Egypt, Saadiah settled in Baghdad. Among his works are halakhic monographs (a genre first developed by him) and defenses of rabbinic Judaism against the Karaites (which provoked fierce responses). His philosophical treatise, *The Book of Beliefs and Opin-*

ions, written in Arabic, was one of the earliest Jewish philosophical works, reflecting Greek and Arabic influence. Here he tried, among other things, to provide rational reasons for the principles of the Oral and Written Law.

Sabbateanism—a movement of followers of Shabbetai Zevi (1626–76), who claimed to be the messiah but later converted to Islam. The term became a pejorative epithet for any kind of false messianism.

Sadducees (Hebrew: Tzedukim)—political-religious party of the Hasmonean period. The Sadducees were a conservative group, composed largely of the upper classes of Jewish society: priests and aristocrats. They controlled the Jerusalem Temple and, much of the time, the Sanhedrin. Their opponents were the Pharisees (see entry); the rivalry endured until the destruction of the Temple. Both parties acknowledged the authority of the Torah, the Written Law, but the Sadducees rejected the Oral Law, refusing to recognize any commandment that they could not find plainly revealed in the text of Scripture.

Salmon b. Jeroham—(Baghdad or Palestine–Syria, 910–c. 960), Karaite scholar. Salmon studied in Egypt, then settled in Jerusalem and later in Aleppo. His main work is the *Book of the Wars of the Lord,* an anti-rabbinic polemic, written in rhyme, aimed directly against Saadiah Gaon (see entry). See also headnote to C7, §20.

Samuel b. Meir; Rashbam—(France, c. 1085–c. 1174), commentator on the Talmud and the Bible. Born in northern France, Samuel was the grandson of Rashi and the elder brother of Jacob Tam (see entries). He was a tosafist of the first generation. Among his main works are his continuation of Rashi's unfinished commentary on the talmudic tractate Bava Batra and his commentary on the Pentateuch, which, more than any other medieval commentary, aims to reveal the literal meaning (*peshat*) of Scripture.

Sasportas, Jacob—(North Africa, c. 1610–98), rabbi, opponent of Sabbateanism. Born and educated in Oran, Sasportas traveled widely, serving as a rabbi in Livorno and Amsterdam, among other places. He was widely known as a talmudic scholar and a firm defender of the traditional *halakhah.* At several points in his life, Sasportas was engaged in fierce disputes with various opponents. His best-known work is

Tzizat Novel Tzevi, which contains his criticism of Sabbatean ideology and practices and of the prophet Nathan of Gaza.

Sephardi—a Jew from Spain; by extension, a Jew fom the Orient. *See also*
Ashkenazi

Shammai. *See* Hillel the Elder

Shemaiah and Avtalyon—(Palestine, late 1st century B.C.E.), the fourth "pair"
(*zugot,* mentioned in tractate *Avot*), who received the tradition from
Yehudah b. Tabbai and Shimon b. Shatah. Talmudic tradition describes Shemaiah and Avtalyon as descended from proselytes. The
first was *nasi* and the second *av bet din* (head of the court). Shammai
and Hillel, the fifth "pair," were their disciples. Shemaiah's dictum
(Avot 1:10) "Love work, hate lordship, and seek no intimacy with
the ruling power" reflects his attitude toward the government of
his time.

Sherira (b. Hanina) Gaon—(Babylonia, c. 906–1006), talmudist and halakhic authority, a leading figure of the gaonic period. Born into the
exilarch's family, Sherira was nominated (at the age of seventy)
to be Gaon of Pumpedita, where he revived an academy in radical decline. Sherira helped to establish the Babylonian Talmud as a
canonical corpus for Jews around the world. Almost half of the responsa preserved from the gaonic period are written, most of them
jointly, by him and his son, Rav Hai Gaon, who succeeded him in
Pumpedita. On his famous "Iggeret Rav Sherira" (The Epistle of
Sherira Gaon), see headnote to €7, §19.

Shomer Hatza'ir—left-wing Zionist socialist youth movement, founded in
Vienna in 1916.

Sofer (Schreiber), Moses; Hatam Sofer—(Germany-Hungary, 1762–1839),
rabbi, halakhic authority, and leader of Orthodox Jewry. Born in
Frankfurt, Sofer was appointed rabbi of Pressburg in 1806; there he
remained for the rest of his life, founding a yeshivah that became
a center of Orthodoxy. Sofer was uncompromising in his struggle
against *haskalah* and the early Reform movement. He wrote commentaries on several tractates of the Talmud and a very large number of responsa.

Spinoza, Baruch—(Holland, 1632–77), philosopher. Born into the Portuguese Jewish community of Amsterdam, Spinoza as a very young man became a critic of the conventional Judaism of his time and soon, in the eyes of the communal elders, a heretic. He was formally excommunicated on July 27, 1656. Four years later, Spinoza left Amsterdam to settle in Rijnsburg, where he entered into a philosophical dialogue with liberal Protestants. His major philosophical work, the *Ethics,* was published posthumously. His *Theological-Political Treatise* is one of the earliest exercises in biblical criticism; it is also a sophisticated critique not only of Judaism but, implicitly, of Christianity as well. (See also headnotes to ℭ1, §15; ℭ2, §6; and ℭ5, §8.)

Tam, Jacob b. Meir; Rabbenu Tam — (France, c. 1100–1171), talmudic scholar, halakhic authority. The grandson of Rashi, Tam was the most prominent scholar of his generation. He settled in Ramepert, a small town, but exercised halakhic authority all over France and Germany. Tam lived through the persecutions and murders of the Second Crusade, which devastated the Ramepert community. Most of the Tosafot are based on his interpretations and rulings. Among his other works is *Sefer ha-Yashar,* which includes responsa and talmudic commentaries.

Yannai, Alexander (c. 126–76 B.C.E.), Hasmonean king of Judea and high priest (103–76). In his reign Judea reached its peak in terms of political power and territorial extent. Yannai ruled like a Hellenistic tyrant, killing his political enemies. Through most of his reign, he was opposed by the Pharisees, who criticized him for claiming both the priesthood and the throne. There was apparently a reconciliation toward the end of his life, perhaps some sort of political alliance. He was succeeded by his widow, Salome Alexandra, a Pharisee supporter.

Glossary of Terms

adam hashuv—lit., "prominent person"; a leading sage or rabbi; on some views, one whom the *kahal* must consult before enacting legislation.

aggadah—lit., "that which is told or conveyed"; the non-halakhic part of Rabbinic literature.

akedah—lit., "binding"; the binding of Isaac upon the altar by his father, Abraham (see Gen. 22).

aliyah—lit., "ascension" or "rising"; the immigration of Jews to the Land of Israel.

am ha-aretz (pl. *amme ha-aretz*)—lit., "people of the land." In Rabbinic Hebrew, a person without knowledge of Torah; applied pejoratively to those who did not belong to the class of the *hakhamim*.

amanah—from the root denoting "truth" and "promise keeping"; a solemn joint agreement and commitment. In modern Hebrew, *amanah* (*hevratit*) is the term for "social contract."

amora (pl. *amora'im*)—sages of the Talmud (Babylonian and Palestinian, roughly 200–600 C.E.); distinguished from the earlier *tanna'im*.

anoos—someone who is forced to act against his or her will, either by human agents or by natural circumstances, and is therefore inculpable; also, a forced convert.

anshe knesset ha-gedolah—lit., "Men of the Great Assembly," a supreme authority of the Jewish people, precursor of the Sanhedrin, traditionally said to have functioned in the early days of the Second Commonwealth.

asham—lit., "guilt, guilt offering"; one of the sacrifices.

azazel—lit., "a rough and rocky mountain." *Azazel* goat—a special sacrifice on the Day of Atonement, sent to *azazel,* an unspecified place in the Judaean Desert.

baraita (pl. *baraitot*)—lit., "external"; traditions and teachings of the *tanna'im,* not embodied in the Mishnah but often quoted in the Gemara (see entries).

bat kol—lit., "echo, reverberating sound"; occasionally in Rabbinic literature, "divine voice," a substitute for "prophecy."

berit—covenant, treaty. In its mundane sense, primarily a political and military treaty, often specifically that between monarch and vassal. In biblical and Judaic religion, the special relationship established between God and, first, the patriarchs, starting with Abraham, and then their descendants, the people of Israel.

berurim—selectmen, local officials elected (or appointed) to govern or represent the *kahal*.

bet din—court, sometimes high court or Sanhedrin.

Bet Yosef—a commentary upon the *Tur* (see entry) written by Joseph Karo, which became an authoritative textbook of *halakhah* and formed the basis for Karo's code, *Shulhan Arukh*.

bimah—dais on which the Torah is read in the synagogue.

da'at torah—lit., "opinion of Torah," which goes along with *emunat hakhamim*, "faith in scholars." In modern ultra-Orthodoxy, these phrases designate the authority of leading scholars to decide in (all) areas of policy that were not traditionally subject to halakhic jurisdiction. Characteristically, pronouncements of *da'at torah* are made with no reasons provided (see also headnote to C6, §24).

dat—lit., "law, ordinance, custom, punishment"; in modern Hebrew, "religion."

de'orayta—laws (*halakhot*) mentioned in or derived from the written Torah; opposite of *derabbanan*.

derabbanan—laws (*halakhot*) ordained by the rabbis (secondary legislation); opposite of *de'orayta*.

derashah—interpretation, argument, homily. *See also* midrash.

devekut—cleaving; in Jewish mysticism and Hasidism, cleaving to God.

dina de-malkhuta dina—lit., "the law of the [secular, usually foreign] kingdom [*malkhuta*, Aramaic equivalent of the Hebrew *malkhut*] is law"—that is, the laws of the kingdom supersede Jewish law, typically in civil affairs.

din torah—(1) law of Torah; opposite of *de'orayta*, law of the sages. (2) strict law; opposite of equity.

elohim—God, the Lord; also judges.

emunat hakhamim—faith in the sages; commitment to follow the opinion of a *hakham*. See also *da'at torah;* headnote to C6, §24.

ephod and *hoshen*—*ephod,* "covering, vest"; *hoshen,* "breastplate," specifically the high priest's breastplate, tied to the *ephod.* On the breastplate twelve precious stones designate the twelve tribes of Israel. See Exodus 28; see also *urim* and *thummim.*

eretz yisrael—Land of Israel.

Gaon (pl. Geonim)—title of the heads of the Babylonian academies in the post-talmudic period (roughly 750–1150 C.E.).

Gemara—from the Aramaic, lit., "to learn or infer"; the main part of the Talmud.

get (pl. *gittin*)—legal document, usually writ of divorce.

hakham (pl. *hakhamim*)—sage, learned person, scholar of the Torah. *Talmid hakham* (pl. *talmide hakhamim*), lit., "student (disciple) of a sage," usually designates a scholar; also, the learned class, opposite of *am ha'aretz.*

halakhah—lit., "practice, accepted opinion"; Jewish law in general or a specific instance of it.

halitzah—lit., "untying, removing"; the ceremony of removing the *yabam's* (levir's) shoe, which exempts him and his brother's childless widow from marrying each other (see Deut. 25:5).

Hanukkah—lit., "inauguration, consecration"; the eight-day festival commemorating the rededication of the Temple in 165 B.C.E. after its desecration under Antioch Epiphanes.

haredim—lit., "those who are anxious [because of fear of God]"; members of the ultra-Orthodox movement, a nineteenth- and twentieth-century response to *haskalah,* Zionism, and reform.

hasid (pl. *hasidim*)—lit., "pious." The term designates members of pietistic groups, notably during the Second Commonwealth and in thirteenth-century Germany. More recently, and most of the time in this volume, it designates members of the movement known as Hasidism, founded by Israel Ba'al Shem Tov (Besht) at the end of the eighteenth century in eastern Europe.

haskalah—lit., "culture, enlightenment"; the Jewish enlightenment in Europe in the eighteenth and nineteenth centuries, initiated in Germany by Moses Mendelssohn. An adherent of *haskalah* is a *maskil*.

hattat—lit., "sin, transgression"; sin offering, one of the sacrifices.

herem—ban, excommunication, strengthened by the use of an oath. Talmudic law knows the punishment of "placing under a ban." Medieval *halakhah* emphasized in addition a more severe penalty called *herem*—which became the ultimate sanction for the rule of the *kahal*. Often, the legislation of the *kahal* took the form of a conditional *herem*: "Anyone who does X shall be placed under *herem*." Thus, *herem* also denotes the acts of legislation and the decrees passed.

hok (pl. *hukkim*)—law, rule, custom; traditionally distinguished from *mishpat*. According to a common view, *hukkim* designates laws whose reasons were not revealed, whereas *mishpatim* designates the rational laws.

Hoshen Mishpat—*hoshen*, "breastplate"; *mishpat*, "law"; the fourth "column" of the *Tur* and the fourth part of the *Shulhan Arukh,* dealing with criminal and civil law.

hukkim. See *hok.*

huppah—canopy, bridal chamber, hence also, wedding.

isura—prohibition, primarily of a ritual nature; also, ritual matters in Jewish law. The term encompasses all realms of *halakhah* not defined as *mamona.*

Kabbalah—lit., "tradition"; the common term for Jewish mysticism.

kahal (pl. *kehillot*)—lit., "gathering, community." In biblical literature, congregation of worship. In medieval Hebrew and thereafter, the local Jewish community, specifically as a political entity; sometimes, the assembly of its members.

kal vahomer—a fortiori; an inference from minor to major, one of the thirteen means defined by the *tanna'im* for the interpretation of the Torah.

karet—lit., "cutting off." In talmudic law, divine punishment through premature or sudden death; distinguished from capital punishment.

kashrut—noun derived from *kasher* (kosher), lit., "propriety, lawfulness"; ritual lawfulness, especially of food.

Kesef Mishneh—a commentary on Maimonides' *Mishneh Torah* written by Joseph Karo.

ketubah (pl. *ketubot*)—marriage contract, fixing, among other things, the amount of money or other goods due to the wife on her husband's death or upon being divorced.

kibbutz medini. See *medini.*

kiddushin—marriage, the act of betrothal.

lehatnot—to stipulate, to make conditions. See *tenai.*

letek—a measure of volume for dry objects; also, a land measure.

lishmah—lit., "for its own sake"; used to indicate purity of intention, excluding any ulterior motive.

lulav—palm branch, one of the four species of plants ritually used on the Sukkot festival.

ma'amad—lit., "standing up, place, status"; committee of *kahal* officials.

mahloket—dispute, controversy, disagreement.

malkhut—kingdom, kingship, monarchy, empire, also government; the name of the tenth *sefirah* in Kabbalah. *Malkhuti*—monarchical, kingly, majestic.

mamlakhtiyut—from the same root as *malkhut;* statehood, sovereignty; also, statism, civic consciousness. See also headnote to C10, §9.

mamona (pl. *mamonot*)—lit., "property or wealth"; civil and fiscal matters in Jewish law, opposite of *isura.*

mamzer (pl. *mamzerim*)—according to biblical law, a *mamzer* (and his or her descendants) is excluded from "the congregation of the Lord." Rabbinic *halakhah* interpreted *mamzer* to mean a child born from incest or adultery, and the "exclusion" as prohibiting marriage to any Israelite (save another *mamzer* or a convert).

mashkanta (pl. *mashkantot*)—mortgage, a loan transaction whereby landed property is transferred to the creditor with the privilege of redemption by returning the loan.

maskil (pl. *maskilim*). An adherent of *haskalah.*

megillah—lit., "scroll"; specifically, the book of Esther. The public reading of Esther is the central ceremony of the festival of Purim, a *mitzvah* ordained by the Rabbis.

medinah. See *medini.*

medini—political. Derived from *medinah,* "state, country," also "province, region"; in medieval Jewish philosophy, a translation of *polis. Kib-*

butz medini—political society/community; a possible translation of "body politic." *Yishuv/siddur medini*—political order.

Mekhilta—lit., "treatise"; name of two tannaitic midrashic works on Exodus attributed to Rabbi Ishmael and Rabbi Shimon b. Yohai.

midrash—commentary, sermon, study, textual interpretation; homiletical interpretation of Scripture (see Michael Fishbane's introductory essay, "Law, Story, and Interpretation: Reading Rabbinic Texts").

minhag—custom. Denotes a binding practice that, unlike, e.g., *mitzvah de'orayta* or *takkanah,* stems from a rooted custom. A custom in this sense usually has the halakhic status of *derabbanan.*

minim—heretics.

minut—heresy. In Rabbinic literature, *minut* refers to early Christianity and Gnosticism; later, the term refers to any rejection of the Jewish faith and more generally the Jewish way of life.

minyan (pl. *minyanim*)—religious quorum, consisting of at least ten Israelite adults.

Mishnah—lit., "repetition"; verbal teaching by repeated recitation; also, study, opinion; hence,, codification of oral laws, compiled in six orders by Judah the Prince in the early third century C.E. A section of the Mishnah is a mishnah.

Mishneh Torah—lit., "repetition of the Torah"; Hebrew name of the fifth book of the Pentateuch, Deuteronomy. Also, in most references here, the name of Maimonides' halakhic code.

mishpat (pl. *mishpatim*)—judgment; justice; social and moral law, ordinance; opposite of *hok.*

mishpat ivri—lit., "Hebrew law"; a construction of twentieth-century jurists who carved out of *halakhah* a body of law without its theological references and ritual codes so that this (secularized) version of the legal tradition could be incorporated, whenever opportunities arose, into Israeli civil and criminal law.

mitnaged (pl. *mitnagdim*)—lit., "opposed, opponent"; opponent of Hasidism.

mitzvah (pl. *mitzvot*)—commandment, precept, law, religious duty, sometimes also obligation. The term usually refers to the precepts of the written Torah, yet there are specific instances in which it is used for rabbinically ordained rituals (e.g., *megillah* and Hanukkah); hence there are *mitzvot de'orayta* and *mitzvot derabbanan.*

moda'a—a legal term for "protest, disclaimer."

nasi (pl. *nesi'im*)—in modern Hebrew, president; in biblical Hebrew, chieftain, ruler, officer; in talmudic Hebrew, head of the Sanhedrin, e.g., Judah the Prince.

ne'ilah—lit., "locking, shutting, closure, conclusion"; the concluding prayer, close to sunset, on the Day of Atonement.

Noahide Code—derived from Genesis 9, which is interpreted as listing laws ordained for Noah and his sons after the flood. From Rabbinic literature on, it denotes universal laws binding on all human beings, among them the prohibitions against murder, theft, incest (adultery), and idolatry—in contrast to the Torah of Moses, which binds Israelites only. According to some Jewish medieval thinkers, the term denotes a Jewish version of natural law.

nomos—from the Greek *nomoi,* "human law," opposite of *physis,* "the law of nature." Used in medieval Hebrew to indicate human law in contrast also to divine law (see headnotes to C2, §§4 and 5).

ohel mo'ed—in the Bible, the tent of congregation (see, e.g., Exod. 33:7–11); according to some biblical sources, the Tabernacle (see, e.g., Exod. 39:32).

parnas (pl. *parnasim*)—lit., "provider"; prominent individual (usually wealthy) functioning as leader of the community.

perutah—lit., "the smallest coin, groat"; used for the minimal amount of value.

peshat—plain meaning (of a text), as distinct from its midrashic exposition.

posek (pl. *poskim*)—lit., "arbiter, decider"; rabbinical scholar who pronounces in disputes about halakhic questions.

prosbul—from the Greek *pros boule;* a declaration made in court, before the execution of a loan, to the effect that the law of the Sabbatical year shall not apply—an innovation of Hillel the Elder (see headnote to C6, §15).

rabbi—lit., "master"; talmudic scholar; an honorific title (see introduction to C6 and the introductory essay by Menachem Lorberbaum and Noam J. Zohar, "The Selection, Translation, and Presentation of the

Texts"). "Rabbi" with a capital *R* is used here to indicate one of the *tanna'im* or *amora'im*.

reshut—lit., "permission, license," opposite of "prohibition"; often used to designate a normatively neutral realm contrasted with the realm covered by *mitzvah* or Torah.

ru'ah hakodesh—the holy spirit; prophetic inspiration.

Sanhedrin—from the Greek *synedrion;* the supreme council of the Jews during the Second Temple period and at some points during the age of the *tanna'im,* sometimes referred to as the high court; also a tractate of the Mishnah and Talmud.

satan—lit., "hostile being, hinderer, accuser"; the Angel of Evil or Death; Satan.

se'ah—a measure of volume for both dry objects and liquids.

sefirah (pl. *sefirot*)—sphere. In Kabbalah, the ten *sefirot* are the ten divine emanations or potencies.

sha'atnez—a mixed weave of wool and linen, the wearing of which is forbidden; figuratively, mixing things together, confusion.

Shabbat—from the root denoting "rest or cessation of labor"; Sabbath, seventh day of the week, day or period of rest; also a week.

shekhinah—divine presence, Godhead; royalty, royal residence.

shevu'ah (pl. *shevu'ot*)—oath, vow, testament; also curse.

shema—lit., "hear, listen, pay heed"; an abbreviation of *"Shema yisrael YHWH elohenu YHWH ehad,"* "Hear O Israel! The Lord is our God, the Lord is one" (Deut. 6:4), the Jewish credo (recited by observant Jews twice daily).

shofet (pl. *shoftim*)—judge, magistrate, political leader.

Shulhan Arukh—lit., "prepared table"; authoritative code of Jewish religious and civil law written by Joseph Karo in the sixteenth century.

siddur medini. See *medini*

Sifra—lit., "book"; halakhic midrash to Leviticus, also known as *Torat Kohanim* (Law of Priests) and *Sifra debei Rab* (Book of the School of Rav), produced by the tannaitic school of Rabbi Akiva.

Sifre—tannaitic halakhic midrash to the books of Numbers and Deuteronomy.

Simhat Torah—lit., "rejoicing of the law"; the festival that falls after the seventh (and last) day of Sukkot, at which the community completes the annual reading of the Torah and starts it once again.

sofer (pl. *sofrim*)—scribe.

sugya (pl. *sugyot*)—talmudic pericope, a unit of talmudic discussion.

sukkah—lit., "booth"; pl. Sukkot, the Feast of Tabernacles, for which booths are erected, where Jews dwell or eat for seven days.

takkanah (pl. *takkanot*)—regulation, remedy, rule, reform, improvement; an ordinance of the rabbis or the *kahal,* opposite of law of the Torah. *Takkanat ha-medinah*—a regulation by the rabbis or the *kahal* for the sake of law and order or for the improvement of the state, society, or community. See also *tikkun*.

talmid hakham. See *hakham*.

Talmud—lit., "study, learning, instruction"; the Mishnah and the Gemara together, the Gemara being the commentaries of the *amora'im* on the Mishnah. The Babylonian Talmud (Talmud Bavli) was compiled about 500 C.E.; the Jerusalem or Palestinian Talmud (Talmud Yerushalmi) was compiled about 375 C.E.

tanna (pl. *tanna'im*)—first generations of Rabbinic sages, distinguished from the later *amora'im.* The tannaitic sayings are recorded in the Mishnah, Tosefta, and the *baraitot.*

tenai—condition, term, stipulation. *Lehatnot*—to stipulate, to make conditions.

terumah—lit., "offering, donation"; priestly tithe on produce.

tikken--lit., "repaired, corrected"; regulated; enacted a *takkanah.*

tikkun—repair, correction, reform, amendment, improvement, regulation. *Tikkun ha-medinah*—establishing law and order in the state or improving its well-being. *Tikkun olam*—lit., "repairing the world"; reforming society. *Tikkun seder medini*—repairing the political order. *Takkanah la'olam*—general improvement to the world or society.

Tishah be-Av—the ninth day of the month of Av, the traditional date of the destruction of the First and Second Temples, a day of fasting and mourning.

Torah—law, doctrine, dogma; instruction, theory; specifically, God's law. In its narrow sense, Torah denotes the law of Moses (the Pentateuch);

more broadly, the entire body of valid instruction in the Jewish tradition.

Tosefta—lit., "supplement"; tannaitic *baraitot* compiled as a supplement to the Mishnah a generation after the Mishnah was written, according to the tradition. It was redacted according to the six orders of the Mishnah.

Tosafot—lit., "additions"; supplements to and commentaries on the Talmud written by rabbinic scholars (the tosafists) in Germany and France in the eleventh to thirteenth centuries. They are printed along with Rashi's commentaries on either side of the traditional talmudic texts.

Tur—abbreviation of *Arba'ah Turim* (Four Columns), an early fourteenth-century codification of rabbinic *halakhah* written by Jacob b. Asher in Spain.

tzaddik (pl. *tzaddikim*)—righteous, virtuous, just, pious, God-fearing. In Hasidism, a leader who has spiritual qualities and magical abilities.

tzedakah—lit., "justness, fairness, righteousness"; charity; also good deed, piety, mercy.

tzibbur—public, community, congregation.

urim and *thummim*—devices referred to in the Bible for producing oracles, attached to the breastplate of the high priest. See also *ephod* and *hoshen*.

yishuv—lit., "population, settlement"; the Jewish population in the Land of Israel, particularly before 1948.

yishuv medini. See *medini*.

Yigdal—Jewish medieval hymn, incorporated in the daily prayers, based on the thirteen articles of the credo composed by Maimonides.

Yom Kippur—Day of Atonement, the culmination of the Jewish High Holidays.

zekhut—right, privilege, prerogative; also merit or acquittal.

Commentators

Peter Berkowitz, Law, George Mason University, Arlington, Virginia

David Ellenson, Jewish Thought, Hebrew Union College–Jewish Institute of Religion, Los Angeles

Menachem Fisch, History and Philosophy of Science, Tel Aviv University

Michael Fishbane, Divinity School, University of Chicago

Amy Gutmann, Politics, Princeton University

Moshe Halbertal, Philosophy, The Hebrew University, Jerusalem

David Hartman, Shalom Hartman Institute, Jerusalem

Moshe Idel, Jewish Philosophy, The Hebrew University, Jerusalem

Lawrence Kaplan, Jewish Studies, McGill University, Montreal

Bernard M. Levinson, Classical and Near Eastern Studies, University of Minnesota, Minneapolis

Sanford Levinson, Law, University of Texas, Austin

Menachem Lorberbaum, Jewish Philosophy, Tel Aviv University

Yair Lorberbaum, Law, Bar Ilan University, Ramat Gan

Jonathan W. Malino, Philosophy, Guilford College, Greensboro, North Carolina

Susan Neiman, Philosophy, Tel Aviv University

Clifford Orwin, Political Science, University of Toronto

Hilary Putnam, Philosophy, Harvard University, Cambridge

Joseph Raz, Law, Balliol College, Oxford University

Avi Sagi, Philosophy, Bar Ilan University, Ramat Gan

Michael J. Sandel, Government, Harvard University, Cambridge

David Shatz, Philosophy, Stern College, Yeshiva University, New York

Allan Silver, Sociology, Columbia University, New York

Suzanne Last Stone, Cardozo Law School, Yeshiva University, New York

Yael Tamir, Philosophy and Education, Tel Aviv University

Michael Walzer, Social Science, Institute for Advanced Study, Princeton

Noam J. Zohar, Philosophy, Bar Ilan University, Ramat Gan

Index of Biblical and Rabbinic Sources

Page numbers of selections in this volume are marked with ∫. Only the first page number is listed.

Index of Names

Page numbers of selections in this volume, listed under their authors' names, are marked with $\mathcal{S}$; commentaries and introductory material are labeled "com" and "intro," respectively. Only the first page number is listed.

General Index

An alphabetical list of legal principles and political sayings frequently invoked in traditional discourse appears under the entry "Maxims."